THE SCHOOLS HISTORY PROJECT · S·H·P · OFFICIAL TEXT

MW01157170

RUSSIA UNDER TSARISM AND COMMUNISM 1881–1953

SECOND EDITION

Chris Corin

Terry Fiehn

HODDER EDUCATION
AN HACHETTE UK COMPANY

In the same series

Fascist Italy	John Hite and Chris Hinton	978 07195 73415
Weimar and Nazi Germany	John Hite and Chris Hinton	978 07195 73439
Britain 1783–1851	Charlotte Evers and Dave Welbourne	978 07195 74825
Britain 1851–1918	Michael Willis	978 07195 74894
The Early Tudors: England 1485–1558	David Rogerson, Samantha Ellsmore and David Hudson	978 07195 74849
The Reign of Elizabeth: England 1558–1603	Barbara Mervyn	978 07195 74863
England 1625–1660: Charles, the Civil War and Cromwell	Dale Scarboro	978 07195 77475
Modern America: The USA, 1865 to the present	Joanne de Pennington	978 07195 77444

Authors' acknowledgement
The authors would like to thank Beryl Williams, Reader in History, Sussex University, for her enormous contribution to this book. Not only have her advice and guidance been invaluable, but much of the material in this book has been drawn from her published work and her own papers and notes, freely and generously made available to us.

The Schools History Project

Set up in 1972 to bring new life to history for students aged 13–16, the Schools History Project continues to play an innovatory role in secondary history education. From the start, SHP aimed to show how good history has an important contribution to make to the education of a young person. It does this by creating courses and materials which both respect the importance of up-to-date, well-researched history and provide enjoyable learning experiences for students.

Since 1978 the Project has been based at Trinity and All Saints University College Leeds. It continues to support, inspire and challenge teachers through the annual conference, regional courses and website: http://www.schoolshistoryproject.org.uk. The Project is also closely involved with government bodies and awarding bodies in the planning of courses for Key Stage 3, GCSE and A level.

Although every effort has been made to ensure that website addresses are correct at time of going to press, Hodder Education cannot be held responsible for the content of any website mentioned in this book. It is sometimes possible to find a relocated web page by typing in the address of the home page for a website in the URL window of your browser.

Hachette UK's policy is to use papers that are natural, renewable and recyclable products and made from wood grown in sustainable forests. The logging and manufacturing processes are expected to conform to the environmental regulations of the country of origin.

Orders: please contact Bookpoint Ltd, 130 Milton Park, Abingdon, Oxon OX14 4SB.
Telephone: +44 (0)1235 827720. Fax: +44 (0)1235 400454. Lines are open 9.00a.m.–5.00p.m., Monday to Saturday, with a 24-hour message answering service. Visit our website at www.hoddereducation.co.uk.

© Chris Corin and Terry Fiehn 2002, 2011

First published in 2002 as *Communist Russia under Lenin and Stalin*

This second edition first published in 2011 by
Hodder & Stoughton Limited
an Hachette UK company
338 Euston Road
London NW1 3BH

Impression number	10 9 8 7 6 5 4 3 2			
Year	2015	2014	2013	2012

Typeset in 10/12pt Walbaum by DC Graphic Design Limited, Swanley, Kent
Artwork by Oxford Designers and Illustrators
Printed and bound in Great Britain by CPI Group (UK) Ltd, Croydon, CR0 4YY

A catalogue record for this title is available from the British Library

ISBN 978 1 444 12423 1

Contents

Using this book   iv
Introduction   v

■ **Section 1**   **Why did the tsarist regime collapse in 1917?**   **1**
    1   What were the challenges facing the tsarist regime at the end of the nineteenth century?   3
    2   1905   28
    3   Could tsarism have survived? 1906–1917   46
    Section 1 Review: Why did the tsarist regime collapse in 1917?   73

■ **Section 2**   **Why were the Bolsheviks successful in October 1917?**   **75**
    4   Was the Provisional Government doomed from the beginning?   75
    5   Was the Bolshevik seizure of power in October 1917 inevitable?   95
    Section 2 Review: Why were the Bolsheviks successful in October 1917?   111

■ **Section 3**   **The consolidation of the Bolshevik state 1917–1924**   **113**
    6   How did the Bolsheviks survive the first few months in power?   115
    7   How did the Bolsheviks win the Civil War?   125
    8   How was the Bolshevik state consolidated between 1921 and 1924?   149
    Section 3 Review: The consolidation of the Bolshevik state 1917–1924   167

■ **Section 4**   **From Lenin to Stalin**   **169**
    9   How significant is Lenin's contribution to history?   172
    10   How did Stalin emerge as the sole leader of Russia?   181

■ **Section 5**   **How did Stalin transform the economy of the USSR in the 1930s?**   **196**
    11   Why did Stalin make the Great Turn?   198
    12   Was collectivisation a success?   204
    13   How well planned were the Five-Year Plans?   219
    Section 5 Review: How did Stalin transform the economy of the USSR in the 1930s?   245

■ **Section 6**   **How did Stalin control the USSR?**   **246**
    14   How far was Stalin responsible for the Great Terror?   249
    15   The cult of the personality   276

■ **Section 7**   **Soviet society in the 1920s and 1930s**   **285**
    16   Were Soviet culture and society transformed by the October Revolution?   285
    17   Culture and society in a decade of turmoil   302

■ **Section 8**   **From pariah to saviour: the Soviet Union and Europe 1921–1945**   **321**
    18   Alone in a hostile world: how did Soviet foreign policy develop between 1921 and 1941?   325
    19   How was the Soviet Union able to turn disaster into victory in the Great Patriotic War?   342

■ **Section 9**   **Stalin's final years and Conclusion**   **564**
    20   Stalin's final years 1945–1953   364
    21   Conclusion   387

Bibliography and Selected Reading   394
Text acknowledgements   397
Photo credits   398
Index   399

Using this book

This is an in-depth study of Tsarist and Communist Russia 1881–1953. It contains everything you need for examination success and more. It provides all the content you would expect, as well as many features to help both independent and class-based learners. So, before you wade in, make sure you understand the purpose of each of the features.

Focus routes

On every topic throughout the book, this feature guides you to produce the written material essential for understanding what you read and, later, for revising the topic (e.g. pages 46, 154, 182). These focus routes are particularly useful for you if you are an independent learner working through this material on your own, but they can also be used for class-based learning.

Activities

The activities offer a range of exercises to enhance your understanding of what you read and to prepare you for examinations. They vary in style and purpose. There are:

- a variety of essays, both structured essays (e.g. pages 112, 193) and more discursive essays (e.g. pages 381, 389)
- source investigations (e.g. pages 106, 138)
- examination of historical interpretations, which is now central to A level history (e.g. pages 180, 267, 269)
- decision-making exercises which help you to see events from the viewpoint of people at the time (e.g. pages 116, 123, 148, 201)

These activities help you to analyse and understand what you are reading. They address the content through the key questions that the examiner will be expecting you to have investigated.

Overviews, summaries and key points

In such a large book on such a massive topic, you need to keep referring to the big picture. Each chapter begins with an overview and each chapter ends with a key-points summary of the most important content of the chapter.

Learning trouble spots

Experience shows that time and again some topics cause confusion for students. This feature identifies such topics and helps students to avoid common misunderstandings (e.g. pages 79, 96 and 98). In particular, this feature addresses some of the general problems encountered when studying history, such as assessing sources (e.g. page 270);

analysing the provenance, tone and value of sources (e.g. pages 169, 267–270); handling statistics (e.g. page 242); and assessing historians' views (e.g. pages 98, 105, 161).

Charts

The charts are our attempts to summarise important information in note or diagrammatic form (e.g. pages 124, 154). There are also several grid charts that present a lot of information in a structured way (e.g. pages 165, 190–1, 316–317). However, everyone learns differently and the best charts are the ones you draw yourself! Drawing your own charts in your own way to summarise important content can really help understanding (e.g. page 135) as can completing assessment grids.

Glossary

We have tried to write in an accessible way but occasionally we have used advanced vocabulary. These words are often explained in brackets in the text but sometimes you may need to use a dictionary. We have also used many general historical terms as well as some that are specific to the study of Tsarist and Communist Russia. You won't find all of these in a dictionary, but they are defined in glossary boxes close to the text in which they appear. The first time a glossary word appears in the text it is in SMALL CAPITALS like this.

Talking points

These are asides from the normal pattern of written exercises. They are discussion questions that invite you to be more reflective and to consider the relevance of this history to your own life. They might ask you to voice your personal judgement (e.g. pages 120, 134); to make links between the past and present (e.g. pages 173, 181, 315); or to highlight aspects of the process of studying history (e.g. pages 141, 177).

Tsarist and Communist Russia is one of the most popular A level history topics. The content is deeply relevant to the modern world. But the actual process of studying history is equally relevant to the modern world. Throughout this book you will be problem solving, working with others, and trying to improve your own performance as you engage with deep and complex historical issues. Our hope is that by using this book you will become actively involved in your study of history and that you will see history as a challenging set of skills and ideas to be mastered rather than as an inert body of factual material to be learned.

Introduction

SOURCE I   Tsar Nicholas II being held captive after the 1917 revolution that deposed him

COMMUNISM
Last stage in Marx's notion of the evolution of history where there would be no state; everybody would be equal and share in an abundance of goods produced by machinery rather than by workers' labour; more leisure and people would take what they needed from central pool of goods.

AUTOCTRAT
All-powerful ruler.

The Russian Revolution of October 1917 is arguably the most important event in the twentieth century, since it led to the creation of the world's first Communist state which lasted for over 70 years and had a huge impact on world affairs for the greater part of the twentieth century. From its very beginning, Communist Russia represented a philosophy and worldview that terrified countries in the West. The governments of Western Europe and the USA regarded COMMUNISM as a kind of virus that could, if unchecked, infect their countries. Fear of Communism affected the internal politics and foreign policies of numerous countries. For example, in Germany, it helped Adolf Hitler come to power. It also made some governments unwilling to stop the aggressive Nazi rearmament programme because they saw a strong Germany in Central Europe as the best bulwark against the expansion of Communism from the East.

After the Second World War, the Soviet Union emerged as a superpower vying with the USA for influence in the post-1945 world. The Cold War between these two great powers – the propaganda, spying, intrigue and interference in the affairs of other countries which this entailed – dominated international relations over five decades and nearly brought the world to the point of self-destruction. The Communist model was exported to Eastern Europe, China, South-Eastern Asia and parts of Africa and the Caribbean. So there is little doubt that the Bolshevik, or Communist, Revolution of 1917 had a major impact on the course of the twentieth century.

The aim of this book is to tell the story of how the Communist state came into being and how it developed during the middle part of the twentieth century. It looks first at the collapse of the tsarist regime that preceded it, focusing on the last Romanov tsar, Nicholas II. It examines the reasons for the revolution that overthew Nicholas in February 1917 and then considers the events that led to the seizure of power in October of that year by the Bolsheviks whose leader was Vladimir Ilyich Ulyanov, better known as Lenin. Next, it looks at how the Bolsheviks consolidated their power and how Joseph Dzhugashvili, better known as Stalin, became the leader of the USSR. It goes on to explore the nature of the Stalinist state that took shape in the 1930s and 1940s and how the USSR was governed by Stalin up until his death in 1953.

Tsar Nicholas II was an AUTOCRAT who had supreme power over his subjects. In the period he ruled he did his best to protect the autocracy because he believed it was the best way of governing Russia. He thought that any moves towards democracy would lead to revolution, chaos and the collapse of the Russian Empire. However, he faced the major challenge of trying to modernise Russia within the framework of an autocratic state. Russia needed to modernise and industrialise so that it could remain a major world power. Unfortunately, Nicholas was not suited to this challenge and neither he nor the ruling élite were prepared to make the political and social transformations that modernisation entailed. Russia slid into revolution, prompted by the stresses and strains created by the First World War.

SOCIALISM
Workers' control of state. Factories, machines owned collectively and run by state; everybody equal, class system brought to an end; wealth and goods shared out fairly; equal entitlement to good housing and standard of living.

TOTALITARIANISM
A state in which power is concentrated in the hands of one man or small group, exercising excessive control of individuals and denying them fundamental civil and political liberties; monitoring and control of aspects of individuals' lives carried out by secret police who are accountable only to the political élite.

CAPITALISM
Economic system based on private enterprise and the profit motive in which the market determines the price of goods and regulates the supply and distribution of raw materials and products.

Lenin was a follower of the teachings of Karl Marx who believed that human history passed through a series of evolutionary stages leading to SOCIALISM and then on to Communism, the highest form of society. Marx thought that this would be achieved by a revolution of the working classes in highly industrialised countries. Lenin brought to Marxism a specifically Russian tradition in revolutionary thought. He developed the notion of a disciplined revolutionary party run by professional, hard-working revolutionaries who would seize power in Russia and set in motion a world revolution. In 1917, Lenin and his party, the Bolsheviks, hijacked a revolution that had been generated by the Russian people desperate to rid themselves of the regime of Nicholas II. Lenin used the momentum of this 'revolution from below' to set up a Communist state which he was sure would be the precursor to Communist revolution throughout the world.

The world revolution never materialised, and Lenin only lived long enough to see his new regime secure in power. The Soviet Union remained isolated from other countries as the only Communist state in the world. After Lenin's death, the mantle of power was taken up by Stalin who was determined to build socialism in one country – Russia. He equated the building of the socialist state with national pride and achievement.

Stalin envisaged nothing less than the complete economic and social transformation of Soviet Russia that would help it catch up with and overtake the industrialised capitalist countries of the West. With the ruling elite of the Communist Party, Stalin planned a 'revolution from above' which would not only change the way people lived but also their fundamental attitudes and values. There was a high price to be paid for this revolution – millions of deaths, including leading figures in the Bolshevik Party, and immense suffering which resulted from Stalin's policies and the operation of the new command economy. In the process of carrying his policies out, Stalin created a TOTALITARIAN state that provided the models for George Orwell's *1984* and Aldous Huxley's *Brave New World*.

By the end of the 1930s, Stalin had changed a backward agricultural country into an industrialised country, one that was able to take on the might of the Nazi war machine and defeat it in the Second World War. He had also given shape and form to the institutions of the Soviet state and economy which remained largely unchanged until the 1980s.

It was Lenin who made the October Revolution happen and it was Lenin who laid the foundations of the Communist state. But it was Stalin who shaped it into the Soviet totalitarian system that competed with the democratic countries of the CAPITALIST world until the collapse of Russian Communism in 1991.

SOURCE 2 Lenin returned to Russia by train in 1917 to start the socialist revolution. Trotsky called Lenin the 'engine driver of the revolution', hence this painting from the 1930s putting Lenin at the controls. Stalin wasn't on the train with Lenin and was not in the welcoming party to greet Lenin on his return. However, in the painting, he appears as the figure in the background

SOURCE 3 Stalin appeared on many posters and paintings leading the workers who were engaged in the transformation of the USSR

Why did the tsarist regime collapse in 1917?

In February 1917 the old regime of the Romanov tsars was swept away by a popular revolution. The Tsar had survived a revolution in 1905 but failed to make the political, social and economic changes necessary to survive the one in 1917. In this section we look at the challenges the tsarist regime faced as it entered the twentieth century and the factors that contributed to the February Revolution.

SOURCE 1   The head of the vandalised statue of Tsar Alexander III lying on the ground

SOURCE 2   A demonstration in Petrograd on International Women's Day, 23 February 1917

ACTIVITY

What is a revolution?

Are revolutions always carried out by masses of people – are they POPULAR REVOLUTIONS? Do they always have leaders and revolutionary parties that organise and direct the people? In this book we are concerned specifically with three revolutions: one in 1905 and two in 1917, which are pertinent to historical debate about what a revolution is, whether it is 'popular', the role of revolutionary parties and whether a revolution deserves that title. At the end of this section, you will be able to reach your own conclusions about these issues.

1 What do you think a revolution is?
2 What ideas about revolution in Russia are suggested by Sources 1–4?
3 Do you think you can have a revolution without leaders?
4 What do you think are the main causes of revolutions? Look at the causes suggested below and rank them in order of importance according to the diagram on the right (a diamond nine). Add any others you can think of.
   a) Wanting more democracy
   b) Economic distress
   c) A revolutionary philosophy or set of ideas
   d) Wanting political change
   e) Wanting a new leader
   f) Losing a war
   g) Lack of confidence in the existing government
   h) Leaders who put forward a different way of running society
   i) Mismanagement of the economy by the government
5 What aspects of society need to change in order to justify the term 'revolution'?

> **POPULAR REVOLUTION**
> A revolution that is accepted and welcomed by the majority of the people in a country. Many of the people may have been involved in carrying out the revolution.

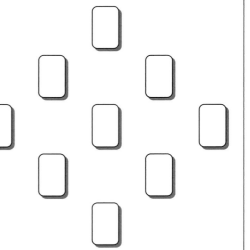

SOURCE 3 A painting of a barricade in a Moscow street, 1905, artist unknown

SOURCE 4 The storming of the Winter Palace – a still from Eisenstein's film *October*, made in 1927

1 What were the challenges facing the tsarist regime at the end of the nineteenth century?

CHAPTER OVERVIEW

This chapter introduces tsarist Russia – the country, society and government – at the end of the nineteenth century. Russia under the tsars was an autocracy. This was epitomised by the reign of Alexander III (1881–94). However, if Russia wanted to remain a major power in the world, it had to modernise. This created serious challenges for the tsars who wanted to manage change within the existing political and administrative framework. These challenges came from different groups in Russian society and, in particular, from a growing political opposition who believed Russia should be governed in a different way.

A The Russian Empire and its people (pp. 4–7)

B How was Russia governed under the tsars? (pp. 8–11)

C Nicholas II – a new hope? (pp. 12–14)

D Modernisation (pp. 14–17)

E Other challenges facing tsarist Russia (pp. 18–27)

The assassination of Alexander II

SOURCE 1.1 An illustration of the assassination of Alexander II

On 1 March 1881, the Russian Tsar, Alexander II, was travelling by coach through the snow to the Winter Palace in St Petersburg. An armed Cossack sat with the coach driver while another six Cossacks followed on horseback. Two sledges carrying the Chief of Police for St Petersburg and other police officers followed on behind. That very day, the Tsar had signed a document that granted the first ever constitution to the Russian people.

Watching the Tsar's journey was a group of radicals called 'Narodnaya Volya' or 'The People's Will'. Eighteen months earlier they had condemned him to death at a secret meeting and had already made six unsuccessful attempts on his life. On a street corner near the Catherine Canal, one of them hurled a bomb to halt the fast moving, iron-clad coach. Despite an explosion under the back axle, the carriage held together and the coachman drove on. But several of the Cossacks had been fatally injured and the Tsar, ignoring advice, ordered the coach to stop. He climbed out to comfort them. When asked how he was, the Tsar replied, 'Thank God I am safe'. Not so. A second assassin threw his bomb, which landed at the Tsar's feet and exploded. The dying Tsar insisted on being taken to the Winter Palace where he died just over an hour later. The bomber, also fatally wounded, died that night in hospital.

Five members of The People's Will were convicted and sentenced to death. The nineteen-year old who had thrown the first bomb had told the police all he knew about his comrades. On 3 April, wearing the word 'TSARICIDE' on a placard on their chests, they were led out for public execution before a vast crowd and ten thousand troops. The four men and one woman were hanged incompetently – one victim had to be re-hanged three times.

The assassination of Alexander II in 1881 marked an important point in Russian history. Tsarist Russia was looking increasingly creaky and vulnerable. This vast Empire was undeveloped in comparison with the industrialised nations of Western Europe. The world was changing and the tsarist regime needed to come to terms with the modern industrial age. The fate of the Romanov tsars rested on their ability to deal with the challenges posed by the modern world. Were they up to the job? To consider this question, we first need to understand:

- why Russia was a difficult country to govern
- who the people of Russia were
- how Russia was governed by the tsars
- why there was so much opposition to the government.

A   The Russian Empire and its people

Tsarist Russia at the end of the nineteenth century occupied a vast area across two continents – Europe and Asia. From west to east it measured over 6400 km and from north to south over 3000 km. It covered about one sixth of the world's total land mass. The USA could fit into it two and a half times and Britain nearly a hundred times. Large parts were (and still are) either uninhabited or sparsely populated. The northern part of Russia, the tundra, is frozen for most of the year. South of the tundra lies endless miles of forest and then the Steppes – open plains and grassland. To the far south there are deserts.

Communications across this huge area were poor. There were few paved roads except in the big cities. Most of the roads were hard packed earth, which turned to mud in heavy rain and became impassable in winter. For longer journeys, rivers were used. Most of Russia's major cities had grown up along important river routes. The other major form of travel was the railway. Although there had been a great expansion of the railway by 1900, Russia still only had as much track as Britain. The most important route was the Trans-Siberian Railway that crossed Russia from Moscow in the west to Vladivostok in the east. This journey took more than a week of continuous travel to complete.

FOCUS ROUTE

Identify aspects of Russia that made it a difficult country to govern at the end of the nineteenth century. Consider: size, landscape, communications, diversity of people and national groups. Make notes on each of these.

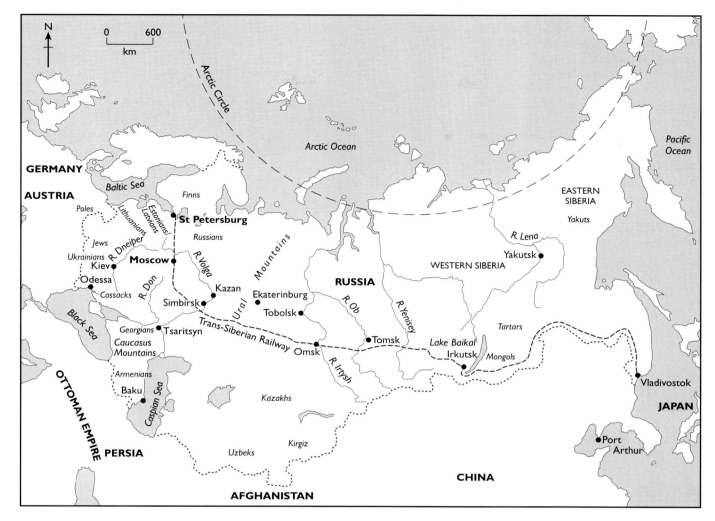

SOURCE 1.2   The major nationalities in Russia by mother tongue in 1897

Nationality	Millions
Russian	55.6
Ukrainian	22.4
Polish	7.9
White Russian	5.8
Jewish	5.0
Kirgiz	4.0
Tartar	3.4
Finnish	3.1
German	1.8
Latvian	1.4
Bashkir	1.3
Lithuanian	1.2
Armenian	1.2
Romanian/Moldavian	1.1
Estonian	1.0
Murdrinian	1.0
Georgian	0.8
Turkmenian	0.3
Tadzhik	0.3

The people

From the fifteenth century onwards, the Russians who lived in the area around Moscow gradually conquered the peoples around them. They were ruled by a leader called the tsar. The area they controlled expanded and developed into the Russian Empire. Large slabs were added only in the nineteenth century. Vladivostok and the most easterly part on the Pacific Ocean became part of the Empire in 1859. The Caucasus region, which included the Georgian and Chechen people, was secured as late as 1864, and the central Asian area of Russia including Turkistan was conquered in the 1860s and 1870s.

Tsarist Russia at the turn of the century was a vast sprawling empire containing a patchwork quilt of different national groups (see Source 1.2). The Russians themselves formed about half of the population, the vast majority of whom lived in the European part of Russia west of the Ural mountains. The diversity of culture and religion and language throughout the Empire was astonishing, from sophisticated European Russians living in St Petersburg to nomadic Muslim peoples living in the desert areas of the south, to the tribes who wandered the vast spaces of Siberia living and dressing very much like native American Indians.

■ **Learning trouble spot**

It is difficult to determine the size of social classes in Russia at the end of the nineteenth century. The 1897 census looks at 'social estates', not classes. There is no category for middle classes. The 'merchants and honoured citizens' category comes nearest, only 0.5 per cent of the population. The 'urbanites' category comprised tradesmen, shopkeepers, white collar workers and artisans. Similarly, there is no category for industrial workers. About 7 per cent of peasants lived in the towns but not all of these were factory workers. The 'others' category covers much of the population of Russian Central Asia. The Cossacks were categorised separately.

The social structure of tsarist Russia

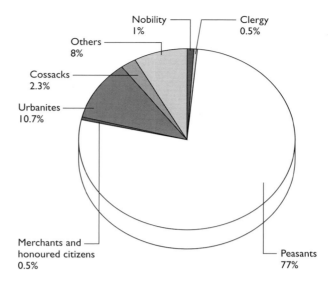

SOURCE 1.3   A breakdown of Russia by class, based on the census of 1897

The most noticeable features of Russian society at the end of the nineteenth century were the high proportion of the population, almost 80 per cent, who were peasants and the small proportion in the professional and merchant classes. The absence of a significant middle class played an important part in the development of Russia during the early twentieth century. Tsarist Russia operated a rigid social hierarchy with the royal family and nobles at the top and the peasants and workers at the bottom. Chart 1B gives some idea of the character of these different groups.

■ 1B The social structure of tsarist Russia

NOBILITY
- Made up just over one per cent of population but owned 25 per cent of all the land. Some were extremely rich, with enormous country estates.
- Few spent much time on their estates. For most of the year they lived in St Petersburg or Moscow doing the round of social events that constituted 'society'.
- Some had important jobs in government or in the army but this was often more because of their position in society than on merit.
- An increasing number of nobles were selling their land to peasants and moving to the cities.

SOURCE 1.4   The ball of the coloured wigs at Countess Shavalova's palace, 1914

MIDDLE CLASSES
- Although small in number, there was a growing class of merchants, bankers and industrialists as industry and commerce developed.
- The more progressive were sitting on town councils, supporting schools and becoming art patrons and founding museums and art galleries.
- There was a burgeoning cultural life (theatres, ballets and operas) in the major cities in which the middle classes participated.
- The lifestyle of the middle class was very good. They owned large houses and enjoyed a wide variety of food.
- The professional class (doctors, lawyers, teachers) was growing and beginning to play a significant role in local government. Lawyers in particular were becoming active in politics.

URBAN WORKERS
- Most workers were young and male. Although many were ex-peasants, by 1900 over a third were young men whose fathers had worked in factories, mines and railways.
- There were large numbers of women working in the textile factories in St Petersburg and Moscow.
- Wages were generally very low and working conditions very poor. There were a high number of deaths from accidents and work-related health problems.
- Living conditions were generally appalling. Many shared rooms in tenement blocks or in barrack-style buildings next to factories or mines. People had no privacy or private space: men, women and children often lived in rooms divided by curtains.

PEASANTS
- Before 1861, Russian peasants had been serfs, virtually owned by their masters, the nobility. In 1861 they had been emancipated (freed) and given plots of land from the estates of the nobility.
- Although emancipated, the peasants were subject to restrictions in the commune or 'mir' in which they lived. These affected the way they farmed and their personal freedom, e.g. they could not leave the village without permission.
- Life for most peasants was hard and unremitting. They slogged out their lives on small patches of land that they owned and worked on the estates of the nobility.
- Most were poor, illiterate and uneducated.
- Some peasants – KULAKS – were quite well off. They hired labour, rented and bought land.
- Most peasants got by in good years, but in years of bad harvests there was widespread starvation, e.g. 400,000 died in 1891.
- Disease was widespread, with regular epidemics of typhus and diphtheria.
- Many peasants lived in debt and squalor, prone to drunkenness and sexually transmitted diseases, especially syphilis.

> **KULAK**
> Rich peasant who hired labour and owned animals.

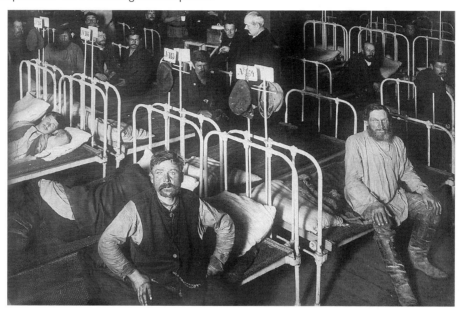

SOURCE 1.5 Inside a workers' lodging house, c. 1900

SOURCE 1.6 Peasants in a village near Nizhny-Novgorod, c. 1891

WHAT WERE THE CHALLENGES FACING THE TSARIST REGIME AT THE END OF THE NINETEENTH CENTURY?

8

WHAT WERE THE CHALLENGES FACING THE TSARIST REGIME AT THE END OF THE NINETEENTH CENTURY?

FOCUS ROUTE

Make notes on:
• how Russia was governed by the tsars
• the three principles underpinning the tsarist system
• the importance of the role of the Orthodox Church
• the difference between the Westerners and Slavophiles.

B How was Russia governed under the tsars?

■ IC The structure of the tsarist state

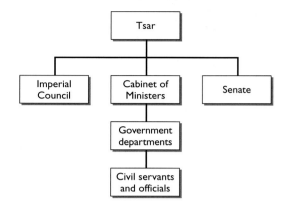

The tsar was an autocrat, an absolute ruler, who had supreme power over his subjects. His position was underpinned by three key principles – autocracy, nationality and orthodoxy (see page 9 below). The tsar had an imperial council, made up of nobles, to advise him, and a cabinet of ministers who ran the various government departments. But they were responsible to him alone, not to a parliament or to a prime minister. They reported directly to the tsar and took instructions from him. This meant that the tsar was the fundamental pivot on which the system rested.

There was a huge bureaucracy of civil servants and officials who ran this enormous empire. It was a rigid hierarchy (orders passed down from above by superiors to lower ranks) marked by inefficiency – it took ages to get things done – and nepotism. The top ranks were dominated by the nobility. The lower ranks that had contact with the people were generally badly paid and there was a culture of corruption in which bribery was common. This, together with the arbitrary nature of decision making, undermined respect for the authorities. The bureaucracy was virtually impenetrable for ordinary citizens who rarely found that their interests were served properly.

The size and diversity of the empire made it extremely difficult to govern. The different regions of the empire were under the control of governors who had their own local bureaucracies. Poor communications meant that it was hard to get decisions from the centre carried out. The regional governors often acted like independent rulers in their own fiefdoms.

Opposition was not tolerated. Political parties were illegal. Newspapers, periodicals and books were censored. Public gatherings of more than 12 people required police permission. The government made use of an extensive secret police network, the Okhrana, to root out dissidents and people likely to cause trouble. There was a system of surveillance with agents in most institutions and in factories. People deemed to be dangerous or hostile to the regime, especially those who organised strikes and protests, were put in prison or exiled to Siberia. By 1898, nearly 300,000 had been sent to Siberia. Large scale protests, demonstrations and riots, which often broke out in times of famine, were suppressed by the army. Tsarist Russia was an oppressive and intolerant regime.

COMPETING MINISTRIES

Ministries competed with each other for control of policy, resources and the tsar's attention. The two biggest ministries were Finance and the Interior. The Ministry of Finance, with staff drawn from the fields of banking and commerce, wanted changes in society to allow enterprise and initiative to flourish. This would entail giving the middle classes more power and freedom. The Ministry of the Interior, with staff drawn from the nobility and landowners, held firm to the autocratic principle and thought Russia should be ruled by an iron hand and they resisted changes that would create a more liberal Russia. So these two ministries were often pulling against each other and this created confusion and lack of clarity in policy.

9

WHAT WERE THE CHALLENGES FACING THE TSARIST REGIME AT THE END OF THE NINETEENTH CENTURY?

The army

The army, the largest in Europe, was crucial to the survival of the tsarist regime. Most officers were from noble backgrounds. Ordinary soldiers were conscripts taken from the villages who were required to serve for seven years actively and eight in reserve. Soldiers had to be completely subservient to officers and had few rights: they were not allowed to ride in first or second class railway carriages or enter most restaurants and cafes. Pay was extremely poor and most soldiers grew their own food and lived mainly on soup, tea and bread. So far they had remained loyal to the regime. The army was used to suppressing disturbances and revolts. However, it was becoming increasingly disenchanted with being used as a police force and morale was suffering badly among officers and soldiers, most of whom where ex-peasants, who did not like having to put down peasant conflicts.

One section of the army the regime could rely on was the Cossacks. They came from the Don area of Russia and were loyal supporters of the tsar. Cossacks could be trusted to act against other peoples in the empire, including the Russians. They formed the best cavalry units in the Russian army and were feared because they could be brutal and ruthless.

Three key principles underpinning tsarist rule

1 Autocracy

As far as the tsars were concerned they had been appointed by God to lead and guide their people. Article 1 of the Fundamental Laws, 1832, makes it clear: 'The Emperor of all the Russias is an autocratic and unlimited monarch; God himself ordains that all must bow before his supreme power, not only out of fear but also out of conscience.' The autocrat could rule the country without constraints according to his own idea of duty and what was right. The tsars rejected any hint that their power rested on the consent of the people.

2 Nationality

There was a strong belief that Russians had a distinctive way of life, values, beliefs and customs that were superior to the people around them and should predominate throughout the Empire. This 'Russianness' was emphasised by the Orthodox Church and practised in the policy of Russification (see page 19). The Tsar had an obligation to preserve and strengthen national identity.

3 Orthodoxy

The Russian Orthodox Church was an offshoot of the Christian Church, which, for historical reasons, had become independent of the Pope and Rome and saw itself as the upholder of the 'true' Christian faith. It supported the divine right of the tsar to rule and exhorted believers to obey the tsar as the agent of God. The Church believed there was a mystical bond between the god-like tsar and the people – he was the father and they were the children.

SOURCE 1.7 A Social Democratic Party cartoon showing the social structure of the Russian state. The text reads, from top to bottom:

We rule you
We govern you
We fool you
We shoot you
We eat instead of you
We work for you. We feed you.

10

WHAT WERE THE CHALLENGES FACING THE TSARIST REGIME AT THE END OF THE NINETEENTH CENTURY?

THE WORLD OF THE SECRET POLICE – KONSPIRATSIA

In 1881, after the assassination of Alexander II, a nationwide police offensive led to 10,000 arrests. A decree of March 1882 allowed the police to declare any citizen subject to surveillance. A murky world of police, spies and double agents – Konspiratsia – operated in and around the big cities. In July 1881, Georgii Sudeikin was given responsibility for maintaining public order in St Petersburg. He recruited revolutionaries as double agents to gain information about terrorist attacks and sow confusion in their ranks. Sudeikin used several aliases and passports and met agents in secret locations.

After a revolutionary had been arrested, Sudeikin had them 'softened up' in solitary confinement. Then, he persuaded them to become a police spy. One such person was Sergei Dagaev, a prominent member of The People's Will. He was arrested in 1882 after an underground printing press was found in his apartment. In 1883, now a police spy, he was released by means of a staged escape. He provided the police with information that led to a wave of arrests. However, The People's Will became suspicious and, under pressure, Dagaev confessed his guilt. As penance he was ordered to murder Sudeikin, a deed he carried out with two accomplices. Dagaev then fled the country with his wife and transformed himself into Alexander Pell, the admired professor of mathematics at the University of South Dakota in the USA. Sudeikin had paid the price for his double dealing.

The Reforms of Alexander II

The Crimean War (see page 15) had confirmed how backward Russia was in comparison with some western European countries. To remedy this, Alexander II had introduced major reforms in Russia during his reign (1855–81).

- In 1861 he had emancipated (freed) the serfs.
- He had brought new ideas to the antiquated judicial system, including better trained independent judges, trial by jury, and Justices of the Peace who took over the judicial powers of the nobility in country districts.
- He started the process of modernising the army.
- He brought in a new form of local government – zemstva – town and district councils, which had some autonomy to manage their own affairs. The councils were elected but the vote was heavily weighted in favour of the nobles.
- He had reformed education, with primary and secondary schools open to a wider section of the population, and he gave greater independence to the universities.

Alexander was in no sense a liberal. He thought his reforms were the best way to maintain tsarist rule in Russia and prevent 'revolution from below'. However, for many in Russia the reforms did not go far enough and in the second part of his reign he had faced mounting criticism and unrest. When he was assassinated in 1881, his son, Alexander III, decided on a different course and Russia entered a period of repression and reaction.

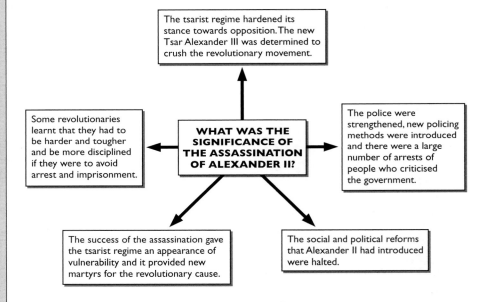

Alexander III

Alexander III represented the very image of an autocrat. He was 6ft 4ins tall, broad-shouldered and extremely strong. His favourite trick was to unbend horseshoes to amuse his children. When he came to the throne, he made it clear that he was going to affirm the principle of autocracy in no uncertain terms. On 29 April 1881, in The Manifesto on Unshakable Autocracy, he announced that the Tsar would 'rule with faith in the strength and truth of the autocratic power that we have been called upon to affirm and safeguard for the popular good from infringement.' He gave the impression of immense power and in this sense fulfilled the role of the autocrat perfectly. Unfortunately, he was limited in intellect and advised by a divided collection of ministers.

Repressive measures

Alexander III rejected his father's reforms as 'ill-advised, tantamount to revolution and pushing Russia on to the wrong road' and considered that they had contributed to his father's assassination. He 'would not grant Russia a constitution for anything on earth' and set about turning the clock back.

1 In 1881 The Statute of State Security was passed giving the government powers to:
   a) prohibit gatherings of more than 12 people
   b) prosecute any individual for political crimes
   c) introduce emergency police rule where public order was threatened
   d) set up special courts outside the legal system
   e) close schools, universities and newspapers.

   Most of these measures remained in force until 1917.
2 He brought in strict controls on the universities, reducing student freedom.
3 In 1890, the independence of the zemstva was reduced and control became more centralised. The number of people eligible to vote in elections was cut drastically, For instance, in Moscow and St Petersburg only 0.7 per cent of the population could vote.
4 Justices of the Peace, an important feature of the previous tsar's reforms, were abolished in 1889 and replaced in the countryside by Land Captains. These were members of the gentry chosen to control the peasants and were deeply resented.

Economic progress

A more progressive approach was adopted on the economy. Bunge, the finance minister and later Prime Minister, laid

Commissioned by Nicholas II, this statue was known as the 'Hippopotamus'. Rather than pull it down the Bolsheviks carved these lines on the pedestal:

'Their well-deserved hangman's fee
My son and sire received.
But, a spectre of ancient slavery,
I ride, through all eternity
Derided by humanity.'

down the basis for future development, encouraging railway building as an economic stimulus and using tariff protection to help several industries to grow. A factory inspectorate was introduced and peasants' redemption payments were reduced. He also established an income tax on businesses. At the end of the reign in 1892, Sergei Witte was appointed Finance Minister and took these policies forward to create the industrial boom of the 1890s (see page 15). Alexander had great faith in Witte, who in turn admired the Tsar.

11

WHAT WERE THE CHALLENGES FACING THE TSARIST REGIME AT THE END OF THE NINETEENTH CENTURY?

C Nicholas II – a new hope?

SOURCE 1.8 Tsar Nicholas II and Tsarina Alexandra and their family. On 14 August 2002, the Russian Orthodox Church canonised the Tsar and his family for bravery when they were executed by a Bolshevik firing squad in July 1918. They were placed on the lowest rung of the sainthood ladder, as 'passion-bearers'

Konstantin Pobedonostsev
Called 'the pace-setter of reaction' by liberals, Pobedonovstsev was a strong influence on Alexander III and Nicholas II as their tutor and Chief Procurator of the Holy Synod, the lay administrator of the Orthodox Church, and a key figure between 1881 and 1905. He was convinced that firmness was the essential characteristic of good government. He warned Alexander III: 'if the direction of policy passes to some kind of assembly, it will mean revolution and the end, not only of government, but of Russia itself.' He called representative democracy 'the great lie of our time'.

He was instrumental in driving Alexander III's repressive measures and the Russification policy (see page 19). He sought to re-educate the people by increasing the number of clergy, churches and church schools, particularly in the outlying parts of the Empire. He was deeply anti-Semitic and encouraged the fierce pogroms launched against the Jews during the 1880s. Alexander's government introduced measures restricting the political and economic activities of the Jews.

Nicholas II came to the throne in 1894, after his father had died unexpectedly, and lacked the training and experience for leadership. He admired his father greatly and was initially rather overwhelmed at the prospect of succeeding him. His private letters and diary are revealing. They provide evidence of his strong religious convictions and his deep affection for his wife and family (he had photographs of them everywhere, including the lavatory) but they also display a remarkable indifference to the world around him. He was deeply moved by the death of his favourite dog but the events of the 1905 revolution received little attention. He was charming and kind to those around him and could command respect and loyalty. He found it difficult to say unpleasant things to people to their face. However, he could also be vicious and merciless. He was very anti-Semitic and praised regiments that put down disorders. Nicholas was particularly attached to the army because of his upbringing and loved the superficialities of military life. He saw it as his personal domain and appointed grand dukes and members of his family to high positions. Often these were incompetents who damaged the army.

13

WHAT WERE THE CHALLENGES FACING THE TSARIST REGIME AT THE END OF THE NINETEENTH CENTURY?

SOURCE 1.9 This haunting image of Nicholas sitting on a tree stump after he had been deposed and the brutal death that he and his family suffered influence our view of him but these circumstances do not make him a good ruler

The problem for Nicholas was that he had to manage Russia through a time of major social and economic change. He was not really equipped for this. His many inadequacies have been well documented: his inability to make decisions; his unwillingness to engage in politics – even to read government reports; his lack of organisational skills ('Unfit to run a village post office' was the comment of an unknown cabinet minister); his weakness; his obstinacy. Yet it was his job to bring Russia into the twentieth century. Would he rule Russia in the same way as his father or would he embrace change and be prepared to modify the institutions of the autocracy?

From the beginning, he made his intentions clear: 'Let it be known to all that I shall devote all my strength, for the good of the whole nation, to maintaining the principle of autocracy just as firmly and unflinchingly as it was preserved by my unforgettable father.' Influenced by his tutor, Pobedonostsev, he believed that democracy, with its elections and parliaments, would bring about the collapse of the Russian Empire. Nicholas was ideologically incapable of accommodating the new middle class let alone a more demanding peasantry and working class.

AN UNFORTUNATE START

Nicholas II's reign got off to a bad start. In May 1896, during the celebrations that accompanied his coronation, 1400 people were killed and 600 injured in Khodynka Field. It seems there was a rush for free commemoration mugs, beer and food, which led to people being trampled and crushed. When, that evening, Nicholas went to a ball organised by the French ambassador, and joined in other coronation festivities, there was public outrage for his apparent lack of concern. He was dogged by this event throughout his reign and did not like to be reminded of his coronation.

What were the views of contemporaries and historians?

SOURCE 1.10 Dominic Lieven, *Nicholas II Emperor of all the Russias*, 1993, p. 52

Comparing the appearance of Nicholas II at his coronation with that of his father thirteen years before, Princess Radzivill remarked that, 'there, where a mighty monarch had presented himself to the cheers and acclamations of his subjects, one saw a frail, small, almost insignificant youth, whose imperial crown seemed to crush him to the ground, and whose helplessness gave an appearance of unreality to the whole scene.' His sister-in-law (Princess Victoria of Hesse) was to comment that 'his father's dominating personality had stunted any gifts of initiative in Nicky'.

SOURCE 1.11 Constantine Pobedonostsev, Nicholas II's tutor, quoted in Orlando Figes, *A People's Tragedy: The Russian Revolution 1891–1924*, 1997, p. 23

He only understands the significance of some isolated fact, without connection and with the rest, without appreciating the interrelation of all other pertinent facts, events, trends, occurrences. He sticks to his insignificant, petty point of view.

SOURCE 1.12 Leon Trotsky, *History of the Russian Revolution*, 1932–3, pp. 65–67

Nicholas II's ancestors did not bequeath him one quality which would have made him capable of governing an empire or even a province or a county . . . Nicholas recoiled in hostility before everything gifted and significant. He felt at ease only among completely mediocre and brainless people, saintly fakirs, holy men to whom he did not have to look up . . . This dim, equable and 'well-bred' man was cruel. At the dawn of his reign, Nicholas praised the Phanagoritsy regiment as 'fine fellows' for shooting down the workers. He always 'read with satisfaction' how they flogged with whips the bob-haired girl-students, or cracked the heads of defenceless people during Jewish pogroms.

14

WHAT WERE THE CHALLENGES FACING THE TSARIST REGIME AT THE END OF THE NINETEENTH CENTURY?

SOURCE 1.13 Orlando Figes, *A People's Tragedy: The Russian Revolution 1891–1924*, 1997, p. 23

Nicholas was the source of all the problems. If there was a vacuum of power at the centre of the ruling system, then he was the empty space. In a sense, Russia gained in him the worst of both worlds: a Tsar determined to rule from the throne yet quite incapable of exercising power. This was 'autocracy without an autocrat.' Perhaps nobody could have fulfilled the role which Nicholas had set himself: the work of government had become much too vast and complex for a single man; autocracy itself was out of date. But Nicholas was mistaken to try in the first place.

SOURCE 1.14 A. Ascher, *P. A. Stolypin: The Search for Stability in Late Imperial Russia*, 2001, pp. 92–3

A narrow-minded, prejudiced man, who was incapable of tolerating people who did not fit his conception of the true Russian. He disliked the national minorities, especially the Jews, and showed little sympathy for proposals to improve their status within the Empire. Nicholas had persuaded himself that all groups of the population except for the intelligentsia (whom he could not abide) were completely devoted to him. He lacked the personal drive and ambition to instil a sense of purpose and direction in the ministers and bureaucracy.

SOURCE 1.15 Dominic Lieven, *Nicholas II Emperor of all the Russias*, 1993, pp. 261–62

Nicholas II was not stupid. On the contrary, his problem tended to be that he could understand many points of view and wavered between them. The dangers Russia faced were very great . . . Nicholas loved his country and served it loyally and to the best of his ability. He had not sought power and he was not by temperament or personality very well equipped to wield it. He was a very kind, sensitive, generous and initially naive man. These traumatic years required something very different and would probably have destroyed any man who sat on the throne.

The Tsarina

Alexandra was never liked by the Russian people or the Russian court. She was born of a German royal house and was a Protestant. She converted to the Orthodox Church and threw herself into learning Russian customs and traditions. However, she was always regarded as an outsider – the 'German woman'. What made it worse was that she was shy and hated grand court occasions, preferring to remain at home with her family. She appeared cold and aloof. Unfortunately, her mother-in-law, Marie, loved court life, which continued to revolve around her. Alexandra kept away as often as she could.

She loved Nicholas and her family deeply and sought to create a private world, demanding that the Tsar spend the evenings with the family. More and more, the family retreated to their palace at Tsarskoe Selo just outside St Petersburg. Although shy, Alexandra was strong-willed and obstinate. She was also very religious. She believed firmly that the Tsar had been appointed by God to be the autocratic ruler of Russia. She was adamant that he should keep his powers and not share them with the people who were his servants. Her influence on him was great and not always helpful. At crucial moments she would always argue against any move towards constitutional monarchy and urge Nicholas to assert his autocratic will without regard for the constraints of the law.

ACTIVITY

Read sources 1.10, 1.11 and 1.12 from contemporaries:

1 What points emerge about Nicholas II as man and ruler from them?

2 To what extent do they agree?

3 How reliable are they for the historian assessing Nicholas II?

Read sources 1.13, 1.14 and 1.15 – historians' judgements of Nicholas II:

4 Which is the most and which is the least favourable to Nicholas II?

5 What view of the Tsar is each extract seeking to convey?

Using all the sources:

6 Which points made by the historians are supported by contemporaries?

TALKING POINT

Do you agree that the canonisation of Nicholas II and his family as martyrs tells us more about Russia in 2002 than about Nicholas II?

GREAT POWER STATUS

In 1815 Russia was the leading power in Europe. Napoleon's invasion in 1812 had been repulsed and the Russian army, the most powerful in the world, had liberated Europe. In 1814, Alexander I had ridden through Paris in triumph and had dominated the Congress of Vienna, which produced a settlement for Europe after twenty years of war. In the hundred years after 1815, maintaining great power status was a high priority for the Russians. However, defeat in the Crimean War (1854–56) was a huge blow to Russian prestige: Russia had been fighting on her own territory against Britain and France. The inadequacies of Russian rifles and supplies highlighted the shortcomings of her industry and communications. The case for modernisation was unanswerable and the reforms of Alexander II followed. Russia had prospective enemies to the west, south and east. The unification of Germany in 1871 created a potential threat from what was one of the fastest growing industrial states. To counter this threat, in 1891 Russia formed an alliance with France with the added bonus of French loans to help finance modernisation. Alec Nove points out that Witte's public statements and papers make it clear that the dominant motive behind his industrialisation policy was to allow Russia to catch up with the more developed powers 'particularly in her potential to produce the means of national power, above all armaments'.

D Modernisation

To be a great power in the twentieth century – and the Tsar and the ruling élite wanted their country to play a major role on the world stage – Russia had to modernise. It lagged far behind its Western competitors in industrial and technological capacity. It had to industrialise to have any hope of matching countries like the USA, Germany, Britain and France. A strong industrial base was needed to provide the weapons, ships, munitions and other military equipment required for modern warfare.

Russia also needed to modernise to raise the standards of living for ordinary people. It was a poor, backward country and had to increase its general wealth to bring the peasants out of poverty and take surplus labour off the overcrowded land and into the towns.

FOCUS ROUTE

As you go through this section fill out a table like the one below to evaluate the policies of Witte.

Policy	Arguments for	Criticisms of
State encouragement for heavy industry		
Massive expansion of railways		
Foreign loans, investment and expertise		
Strong rouble, adoption of gold standard		
High tariffs on foreign industrial goods		
Raised levels of taxation		

Industrialisation

Sergei Witte, Finance Minister from 1892 to 1903, was the architect of Russian industrialisation. Russia had huge reserves of oil, iron, coal and timber – the problem was how to exploit them. Witte believed that, because Russia was so far behind other countries, the state had to play a large role in stimulating industrial growth. He launched Russia into an age of heavy industry, using the railways as a springboard. Witte had 'a kind of holy passion for railways' and saw them as agents of civilisation and progress. The railways would not only provide better communications between cities for the movement of people and goods but they would also stimulate demand for iron, steel, coal and other industries. There was a railway boom in the 1890s and the extent of railway tracks nearly doubled:

Railway growth (in miles of track)	
1866	3,000
1881	13,270
1891	19,510
1900	33,270
1913	43,850

By the end of the 1890s, nearly 60 per cent of all iron and steel was consumed by the railways. Witte's most famous project was the Trans-Siberian Railway, which was of more symbolic than economic importance, although it did help to develop western Siberia.

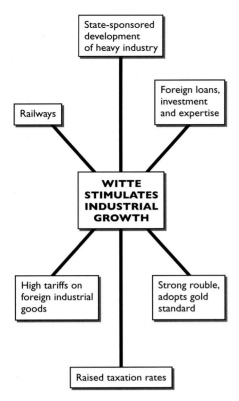

THE WELSH CONNECTION

In 1868, a Welsh businessman, John Hughes, took up a concession from the Russian government and bought land and mineral rights in the Donbass (part of the Ukraine). He sailed to Russia in 1870 accompanied by about 100 mostly Welsh ironworkers and miners. There he built a steel works and developed coal and iron ore mines. The settlement was called Yuzovka (Hughesovska). Hughes died in1889 but his sons took over and the works expanded rapidly in the 1890s. At the beginning of the twentieth century the population of Yuzovka had reached about 50,000 and it was the largest steel works in Russia and the showplace of the Witte era.

The government needed a lot of money to invest in the railways and in expensive capital equipment (machinery used to manufacture goods) in order to establish a sound engineering and manufacturing base. The big question was: where was the money going to come from? Witte came up with two sources:

1 foreign investment – he negotiated huge loans, particularly from the French. Also, to encourage the influx of foreign money, Witte adopted the gold standard, which meant that the rouble had a fixed gold content. This gave it strength when exchanged with other currencies. However, paying the interest rates to service foreign debt was a major drain on resources

2 the Russian people themselves, who of course were mainly peasants. He increased their direct taxes and also indirect taxes on everyday items such as salt, kerosene and alcohol. Peasants had to sell more grain to pay their taxes, which allowed Witte to increase grain exports. Also, to protect her developing industry, Russia imposed extremely high tariffs on foreign industrial commodities. This made many goods very expensive for Russians to buy – notably agricultural machinery. Workers' wages were kept low so that money went back into industrial development rather than into wage bills. He was squeezing the people very hard, especially the peasants, in order to pay the interest on the loans and protect fledgling industry.

The drive for industrialisation was a top down, state-sponsored model to an extent unequalled by any Western country. By 1899, the state had bought almost two thirds of all metallurgical production, controlled 70 per cent of the railways and owned numerous mines and oil fields. Critics argue that the emphasis on heavy industry meant that light industry, like textiles, was neglected, as was the development of smaller, sophisticated machine tool and electrical industries that would have reduced the need for imports and helped modernise manufacturing. Furthermore, Witte also neglected agriculture, which suffered from underinvestment.

Witte relied not only on foreign loans but also on foreign expertise. He brought in a large number of foreign companies, engineers and experts to help kick-start Russian industry into the modern age. They came from France, Britain, Germany, Sweden and other European countries. They were particularly evident in the new industrial areas in the south and the west, in the metallurgical industries of the Donbass, and in the oil industry around Baku. Witte encouraged the growth of private enterprise and, although his critics accused him of creating a dangerous and shameful dependence on foreigners, a new class of go-ahead Russian industrialists, entrepreneurs and businessmen began to emerge, especially in Moscow.

Witte hoped that industrial growth would take off and create more wealth for everyone before the squeeze on the workers and peasants hurt too much. Up to 1900, his plan seemed to be working. The growth in industry was remarkable. For example, between 1890 and 1900, the production of iron and steel had risen from 9 to 76 million poods a year (1 pood = 36.11 pounds); coal output tripled and the production of cotton cloth increased by two thirds. The growth rate in the 1890s hit nine per cent. Towns increased in size. By 1897, Moscow had one and a half million inhabitants and St Petersburg over two million. Moscow by the turn of the century was the fastest growing city east of New York and one of the ten biggest cities in the world.

ACTIVITY

Answer this question in a short essay of three to four paragraphs: Why was it important for Russia to modernise and why did this pose a threat to the tsarist regime?

The contradictions of modernisation

The dilemma for Nicholas II was that while modernisation was desirable in many respects, it also posed a serious threat to the tsarist regime.

- When millions moved from the countryside to the cities to work in factories there was bound to be an increase in social tensions and instability within society. The working classes, living and working in poor conditions, could become volatile and discontented. They would find it easier than the peasants to take concerted action because they were concentrated in large numbers in the cities.
- A more educated workforce (and Witte favoured the spread of technical education) would create people who were more able to challenge the government.
- The growth of the middle classes would create pressure for political change, for more accountable and representative government. Most modern industrial countries had democracies and parliaments in which the middle classes featured strongly and the power of monarchs was limited.

SOURCE 1.16   H. Rogger, *Russia in the Age of Modernisation and Revolution 1881–1917*, 1983, p. 108

Witte hoped and believed that industrialisation would transform Russian society, but to become industrialised Russia had first to be transformed. At the least both processes had to move at comparable speeds, but this demanded that the country, its people and indeed the world hold still, so to speak, for an unknown length of time while industry performed its work of transformation. Tranquillity at home and peace abroad were essential, and the former especially would be difficult to maintain in the midst of the strains to which the country was being subjected. Even if there had been a greater supply of political intelligence or flexibility on the part of Russia's rulers, industrialisation was bound to threaten political stability, and instability to endanger Witte's policies.

MODERNISATION 40 YEARS ON

Stalin, like Witte, faced the same problem of how to bring an underdeveloped Russia to the same level as the advanced nations. There are some similarities in their solutions. Both drove change from above, focusing on heavy industry and squeezing the peasants, though in Stalin's case infinitely harder. But there was a crucial difference: there was no foreign capital for Communist Russia. Witte would have appreciated why, as indicated in a memo he sent to the Tsar. 'What sense is there for foreign states to give us capital? Why create with their own hands an even more terrible rival? For me it is evident that, in giving us capital, foreign countries commit a political error, and my only desire is that their blindness should continue for as long as possible.'

Sergei Witte 1849–1915

Witte was born in Tiflis in Georgia in 1849 and spent his early years in the Caucasus. After graduating from the University of Odessa, he worked for the Odessa Railway and became an expert in railway administration. This led to his appointment in 1889 to the railway department of the Ministry of Finance. His growing reputation saw him soon promoted in 1892 to the post of Minister of Communications and then to Minister of Finance in 1893. It was in this role that he drove the push for industrialisation. He was by far the most able minister in the government and the best hope for the Tsar of peacefully modernising Russia before 1905. However, he was opposed by the more conservative elements in the government and court circles who would not support his programme for change – their antagonism and criticism contributed to his dismissal in 1903. He was an outsider with a background in business who was married to a Jewish divorcee and they did not trust or like him. This was in part because he was a difficult personality to deal with, described variously as tricky, evasive, boastful and quarrelsome. However, he was also very energetic, highly organised and, intellectually, towered above the officials and politicians of the time.

Although Witte was a firm supporter of the autocracy, by 1905 he had come to believe that some constitutional reform was necessary as part of the process of modernising Russia. Nicholas brought him back in the midst of the chaos of 1905 to negotiate a successful peace settlement with Japan to end the Russo-Japanese War. Witte was then made Prime Minister, in which role he secured vital loans that kept the regime from bankruptcy. He persuaded Nicholas to sign the October Manifesto granting concessions to the middle classes and establishing a duma or parliament. However, in 1906, when he discovered that Nicholas never intended to honour these concessions, he resigned. For his part, Nicholas never forgave Witte for pushing through constitutional change and Witte was ostracised from the Russian establishment until his death in 1915.

18

WHAT WERE THE CHALLENGES FACING THE TSARIST REGIME AT THE END OF THE NINETEENTH CENTURY?

FOCUS ROUTE

Make notes of the challenges facing the tsarist regime from different groups:
1 The peasants
2 The national minorities
3 The urban workers
4 The political opposition
   a) Liberals
   b) Socialist Revolutionaries
   c) Social Democrats

E Other challenges facing tsarist Russia

The government also faced challenges from four social groups: the peasants, the workers, the national minorities, and the intelligentsia from the middle classes and gentry.

1 The peasants

The peasants made up the vast bulk – almost 80 per cent – of the population. In the main, they were poor and life was hard and unremitting (see page 7). They harboured a whole raft of grievances dating back to their emancipation of 1861. Although they had been freed and given plots of land, the peasants were forced to pay for these by making yearly redemption payments to the government. Many could not afford the payments and were driven into debt. What made things worse was that the plots they had were often too small to make a reasonable living so many had to supplement their earnings by working on the estates of the nobility. This was exacerbated in the second half of the nineteenth century when a huge increase in population put even greater pressure on the land.

The peasants felt betrayed by the emancipation. They believed that the land really belonged to the people who worked it – them! They wanted the rest of the big estates to be given to them to work freely as independent land owners. There was always a threat of peasant uprisings, which made the tsarist regime unstable. These uprisings usually took place when harvests were bad and the peasants were starving; at these times they had little to lose.

The peasants were also subject to restrictions placed on them by their own village commune or 'mir' which could be a blessing and a curse. The mir was generally run on a co-operative basis and offered mutual support. Village assemblies were quite democratic allowing for views to be voiced before decisions were reached, although older or richer peasants tended to be more influential. It was an egalitarian institution in which strips of land were allotted to a household according to its size and this could be reviewed if the size of the household changed. Whilst fair, this did not usually lead to efficient agriculture (see below). The mir could be very restrictive. Peasants could not move freely from place to place without the mir's permission and could be flogged and imprisoned without trial. It found ways to punish those who did not toe the line, for instance it selected the conscripts for the army.

Agriculture was central to the development of the Russian economy. It was essential that it was modernised and mechanised in order to produce enough grain to feed the people of Russia and to sell abroad to earn foreign currency. Many peasants were still using the outdated strip system of farming with a few animals and antiquated tools, e.g. wooden ploughs. This led to subsistence farming rather than production for the market. The picture was not the same all over Russia. Some parts were doing well, particularly in the south and west. Recent evidence suggests that agriculture was in a much better state than historians had previously thought. It is argued that some more entrepreneurial peasants, called kulaks, were buying up and renting land from the nobility, experimenting with crops and cultivating market gardens to feed the expanding towns. There is also evidence to suggest that some communes were progressive and anxious to put new farming methods into practise. Agricultural output at the end of the nineteenth century was going up year on year.

2 The urban workers

Even by 1900, the urban workers only numbered around 3 million, 2.5 per cent of the population. Most of the workers were ex-peasants although by 1900 almost one third had fathers who had been workers in the mines or factories or on the railways. Many retained close links to their villages and often returned, particularly at harvest times, to work on the land.

Working conditions were grim. Long hours, normally over 11 hours a day but often longer, were compounded by a harsh environment where workers were disciplined and fined for the smallest infractions. Accidents, causing death or serious injury, were common and there was a high rate of disease and illness related to the conditions in the workplace. Wages were very low, barely enough to live on. Living conditions were no better. Large numbers of workers lived in barrack-style accommodation next to the factories or mines in which they worked. This was usually dirty and unsanitary. It was not unknown for workers coming off shift to get into the beds of the workers going on shift when the factories were kept going 24 hours a day. Privacy was a luxury, with men, women and children living alongside each other, separated only by a curtain – cooking, eating, sleeping and having sex. Others lived in huge tenement blocks where things were no better.

Although they did not form a large proportion of the population, the urban workers were militant and posed a real threat to the authorities. There were several reasons for this.

- They resented deeply the harsh conditions in which they found themselves, seeing themselves as slaves rather than workers.
- Exploitation was especially bad in small workshops that were not subject to government legislation.
- They had a high literacy rate (57.8 per cent) compared with the peasantry. They were able to read political literature and articulate their views and were generally more receptive to revolutionary ideas.
- A significant section of Russian industry was concentrated in large complexes and huge factories. This was partly because of the heavy state involvement and partly because, since Russia had been late to industrialise, it used the latest mass production techniques. Some factories, like the Putilov engineering works in St Petersburg, employed thousands of workers. This made it easier to organise politically and to create unity of purpose and action. If the workers from these big plants went on strike, thousands of people hit the streets.

There was a significant level of labour unrest in the 1890s. Although phenomenal industrial growth benefited some of the more skilled workers, not much of this new wealth found its way to the great mass of workers. St Petersburg, growing very fast, was also regarded as the most overcrowded and unhealthy city in Western Europe. The number of strikes increased in the last decade of the nineteenth century even though to participate in a strike could lead to a prison sentence of one to three weeks. The textile workers in St Petersburg mounted massive strikes in 1896 and 1897.

3 The national minorities and Russification

Many of the nationalities in the Russian Empire resented Russian control, particularly the policy of Russification that had been imposed more rigorously in the second part of the nineteenth century. It was promoted by Alexander III and carried on by Nicholas II. This policy involved making non-Russians use the Russian language instead of their own and adopt Russian customs and habits. Russian officials were brought in to run regional governments in non-Russian parts of the Empire like Poland, Latvia and Finland. The Russian language was used in schools, law courts and regional government. For instance, in Poland, it was forbidden to teach children in the Polish language. Poles could not be employed in government positions. Usually it was Russians who got the important jobs in government and state sponsored industry. What made it worse was that the minorities had to pay large sums to the imperial treasury.

The emphasis on the superiority of the Russian way of life infuriated the national minorities who saw Russification as a fundamental attack on their way of life, their national and cultural heritage, and a monstrously unfair policy that discriminated against them. This was especially true in respect of religion. The Catholic Church in Poland, the Georgian Orthodox Church, the Lutherans in Lithuania and other religious sects all resented government interference in their religious practices. The Jews, who formed a sizeable ethnic group, were forced to live in an area known as the Pale of Settlement. They suffered from a deliberate policy of anti-Semitism which placed social, political and economic restrictions upon them. Encouraged by the authorities, they were subject to

19

WHAT WERE THE CHALLENGES FACING THE TSARIST REGIME AT THE END OF THE NINETEENTH CENTURY?

20

WHAT WERE THE CHALLENGES FACING THE TSARIST REGIME AT THE END OF THE NINETEENTH CENTURY?

frequent pogroms – organised attacks on their homes and businesses by ultra-conservative nationalists.

During the nineteenth century there were a number of uprisings and protests from national groups seeking greater personal freedom and more autonomy (self-government) in their parts of the empire. These tended to occur in one region at a time and the tsarist government was able to suppress them. It seems strange that the government sought to antagonise and alienate such a large section of its population. It drove many into the ranks of the revolutionaries. For instance, many Jews were found in revolutionary groups and in 1897 they formed their own 'Bund' or union.

4 Political opposition

Substantial opposition had grown towards tsarism during the later part of the nineteenth century. Amongst the Russia intelligentsia (writers, artists, philosophers and political activists), many believed the regime was oppressive and that Russians lacked basic freedoms present in Western European countries. Some felt that change could be achieved through reform; others that the only way to bring change to Russia was to overthrow the tsarist regime by revolution.

THE LIBERALS

The liberal movement had grown significantly after the local government reforms of Alexander II in 1864, which had set up town and district councils called zemstva (singular zemstvo). These gave local areas a small degree of autonomy to run their own affairs, manage schools and hospitals, build and maintain roads, etc. These councils had proved to be very effective and created a class of people who became skilled in local politics. This included liberal leaning members of the Russian nobility as well as representatives of the middle classes, many of whom worked for the zemstva, including Chekhov (the playwright) who was employed as a doctor. They gained a taste for greater participation in government. The zemstva have been called 'the seedbeds of liberalism'.

The idea of 'liberalism' prevalent in Western Europe was not very Russian and it took a different form in Russia. What Russian liberals agreed on was that reform rather than violence was the way to change the tsarist system and limit the tsar's powers. Many others wanted an extension of freedoms and rights (see right). Before 1905, there was no liberal party to

speak of. Liberalism took on a more organised form at the beginning of the twentieth century. In 1903, the Union of Liberation was formed demanding economic and political reform. The Liberals were the major opposition to tsarism before 1905 and indeed up to the 1917 revolution.

Main beliefs: civil rights and freedom of the individual, the rule of law, free elections, parliamentary democracy and limitation of the tsar's powers, and self-determination for the national minorities. Some believed that the concept of the zemstvo should be extended to regional and perhaps national level.

Methods: reform rather than violent action, political channels through zemstva, articles in newspapers, meetings and reform banquets.

Support: they did not have a large popular base and had few active supporters outside Moscow, Petrograd and a few other large cities. Their main support came from the middle class intelligentsia: lawyers, doctors, professors, teachers, engineers and other professional groups. They also had support amongst progressive landowners, industrialists and businessmen.

REVOLUTIONARIES
Populism and The People's Will

In the later part of the nineteenth century, the main revolutionary movement was Populism. Populists put their trust in and sought support from ordinary people. From the 1860s to the 1880s the populists or Narodniks, largely well-to-do intellectuals, believed that the peasants in Russia could develop their own form of socialism. Life would be based around co-operation and sharing in peasant communes on a fairly small scale. This would avoid capitalism and the evils of industrialisation. However, it was not really clear how this would be achieved and did not amount to a coherent programme. They believed in 'going to the people' and spreading their socialist ideals to the peasantry by peaceful propaganda. Many populists, particularly students and young people, did

'go to the people' in the 1870s, moving out to the countryside to live with peasants and convince them of their revolutionary potential. But the peasants had nothing in common with these middle class youngsters with their strange ideas and rejected them.

After the failure to get a response from the people, in 1879 some Populists formed The People's Will. Peaceful propaganda gave way to violent action – they turned to terrorism to bring down the tsarist regime. Their most spectacular success was the assassination of Alexander II (see page 4). This prompted a fierce reaction from the tsarist regime and led to a period of repression. The People's Will and Populism in general helped create a revolutionary tradition and more directly gave birth to the Socialist Revolutionary Party.

THE SOCIALIST REVOLUTIONARIES (SRs)

The Socialist Revolutionary Party, formed in 1901, was a loose organisation accommodating groups with a wide variety of views and did not hold its first congress until 1906. It was never well co-ordinated or centrally controlled. There was a split between moderates and radicals (who supported extreme terrorism) that persisted into the 1917 revolution.

Main beliefs: SRs placed their central hope for revolution with the peasants who would provide the main support for a popular rising in which the tsarist government would be overthrown and replaced by a democratic republic. Land would be taken from landlords and divided up amongst the peasants. Unlike the populists, the SRs accepted that the development of capitalism was a fact. The leading exponent of their views was Victor Chernov. He accepted that the growth of capitalism would promote the growth of a proletariat (working class) who would rise against their masters. But he saw no need for the peasants to pass through capitalism; he believed they could move

straight to a form of rural socialism based on the peasant commune that already existed. He saw SRs as representing 'all labouring people'.

Methods: Agitation and terrorism, including assassination of government officials.

Support: Peasants provided a large popular base but by 1905 industrial workers formed perhaps 50 per cent of the membership. This is probably because many workers were recently arrived ex-peasants who recognised the SR Party and supported its aims of land and liberty. Most had regular contact with their villages. It also attracted intellectuals who wanted to make contact with the mass of the population. The SRs often bemoaned their lack of strength in villages because most SR committees were run by students and intellectuals in towns and communication was difficult. Most peasants could not read the leaflets the SRs produced. Nevertheless they were the party the peasants recognised as representing them, especially its pledge to return the land 'to those who worked it'.

The Marxists

In the 1880s, it seemed to some Russian intellectuals that there was no hope of a revolutionary movement developing amongst the peasantry. Instead they turned to the latest theories of a German philosopher, Karl Marx. The 'scientific' nature of Marxism appealed to them – it was an optimistic theory which saw progress through the development of industry and the growth of the working class to the ultimate triumph of socialism. Marxist reading circles developed and societies and groups were formed. They believed in action and soon became involved in organising strikes in factories. The working class, not the peasants, were the key to the revolution. See chart 1E on pages 22–23.

Karl Marx (1818–83)

Marx was a German philosopher who spent the last years of his life in London. He wrote the *Communist Manifesto* which encouraged workers to unite to seize power by revolution. He also wrote *Das Kapital* which explained his view of history. His views became known as 'Marxism' and influenced the thinking of socialists throughout Europe in the late nineteenth and twentieth centuries.

Marxism

Marxism was attractive because it seemed to offer a 'scientific' view of history, similar to the evolutionary theories of Charles Darwin. According to Marx, history was evolving in a series of stages towards a perfect state – Communism. Each stage was characterised by the struggle between different classes. This was a struggle over who owned the 'means of production' (resources used to produce food, goods, and so on) and so controlled society. In each stage, Marx identified a ruling class of 'haves' who owned the means of production and exploited an oppressed class of 'have-nots' who sweated for them for little reward. He saw change as being brought about by a revolutionary class who would develop and contest power with the existing ruling class. Economic change and development (economic forces) would bring this new class to the fore and eventually allow it to overthrow the ruling class in a revolution (see Chart 1E on pages 22–23).

Marx was a determinist: he thought that there were certain forces (economic forces, e.g. changes in technology) driving history which would lead to the changes he predicted. However, he did give individuals a role in history. He believed that they could affect the course of events, though not the general pattern: 'Men make their own history but do not make it just as they please; they do not make it under circumstances chosen by themselves but under circumstances directly encountered, given or transmitted from the past.'

His theory gave middle-class revolutionaries an important role in that they saw what the true nature of history was and could help to bring it about.

Marx did not think his theories were the final word and he did not think all countries would go through the pattern described; he thought it applied particularly to countries in Western Europe. He expected that experience would lead to changes in his theories; he even had a name for this – *praxis*.

FEUDALISM

Government: Absolute monarchy

Means of production: Land; land ownership gives power.

Social organisation: Aristocracy is the dominant group controlling the mass of the population – peasants – who work on their estates. Peasants are virtually owned by their lords and masters.

Revolutionary change: The revolutionary class is the middle class (merchants, traders, manufacturers). As this group gets wealthier, it begins to break down the rules of feudal society which hinder its development, e.g. wants an economy based on money and labourers free to work in towns.

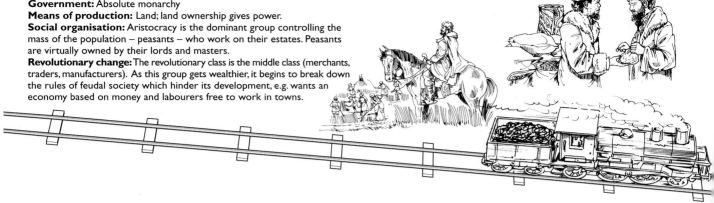

COMMUNISM

Government: There is no state, just people who are interested in managing the day-to-day business of keeping society going.

Social organisation: Everybody is equal. There is an abundance of goods produced by machinery rather than by workers' labour, so everyone has much more leisure time. People work on the principle, 'From each, according to their ability, to each according to their needs' – they take out what they need from a central pool and contribute to society in whatever way they can. (Marx's view of Communist society is not very clear.)

THE TRANSITION TO COMMUNISM
The need for government declines because there are no competing classes.

SOCIALISM

Government: Workers control the state. At first, government is exercised through the **dictatorship of the proletariat**, a period of strict control necessary to deal with counter-revolution (old capitalist enemies trying to recover power) and to root out non-socialist attitudes.

Means of production: Factories, machines, etc., as in the capitalist period but not owned by individuals. They are owned collectively by everybody.

Social organisation: Everybody is equal, the class system is brought to an end. Wealth and goods produced by industry are shared out fairly. Everybody has an equal entitlement to good housing and decent standards of living.

BOURGEOIS (MIDDLE-CLASS) REVOLUTION

The growth of trade and industry sees the middle classes becoming larger and more powerful. Eventually, they want to reshape society and government to suit their interests, e.g. they want to have a say in how the country is run and do not want landed aristocrats determining national policy. The middle classes take power from the monarch and aristocracy. The bourgeois revolution can be violent, as in France in 1789, or more peaceful and gradual, as in Britain during the eighteenth and nineteenth centuries.

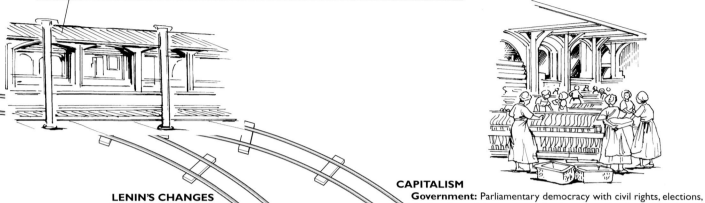

CAPITALISM

Government: Parliamentary democracy with civil rights, elections, freedom of the press, etc., but largely run by the middle classes.

Means of production: Industrial premises, factories, capital goods like machinery, banks owned by **capitalists**. Land becomes less important as industry and trade create greater share of national wealth.

Social organisation: Middle classes or **bourgeoisie** are the dominant or ruling class although the aristocracy may still hold on to some positions of power and prestige. The mass of the population move from being peasants to being industrial workers – the **proletariat**, who are forced to work long hours in poor conditions for little reward.

Revolutionary change: As capitalism grows so does the proletariat, since more workers are needed to work in factories and commercial premises. Great wealth and material goods are produced, but these are not shared out fairly. A small bourgeoisie gets increasingly wealthy while the proletariat remains poor. Gradually, the proletariat develops a class consciousness and realises that it is being oppressed as a class.

LENIN'S CHANGES TO MARXIST THEORY (MARXISM–LENINISM)

1 Revolution would be accomplished by a small group of highly professional, dedicated revolutionaries. They were needed to develop the revolutionary consciousness of workers and focus their actions.

2 Lenin believed that the revolution would occur during a period of conflict between capitalist powers. He accepted Trotsky's 'weakest link' theory – revolution would start in an underdeveloped country (just like Russia) where the struggle and conflict between proletariat and bourgeoisie was very great, then spread to more advanced industrial countries.

3 He did not think that the middle classes in Russia were strong enough to carry through a bourgeois-democratic revolution. He believed that the working class could develop a revolutionary government of its own in alliance with poor peasants who had a history of mass action in Russia – the bourgeois and socialist revolution could be rolled into one.

SOCIALIST REVOLUTION

The proletariat moves from class consciousness to a revolutionary consciousness aided by revolutionary leaders (often from the middle classes). They now form the great bulk of the population whilst the bourgeoisie are a tiny minority. They rise up and seize power, ousting their class enemies – the bourgeoisie. The socialist revolution starts in a highly industrialised country.

THE SOCIAL DEMOCRATS (SDs)

In 1898, Marxists formed the Russian Social Democratic Labour Party. The leading light was George Plekhanov who had translated Karl Marx's work into Russian. However, some people found him a little too intellectual and not revolutionary enough. There were serious disputes about the direction of the party. Some wanted to encourage trade unions to improve the conditions of the workers. Others wanted the focus to be on revolutionary tactics and the preparation of the working class for revolution.

At the Second Party Congress in 1903, the SDs split into two factions – the Bolsheviks (Majoritarians)

and the Mensheviks (Minoritarians). This was largely caused by the abrasive personality of Vladimir Ulyanov or Lenin (see page 26) who was determined to see his idea of the revolutionary party triumph. During the congress the votes taken on various issues showed the two groups were roughly equal. But in a particular series of votes Lenin's faction came out on top (mainly because some delegates had walked out of the conference) and he jumped on the idea of calling his group the majority party (Bolsheviki) which gave them a stronger image. In fact, until 1917, they always had fewer members that the Mensheviks for reasons that will become apparent below.

Main beliefs: Both factions accepted the main tenets of Marxism but they were split over the role of the party.

Bolsheviks

Lenin believed that a revolutionary party should:
- be made up of a small number of highly disciplined professional revolutionaries
- operate under centralised leadership
- have a system of small cells (made up of three people) so that it would be more difficult for the police to infiltrate.

It was the job of the party to bring socialist consciousness to the workers and lead them through the revolution. Critics warned that a centralised party like this would lead to dictatorship.

Mensheviks

They believed that the party should:
- be broadly based and take in all those who wished to join
- be more democratic, allowing its members to have a say in policy making
- encourage trade unions to help the working class improve their conditions.

Mensheviks took the Marxist line that there would be a long period of bourgeois democratic government during which the workers would develop a class and revolutionary consciousness until they were ready to take over in a socialist revolution.

Support: Their support came mainly from the working class. The Bolsheviks tended to attract younger more militant peasant workers who liked the discipline, firm leadership and simple slogans. The Mensheviks tended to attract different types of workers and members of the intelligentsia, also a broader range of people – more non-Russians, especially Jews and Georgians.

25

WHAT WERE THE CHALLENGES FACING THE TSARIST REGIME AT THE END OF THE NINETEENTH CENTURY?

ACTIVITY

1 Sources 1.17–1.20 contain views and ideas associated with the various parties.
   a) Identify the party.
   b) Explain what points about the party the writer of each source is making.
2 Source 1.21 has a very different message. What warning does it contain and for which party?

SOURCE 1.17

And thus I confirm that:

1 no revolutionary movement can be firm without a solid and authoritative organisation of leaders;

2 that the wider the masses spontaneously drawn into the struggle, acting as a basis of the movement and participating in it, all the more urgent is the necessity of such an organisation . . . ;

3 that such an organisation should consist primarily of people who are professional revolutionaries;

4 that in an autocracy, the more we restrict the membership of such an organisation to those who are professional revolutionaries and who received professional training in the art of struggle against the political parties, the harder it will be to 'draw out' such an organisation.

SOURCE 1.18

Fundamental Civil Rights

1 All Russian citizens, irrespective of sex, religion or nationality, are equal before the law . . .

2 Each citizen shall have freedom of conscience and religious belief . . .

3 Each individual is free to express himself orally, in writing and in published works . . . censorship will be abolished . . .

The state structure

1 Popular representatives shall be elected by universal, direct, equal and secret ballot . . .

2 No resolution, regulation, edict or similar act can become law without the approval of the representatives . . .

3 Ministers are responsible to the assembly of popular representatives.

SOURCE 1.19

A great peasant upheaval must come, such as would enable the peasantry to confiscate all land not already held by the communes. The land would be socialised and made available to the peasant toiler in accordance with his needs. The peasants might either become members of a co-operative or till the soil as small 'proprietors' . . .

The combat organisation ought first to disorganise the enemy; second, terrorism would serve as a means of propaganda and agitation, a form of open struggle taking place before the eyes of the whole people, undermining the prestige of government authority.

SOURCE 1.20

A man can be sincerely devoted to a cause but quite unsuited for a strongly centralised militant organisation consisting of professional revolutionaries. For this reason the party of the proletariat must not limit itself to the narrow framework of a conspiratorial organisation because then hundreds, and even thousands, of proletarians would be left outside the party. We can only be glad if every striker, every demonstrator . . . can describe himself as a party member.

SOURCE 1.21 Leon Trotsky, *Our Political Tasks,* 1904

In the internal politics of the party these methods lead, as we shall yet see, to this: the party organisation is substituted for the party, the central committee is substituted for the party organisation, and finally a 'dictator' is substituted for the central committee.

26

WHAT WERE THE CHALLENGES FACING THE TSARIST REGIME AT THE END OF THE NINETEENTH CENTURY?

Lenin

Vladimir Ilyich Ulyanov, later known as Lenin, was born in Simbirsk in 1870 into a privileged professional family. His father was a Chief Inspector of Schools, his mother the daughter of a doctor and a landowner. They were a family of mixed ethnic origin (Jewish, Swedish, German and Tartar) and Lenin may not have had much Russian blood in his ancestry. According to Robert Service in *Lenin, A Biography* (2000), new archival evidence about Lenin's early life suggests he was a raucous, self-centred little boy who gave his brothers and sisters a hard time. He had tantrums and would beat his head on the floor. However, he was a gifted school pupil, doing exceptionally well in exams.

Service suggests that the Ulyanovs were a self-made, upwardly mobile family, anxious to succeed. However, the involvement of Lenin's elder brother in a plot to assassinate Tsar Alexander III saw the family ostracised: people refused to speak to them. Service thinks that Lenin may have learned to hate at this time. Certainly he was deeply affected by his brother's execution and seemed, by some accounts, to have become harder and more disciplined.

Lenin went on to university at Kazan where he studied law and soon became involved in student revolt. This led to his expulsion but he was eventually allowed to sit his exams and, for a short time, practised as a lawyer. He was becoming more interested in revolutionary ideas and, after flirting with populism, was drawn to the scientific logic of Marxism.

In 1893, he moved to St Petersburg and joined Marxist discussion groups where he met his future wife, Nadezhda Krupskaya. He became involved in propaganda for a strike movement in 1895 and was arrested. He spent the next four years first in prison and then in exile in Siberia, where he married Krupskaya, a kind of revolutionary working relationship, and enjoyed with her possibly the happiest years of his life, writing, walking and hunting.

After his release from exile in 1900, Lenin moved to London with Krupskaya. He founded a newspaper, *Iskra* ['The Spark'], with his friend Martov (Julius Tsederbaum). He wanted to establish it as the leading underground revolutionary paper which would drive forward the revolutionary movement. In 1902, he published his pamphlet *What Is To Be Done?* which contained his radical ideas about the nature of a revolutionary party (see right). He wanted to put forward his ideas at the Second Congress of the Social Democratic Party which met in 1903 (first in Brussels and then in London). His abrasive personality helped to cause the split in the party into Bolsheviks and Mensheviks. He lost control of *Iskra* to the Mensheviks.

The Bolsheviks played a relatively minor role in the 1905 revolution and Lenin returned to St Petersburg only in October. But when the revolution failed, he left for exile abroad once more. The years from 1906 to 1917 were frustrating. There were arguments and splits in the Bolshevik Party and membership collapsed. Lenin seemed destined to remain a bit player in history.

Political theorist

Lenin is regarded as an important political theorist. The body of his work, including adaptations of Marxist theory, has been called Marxism–Leninism. But he really saw his writings as plans for action. His principal writings include:

- *What Is To Be Done?* (1902) – here he argued for his idea of a revolutionary party:
  - it was to be highly centralised; a clear line of policy would be laid down by the central committee of the party
  - there would be a network of agents who would be 'regular permanent troops'
  - it would be a small, conspiratorial party made up of professional, dedicated revolutionaries
  - it would act as the vanguard of the working class who would not attain a revolutionary consciousness without clear guidance from the revolutionary élite.

  Lenin encouraged the individual revolutionary to be hard with himself and others to achieve his aims; there was no room for sentiment.
- *Imperialism: the Highest Stage of Capitalism* (1916) – here he claimed that capitalism was a bankrupt system and would collapse in a series of wars between capitalist countries over resources and territory. This would lead to civil war and class conflict within countries, which would facilitate the socialist revolution. This could start in a relatively undeveloped country – the weakest link in the capitalist chain – and then spread to other industrialised countries. Russia seemed to be this weakest link.
- *The State and Revolution* (1917) – this book discussed what the state would be like after revolution and dismissed the need for constitutional government. Existing state structures should be taken over and smashed by revolutionaries. The transformation of the economy and society would be relatively easy – the spontaneous will of the people would support revolution and they would play a large part in managing their own affairs in industry and agriculture.

27

WHAT WERE THE CHALLENGES FACING THE TSARIST REGIME AT THE END OF THE NINETEENTH CENTURY?

REVOLUTIONARY NAMES

Many of the revolutionaries adopted pseudonyms or aliases to protect their families and confuse the tsar's secret police so that they would have trouble tracking down their associates. Vladimir Ulyanov's pseudonym 'Lenin' was probably derived from the River Lena in Siberia and was first used in 1901. The name Trotsky was taken from a prison guard during Trotsky's escape from Siberia in 1902. Other well-known pseudonyms are Stalin meaning 'Man of Steel' which Joseph Dzhugashvili was supposed to have acquired whilst in prison camps; Martov (Julius Tsederbaum) leader of the Mensheviks; and Parvus (Alexander Helphand).

Trotsky

Lev Bronstein was born in 1879 in the Ukraine, the son of a well-to-do Jewish farmer. He had a flair for writing and for foreign languages. He, too, was dissatisfied with the society he lived in, particularly its treatment of Jews. He was drawn to Marxism in his teens and had joined a Marxist discussion group by the age of sixteen. He fell in love with the leader of the group, Alexandra Sokolovska, and they were soon involved in inciting strikes. They were both arrested in 1900, got married in prison and were exiled together to Siberia. Aided by his wife, he escaped dramatically in 1902 by using a false passport signed with the name of a prison warder – Leon Trotsky.

Arriving in Paris he met a young Russian art student, Natalia Sedova. He was to live with her for the rest of his life and have two sons by her. He soon made the journey to London, where he got on well with Lenin and his wife Krupskaya, who were busy writing and editing the Social Democratic journal, *Iskra*. They admired his writing skills, giving Trotsky the nickname 'The Pen'. But at the 1903 Social Democratic conference he would not side with Lenin. He prophesied that Lenin's concept of a revolutionary party would lead inevitably to dictatorship. He remained in the Social Democratic Party somewhere between the Bolsheviks and Mensheviks but not in either camp.

He first made his mark in the 1905 revolution, where his oratorical talents led to his becoming deputy chairman of the St Petersburg Soviet. His subsequent arrest and escape established his credibility in revolutionary circles. His analysis of the situation in Russia moved closer to Lenin's when, with 'Parvus' (Alexander Helphand), he developed the theory of the weakest link (see page 23) concerning the weakness of the Russian bourgeoisie and how revolution might begin. He was in the USA when the revolution broke and arrived back to find the Mensheviks collaborating with the Provisional Government. This horrified him as much as it did Lenin and it was not long before he threw in his lot with the Bolshevik Party. Like Lenin, he was anxious for a workers' government to be put in place at the earliest possible opportunity.

KEY POINTS FROM CHAPTER 1

What were the challenges facing the tsarist regime at the end of the nineteenth century?

1 Tsarist Russia was a vast country with a diverse population, making it a very difficult country to govern.

2 Russia was an autocracy, ruled by a tsar who was at the head of a large, unresponsive and inefficient bureaucracy.

3 The tsars used repressive measures and secret police to keep control.

4 Russia needed to modernise and industrialise if it was to compete with the developed countries of Western Europe and maintain its position as a major world power.

5 The task of modernising Russia was one that even the most able leader would have found difficult. Nicholas II was not a good leader for these circumstances – he was not able, competent or decisive. He had little idea of the needs of his subjects. He resisted change and tried to preserve as much of the autocracy as he could.

6 Sergei Witte set in motion a process of modernisation but he was forced from office by conservative court influences and the problems engendered by rapid industrialisation and then recession.

7 Tsarist Russia faced challenges from different groups in Russia: the peasants, urban workers, national minorities and the intelligentsia engaged in forming political opposition to the government. All these groups had different and specific demands which the tsars were not able or willing to accommodate.

CHAPTER OVERVIEW

At the beginning of the twentieth century, Russia was unsettled and volatile. This instability was heightened by an economic depression, which started after 1900, and a war with Japan in 1904. Opposition to the Tsar was growing stronger, particularly from the liberal intelligentsia. At the beginning of 1905, when feelings were running high, the murder of protestors on 9 January, 'Bloody Sunday', led to an explosion of popular discontent. For over a year Russia was out of control and the survival of the tsarist regime was threatened. The Tsar survived mainly because the army remained loyal and he made concessions. There followed a period of brutal suppression that changed the relationship between the Tsar and his people.

A What were the causes of the revolution of 1905? (pp. 28–32)

B The 1905 revolution (pp. 32–39)

C Why did the Tsar survive the 1905 revolution? (pp. 39–42)

D Interpreting 1905 (pp. 42–45)

A What were the causes of the revolution of 1905?

FOCUS ROUTE

1 Make notes on the following key factors that pushed Russia into revolution in 1905:
   a) rapid social and economic change
   b) economic depression
   c) failure of government attempts to improve conditions for workers
   d) Russo-Japanese War
   e) increasing opposition from the liberal intelligentsia.
2 Collect evidence/information which tells you about:
   a) whether 1905 was a popular revolution
   b) the role of revolutionary parties
   c) whether it deserves to be called a 'revolution'.

In the last decade of the nineteenth century, Russia was experiencing rapid social and economic change. As the economy grew, peasants poured into overcrowded cities and towns to take up industrial jobs. Living conditions were squalid, pay was low and hours were long. Militancy amongst workers was evident in strikes throughout the 1890s. In rural areas, some peasants were prospering but most still lived in poverty under burdensome restrictions and there were frequent disturbances and outbreaks of violence. The only response the government could come up with to deal with these expressions of discontent was repression.

The nature of civil society in Russia was changing. The nobility did not have the firm hold on the countryside they once had. They were selling their estates and renting land to enterprising peasants. Many were moving to the cities and their children were entering the liberal professions. Ex-peasants could become landowners and merchants. A new class of businessmen was emerging, looking hard at how the government managed its affairs. The zemstva had been active in towns and a growing class of professional people believed they should play

SOURCE 2.1 Extract from a letter sent to the Tsar in 1902 by Leo Tolstoy concerning the state of the nation at the beginning of the century. Quoted in M. Ferro, *Nicholas II, The Last of the Tsars*, 1990, pp. 73–4

One third of Russia is under a regime of reinforced surveillance... The army of policemen, regular and secret, grows continually. The prisons and places of deportation are filled with persons sentenced for political reasons, not to mention the hundreds of thousands of ordinary prisoners to whom the workers must now be added. The censorship has attained a level of oppressiveness unknown even in the abominable period of the 1840s. Religious persecution has never been so frequent and so cruel, and grows worse every day. Troops with weapons loaded ready to fire on the people have been sent into every city... And the peasants, all one hundred million of them, are getting poorer every year... Famine has become a normal phenomenon. Normal likewise is the discontent of all classes of society with the government.

Alexis de Tocqueville (1805–59) French political thinker and historian, best known for his book *Democracy in America* (1835).

BOSSES AND WORKERS

Historian Beryl Williams points out that many industrial enterprises were run along paternalistic lines, with bosses 'seeing themselves as father figures to their workforce rather than employers'. It seems that many workers before 1905 co-operated with employers they saw as 'good'. They protested against undignified treatment by supervisors and managers and wanted better conditions and opportunities for education. Williams adds: 'The vast majority of workers before 1905 never saw a revolutionary.'

a more active part in running society. But the government would not work with them, dismissing hundreds of liberals from the zemstva in 1900. The liberal intelligentsia were tired of this backward and cumbersome regime and began to think in terms of civil rights rather than service to the Tsar. During 1899–1901 in St Petersburg, Moscow and other cities, after brutal police suppression, student disturbances resulted in the closure of universities and higher education institutions.

It is in this unsettled situation that we can look for the explanation of the 1905 revolution. Alexis de Tocqueville commented that revolutions tend to happen in times of rapid change when things are improving and expectations are rising. What makes the situation especially revolutionary is when things take a turn for the worse and those expectations are frustrated. In Russia, things certainly took a turn for the worse.

From 1900, Russia entered a deep depression brought on by an international recession. All areas of the economy were affected. Any gains that might have been made by the industrial workers were wiped out by the slump. Wages fell and there was increasing unemployment. The areas that had been growing fast were the areas that were particularly hard hit: in the Donbass region, by 1903, only 23 of the 35 blast furnaces were working and mines were closing. There was also a slump in the oil industry. The railway industry was badly hit and the metal working industry in St Petersburg suffered from falling government orders resulting in the closure of many small firms. In 1902 and 1903, across Russia there was growing worker discontent and industrial action. The peasants were also affected. A poor harvest in 1901 against a backdrop of increasing rents led to a peasant revolt in 1902–3. Many ex-peasant workers went back to their villages to join the revolt. There was an air of growing internal disorder.

Amidst this turmoil, the revolutionary parties – the Social Democrats and Socialist Revolutionaries – were taking shape (see pages 20–24). However, it would be wrong to think that the parties recruited workers and peasants in large numbers (see Bosses and Workers below). The workers were more likely to join trade unions set up by the police (see below). The peasants in the countryside were not rushing to sign up to the SRs. In fact, it is now acknowledged that the SR Party was an urban rather than a rural party at this time. It was newly urbanised peasants and students who were attracted to their programme of armed struggle and terrorism.

Police trade unions

Sergei Zubatov, head of the Moscow Okhrana, believed that repressive measures alone could not combat the appeal of socialism and the spread of revolutionary ideas. The workers had to be convinced that their lives could be improved within the existing system. He thought this could be achieved by giving them trades unions and educational and self-help organisations – supervised and partially funded by the police. Starting in 1901, Zubatov set up three unions in Moscow, which submitted demands to their employers who were then pressured by police representatives into making concessions to the workers. The Zubatov movement spread rapidly across the south and west of the Empire in towns like Odessa. It provided workers with a mechanism to voice their criticism and demands legally. Concerned by his success, *Iskra*, the revolutionary newspaper, denounced Zubatovism, saying: 'It was more terrible to us than is police brutality.' Some of the government and the business community were also not keen, fearing the unions would politicise the workers and harm the economy irreparably. When, in 1903, a strike organised by police unions in Odessa escalated into a general strike, Zubatov was dismissed.

Historians have differing views on Zubatov's programme. Chris Read regards it as a government own goal, one of the self-inflicted blows that caused the 1905 revolution: 'Wherever they were set up, Zubatov unions became a cover for radicals and blew up in the face of their sponsors.' However, Jeremiah Scheidermann points out that it was the only coherent labour policy coming from government quarters.

SOURCE 2.2 A cartoon drawn during the Russo-Japanese war. The sailor is saying: 'Oh you funny Japs, always making mistakes. Thank you for the badly aimed shells which help me light my pipe!'

ACTIVITY

1 What does Source 2.2 reveal about the Russian attitude towards the Japanese?
2 How might this help explain why the war started?

The Russo-Japanese War 1904–5

By the end of 1903, the situation in Russia was volatile and potentially explosive. And then war was added to the mix.

The war with Japan arose out of Russia's expansionist policy in the Far East. Russia wanted to exploit the area because it was rich in resources and markets. It also wanted control of the ice-free port of Port Arthur in Manchuria. It came into conflict with Japan over Korea, which the Japanese had already marked out for themselves for economic expansion. When Japan proposed a compromise whereby Russia would be ceded predominance in Manchuria if it agreed that Japan could control Korea, the Russians treated the Japanese with disdain. Not long afterwards, Japan launched a surprise attack on Russian ships at Port Arthur on 26 January 1904, and the war was on.

It has been claimed that the Tsar and his Minister of Internal Affairs, Plehve, had sought the war as a convenient way of diverting attention from the problems at home – a successful war would rally the people behind the Tsar. However, recent evidence suggests that the Tsar and his chief ministers did not want a war. It is more likely that they saw Japan as a third-rate power that could be bullied easily and it was this that led to their high-handed manner in refusing to negotiate a settlement.

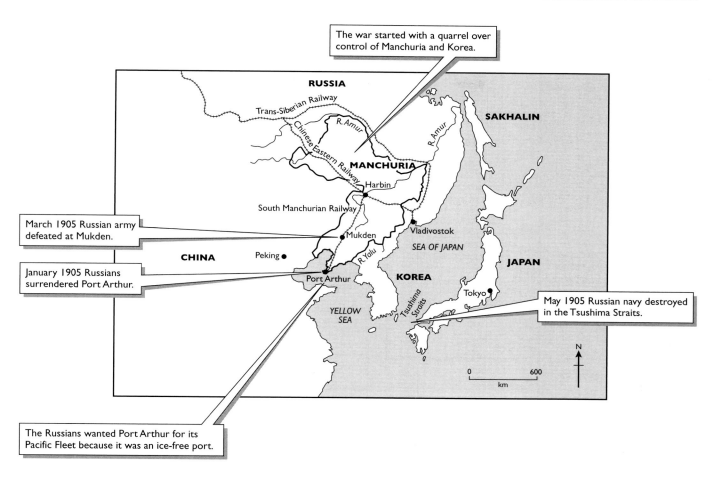

The war started with a quarrel over control of Manchuria and Korea.

March 1905 Russian army defeated at Mukden.

January 1905 Russians surrendered Port Arthur.

May 1905 Russian navy destroyed in the Tsushima Straits.

The Russians wanted Port Arthur for its Pacific Fleet because it was an ice-free port.

What is clear is that the Russians completely underestimated Japan and overestimated their own superiority. Japan had a better trained army and navy and more effective intelligence. They were also much closer to the action. The Russians were operating a very long way from European Russia and had not completed the Trans-Siberian Railway which made it difficult to send reinforcements and supplies. The Russians suffered several defeats in early 1904 and had to retreat. Public support for the war quickly turned to dismay. In January 1905, Port Arthur fell to the Japanese and the following March, the Russian army was defeated at Mukden. The final humiliation was the naval defeat of the Russian Baltic fleet in May. It had sailed almost half way around the world to join the battle, a journey which took over six months, and on the way firing on British fishing trawlers thinking they were Japanese warships. When they finally met the Japanese navy in the Tsushima Straits, most of the ships were destroyed or put out of action in under an hour. These disastrous defeats on land and sea led to Witte being sent off to negotiate the Treaty of Portsmouth under the auspices of the USA. The Russians agreed to withdraw from Manchuria and ceded control of Korea and Port Arthur.

Abraham Ascher suggests that Russia might have avoided revolution in 1905 if it had not provoked a war with Japan – the catastrophic defeats, he says, justified the opposition claims that the autocratic government was 'irresponsible, incompetent and reckless'. The war acted as a catalyst for meltdown in 1905.

LONG-TERM DISCONTENT

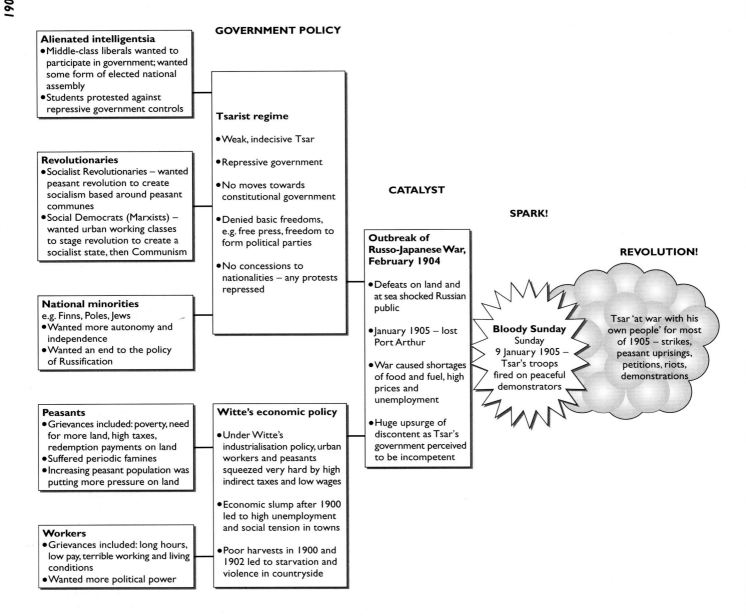

GOVERNMENT POLICY

Alienated intelligentsia
- Middle-class liberals wanted to participate in government; wanted some form of elected national assembly
- Students protested against repressive government controls

Revolutionaries
- Socialist Revolutionaries – wanted peasant revolution to create socialism based around peasant communes
- Social Democrats (Marxists) – wanted urban working classes to stage revolution to create a socialist state, then Communism

National minorities
e.g. Finns, Poles, Jews
- Wanted more autonomy and independence
- Wanted an end to the policy of Russification

Peasants
- Grievances included: poverty, need for more land, high taxes, redemption payments on land
- Suffered periodic famines
- Increasing peasant population was putting more pressure on land

Workers
- Grievances included: long hours, low pay, terrible working and living conditions
- Wanted more political power

Tsarist regime
- Weak, indecisive Tsar
- Repressive government
- No moves towards constitutional government
- Denied basic freedoms, e.g. free press, freedom to form political parties
- No concessions to nationalities – any protests repressed

Witte's economic policy
- Under Witte's industrialisation policy, urban workers and peasants squeezed very hard by high indirect taxes and low wages
- Economic slump after 1900 led to high unemployment and social tension in towns
- Poor harvests in 1900 and 1902 led to starvation and violence in countryside

CATALYST

Outbreak of Russo-Japanese War, February 1904
- Defeats on land and at sea shocked Russian public
- January 1905 – lost Port Arthur
- War caused shortages of food and fuel, high prices and unemployment
- Huge upsurge of discontent as Tsar's government perceived to be incompetent

SPARK!

Bloody Sunday
Sunday 9 January 1905 – Tsar's troops fired on peaceful demonstrators

REVOLUTION!

Tsar 'at war with his own people' for most of 1905 – strikes, peasant uprisings, petitions, riots, demonstrations

B The 1905 revolution

Some historians maintain that the 1905 revolution really started at the end of 1904. In the summer of 1904, Plehve, the Minister of the Interior, was assassinated by the Socialist Revolutionaries. Deeply unpopular, he was not much mourned by the public or even, it seems, by his colleagues. The assassination seemed to be a turning point and released a flood of criticism against the government. This was largely to do with the disastrous conduct of the war but it also reflected disenchantment with the regime. Activity by opposition groups increased dramatically in the last four months of 1904 and the autocracy started to look fragile.

When, in early November, the liberals decided to hold a national zemstvo congress, the government allowed it to go ahead. Over 5000 telegrams poured in urging the delegates to press for fundamental changes – and they did. They called for civil liberties, the rule of law, an extension of voting rights, and a representative body that would participate in the running of the country.

This was accompanied by a series of 'banquets' around the theme of reform organised by the Union of Liberation. The banquets could be passed off as 'private' events but really they were political meetings in which the liberal intelligentsia discussed their ideas for changing the tsarist regime. That the government let them go ahead unchallenged shows its weakness. The press, uncensored, reported the meetings and was becoming increasingly hostile towards the government.

The Russo-Japanese War had been a disaster for the economy, which had been emerging from depression. Trade to the East was curtailed as the use of the Trans-Siberian Railway for military purposes meant that other goods could not be carried on it. Industries such as silk, cotton and chemicals were hit hard and factories, short of raw materials, closed. Large numbers of young peasants were mobilised into the army and so agricultural work and production suffered. The overall result was a rise in food prices and high levels of unemployment. In the winter of 1904–5, there was growing discontent.

1905

In the capital, St Petersburg, a charismatic priest named Gapon took on a leading role. Father Gapon ran the Assembly of Russian Factory Workers, an offshoot of a Zubatov union. The police allowed this because they considered him loyal and indeed he was a monarchist who believed in the bond between the Tsar and his people. However, despite his police links he was becoming more radical and his association was becoming dominated by skilled workers, some of whom were ex-Social Democrats. A strike at the giant Putilov engineering works on 7 January, sparked by the sacking of four members of Gapon's association, led to a strike of over 100,000 workers. It was an economic strike with demands for minimum wages and a limited working day. Other large industrial enterprises joined in and tens of thousands were involved. The situation in the city was becoming tense.

Beryl Williams has argued that Gapon 'had a real conviction of his destiny to improve the lot of the Russian working class . . . but he had no political strategy other than a reliance on the Tsar to help him'. Gapon decided to do just that – ask the Tsar for help. This was to have a dramatic impact and kick start the events of 1905.

1905 was a tumultuous year and events pushed the regime to the edge of the abyss. You can see the course of the revolution through 1905 in Chart 2C on page 37. Four events, which were particularly significant, are described in more detail below. These are Bloody Sunday, the mutiny of the Battleship *Potemkin*, the formation of the St Petersburg Soviet and the October Manifesto.

1 Bloody Sunday

Gapon, urged on by the more radical workers in his union, organised a petition to the Tsar and a march to the Winter Palace. The petition is a moving document (see Source 2.3, page 34). It called for an eight-hour day, minimum wages and more dignified treatment. More radically, it also called for freedom of speech and assembly, the right to form trade unions and an elected parliament. Although it contained radical demands, it was not aggressive in tone and did not attack the Tsar.

The march set off peacefully on the morning of 9 January, a Sunday. The crowd, estimated at between 50,000 and 100,000, included women and children and everybody was in their best clothes. They were carrying icons and pictures of the Tsar. In fact, the Tsar was not even in St Petersburg. It seems that the authorities, who were well informed about the march, assumed that it would disperse before it got to the Winter Palace. The troops guarding the Palace had orders to stop the marchers reaching it. As the crowd approached they were charged by cavalry and the troops opened fire. It is difficult to know how many were killed and wounded. Ascher puts it at 130 killed and 300 seriously wounded although Soviet sources put deaths at up to 200 and the wounded up to 500.

WHAT HAPPENED TO FATHER GAPON?

When the firing started, Gapon was thrown over a fence by his bodyguards and then was hidden in different locations, including the apartment of Maxim Gorky. Shocked by the violence, he is reported to have shouted: 'There is no God! There is no Tsar!'

Gapon later fled abroad where he declared himself a Socialist Revolutionary. He returned to St Petersburg in the autumn of 1905 and attempted to resurrect his workers' organisation. This was unsuccessful and he seems to have become caught up in a conspiracy to betray the SRs to the secret police, the Okhrana. This resulted in his murder in March 1906. The strange thing is that the leader of the SR combat organisation, Evno Azef, who probably ordered his murder, was in fact an Okhrana agent. (For more on Evno Azef, see page 58.)

The response to this event was dramatic. Strikes broke out in St Petersburg and quickly spread to other cities and towns. By the end of January, over 400,000 people were out on strike. Order broke down and Russia descended into chaos – the 1905 revolution was under way. For the rest of the year the government had little control of events. Strikes, demonstrations, petitions, terrorist acts and peasant uprisings were commonplace – the Tsar was 'at war with his own people'.

The importance of Bloody Sunday cannot be overestimated. It not only sparked the uprisings of 1905, it also broke the bond between the Tsar and his people. The people had gone to the 'Little Father' for help and they had got bullets in return. They would never trust him in the same way again (see Source 2.5).

SOURCE 2.3   Extracts from the workers' petition to the Tsar

Sire,
We, the workers and inhabitants of St Petersburg, of various estates, our wives, our children, and our aged, helpless parents, come to You, Sire to seek justice and protection. We are impoverished; we are oppressed, overburdened with excessive toil, contemptuously treated . . . O Sire we have no strength left and our endurance is at an end. We have reached that frightful moment when death is better than the prolongation of our unbearable sufferings . . . We ask but little: to reduce the working day to eight hours, to provide a minimum wage of a rouble a day . . .

Officials have brought the country to complete ruin and involved it in a shameful war. We working men have no voice in how the enormous amounts raised from us in taxes are spent . . . We are seeking here our last salvation. Do not refuse to help Your people.

ACTIVITY

1 What message do you think the artist intended to convey in Source 2.4?
2 What does Source 2.5 tell us about changing attitudes towards the Tsar and the impact of Bloody Sunday?

SOURCE 2.4   A painting of the Bloody Sunday massacre, Makovsky (1846–1920)

'I observed the faces around me,' recalled a Bolshevik in the crowd, 'and I detected neither fear nor panic. No, the reverend and almost prayerful expressions were replaced by hostility and even hatred and vengeance on literally every face – old, young, men and women. The revolution had been truly born, and it had been born in the very core, in the very bowels of the people.' In the one vital moment the popular myth of a Good Tsar which had sustained the regime through the centuries was suddenly destroyed. Only moments after the shooting had ceased an old man turned to a boy of fourteen and said to him, with his voice full of anger: 'Remember, son, remember and swear to repay the Tsar. You saw how much blood he spilled, did you see? Then swear son, swear!'

2 Mutiny on the Battleship *Potemkin*

In the final analysis, the Tsar's fate depended on the loyalty of the armed forces. If they went over to the side of the peasants and workers, the regime would fall. On 14 June, the Tsar and his regime got a huge shock – the crew of the Battleship *Potemkin* mutinied. Conditions in the Russian navy were harsh and morale was low following the recent naval disasters. When the crew of the *Potemkin* found that they were being given rotten meat to eat, they complained. An officer shot one of the complainers whereupon he was thrown overboard. The crew killed several officers and seized control of the ship. They sailed to Odessa, which was in a state of turmoil with strikes and demonstrations taking place daily. The arrival of the ship was warmly received and radicals were invited on board. The police and troops had to withdraw when the *Potemkin* threatened to open fire on them. Crowds gathered and this degenerated into looting and arson with large parts of the harbour set on fire.

The Tsar ordered troops to go in and they opened fire indiscriminately, killing perhaps as many as 2000 citizens. Odessa was brought under control. Meanwhile the *Potemkin* escaped hoping to stir up mutiny on other ships. But failing to find support, the sailors surrendered the ship in a Romanian port in exchange for safe refuge. The episode was an embarrassment for the government and a matter of grave concern.

3 The St Petersburg Soviet

On 17 October 1905, prompted by Mensheviks, the Soviet of Workers' Deputies met to co-ordinate the activities of workers in the general strike, which had started in September. It was mainly made up of representatives elected from a variety of factories. It tried to be neutral and non-partisan. The St Petersburg Soviet, as it became known, not only directed the general strike, informing workers what was going on through its newspaper *Izvestia*, but it also sorted out food supplies and other essential tasks. The most famous revolutionary leader involved was Leon Trotsky who became deputy chairman.

Soviets, which had sprung up elsewhere even before October, spread to a number of cities and into the countryside – there were around 80 in operation by the end of November. The creation of the soviet was a strong indication of the power of the urban workers to develop an effective form of organisation and run their own affairs.

SOVIET

The word 'soviet' in Russian simply means 'council'. Factories sent representatives to the council to look after their interests and put their point of view to the wider community. In principle any deputy could be recalled at any time if he failed to satisfy his constituents and he could be replaced by someone else.

At the time, the word 'soviet' did not have the political connotation that it later assumed under the Bolshevik regime. It provided a model of working class organisation for the revolution of 1917.

SOURCE 2.6 A painting of a barricade in a Moscow street, 1905, artist unknown

SOURCE 2.7 O. Figes, *A People's Tragedy: The Russian Revolution 1891–1924*, 1997, p. 191

Nicholas remained unconvinced and asked his uncle, the Grand Duke Nikolai, to assume the role of dictator. But the Grand Duke, an excitable and outspoken man, took out a revolver and threatened to shoot himself there and then if the Tsar refused to endorse Witte's memorandum . . . The Grand Duke was the one man capable of playing the role of dictator and it was only when he took the side of reform that it finally dawned on the Tsar that repression was no longer an option and he agreed to sign the manifesto.

4 The October Manifesto

The general strike put the Tsar and the regime under an enormous amount of pressure. Nicholas' first reaction was to suppress it but the people defiantly occupied the streets. Witte, recently returned from successful peace negotiations following the war, now presented Nicholas with a choice – to put down the uprising in bloodshed or introduce reforms. Nicholas was not against the former, preferring a military dictatorship to constitutional government. But his main advisors agreed with Witte and Nicholas was dragged, very reluctantly, as Source 2.7 shows, to make concessions in what came to be known as the October Manifesto. This conceded:

- freedom of speech and conscience
- freedom of association and unwarranted arrest
- an elected duma (parliament) which could block laws coming into force although it could not enact laws.

It seemed that the principle of autocracy had been abandoned. The liberals hailed it as the first step towards constitutional government and for them the main aim of the campaign had been achieved. The St Petersburg Soviet also voted to end the general strike since most workers were suffering severe hardship. The revolutionary groups and some left-wing liberals dismissed the Manifesto as a trick. Witte had achieved what he had set out to do – isolate the radicals by accommodating the liberals.

January, February

- 9 January – Bloody Sunday: a wave of strikes soon spread to other cities and towns.
- Censorship collapsed and newspapers became increasingly hostile towards the government.
- 4 February – The assassination of the Tsar's uncle, the Grand Duke Sergei, shocked the government. The Tsar invited petitions containing suggestions for reform. Thousands poured in over the following months from all sectors of society.
- Workers started forming factory committees to represent them. Their demands were mainly economic rather than political.
- Right-wing groups and hooligans known as the Black Hundreds, supporting the Tsar, attacked people deemed to be anti-government.

March, April, May

- The police were becoming increasingly ineffective. Citizens formed militias or vigilante groups to protect themselves from roving bands of criminals.
- 10 March – The Russian army was defeated at Mukden.
- April – At the Second Zemstvo Congress there was a growing demand for civil freedoms and a legislative assembly elected by universal adult suffrage.
- May – The Union of Unions was formed – a non-party organisation that acted as an umbrella group for a range of trade and professional organisations. All sections of society were united against the government – liberals, workers, students, lawyers and professional groups – to force reform.
- 14 May – The Russian Baltic fleet was wiped out at Tsushima.

June, July, August

- In the countryside, peasant disturbances started rising significantly in June and July (there had not been much activity in the spring). They fell in August at harvest time. Incidents included: peasants seizing land, grain and animals; burning landlord's houses; illegal cutting of timber; and refusal to pay rents and taxes. Their general demands were land, the end of redemption payments and a reduction in rents. There was no co-ordinated peasant movement. It was largely spontaneous and a response, in part, to economic distress, including food shortages in the summer of 1905.
- 14 June – The mutiny of the Battleship *Potemkin*.
- 31 July – The All-Russian Peasants Union met secretly near Moscow – the voice of the peasants was taking shape demanding the handover of land and a constitutional assembly.
- 27 August – Universities and institutes were given autonomy to control education within their institution and run their own affairs. They became focal points for political meetings.
- 29 August – The Treaty of Portsmouth was signed between Russia and Japan. This released Russian troops who could be returned to European Russia to re-establish control.

September, October

- Labour unrest reached a new level of intensity in the autumn, putting a lot of pressure on the government. In September, a strike in Moscow called by railway workers caused chaos since Moscow was a railway hub. The strike spread to other areas of Russia as other railway workers joined it. This then turned into a general strike attracting support from industrial and utility workers, shop assistants, bank employees and staff from government offices – up to two million from almost every area of employment. The strike caused real hardship in cities and towns: food and medical supplies ran short and unburied bodies piled up.
- All opposition groups – workers, students, liberals and revolutionaries – united in demanding radical change. The middle classes, even some industrialists, supported the strikers and gave money. The regime did not dare use violence as the strike was supported by so many different social groups.
- 12–18 October – The Kadet Party (liberal) was formed.
- 13 October – The St Petersburg Soviet was formed. The urban workers had emerged as an organised and dynamic force confronting the autocracy.
- 17 October – The Tsar was persuaded that concessions were necessary and agreed to the October Manifesto, granting civil liberties and an elected assembly. Liberals and the middle classes felt they had achieved their main aims.
- There was a short period of freedom in which opposition groups and anti-government newspapers flourished. Political meetings and celebrations were held in the streets. New political parties were formed.
- At the end of October there was an explosion of violence. Much of this was initiated by supporters of the Tsar angry that the liberals and left had won the Manifesto. There was fighting between right and left on the streets. It seems that the police, and possibly elements in the government, were involved in organising violent revenge attacks.

November, December

- Throughout November tension was building as the soviets, particularly the St Petersburg Soviet, became more militant. It had an armed militia of over 6000.
- 3 December – Leaders of the St Petersburg Soviet were arrested.
- Armed uprisings were common, particularly in Moscow, where the Bolsheviks took the lead. The army moved into cities and towns to re-establish control.

The national minorities in the 1905 revolution

The national minorities took advantage of government disarray in Russia to demand autonomy, democratic government and the end of Russification. The Poles and the Finns demanded outright independence. The Jews wanted civil rights. In many areas, particularly on the edges of the empire, the struggle became very violent – for example in parts of the Caucasus where peasants ignored the authorities and attacked officials. There was a strong nationalist character to demands, e.g. for local language and culture to be taught in schools. There was a racial edge to demonstrations, e.g. in Tbilisi and Odessa. Also, 10,000 troops were dispatched to Georgia to try to keep it under control.

In Poland, trouble started as early as January, where there were clashes between strikers and troops. In February students and pupils joined demonstrations. It expanded to include professional groups and then to smaller cities and the countryside. In a state of almost civil war, the tsarist regime had to keep a force of 300,000 soldiers in Poland who were badly needed in the Russo-Japanese war. Popular unrest in the Baltic states followed a similar pattern, where workers and peasants were in a virtual state of civil war with the authorities by the summer of 1905.

The army

The role of the army was a crucial factor in the 1905 revolution. Most of the soldiers were peasants and many were not happy about being used to suppress revolts in the countryside. From late October to mid-December 1905, there were over 200 mutinies in the army. Mostly this involved holding meetings, not obeying orders and talking back to officers. There was also trouble from soldiers in the Far East anxious to be demobilised after the end of the war. About a third of infantry units were affected by some kind of disturbance. It seemed that they felt that the old rules did not apply after the October Manifesto. John Bushell maintains that soldiers mutinied when they believed the regime had lost its authority but repressed civilians when they thought the regime was back in charge.

On 6 December military reforms seemed to meet the soldiers' key demands. Their pay was increased and their terms of service reduced, e.g. from four to three years for infantrymen and from seven to five years for sailors. They had demanded better food and now, for the first time, they were promised increased meat rations and tea and sugar. Also, they would no longer be required to do forced labour in the civilian economy. So, although there were mutinies up to the summer of 1906, the army came back on side and remained loyal. The élite army units and the Cossacks had not been touched by mutinies and were rewarded with money and privileges. It was to these loyal troops that the regime turned to restore order at the end of 1905.

What part did the revolutionary parties play?

The Socialist Revolutionaries had some influence among the newly urbanised workers, the railway workers and students. Most of their activity was in towns and SRs bemoaned their lack of impact on the peasants in rural areas. Their terrorist wing called for rural terror against landlords and advocated violence and arson. The Social Democrats, especially the Mensheviks, were influential in the larger factories among more organised workers. But the scope of the activity of SDs and SRs was very limited.

All sources say that the revolutionary parties were unprepared for the revolt that broke out in 1905. Workers and peasants were apathetic and sometimes downright hostile towards them. As late as September, in St Petersburg and Moscow, socialist speakers were often interrupted, especially when they squabbled over political methods and party ideology. Workers and peasants were irritated by this and listened more to local leaders who reflected their needs, demands and attitudes.

The Mensheviks played a significant role in the creation of the St Petersburg Soviet and came to dominate it although there were SR and Bolshevik representatives. The Bolsheviks distrusted independent working class bodies and Lenin, who returned from exile in early November, never spoke in the Soviet. The supreme orator here was Trotsky, who became deputy chairman and was looking to widen the revolution and challenge the government. At this point he was not firmly in either the Menshevik or the Bolshevik camp. The Social Democrats played a much more active role in radicalising the soviets in St Petersburg and Moscow in November, and the Bolsheviks were particularly active in organising and taking part in the Moscow uprising in December.

TERRORISM

During 1905, 3600 government officials were killed or wounded. This wave of terrorism differed from the attacks in the 1870s and 1880s in that the terrorists' targets were indiscriminate – rather than concentrating on high-level figures they threatened any servant of the state. They had an effect. Terrorism produced fear in the minds of officials and played its part in destabilising the tsarist regime politically and psychologically.

SOURCE 2.8 The cover of the magazine *Raven* (1906) showing tsarist ministers being blown up

TALKING POINT

It can be argued that these terroists were the forerunners of modern extremists. How effective do you think terrorism is as a political weapon to bring about change?

SOURCE 2.9 An official quoted in Peter Waldron, *Governing Tsarist Russia*, 2007, p. 124

Every day there are several assassinations, either by bomb or revolver or knife, or various other instruments, they strike and strike anyhow and at anybody . . . and one is surprised that they have not yet killed all of us.

C Why did the Tsar survive the 1905 revolution?

Restoring order

In the period of freedom after the October Manifesto, the soviets became more militant and a little too overconfident. The St Petersburg Soviet interfered in the running of the railways, supported strikes and organised an armed militia of some 6000 men. This led to a showdown between the Soviet and the government. The new Minister of the Interior, P. N. Durnovo, an uncompromising reactionary, was determined to re-establish government control (see Source 2.11). The government made the first move on 3 December by arresting the leaders of the St Petersburg Soviet and hundreds of its deputies. This caused an armed uprising in Moscow led by the Social Democrats and barricades were erected. On 15 December, troops bombarded the workers' district of Presnia, the centre of resistance. The uprising was crushed, followed by a brutal crackdown with mass arrests, beatings and summary executions.

This proved to be a turning point. The violence of November and the Moscow uprising had split the opposition movement. The liberals felt that the aims of the opposition had been achieved in October and withdrew from further action. The middle classes, terrified of further violence and frightened by the coarse proletarians on the streets, wanted order restored. The government now felt confident to take control. From mid-December the government decided to move against any civilians defying authority. In the cities, the Ohkrana and the police arrested hundreds of people. Peter Struve, an ex-Marxist remarked: 'Thank God for the Tsar, who has saved us from the people'.

In the countryside it took longer to bring things under control. A wave of peasant unrest and violence had reached its peak in November. For instance, in the Tambov region, 130 estates had buildings that were burned down. The deterioration in economic conditions in the countryside (the harvest of 1905 was poor) played a role in this but the peasants were also angry that they had not received any land deal in the October Manifesto (see Source 2.10). The government did promise to cut redemption payments in half by January 1906 and end them completely by January 1907; it also announced the setting up of the Peasants' Bank to help them buy land. But this was not enough and peasant disturbances broke out again early in 1906. For much of that year the countryside was in revolt. There was widespread lawlessness and hundreds of government officials were assassinated by the Socialist Revolutionaries.

Troops were sent out on punitive expeditions to re-establish order. Brutal and repressive measures – beatings, rape, flogging and executions – were employed to intimidate the peasants and beat them into submission. Between mid-October 1905 and April 1906, as many as 15,000 people were executed and 45,000 deported. The prisons overflowed with political prisoners. The troops worked their way through the Baltic provinces, the Ukraine and the Caucasus. In the summer of 1906, field court martials were introduced to deliver fast trials and fast executions (within 24 hours of sentencing). Peasants were hanged in their hundreds. The noose used in the hangings became known as 'Stolypin's necktie', after Peter Stolypin, the new Minister of the Interior (see page 47). This cold-blooded repression had its effect and the resistance to the authorities was everywhere in retreat. The old order was back.

SOURCE 2.10 Quoted in A. Ascher, *The Revolution of 1905*, 2004, p. 142

Petition to the Duma 8 Feb 1906 by peasants and townspeople of Sviatii Krest: '*God created the world and gave human beings full control (on the land); (but) God created neither nobles nor peasants; we are all God's children and have the right to demand out father's inheritance . . . Are we peasants really only his stepsons, and the nobles his sons? This is gross injustice. Whoever works the land should have as much of it as he and his family cultivate.*'

SOURCE 2.11   Quoted in A. Ascher, *The Revolution of 1905*, 2004, p. 109

Durnovo to the regional governor of Kiev:
*'I urgently request . . . that you order the use of armed force without the slightest
leniency and that insurgents be annihilated and their homes burned in the event
of resistance. It is necessary once and for all to stop, with the most severe measures,
the spreading wilfulness that threatens to destroy the entire state.'*

SOURCE 2.12   'Now at last my people
are free' says the Tsar

SOURCE 2.13   Nicholas as a skeleton on
horseback – a cartoon captioned *Peace and
Quiet*, 1906

SOURCE 2.14   The record of repression
between 1906 and 1910 (the first five years
of the constitutional era) compared with the
previous 80 years, compiled by the German
socialist Karl Liebknecht for the Second
International, an organisation of socialist and
labour parties

1906–1910	1825–1905
5735 persons sentenced to death for political crimes of whom 3741 were executed.	625 persons sentenced to death for political crimes of whom 192 were executed.
37,620 condemned by the courts for political offences.	

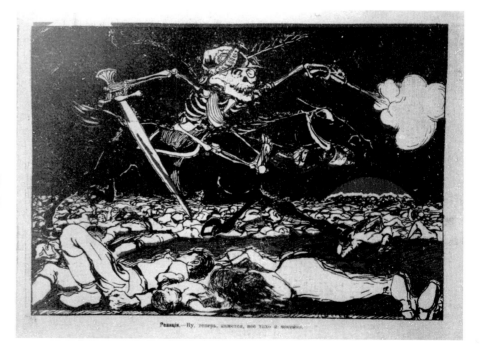

Nicholas the Bloody

Before the revolution of 1905, Nicholas II had been called 'Nicholas the Unlucky'. Following the repression after 1905, he was called 'Nicholas the Bloody'. He wore the Union of Russian People's badge and supported the attacks on the Jews. He gave his full support to the punitive expeditions and executions. The Tsar said he was delighted by one campaign in the Baltic States where about 1200 people were executed, and he praised its commander for 'acting splendidly'. He thoroughly approved of the field court martials and officials were instructed to make sure that no pleas for clemency were sent to the Tsar.

SOURCE 2.15   Konstantin Balmont's poem, *Our Tsar*, written in 1906

Our Tsar means Mukden; our Tsar is Tsushima.
Our Tsar is a bloody stain,
A stench of gunpowder and smoke.
Black is his soul.
Our Tsar, sickly and blind,
Is prison and knout, shooting and hanging,
Tsar! You are the gallows-bird . . .
The hour of retribution awaits you,
Tsar, who began where? At Khodynka.
And will end where? On the scaffold.

> Note: Mukden and Tsushima were Russian defeats in 1905 in the Russo-Japanese war. Khodynka is a reference to the deaths of over 1350 people in a mass panic that occurred on Khodynka Field in Moscow during the festivities following Nicholas II's coronation (see page 13).

Why was the Tsar able to survive the 1905 revolution?

1   The crucial factor was that the army remained loyal, despite a rash of mutinies. Once it had received pay and changes to conditions of service, it supported the Tsar and could be employed in putting down the revolution in the cities and later revolts in the countryside.

2   The various groups opposing the Tsar – the workers, the peasants, the liberal middle classes, students and wider public in the cities and the national independence movements – did not combine to provide a co-ordinated and effective opposition. They had different aims and purposes and did not act together to bring him down.

3   The October Manifesto split the liberals and socialists. The liberals wanted political reform and movement towards a constitutional democracy; the socialists wanted a social revolution. Many liberals felt they had got what they wanted out of the Manifesto and urged that the Tsar be supported.

4   The middle classes feared the continuation of violence and disorder. They wanted the revolution to stop and a return to authority and control.

5   The government used brutal, repressive measures, especially punitive expeditions, to bring the populace into line and beat them into submission. These methods were effective in re-establishing government control across the Empire.

6   By the end of 1905, the government was in deep financial trouble. The cost of the war and falling tax revenues were driving the government to the brink of financial collapse. However, Witte secured a huge loan, largely from French bankers, in April 1906. This loan stabilised the economy and gave the government money to pay for its functions for a year. It paid for the troops who were needed to put down uprisings and restore order.

D Interpreting 1905

Traditionally, historians have seen the 1905 revolution as the result of the impoverishment and increasing misery of workers and peasants, exacerbated by war, leading to an explosion of popular discontent. According to Beryl Williams, recent evidence suggests that it is more complicated than this. She maintains that it was a popular protest, but one stemming from a period of economic growth rather than increasing misery, and from a period when some individuals and areas benefited but others did not. Also, this was a time when attitudes and society were undergoing rapid change. In her view it was initiated by sudden depression and war rather than fundamental economic causes and was more to do with freedom and dignity than the policies of political groups or socialist parties whose activists were often seen as outsiders divorced from local concerns. There was a huge demand for reform and institutional change. Liberals, progressive landowners and nobility, businessmen and entrepreneurs wanted more freedom of action, civil rights and to escape the heavy hand of the tsarist state. Some wanted more self-government and local autonomy and some, in the case of the nationalities, wanted independence. Workers were looking for fundamental improvements in their living and working conditions and, importantly, dignity. Peasants wanted the land and relief from redemption payments and local bureaucracy.

The tsarist regime had managed to survive 1905 with its institutions intact. But society had changed in many ways, as Source 2.16 indicates. The brutal way in which the protest had been suppressed had broken the bond between the Tsar and his people – he lost their affection. Fear and respect for the Tsar had been replaced by fear alone. The people had also experienced political freedoms – the growth of free speech and critical newspapers, the formation of political parties, the soviets and the forthcoming dumas – which could not just be put back in a box. The attitude of the workers and peasants had also changed. They were more inclined towards social revolution than liberal reform; the liberals had let them down after October. After 1905 appalling living and working conditions and lack of dignity seemed even more intolerable to workers. Landowners noticed that the mood of the peasants had changed and that deference had been replaced by sullen resentment and hatred. Much would depend on how Nicholas acted and whether he would take the chance to restore relations with the people.

SOURCE 2.16 Peter Waldron, *Between Two Revolutions: Stolypin and the Politics of Renewal in Russia*, 1997, p. 184

While the troubles of 1905 should have alerted the state apparatus to the deep crisis that faced it, the regime's ability to come through the year relatively unscathed served to reassure the Tsar and his advisers that they were secure. They had vanquished the most serious threat to their position for generations. This was, however, a superficial view of the security of the tsarist state. The experience of 1905 served to accelerate the disillusionment of much of Russian society and government. The regime had not flinched from setting its troops against the population when revolt threatened and had used great brutality to put down rebellion in both city and countryside. Society's sympathy with tsarism was rapidly diminishing as its patriarchal structures disintegrated. The emancipation of the serfs had severed the link between noble and peasant and the rapid decline in noble landowning after 1861 had accelerated the process. The inhabitants of the growing cities of the Empire felt little loyalty to any other social group.

ACTIVITY

What do Sources 2.16 and 2.17 tell us about the significance of the 1905 revolution in Russian history?

SOURCE 2.17 A. Ascher, *The Revolution of 1905*, 2004, pp. 216–7

If one takes a long-range view of Russian history, then the Revolution of 1905 can be seen not simply as a failure or as an event that was important because it led inexorably to 1917. On the contrary, 1905 should be viewed as an upheaval that opened up new possibilities for the country that was suppressed by the Bolshevik revolution of 1917. Seventy-four years later, in 1991, it turned out that even that cataclysmic event did not introduce a political system of very long duration. Over the last thirteen years, the country has found itself in the throes of yet another upheaval, inspired to a large extent by the same ideals that had animated much of the opposition of 1905: the rule of law; government by the people; individual rights; and respect for the ethnic and religious minorities. Though aborted, the Revolution of 1905 left an enduring legacy: it initiated a process of political, economic, and social change that even now still has not run its course.

Was 1905 really a revolution?

There has been a tendency for historians to see 1905 as simply part of the build up to the revolution of 1917. This is partly due to Lenin's description of 1905 as a 'dress rehearsal' for the main event. Some would say it does not really qualify as a 'revolution' at all because no fundamental changes took place in the political and social fabric of Russia; the old order remained and was largely intact. But some historians, including Abraham Ascher, claim that there is a good case for considering it as a revolution and that it deserves consideration in its own right (see Source 2.17). The challenge to the established order in Russia came from mass movements and popular protest affecting most parts of Russia and there was a real chance that if all the unrest had occurred simultaneously the government could have fallen. Ascher makes the point that the people who participated in 1905 were trying to bring about real and far reaching changes then and there, not preparing for a future event. The happenings of 1905 opened up several paths and possibilities including more democratic government through elected dumas and political parties and the expansion of civil rights – alternatives to autocratic rule. We might, more generously, call it a genuine but uncompleted revolution.

ACTIVITY

Essay: What were the causes of the 1905 revolution and why did the Tsar survive?

This is a straightforward essay where you are asked to deploy the information in a direct way. You could put the points in order of importance or chronologically. Use the information you have collected in the Focus Route tasks for this section.

Introduction – set out very briefly your main line of argument mentioning some of the major points but not going into any detail about them.

Conclusion – sum up the main points of your argument for the first part of the essay, bringing in issues of interpreting 1905. For the second half, stress the most important factors in survival.

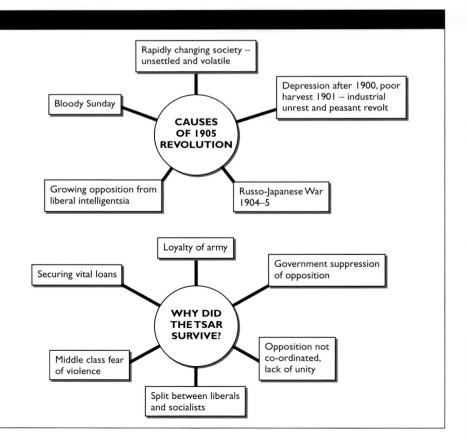

KEY POINTS FROM CHAPTER 2

1905

1 At the beginning of the twentieth century Russia was undergoing rapid social and economic change and old societal relationships were breaking down.

2 A deep depression starting in 1900 made life worse for workers and peasants leading to industrial discontent and peasant revolt.

3 There was growing opposition from the liberal intelligentsia to what they saw as an incompetent and out-dated style of government.

4 When the war with Japan went disastrously wrong, the government began to look increasingly vulnerable.

5 Bloody Sunday sparked off a series of strikes, uprisings, demonstrations and disturbances. The Tsar and his government lost control of the country for most of 1905. By October, a general strike put the regime under a lot of pressure.

6 In the October Manifesto, the Tsar agreed concessions, notably an elected duma and civil rights, whereupon the liberals stopped supporting revolution, as did the middle classes, frightened by the violence on the streets.

7 The government arrested leaders of the workers' movement in St Petersburg and crushed an armed uprising in Moscow.

8 Throughout 1906, troops were used to suppress the peasants in the most brutal way in the countryside and the national minorities on the periphery of the Empire.

9 The events of 1905 marked a watershed in which attitudes towards the Tsar and the tsarist regime changed. The tsar had lost a lot of respect and different sections of society wanted to see change.

10 There is a debate over whether 1905 deserves to be called a revolution. But it did open up different possibilities and alternatives to autocratic rule.

3 Could tsarism have survived? 1906–1917

CHAPTER OVERVIEW

The Tsar had survived the 1905 revolution with the institutions of tsarism largely intact but the underlying issues and problems associated with reform and modernisation remained. Peter Stolypin seemed to offer the best chance of achieving reform after 1905 but he was assassinated in 1911. Stolypin's major reforms were in agriculture but it is not clear how successful these were. Industry continued to grow but growth was uneven and unbalanced. Little was done to improve life for workers and there was considerable industrial unrest in the years leading up to 1914. The impact of the First World War was devastating and Russia slid towards revolution in 1917. The Tsar himself contributed to this by a series of misjudged actions and policies.

A Could Stolypin be the saviour of the Tsar? (pp. 46–48)

B The constitutional experiment (pp. 48–52)

C How far had the economy improved by 1914? (pp. 52–55)

D How revolutionary was Russia in 1914? (pp. 55–58)

E The impact of the First World War (pp. 59–64)

F How popular was the February Revolution? (pp. 65–69)

G Could tsarism have survived? (pp. 70–72)

A Could Stolypin be the saviour of the Tsar?

FOCUS ROUTE

Draw up a chart to evaluate whether Stolypin could have saved the Tsar. You will need to continue this into Section C for his agrarian reforms.

Stolypin	Positive contribution	Negative contribution	Difficult to tell
Stolypin's abilities			
Restores order in 1906			
Relationship with the Dumas			
Relationship with the Tsar			
Agrarian reforms			

SOURCE 3.1 Since the collapse of Communism, Stolypin's reputation has grown. In a poll taken in Russia at the end of 2008 to name Russia's greatest historical figure, Stolypin was in second place behind Alexander Nevsky and ahead of Stalin. Vladimir Putin praised Stolypin as a role model whose attempts to achieve stability he would like to emulate

VIEWS OF STOLYPIN

Sir Arthur Nicolson, the British Ambassador to St Petersburg and a distinguished diplomat, said he 'was the most notable figure in Europe'. Dominic Lieven describes him as 'radiating vigour, forcefulness and self-confidence', with 'a talent for acting, oratory and public relations rare among senior officials'. According to Richard Pipes, 'Stolypin stood head and shoulders above his immediate predecessors and successors in that he combined a vision of the desirable with a sense of the possible; he was a rare blend of statesman and politician. Witte, his closest competitor, was a brilliant and realistic politician, but a follower rather than a leader and something of an opportunist.'

Peter Stolypin dominated the Russian government from July 1906, when he became Prime Minister, until his assassination in September 1911. He first came to notice as a provincial governor in Sartov due to his vigorous suppression of peasant unrest. A St Petersburg outsider, he was appointed Minister of the Interior and soon after Prime Minister, although he kept his former post also. He thus wielded a considerable amount of power.

Stolypin was a strong supporter of the autocracy and opponent of revolution and disorder. He set up field court martials in 1906 to crush peasant uprisings (see page 40). 'Stolypin's neckties' (the hangman's noose) dealt with thousands of peasants and nearly 60,000 political detainees were executed or sent into exile or penal servitude in 'Stolypin carriages' (railway cars). He was appointed by, and utterly beholden to, the Tsar and he never attempted to build a political base of his own. However, like Witte before him, he also believed that reform was essential to solve Russia's problems. He believed that industrial progress alone was not sufficient to take Russia forward and gave his attention to agriculture. He had two objectives:

1 to feed the rapidly growing population and avoid the cycle of famine and revolt
2 to create a strong conservative peasantry who would support the regime.

Stolypin was virtually the only Prime Minister of the constitutional decade to see the Duma as a partner in building a strong Russia (see pages 49–52). He did not consider that he was limiting the monarch's authority but rather giving it a broader social base. In particular, he developed an understanding with the Octobrists (more conservative liberals) which allowed him to push through his reforms. His success suggested the possibility of a working relationship between government and elected assembly. Yet he was only really prepared to work with it on his terms:

- When the Second Duma would not do his bidding, he changed the electoral system drastically to create one he hoped would be much more amenable. The liberals called this Stolypin's *coup d'état*.
- When he was having trouble getting measures through, he cynically used Article 87 of the Fundamental Laws which allowed him to pass emergency measures by decree when the Duma was not sitting.

In the end it was this last point that brought him down. He wanted to introduce zemstva in the western provinces to make local government more democratic. However, the upper chamber of the Duma opposed this as landowners feared they would lose their authority. In March 1911, he persuaded the Tsar to suspend both chambers of the Duma to allow him to force his measure through by decree.

STOLYPIN'S ASSASSINATION

On 1 September 1911, Stolypin went to the opera in Kiev at which Tsar Nicholas was also present. During the interval a young man, a Socialist Revolutionary but also a police informer, came up to him and shot him twice. It is reported that Stolypin turned to the Tsar and made the sign of the cross, saying, 'I am happy to die for the Tsar.' It took him five days to do so. It was the eighteenth attempt on his life.

This alienated both houses of the Duma including the majority of the Octobrists who had hitherto supported him.

The Left condemned Stolypin for his policy of repression while the Right considered that his dangerous reform policies undermined the principles of autocracy or, in the case of the land reforms, the power of the gentry in the countryside. He proposed a series of reforms to extend civil rights, reform local government and local justice, and improve education. In the event, he was only able to implement his programme of agrarian reform using emergency laws. The enmity which confronted him from all sides demonstrated the difficulty of taking a middle road in Russia. By 1911 his star was waning and had he not been assassinated, it is likely that he would have been dismissed.

Stolypin was a man of contradictions. On the one hand he supported the autocracy, using fierce and relentless repression to deal with dissidents; on the other he championed reform. In 1906, he commented to Bernard Pares, a British historian: 'I am fighting on two fronts. I am fighting against revolution, but for reform. You may say that such a position is beyond human strength and you may be right.' He wanted citizens to participate in political life and build a state based on the rule of law. However, some of his actions contradicted this – particularly his field court martials, his *coup d'état* and the use of Article 87. Perhaps this expressed the problems of trying to modernise Russia within the framework of an autocracy.

Whether Stolypin could have saved tsarism is a matter for conjecture but it is probably fair to say that he was the Tsar's last, best hope. Abraham Ascher argues that he had a vision for the transformation of Russia and that his reform proposals were 'more feasible and more likely to lead Russia out of the abyss than any other'. Other historians, however, would maintain that there was no hope of reforming the archaic regime and he was bound to fail. But in failing to support Stolypin, Nicholas showed his stubborn opposition to reform. After Stolypin he made a series of disastrous appointments to the government – people at best inefficient, at worst incompetent.

B The constitutional experiment

The October Manifesto had offered the chance of political change. The setting up of an elected duma was a major step towards some sort of constitutional government. Was the Tsar willing to take up the constitutional challenge? The initial signs were not good. The Tsar made it clear in the Fundamental Laws, issued in April 1906, that the autocracy was still in the ascendancy: 'The Sovereign Emperor possesses the initiative in all legislative matters . . . The Sovereign Emperor ratifies the laws. No laws can come into force without his approval.' It seemed that the Duma was to have little real power to initiate or enact legislation. This was confirmed when it was announced that there would be a second chamber, the State Council, with equal powers to the Duma. Half of the State Council's members would be chosen by the Tsar. Only if both agreed to a legislative proposal would it go forward to the Tsar for approval. Also, Article 87 of the Laws gave the Tsar the right in 'exceptional circumstances' to pass his own laws without consulting the Duma at all. The Tsar also retained control of the military, foreign policy and the appointment of ministers. To many liberals it seemed the Tsar had reneged on his promises in October.

The elections for the Duma employed a complicated system of electoral colleges designed to represent the different social classes. It was profoundly weighted towards the upper classes. For instance, 2000 landowners were represented by one deputy and 90,000 workers were represented by one deputy. Despite this, the elections returned the Kadets as the largest party and there was significant representation on the Left despite the fact that the revolutionary parties had boycotted the elections. The home of the Duma was the Tauride Palace.

FOCUS ROUTE

As you work through sections B–F keep a running list of:
- points at which Nicholas repulsed moves to constitutionalism in favour of maintaining the autocracy
- mistakes and misjudgements by Nicholas.

Draw up a chart to record what happened in the four Dumas under the following headings:
- dates of each duma, e.g. First Duma, April–June 1906
- composition (main parties or groupings)
- main achievements (if any)
- key events
- notes and comments (anything else you want to add)

New Liberal parties

The Kadets – The Constitutional Democrats – were formed in October 1905 just before the October Manifesto was signed. The Kadets were not a liberal party in the Western sense. They called themselves 'the Party of Popular Freedom' and saw themselves as a national party, not a class party, although they did draw support mainly from the liberal intelligentsia – academics, lawyers, progressive employers, doctors and zemstvo employees. The leader of the Kadets was Paul Milyukov, a professor of history. They wanted a democratically elected assembly, full civil rights for all citizens, the end of censorship, recognition of trade unions and free education. There were tensions in the party between the right wing, which supported monarchy, and the left wing, which wanted Russia to be turned into a republic.

The **Octobrists** took their name from the October Manifesto, which they saw as the definitive statement of reform – it should go no further. They were more conservative than the Kadets and did not want full constitutional government. They wanted the Tsar to exercise strong government and were nationalists who supported the maintenance of the Russian Empire. They were more an association of different groups rather than a defined political party. Their support came from industrialists, landowners and those with commercial interests. Two key leading members were Mikhail Rodzianko, a powerful landowner, and Alexander Guchkov, a factory owner.

First and Second Dumas

When the First Duma met in April 1906, there was immense hostility towards the Tsar (see Source 3.2). The deputies demanded that the powers of the Duma should be increased and that elections should be universal and secret. They also wanted guarantees of certain freedoms, e.g. speech and assembly. There followed two months of bitter disagreement. The Tsar, horrified by the hostility and lack of respect, dissolved the Duma. It is reported he said: 'Curse the Duma. It is all Witte's doing.' Two hundred Kadet and Trudovik deputies went to Vyborg in Finland from where they urged the Russian people not to pay their taxes. Later they were arrested and disbarred from re-election.

In the elections for the Second Duma, which met in February 1907, the Kadets and the moderates lost out to increased representation on the Left. There were over 200 left-wing deputies, partly because the revolutionary parties had ended their boycott. It was much more radical than the First Duma and was called 'The Duma of National Anger'. The Second Duma was riven by division and deputies made fierce attacks on the government (see Source 3.2). As a result it lasted only three months. You can see a more detailed description of the work of the dumas in Chart 3A, page 51.

■ **Learning trouble spot**

You need to consider the early dumas in the context of the times to make sense of what was going on and of the regime's response. Russia was still very unsettled in 1906. There was a major upsurge in peasant disturbances and, to a lesser degree, industrial unrest among workers. Also, 141 mutinies took place in the armed forces from May to July 1906. What was worrying for the regime was that much of this was political. The peasants were very aware of the First Duma and sent in a large number of petitions. The Kadets felt there was a chance of winning concessions on key issues and were pitting themselves against the government. After the First Duma, the government cracked down hard on the Kadets, closing down their offices and dismissing members of the party from government service. However, the peasants and workers had confidence in and great hopes for the Second Duma and flocked to the polls in huge numbers. In St Petersburg over 70 per cent of eligible workers voted.

Use the information in this section and Source 3.2 to answer the questions below:

1 Do you think the hostility in the Duma was more the fault of the Tsar or the deputies?

2 Why was it unlikely that the First and Second Dumas would be able to collaborate with the government?

SOURCE 3.2 Lionel Kochan, *Russia in Revolution, 1890–1918*, 1971, pp. 120–1 and 128–9

On the First Duma

The Duma was solemnly opened by the Tsar in the throne room of the Winter Palace. Had its walls ever enclosed such a strange scene, one ministerial onlooker wondered to himself. To one side stood the uniformed members of the Imperial Council and the Tsar's retinue, the ladies of the court liberally bedecked with pearls and diamonds. To the other stood the members of the duma, dressed overwhelmingly in the garb of workers and peasants. Prominent among the latter stood a tall workman named Onipko; he surveyed the throne and those about it 'with a derisive and insolent air' . . . So threatening was his mien already that one minister turned to his neighbour, whispering: 'I even have the feeling that this man might throw a bomb.' The dowager empress also felt herself surrounded by enemies, 'so much did they seem to reflect an incomprehensible hatred for all of us,' she confessed.

On the Second Duma

(quoting Bernard Pares, 1923–4, SEER 11, 48–9)

Right-wing members were openly provocative. They told an English liberal, Bernard Pares, that 'they aimed at dissolution and the curtailment of the franchise' . . . Shulgin introduced a cleverly worded mock bill for the socialization of all brains and once began a speech by asking the Socialist Revolutionaries if any of them happened to have a bomb in his pocket . . . On the other hand, ministers speaking in the duma were interrupted by the lefts; sometimes at unsatisfactory answers to abuses of official or police authority . . . A genuine thrill ran through the house when an old SR peasant, Kirnosov (from Saratov), with flaming eyes and shaggy hair and beard, intervened in a debate which touched on the rights of property. 'We know all about your property,' he said, 'we were your property. My uncle was exchanged for a greyhound.'

Third and Fourth Dumas

For the Third and Fourth Dumas, Stolypin decided to change the electoral system to favour the upper and propertied classes. The peasants and workers were virtually excluded and non-Russian national groups much reduced. As a result, the Octobrists and right-wing parties predominated. Even so, the Third Duma was not subservient and questioned the government hard, particularly on state finances. Stolypin was able to work with the more moderate centre parties to achieve progress in his social and economic reforms. However, this time he found that it was the right-wing groups and nationalists who tried to put a brake on his reforms, probably with the support of the Tsar. At least it showed the Duma could work positively with the government and it did provide a training ground in constitutionalism.

The Fourth Duma was interrupted by the outbreak of the First World War and met intermittently during the war. Before the war, it attempted some reform of the Orthodox Church and supported the law of 1908 providing for universal education – but progress was slow. It was also critical of the government's handling of increasing social unrest, especially the Lena Goldfields Massacre (see page 55). On the outbreak of the war the Duma threw itself behind the Tsar and the national war effort. It agreed to suspend itself for the duration of the war. However, when it became apparent that the government was managing the war very badly, the Duma pressurised the Tsar into recalling it in July 1915. It offered the Tsar one last opportunity to agree to limited constitutional government (see pages 62–63).

Why might Stolypin have approved of the future British Prime Minister Lord Liverpool's statement of 1793: 'We ought not to begin first by considering who ought to be the electors, and who ought to be elected; but we ought to begin by considering who ought to be elected, and then constitute such persons, electors, as would be likely to produce the best elected.'

■ 3A The dumas

First Duma

Duration: April–June 1906 (2 months)
Representation: Of the 478 seats, the Kadets with 185 seats and the Trudoviks (left-wing labourists) with 94 were dominant along with moderate business interests. 112 were non-partisans, generally sympathetic to the liberals.

Main events/achievements
· Deputies demanded increased powers.
· Little in practice achieved though there were fierce debates on a range of issues, such as civil rights, amnesty for political prisoners and land ownership.
· Tsar claimed Duma unworkable and dissolved it.

Second Duma

Duration: February–June 1907 (4 months)
Representation: The number of Kadets halved to under a 100 but they were still significant. The Trudoviks were the largest group with 104 deputies. Also, there were 47 Mensheviks and 37 SRs who joined the elections for the first time. In all there were well over 200 deputies on the Left. The National parties had 93 deputies. However the right-wing groupings had also increased their number with over 60 deputies from various factions; the Octobrists had increased their number to 44.

Main events/achievements
· Left- and right-wing deputies attacked each other, debates frequently ending in brawls.
· Left-wing deputies made fierce attacks on Stolypin and his land reforms.
· The Duma co-operated with the government over famine relief.
· The government claimed Menshevik and SR deputies were subversive and, amid scenes of disorder, the Duma was dissolved.

Third Duma

Duration: November 1907–June 1912 (four and a half years)
Representation: Electoral system changed restricting franchise; peasant and working class vote radically reduced (only one in six able to vote). As a result the parties on the Right dominated: the Octobrists with 154 deputies and the Rightists with 147 out of a total of 441 seats. The Kadets had been cut down to 54, the national parties to 26 seats and the Trudoviks to 14.

Main events/achievements
· Relations with the government were more harmonious now that the Duma was biased towards the Right but it was by no means servile.
· Stolypin was able to work with it and put through his land reforms although he faced a lot of opposition.
· A law on universal education was passed aiming at a minimum of four years compulsory primary school education.
· Steps were taken to modernise the army.
· Justices of the Peace were restored, replacing the hated land captains.
· The Duma developed a progressive national health insurance scheme for workers to cover sickness and accidents.

Fourth Duma

Duration: November 1912–August 1914, suspended but also met in 1915 and 1916.
Representation: Similar to Third Duma.
Main events/achievements
· This was a period of some tension as the Lena Goldfields Massacre heralded in industrial unrest and strikes.
· Some reform of Orthodox Church reducing state control and broadening education in church schools.
· Progress in education, supporting 1908 law which had provided for universal education; increased spending on teacher's salaries.
· Discussion of the health of people, in particular ways to reduce drunkenness.

WHY DIDN'T THE TSAR JUST GET RID OF THE DUMA ALTOGETHER?

1 He was bound by the agreement in the October Manifesto. He feared a popular reaction if he ditched it.
2 Britain and France were Russia's allies in the international arena and the Tsar wanted to give the appearance of a more democratic Russia.
3 The electoral system was changed to make the Duma more docile.

FOCUS ROUTE

As you work through this section:

1 Assess whether Stolypin's agrarian reforms could have helped save the Tsar and enter your thoughts on Stolypin in the table that you constructed for Section A.
2 Make notes in preparation for the essay at the end of this section.

Summary

Nicholas had shown that he was never really willing to work with or listen to the Duma. He looked for excuses to close down sessions. He was only concerned with preserving the autocracy, largely because he believed it was a better way of running Russia. He did not accept that democratic government could be effective and did not understand that, by passing some of his responsibilities to an elected assembly, he could avoid the criticism and hostility directed at him from various sections of Russian society. Not all the blame should be attached to the Tsar. The Kadets' demands in the First Duma were very radical and they were not prepared to compromise or be patient. As a result, the Duma degenerated into quarrels and a bitter struggle between the Tsar and his supporters on the Right, and the liberals and other parties on the Left. This did not allow for any relationship of trust and co-operation to develop.

C How far had the economy improved by 1914?

Agrarian reforms

Stolypin saw his land reforms as the key to transforming Russia into a stable and prosperous country. Peasants were allowed to leave the mir (commune), to consolidate their strips of land into a single unit and build a farmhouse on it. He called it 'a gamble not on the drunken and feeble but on the sober and strong'. A land bank was set up to help the independent peasant buy land. Stolypin believed that the mir with its antiquated farming methods 'paralysed personal initiative'. Also, making peasants into independent property owners and giving them full civil rights would give them a stake in the country and lead to them becoming supporters of the regime. There were also schemes to re-settle peasants in Siberia which had been opened up by the Trans-Siberian Railway. This was in order to use peasants to create new food-growing areas.

The view of Abraham Ascher in his major study of Stolypin is that, 'given more time for implementation, the agrarian reforms might have contributed to a more moderate revolution than the one of 1917.' However, by 1914 only about 10 per cent of households in European Russia lived on farms separated from the commune. Only a minority lived on farms in the West European sense with a cottage and fields fenced off from their neighbours. Communal institutions remained strong, embodying the peasants' notions of social justice, and the mir was appreciated by many peasants as a 'life jacket'. Those who left – the 'Stolypin separators' – were seen as traitors to the peasant tradition. The reform was more successful in the west – in the Ukraine and Belorussia – than in other parts of Russia where reform was most needed.

Judith Pallot argues that, 'Stolypin's reform was "in essence a utopian project", and too narrowly conceived to create a loyal peasantry and modernise peasant farming – there were alternatives which could have done as much if not more to increase peasant farm productivity.' (J. Pallot: *Land Reform in Russia 1906–1917*, 1999, pp. 30–31). She points out that the commune was not always backward: new crops, seeds, crop rotations and fertilisers were being employed in some go-ahead communes. Also, some 'separators', eager to make a quick profit, used poor farming methods that exhausted the soil.

SOURCE 3.3 Number of peasant households becoming independent 1907–1914 (out of an estimated total of 10–12 million households)

1907	48,271
1908	508,334
1909	579,409
1910	342,245
1911	145,567
1912	122,314
1913	134,554
1914	97,877

SOURCE 3.4 A peasant in a Soviet prison after collectivisation talking to a companion, quoted in S. Williams, *Liberal Reform in an Illiberal Regime: The Creation of Private Property in Russia, 1906–1915*, 2006, pp.1–2

I had 20 desiatines (about 54 acres). This means I was a kulak by their ideas. I worked hard, but got little from it. At least until the Stolypin booklet (booklet on soil management and crop production distributed to accompany the reforms) fell into my hands. When I applied what was written there to my land, I got rich directly. But of course, when it (the Revolution) began they took everything away and threw me out into the forest. There they set aside 4 desiatines for my family and me . . . They took away everything but I brought my Stolypin booklet. And then the years passed, and again I did things according to Stolypin, and again I was rich – not rich, but well enough off. And again they were envious, and again took everything and threw me out.

By 1914, the vast majority of agricultural production, in what was still an overwhelmingly agricultural country, was the responsibility of 20 million peasant households, most of whom were still organised in rural communes using the inefficient strip system. Helped by loans from the state bank and migration to new farms in Siberia, the amount of land held by peasants increased, and by 1916 less than 10 per cent of the sown area was directly cultivated as landowners' estates.

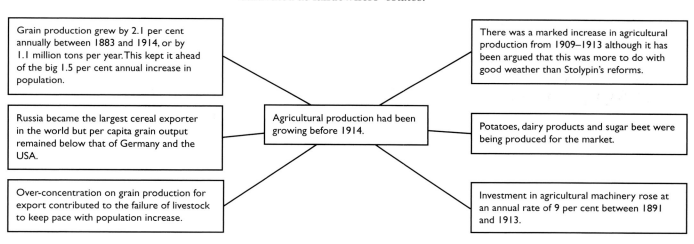

Grain production grew by 2.1 per cent annually between 1883 and 1914, or by 1.1 million tons per year. This kept it ahead of the big 1.5 per cent annual increase in population.

Russia became the largest cereal exporter in the world but per capita grain output remained below that of Germany and the USA.

Over-concentration on grain production for export contributed to the failure of livestock to keep pace with population increase.

Agricultural production had been growing before 1914.

There was a marked increase in agricultural production from 1909–1913 although it has been argued that this was more to do with good weather than Stolypin's reforms.

Potatoes, dairy products and sugar beet were being produced for the market.

Investment in agricultural machinery rose at an annual rate of 9 per cent between 1891 and 1913.

Progress in industry

After 1907, industrial production grew steadily at a rate around 6 per cent per annum until 1914, although this high rate was largely due to the fact that it started from a low base. Although well behind the major Western industrial powers, the achievements were impressive. By 1914, Russia was the world's fourth largest producer of coal, pig-iron and steel, and the Baku oilfields were only rivalled by Texas. Heavy industry was still the driving force. This was in large part due to the government's rearmament programme with huge orders for metallurgical companies to rebuild the Baltic fleet after the losses of the Russo-Japanese War and also to re-stock with weapons generally. The downside of this focus on rearmament was that industry could not meet the demand for agricultural tools and machinery.

Industrial development was still largely state sponsored with companies dependent on government contracts. Foreign loans were still important but less so than they had been. In Russia there was a growing internal market and the production of consumer goods rose. Demand was coming from the peasants as the agricultural sector became more successful and prices for farm produce increased. However, as a proportion of total industrial production, the share of consumer goods actually fell from 52 per cent to 45 per cent.

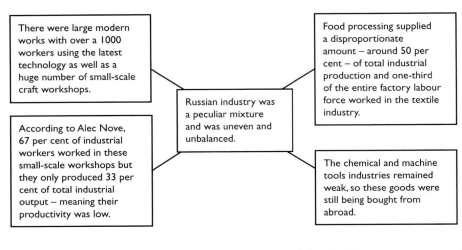

There were large modern works with over a 1000 workers using the latest technology as well as a huge number of small-scale craft workshops.

According to Alec Nove, 67 per cent of industrial workers worked in these small-scale workshops but they only produced 33 per cent of total industrial output – meaning their productivity was low.

Russian industry was a peculiar mixture and was uneven and unbalanced.

Food processing supplied a disproportionate amount – around 50 per cent – of total industrial production and one-third of the entire factory labour force worked in the textile industry.

The chemical and machine tools industries remained weak, so these goods were still being bought from abroad.

Comparing Russia with other countries:

- Per capita income in Russia in 1913 was one-tenth that of the USA and one-fifth that of Britain.
- Per capita output was only half that of the Austro-Hungarian empire.
- Industrial growth was still less rapid than in the USA and Germany so the gap in productive capacity widened.

SOURCE 3.5 The Tsarist economy: annual production (million tons)

	Coal	Pig iron	Oil	Grain
1870	0.68	0.33	0.03	
1880	3.24	0.42	0.5	
1890	5.90	0.89	3.9	
1900	16.10	2.66	10.2	56
1910	26.80	2.99	9.4	74
1913	35.40	4.12	9.1	90
1916	33.80	3.72	9.7	64

SOURCE 3.6 Growth of St Petersburg

Year	Inhabitants (millions)
1812	0.308
1830	0.435
1863	0.539
1869	0.667
1881	0.861
1897	1.260
1914	2.20

Writing an essay to answer a specific question:

How far do you agree that the economy of Tsarist Russia was transformed in the years to 1914?

To answer this question you have to look carefully at what it is asking you to do. 'Transformed' means changed fundamentally. 'How far do you agree' suggests there is a debate on this issue and that you have to make a judgement. You need to:

- look at the development of agriculture and industry in 1881–1914. Some figures, but not many, will be required as supporting evidence
- look particularly at Witte's industrialisation drive and Stolypin's land reforms
- acknowledge ups and downs – growth in the 1890s, depression after 1900, effect of Russo-Japanese War and 1905 revolution, boom after 1909
- survey the economic situation in 1914 and make some international comparisons
- consider the views of historians about the state of the economy before 1914.

Some historians consider that the economy was stabilising and set to do well if growth rates had continued at the same pace. Alexander Gerschenkron, a Russian-American economist, thought that the signs were so encouraging that, if the First World War had not occurred, Russia was well on the way to developing into a successful modern industrial state. Others, more pessimistic, contend that, despite her growth, Russia was still backward in many respects and falling behind more advanced industrialised countries, especially in terms of production per head of the population. A third view is that the boom was likely to be short-lived and that Russia would soon face another crisis. Alec Nove, one of the most highly regarded historians of the Russian economy, highlights the uneven nature of Russian industry and points out that the question of whether Russia would have become a modern industrial state had it not been for war and revolution is, in essence, meaningless. It assumes that the regime would have proceeded on an orderly path and adjusted to the strains of a changing society. Nove quotes Gerschenkron: 'Industrialisation, the cost of which was largely defrayed by the peasantry, was itself a threat to political stability and hence to the continuation of the policy of industrialisation.'

D How revolutionary was Russia in 1914?

FOCUS ROUTE

Assess each group as you read through this section:

	How far a potential revolutionary threat?	Reality in 1914
Workers		
Peasants		
Liberals		
Revolutionaries		
Army		

The workers

By 1914, the industrial workforce had established itself as a distinct section of the population: a majority of workers who began employment between 1906–13 were the children of workers. The level of literacy among workers was high, reaching 64 per cent in 1914 compared with less than 40 per cent for the adult population in general. Things had not improved much for most of them since 1905; they had seen very little reward from the growth in industrial production. Workers' wages were less than one-third the average in Western Europe and the Russian government had made no real attempt to improve their conditions in contrast to the social reforms enacted elsewhere in Europe. In 1912, limited insurance had been introduced for accidents and sickness but this covered only a minority of the workforce. People still worked long hours for low pay. In some workplaces their hours had actually been increased since 1905 and others had been put onto piece work. For old age, occupational disease and unemployment there was little or no support.

After 1905 the labour movement had retreated due to the repression of trade unions and strikes, but there was a revival of militancy from 1912. It started with the Lena Goldfields Massacre in April 1912. Striking workers, protesting about degrading working conditions, low wages and a 14-hour working day, clashed with troops and over 200 people were killed and many injured. This opened the floodgates to workers' protests.

Strikes grew in militancy from 1912 to 1914. July 1914 saw a general strike in St Petersburg involving barricades and street fighting. However, only a quarter of the work force were involved, compared with four-fifths in February 1917. Students, whose relationship with the government had become increasingly embittered in the years leading to 1914, supported the workers. The regime was right to be worried by industrial and urban unrest but was not likely to be toppled by it in 1914.

SOURCE 3.7 Strikes 1908–1914

Year	Total strikes	Strikes regarded as political
1908	892	464
1909	340	50
1910	222	8
1911	466	24
1912	2032	1300
1913	2404	1034
1914 (Jan–July)	3534	2401

Year	No. of strikers
1911	105,110
1912	725,491
1913	861,289
1914 (Jan–July)	1,448,684

Some historians argue that workers in larger factories were turning towards the Bolsheviks who supported violent upheaval and armed struggle and that this indicated a similar situation building to that of 1905. However, R. B. McKean in his study of *St Petersburg Between the Revolutions: Workers and Revolutionaries June 1907–February 1917* argues that most workers did not work in the larger factories targeted by the socialists but in the domestic and service sectors. He maintains that most workers were not socialists and the strikes were mainly about pay and working conditions; only a relatively small number, predominantly male metal workers, were engaged in radical activity before 1917.

The peasants

Some historians contend that recent evidence suggests that living standards were rising amongst peasants in the years leading to 1914. Several years of good harvests certainly helped. They point out that the villages were relatively quiet before 1914 and militancy was to be found in the cities rather than the countryside. However, it is difficult to generalise about the standard of living for peasants because there was so much variation between and even within regions. It seems likely that while a minority prospered, others remained impoverished.

Although there had been no major upheavals and disturbances, some historians have noted simmering resentment in the countryside. The divisive nature of the Stolypin reforms was shown by conflicts over enclosure between 1906 and 1914. In some instances, the separators faced violence and intimidation from the older entrenched peasants and troops had to be brought in to make sure the reforms went ahead. The peasants had not been tied closer to the Tsar as Stolypin hoped. Their expectations of change had been dashed after 1905 and the growth in population had only increased their hunger for land, particularly in the central agricultural province. Their main aims had not changed: getting their hands on the nobility's land and farming it free from government interference. Orlando Figes' research suggests that landowners felt that, 'the next – and imminently more powerful revolutionary outburst by the peasantry would only be a question of time.'

Stolypin's reforms had other consequences

The peasants who had left the land as a result of the reforms were often full of resentment and many of these had gone into the towns and cities to become industrial workers. Also thousands of peasants who had been encouraged to go to Siberia returned home, having found the land inhospitable or been cheated by land speculators. They also were resentful. The net result was to increase a section of the labour force that was rootless and disoriented and who provided good material for revolutionary propaganda.

The liberals

The liberals were in a weak and uncomfortable position sandwiched between the Right, who firmly supported the autocracy, and the radical workers and peasants. The liberals were divided and no real threat. The Octobrists and the Kadets distrusted each other, were out of touch with the masses and refused to seek their support. They feared mass anarchy and did not support the strike movement. They depended on the government to implement their programmes so they needed the Tsar more than he needed them. However, Guchkov, the Octobrist leader, told his followers in November 1913 that he was reminded of 1905 but this time the danger came from a government whose actions were revolutionising society and the people. 'With every day, people are losing faith in the state and in the possibility of a normal, peaceful resolution of the crisis' the probable outcome of which was 'a sad unavoidable catastrophe'.

How strong were the revolutionaries?

The SRs and the Mensheviks had both been weakened in the years before 1914. The SRs were in turmoil after 1908 as a result of the exposure of Azef (see below), especially as the party's terrorist wing had such prestige within the party. The SRs became obsessed with the issue of double agents and party organisation broke down. There were divisions amongst the leadership, and between the leadership and the rank and file. The party was unable to take advantage of the revival in militancy after the Lena Goldfields Massacre. Until that event the Mensheviks, with their emphasis on the creation of a legal labour movement taking advantage of the new political freedoms won in 1905, enjoyed more support inside Russia. Lena was a blow to any illusions about the regime and peaceful change, and gave the more radical Bolsheviks their opportunity. By 1914 the Bolsheviks had more influence in the trade unions than the Mensheviks, gaining control of some of the biggest unions in St Petersburg and Moscow, like the Metalworkers Union. The Bolshevik paper, *Pravda*, had achieved a national circulation of 40,000 copies per issue, over twice that of its Menshevik rival. However, the workers were generally not housed in large factories, radicalised and under Bolshevik control as some Soviet historians claimed them to be. The leadership was either in exile or, like Lenin, isolated abroad. Lenin had failed to build a national illegal party organisation. Even in January 1917 Lenin said, 'We, the old people, perhaps won't survive until the decisive battles of the forthcoming revolution.' A huge problem for the Bolsheviks as well as the SRs was that they were thoroughly infiltrated by the Okhrana.

How reliable was the army?

The events of 1905 had shown that the regime could survive if it could rely on the army, and in 1914 the army remained loyal. However, Edward Acton points out that the experience of 1905–6 and the subsequent reforms had weakened the reliability of the army as an instrument of control. The mutinies in 1905 and 1906 could not be easily forgotten. Cutting the period of service to three years brought the army into much closer contact with the stresses and strains of civilian society. Also, as the officer corps became more professional, it became more determined not to be used for crushing civilian disturbances.

POLICE, SPIES AND THE REVOLUTIONARY PARTIES: AZEF AND MALINOVSKY

Evno Azef has been called the greatest double agent of them all. He had a remarkably long 15-year career and by 1903 he had risen to become the overseer of the SR's Combat Organisation when it was at its most active, assassinating in 1904 Plehve, the Minister of the Interior, and in 1905 Grand Duke Sergei. Anna Geifman, using newly available Okhrana archive material, sees Azef's role as that of a typical spy and informer. She claims the assassination of Plehve was due to police incompetence since Azef had provided enough information to foil the attempt.

After the assassination of Grand Duke Sergei, Azef met the new police chief regularly in a flat in St Petersburg and together they prevented any further assassination attempts on major figures – including one on the Tsar – until Azef's exposure in 1908 (he fled abroad with his mistress and settled in Germany). The unmasking of Azef was a devastating blow to the SR's Combat Organisation. One member wrote: 'If the person we believed in as the best of friends, as a brother, turns out to be such a base traitor, does this not mean that it is no longer possible to believe in man altogether, that there is no truth in the world, that there is nothing worth living for?' Almost two dozen more informers were exposed in the next four years and the debilitating effect on the SRs contributed to their failure in 1917.

For their Bolshevik rivals, Lenin insisted that the revolutionary movement would triumph only if a 'few professionals as highly trained and experienced as our [security] police' were allowed to organise it: hence the secret meeting places, forged passports, secret codes and aliases – Lenin himself had 150 of them. Despite this, four out of five of the party's St Petersburg committee in 1908-9 were Okhrana agents. In 1911, the Bolsheviks set up a special three-man commission 'to expose and isolate provocateurs'. It included Roman Malinovsky, an SD member of the Duma, who became Lenin's closest political confidant inside Russia. But Malinovsky was an Okhrana agent, ordered by the Director of the Police Department to attach himself closely to Lenin. Lenin refused to consider suspicions that he was a police agent.

Police files opened after the February revolution finally established Malinovsky's guilt, showing drafts of his speeches in the Duma with amendments in the handwriting of both Lenin and the police chief. He submitted 88 reports on his SD colleagues between 1910 and 1913 which wreaked havoc on the Bolshevik underground. Stalin, Sverdlov, Bukharin and Ordzhonikidze were among those Malinovsky had arrested. He even persuaded Lenin to appoint an Okhrana agent editor of *Pravda*. In 1914, a new police chief decided that rising Bolshevik support might be undermined by exposing their best known spokesman as an agent provocateur. Malinovsky fled Russia. When Lenin returned to Russia in 1917 and read of Malinovsky's guilt, Zinoviev tells us he went white with astonishment and said, 'What a scoundrel! He tricked the lot of us. Traitor! Shooting's too good for him!' After the revolution Malinovsky returned to Russia voluntarily, was put on trial and shot.

The Okhrana were the best secret service of their day: Molotov, a leading Bolshevik, admitted that, 'they had smarter people than ours'. Typically, when SR terrorists considered flying a dynamite-packed biplane into the Winter Palace in 1909, the Okhrana ordered the monitoring of all flights as well as people learning to fly. Even so, the Okhrana could not prevent the major upsurge in terrorism during Nicholas II's reign. Nevertheless, their widespread penetration of the Social Democrats destroyed morale and comradeship. Simon Sebag Montifore argues that the Okhrana were so successful in poisoning revolutionary minds that, 'thirty years after the fall of the tsars, the Bolsheviks were still killing each other in a witch-hunt for non-existent traitors'. Molotov, justifying Stalin's terror in his retirement, said, 'We never forgot the agent provocateur Malinovsky.'

Evno Azef

Roman Malinovsky

E The impact of the First World War

FOCUS ROUTE

As you read through this section make notes on how the war contributed to the problems facing the Tsar.

When war broke out in July 1914, Russia's internal divisions were temporarily forgotten and Nicholas rode a wave of popular support. Paintings of the Tsar were carried in processions and crowds sang the national anthem. The *Times* correspondent wrote: 'For perhaps the first time since Napoleon's invasion of Russia, the people and their Tsar were one, and the strength that unity spreads in a nation stirred throughout the Empire.' But the enthusiasm did not last long.

At the Front

The Russians had the largest army and gained some early successes against the Austro-Hungarians. But it was a different story against the Germans. In August 1914, at the battle of Tannenberg, and in September at the Masurian Lakes, the Russians took heavy losses and were driven back. There followed a long retreat throughout 1915. By the autumn of 1915 they had been forced out of Poland, Lithuania and Latvia. Between May and December of that year one million Russians were killed and a similar number were taken prisoner. The Russians recovered during the winter of 1915–16 and in the summer of 1916 General Brusilov launched a brilliant offensive, which brought the Austrians to their knees with over half their army killed or captured. But the Germans moved troops to reinforce them and the Russians were pushed back once more.

The real problem for the Russians was at the top: the quality of leadership was poor, with notable exceptions like Brusilov. Many of the top officers had been appointed because of their loyalty to the Tsar. They had no experience of fighting and little military expertise. There was no clear command structure and no war plan was developed. The performance of the War Ministry was dire, compounded by the breakdown of the distribution system (see The home front, page 61): there was a lack of supplies and equipment, especially rifles, ammunition and boots. The shortage of rifles was so bad on some parts of the Front that soldiers had to rely on picking up the rifles of men shot in front of them. Often the war materials were available but they were not where they were needed.

■ 3B Russian battle lines, 1914–17

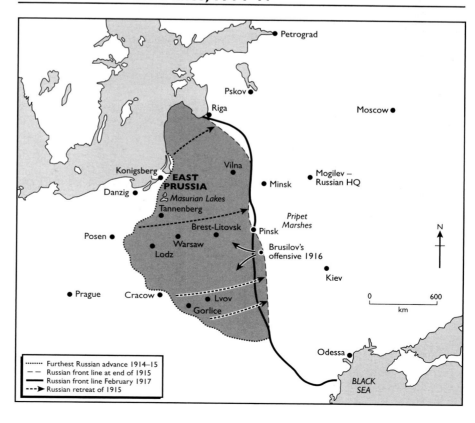

- .... Furthest Russian advance 1914–15
- – – – Russian front line at end of 1915
- —— Russian front line February 1917
- ▶▶▶ Russian retreat of 1915

SOURCE 3.8 Mikhail Rodzianko, A report from the Front

The army had neither wagons nor horses nor first aid supplies . . . We visited the Warsaw station where there were about 17,000 men wounded in battles. At the station we found a terrible scene: on the platform in dirt, filth and cold, in the rain on the ground even without straw, wounded, who filled the air with heart rending cries, dolefully asked: 'For God's sake order them to dress our wounds, for five days we have not been attended to.'

SOURCE 3.10 Russian troops awaiting German attack, 1917

When Mikhail Rodzianko, the President of the Duma, went on a special fact-finding tour, he received a lot of complaints about poor administration and the lack of basic supplies. He also found that provision for dealing with wounded soldiers was abysmal (see Source 3.8). The morale of the soldiers was hard hit by the incompetence of their officers and the lack of regard for their welfare – tens of thousands deserted.

SOURCE 3.9 Rodzianko's son, who was in the army, told of criminal incompetence and lack of co-operation in the high command. He reported the following attack on the Rai-Mestro Height to his father. It had been ordered by the Grand Duke who had been warned about a swamp which lay in the way, but he still ordered the advance

The troops found themselves in the swamp, where many men perished. . . . My son sank up to his armpits and was with difficulty extricated. . . . The wounded could not be brought out and perished in the swamp. Our artillery fire was weak . . . and the shells fell short and dropped among our own men. . . . Nevertheless, the gallant guards fulfilled their task, WHICH THEY WERE THEN ORDERED TO ABANDON.

SOURCE 3.11 Wounded Russians during the First World War at a temporary field hospital in a Russian church

However, the Russian war effort was not the total disaster it has sometimes been portrayed as, by mostly Soviet historians. Norman Stone has pointed out that by 1916 the Russians were matching the Germans in shell production and there had been a 1000 per cent growth in the output of artillery and rifles. They had success against the Austrians and contributed significantly to the Allied victory by mounting attacks on the Eastern Front to relieve pressure on the Western Front. In 1916, Brusilov saved the French at Verdun when the Germans had to pull out 35 divisions to counter his offensive. The Eastern Front engaged enormous numbers of German troops. Also, according to Stone, the army was not on the verge of collapse at the beginning of 1917; it was still intact as a fighting force.

The home front

The strain of equipping and feeding millions of soldiers proved too much for the Russian economy and revealed its structural weaknesses. Military needs had priority and the railways, which were barely able to cope with freight traffic in peacetime, were now overloaded. There were bottlenecks at Moscow. The signalling system collapsed and trains were left stranded on lines due to engine failure. Early in the war, goods and supplies were available but trucks ended up in sidings waiting for engines or lines to be unblocked.

The loss of land in Poland and the West knocked out the more important of the two main lines from northern to southern Russia. As a result, there was a major problem moving grain from the south to the cities, and Petrograd suffered particularly. Making matters worse was the lack of grain coming onto the market. The peasants were not selling it as there was little incentive for them to do so. The government would not pay higher prices and the conversion of factories to military work meant there was little for peasants to buy – the production of agricultural implements was only 15 per cent of the pre-war level.

Inflation compounded these problems. Russia abandoned the gold standard and started printing money to pay wages, and so government spending rose. With people desperately seeking goods in short supply, inflation kicked in. Whilst wages more or less doubled between 1914 and 1916, the price of food and fuel quadrupled.

The expansion of the workforce in factories and mines servicing military needs and the influx of refugees from German occupied areas led to very serious overcrowding in the towns and a deterioration in living standards. There were food and fuel shortages and endless queues. Petrograd suffered more than other places because it was remote from food-producing areas. By 1916, it was receiving barely a third of the food and fuel it required. The shortage of food was a major source of anger, matched only by the ban on vodka sales. Strikes had broken out in 1915 and they increased in number, frequency and militancy during 1916. The war also took its toll in a more personal way. As the list of casualties mounted there was hardly a family that had not been affected by a son killed or captured.

The role of the Tsar in the war

The support the Tsar enjoyed at the beginning of the war faded as the military defeats piled up. As in 1905, confidence in the government evaporated as its incompetence and inability to effectively organise supplies for the military at the Front and the people in the cities became apparent. The zemstva and municipalities started forming their own bodies to provide medical care, hospitals and hospital trains for the thousands of wounded soldiers. These bodies eventually united to form one organisation – Zemgor. They went on to supply uniforms, boots and tents. Professional groups and businessmen formed War Industries Committees (WICs) to shift factories over to military production. Leading liberals played an important role in these non-governmental organisations that seemed to offer an alternative – and much more effective – form of government. So, even though these organisations were fully supportive of the war, the autocracy regarded them with suspicion and would not co-operate with them. The Tsarina, in particular, saw them as revolutionary bodies undermining the autocracy; and indeed they did act as a focus for criticism of the bureaucracy's failings.

The Tsar was pressurised into reconvening the Duma in July 1915. Progressive elements in the Duma (about two-thirds of the total deputies) formed the 'Progressive Bloc'. They wished to be fully involved in the war effort and wanted to prevent the country slipping into revolution and anarchy, which frightened them as much as anybody else. The Bloc called for a 'ministry of national confidence' in which elected members of the Duma would replace incompetent ministers to form a new government. This offered a real chance for the Tsar to be seen to be working with the people and offload some of the responsibility for the war. But the Tsar would not countenance it and suspended the Duma, which only met again briefly in 1916 and 1917. The Progressive

Bloc became frustrated by his intransigence. In November 1916, Milyukov, the Kadet leader, made a speech listing the government's shortcomings around the question: 'Is this stupidity or treason?' (see Source 3.12). He also declared that the Duma would fight the government 'with all legitimate means until you go'.

SOURCE 3.12 Speech by Paul Milyukov to the Duma, November 1916, quoted in John Laver, *Russia 1914–41*, pp. 6–7

We now see that we can no more legislate with this government than we can lead Russia to victory with it. When the Duma declares again and again that the home front must be organised for a successful war and the government continues to insist that to organise the country means to organise revolution, and consciously chooses chaos and disintegration – is this stupidity or treason? [Voices from the left: 'treason'.] *. . . We have many reasons for being discontented with this government. But all these reasons boil down to one general one: the incompetence and evil intentions of the present government . . . And therefore in the name of the millions of victims and their spilled blood . . . we shall fight until we get a responsible government which is in agreement with the general principles of our programme. Cabinet members must agree unanimously as to the most urgent tasks, they must agree and be prepared to implement the programme of the Duma. A Cabinet which does not satisfy these conditions does not deserve the confidence of the Duma and should go.* [Voices: 'bravo'; loud and prolonged applause.]

In August 1915 the Tsar made a huge mistake: he decided to take direct control of the army and went off to military headquarters in Mogilev, 600 kilometres from Petrograd. This had a number of serious consequences for him:

1 He now became personally responsible for the conduct of the war. If things went badly he would be directly to blame. He could not pass off the responsibility to his generals.
2 He was away from Petrograd for long periods of time, leaving the Tsarina and Rasputin (see opposite) in control of the government. 'Lovy,' she wrote to her husband, 'I am here, don't laugh at silly old wifey, but she has "trousers" on unseen.'

This created chronic instability in the government. There were constant changes of ministers – a game of ministerial leapfrog (see box) in which the hand of the Tsarina can be detected. Competent people were dismissed: for instance, the War Minister, Polivanov, who was rebuilding the army and supply system with some success after the disasters of 1915, was discharged. The Tsarina regarded him as a traitor and a 'revolutionist' because of his willingness to work with Zemgor and the WICs. Incompetent people were appointed, often because they flattered the Tsarina or because they were recommended by Rasputin. The appointment of Sturmer as Prime Minister in February 1916 caused great disquiet: not only was he incompetent and dishonest but he also had a German name.

It is not surprising that by the end of 1916 support for the Tsar was haemorrhaging fast. All classes in society were disillusioned by the way the government was running the war and since the Tsar embodied the government and had taken direct control of the armed forces it was towards him that the finger of responsibility was pointed. The governing élite was in disarray and even some of the nobility were supporting the Progressive Bloc in the Duma. People were talking about an impending revolution.

The situation in Petrograd was becoming tense. A secret police report at the end of 1916 said that the workers in Petrograd were on the verge of despair, with the cost of living having risen by 300 per cent, food almost unobtainable and long queues outside most shops. The secret police reported a rising death rate due to inadequate diet, unsanitary and cold lodgings and 'a mass of industrial workers quite ready to let themselves go to the wildest excesses of a hunger strike'.

MINISTERIAL LEAPFROG: SEPTEMBER 1915 TO FEBRUARY 1917

- 4 Prime Ministers
- 5 Ministers of Internal Affairs
- 3 Ministers of Foreign Affairs
- 3 Ministers of War
- 3 Ministers of Transport
- 4 Ministers of Agriculture

ACTIVITY

1 Why do you think Sources 3.14 and 3.15 might have serious consequences for the Tsar?
2 In what ways do you think that Rasputin contributed to the Tsar's downfall?

THE IMPACT OF RASPUTIN

SOURCE 3.13 Grigory Rasputin surrounded by ladies of the aristocracy

Grigory Yefimovich, born into a Siberian peasant family, gained a reputation as a holy man, or 'starets', and the name Rasputin. It was rumoured that he belonged to the Kylysty, a sect that found religious fulfilment and ecstasy through the religious senses and, in particular, sexual acts. In 1905, Rasputin was introduced into polite society in St Petersburg and became known to the royal family. The Tsar's son, Alexis, suffered from haemophilia, and doctors found it difficult to stop the bleeding that resulted from this. In 1907, when Alexis was experiencing a particularly bad episode, Rasputin was called in and Alexis recovered. This happened on other occasions. It is not known how Rasputin did this: he may have had some skill with herbal remedies or some ability in hypnosis that calmed Alexis. The Tsarina, a deeply religious woman, believed that Rasputin had been sent by God to save her son. This gave him an elevated position at the Russian court with direct access to the royal family. Women from the higher social circles flocked to him to ask for advice and healing or to carry petitions to the Tsar to advance their husbands' careers. There were rumours that Rasputin solicited sexual favours for this help and stories of orgies emerged. However, secret police reports and subsequent investigations seemed to show that his sexual activity – and he was very active – was restricted mainly to actresses and prostitutes rather than society women.

Whatever the truth about Rasputin's relationships, his reputation for debauchery played a significant role in damaging the standing of the royal family and caused the Tsar political problems. The Tsar had newspaper reports about Rasputin censored. He fell out with the Duma over this and Rasputin's influential position at court. Ministers like Stolypin profoundly disapproved of Rasputin, but any mention of the problems he caused brought short shrift from the Tsar.

The impact of Rasputin became even more damaging during the war. When the Tsar went to the Front, he left the Tsarina and Rasputin effectively in control of domestic matters. They played havoc with ministers and contributed to the government's instability. As a result, they became the focus of growing public anger and antagonism towards the regime. She was portrayed as a German spy, deliberately conniving with Rasputin to betray Mother Russia. Pornographic cartoons (see Source 3.15) and letters found their way into the press and implied that she was having an illicit relationship with Rasputin and was under his control. Even the rapidly diminishing supporters of the Tsar could not put up with the degenerate monk and the 'German woman' running the country. In December 1916, a member of the royal family, Prince Yusupov, arranged to murder Rasputin in a last ditch effort to save the autocracy. But the damage had been done: many were now convinced the regime was not worth saving.

SOURCE 3.14 One of the letters from the Tsarina to Rasputin that was leaked to the press. Some historians think these letters were edited to the detriment of the Tsarina. Others point out that she used gushing, over-the-top language in all her letters. There is no evidence that she had a sexual affair with Rasputin

My beloved, unforgettable teacher, redeemer, mentor! How tiresome it is without you. My soul is quiet and I relax only when you, my teacher, are sitting beside me. I kiss your hands . . . I wish only one thing: to fall asleep . . . forever on your shoulders and in your arms . . . will you soon be again close to me? Come quickly, I am waiting for you and I am tormenting myself for you . . . I love you forever.

SOURCE 3.15 Postcards like this circulated freely during 1917

Military failures

● Heavy defeats and the huge numbers of Russians killed in 1914 and 1915 led to disillusionment and anger about the way the Tsar and the government were conducting the war. Losing a war is always bad for a government.

● In August 1915, the Tsar assumed command of the army and went to the Front to take personal charge; from then on he was held personally responsible for defeats.

Difficult living conditions

The war caused acute distress in large cities, especially Petrograd and Moscow. Disruption of supplies meant that food, goods and raw materials were in short supply; hundreds of factories closed and thousands were put out of work; prices rocketed and inflation was rampant; lack of fuel meant that people were cold as well as hungry. Urban workers became very hostile towards the tsarist government. In the countryside, the peasants became increasingly angry about the conscription of all the young men, who seldom returned from the Front.

Role of the Tsarina and Rasputin

● The Tsar made the mistake of leaving his wife, the Tsarina Alexandra, and the monk Rasputin in charge of the government while he was at the Front. They made a terrible mess of running the country, dismissing able ministers in favour of friends or toadies who performed poorly. Ministers were changed frequently. As a result, the situation in the cities deteriorated rapidly with food and fuel in very short supply.

● The Tsarina and Rasputin became totally discredited. The odium and ridicule they generated (cartoons were circulated showing them in bed together) also tainted the Tsar, who was blamed for putting them in charge. The higher echelons of society and army generals became disenchanted with the Tsar's leadership and support for him haemorrhaged away. By the beginning of 1917, few were prepared to defend him.

Failure to make political reforms

During the war the Tsar had the chance to make some concessions to political reform that might have saved him. Russia could have slipped into a constitutional monarchy and the pressure would have been taken off him personally. The Duma was fully behind the Tsar in fighting the war. A group called the 'Progressive Bloc' emerged who suggested that the Tsar establish a 'government of public confidence', which really meant letting them run the country. However, the Tsar rejected their approach. He had opted to retain autocracy and was to pay the price for it.

FOCUS ROUTE

Draw an annotated diagram as you read through this section and the next chapter. Mark on key dates and use brief notes to show how the revolution developed. Identify key turning points.

F How popular was the February Revolution?

In February 1917, a wave of popular unrest swept Nicholas II from office and the Romanov dynasty to oblivion. By the time he abdicated it was clear that support for him had almost universally collapsed and that there were few people left who wanted to see him continuing to run the country. The final push came from the workers in Petrograd, who came out of the winter with little prospect of any improvement on the horizon. Strikes and lock-outs had created high levels of tension. The Tsarina ignored warnings from the secret police, condemning strikers as hooligans and fulminating against leading members of the Duma for undermining the government.

■ **Learning trouble spot**

The Russian calendar

The tsarist Russian calendar was based on the Julian calendar (introduced by Julius Caesar in 46BC). Although a new calendar had been introduced by Pope Gregory in 1582 and gradually adopted throughout Europe – Britain had changed to the Gregorian calendar in 1752 – Russia had kept the old Julian calendar. By 1918, there was a difference between the two calendars of thirteen days. The Bolshevik government adopted the Gregorian calendar on 31 January 1918; the next day was declared to be 14 February.

Some books (including this one) use the old-style calendar, which was in use in Russia at the time, to date the events of 1917. Others use the Gregorian calendar, which was used in the rest of Europe.

Event	Date under old-style calendar	Date under Gregorian calendar
First revolution of 1917	23 February	8 March
Second revolution of 1917	25 October	7 November

CENTRES OF RADICALISM: VYBORG AND THE PUTILOV ENGINEERING WORKS

The Vyborg district of Petrograd was a working-class area that had a history of radical action. The Putilov engineering works in the Narva district had as many as 40,000 men working in several huge factories. If the Putilov workers went on strike then the authorities had a sizeable demonstration on their hands. A strike by the Putilov workers had contributed to the beginning of the 1905 revolution.

Workers who had been laid off wandered the streets. Some women spent almost 24 hours in queues for food and other goods. When the news of the introduction of bread rationing hit the streets towards the end of February 1917, the flood gates opened. Queues and scuffles over remaining bread stocks turned into riots. Anti-government feelings in Petrograd were running high.

On Thursday 23 February, International Women's Day, the discontent became more focused. What started off as a good-humoured march in the morning – 'ladies from society; lots more peasant women; student girls' – took on a different mood in the afternoon. Women, many of them textile workers on strike, took the lead in politicising the march. They went to the factories in the Vyborg district of Petrograd and taunted the men, calling them cowards if they would not support them. Women tram drivers went on strike and overturned trams, blocking streets. Women took the initiative while men were more cautious. Local Bolshevik leaders actually told the women to go home because they were planning a big demonstration for May Day, but the women took no notice.

By the afternoon, the women had persuaded men from the highly politicised Putilov engineering works and other factories to join them. A huge crowd began to make its way towards the centre of the city. They crossed the ice of the frozen River Neva and burst on to Nevsky Prospekt, the main street in Petrograd. The protest started to gather momentum.

■ **3D Map of Petrograd, 1917**

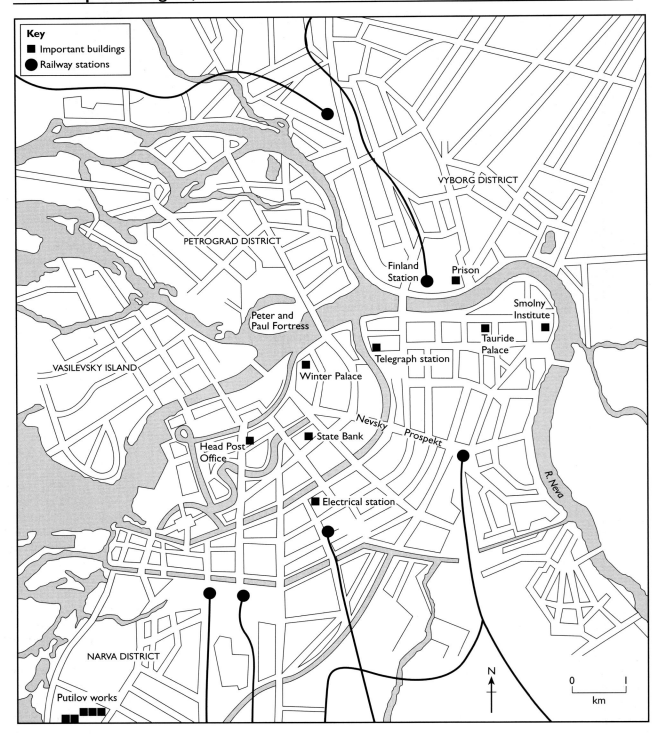

Key
- ■ Important buildings
- ● Railway stations

VYBORG DISTRICT

PETROGRAD DISTRICT

Peter and
Paul Fortress

Finland
Station

Prison

Smolny
Institute

Telegraph station

Tauride
Palace

VASILEVSKY ISLAND

Winter Palace

Head Post
Office

State Bank

Nevsky Prospekt

R. Neva

Electrical station

NARVA DISTRICT

Putilov works

N

0   1
km

SOURCE 3.17   O. Figes, *A People's Tragedy: The Russian Revolution 1891–1924*, 1997, p. 310

The first symbolic battle of this war of nerves was fought out on the Nevsky Prospekt – and won decisively by the people – on the afternoon of the 25th. Part of the crowd was brought to a halt by a squadron of Cossacks ... not far from the spot where, twelve years before, on Bloody Sunday 1905, the Horseguards had shot down a similar crowd. A young girl appeared from the ranks of the demonstrators and walked slowly towards the Cossacks. Everyone watched her in nervous silence: surely the Cossacks would not fire at her? From under her cloak the girl brought out a bouquet of red roses and held it towards the officer. There was a pause. The bouquet was a symbol of peace and revolution. And then, leaning down from his horse, the officer smiled and took the flowers. With as much relief as jubilation, the crowd burst into a thunderous 'Oorah!' From this moment the people began to speak of the 'comrade Cossacks', a term which at first sounded rather odd.

FOCUS ROUTE

1 As you read pages 65–69, note down evidence using this grid:

	Evidence for	Evidence against
The revolution was spontaneous		
The revolution was popular		

2 Why was the role of the army so important in the February Revolution? Make a note of your answer to this question.

The protest grows

Over the next three days, the demonstrations grew and took on a more political nature. Demands for bread were accompanied by demands for an end to the war and an end to the Tsar. Observers reported that there was almost a holiday atmosphere in the city as all classes of people – students, teachers, shopkeepers, even well-dressed ladies – joined the ranks of the workers marching towards the centre of the city. There seemed to be no general organisation of events. Certainly no political party was in charge: all the main leaders of the revolutionary parties were abroad or in exile. But socialist cells, particularly from the Bolshevik revolutionary party, were active in spreading protest and getting the workers out on the streets with their red flags and banners. By Saturday, there was virtually a general strike as most of the major factories shut down and many shops and restaurants closed their doors.

The weekend of 25 and 26 February was the testing time. There had been demonstrations in the past and these had been dealt with effectively by the Cossacks and other troops. The difference this time was that the soldiers joined the demonstrators. The NCOs in the army, like the sergeant in Source 3.18 on page 68, played a key role in this. These men had a more direct relationship with the soldiers than their senior officers did and it seems that the NCOs had decided that the time had come when they would no longer fire on the crowds. Also, many of the soldiers in the Petrograd garrison were young reservists, some fresh from the villages, who identified more easily with the people on the streets. They were desperate not to be sent to the front line where the Russian army was suffering huge losses, and they shared the dissatisfaction with the way the war was being conducted and the impact it was having on the living conditions of ordinary Russians in the cities.

Revolution!

It was, paradoxically, Tsar Nicholas himself who initiated the mutiny of his own soldiers. Hearing about the trouble in Petrograd, he ordered that troops put down the disorders. On Sunday 26 February, some regiments opened fire on the crowds, killing a number of demonstrators. This tipped the scales. The crowds became hostile and the soldiers now had to decide which side they were on: were they going to join the people or fire on them? One by one, regiments moved over to the side of the people. There was some fighting between the soldiers in different regiments and a number of officers were killed, but this was largely over by 27 February. As Orlando Figes puts it, 'The mutiny of the Petrograd garrison turned the disorders of the last four days into a full-scale revolution.'

The main struggle now took place between the soldiers and the police. The police had taken the main role in attacking demonstrators and had a habit of putting snipers on rooftops to fire down on the crowds. Soldiers rooted them out, throwing them off the roofs on to the streets to the cheers of the crowds below. Police stations were attacked and police records destroyed. The prisons were thrown open and the prisoners released.

The revolution of February 1917 was not a bloodless revolution. Some estimates put the death toll at around 1500 with several thousands wounded. Also, by 28 February the situation in the capital was starting to get out of control. Although in many ways the people showed remarkable self-restraint, crime was beginning to grow (partly because of all the criminals released) and there was increasing violence. Armed gangs looted shops, and private houses of the well-to-do were broken into (see Source 3.20). Somebody had to take control of the situation. Most people looked to the Duma, the Russian parliament, although the socialists were already forming their own organisation to represent the interests of the workers – the Soviet.

SOURCE 3.18   O. Figes, *A People's Tragedy: The Russian Revolution 1891–1924*, 1997, pp. 313–14, quoting a young peasant sergeant, Kirpichnikov

I told them that it would be better to die with honour than to obey any further orders to shoot the crowds: 'Our fathers, mothers, sisters, brothers, and brides are begging for food,' I said. 'Are we going to kill them? Did you see the blood on the streets today? I say we don't take up positions tomorrow. I myself refuse to go.' And as one, the soldiers cried out: 'We shall stay with you!'

SOURCE 3.19   B. Williams, *The Russian Revolution 1917–21*, 1987, pp. 8–9

The fall of the Russian monarchy was accomplished over a ten-day period from 23 February to 4 March 1917. Ten days of popular demonstrations, political manoeuvring and army mutiny developed imperceptibly into a revolution which no one expected, planned or controlled … Moreover, there was no doubt that the initiators of the revolution were the workers and the reserve troops in the capital … All the major leaders of the revolutionary movement were in Siberia or abroad when the movement started, and certainly no political party organized the revolution.

SOURCE 3.20   B. Moynahan, *The Russian Century*, 1994, p. 81

Countess Kleinmikhel was dining with the Prince and Princess Kurakin. They had started the first course when servants burst into the dining room. 'Run! Run!' they cried. Bandits had broken into the building, wounding two doormen, and were making their way through the rooms. The countess led her guests out into the night to refuge in the house opposite. From there they watched fascinated as a group of soldiers and sailors were served their meal on silver plate and ordered up dozens of bottles of wine from the countess's cellar.

ACTIVITY

1 To what extent do you think the February Revolution was both a spontaneous and a popular revolution? Use the evidence you have collected in the Focus Route on page 67 to answer this question.

2 How do Trotsky (Source 3.21) and Chamberlain (Source 3.22) disagree about the question of who led the revolution? Is one right and the other wrong? Or could both be true in certain ways?

3 What do you think were the main reasons why the revolution was successful?

SOURCE 3.21 A quotation attributed to Trotsky

To the question 'Who led the February uprising?' we can answer definitely enough: conscious and tempered workers educated in the main by the party of Lenin.

SOURCE 3.22 W. H. Chamberlain, *The Russian Revolution, 1917–1921*, 1935

The collapse of the Russian autocracy . . . was one of the most leaderless, spontaneous, anonymous revolutions of all time.

The end of the Romanovs

While these events unfolded, the Tsar was still at Mogilev and did not comprehend the seriousness of the situation. Rodzianko sent him a telegram explaining how bad things were and suggesting that a new government be formed with more power being given to elected representatives (i.e. the first moves towards a constitutional monarchy). Nicholas' answer was to suspend the Duma and send loyal troops to march on the capital to restore order. But the Duma members remained in the Tauride Palace and held informal meetings. Meanwhile, crowds of people milled around outside demanding that the Duma take control of the situation.

On Monday 27 February, the Duma formed a special committee made up of representatives of the main political parties. It soon became clear to the committee that the revolution had gone too far for the Tsar to be involved in any kind of government. The Russian Army High Command had come to the same conclusion and put a stop to the troop movements on Petrograd. The Tsar had made a last ditch effort to get back to the capital but his train had been stopped outside the city. When the generals told the Tsar they would not support him, he knew the time to go had come. On 2 March he abdicated in favour of his brother Michael; but Michael, realising the extent of anti-monarchical feeling, refused and the Romanov dynasty came to a swift end. The Duma committee set about forming a new government.

The army

Whereas the army remained loyal in 1905, they went over to the side of the people in 1917. The army of February 1917 was a very different army to the one at the beginning of the war in 1914. Fourteen million men had been mobilised and approximately half of them had been killed, wounded or taken prisoner. A fundamental change had taken place in the officer corps with the promotion of peasant and lower middle class men who were often liberals or socialists, replacing aristocratic and conservative officers. More importantly, many of the soldiers in Petrograd were young reservists who were about to be deployed to the front line and who were often reluctant to go to war because of the huge losses of personnel. They were more sympathetic to the people on the streets and unwilling to suppress disorders. At the other end of the scale, the generals also played a crucial role. When Guchkov, leader of the Octobrists, asked the generals in the winter of 1916–17 about their support for some sort of *COUP D'ÉTAT* to get rid of Nicholas, he understood that they would not intervene to save the monarch. At the beginning of 1917, the generals considered that Nicholas was a liability and were happy to see him go although they hoped to retain the monarchy.

COUP D'ÉTAT
Violent seizure of power, usually by a relatively small number of people.

FOCUS ROUTE

The rest of this chapter and the Section
I review concentrates on answering key
questions about the downfall of tsarism.
As you work through the section note the
views of historians and use the guidance
in the section review to develop your own
interpretation.

G   Could tsarism have survived?

There are many different interpretations of the Russian revolution of February
1917 and the factors that brought the tsarist regime down, especially the role of
the First World War. The background of Western historians predisposed them
to hope that Russia might be developing into a parliamentary democracy. Some
have argued that the tsarist regime was making progress on the political and
economic front and was beginning to stabilise before 1914 but the First World
War produced strains that the tsarist state could not survive. Others have taken
the line that the revolution of 1905 opened up possibilities for change and that
for various reasons the tsarist regime, and particularly the Tsar, was unable or
unwilling to seize them. George Kennan is an interesting bridge between the two
views (see Source 3.22). He argues that the regime would have collapsed sooner
or later, war or no war.

The Soviet view stressed the importance of the development of a genuine
revolutionary Marxist party under Lenin confronting the tsarist regime with
a challenge it could not withstand – the number of strikes had grown rapidly
after the Lena Goldfields Massacre, were increasingly political in nature, and
culminated in the St Petersburg general strike of July 1914. Soviet historians
argue that the outbreak of the war merely delayed the onset of revolution.

Increasingly, revisionist historians have contended that tsarism could not
have survived. They give more attention to social, economic and institutional
factors. Most revisionist historians point to the underlying weaknesses in the
structure of the tsarist regime – its administration, bureaucracy and political
institutions. In their view, the autocratic regime could not cope with the
problems resulting from industrialisation and modernisation. Although some
in the ruling élite, like Witte and Stolypin, saw the need for reform, the Tsar
and his most reactionary supporters were hostile to the political demands
and social transformations that reforms entailed and obstinately stuck to an
outdated vision of autocracy. The roots of revolution, therefore, can be found
in the conflict between society becoming more educated, more urban and
more complex and a fossilised autocracy that would not concede its political
demands. The war was not responsible for the collapse of the regime though
it revealed its inadequacies and hastened its collapse. Sheila Fitzpatrick
argues that Russian society on the eve of the war was so deeply divided and
the political and bureaucratic structure so fragile and overstrained that it was
vulnerable to any kind of jolt, even without the war.

Dominic Lieven, Nicholas II's biographer, does not apportion so much
personal blame to the Tsar. He feels that no Tsar, however strong and capable,
would have been able to cope with the problems of modernising Russia within
the framework of an autocracy. This reinforces the view that the real problem
lay in the structural weaknesses and inflexibility of the autocratic state, which
was not fit for the modern world. It was not only the Russian Empire that
collapsed after the First World War, the German and Austrian Empires shared
the same fate.

Richard Pipes is a conservative historian and often critical of revisionists
but he too stresses the weaknesses of the regime in the face of the challenge
of modernisation in a deeply divided country. The prevalence and intensity
of hatred: ideological, ethnic, and social was such that sooner or later there
would again be recourse to violence. He quotes the poet Alexander Blok,
writing in 1908, who refers to a bomb ticking in the heart of Russia: 'In all of
us sit sensations of malaise, fear catastrophe, explosion . . . We do not know yet
precisely what events await us, but in our hearts the needle of the seismograph
has already stirred.'

Christopher Read has written an article on whether tsarism might have successfully modernised itself (C. Read, *In Search of Liberal Tsarism: the historiography of autocratic decline*, Historical Journal, 45, 1 (2002), pp. 195–210). He argues that even those who think that Russia was developing rapidly saw little chance of the autocracy surviving the process. For Read the real question is not whether tsarism could have survived but what kind of revolution Russia faced: would it be a bourgeois revolution focused on institutional reform and led by what was still a weak middle class or a radical populist revolution, which would lead to widespread property redistribution and extensive social transformation? For Robert Service the war answered this question. As he says in Source 3.23, it made possible a radical upheaval. But elsewhere he argues that even before the war, as things stood, some kind of revolutionary clash was practically inevitable.

SOURCE 3.23   R. Service, *The Russian Revolution* 1900–1927, 4th edn, 2009, p. 16

The empire as it was developing by 1914 was a sensitive plant, but it was not doomed to undergo the root-and-branch revolution of 1917. What made that kind of revolution possible was the protracted, disruptive, exhausting conflict of the First World War. No First World War, no October Revolution. Lenin and his Bolsheviks were donated a revolutionary opportunity they would probably never have created for themselves.

SOURCE 3.24   P. Waldron, *The End of Imperial Russia*, 1855–1917, 1997, p. 37 and p. 164

All the problems that had accumulated over the previous half-century came into sharp focus during the war. Poor military performance engendered even greater scepticism about the political capabilities of tsarism. The unmodernised Russian economy was too weak to both supply the army and to maintain the standard of living of the peasantry and of working people. The government proved incapable of recognising the strains that a war economy placed upon the ordinary people of the empire and failed to understand that it needed actively to win their support to ensure the success of the war effort. By 1917 the Russian people had no will to support either the person of the monarch, nor the system which he represented.

SOURCE 3.25   G. Kennan, 1969, quoted by C. Read: *In Search of Liberal Tsarism: The historiography of autocratic decline*, Historical Journal, 45, 2002, p. 195–6

I was inclined to feel that, had the war not intervened, the chances for survival of the autocracy and for its gradual evolution into a constitutional monarchy would not have been bad. On reviewing once more the events of these last decades, I find myself obliged to question that opinion. Neither the tardiness in the granting of political reform, nor the excesses of an extravagant and foolish nationalism, nor the personal limitations of the imperial couple began with the war or were primarily responses to the existence of the war. None of the consequences of these deficiencies were in the process of any significant correction as the war approached.

SOURCE 3.26   M. Harrison, The Second World War, in R. W. Davies, M. Harrison and S. G. Wheatcroft (eds) *The Economic Transformation of the Soviet Union 1913–1945*, 1994, p. 266

Peasant farmers preferred own consumption of their food surpluses to sale of food in return for useless cash, given the prevailing shortage of industrial goods. Urban–rural trade broke down, and the countryside disintegrated into self-sufficient regions, withholding food surpluses from the food-deficit sectors of towns and industries. A weak transport system and administrative infrastructure made it more difficult for government to intervene, impose rationing and controls, and direct food resources where they were needed. When the full extent of consumer shortages were revealed, the ensuing crisis toppled the old regime.

SOURCE 3.27 S. Badcock, *Autocracy in Crisis: Nicholas the Last*, in I. D. Thatcher (ed.) *Late Imperial Russia: Problems and Perspectives*, 2005, p. 23

The breakdown of cordial relations between government and Duma, and the formation of the Progressive Bloc in August 1915 demonstrated the regime's inability to co-operate with society even in favourable conditions, and was testament to its increasingly incompetent handling of the war effort.

SOURCE 3.28 R. B. McKean, *The Russian Constitutional Monarchy, 1907–1917*, 1977, p. 30

From the point of view of the monarchy, the impact of the war upon the Imperial army was the most disastrous consequence of the three years' hostilities. Despite the defeats in the Far East, the efforts of the revolutionary parties to establish links with the troops and the attraction of looting the gentry estates, the peasant-soldiers had kept their oath in the revolution of 1905 and 1906 and suppressed all workers' and peasants' disturbances. In a variety of ways the Great War gradually broke the army's loyalty.

KEY POINTS FROM CHAPTER 3

Could tsarism have survived? 1906–1917

1 Peter Stolypin attempted to preserve the autocracy by bringing in reforms but he was attacked by left- and right-wing politicians, indicating the difficulty of modernising Russia within the framework of an autocracy.

2 Stolypin's reforms in agriculture attempted to create more productive independent peasants who would support the regime but the reforms had only limited success. Agricultural production grew, but despite some innovation, farming methods were still largely antiquated, using the strip system, and organised by rural communes. Some peasants prospered while others remained impoverished. A rootless and discontented class of landless peasants was growing, with many moving to the towns and cities.

3 Industrial production grew steadily over the period but Russian industry was uneven and unbalanced.

4 The working classes were becoming more radical after the Lena Goldfields Massacre in 1912. Militancy and strikes increased in 1912–14.

5 The revolutionary parties were not in a strong position in 1914 although support for the Bolsheviks had revived after 1912.

6 The First World War had a devastating impact on Russia with millions killed and wounded. Incompetent administration and the collapse of the distribution system resulted in a lack of supplies, weapons and medical services at the Front and shortages of food and fuel in major cities, especially Petrograd. Confidence in the government plummeted.

7 The professional classes and businessmen set up non-governmental organisations to improve supplies of war materials, which seemed to offer an alternative form of government.

8 The Tsar made several bad mistakes. He went to the Front, taking personal responsibility for the war. He would not work with the Progressive Bloc in the Duma or co-operate with the non-governmental organisations. He left the Tsarina and Rasputin in charge of government.

9 The Tsarina and Rasputin created instability by changing ministers continually and became a focus for criticism and antagonism towards the regime. The ruling élite lost confidence in the Tsar.

10 By the beginning of 1917 there was little support left for the Tsar and his government. A spontaneous eruption of discontent in February 1917 saw him swept from power when the army and its generals deserted him.

Section 1 Review: Why did the tsarist regime collapse in 1917?

Writing an essay about the revolution of February 1917

Often questions about the 1917 revolution take a particular line to which the essay writer has to respond. For example: the war was the main factor in bringing about the revolution, or, the Tsar was the main contributor to his own downfall.

Sometimes, a question asks 'how far' one of these factors (e.g. war, Tsar) caused the revolution. Usually the same information is required but the writer has to be able to organise or 'deploy' it in different ways. It can be helpful to think of the information as blocks that can be used flexibly. Here are some of the main blocks of information you might deploy in any essay looking at the cause of the February 1917 revolution. You would give more weight to some information than to others depending on the essay question.

■ A How the Tsar contributed to his own downfall

Personality and leadership

- Personality – weak but obstinate, indecisive, lack of interest in world around him.
- Did not have the skills (e.g. organisational) or capabilities (e.g. unwilling to address people directly) to do the job of ruling Russia.
- Used repression as the main weapon in dealing with problems, relying on the army, which did not like to be used as a police force.

Reform

- Never willingly supported Witte's or Stolypin's reforms: did not want the changes in society these would entail. Wanted to protect court power and power of landowning classes. Sided where he could with right-wing groups who resisted reform.
- Half-heartedly supported Stolypin's land reforms. Resisted extension of zemstva to western provinces.
- No real concessions to workers on limiting working day or improving working conditions. Rejected trade unions or bodies representing workers.

Attitude to political change

- Resisted all forms of change pre-1905 – confirmed believer in autocracy. Not keen on zemstva or allowing local self-government.
- October Manifesto wrenched out of him – never committed to it and subsequently reneged on promises. Missed opportunity to bring liberal intelligentsia onto his side.
- Did not really want the Duma or representative body in first place and in Fundamental Laws showed his unwillingness to share power.
- Would not co-operate with the dumas during 1906–14 or with Progressive Bloc during war.

Misjudgements and mistakes

- Nicholas failed to realise seriousness of the situation building in 1904 and the need to respond to the demands of liberals and workers. Bloody Sunday 1905 resulted in massive loss of respect for Tsar.
- Appointment of nonentities and incompetents to run government after Stolypin's death.
- His and Tsarina's support for Rasputin damaged the reputation of royal family.
- Going to the Front in 1915, taking on personal responsibility for war.
- Leaving government in hands of Tsarina and Rasputin.
- Rejected the proposals of the Progressive Bloc in 1916.
- February 1917 – still not really aware of the dangers to the regime and took no action until too late.

74

SECTION I REVIEW: WHY DID A REVOLUTION TAKE PLACE IN RUSSIA IN FEBRUARY 1917?

■ B The problems facing Russia that even the most gifted of tsars would have had difficulty coping with

Problems thrown up by industrialisation and modernisation

- The ruling élite knew that Russia needed to modernise to compete with other world powers and remain a major military power. But the majority were determined to resist any challenge to autocracy and the social transformation modernisation entailed.
- The growing professional middle class wanted a greater role in national government and felt they could do a better job than the autocracy.
- Rapid industrialisation generated a new strata of society – a working class extremely isolated and hostile to the existing situation and able to organise itself.

Opposition groups

- The development of the liberal parties pre-1914 and middle-class pressure for reform.
- The development of the revolutionary parties, their relative strength and importance pre-1914, the extent to which the Bolsheviks were articulating the interests and aspirations of the working classes.

Political change

- Problems to do with constitutional change – relations between the Tsar, his ministers and the Duma.
- Problems of bringing in reforms. The hostility to Stolypin's reforms from all sides demonstrated the difficulty of taking a middle road.
- Attitudes of parties on right and left partly responsible for problems: 'a deadlocked political system, drifting helplessly toward destruction'.
- Possibilities opened up by Progressive Bloc in war.

Degree of support for the tsarist regime

- Contraction of the social bases of support for the regime.
- Developments after 1905–6 increased concerns about the reliability of the army in a crisis.

Social and economic divisions and strains

- Lack of improvement in living and working conditions of the working classes.
- Strikes and militancy pre-1914 and during the war.
- Impact of Stolypin's reforms on peasants and attitudes of peasants pre-1914.

Impact of First World War

- Effect of defeats and losses on the army and its morale, the changing composition of the army.
- Effect of economic disruption and distribution problems on people back home.
- Effect on the confidence in government.
- The actions of opposition politicians in the Duma and the development of the War Industries Committees.

ACTIVITY

Essay writing: Beginning essays

The beginning of an essay is difficult but very important. In your first paragraph you need to make an impression on the reader. This will not happen if the first paragraph just sets the scene without reference to the question or merely re-states the question. The first paragraph should show that you understand the question and have an answer to it. It is worth developing your skills in this respect. You can consider how historians tackle the problem by studying articles in A level history journals.

Essay: How far did the Tsar contribute to his own downfall?

One way of meeting the challenge of starting the essay is by using quotations, particularly contemporary quotations. The example below shows, at the outset, the gap between the Tsar's perception of the situation and reality. It makes an arresting start and shows that you are addressing the question – which is very important. It would work very well if you wanted to argue that Nicholas was largely responsible for his own downfall, but it could still be used if you wanted to argue that other factors were more important.

In January 1917, two months before he was compelled to abdicate, the Tsar received the British Ambassador, Sir George Buchanan, who asked for and was granted permission to speak frankly: 'Your majesty, if I may be permitted to say so, has but one safe course open to you – namely to break down that barrier that separates you from your people and to regain their confidence.' Drawing himself up and looking hard at me, the Emperor asked: 'Do you mean that I am to regain the confidence of my people or that they are to regain my confidence?' This shows just how strongly Nicholas II believed in the autocracy and how out of touch he was with reality. He made important mistakes and misjudgements but the central problem he faced was how to modernise Russia within the framework of an autocracy. It will be argued that even the most gifted of tsars could not have done that successfully.

CLASS ACTIVITY

Each student should write their own first paragraph for this essay. Then in groups, compare what has been written and within each group decide which is the most effective paragraph and why. Share this with the rest of the class.

Why were the Bolsheviks successful in October 1917?

At the beginning of 1917, Lenin had commented that he did not expect to see a revolution in his lifetime. Yet in 1917 two revolutions took place. The first had removed the Tsar. In the second, the Bolsheviks seized power. In this section we look at why the Bolsheviks were successful and how Lenin became the leader of the USSR.

4 Was the Provisional Government doomed from the beginning?

CHAPTER OVERVIEW

After the Tsar had abdicated, a Provisional Government took on the role of running Russia. But it had to share power with the Petrograd Soviet (a council representing workers and soldiers) which controlled the capital. Across the rest of Russia a mixture of committees and soviets sprang up to run the affairs of cities, towns and rural areas. The Provisional Government was faced with a range of issues – the war, land, social reform, food supplies, the status of the national minorities – on which it could not satisfy the huge wave of expectations building in the Russian people. Lenin, who returned in April, offered radical alternatives which many people found more attractive.

A Which was more powerful: the Provisional Government or the Soviet? (pp. 76–79)

B The honeymoon of the revolution (pp. 79–80)

C What were the policies of the key players in March 1917? (pp. 80–81)

D What difference did the return of Lenin make? (pp. 82–84)

E What problems faced the Provisional Government? How well did it deal with them from April to August? (pp. 85–89)

F What was the position at the end of August 1917? (pp. 90–93)

G Review: Was the Provisional Government doomed from the beginning? (p. 94)

A # Which was more powerful: the Provisional Government or the Soviet?

FOCUS ROUTE

1 Draw a table like the one below and complete it as you work through this section.

	Provisional Government	Soviet
Who were its members?		
How was this body formed?		
What powers did it have?		

2 Make notes to explain why:
   a) the Soviet did not take power when it had the opportunity
   b) the Soviet co-operated with the Provisional Government.

CONSTITUENT ASSEMBLY

When an old system of government collapses (in this case, the tsarist autocracy), a new system of government has to be set up. But somebody has to work out what the new system will consist of: will there be a president? will there be one house of representatives or two? how will these be elected? and so on. The constituent assembly, a parliament elected by everyone, would have the authority to do this. For instance, it writes the new constitution.

ACTIVITY

Look at Sources 4.1 and 4.2. What can you learn from these photographs?

On 2 March a Provisional Government was declared, made up largely of leading figures of the various liberal parties. It was dominated by the Kadets and their leader, Milyukov, who became Foreign Minister. There was one socialist minister, Alexander Kerensky, who became Minister of Justice; he was soon to become a major player in the events that unfolded during 1917. The new Prime Minister, Prince G. E. Lvov, was a strange choice but a popular one. He had headed the union of zemstva (town and district councils), and had been widely praised for his efforts in providing support and medical help for soldiers at the Front. The avowed job of the Provisional Government, and hence its title 'provisional', was to run Russia until elections to a Constituent Assembly could take place.

Another important body was taking shape at the same time in the same building – the Tauride Palace – where the Duma members were meeting. The Petrograd Soviet was formed on Monday 27 February. The idea for this seems to have come from Menshevik intellectuals. It quickly became the focus of working-class aspirations. Factories were asked to elect delegates to attend a full meeting of the Soviet. When it met, an Executive Committee was chosen. This was dominated by Mensheviks and non-party socialist intellectuals. Its first chairman was a leading Menshevik, Chkheidze.

Soldiers were also anxious to protect their own interests. On Wednesday 1 March, they went to the Soviet and demanded representation. They gained the famous Order No. 1 (see Source 4.3). Each regiment was to elect committees that would send representatives to the Soviet. It was now called the 'Soviet of Workers' and Soldiers' Deputies'.

SOURCE 4.1 Members of the first Provisional Government

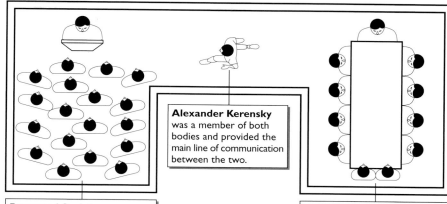

Alexander Kerensky was a member of both bodies and provided the main line of communication between the two.

The Petrograd Soviet and Provisional Government held meetings in different wings of the Tauride Palace

SOVIETS

Soviets were set up in different towns and cities all over Russia after February 1917. The Petrograd Soviet was the most important one and is referred to here as the Soviet. By 3 March it had 1300 members; a week later it had 3000, of whom only 800 were workers. The rest represented various army units. The huge numbers could not make decisions easily, so they chose an Executive Committee to do this. This committee was dominated by socialist intellectuals.

Petrograd Soviet

Made up of:
• Workers' and soldiers' representatives
• Socialist intellectuals, mainly Mensheviks and Socialist Revolutionaries
Chairman of executive committee:
Chkheidze
Role:
To protect the interests of the working classes and soldiers
NB Socialist intellectuals formed the leadership of the Soviet.

Provisional Government

Made up of:
Leading figures from the Kadets and other liberal parties
Leader:
Prince Lvov
Role:
To run the country until a Constituent Assembly had been elected
NB The Provisional Government had been chosen by a committee of the Duma; it had not been elected by the people.

SOURCE 4.2 A meeting of the Petrograd Soviet in the Tauride Palace

■ 4B The power of the Petrograd Soviet

Railways

Telegraph station

Soldiers in the Petrograd garrison

The Soviet controlled ...

Factories

Power supplies

COUNTER-REVOLUTION

A counter-revolution is when the supporters of the old system of government try to take back power and re-establish the old system, if not the old ruler.

SOURCE 4.4 Mstislavsky, a Socialist Revolutionary leader

Oh, how they feared the masses! As I watched our 'socialists' speaking to the crowds ... I could feel their nauseating fear ... As recently as yesterday it had been relatively easy to be 'representatives and leaders' of these working masses; peaceable parliamentary socialists could still utter the most bloodcurdling words 'in the name of the proletariat' without blinking. It became a different story, however, when this theoretical proletariat suddenly appeared here, in the full power of exhausted flesh and mutinous blood.

SOURCE 4.3 Extracts from Order No. 1, adapted from *A Source Book of Russian History*, Vol. 3, by G. Vernadsky, 1972, p. 882

The Soviet of Workers' and Soldiers' Deputies has decided:

- *In all companies, battalions, squadrons and separate branches of military service of all kinds and on warships, committees should be chosen immediately.*
- *The orders of ... the State Duma [Provisional Government] shall be carried out only ... [when] they do not contradict the orders and decisions of the Soviet of Workers' and Soldiers' Deputies.*
- *All kinds of arms, such as rifles and machine guns, must be under the control of the company and battalion committees and must in no case be handed over to officers even at their demand.*
- *The addressing of officers with titles such as 'Your Excellency', 'Your Honour', etc., is abolished and these are replaced by 'Mr General', 'Mr Colonel' and so on.*

Order No. 1 was extremely significant. It not only gave the soldiers representation but also gave their committees control of all weapons. It stated that soldiers would only obey the orders of the Provisional Government if the Soviet agreed. Thus a situation known as 'dual power' was created. The Provisional Government was the popularly accepted, although unelected government but the real power lay quite clearly with the Soviet. Chart 4B shows the areas the Soviet controlled through its soldier and worker representatives. The Provisional Government could not move around or send a message without the Soviet's knowing. The Soviet could determine which factories stayed open and which services, such as electricity, would be provided.

The policy of the Soviet was to keep its distance from the middle-class Provisional Government, to act as a sort of watchdog to make sure that it did nothing to damage the interests of the working class. It decided not to participate directly in the government. There was one exception – Alexander Kerensky. He was vice-chairman of the Soviet and Minister of Justice in the Provisional Government (see pages 90–93). He served a useful role, running, sometimes literally, between the two to make sure there were no misunderstandings.

Why did the Soviet not take power?

The obvious question here is: why didn't the Soviet simply take over and form its own government? There are a number of answers to this:

1 The leaders of the Soviet did not think the time was right for the workers to form the government. The Mensheviks and the Socialist Revolutionaries believed that Russia had to go through a 'bourgeois revolution' before the workers could assume power. They were following the classical Marxist line (see pages 22–23) and believed that there had to be a long period in which capitalism developed more fully, society became more industrialised and the proletariat became much larger. During this time, Russia would be run by a democratically elected government. They believed the workers needed a period of education before they could play a role in running a country, though they did see a powerful role for the soviets in local government.

2 There was a practical reason behind this theoretical position: they wanted to avoid a civil war and COUNTER-REVOLUTION. They needed to keep the middle classes and the army commanders on their side. The Russian High Command had kept their troops outside the city because they were reassured that the Duma politicians (solid middle-class citizens) were in control of the situation. If they thought that a socialist government hostile to them and to military discipline was going to assume power, then they might well send in their troops.

3 The leaders of the Soviet, mainly intellectual socialists, were scared; they were not sure they could control the masses. They thought all the anger in the streets might be turned against them if they became the government (see Source 4.4).

Therefore, the leaders of the Soviet, most of whom had little experience of government, decided to step back and let others steer the ship in the dangerous waters of February–April 1917, while they kept a close eye on events.

■ **Learning trouble spot**

Dangerous times and difficult decisions
When looking back at events like the February Revolution, students can make the error of thinking that it was bound to be successful and that it all happened relatively smoothly. But it was a period of great turmoil, when people could not see the future and so were fearful. The members of the Duma were acting illegally and would have been arrested if the Tsar had returned with loyal troops. Trapped between a vengeful tsar and the noisy crowds outside who might turn violent, they argued about what they should do. Some slipped out of the back door and went home. It was only when the Soviet formed itself that they thought they had better do something.

Similarly, the meetings in the Soviet were chaotic with people running in and out while, outside, groups of soldiers and workers, many of whom were drunk, roamed the streets. The situation in Petrograd was very worrying for the middle classes and for socialist intellectuals. The socialist writer Maxim Gorky, for instance, was very depressed by the looting and violence (see page 315). He said that it was 'chaos', not revolution at all. So, people were trying to make decisions that held the situation together and the best policy to them seemed to be one of co-operation between the Provisional Government and the Soviet.

TALKING POINT

Why do the middle classes and intellectuals get frightened in times of unrest and fear the growth of working-class action? Is this still an issue in our society today and in other societies?

THE FREEST COUNTRY IN THE WORLD

When we look at the Provisional Government, we often think of it as a group of rather staid middle-class liberals compared with the radical left-wing revolutionaries. But if all of their ideas had been put into practice Russia would have been the most radical liberal democracy in Europe in 1917. At the same time, in Britain, women did not have the vote at all and trade unionists would have looked in envy at the rights that their Russian counterparts had won.

B The honeymoon of the revolution

For the first two months of the revolution, there was little to bring the Provisional Government and the Soviet into conflict. The first measures taken by the Provisional Government met with Soviet and public approval:

- Tsarist ministers and officials were arrested and imprisoned. The police, on the whole, put themselves under arrest; this was a desperate move to stop the workers and soldiers from literally pulling them to pieces.
- The secret police were disbanded.
- The first decree of the Provisional Government (worked out with the Soviet) granted an amnesty for political and religious prisoners and established freedom of the press and freedom of speech. The death penalty was abolished. Discrimination on social, religious or national grounds was made illegal.
- The Provisional Government promised it would arrange for elections for a Constituent Assembly that would determine the future government of Russia. These elections were to be by secret ballot and universal suffrage.

Support for the new government flooded in from outside the capital and harmony was maintained between the Provisional Government and the Soviet. The soldier representatives on the Soviet were happy since it was agreed that soldiers in the Petrograd garrison would not be sent to the Front. The workers were happy because they had secured the right to strike and to organise trade unions, an eight-hour working day and the recognition of the factory committees. It was an optimistic time, when it seemed that the worst aspects of tsarism had been ditched and a bright future beckoned. Lenin remarked in the summer of 1917 that Russia was the freest country in the world.

Make a note of your answers to the following questions:

1 How much control did the central government have over the rest of Russia?
2 What kinds of organisation sprang up to run local areas?

What was happening in the rest of Russia?

There is a tendency to focus on Petrograd in 1917 and ignore what was happening in the rest of Russia. The tsarist administrative order was being dismantled: what would take its place? The Provisional Government dismissed the old tsarist governors and replaced them with commissars. These were usually the old zemstvo (town council) chairmen, some of whom were landowners. But they were largely ignored and were given little respect.

In many areas 'Committees of Public Organisations' were set up. At first, these tended to be multi- or non-party bodies run by middle-class zemstvo members, but their membership rapidly expanded to take in representatives of various workers', soldiers', trade union and other popular committees that mushroomed at the time. However, these bodies were being outstripped by the growth in towns and districts of soviets that were set up to represent workers' interests. As news of the revolution spread into the countryside, peasants also started to set up committees and give voice to their opinions and demands. The Prime Minister, Lvov, who was more radical and populist than other liberals in the Provisional Government, encouraged localities to run their own affairs.

Things were moving fast and a great wave of expectation was building up. The honeymoon of the revolution was coming to an end and some hard decisions had to be taken. The main issue that was causing problems was the war. The war was still being fought and soldiers were dying in large numbers; there were still shortages of food and fuel, too. And, soon, the capital was to be shaken up by the arrival at the beginning of April of a new personality – Lenin!

C What were the policies of the key players in March 1917?

The honeymoon of the revolution did not last long. Different groups in society started to make conflicting demands, which the Provisional Government found hard to meet. The situation was becoming highly charged as groups began to argue about the policies the new government should adopt. You can see a summary of the key issues in Chart 4C and the policies of the main groups in Chart 4D.

■ 4C Key issues in March 1917

War
Should Russia sue for an immediate peace, with all the national shame, humiliation and loss of territory that this implied? If not, should Russia fight a defensive war (i.e. seek only to defend its own existing territory), or should it continue to fight alongside the Allies in the hope of winning more territory?

Land
Should land be taken from the nobility and big landowners and handed over immediately to the peasants for them to divide amongst themselves? Or should the issue of land redistribution be left to an elected government of Russia to organise in a more controlled way?

Social reform
How quickly could a programme of social reform for the workers (e.g. greater power in the workplace, improvements in working and living conditions) be put into action and how far should it go?

KEY ISSUES IN MARCH 1917

National minorities
Many national groups, such as the Finns, the Poles and the Ukrainians, were clamouring for independence or more self-government now that the tsarist regime had collapsed. Should the old Russian empire be allowed to break up?

Economy
How could the economic situation be improved, particularly the supply of food and fuel?

THE LIBERALS

The Kadets (Constitutional Democratic Party) were the dominant liberal force in the Provisional Government but there were liberal groups that were more right wing, such as the Octobrists (see page 49).

The Kadets were not united:

- Some of the Kadets – including their leader, Milyukov – had moved further to the right. They believed that the revolution was over in March and should go no further. They wanted to set up a sound constitutional framework, with a democratically elected government, but in a centrally controlled state.

- Left-leaning Kadets wanted much greater social reform, with a larger role for people in government, and more power to regional and local centres.

Main policies
- **War**   They were committed to continuing the war on the side of Britain and France. After the war they wanted Western help for their fledgling democracy and to remain an important power internationally. Milyukov (who was the War Minister as well as the leader of the Kadets) wanted to make territorial gains if the Allies won.

- **Land issue**   They wanted the problem of land redistribution to be sorted out by the elected Constituent Assembly.

- **National minorities**   They did not want the old empire broken up; they wanted to maintain the integrity of the state.

- **Elections to Constituent Assembly**   They realised that the majority of the population were not going to vote for them, and therefore sought to delay the elections until the war was over, when a more settled atmosphere might improve their chances.

SOCIALISTS

The socialists were a very mixed grouping. The main socialist groups in Petrograd were the Socialist Revolutionaries, the Mensheviks and the Bolsheviks. The first leading Bolsheviks to arrive, in mid-March, were Stalin and Kamenev. Like the Mensheviks, they assumed that this was the 'bourgeois' stage of the revolution. There was even talk that the Bolsheviks and Mensheviks would reunite. There were also many socialists who did not belong to any party but could be powerful on local soviets.

Main policies
The main socialist parties shared broadly the same policies in March 1917:

- **Co-operation**   They were prepared to co-operate with the Provisional Government while acting as a watchdog to ensure that the people's interests were not jeopardised.

- **War**   They wanted to fight a defensive war only, to prevent defeat by the Germans; they did not want to fight to gain territory.

- **Land issue**   They wanted to leave this to the Constituent Assembly. The Socialist Revolutionaries were anxious to redistribute land as soon as possible but were prepared to wait until the Assembly met.

- **National minorities**   They wanted to accede to the national aspirations of non-Russian people, offering more self-government and local control; in particular, they wanted to grant self-government to the Ukraine.

Both the Mensheviks and the Socialist Revolutionaries (SRs) were split over the war:

- **Socialist Revolutionaries**   Chernov and moderate SRs favoured continuation of a defensive war while left-wing SRs opposed war.

- **Mensheviks**   Tsereteli and moderate Mensheviks supported continuation of the war but Menshevik-INTERNATIONALISTS led by Martov opposed it.

The liberals were dominant in the Provisional Government.

The moderate wings of both the Socialist Revolutionaries and the Mensheviks were dominant in the Petrograd Soviet.

INTERNATIONALISTS
Socialists opposed to the First World War who campaigned for an immediate peace through international socialist collaboration.

■ **Learning trouble spot**

Making policy in the political parties
It is easy to fall into the trap of thinking that the political parties in Russia had fixed policy lines and stuck with these all the time. But if you think of parties today, you know that there are various groups inside a party that disagree with each other. This was particularly the case in Russia in 1917. Many of the parties were loose-knit organisations, particularly the Socialist Revolutionaries, and there were many internal disagreements. They had not expected to be in the position they were in in 1917 and were working things out as they went along.

D What difference did the return of Lenin make?

It was into this highly charged situation that Lenin arrived at the beginning of April. Lenin had been in Switzerland and the events of February 1917 had taken him completely by surprise. As soon as he realised what was happening, he hurriedly made preparations to get to Petrograd. However, the journey involved crossing German territory and Lenin had no desire (as a Russian and a revolutionary) to end up in a German prison. In the event, it was the Germans who helped him. They provided him with a railway carriage which was sealed when the train entered German territory and unlocked on the other side. The German authorities hoped that he would cause some mischief in Russia and hinder the Russian war effort.

Lenin's train pulled in at Finland Station in Petrograd, where an excited crowd was waiting for him. He was greeted by the Menshevik chairman of the Soviet, Chkheidze, who told Lenin politely, but firmly, that the revolution was going very well and that they did not need him, Lenin, to rock the boat. But that was exactly what Lenin intended to do. He brushed Chkheidze aside and immediately made a speech welcoming the revolution, but saying that it was far from complete. He called for:

- a worldwide socialist revolution
- an immediate end to the war
- an end to co-operation with the Provisional Government
- the Soviet to take power
- land to be given to the peasants.

ACTIVITY

What questions do you need to ask about the painting in Source 4.5 before you can decide whether it is useful evidence for historians?

SOURCE 4.5 After Lenin had brushed aside the welcoming committee, he jumped onto an armoured car and made a speech calling for a worldwide socialist revolution. This painting of the occasion was made in the 1930s

N. N. Sukhanov
In this section of the book, we use the eyewitness accounts of Sukhanov several times. Sukhanov was the diarist of the revolution. He was in a unique position. He knew the Bolshevik leaders well and his wife was a Bolshevik. Indeed, the very meeting at which Lenin and the Bolsheviks decided to seize power was held in his flat (he was out and his wife had not told him about the meeting). He was a Menshevik-Internationalist, one of a small group headed by Martov, Lenin's old friend and eventual antagonist. So his observations about the Bolsheviks and what was going on amongst the masses are often acute and extremely useful. He published his eyewitness testimony of the five years of the revolution in seven volumes in 1922.

TALKING POINT

What are the likely strengths and weaknesses of Sukhanov's diary as a source?

These demands were set out in the so-called 'April Theses', which he had jotted down on the journey from Switzerland. The day after his arrival he delivered his Theses at a meeting of the Social Democrats. They were received with boos and whistles from the Mensheviks, who claimed he was ignoring the lessons of Marx. One called the Theses 'the ravings of a madman'; another said, 'Lenin is a has-been'. The Bolsheviks, too, reacted with astonishment. The Theses went beyond anything that even the most radical had imagined. Some believed that Lenin had lived abroad for too long and was out of touch. His ideas were opposed by some members of the Bolshevik Central Committee. But, by the end of the month, Lenin's personality and power of argument ensured that the April Theses were party policy.

The Bolsheviks now provided a radically different alternative to the Provisional Government and the moderate socialists in the Soviet. The main points of the Theses were turned into slogans: 'Bread, Peace and Land!', and 'All Power to the Soviets!' These appealed to the soldiers and workers whose expectations and demands were becoming more radical and were moving ahead of the ability of the Provisional Government and the Soviet to satisfy them.

SOURCE 4.6 J. Carmichael, *A Short History of the Revolution*, 1967, pp. 80–81. Here, Carmichael is quoting extracts from N. N. Sukhanov's diary in which Sukhanov describes the impact of Lenin's speech at the Finland Station

'Dear Comrades, soldiers and sailors and workers! I am happy to greet in your persons the victorious Russian Revolution, and greet you as the vanguard of the worldwide proletarian army ... long live the worldwide Socialist Revolution!'

... Suddenly, before the eyes of all of us, completely swallowed up by the routine drudgery of the Revolution, there was presented a bright, blinding beacon ... Lenin's voice, heard straight from the train, was a 'voice from outside' ...

I shall never forget that thunderlike speech, which startled and amazed not only me, a heretic who accidentally dropped in, but all the true believers. I am certain that nobody expected anything of the sort.

How did Lenin justify the April Theses?

Lenin believed that the bourgeoisie (middle classes) were too weak in Russia to carry through the democratic revolution. He said that the proletariat had already assumed power in the soviets – they were driving the Russian Revolution in the form of the Petrograd Soviet. It was therefore a backward step to move to a middle-class-dominated parliamentary democracy. He claimed that in Russia the poorer peasants could be treated as proletarians because they had a consciousness of their class position and were active players in the revolution.

But Lenin saw this as part of a wider picture. Along with Trotsky, he believed that a worldwide socialist revolution would start, not in a highly industrialised society as Marx had suggested, but in a backward country where capitalism was just developing and the conflict between the industrialists and the employees was more acute (as a result of low wages, bad conditions, etc.). Trotsky and Lenin thought that 'the weakest link' in the capitalist chain would break first and that once the revolution had begun it would spread to the proletariat in other countries. They considered that Russia was the weakest link and that the war had acted as a catalyst to bring Europe to the brink of a socialist revolution. Lenin was sure that Germany, at least, was about to explode into revolution. Both thought that once the revolution started, the proletariat of the advanced capitalist countries would come to the aid of the Russian proletariat and help them to develop the conditions in which socialism could be built.

■ 4E How Lenin's radical policies distinguished the Bolsheviks from other socialist parties

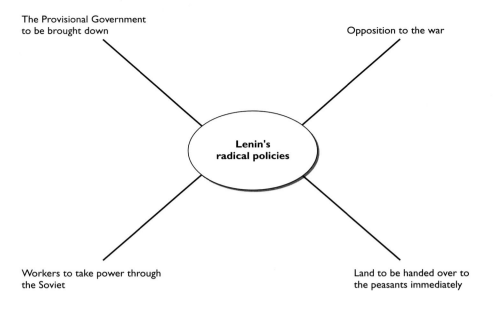

The Provisional Government to be brought down

Opposition to the war

Lenin's radical policies

Workers to take power through the Soviet

Land to be handed over to the peasants immediately

FOCUS ROUTE

1 Use the table below to summarise the positions of the key players at the end of April 1917 and the alternatives they presented to the populace. You will need to refer to sections C and D.

	Provisional Government	Petrograd Soviet	Bolsheviks
Who were they?			
What general policy statements did they make?			
What were their attitudes to each other?			
What were their attitudes to the war?			
What were their attitudes to the land question?			

2 a) Why did Lenin's arrival in Petrograd have such an impact?
   b) Draw an annotated diagram showing and explaining the main ways in which he distinguished the Bolsheviks from the other socialist parties.
   c) How did Lenin justify his April Theses?

■ Learning trouble spot

Political parties

It is easy to get confused about the various parties. Here's a brief summary:

- Liberals, mainly from the Kadets, dominated the Provisional Government.
- Moderate socialists from the Menshevik and Socialist Revolutionary parties were running the Petrograd Soviet.
- Both of these parties had radical wings: Menshevik-Internationalists and left-wing SRs.
- The Bolshevik party, led by Lenin, was more disciplined and centrally controlled, but at this time did not have a strong presence in the Soviet.

FOCUS ROUTE

1 As you work through this section, fill out a table like the one below to evaluate the policies and actions of the Provisional Government.

Issue	How the Provisional Government dealt with it	How successful its response was

2 Look closely at the moderate socialists. Make notes on how:
   a) the socialist groups (apart from the Bolsheviks) became associated with the policy of continuing the war
   b) the moderate socialist leaders of the Soviet were losing the support of the workers
   c) the Socialist Revolutionary leaders were losing touch with the mood of the peasants.

Four key issues faced the Provisional Government. These were:

- the war
- the land
- national minority demands
- the deteriorating economic situation.

1 The war

It was clear from early on that the conduct of the war would be a crucial factor and would determine the way in which the revolution developed. It is central to understanding why the Provisional Government failed.

Matters came to a head at the end of April when it was apparent that Milyukov, Minister of War, not only wanted to defend Russia but also hoped to make territorial gains if the Allies won; in particular, he was after Constantinople and control of the straits into the Black Sea, which the Russians had wanted for centuries. This outraged the socialists in the Soviet who were committed to a defensive war only. Milyukov was forced to resign and the Provisional Government was in crisis.

The crisis ended when the Provisional Government was reformed on 5 May. Five socialist leaders joined the new COALITION government. The most important of these were the Menshevik leader Tsereteli and the leader of the Socialist Revolutionaries, Chernov. The significance of this cannot be underestimated. From now on, the Menshevik and Socialist Revolutionary leaders would be associated with the conduct of the war and therefore would be criticised and risk losing support if the war went badly.

> **COALITION**
> Combination government formed by people drawn from different political parties.

The summer offensive, 1917

At the beginning of the summer of 1917, the Provisional Government decided to launch a major offensive against the Germans. The reasons are not altogether clear, but it seems to have resulted from the following factors:

- Britain and France had requested strongly (even desperately) that Russia attack on the Eastern Front to take the pressure off their forces in the West. The Provisional Government was responding to its treaty obligations to the Allies.

A SEPARATE PEACE

Some commentators believe that if the Russians had negotiated a separate peace treaty with the Germans in May or June 1917, the Bolshevik Revolution of October would probably not have taken place. Such a treaty would have offended Britain and France but Russia would have been able to focus on its internal problems. The socialists in the new coalition did try to set up an international peace conference, but they failed to get anywhere. However, peace would have meant the loss of territory and, even in March 1918, would have been very unpopular.

- There was still a strong nationalist and patriotic element in Russian society, across classes, that did not like to surrender to the Germans. For them, defeat, which would probably mean giving up Russian land in any negotiation, would be a national humiliation.
- The Kadets and other conservative forces in Russia thought that a successful offensive might put the generals and officers back in control of the armed forces and that they might then be able to bring the revolution under control. Joined by the liberal press, they called for the masses to unite under the banner of Russia.
- Some socialists felt that a successful offensive would put them in a better bargaining position with the Germans in peace negotiations.

In the event, the socialists allowed themselves to be persuaded by their liberal coalition partners that a summer offensive should be undertaken. The new Minister for War, Alexander Kerensky, threw himself into a propaganda campaign to mobilise the armed forces and the people for a massive attack. Kerensky, who was still immensely popular, made patriotic speeches and toured the Fronts. To some extent it worked. Middle-class civilians volunteered to fight in shock battalions designed to raise the army's morale. However, Kerensky was not so successful with the soldiers, who were increasingly unwilling to fight. Soldiers' committees argued that they could see little point in fighting for territory when everybody wanted peace. There was considerable fraternisation between German and Russian troops and thousands ran away before the offensive began.

SOURCE 4.7   O. Figes, *A People's Tragedy: The Russian Revolution 1891–1924*, 1997, p. 419

The crucial advance towards Lvov [a town] soon collapsed when the troops discovered a large store of alcohol in the abandoned town of Koniukhy and stopped there to get drunk. By the time they were fit to resume fighting three days and a hangover later, enemy reinforcements had arrived and the Russians, suffering heavy casualties, were forced to retreat . . .

. . . Bochareva's Battalion of Death did much better than most. The women volunteers broke through the first two German lines, followed by some sheepish male conscripts. But then they came under heavy German fire. The women dispersed in confusion, while most of the men stayed in the German trenches, where they had found a large supply of liquor and proceeded to get drunk. Despite the shambles around her, Bochareva battled on. At one point she came across one of her women having sexual intercourse with a soldier in a shell-hole. She ran her through with a bayonet; but the soldier escaped. Eventually, with most of her volunteers killed or wounded, even Bochareva was forced to retreat. The offensive was over. It was Russia's last.

The offensive began on 16 June and lasted for about three days. Then it began to fall apart. The rate of desertion was extremely high. Soldiers killed their officers rather than fight. The result was that hundreds of thousands of soldiers were killed and even more territory was lost. The failure of the offensive produced an immediate effect in Petrograd – an armed uprising in early July, known as the July Days (see page 96). Although the Provisional Government survived this, in the longer term the effect of their war policy was that the moderate socialist leaders in the government lost their credibility with the soldiers and workers.

TALKING POINT

Russians wanted the war to end but many did not want to see it end in a humiliating defeat. What if your country were in a situation where your enemies were about to be your conquerors and take much of your best territory? Would you carry on fighting even though you knew defeat was certain?

THE WOMEN'S DEATH BATTALION

Maria Bochareva, who had fought in the war and been twice wounded, was given permission to form a women's volunteer unit. Shocked by the breakdown of military discipline, she hoped that a women's unit would shame male soldiers into fighting. The women shaved their heads and put on standard army uniform. It did not have the intended effect. Some soldiers refused to fight alongside the women and others saw it as an indication of how desperate the army had become.

SOURCE 4.8 Members of the Women's Death Battalion, formed in July 1917 by Maria Bochareva. The top photo shows the battalion being blessed by Patriarch Nikon, a Russian Orthodox Church leader

2 The land

By May 1917, there was significant unrest in the countryside. The peasants were hungry for land and the collapse of central authority meant there was no one to stop them taking it. They had always believed that the land belonged to them and had felt betrayed by the emancipation of 1861 (see page 18). Now they saw a chance to complete the process that had been started then. However, they wanted government approval to give legitimacy to their actions.

But the liberals in the Provisional Government were not willing simply to hand over the land to the peasants. They were not against land redistribution, but they wanted it to be done within the framework of law set down by the Constituent Assembly and they wanted landowners (often their supporters) to be compensated. They were also concerned that a land free-for-all would lead to the disintegration of the army as peasant soldiers rushed back to claim their share. This seemed a reasonable position, but not to the peasants. As the summer wore on they began taking more and more land, as well as livestock, tools, timber and anything they could grab from private estates.

When the Socialist Revolutionaries joined the Provisional Government in May, it seemed that a better relationship might develop between government and peasants. Chernov, their popular leader, was Minister of Agriculture and the Socialist Revolutionaries had played a leading part in helping to organise peasant soviets. But, broadly, the Socialist Revolutionaries, too, urged that the land problem be resolved by the Constituent Assembly. Chernov did want to try a radical alternative whereby peasants would be empowered to use land from private estates (with ownership to be sorted out later), but the liberals in the Provisional Government blocked this.

During the summer, land seizures increased (237 cases were reported in July) and local Socialist Revolutionary activists encountered resistance only if they tried to restrain the peasants. Socialist Revolutionary leaders failed to understand that the peasant demand for fundamental land reform could not be put off until the Constituent Assembly met. The peasants were going to take the land with or without permission.

3 National minority demands

Another issue that emphasised the splits in the Provisional Government was the demands of the national minorities. When the centralised tsarist state collapsed, the Finns and the Poles called immediately for outright independence. Other areas in the old Russian empire wanted more autonomy, particularly in the Caucasus region. One of the biggest problems arose in the Ukraine, an area of immense value to the Russians, containing the most valuable farmland in the old empire and very near the Front. The Ukrainians demanded self-government and the moderate socialists in the government made concessions to them. This outraged the liberals, who saw it as the first step towards the break-up of Russia. They believed that for Russia to stay a great power, it had to keep all the regions together in one centrally governed state.

4 The deteriorating economic situation

Food shortages, unemployment and high prices had been important factors in bringing about the February Revolution. These problems did not go away when the Provisional Government took power. The downward spiral in the economy continued, affecting the workers badly. The railway system, already badly dislocated by the war, showed signs of breaking down. Shortages of fuel and raw materials led to factories cutting output or closing and laying off workers; 568 factories in Petrograd closed between February and July with the loss of 100,000 jobs. The scarcity of manufactured goods caused prices to rise rapidly.

Food shortages were a major issue. There was a temporary respite in the grain crisis after February, but by the end of the summer the situation was critical again. The harvest of 1917 was very poor. In August the government increased the price it paid for grain by 100 per cent but this did not persuade peasants to bring grain into the cities. They were unwilling to sell their grain because there were few goods to buy and those that were available were on sale at inflated prices. In Petrograd, grain prices doubled between February and June and rose again in the autumn. The Provisional Government seemed unable to do anything about the food shortages. It sent out punishment brigades into the countryside to requisition grain, but this served only to make the peasants more hostile.

As long as the war continued, and resources were channelled towards the army, there was not much the government could do. The result in the cities was growing class antagonism between workers and employers. The workers had expected social reform after February, with higher wages, better working conditions, shorter hours and more influence in the workplace. But wages were becoming worthless and employers were using lock-outs to bring the workers to heel.

Strikes began to increase and workers' committees began to take over the running of some factories completely. Workers turned their antagonism on the government, demanding price controls, a halt to speculation and the arrest of profiteers. However, the liberals in the Provisional Government were under pressure from industrialists not to interfere or fix prices and would not act against them. The moderate socialist leaders in the government and the Soviet found themselves increasingly unable to meet the needs of their natural supporters, the workers.

■ 4F Wages and the cost of living before and during the Revolution

SOURCE 4.9   Daily wages (roubles and kopeks)

Trade	July 1914	July 1916	August 1917
Carpenter, cabinetmaker	1.60–2.00	4.00–6.00	8.50
Painter, upholsterer	1.80–2.00	3.00–5.50	8.00
Blacksmith	1.00–2.25	4.00–5.00	8.50
Chimney sweep	1.50–2.00	4.00–5.50	7.50
Locksmith	0.90–2.00	3.50–6.00	9.00

SOURCE 4.10   Cost of food (roubles and kopeks)

	August 1914	August 1917	Percentage increase
Black bread	0.02	0.12	500
White bread	0.05	0.20	300
Pork	0.23	2.00	770
Herring	0.06	0.52	767
Cheese	0.40	3.50	754
Butter	0.48	3.20	557
Eggs (dozen)	0.30	1.60	443
Milk	0.07	0.40	471

SOURCE 4.11   Cost of other basic commodities (roubles and kopeks)

	August 1914	August 1917	Percentage increase
Cotton cloth	0.15	2.00	1,233
Men's shoes (pair)	12.00	144.00	1,097
Men's suits	40.00	400.00–555.00	900–1,109
Tea	4.50	18.00	300
Matches (carton)	0.10	0.50	400
Soap	4.50	40.00	780
Gasoline	1.70	11.00	547
Candles	8.50	100.00	1,076
Firewood (per load)	10.00	120.00	1,100
Charcoal	0.80	13.00	1,523

All figures taken from J. Reed, *Ten Days that Shook the World* (illustrated edition), 1977

ACTIVITY

Making sense of statistics.

1 Using Excel, calculate the average increase in daily wages between July 1914 and August 1917 for each of the five trades in Source 4.9.
2 Calculate the average percentage increase from these figures.
3 Using Source 4.10, calculate the average percentage increase in the cost of food between August 1914 and 1917.
4 Using Source 4.11, repeat this same calculation for other basic commodities.
5 Draw a bar chart comparing the increases in all three areas covered by Sources 4.9–4.11.

What was the position at the end of August 1917?

Disagreements grew within the Provisional Government as it became harder to find solutions to the problems facing Russia. On 2 July, three Kadet (liberal) ministers resigned from the Provisional Government over the concessions given by socialist ministers to Ukrainian demands for self-government and land reform. The liberals also blamed socialist leaders for the militant strikes in the cities. A day later, Lvov resigned as Prime Minister, equally fed up with both liberals and socialists.

Alexander Kerensky became Prime Minister. He was seen as the only man who could unite the country – since he was acceptable to workers, the middle classes and the military – and stop the drift into civil war. He was therefore keen to keep a coalition government which included Kadets, although the balance had shifted in favour of the socialists. However, the people in the streets saw the Kadets and other liberals as reactionaries working in the interests of landowners and industrialists. Urban workers, peasants and soldiers were demanding more radical action from the government over land reform, the economy and the war, and were becoming increasingly impatient.

■ **Learning trouble spot**

The changing Provisional Government
The changes in the Provisional Government coalition can be confusing. There are three key ones:

1 In March 1917, it was dominated by the liberals (Kadets). The only socialist was Kerensky.
2 In May, five socialists joined but the liberals still dominated.
3 In July, Kerensky became Prime Minister and the balance shifted in favour of the socialists, although there was still a strong liberal presence.

Who was Alexander Kerensky?
Alexander Kerensky was a lawyer. Like Lenin, he was born in Simbirsk. Both had fathers who became Chief Inspectors of Schools (strangely enough, Kerensky's father was Lenin's headmaster) and both trained in the law. Kerensky became involved in radical politics in his teens but did not favour Marxism or terrorism. He set up an office in St Petersburg to advise workers on their rights and represent them free of charge. In the 1905 Revolution he published a socialist newspaper and was arrested. The four months he served in prison cemented his position in radical socialist circles and in 1912 he was elected to the Duma. He joined the Trudoviki group, left-wing socialists on the edge of the Socialist Revolutionary party.

Kerensky was a master of the art of twentieth-century political communication. In his biography of Lenin, Robert Service refers to Kerensky as 'the real master of the modern technology of politics in 1917' (R. Service, *Lenin*, 2000, page 277). In comparison, the propaganda techniques of the Bolsheviks were not very imaginative and posters of Lenin were not made until after the October Revolution. Kerensky had great skills as an orator and was famous for his passionate speeches which left his 'whole body trembling with sweat pouring down the pale cheeks'. At the end of his dramatic speeches, he would collapse in a faint through nervous exhaustion. An English nurse marvelled as people 'kissed him, his uniform, his car and the ground on which he walked. Many of them were on their knees' (F. Farmborough, *Nurse at the Russian Front*, 1977, pages 269–70). He was very popular with women.

He was the ideal man for February 1917, the link man between the Provisional Government and the Soviet because he was generally liked in all circles and the workers trusted him. In the early months after February, he

was referred to as 'the first love of the revolution', the 'poet of freedom' and the 'saviour of the fatherland'. He was a popular choice for Prime Minster in July 1917. He was seen as the 'human bridge' between socialists and liberals, acceptable to the workers and soldiers as well as to the military leaders and the bourgeoisie.

Kerensky was energetic and tenacious, but he was also temperamental and vain. He had a picture of himself at his huge desk printed on tens of thousands of postcards (see Source 4.12) and newsreels made of his public appearances. He deliberately struck a Napoleonic pose, making tours of the Front in a smart military uniform with his arm in a sling. When he became Prime Minster he seemed to see himself as the man destined to save Russia and adopted a self-important air. He moved into Tsar Alexander III's rooms in the Winter Palace. He kept on the old palace servants and had the new red flag on the palace raised and lowered as he came and left, just as the old flag had been for the tsars.

SOURCE 4.12   A photograph of Kerensky at his desk

SOURCE 4.13   Kerensky (right) reviews the troops at the Front in mid-May 1917

SOURCE 4.14 O. Figes, *A People's Tragedy: The Russian Revolution 1891–1924,* 1997, p. 337, describing Kerensky's speech to the Soviet on 2 March 1917, in which he asked for approval of his decision to join the Provisional Government as Minister of Justice

'Comrades! Do you trust me?' he asked in a voice charged with theatrical pathos. 'We do, we do!' the delegates shouted. 'I speak, comrades, with all my soul, from the bottom of my heart, and if it is needed to prove this, if you do not trust me, then I am ready to die.'... He told them that 'his first act' as the Minister of Justice had been to order the immediate release of all political prisoners and the arrangement of a hero's welcome for their return to the capital. The delegates were overcome with emotion and greeted this news with thunderous cheers. Now Kerensky turned to ask them whether they approved of his decision to join the government, offering to resign from the Soviet if the answer should be no. But there were wild cries of 'We do! We do!' and, without a formal vote, his actions were endorsed. It was a brilliant coup de théâtre. What might have been the moment of his downfall had in fact become the moment of his triumph. Kerensky was now the only politician with a position in both the government and the Soviet. He was the undisputed leader of the people.

SOURCE 4.15 A hostile cartoon mocking Kerensky's 'Napoleon Bonaparte' image

SOURCE 4.16 Sir Robert Bruce Lockhart, British Consul in Moscow 1911–17, quoted in R. Abraham, *Alexander Kerensky, The First Love of the Revolution,* 1987, p. 207. Lockhart describes an address given to a packed meeting in the Bolshoi Theatre in Moscow on 11 June 1917

The whole theme of his speech was built around the idea that without suffering nothing that was worth having could be won. He himself looked the embodiment of suffering. The deathly pallor of his face, the restless movements of his body as he swayed backwards and forwards, the raw, almost whispering tones of his voice ... all helped to make his appeal more terrible and more realistic.... And, when the end came, the huge crowd rose to greet him like one man. Men and women embraced each other in a hysteria of enthusiasm. Old generals and young praporshicks *wept together over the man who all Russia feels can save the country from ruin. Women gave presents of jewellery, officers sacrificed their orders. An autographed photogravure of [M.] Kerensky was sold for 16,000 roubles and the whole theatre rained roses.*

ACTIVITY

1 **a)** What impression of Kerensky do you get from Sources 4.12, 4.13 and 4.15?
   b) He had many copies of Source 4.12 made and sent out to people. Why?
2 What do Sources 4.14 and 4.16 reveal about Kerensky's abilities and why he was a popular leader?
3 What aspects of Kerensky's character and history made him the ideal man for February 1917 and the popular choice for Prime Minister in July 1917?

The **liberals** in the Provisional Government were moving to the right. They wanted:
- no land reform
- defence of property
- military discipline restored
- law and order re-established.

The **Soviet** was declining in influence. The moderate socialist leaders of the Soviet were increasingly out of touch with workers and soldiers in the streets. It also lacked decisive leadership.

The **army** was **disintegrating**. The process had begun after the collapse of the June–July offensive and was accelerating. Whole regiments were deserting and making their way back home. Soldiers were commandeering trains, throwing the transport system into disarray. There was widespread violence and drunkenness on the trains, e.g. in one incident, officers were thrown out of the window of a train as it crossed a bridge.

The **economic situation in the cities** was deteriorating. Grain was not getting in from the countryside, and the peasants were being extremely unco-operative. Shortages of raw materials were causing factory closures and unemployment. The price of goods and food was rising.

Control was breaking down in the countryside. After the harvest was gathered in, **land seizures** continued. The level of **violence** was increasing. Country houses were burned down and some landlords were killed. Robbery was rife.

Support for the **Bolsheviks** was increasing. Workers, soldiers and sailors were becoming more radicalised. Workers, in particular, were looking to the Bolsheviks for reform in their workplaces and improvements in living standards.

There was **increasing lawlessness** in the cities. Robbery and housebreaking were very common. Well-dressed people were beaten in the streets.

ACTIVITY

Alexander Kerensky, the Prime Minister, has a few headaches at the end of August. Can he and the Provisional Government survive?

a) Using Chart 4G and other information in this chapter, list the main problems and challenges to his government's authority.

b) Four courses of action are identified below; these were all realistic choices for Kerensky.

   i) Negotiate an immediate peace treaty with the Germans.

   ii) Find a loyal general to help you to restore discipline, law and order.

   iii) Suppress the Bolsheviks who present a continuing threat by demanding the overthrow of the government and attracting growing support in the cities.

   iv) Hold immediate elections for the Constituent Assembly.

Draw a table like the one shown below. Give each course of action a mark out of ten showing whether you think it is a good idea or not and note down how it might help. Then work out the risks or problems involved. Discuss your decisions with the rest of the class.

Course of action	Mark out of ten	How this might help	Risks or problems involved
Negotiate immediate peace treaty with Germany			
Find a general to restore law and order			
Suppress the Bolsheviks			
Hold elections to the Constituent Assembly			

Review: Was the Provisional Government doomed from the beginning?

Any government faced with the sort of demands confronting the Provisional Government – complete redistribution of land, radical social reform, autonomy and independence for national minorities, conflicting views about the conduct of the war – would have been in trouble. In addition to this, the Provisional Government was a temporary body and it did not have the power to enforce its decisions. So we might say that it was in an impossible position and that too much was being expected of it in too short a time.

On the other hand, the Kadets in the government had effectively blocked the government from taking measures that would have gained it popular support. They had:

- blocked the land deal and Chernov's suggestions for a compromise, thereby siding with the landowners and antagonising the peasants
- supported the war and wanted to continue it aggressively, to the dismay of the soldiers and many other citizens
- sided with the employers against the workers over workers' power and working conditions. They had refused to intervene in the running of the economy, for example by preventing further price rises, to the increasing frustration of the workers.

By the summer of 1917, it was clear that the liberals did not want the revolution to go any further. They wanted it reined in and would prefer military control to soviet control.

ACTIVITY

Do you think the Provisional Government was doomed from the beginning? Given its status and the situation in Russia, could it have met the expectations of the mass of the people?
a) Note down reasons for and against the idea that it was doomed from the start.
b) What would you identify as the most significant or important factors in deciding whether it was doomed or not?

KEY POINTS FROM CHAPTER 4

Was the Provisional Government doomed from the beginning?

1 A Provisional Government was formed to rule Russia until a Constituent Assembly could be called to set up a new system of government.
2 The Provisional Government had to share power with the Petrograd Soviet, which controlled the armed forces, industries and services in the capital.
3 In the rest of Russia, all sorts of bodies – committees, councils and soviets – were set up to run local government. These were managed by local people of repute, including non-party socialists.
4 The honeymoon of the revolution did not last long as people's expectations of change developed.
5 Lenin offered a radically different programme from that of the Provisional Government and more moderate socialist leaders.
6 The leaders of the Mensheviks and the Socialist Revolutionaries were drawn into the Provisional Government and thereafter became associated with its weaknesses and failures.
7 The Provisional Government would not end the war or legitimise the right of peasants to redistribute the land amongst themselves and this lost them a lot of support.
8 There were splits between the liberals and socialists in the government and it was difficult to develop a coherent programme on key issues.
9 The workers were becoming increasingly radicalised as the economic situation deteriorated.
10 By the end of August, the new socialist Prime Minister, Alexander Kerensky, faced a formidable range of problems.

5 Was the Bolshevik seizure of power in October 1917 inevitable?

CHAPTER OVERVIEW

The popularity of the Bolshevik Party grew in the summer of 1917 as the workers became more disillusioned with the policies of the Provisional Government and the moderate socialist leaders in the Soviet. At the beginning of July there was an explosive rising – the July Days – in Petrograd which reflected the frustration of workers, soldiers and sailors. The Bolsheviks were drawn into this but the rising collapsed and leading Bolsheviks were arrested. Kerensky tried to assert his authority by taking military control of the capital, with the help of General Kornilov, but the plan backfired on him and he was discredited. The Bolsheviks exploited this situation to seize power in October 1917.

A Why did the Bolsheviks become so popular and how did they almost ruin their chances of taking power? (pp. 96–98)

B The Kornilov affair and its consequences (pp. 99–100)

C The October Revolution – did Kerensky hand power to the Bolsheviks? (pp. 101–103)

D Popular revolution or *coup d'état?* (pp. 104–109)

E Review: Was the Bolshevik seizure of power inevitable? (p. 110)

Note: Section A of this chapter looks at the fortunes and misfortunes of the Bolsheviks from April to August 1917. This covers the same time period described in sections E and F in Chapter 4. The story of the Revolution from September to October starts in section B (page 99).

FOCUS ROUTE

1 As you work through this chapter, follow the ups and downs of the Bolshevik Party from April to October. The timeline in Chart 5A will help. Annotate your copy of the graph to explain key points in their progress, showing why their popularity increased from May to November.

2 Throughout this chapter you are going to think about the question of whether the Bolshevik seizure of power was always the most likely outcome. At various points, you will be asked to note down your opinions. Then at the end you will be asked to reach a final judgement.

Support for the Bolshevik Party

April May June July August September October

96

WAS THE BOLSHEVIK SEIZURE OF POWER IN OCTOBER 1917 INEVITABLE?

■ 5A Timeline of the revolutions in 1917

FEBRUARY
23 Women's Day parade
25 General strike
27 Duma committee and Petrograd Soviet formed

MARCH
1 Order No. 1 issued
2 Provisional Government formed (Tsar abdicates)

APRIL
3 Lenin returns to Petrograd

MAY
2 Milyukov resigns as Minister for War; Provisional Government in crisis
5 Coalition government of socialists and Kadets formed

JUNE
3 First All-Russian Congress of Soviets begins
16 Launch of military offensive

JULY
3–4 'July Days'
5–6 Bolsheviks arrested in Petrograd; Lenin flees to Finland
8 Kerensky becomes Prime Minister, at head of new coalition government

AUGUST
26–30 Kornilov affair

SEPTEMBER
9 Bolshevik majority in Petrograd Soviet
15 Bolshevik Central Committee rejects Lenin's first call for insurrection

OCTOBER
7 Lenin returns to Petrograd
10 Bolshevik Central Committee confirms decision to seize power
25–26 Bolsheviks seize power

 A # Why did the Bolsheviks become so popular and how did they almost ruin their chances of taking power?

The Bolshevik Party became the main focus for the masses dissatisfied with the government's performance. Their programme of ending the war, controlling employers, social reform for workers and prioritising food supplies was appealing. During May and June the workers and soldiers in Petrograd and Moscow began to differentiate between the Bolsheviks and the other socialist groups. Left-wing members of the Socialist Revolutionary and Menshevik parties were increasingly drawn towards the Bolshevik camp. Support for the party grew and membership increased enormously (see Source 5.11, page 107). Probably the most famous recruit to the Bolshevik Party in the summer of 1917 was Leon Trotsky.

■ Learning trouble spot

The workers and political parties

It is easy to think that workers supported one or other of the socialist parties in the same way as people support political parties today. But in *The Russian Revolution 1917–21* (1987), Beryl Williams has pointed out that workers in the first months after the February Revolution in 1917 did not tend to think in party terms. Most would not have known the difference between a Menshevik and a Bolshevik. Workers tended to identify more with their own craft or industry and placed most of their trust in their workplace committees and local soviets, most of which were multi-party or non-party organisations. However, it seems that by June many workers were becoming aware of the Bolsheviks as a separate party with a different programme – one which tied in with their own demands and aspirations.

The July Days

The mounting frustration of workers and soldiers erupted at the beginning of July in what became known as the July Days, several days of uncontrolled rioting on the streets. This was sparked by the failure of the summer offensive against Germany, workers' anger at their economic plight and the Petrograd garrison's fear that its regiments were to be sent to the Front.

For two days the capital was defenceless. On 3 July, Sukhanov, the diarist of the revolution, reported lorries and cars rushing about the city full of 'fierce-faced' civilians and soldiers, and armed groups marching in the streets. On 4 July, events took a more violent turn when 20,000 armed sailors from the Kronstadt naval base arrived in Petrograd. Red Kronstadt, as it was known, was a hotbed of revolutionary activity. The sailors marched to the Tauride Palace where they demanded that the Soviet take power. Chernov, the Socialist Revolutionary leader, was sent out to calm them down but was seized and bundled into a car. He was rescued by Trotsky who barely escaped with his own life (see Source 5.2).

KRONSTADT

Kronstadt was a naval base on an island just off the coast near Petrograd. The sailors who lived in the base were, in 1917, extremely radical and supported revolutionary change. However, there is a common misconception that they were, to a man, Bolsheviks. Many were Bolsheviks, but anarchists and Socialist Revolutionaries were also very influential. The sailors had their own fiercely independent soviet which was multi-party and chaired by a Socialist Revolutionary.

97

WAS THE BOLSHEVIK SEIZURE OF POWER IN OCTOBER 1917 INEVITABLE?

SOURCE 5.1 Troops fire on demonstrators in Petrograd during the July Days

SOURCE 5.2 J. Carmichael, *A Short History of the Revolution*, 1967, p. 116, quoting from Sukhanov's diary

A group of workers rushed [into the room where the Soviet leaders were meeting] ... shouting out: 'Comrade Chernov has been arrested by the mob! They're tearing him to pieces right now! To the rescue! Everyone out into the street!'

Chkheidze, restoring order with difficulty, proposed that Kamenev, Martov and Trotsky should hasten to rescue Chernov. [Trotsky and several others went out to help] ... The mob was in turmoil as far as the eye could reach. A number of sailors with rather savage faces around the motor car were particularly violent. Chernov, who had plainly lost all presence of mind, was in the back seat.

[Trotsky climbed on to the bonnet of the car.]

All Kronstadt knew Trotsky and, one would have thought, trusted him. But he began to speak and the crowd did not subside. If a shot had been fired nearby at that moment by way of provocation, a tremendous slaughter might have occurred, and all of us, including Trotsky, might have been torn to shreds.

[Trotsky said:]

'You hurried over here, Red Kronstadters, as soon as you heard the revolution was in danger ... Long live Red Kronstadt, the glory and pride of the revolution ... You've come to declare your will and show the Soviet that the working class no longer wants to see the bourgeoisie in power. But why hurt your own cause by petty acts of violence against casual individuals? ... Every one of you is prepared to lay down his life for the revolution. I know that. Give me your hand, comrade! Your hand, brother!'

Trotsky stretched his hand down to a sailor who was protesting with especial violence. The latter moved his hand out of reach.... But I think they were Kronstadt naval ratings who had, in their own judgement, accepted Bolshevik ideas. It seemed to me that the sailor, who must have heard Trotsky in Kronstadt more than once ... was confused. Not knowing what to do, the Kronstadters released Chernov. Trotsky took him by the arm and hurried him into the Palace. Chernov sank nervelessly into his chair.

[Later a worker jumped on to the platform of a Soviet executive committee meeting and shouted:]

'Comrades! How long must we workers put up with treachery? You're all here debating and making deals with the bourgeoisie and the landlords ... You are busy betraying the working class. Well, just understand that the working class won't put up with it! There are 30,000 of us all told here from Putilov. We're going to have our way. All power to the soviets! We have a firm grip on our rifles! Your Kerenskys and Tseretelis are not going to fool us!'

FOCUS ROUTE

Make a note of your answers to the following questions:

1 How did the Bolsheviks differentiate themselves from other socialist parties?
2 **a)** What was the significance of the July Days?
   b) How involved were the Bolsheviks in the uprising?
   c) Why did they look weaker after the July Days?
3 Were the Bolsheviks really a highly disciplined and organised party?

ACTIVITY

1 What do Sources 5.1 and 5.2 and the incidents described above show about:
   a) the feelings of the workers and soldiers
   b) their attitudes towards the Provisional Government
   c) the position of revolutionary leaders in July 1917
   d) the situation in Petrograd regarding control and order?

■ Learning trouble spot

What was the position of the Soviet at this time?

In the summer of 1917, the Petrograd Soviet was controlled by the moderate leaders of the Mensheviks and the Socialist Revolutionaries. However, it was becoming increasingly weak and identified with the Provisional Government.

FOCUS ROUTE

Did it look at this point as if the Bolshevik seizure of power was inevitable?

Some historians have seen the July Days as an early attempt by the Bolsheviks to take power. There is little doubt that the rising was encouraged by middle-ranking Bolshevik officials, and Sukhanov talks of armed groups led by 'Bolshevik lieutenants', but it seems that the Bolshevik leadership were far from committed. In fact, when the rioting began and the Kronstadt sailors marched into Petrograd, Lenin was on a short holiday. When he returned on 4 July he appealed for restraint and the Bolshevik Central Committee called off the demonstration it had planned for early the next day. Lenin adopted a 'wait and see' policy. He did not dissociate himself from the demonstrations but he did not provide coherent leadership or make a concerted attempt to seize power.

This lack of leadership proved the undoing of the July rising. Without a clear purpose, the rising lost momentum. Troops loyal to the Soviet arrived and the crowds were dispersed. The steam was also taken out of the demonstrations by the leaking of a letter by the Provisional Government which appeared to show that Lenin was in the pay of the Germans and had come back to Russia to undermine the Russian war effort. Several leading Bolsheviks and Trotsky were arrested; Lenin was forced into hiding in Finland. The Soviet newspaper, *Izvestia*, denounced the role of the Bolsheviks in the July Days and it seemed that the Bolshevik cause had been dealt a blow from which it might not recover.

LENIN'S ESCAPE

Lenin, dressed as a working man, had to shave off his beard to escape. You can tell if a Soviet film of the events of October 1917 is genuine by looking to see if Lenin has a beard, as it had not grown back by the time the Bolshevik seizure of power took place. Lenin's hiding place was just on the other side of the Finnish border.

■ Learning trouble spot

Lenin and the Bolshevik Party

One important historical question during this period concerns the relationship between Lenin and the Bolshevik Party:

- Was it Lenin's conviction and force of personality alone that was driving them forward?
- Was Lenin in control of a highly disciplined party that obeyed orders?

Lenin had certainly changed party policy in April from co-operation with the Provisional Government to outright opposition and had called for the Soviet to take power. But revisionist historians like Edward Acton (*Rethinking the Russian Revolution*, 1990, page 196) point out that Bolshevik Party activists had been calling for these changes before Lenin's return. Lenin was more in tune with grassroots Bolsheviks than other Bolshevik leaders were. Lenin himself remarked that the body of the party was more radical than the leadership.

Acton goes on to say that Lenin was not in a position to impose control over the party. Membership soared, cells sprang up, elections and meetings took place, committees operated at different levels and communications were poor – all of which made close supervision difficult, especially outside Petrograd. The party's policy was fiercely debated at every level and there were often divisions even at the top. According to Acton, 'Formal policy directives from the centre were followed only in so far as they corresponded to local Bolshevik opinion.' The July Days appear to be an example of lower-ranking party members running ahead of their leaders.

99

WAS THE BOLSHEVIK SEIZURE OF POWER IN OCTOBER 1917 INEVITABLE?

B The Kornilov affair and its consequences

FOCUS ROUTE

Make notes to explain how the Kornilov affair helped the Bolsheviks.

The arrests of leading Bolsheviks and the closure of Bolshevik newspapers after the July Days gave the moderate socialists and the liberals in the Provisional Government a boost, but not for long. You know from Chapter 4 that their problems – war, pressure for land reform, pressures from the national minorities, and a deteriorating economic situation – got worse as August progressed. (See Chart 4G and the Activity on page 93.)

■ 5B How did Kerensky respond to his problems?

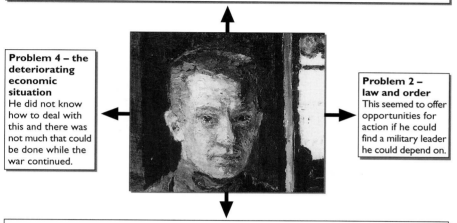

Problem 1 – the war
He was still unwilling to make a separate peace with Germany. The moderate socialists and liberals in the Provisional Government agreed with him because they knew it would cost Russia dearly in territory and they did not want to be defeated by Germany.

Problem 4 – the deteriorating economic situation
He did not know how to deal with this and there was not much that could be done while the war continued.

Problem 2 – law and order
This seemed to offer opportunities for action if he could find a military leader he could depend on.

Problem 3 – the Bolsheviks
Along with other moderate socialists, he did not want to go for full-scale suppression of the Bolsheviks. He thought such a move might lead to rioting and violence.

By the end of August, Kerensky had come to the conclusion that the only course open to him was to restore law and order in the cities and discipline in the army. He desperately needed troops he could count on to carry out his orders and deal with any threat presented by the Bolsheviks. Kerensky appointed a new Supreme Commander of the Russian forces, General Kornilov, and entered into an agreement with him, as he saw it, to bring trustworthy troops to Petrograd. But Kornilov, who was fast becoming the middle-class hope for salvation, saw it as an opportunity to crush the radical socialists, prevent the worst excesses of the revolution, and restore order and authority in Petrograd. He sent his troops marching towards the city in what was the beginning of an attempt to seize control of the government and establish military control.

Kerensky panicked when he realised what was happening. He denounced Kornilov and called on the Soviet to help to defend Petrograd from counter-revolution. Whilst some of the middle classes would undoubtedly have welcomed Kornilov and the restoration of order that would protect their property and interests, the mass of the people were terrified by the prospect. To them it meant the return of the old order, the loss of the gains of the Revolution, and bloodshed in the fighting that would inevitably result. The soldiers in Petrograd were also alarmed: they might lose the power they had gained over their officers, old-style discipline would be restored and they might be forced to go to the Front to fight. In their alarm and panic, the people desperately wanted help – and it was the Bolsheviks that provided it. Soldiers, workers and sailors prepared to defend the city, but much of this defence was organised by the Bolsheviks. The Bolshevik Red Guard (militia trained secretly by the Bolsheviks) appeared on the streets and Kerensky was good enough to supply

100

WAS THE BOLSHEVIK SEIZURE OF POWER IN OCTOBER 1917 INEVITABLE?

them with weapons. In the event, Kornilov's troops did not arrive. Railway workers halted the trains carrying them to Petrograd and Bolshevik agents persuaded them to desert their officers. Kornilov was arrested.

The consequences of Kornilov's ill-judged intervention were very significant:

1 Kerensky's reputation was irretrievably damaged. Kerensky's wife wrote: 'The prestige of Kerensky and the Provisional Government was completely destroyed by the Kornilov affair; and he was left almost without supporters.'
2 The Menshevik and Socialist Revolutionary leaders were discredited by their association with Kerensky. Their inability to change their policies also condemned them in the eyes of the people. All that the moderate socialist leaders could do was to place their hopes on the forthcoming Constituent Assembly.
3 The mass of the people completely distrusted the Kadets and other liberals as the agents of the industrialists and large landowners.
4 Soldiers, infuriated by what they thought was an officers' plot, murdered hundreds of officers. It became clear that generals could not rely on 'loyal' troops to carry out their orders. Officers, for their part, felt that Kerensky had betrayed Kornilov and were not prepared to fight for him in the coming confrontation with the Bolsheviks.
5 The Bolsheviks rode back on a wave of popular support as the saviours of the city, the true defenders of the Revolution. They were elected in huge numbers on to soviets. On 9 September, the Bolsheviks gained overall control of the Petrograd Soviet and on 25 September Trotsky was elected its President. They also took control of the Moscow Soviet and dominated the executive committees of soviets throughout urban Russia.

Kornilov

Kornilov, the son of a Siberian Cossack, had shown some sympathy towards revolutionary change, even approving soldiers' committees in the army. He was liked and supported by his own soldiers, and did not seem to have political ambitions. He seemed a good choice as Supreme Commander for Kerensky, who desperately needed stability in the army and loyal troops. But Kornilov quickly became the darling of right-wing conservative forces (industrialists, army officers and landowners) who saw in him their main hope for turning the tables on the revolutionaries. This may have swayed him to make his move on Petrograd. It is not clear whether he wanted to set up a military dictatorship or not. He said he would not move against the Provisional Government but he did want it 'cleansed and strengthened'. What Kornilov was clear about was that his main aim was to 'Hang the German spies, headed by Lenin ... and disperse the Soviet'.

FOCUS ROUTE

Did it look as if the Bolshevik seizure of power was inevitable at this point? Note your opinion, explaining any pointers that suggest it was increasingly inevitable and any reasons why it was still not inevitable.

■ **Learning trouble spot**

Was the rise in support for the Bolsheviks in September due only to the Kornilov affair?

In *From Tsar to Soviets: The Russian People and their Revolution 1917–21* (1996, page 147), the historian Chris Read makes the point that support for the Bolsheviks was rising again even before Kornilov's attempted coup. In August in the elections to the Petrograd City Duma, the Bolsheviks polled 33 per cent of the votes, coming a close second to the Socialist Revolutionaries. Menshevik supporters, in particular, were moving to the Bolsheviks because of, as one Menshevik paper put it, a 'lack of concrete results' for the masses. The Kornilov affair hastened this process.

101

WAS THE BOLSHEVIK SEIZURE OF POWER IN OCTOBER 1917 INEVITABLE?

C The October Revolution – did Kerensky hand power to the Bolsheviks?

FOCUS ROUTE

As you work through this section make notes on the following:

a) how the actions of Kerensky helped the Bolsheviks
b) how the Bolsheviks actually seized power.

WHO WERE ZINOVIEV AND KAMENEV?

Zinoviev (top) and Kamenev were important Bolshevik leaders who had been close to Lenin while he was in exile abroad before 1917. Zinoviev had been in hiding with Lenin in Switzerland. He had returned with Lenin on the train from Switzerland in April 1917. Both men had consistently opposed the idea of the Bolsheviks seizing power on their own, and wanted to work with other socialist groups.

ACTIVITY

1 What is the case made by Zinoviev and Kamenev in Source 5.3 against the uprising?
2 Is there evidence to support the notion that Lenin's proposed seizure of power might be premature?

Lenin had been in hiding in Finland watching events unfold. He judged that the time was now right for the Bolsheviks to seize power. He thought that a number of factors were working in their favour:

- the Bolsheviks had control of the Soviet
- their popularity was at an all-time high and they had done very well in elections to soviets across Russia
- the liberals and other conservative forces were demoralised after the Kornilov affair
- the Provisional Government was helpless.

A power vacuum had been created after the Kornilov débâcle and Lenin was determined to fill it. He was worried that events might turn against the Bolsheviks, particularly if the Germans made a sudden move and a separate peace was negotiated.

On 12 September, he wrote to the Bolshevik Central Committee urging action. He wrote: 'History will not forgive us if we do not assume power now.' But the other leading Bolsheviks in the Party Central Committee thought his plans were premature and remained unconvinced. They rejected his initial demands and it was only after he had come secretly to Petrograd and talked to them all night on 10 October that they finally agreed. Even then Zinoviev and Kamenev thought that it was too risky and opposed the seizure of power. To Lenin's intense displeasure, they publicised their views in a letter published in Gorky's newspaper, *Novaia zhizn*.

SOURCE 5.3 A letter from Zinoviev and Kamenev, published in *Novaia zhizn* on 18 October 1917

To call at present for an armed uprising means to stake on one card not only the fate of our Party, but also the fate of the Russian and international revolution ... A majority of workers and a significant part of the army is for us. But the rest are in question. We are convinced, for example, that if it now comes to elections for the Constituent Assembly, then the majority of peasants will vote for the Socialist Revolutionaries ... If we take power now and are forced into a revolutionary war, the mass of the soldiers will not support us.

Zinoviev and Kamenev feared civil war and believed the Bolsheviks would end up isolated and defeated by other forces combining against them. There was a real danger for the Bolsheviks that they did not have enough support in the army or amongst the workers to make a success of their rising. Trotsky urged Lenin to wait until the meeting of the Second Congress of All-Russian Soviets on 26 October. He thought that the Bolsheviks could use this as an opportunity to take control since it would appear that the seizure of power was done with the support of the soviets rather than by the Bolsheviks on their own.

Kerensky's response to the growing crisis

Once again Kerensky played into the Bolsheviks' hands. He tried to send the most radical army units out of the capital and there were rumours that he planned to abandon Petrograd to the Germans. This allowed the Soviet (now under Bolshevik control) to set up a Military Revolutionary Committee (MRC) in case there was another attempted right-wing coup. The MRC, dominated by the Bolsheviks and controlled by Trotsky, now had more direct control over soldiers in the capital and seized great quantities of arms and ammunition.

It was now an open secret that the Bolsheviks intended to seize power. Kerensky, in a last-ditch attempt to recover the situation, tried to close down two Bolshevik newspapers, restrict the power of the MRC and raise the bridges

102

WAS THE BOLSHEVIK SEIZURE OF POWER IN OCTOBER 1917 INEVITABLE?

FOCUS ROUTE

Did the Bolshevik seizure of power seem inevitable at this point?

SEIZING POWER

From our viewpoint the Bolshevik seizure of power looks very easy, with little risk involved. But it would not have appeared so to the Bolsheviks. Lenin and Trotsky were quite gloomy on the night of the take-over. They were concerned that Kerensky might turn up with troops loyal to the Provisional Government and they had no idea how the mass of the working class and other socialists would receive the news of their actions. Just a few days earlier, Bolshevik activists had reported that workers would not come out *en masse* in support of the Bolsheviks alone.

■ **Learning trouble spot**

Why did the Bolsheviks want to use the All-Russian Congress of Soviets in their bid for power?

The first congress, held at the beginning of June 1917, was dominated by the Mensheviks and Socialist Revolutionaries. Delegates were sent from soviets across Russia.

The congress was an important forum and, as such, it was potentially very powerful. The Second All-Russian Congress was called for 25 October. It was not entirely representative but reflected the Bolshevik success in elections to the soviets. The Bolsheviks had the most delegates but not a majority until the other parties walked out. Trotsky used the congress to claim that they were taking power in the name of the soviets.

linking the working-class districts to the centre of Petrograd. This was a blunder – it gave the Bolsheviks an excuse for action. They could now say that Kerensky was attacking the Soviet and the Revolution. Kerensky, dosing himself on brandy and morphine, sought loyal troops to help him deal with the Bolshevik threat but, finding none in the city, he left for the Front. He even had to borrow a car from the American embassy to get him there.

The Bolsheviks seize control

At the Smolny Institute, the Bolsheviks' headquarters, Trotsky and Sverdlov organised the final stages of the revolution. On the night of 24–25 October, units of the Red Guard, sailors and garrison soldiers were sent out to seize key points in the city – the bridges, telephone exchange, the main railway stations and the power stations. There was a bit of trouble at the main telegraph office but on the whole any troops on duty just faded away as the Red Guards appeared.

The next day in Petrograd began as normal and indeed, to a casual observer, it might have appeared that nothing special was happening. The shops opened as normal, the trams were running and people went about their everyday business. There was no furore in the streets. Many of the foreign observers in the embassies expected the Bolshevik move to crumble when people realised what was happening. Meanwhile, the Bolsheviks had decided to move in on the Provisional Government in the Winter Palace. On the night of 25–26 October, Bolshevik soldiers entered the Palace and at 2am arrested what remained of the government. The storming of the Winter Palace was to become a great Bolshevik myth defining the heroism of the revolutionaries and the popular nature of the revolution (see pages 104–109).

The same evening the All-Russian Congress of Soviets met. Socialists from other parties denounced the actions of the Bolsheviks. They argued first, that the Bolsheviks did not represent the ordinary Russian people – only a broadly based coalition of socialist parties could do that – and, second, that the Bolshevik action would set in motion a backlash which would set back the cause of socialism for decades. Trotsky replied:

'A rising of the masses of the people needs no justification ... The masses of the people followed our banner and our insurrection was victorious. And now we are told: renounce your victory, make concessions, make compromise. With whom? ... to those who tell us to do this we must say: you are miserable bankrupts, your role is played out; go where you ought to be – into the dustbin of history!'

The main socialist parties stormed from the hall. Only the left-wing Socialist Revolutionaries remained. This was fortunate for the Bolsheviks as it gave them a majority in the congress. Later, Lenin arrived and announced the formation of a Bolshevik government, immediate moves to end the war and a decree transferring land to the peasants.

Whilst the insurrection in Petrograd was relatively bloodless, this was not the case in Moscow and in some other towns. There were ten days of bloody fighting in Moscow between the Bolsheviks and forces loyal to the Provisional Government before a truce was agreed. There was an immediate threat to Petrograd by forces under General Krasnov, organised by Kerensky. But they got no nearer than the edges of the city where a mixed force of workers, sailors and soldiers repulsed them. However fragile their hold was for the moment, the Bolsheviks were in power in Russia.

THE ROLE OF TROTSKY

Trotsky had finally joined the Bolsheviks in August, although in spirit he had been with them for longer and was anxious for the Soviet to seize power. He had been a valuable addition to the party. He was by far the best orator and could really sway crowds. He was probably better known than Lenin because of his role in the 1905 Revolution when he had been deputy chairman of the St Petersburg Soviet. Trotsky's role in the preparations for the October Revolution – persuading Lenin to wait until October; setting up and controlling the Military Revolutionary Committee; reacting to Kerensky's blunders; planning the details of the take-over – has led some to suggest that he was more important than Lenin in the actual seizure of power.

SOURCE 5.4   Bolsheviks outside the Smolny Institute

Does anything you have read in this chapter change your ideas about whether the Provisional Government was doomed from the beginning?

ACTIVITY

Assessing the role of Kerensky

After August, the pressure of leadership seems to have affected Kerensky. One commentator said, 'He is like a railroad car that has left the rails. He sways and vacillates, painfully and without any glamour.' Rumours spread of his love affair with his wife's cousin and of his drunkenness and addiction to morphine and cocaine.

Kerensky has been criticised for poor political judgement in 1917 which made it easier for the Bolsheviks in October and hastened the revolution. The best examples of this are:

- his involvement with Kornilov (Kerensky did appoint Kornilov) and the subsequent débâcle, leading to his loss of credibility, and the creation of a power vacuum which Lenin was only too willing to fill (see pages 99–100)
- his disastrous underestimate of the support for Lenin in October. He believed that any Bolshevik rising would be a repeat of the July Days and easily crushed
- his actions on 24 October, closing two Bolshevik newspapers and announcing his intention of acting against the party, gave Trotsky the excuse to say the soviets were under attack and thereby ensure popular support for the Bolsheviks. Beryl Williams has called this an act of 'unbelievable ineptitude' (*Lenin*, 2000, page 76).

1 Why do you think the Kornilov affair was so damaging to the Provisional Government?
2 How far do you think Kerensky was responsible for the collapse of the Provisional Government in October 1917?
3 Did he hand power to the Bolsheviks?

Before answering these questions, you might like to look back at the material on Kerensky on pages 90–93).

104

WAS THE BOLSHEVIK SEIZURE OF POWER IN OCTOBER 1917 INEVITABLE?

HISTORIOGRAPHY
The study of history writing, talking about the different schools of thought on a historical subject, how the circumstances in which history is written affect what historians say about a subject.

D Popular revolution or *coup d'état?*

The HISTORIOGRAPHICAL debate about whether the October Revolution was a popular revolution or a *coup d'état* has often been sharp and caustic. This is because it reflects the political views of historians about whether Communism is a good or an evil system.

The range of interpretations and the shades of difference between the two positions stated in Chart 5C are enormous, but we can establish some broad schools of thought.

■ 5C Views of the nature of the October Revolution

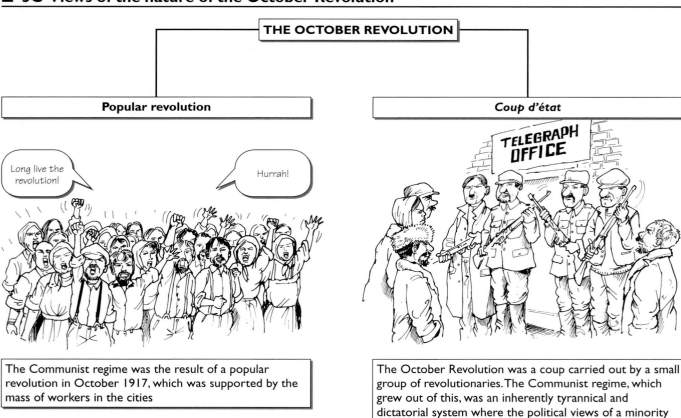

THE OCTOBER REVOLUTION

Popular revolution

Long live the revolution!

Hurrah!

The Communist regime was the result of a popular revolution in October 1917, which was supported by the mass of workers in the cities

Coup d'état

TELEGRAPH OFFICE

The October Revolution was a coup carried out by a small group of revolutionaries. The Communist regime, which grew out of this, was an inherently tyrannical and dictatorial system where the political views of a minority were imposed on the unwilling majority of Russians

The Soviet view (1917–91)

By the Soviet view here we mean the historians and writers who produced their work in Soviet Russia before its collapse in 1991. This view followed the line laid down by the Soviet leadership and writers were not allowed to deviate from it. The Soviet interpretation claims that the October Revolution was a popular uprising which was led and carried out by the working class, supported by the poorer peasants. According to this view, the working class created the soviets, which acted as the power bases through which the revolution was accomplished. They were able to do this because of the weakness of the bourgeoisie in Russia. The Bolshevik Party played a key role in guiding the working classes to success in October. Lenin is given a key role as the leader who directed the party and had the insight to make crucial decisions.

105

WAS THE BOLSHEVIK SEIZURE OF POWER IN OCTOBER 1917 INEVITABLE?

The predominant Western view after 1945

After the Second World War, the West was engaged in a COLD WAR with the
Soviet Union. The USA funded a great deal of historical research (called
Sovietology) to understand the enemy. The predominant view amongst large
numbers of historians was therefore, not surprisingly, hostile to the USSR.
They saw a straight line from Bolshevism to Stalinism and totalitarianism.
They identified the October Revolution as the starting point for this process,
when a 'tiny minority' seized power in a *coup d'état* and then imposed their
evil ideology on an unwilling population. In this view, Lenin controlled a
well-organised and disciplined revolutionary party who directed the masses.
He had the will, the personality and the clear-cut policies that brought about
the revolution; the party operated at his command. In recent years, the most
vociferous proponent of these views has been Richard Pipes. Other Western
historians who have seen the October Revolution as a disaster are Leonard
Schapiro and Robert Conquest. This is also called the 'liberal' view, mainly
referring to Western liberal historians who took this line during the Cold War
when the West feared the aggressive intentions of the Soviet Union.

The revisionists

In the 1970s, a new generation of historians challenged the 'totalitarian' view
of the historians they called 'cold warriors'. Influenced by the Vietnam War,
they became more critical of American policies. They suspected that the
hostile accounts of the October Revolution were part of the Cold War politics
of the post-war period. They looked more closely at the role of Lenin and the
Bolshevik Party in the revolution. They also wanted to look at history 'from
below' as well as 'from above': to put people back into accounts of the October
Revolution. Historians like Stephen Smith (*Red Petrograd: Revolution in the
Factories 1917–18*, 1983) saw a much more active role for the lower ranks of
the Bolshevik Party in pushing forward the revolution. They were not just
the instruments of Lenin. Indeed, such historians have suggested that Lenin
was not so firmly in control and that the Bolsheviks were not so disciplined
as Western historians had previously claimed. Sheila Fitzpatrick went further.
In *The Russian Revolution 1917–1932* (1994) she suggested that it was people
– workers, soldiers and peasants – who created the circumstances in which
the Bolsheviks could operate. They formed soviets and committees before the
Bolsheviks were on the scene. This veers back towards the popular view of the
October Revolution.

Recent views

Historians in more recent years, such as Robert Service and Chris Read, have
acknowledged that there is room to accept the scholarship of the Cold War
historians and of the revisionists. They argue that Lenin was a key figure, saying
that without his drive and persistence there probably would not have been an
October Revolution. They also say that all the hallmarks of a *coup* are present
in the way that the Bolsheviks seized power. However, they maintain that there
was a lot of independent action at local levels in the party and in the soviets
and that the situation greatly facilitated the take-over: the increased radicalism
of the workers, soldiers, sailors and peasants cannot be ignored. The extent of
their involvement is crucial in assessing whether the events of October 1917
constitute a popular revolution or not.

■ **Learning trouble spot**

Pigeon-holing historians
Students sometimes want to put
historians into particular camps
and then assume that within
those camps everyone is saying
roughly the same thing. Although
it is helpful to identify some broad
trends of thought in discussing
the historiography of this or other
topics on Russia, you must be
careful about lumping historians
together. Historians may take
broadly similar positions but take
different lines about particular
events or developments, that is,
their interpretations are varied. For
example, there are many differences
in interpretation amongst the
historians we have grouped together
as 'the revisionists'.

TALKING POINT

What do you think are the main issues about the nature of the evidence on which the
interpretations are based? Could interpretations change in the future?

106

WAS THE BOLSHEVIK SEIZURE OF POWER IN OCTOBER 1917 INEVITABLE?

SOURCE 5.5   B. N. Pomomarev, *History of the Communist Party of the Soviet Union*, 1960

The working class led the struggle of the whole people against the autocracy and against the dictatorship of the bourgeoisie. The other sections of the working class had convinced themselves that in the proletariat they had the champion of the interests of the whole people ... The proletariat were the prime motive force of the entire social and political development of the country ... The October Revolution differed from that of all other revolutions in that the workers created their own organs of power – the Soviets of Workers' Deputies. The Soviets of Workers', Soldiers' and Peasants' Deputies were organs of alliance of the workers and peasants under the leadership of the workers.

SOURCE 5.6   R. Pipes, 'The Great October Revolution as a Clandestine *Coup d'Etat*', *Times Literary Supplement*, November 1992

October was not a revolution but a classic coup d'état *planned in the dead of night on October 10th, and executed two weeks later ... The last thing the conspirators wanted was to attract attention. The 'masses', so much in evidence in the bourgeois revolution of February, were not told that they were taking over until after the event.*

The seizure of power, masterminded by Trotsky, was a model putsch *... Conceived and carried out in strictest secrecy, it eschewed barricades and mob actions in favour of surgical strikes against the organ of the state. It was so successfully camouflaged as a transfer of power to the All-Russian Congress of Soviets that virtually no one, including the rank and file of the Bolshevik Party, had any inkling of what had happened.*

These facts require emphasis because of the entrenched myth that the Bolsheviks rose to power in the wake of an explosion of popular fury. No such explosion is apparent in contemporary sources. Eyewitnesses, including the best chronicler of 1917, the Menshevik Nicholas Sukhanov, are virtually unanimous in depicting October as a coup d'état; *so too are such historians as S. P. Melgunov who had lived through it.*

SOURCE 5.7   O. Figes, *A People's Tragedy: The Russian Revolution 1891–1924*, 1997, pp. 460–61

One of the most basic misconceptions of the Russian Revolution is that the Bolsheviks were swept to power on a tide of mass support for the party itself. The October insurrection was a coup d'état, *actively supported by a small minority of the population (and indeed opposed by several of the Bolshevik leaders themselves). But it took place amidst a social revolution, which was centred on the popular realization of Soviet power ... as the direct self-rule of the people ... The political vacuum brought about by this social revolution enabled the Bolsheviks to seize power in the cities ... The slogan 'All Power to the Soviets!' was a useful tool, a banner of popular legitimation covering the nakedness of Lenin's ambition ... Later, as the nature of the Bolshevik dictatorship became apparent, the party faced the growing opposition of precisely those groups in society who had rallied behind the soviet slogan.*

LIBERTARIAN
An interpretation that focuses on the free will of the people.

SOURCE 5.8   A. Berkman's LIBERTARIAN view summarised in E. Acton, *Rethinking the Russian Revolution*, 1990, p. 177

The Revolution was truly popular and profoundly democratic. Lenin and his comrades were the illegitimate beneficiaries of the autonomous action of the masses. The revolution of 1917 was the product of popular revolt against oppression. It was accomplished 'not by a political party, but by the people themselves'. Time and again the self-proclaimed leaders of the revolution were taken by surprise by the initiative welling up from below – in January 1905, in February, April and July 1917. The masses were not enticed into revolt by superior leaders. Their extreme radicalism was not the product of manipulation or brainwashing by the Bolsheviks, as the liberal view would have it, nor was it the fruit of enlightenment brought to them by the Bolsheviks as the Soviet view contends. The goals for which they strove were their own.

107

WAS THE BOLSHEVIK SEIZURE OF POWER IN OCTOBER 1917 INEVITABLE?

SOURCE 5.9 B. Williams, *The Russian Revolution 1917–1921*, 1987, pp. 46–47

In striking contrast to February and to later film portrayals, this was not a mass uprising. Relatively few people were actively involved. If it were a coup – and Lenin denied this, calling it an armed uprising of the urban masses – it was one enthusiastically supported by the proletariat and accepted by the peasantry.

SOURCE 5.10 E. Acton, *Rethinking the Russian Revolution*, 1990, pp. 203–24

In the light of revisionist research the October revolution emerges as very much more than a conspiratorial coup d'état. *By then the central political issue was that of soviet power. It was popular support for this cause which doomed Kerensky and the Provisional Government and explains the ease with which armed resistance to the new order was overcome . . .*

The Bolshevik victory in the struggle for power owed less to effective organization and military manoeuvre than Soviet, liberal or libertarian accounts would have it. The party owed its strength to its identification with the cause of Soviet power. By October that cause enjoyed overwhelming support in the cities and the army, and tacit support in the villages. By virtue of its relatively flexible, open and democratic character, its sensitivity to mass opinion, its ability to respond to pressure from below, the party had established itself as the prime vehicle for the achievement of popular goals.

FOCUS ROUTE

Using the information on pages 107–109, collect notes for a short piece of writing (three or four paragraphs) in answer to the question: Do you think the Bolshevik revolution was a popular revolution or a *coup d'état*? In your answer, refer to the views of different historians in Sources 5.5–5.10 on pages 106–107.

What evidence is there for Bolshevik popularity?

You have looked at the ideas of historians, but what about the evidence? The problem is, of course, that it is very difficult to gauge the extent of Bolshevik popularity. This accounts for some of the differences in interpretation. We do not know how many people would have turned out on to the streets for them. But it is clear the party was attracting a great deal of support. The figures in Sources 5.11–5.13 give us some indications.

The November elections (Source 5.13 on page 108) could be interpreted as a disaster for the Bolsheviks because they got less than a quarter of the seats in the Constituent Assembly. However, the Bolsheviks did very well in the cities (as much as 70 per cent of those voting in some working-class districts of Petrograd voted for them). So urban working-class support does seem quite high – look at the figures for the municipal elections in Source 5.12. Also, a lot of the peasants would have been voting for the left wing of the Socialist Revolutionaries who were collaborating closely with the Bolsheviks at this time.

There is a tendency to focus on the political events leading up to the insurrection, but you also need to be aware of the attitudes of the workers and peasants in September and October. The workers had become highly politicised and radicalised in these months when food was very short, wages could not keep pace with rampant inflation and unemployment was rising. Strikes were frequent and militant. Where employers staged lock-outs, workers' committees seized control of the premises. This was usually a desperate attempt to save jobs more than anything else. Employers were assaulted and crowds broke into the houses of the middle classes, accusing them of hoarding food. Hunger was a crucial factor in October. Workers had given up hope of receiving help from the Provisional Government and were tired of the Mensheviks who tried to mediate between them and employers. Only the Bolsheviks offered the chance of real change.

Similarly, in the countryside from September onwards there was an upturn in violence. Estates were raided, land seized, landowners murdered and their houses burned. The peasants would not wait for the Provisional Government any longer. They might not support the Bolsheviks, but they willingly accepted the Bolshevik promise that land would be handed to them, and there was a lot of support for the left wing of the Socialist Revolutionaries who were collaborating with the Bolsheviks.

SOURCE 5.11 Membership of the Bolshevik Party 1917

The bulk of the support came from the industrial proletariat but during the summer cells sprang up in the army and navy. It seems that a high proportion, as much as twenty per cent, of those who joined in 1917 were aged under 21. Accurate figures are unavailable but estimates suggest that membership leaped during the summer:

February   10,000
October   250,000

SOURCE 5.12 Moscow municipal elections 1917 (figures rounded to nearest thousand)

	July	October
Socialist Revolutionaries	375,000 (58%)	54,000 (14%)
Mensheviks	76,000 (12%)	16,000 (4%)
Bolsheviks	75,000 (11%)	198,000 (51%)
Kadets	109,000 (17%)	101,000 (26%)

108

WAS THE BOLSHEVIK SEIZURE OF POWER IN OCTOBER 1917 INEVITABLE?

SOURCE 5.13   Constituent Assembly elections, November 1917. The elections for the Constituent Assembly went ahead in November because the Bolsheviks were not in a position to stop them (see page 120). They seem to have been fairly freely conducted

	Votes cast (in millions)	Number of seats won	Percentage share of the vote
Socialist Revolutionaries	21.8	410*	53
Bolsheviks	10.0	175	24
Kadets	2.1	17	5
Mensheviks	1.4	18	3
Others	6.3	62	15

*includes 40 Left SRs

SOURCE 5.14   Daily bread rations (grams) per person in Petrograd in 1917

	March	April	September	October
Manual workers	675	335	225	110
Others	450	335	225	110

■ **Learning trouble spot**

Soviet power

Many workers and soldiers wanted the soviets to run government locally and nationally. These soviets represented ordinary people, and in October 1917 were not necessarily controlled by the Bolsheviks. Many were run by Mensheviks, Socialist Revolutionaries and other socialists. The Petrograd Soviet had become the most important national soviet and many people were in favour of it taking power from the Provisional Government.

Support for the Bolsheviks or for Soviet power?

One of the problems in deciding whether the Bolshevik take-over was popular or not is working out whom exactly the people (i.e. the 'popular' element in this) were supporting. The historian Beryl Williams makes the point that: 'Workers and soldiers might support October and vote for the Bolsheviks in elections, but this did not necessarily imply support for one-party rule, or indeed for Bolshevik policies once they had become known' (*The Russian Revolution 1917–1921*, 1987, pages 49–50). Sukhanov, in Source 5.15, also expresses this ambiguity of feeling from his contact with the 'masses' at the time.

Workers and soldiers supported the Bolsheviks because they were making the move to soviet power. But they wanted a coalition government of the socialist parties and they did not expect the Bolsheviks to run the state on their own. Some commentators believe that power would have passed to the Soviet anyway without the uprising and that Lenin had hijacked the process to grab power for himself. You can see why this is a complicated issue and why historians can disagree about the 'popular' nature of the revolution.

SOURCE 5.15   J. Carmichael, *A Short History of the Revolution*, 1967, p. 193, quoting N. N. Sukhanov

It may be asked whether the Petersburg proletariat and garrison was ready for dynamic action and bloody sacrifice? ... Was it burning, not only with hate, but with real longing for revolutionary exploits?

There are various answers to this. It is quite fundamental, not because the outcome of the movement depended on it – the success of the overturn was assured because there was nothing to oppose it. But the mood of the masses who were to act is important because in the eyes of history this is what determined the character of the overturn.

Personally, as a witness and participant in the events, I have no single answer. There were various moods. The only common ones were hatred for 'Kerenskyism', fatigue, rage and a desire for peace, bread and land ... During these weeks I made the rounds and spoke to the 'masses'. I had the definite impression that the mood was ambiguous, conditional. The Coalition and the status quo could no longer be endured; but whether it was necessary to come out, or necessary to pass through an uprising, was not clearly known ... On the average, the mood was strongly Bolshevik, but rather slack and wavering with respect to action and rising.

109

WAS THE BOLSHEVIK SEIZURE OF POWER IN OCTOBER 1917 INEVITABLE?

SOURCE 5.16 O. Figes, *A People's Tragedy: The Russian Revolution 1891–1924*, 1997, p. 484

The great October Socialist Revolution, as it came to be called in Soviet mythology, was in reality such a small-scale event, being in effect a military coup, that it passed unnoticed by the vast majority of inhabitants of Petrograd. . . . The whole insurrection could have been completed in six hours, had it not been for the ludicrous incompetence of the insurgents themselves, which made it take an extra fifteen. The legendary storming of the Winter Palace, where Kerensky's cabinet held its final session, was more like a routine house arrest, since most of the forces defending the palace had already left for home, hungry and dejected before the final assault began. The only real damage done to the imperial residence in the whole affair was a chipped cornice and a shattered window on the third floor.

Trotsky himself claimed that 25,000 to 30,000 people 'at the most' were actively involved – about 5 per cent of all the workers and soldiers in the city . . . The few surviving pictures of the October Days . . . depict a handful of Red Guards and sailors standing around in the half-deserted streets. None of the familiar images of a people's revolution – crowds on the streets, barricades and fighting – were in evidence.

ACTIVITY

1 What impression of the October insurrection is suggested in the image in Source 5.17?
2 How does this compare with the account in the text and in Source 5.16?
3 Why would the Bolsheviks want Russians in later years to believe their version of events?

Why did the Bolsheviks present the October Revolution as a mass uprising?

The events of 24–26 October constitute the October Revolution. You have read (on pages 102–103) how on the night of 24–25 October the soldiers and Red Guard had taken key points in Petrograd with no opposition. The next day life went on as normal. On the evening of 25 October, the cruiser *Aurora* fired a blank shot at 9.40pm. This was the signal for the beginning of the attack on the Winter Palace, where the Provisional Government was in emergency session. According to the Bolsheviks, Red Guards, supported by the masses, heroically stormed the Palace, broke in and arrested the ministers. It was shown graphically in Eisenstein's film *October* (Source 5.17) and in pictures painted mainly in the 1930s.

In fact, the story was quite different. Bolshevik Red Guards, soldiers and sailors arrived in the square in front of the Winter Palace around noon on 25 October. The palace was defended by cadets from a military school, 200 members of the Women's Death Battalion and two divisions of Cossacks grumbling about having to fight alongside 'women with guns'. Due to Bolshevik inefficiency, no attack took place in the afternoon. The soldiers inside, faced with the prospect of an overwhelming onslaught, began to get panicky and drunk. By the time early evening had arrived, most of the demoralised defenders had left, slipping out of the palace. Meanwhile the members of the Provisional Government in the Palace held emergency meetings and sent out messages for help. When the cruiser *Aurora* fired its shell to signal the beginning of the attack and a few guns were fired, the Women's Battalion became hysterical whereupon it was agreed by everybody that they should be allowed to leave unharmed. The guns of the Peter and Paul Fortress opened up but most of the shots fell short into the River Neva, although one scored a hit. In the next few hours, Bolshevik soldiers filtered into the palace by various entrances and wandered the corridors disarming the few remaining cadets, who put up little resistance. Eventually, a group forced their way into the room where the last members of the Provisional Government were assembled and arrested them. Such was the heroic storming of the Winter Palace.

SOURCE 5.17 The storming of the Winter Palace – a still from Eisenstein's film *October*, made in 1927

110

WAS THE BOLSHEVIK SEIZURE OF POWER IN OCTOBER 1917 INEVITABLE?

E **Review: Was the Bolshevik seizure of power inevitable?**

■ 5D The ups and downs in support for the Bolshevik Party during 1917

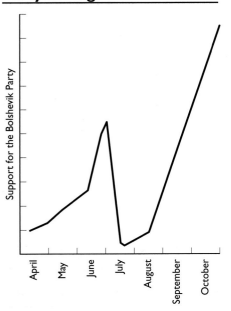

Support for the Bolshevik Party

April May June July August September October

ACTIVITY

If you have completed a graph of Bolshevik fortunes (see the Focus Route on page 95), it might look something like the one shown in Chart 5D.

1 Which of these statements do you think is true? Explain your choice by referring to evidence in this chapter.

a) The Bolshevik seizure of power was inevitable once they became the only party to provide opposition to the policies of the Provisional Government and the moderate socialists. This was the case from June onwards. They were the only group to express the genuine aspirations of the workers and soldiers.

b) There were no points at which the Bolshevik seizure of power was inevitable. Right up to the last moment things could have gone wrong. The Bolsheviks were extremely lucky that Kerensky's blunders played into their hands.

c) Support for the Bolsheviks was growing consistently from May onwards despite the hiccup of the July Days. It looked increasingly likely that they would seize power since they were in tune with the demands of the masses. But there were points at which things could have changed and their bid for power could have been stopped. In the end it was successful because of Lenin's persistence, Trotsky's organisation and Kerensky's mistakes.

KEY POINTS FROM CHAPTER 5

Was the Bolshevik seizure of power in October 1917 inevitable?

1 The Bolshevik Party and its programme became the focus for all opposition to the Provisional Government and support for them grew rapidly during the summer.

2 The frustration of soldiers and workers exploded in the July Days, partly engineered by middle-ranking Bolsheviks. But the Bolshevik leadership was not ready to take power and the uprising fizzled out.

3 The Bolsheviks were not the tightly disciplined, unified body that some have supposed, although its organisation was better than that of other parties.

4 Kerensky tried to use Kornilov to gain control of Petrograd but Kornilov had his own agenda.

5 The Kornilov affair was disastrous for right-wing forces and the Provisional Government but gave the Bolsheviks a boost.

6 Lenin urged his party leadership to stage an immediate uprising but, initially, they were reluctant.

7 Trotsky persuaded Lenin to put off the uprising until the All-Russian Congress of Soviets so that the Bolsheviks could claim to have taken power in the name of the soviets.

8 Kerensky's inept attempts to ward off the Bolshevik coup played into their hands.

9 During 24–26 October, the Bolshevik take-over was carried out successfully.

10 Large numbers of ordinary people supported the idea of the soviets taking power, but not the idea of the Bolsheviks taking power in a one-party state.

Section 2 Review: Why were the Bolsheviks successful in October 1917?

The main focus of Section 2 is the key question: Why were the Bolsheviks successful in October 1917? The two diagrams on pages 111 and 112 summarise the main points relating to this question that have been covered in the last two chapters and add one or two new ideas. You can use these diagrams to help you to write an essay, as suggested on page 112, or for revision in an exam.

■ A The weaknesses and failures of the Provisional Government

The nature of the Provisional Government

- Its scope for action was limited because real power was held by the Soviet.

- It saw itself as a temporary body that could not make binding decisions for the long-term future of Russia; such decisions were to be made by the Constituent Assembly.

- Divisions between socialists and liberals led to a lack of clear policies, as the two groups often blocked each other.

Policies

- The decision to continue the war created a huge amount of opposition, and other problems stemmed from it. If the Provisional Government had made a separate peace with Germany, it might have survived.

- The failure to legitimise the peasant take-over of land created a rift with the peasants, who were then less willing to supply food to the cities.

- It lost the support of the national minorities by refusing to give them a degree of autonomy.

- It did nothing about the deterioration of the economy; together with the lack of social reform this contributed to the radicalisation of the workers.

Mistakes by Kerensky

- He decided to launch a new offensive against Germany in June.

- The Kornilov affair left him discredited. Officers would not fight for him or the Provisional Government because they felt he had betrayed Kornilov and might betray them.

- He underestimated the strength of the Bolsheviks. By moving against them in October, he gave them an excuse for seizing power, thereby increasing their popularity and allowing them to claim that they were seizing power in the name of the Soviet.

Other factors

- Moderate socialists lost contact with their supporters – the workers and peasants.

- The government failed to call the Constituent Assembly early enough.

- Alarmed by violence and the power of the working class, the Kadets moved further to the right and became identified with reactionary military officers, industrialists and landowners.

Summary: By October 1917, the Provisional Government was thoroughly discredited and attracted hatred and contempt.

■ B Bolshevik strengths and factors in their favour

Policies

- Bolsheviks opposed the Provisional Government and urged its overthrow. The identification of other socialist parties with the discredited government was fatal for them. It meant that opposition to the Provisional Government became focused around the Bolsheviks.

- The Bolsheviks were the only party that opposed continuing the war – this greatly increased their popularity.

- They secured the tacit, if not active, support of the peasants with the promise of land redistribution.

- Their radical policies were in tune with workers' and soldiers' aspirations; their slogans of 'Peace, Bread and All Power to the Soviets' fitted in perfectly with what the workers and soldiers wanted (even if the Bolsheviks had a different idea about what these policies actually meant).

The party

- The role of Lenin was crucial – his strong, determined leadership and prestige in the party meant he could force through key policy decisions (such as the April Theses) and the October Revolution. There would probably have been no October Revolution without Lenin.

- Although it was probably not the well-disciplined body it was once thought to be, its organisation was better than that of other parties and it broadly followed directives from the party leadership.

- Trotsky's role in persuading Lenin to postpone the date of the uprising and organising the take-over was very important. It was a good tactic to use the All-Russian Congress of Soviets as the vehicle for the seizure of power.

Luck

- The military and economic collapse in September/October offered a unique opportunity that the Bolsheviks seized. The army was not in a position to do much, and hunger was an important factor in October.

- Radicalised workers who favoured soviet power were prepared to support the party that seemed to offer this.

- The Provisional Government, particularly Kerensky, played into the Bolsheviks' hands with its half-hearted attempt to counter the rising.

Other factors

- The Bolsheviks had their greatest number of active supporters, particularly soldiers and sailors, around Petrograd and Moscow, key places in the revolution.

- Whilst only a small minority of the Petrograd garrison actively supported the Bolsheviks, the majority of soldiers remained neutral and refused to oppose them; this guaranteed their success in October.

Summary: By October, the Bolsheviks had become the focus of opposition to the Provisional Government. The people wanted soviet power and the Bolsheviks became identified with this aim. Some historians have suggested that it was not so much what they did as the situation in which they found themselves – the revolution literally fell into their hands because of profound disillusionment with the existing government, the dire economic situation and the radicalised nature of the workers. Nevertheless, it is clear that Lenin played a key role in forcing through the October insurrection.

ACTIVITY

You could use Charts A and B (pages 111 and 112) to help you write an essay:
1 Why were the Bolsheviks successful in October 1917? or
2 It was the weakness of the Provisional Government that brought about the October Revolution rather than the strengths of the Bolsheviks.
Use the points in the charts as a guide. Decide what your main points are and which point could be used to support these main points. Go back to the notes you have made on your Focus Route activities (or the main text) for help in developing your arguments.

The consolidation of the Bolshevik state 1917–1924

The Bolshevik seizure of power in October was the beginning rather than the end of the revolution. The Bolshevik government had a tenuous grip on power and some observers thought that it would survive only for a few weeks. In this section we look at how the Bolsheviks survived the first months and won the civil war that followed. We examine the impact of this struggle on the emerging state and the problems Soviet Russia faced after seven years of conflict. The final chapter deals with the recovery of the Soviet Union between 1921 and 1924 and considers how centralised and authoritarian the Communist state had become by the time of Lenin's death in 1924.

ACTIVITY

What do Sources 1–7 tell you about:

a) the immediate problems facing the new government
b) the problems the Bolsheviks were likely to have in the longer term?

SOURCE 1   O. Figes, *A People's Tragedy: The Russian Revolution 1891–1924*, 1997, p. 500

Five days after the Bolshevik seizure of power, Alexandra Kollantai, the new People's Commissar of Social Welfare, drove up to the entrance of a large government building on Kazan Street ... she was coming to take possession of it. An old liveried doorman opened the door and examined Kollantai head to foot [but would not let her in] ... Kollontai tried to force her way through, but the doorman blocked her way and closed the doors in her face ... The employees of the Ministry had joined a general Civil Servants' strike in protest at the Bolshevik seizure of power ...

The early weeks of the new regime were frustrated by similar strikes and campaigns in all the major ministries and government departments, the banks, the post and telegraph office, the railway administration, municipal bodies ... and other vital institutions ... Trotsky was greeted with ironic laughter when he arrived at the Ministry of Foreign Affairs and introduced himself to a meeting of officials as their new Minister; when he ordered them back to work, they left the building in protest ... The refusal of the State Bank and the Treasury to honour the new government's cash demands was the most serious threat of all. Without money to pay its supporters, the Bolshevik regime could not hope to survive for long.

SOURCE 2   R. Pipes, *Russia under the Bolshevik Regime 1912–24*, 1994, p. 5

The Bolsheviks were masters only of central Russia, and even there they ruled only the cities and industrial centres. The borderlands of what had been the Russian Empire, inhabited by peoples of other nationalities and religions, had separated themselves and proclaimed independence … The Bolsheviks, therefore, had literally to conquer by force of arms the separated borderlands as well as the villages in which lived four-fifths of Russia's population. Their own power base was not very secure, resting on at most 200,000 party members and an army then in the process of dissolution.

SOURCE 3   Striking workers in the Sormovo factory, June 1918

The Soviet regime, having been established in our name, has become completely alien to us. It promised to bring the workers socialism but has brought them empty factories and destitution.

SOURCE 4   C. Read, *From Tsar to Soviets: The Russian People and their Revolution 1917–21*, 1996, p. 178

There was significant opposition to the uprising from within the Soviet itself. No major Soviet leader or group rallied to the Bolsheviks … The Menshevik leaders organized forces loyal to themselves to put pressure on the Bolshevik leaders to relinquish their power and to share it more broadly. In particular, through the railwaymen's union, they threatened a paralysing strike.

SOURCE 5   Bolshevik moderates

It is vital to form a socialist government from all parties … We consider that a purely Bolshevik government has no choice but to maintain itself by political terror … We cannot follow this course.

SOURCE 6   A speech by Lenin, 14 September 1917

Power to the Soviets means the complete transfer of the country's administration and economic control into the hands of workers and peasants, to whom nobody would offer resistance and who, through practice, through their own experience would soon learn how to distribute land, products and grain properly.

SOURCE 7   O. Figes, *A People's Tragedy: The Russian Revolution 1891–1924*, 1997, p. 494, describing what happened when the crowds found thousands of bottles of alcohol in the Tsar's wine cellars in the Winter Palace

The drunken mobs went on the rampage … Sailors and soldiers went round the well-to-do districts robbing apartments and killing people for sport … The Bolsheviks tried to stem the anarchy by sealing off the liquor supply … They posted guards around the cellar – who licensed themselves to sell off the bottles of liquor. They pumped the wine on the street but crowds gathered to drink it from the gutter … Machine guns were set up to deter the looters – but still they came. For several weeks the anarchy continued – martial law was even imposed – until, at last, the alcohol ran out with the old year, and the capital woke up with the biggest headache in history.

How did the Bolsheviks survive the first few months in power?

CHAPTER OVERVIEW

Lenin found that running a government after the October Revolution was beset with problems. There was a great deal of opposition to one-party rule and the emerging Bolshevik dictatorship. The working classes in the cities supported soviet power but not necessarily Bolshevik power. Most people, including some leading Bolsheviks, expected a socialist coalition to emerge from the ruins of the discredited Provisional Government. But Lenin had always intended to rule alone and the Bolsheviks were prepared to be ruthless in establishing their power base. The newly elected Constituent Assembly posed a serious threat to the government, as did the knotty problem of reaching an acceptable peace settlement with Germany.

A How did Lenin get his new government on its feet? (pp. 117–118)

B How did the Bolsheviks deal with the threat from people who opposed them? (p. 119)

C How did Lenin deal with the threat posed to his government by other socialists? (p. 120)

D How did Lenin deal with the problems posed by ending the war? (pp. 121–122)

E Review: How did the Bolsheviks stay in power in the first few months? (pp. 123–124)

ACTIVITY

What do you think Lenin would do to try to consolidate his position and stay in power in the months immediately following the October Revolution? His opponents thought that he would stay in power for only a few weeks at most.

Decide which of the alternatives in the table below you would expect him to follow. Be prepared to explain your choice.

Issue	Radical option	Cautious option
a) Main instrument of government	Form his own new government	Govern through the Soviet in the name of which he had taken power
b) Elections to Constituent Assembly	Call them off as his party might not be in the majority	Allow them to go ahead
c) Press	Ban newspapers of opposition parties	Allow them to be published
d) Role of other socialist parties in government	Rule alone	Bring other socialist parties into the government
e) Peace with Germany	Agree a separate peace straightaway, whatever the Germans demand	Hold out for a peace deal which would not require giving up too much territory
f) Land	Give land to peasants immediately to parcel out amongst themselves to secure their support	Set up state agencies to allocate land fairly and keep some large estates for government control
g) Political parties	Ban other parties: go for one-party state	Ban Kadets and right-wing parties but allow other socialist parties
h) Trade unions	Ban trade unions	Allow them to continue but with reduced power
i) Army	Democratise army: no ranks, saluting, etc. Power to committees	Keep army structure intact against attacks from outside or inside Russia
j) Women	Introduce full equality immediately	Introduce equal opportunities measures slowly
k) Banks	NATIONALISE banks	Introduce measures to control the banking system but leave banks in private hands
l) Industry	Allow workers' committees to run factories	Give power to workers, eight-hour day, etc., but leave control of factories in private hands
m) National minorities	Grant right of SELF-DETERMINATION to non-Russian groups (Georgians, Ukrainians) in old Russian Empire	Retain the boundaries of the old Russian empire but give more rights to non-Russian minorities

NATIONALISE
To take industries and banks out of private ownership and put them under the control of the state.

SELF-DETERMINATION
Principle of nation states ruling themselves.

FOCUS ROUTE

How well did Lenin deal with the problems and threats facing his new government in the early months? As you read through this chapter, fill in a table like the one below or use the headings to make your own notes and evaluation.

Problems	What was the problem?	How did Lenin deal with it?	How effectively did he deal with it? (Give a mark out of ten.)
Getting new government on its feet			
Land ownership			
Running industry			
Opposition			
Other socialist parties			
Peace with Germany			

A # How did Lenin get his new government on its feet?

Lenin had proclaimed Soviet power but he did not exercise power through the Soviet. The Soviet could easily have become the main body of the government and many people expected it to be so. But Lenin formed an entirely new body – the Council of the People's Commissars, or the SOVNARKOM. It was exclusively made up of Bolsheviks (although some left-wing Socialist Revolutionaries were invited to join later). The reason for this was clear: Lenin had no intention of sharing power with the Mensheviks, Socialist Revolutionaries and other socialist groups in the Soviet.

> **SOVNARKOM**
> Council of the People's Commissars; the Bolshevik governing body (30–40 members) set up after the October Revolution in 1917. It operated until 1941 but became much less influential after the Politburo was formed in 1919 (7–9 members). The Commissars in Sovnarkom ran commissariats.

> **Yakov Sverdlov (1885–1919)**
> Another key Bolshevik at this time was Sverdlov, a great organising genius. Born into a working-class Jewish family, he became a Social Democrat in 1905. He was exiled to Siberia with Stalin but they did not get on. He played an important part in organising the October uprising with Trotsky. He was totally loyal to Lenin, who valued Sverdlov's reliability and dependability. After the revolution he was given the job of building up the party secretariat and establishing a network of party officials and local secretariats throughout Russia, all reporting to Moscow. He would almost certainly have been made General Secretary of the party in 1922 – the job which gave Stalin so much power – but he died of flu in 1919.

■ 6A Some key posts in the Sovnarkom

Chairman	Lenin
Commissar for Foreign Affairs	Trotsky until February 1918, then Chicherin
Commissar for War	Trotsky from February 1918
Commissar for Internal Affairs	Rykov, later Dzerzhinsky
Commissar for Nationalities	Stalin
Commissar for Social Welfare	Alexandra Kollantai
Commissar for Popular Enlightenment (Education and Culture)	Lunacharsky

The government's position was extremely precarious – one Socialist Revolutionary leader gave it 'no more than a few days', the Menshevik leader Tsereteli gave it three weeks. Its power was strictly limited: many soviets and bodies such as public safety committees were still in the control of Mensheviks, Socialist Revolutionaries or non-socialists, and in the countryside the Bolshevik presence was virtually non-existent. Even in the soviets controlled by the Bolsheviks, there was no guarantee that the central government could get its decisions carried out; some were a law unto themselves. All over the capital, civil servants mounted protest strikes and, even worse, the State Bank refused to hand over any money. It took ten days and armed force to make the bank staff open the vaults so that the government could get its hands on much needed roubles (Russian currency).

So how did Lenin and his government manage to survive the first few months? Lenin could not afford to ignore the tide of popular aspiration that had swept away Kerensky and the Provisional Government, so he gave the workers and peasants what they wanted. Edward Acton says: 'No Russian government had ever been more responsive to pressure from below or less able to impose its will upon society.' Power was thrown out to local soviets to manage their own affairs, even though at this stage they were not, in the main, under central control.

The Sovnarkom ruled by decree without going to the Soviet for approval. The early decrees are summarised in Chart 6B (page 118). In key areas, the Bolsheviks compromised their principles to keep popular support:

SOURCE 6.1 Lenin to a delegation of workers and peasants

You are the power – do all you want to do, take all you want. We shall support you.

- **Land decree** This gave peasants the right to take over the estates of the gentry, without compensation, and to decide for themselves the best way to divide it up (since they were doing this anyway). Land could no longer be bought, sold or rented; it belonged to the 'entire people'. It was not what the Bolsheviks wanted. Privately owned land was not part of their socialist vision.
- **Workers' control decree** Factory committees were given the right to control production and finance in workplaces and to 'supervise' management. This decree did not give direct management to the workers but some committees took it to mean that. This went far beyond what many Bolshevik leaders wanted, but they could not resist the strength of workers' pressure for reform.
- **Rights of the People of Russia decree** This gave the right of self-determination to the national minorities in the former Russian Empire. Of course, the Bolsheviks did not have control of the areas in which most of these people lived, so this was nothing more than a paper measure.

■ 6B Early decrees issued by the Sovnarkom

October 1917
- Maximum eight-hour day for workers
- Social insurance (old age, unemployment, sickness benefits, etc.) to be introduced
- Opposition press banned
- Decree on Peace
- Decree on Land

November 1917
- Right of self-determination granted to all parts of the former Russian empire
- Abolition of titles and class distinctions
- Workers to control factories
- Abolition of justice system
- Women declared equal to men and able to own property

December 1917
- CHEKA set up (see page 119)
- Banks nationalised
- Democratisation of army – officers to be elected, army to be controlled by army soviets and soldiers' committees, abolition of ranks, saluting and decorations
- Marriage and divorce became civil matters, no longer linked to the Church
- Church land nationalised

January 1918
- Workers' control of railways
- Creation of Red Army
- Church and state separated

February 1918
- Nationalisation of industry
- Socialisation of land

CHEKA

The All-Russian Extraordinary Commission for Struggle against Counter-Revolution and Sabotage; the Soviet secret police from 1917–22.

■ Learning trouble spot

What happened to the Soviet?

The passing of decrees by the Sovnarkom without seeking the approval of the Soviet was a clear breach of soviet power. But Lenin had no intention of discussing his policy initiatives with non-Bolshevik socialists. Important measures, such as the initiation of peace talks, were passed without consulting the Soviet at all. The Soviet Executive began to meet less frequently, whereas the Sovnarkom met once or twice a day. As the main source of power the Soviet was a dead duck, although it continued to meet well into the 1930s. The local soviets did form the basis of the governmental structure in the Soviet Union but were increasingly dominated by the Communist Party (see pages 160–166).

TALKING POINT

Look back at your choices on issues a), c), f), j), k), l) and m) in the Activity on page 116. Compare them with the measures the new government took, as shown in the text and in Chart 6B. Did you predict Lenin's choices correctly? What have you learned from discovering that Lenin made different choices? Did Lenin's choices surprise you?

WHAT DID LENIN THINK WOULD HAPPEN AFTER THE REVOLUTION?

In *State and Revolution*, finished just before October, Lenin suggested that the general will of the people would support the revolutionary government. Problems would be solved fairly easily because the people would recognise that the party was ruling in their interests. He thought that there would be a vast expansion of democracy and that the people would be able to run their own affairs (see Source 6 on page 114). Therefore there would be less need for bureaucracy. This view seems to be reflected in the decrees giving workers control of the factories and peasants control of the land.

Some historians, however, feel that Lenin let people take control of factories and the land initially because he had no means of preventing them from doing so, and always intended to exercise strong central control over these areas when he was able.

Lenin also stressed in *State and Revolution* the need for a strong and repressive party state to crush the remnants of bourgeois power. There would be a period, called 'the dictatorship of the proletariat', during which the bourgeois state would be crushed and bourgeois attitudes and values squeezed out of society.

B How did the Bolsheviks deal with the threat from people who opposed them?

It is important to understand how chaotic life in Russia was after the October Revolution. The urban revolution had degenerated into violence and lawlessness. A good example is described in Source 7 on page 114. A hooligan and criminal element joined in the social revolution and there was little the Bolsheviks could do about the situation. Maxim Gorky (the famous Russian novelist, socialist and friend of Lenin), in particular, spoke out against the urban violence which he associated with the Bolsheviks, condemning it as a 'pogrom of greed, hatred and violence' rather than social revolution. He pleaded with Bolshevik leaders to save buildings and works of art from being destroyed.

Outside the capital, in the provinces, the establishment of Bolshevik power was often accompanied by violence and the plundering of the houses and shops of the bourgeoisie. Lenin's class war gave Bolshevised soldiers and sailors free licence to loot the *burzhui* and sometimes carry out unspeakable acts of violence. In one town, Red Guards threw 50 military cadets one by one into the blast furnace of a metal factory.

■ **Learning trouble spot**

Who was a *burzhui* (bourgeois)?
This term did not apply only to the middle classes. It was a form of abuse used against employers, officers, landowners, priests, Jews, merchants or anybody seemingly well-to-do. It referred not so much to a class as to any internal enemy, whom workers and peasants blamed for their problems. It later became synonymous with people suspected of speculating or hoarding food.

While one element of the Bolsheviks' strategy to stay in power was to go along with the popular demands, the other was to build its forces of terror and wipe out opposition. One of the first measures of the new Bolshevik regime was to close down the opposition press: first the newspapers of the centre and the right, and later the socialist press. The Bolsheviks, who had pumped enormous amounts of money into their papers and periodicals during 1917, knew the problems that a hostile press could cause them.

Next, attention was turned on opposition political parties. The Kadet Party, which had done quite well in the Constituent Assembly elections, was denounced and outlawed. Leading Kadets were arrested and two were brutally beaten to death by Bolshevik sailors. They were soon followed into prison by leading right-wing Socialist Revolutionaries and Mensheviks – all this before the end of 1917. The engine of political terror was being cranked up.

On 7 December, Lenin set up the main instrument of terror – the Cheka, or Extraordinary Commission for Combating Counter-Revolution and Sabotage. This force of dedicated Bolshevik supporters provided dependable security, bringing units of the Red Guard and military units under its control. It soon proved itself an effective mechanism for dealing with any opposition (see pages 143–147).

Lenin actively encouraged class warfare as a means of intimidating the middle classes and terrorising them into submission. It started with attacks on the Kadets, as the leaders of the bourgeois counter-revolution, but the net soon widened. The legal system was abolished and replaced by revolutionary justice, which was arbitrary and violent in character. Anybody accused of being a *burzhui* (bourgeois) was liable to be arrested, and any well-dressed person found on the streets (including Bolshevik leaders until they could prove who they were) was at risk of being labelled a *burzhui*. Even if not arrested, *burzhui* could be beaten and robbed.

Lenin's use of class warfare played well in Russia. Workers, soldiers and peasants supported the end of privilege and the moves to a more egalitarian society. The abolition of titles and the use of 'comrade' as the new form of address gave power and dignity to the once downtrodden. Workers and soldiers became more cocky and assertive, rude to their 'social betters'. The socialist press encouraged the perception of the *burzhui* as the 'enemies of the people'. They were condemned as 'parasites' and 'bloodsuckers'. The state licensed and encouraged the people to plunder the houses of the middle classes, to 'loot the looters'. There were elements in Russian society that did not need much encouragement to do this.

Striking civil servants, who were causing the emerging Bolshevik government so many problems, were arrested and the civil service was thoroughly purged. Junior officials willing to support the Bolsheviks were promoted and Bolshevik officials were brought in. Often third-rate people or corrupt opportunists were put into positions of real power. The bureaucracy that developed was of poor quality but it was obedient.

There was some opposition to the Bolsheviks and there were demonstrations. But the opposition was weak and unco-ordinated. Mensheviks and right-wing Socialist Revolutionaries did not want to get involved in organised violence because they were still acutely aware of the dangers of civil war. Moreover, they still had hopes for the Constituent Assembly and an all-socialist government. They did not really expect the Bolsheviks to survive.

120

HOW DID THE BOLSHEVIKS SURVIVE THE FIRST FEW MONTHS IN POWER?

How did Lenin deal with the threat posed to his government by other socialists?

TALKING POINT

Was Lenin wrong not to enter a coalition? It meant that the new government lost a democratic base of support which might have ensured less dictatorial government and a shorter civil war. Socialist leaders outside Russia criticised Lenin. The leading German socialist Rosa Luxembourg warned that press censorship and the suppression of democratic elections would lead to dictatorship. What do you think about Lenin's actions?

There was enormous pressure on the Bolsheviks to form a democratic government representing all the socialist parties. Hundreds of resolutions and petitions flooded in from factory committees, army units, and Moscow and provincial towns, demanding that there be co-operation between the parties to avoid factional strife and civil war. A petition from the 35th army division made this clear: 'Among the soldiers there are no Bolsheviks, Mensheviks or Socialist Revolutionaries, only Democrats.' People did not want to lose the gains of the revolution because the socialist parties were fighting amongst each other. They were in favour of Soviet power, not one-party rule.

The railwaymen's union, backed by the post and telegraph union, threatened to cut off communications if the Bolsheviks did not hold talks with other parties. They could paralyse food supplies to Petrograd as well as contact with other cities. This pressure forced Lenin, unwillingly, to send representatives to talks with other parties about a power-sharing government. It also persuaded Lenin, again unwillingly, to allow the planned elections to the Constituent Assembly to go ahead at the end of November. The Bolsheviks knew that there would be an unstoppable backlash if they did not go ahead with the elections, particularly as before October they had attacked Kerensky for postponing them.

Quite a few leading Bolsheviks, including Kamenev and Zinoviev, were in favour of a socialist coalition government. They believed that an isolated Bolshevik Party would have to maintain itself by terror and would almost certainly be destroyed by the civil war that would inevitably follow. So they were happy to be involved in talks with other parties. It seems likely that they were duped by Lenin into thinking he was serious about a coalition, and they temporarily resigned when they found out he was not.

Lenin had always intended the Bolsheviks to rule alone and he engineered the collapse of the talks. He did, however, make an alliance with the Left Socialist Revolutionaries and brought them as junior partners into the Sovnarkom. He saw this as useful because, with them in his government, he could claim to represent a large section of the peasantry. The Left Socialist Revolutionaries had, for some time, been closest to the Bolsheviks, particularly on the land issue; indeed they claimed, with justification, that Lenin had stolen this policy from them.

The Constituent Assembly

The Constituent Assembly posed a bigger threat to Lenin. Elected by the people in the first free elections in centuries, it could claim to be the legitimate body to decide the make-up of the future government of Russia. When the election results became known (see Source 5.13 on page 108), the Bolsheviks found they had won only 175 seats against 410 for the Socialist Revolutionaries (including 40 Left SRs) and nearly 100 for other parties. However, Lenin asserted that his Soviet government represented a higher stage of democracy than an elected assembly containing different political parties. He said that the Constituent Assembly smacked of bourgeois parliamentary democracy and declared it redundant. The Assembly was allowed to meet for one day – 5 January 1918 – then the doors were closed and the deputies told to go home. A crowd which demonstrated in favour of the Assembly was fired on by soldiers loyal to the Sovnarkom, the first time that soldiers had fired in this way on unarmed demonstrators since February 1917.

■ 6C Timeline of Brest-Litovsk peace negotiations

1917
October
26 Decree on Peace
November
13 Trotsky applies to the German High Command for an armistice
19 Armistice negotiations begin at Brest-Litovsk, deep behind German lines in occupied Poland
December
2 One month armistice signed at Brest-Litovsk
9 Negotiations for a peace settlement begin

1918
January
8 On Trotsky's return to Petrograd, 63 leading Bolsheviks meet: • 32 favour a revolutionary war   • 16 favour Trotsky's position of no war but no peace on German terms   • 15 favour Lenin's policy of peace at any price
11 Bolshevik Central Committee vote 9–7 to accept Trotsky's policy 'neither war nor peace'
17 Negotiations resume at Brest-Litovsk
28 Trotsky tells the Germans that Russia is leaving the war but refuses to sign an annexationist peace. Soviet delegates leave
February
1/14 Adoption of Gregorian calendar
18 German troops resume their advance. Central committee vote 7 – 5 to sign the original German terms and request fresh negotiations. (Trotsky abstains)
23 In five days the Germans advanced 150 miles – further than in the previous three years of fighting. Harsher peace terms accepted only after further debate and Lenin's threat of resignation. Trotsky resigns as Foreign Commissar
March
3 Treaty of Brest-Litovsk signed

(When writing about pre-revolutionary Russia, historians cite dates according to the calendar of the time. Russia adopted the Western (Gregorian) calendar in February 1918. Before that they used the Julian calendar.)

D How did Lenin deal with the problems posed by ending the war?

The promise that had brought so many people to the Bolshevik banner was the pledge to end the war. The Decree on Peace, the first signed by the Bolsheviks on 26 October, was a plea to other nations for an immediate truce and a just peace with 'no annexations, no indemnities'. Lenin was convinced that revolutions in Europe would ensure that equitable peace settlements would be reached.

But the practical resolution proved more difficult. The Russian army at the Front disintegrated rapidly; the soldiers had no desire to die in futile last-minute fighting and wanted to get back home. This represented both good and bad news for the Bolsheviks. The good news was that Russian generals could not use the army against them. The bad news was that the German army was free to walk into Russia and take what it wanted.

The Western allies ignored the Decree on Peace and Lenin now faced the fiercest struggle of his career. Most Bolsheviks and Left SRs, relentlessly hostile towards the imperialist powers, felt that to make a separate peace with 'the German bandits' would be to stain the banner of Bolshevism and undermine revolution abroad. Lenin was in a minority and it took all his powers of persuasion and the renewed advance of the increasingly impatient German army to achieve reluctant agreement (see the timeline left).

The Bolsheviks were split three ways

- Lenin believed that he had to have peace at any price to ensure the survival of the regime. There was no army to fight the Germans and when they began to advance into the Ukraine, Lenin feared that they might move on to Petrograd and throw the Bolsheviks out. 'Germany is only pregnant with revolution and we have already given birth to a healthy child. In Russia', he continued, 'we must make sure of throttling the bourgeoisie, and for this we need both hands free.' In January Lenin had few supporters, but one of them was Stalin. He argued, 'There is no other way out: either we obtain a breathing space or else it's the death of the revolution.'

- Bukharin and the Left Communists wanted to turn the war into a revolutionary war to encourage a European socialist revolution. Bukharin believed that the majority of the party supported him and that Lenin's policy was 'fatal for the revolution'. He was not thinking of a conventional army but (unrealistically) of 'a partisan war of flying detachments' with irregular guerrilla forces encircling and defeating the German troops. Even if the revolutionary war failed, militarily it would rouse the proletariat to revolution in the west.

- Trotsky, the Bolshevik negotiator, kept negotiations going as long as he could, hoping that revolution would break out in Germany and Austria. When the Germans grew impatient, he withdrew from the negotiations saying there would be 'neither war nor peace', meaning that the Russians would not fight the Germans but would not sign the treaty either. Lenin saw Trotsky's slogan as 'a piece of international political showmanship', which would not stop the Germans advancing. Stalin said, 'Comrade Trotsky's position is not a position at all.' It was his first major disagreement with Trotsky.

> ### ■ Learning trouble spot
>
> ### The Bolsheviks and world revolution
> The Bolsheviks were sure that other countries in Europe would follow their lead. They believed that the war would collapse into a series of civil wars in European countries as the working class fought with the bourgeoisie. They also believed that revolution in Russia could not survive without the support of workers' revolutions in advanced capitalist societies. This is why Lenin's pleas for a separate peace with Germany were vigorously opposed. Revolutions did not materialise and Lenin's decision to put the international revolution on hold and save his revolution in Russia proved to be a realistic one.

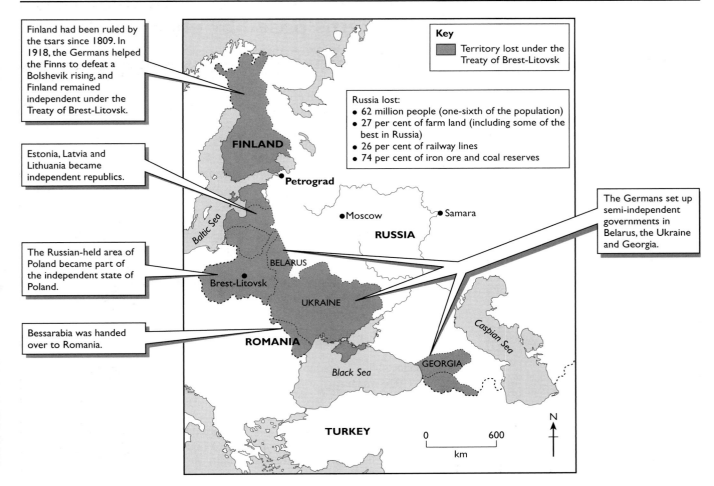

Finland had been ruled by the tsars since 1809. In 1918, the Germans helped the Finns to defeat a Bolshevik rising, and Finland remained independent under the Treaty of Brest-Litovsk.

Estonia, Latvia and Lithuania became independent republics.

The Russian-held area of Poland became part of the independent state of Poland.

Bessarabia was handed over to Romania.

Key
Territory lost under the Treaty of Brest-Litovsk

Russia lost:
- 62 million people (one-sixth of the population)
- 27 per cent of farm land (including some of the best in Russia)
- 26 per cent of railway lines
- 74 per cent of iron ore and coal reserves

The Germans set up semi-independent governments in Belarus, the Ukraine and Georgia.

PEACEMAKING AND THE PEASANT

The Bolsheviks were keen to show the Germans they were a revolutionary democracy by including a representative from the soldiers, sailors, workers, women and peasants in the delegation. On their way to the railway station they realised they did not have a peasant. When they saw a likely looking old man they stopped and whisked Roman Stashkov, a simple village man, into the car. He was not a Bolshevik but as 'Left a SR as possible', which was good enough for the Bolsheviks and despite his initial protest they took him straight to Brest-Litovsk. His primitive table manners stood out at the lavish diplomatic banquets, but he soon began to thoroughly enjoy himself – his response when asked whether he preferred claret or white wine with his main course was, 'which one is the stronger?'

Consequences of the Treaty of Brest-Litovsk

Brest-Litovsk was seen throughout Russia as a 'shameful peace'. No other political party would have acceded to such terms; indeed no leading Bolshevik was prepared to put their name to it. Half the human, industrial and agricultural resources of Nicholas II's empire were lost. This encouraged patriotic Russians to join anti-Bolshevik forces and made civil war almost inevitable.

The Left SRs favoured a revolutionary war and resigned from Sovnarkom in protest at the treaty. In July they assassinated the German ambassador in Moscow in order to provoke a resumption of the war against Germany and attempted to seize power. The situation was serious. Dzerzhinsky, head of the Cheka, was captured and Lenin asked Vatsetis, the commander of the Latvian riflemen, the only reliable troops available to the Bolsheviks, if the regime could last to the following day. The uprising was crushed and mass arrests and reprisals followed. The Left SRs were broken as a party. Vatsetis later became commander of the Red Army.

There had been a short period of intense and quite free debate within the party. However after Brest-Litovsk had been ratified at the Seventh Party Congress, the Left Communists faded and a potentially disastrous split in the party was prevented. The Party Congress resolved that a general tightening up was essential. In the historian Mawdsley's view, 'never again would such a major issue be fought out in public, never again would Lenin be so deeply challenged'.

ACTIVITY

1 Look at the statements in the speech bubbles. Match each comment to one of the people to show how you think the people shown might have responded to the first measures and actions of the new regime.

2 What does this suggest about:
   a) which groups would be likely to support the Bolshevik government
   b) which groups might oppose the Bolsheviks?

(i) Worker at the Putilov engineering works

(ii) Army officer

(iii) Peasant

(iv) Railway worker

(v) Owner of a small factory

(vi) Left-wing Socialist Revolutionary leader

(vii) Moderate socialist leader

(viii) High-ranking civil servant

A I was in favour of the Bolsheviks taking power and I am pleased that we have more power to control our workplaces. No more 'bowing and scraping' before our lords and masters. The tables have turned.

B They won't be able to run the country without us; they have no experience of government. They need the middle classes and they shouldn't encourage the mobs to attack us in the streets and plunder our houses.

C I supported the Soviet, not the Bolsheviks. I don't want one party to run everything. I demand that the different socialist parties get together to form a government that represents everybody.

D You can't put the workers in control of the factories. They don't have the know-how to buy materials and sell them in the marketplace. Already they are giving themselves huge pay rises. It will all end in disaster.

F The Bolsheviks have betrayed the revolution. They have helped the German empire when German workers are crying out for revolution. The Brest-Litovsk Treaty is a shameful peace.

G The army really will fall apart without ranks and discipline. And they have sold Russia to the Germans. Our country must remain 'one and indivisible'.

H Now we have what has always been ours. The land, it belongs to us. I don't know who the Bolsheviks are and I don't much care, but they have done what we wanted and now they can leave us alone to mind our own affairs.

E The behaviour of the Bolsheviks has been disgraceful. They have closed the newspapers. They have arrested Kadets and Socialist Revolutionaries and closed the Constituent Assembly, the legitimate government of Russia. The Bolsheviks are tyrants.

124

HOW DID THE BOLSHEVIKS SURVIVE THE FIRST FEW MONTHS IN POWER?

■ **6E How did the Bolsheviks stay in power?**

Weak opposition
The opposition was unable to co-ordinate action against the government. The power of the Soviet had declined, so there was no serious contender on the left to challenge Bolshevik power.

Political misjudgements
The Socialist Revolutionaries and Mensheviks did not take action, particularly violent action, because they thought the Bolshevik government would collapse quickly and the Constituent Assembly would triumph. They underestimated the Bolsheviks' capacity to survive.

Collapse of army
This meant that officers and conservative forces could not count on any loyal troops to attack the Bolsheviks.

Workers and peasants distracted
Declining living conditions and disillusion with revolution made it difficult to rouse anybody to action. The attention of urban workers was more focused on keeping their own factories going and keeping their jobs. The peasants were only concerned with the land – what was going on in the cities was largely irrelevant to them.

Attacks on opposition
The Bolsheviks moved quickly to deal with opposition. They:
- closed down the opposition press
- arrested key figures in other political parties
- closed down the Constituent Assembly by force before it could get underway
- set up the Cheka to make arrests and deal with demonstrators and protestors.

Use of class warfare
This tactic was effective in deflecting antagonism onto the bourgeoisie. It brought support from large sections of the working class who revelled in turning the tables on the rich and wealthy.

Concessions to urban workers and peasants
Lenin initially gave urban workers and peasants what they wanted – workers' control, eight-hour working days, land and peace, etc., so there were real gains for these groups after the October Revolution.

ACTIVITY

Look at Chart 6E and the table you have completed for the Focus Route activity on page 116. Write a short essay of four or five paragraphs weighing up how well Lenin dealt with the problems and threats facing him in the first months in power. In each paragraph:

a) identify the problem or threat

b) explain what Lenin did

c) evaluate his performance – did his actions achieve what he wanted and what, if any, were the drawbacks/disadvantages?

KEY POINTS FROM CHAPTER 6

How did the Bolsheviks survive the first few months in power?

1 The Bolshevik government was in a fragile condition in the first few months, facing strikes and protests from other socialists over one-party rule.

2 There were divisions within the party over a proposed socialist coalition. Some leading Bolsheviks temporarily resigned in protest at Lenin's failure to support the coalition idea.

3 Lenin always intended to rule on his own and asserted this in his own party and in government.

4 Lenin's early policies had to be modified in response to pressures from the masses.

5 The Bolsheviks crushed opposition and developed forces of terror and coercion, especially the Cheka.

6 Lenin persuaded the Bolsheviks to sign the unfavourable Treaty of Brest-Litovsk. He knew he had to have peace for his government to survive.

7 How did the Bolsheviks win the Civil War?

CHAPTER OVERVIEW

For three years between 1918 and 1920, a bitter civil war was fought between the Bolsheviks and their enemies. Following on immediately from the First World War, which had already brought Russia to its knees economically, it was fought in conditions of extreme hardship and deprivation. The overall death toll, including civilian deaths from hunger and epidemics as well as those caused by military action, may have been as high as ten million. The Bolsheviks won the war largely due to the geographical advantages of the Red Army, the lack of unity among the opposition forces and the organisational abilities of Leon Trotsky. Lenin pursued a ruthless policy of War Communism to keep the Bolshevik state afloat.

A Who was on each side? (p. 126)

B The course of the Civil War (pp. 127–129)

C What was the role of other countries in the Civil War? (p. 130)

D How important was the role of Trotsky in the Civil War? (pp. 131–133)

E Why were the Whites divided and lacking in support? (pp. 134–135)

F Why did the Reds win? (pp. 136–139)

G What was life like in Russia during the Civil War? (pp. 140–141)

H Why did Lenin adopt War Communism? (pp. 141–145)

I What was life like in Bolshevik cities under War Communism? (pp. 146–148)

FOCUS ROUTE

1 Draw a spider diagram to show the sides in the Civil War and their different aims.
2 Can you identify any problems you think the Whites are going to have in the war?

The Greens

The Greens were peasant armies, often made up of deserters from other armies. Some of these armies fought for the Bolsheviks, some against. Most were more concerned with protecting their own area from the ravages of other marauding armies. Some were little more than groups of bandits who did well out of raiding and looting their neighbours. Probably the most famous of the Green armies was that of Nestor Makhno, an anarchist, in the Ukraine. He was a skilled guerrilla leader who at various times fought the Reds, the Whites and the Germans, but became an ally of the Bolsheviks. The Ukrainians, like many of the peasant armies, were fighting for their independence.

■ Learning trouble spot

The sides in the Civil War

If you are confused by the different sides, particularly the Whites, then so were people at the time. When we talk about the White armies, we are mainly referring to Denikin's army in the south, Kolchak's army in the east and Yudenich's army in the north-west. These were largely made up of tsarists, army officers and liberals, with peasants forming a large proportion of the soldiers. The Socialist Revolutionaries and other socialists were involved with White armies at times, but usually operated independently.

A Who was on each side?

The Civil War in Russia from 1918 to 1920 was very complex, as different groups emerged to challenge the Bolsheviks' claim to be the government of Russia. It involved many contestants spread out over an immense area. At one point, there were some eighteen anti-Bolshevik governments in Russia. We can divide the participants in the Civil War into three rather ill-defined sides:

- the Reds – the Bolsheviks
- the Whites
- the Greens.

The Reds – the Bolsheviks

The great strength of the Reds was that they had one clear aim – to stay in power. The 'Workers' and Peasants' Red Army' was formed from Kronstadt sailors and Red Guards, plus workers who volunteered and soldiers from the disintegrating former imperial army.

The Whites

Under this broad banner, there were liberals, former tsarists, nationalists and separatists, Socialist Revolutionaries and other moderate socialists. Few Whites wanted to see the tsar back but many, including liberals, supported military dictatorship until the Bolsheviks were defeated and law and order re-established. Other groups, especially the Socialist Revolutionaries, were keen to see the Constituent Assembly running Russia. Probably the only thing that they all had in common was that they were anti-Bolshevik. The Whites were deeply divided and it was not uncommon for White armies to fight each other. It was very difficult, for instance, for Socialist Revolutionaries to fight alongside former tsarist officers and monarchists (called 'Rightists') who favoured military dictatorship and the return of the land to its former owners. Four White armies were particularly significant (see Chart 7A).

■ 7A Main forces of the Whites

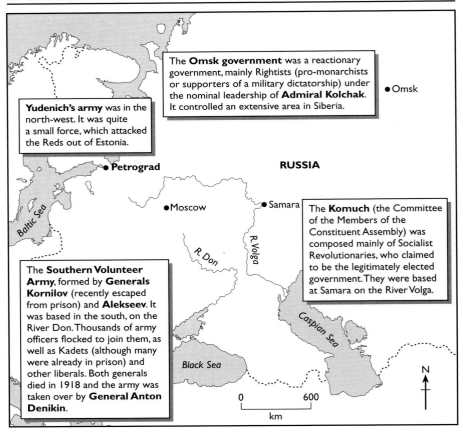

The **Omsk government** was a reactionary government, mainly Rightists (pro-monarchists or supporters of a military dictatorship) under the nominal leadership of **Admiral Kolchak**. It controlled an extensive area in Siberia.

Yudenich's army was in the north-west. It was quite a small force, which attacked the Reds out of Estonia.

The **Komuch** (the Committee of the Members of the Constituent Assembly) was composed mainly of Socialist Revolutionaries, who claimed to be the legitimately elected government. They were based at Samara on the River Volga.

The **Southern Volunteer Army**, formed by **Generals Kornilov** (recently escaped from prison) and **Alekseev**. It was based in the south, on the River Don. Thousands of army officers flocked to join them, as well as Kadets (although many were already in prison) and other liberals. Both generals died in 1918 and the army was taken over by **General Anton Denikin**.

B The course of the Civil War

FOCUS ROUTE

1 Look at pages 128–129. Focus on the geographical position of the forces shown on the map in Chart 7C.
   a) What advantages/disadvantages did the Reds have?
   b) What advantages/disadvantages did the Whites have?
2 What key reasons do the map and text suggest for the defeat of the Whites?

WHAT HAPPENED TO THE CZECH LEGION?

The Czech Legion fought for the Whites for a while, but after the declaration of Czech independence in October 1918 it was weakened by mutinies and desertion and largely withdrew from the fighting.

Although there were some minor clashes in late 1917, the war began in earnest in the spring of 1918. By this time it was clear that the Bolsheviks wanted to run Russia as a one-party state. They had alienated other socialist groups (Socialist Revolutionaries and Mensheviks) as well as the liberals and more conservative right-wing elements in society. It was the Bolsheviks against the rest.

Hostilities were sparked off in the east by the rather bizarre events surrounding the Czech Legion. The Legion had been formed by Czech nationalists hoping to win recognition for an independent Czech state (previously it had been part of the Austrian empire). It had been significantly enlarged by Czech prisoners of war and deserters from the Austrian army. The idea was that it would fight with the Russian army against the Austrians and Germans. When the Treaty of Brest-Litovsk took Russia out of the war, the Legion decided to fight with the Allies on the Western Front. But they did not want to cross enemy lines and it was agreed with the Soviet authorities that they would be transported along the Trans-Siberian railway to Vladivostok, from where they would be taken by ship to Western Europe. The Czechs mistrusted the Bolsheviks and there were clashes with local Bolshevik soviets along the Trans-Siberian railway. When the Bolsheviks tried to disarm them, the Czechs resisted and took control of large sections of this important railway (the main route to the east) and large parts of western Siberia. Substantial White forces then grew up around them.

The full-scale Civil War was underway by the summer of 1918. We shall consider the course of the war by looking at the three White forces that posed the biggest threat to the Bolsheviks. These are shown on the map in Chart 7C on pages 128–129. The Civil War was fought mainly in the east and the south.

■ 7B Key events of the Civil War

1918			Loss of Kharkov and Tsaritsyn leads to criticism of Trotsky.	
Jan	Red Army is established.		He resigns but his resignation is refused.	
March	Treaty of Brest-Litovsk First British troops land at Murmansk.	September	Allies evacuate Archangel.	
May	Czech Legion rebels and captures a large section of the Trans-Siberian railway. Conscription into Red Army is introduced.	October	Denikin takes Orel but is forced back later in the month. Yudenich reaches the outskirts of Petrograd.	
June	Socialist Revolutionary government is established at Samara. Murder of the Tsar and his family.	November	Yudenich is defeated; Denikin is pushed back.	
August	Americans arrive in northern Russia and in the east. British land at Archangel and establish an anti-Bolshevik government.	**1920** February	Kolchak (captured in January) is executed by the Bolsheviks. Red Army invades Georgia.	
November	Kolchak assumes control in Omsk.	April	Denikin, having been pursued to the Crimea, is succeeded by Wrangel.	
December	French land at Odessa.	May	Polish army invades Russia and occupies Kiev.	
1919 February	Denikin assumes supreme command in the south-east. Red Army occupies Kiev.	July	Tukhachevsky mounts Red Army counter-offensive against Poles.	
March	Kolchak's forces cross the Urals but are repulsed by the Red Army. Growing discontent in French and British forces.	August	Red Army defeated by Poles outside Warsaw.	
April	French evacuate Odessa.	November	Wrangel, last surviving White general, is defeated in the Crimea.	
June	Denikin and southern army take Kharkov.	**1921** March	Treaty of Riga: peace between Poland and Soviet Russia.	
July	Denikin advances from the Caucasus and captures Tsaritsyn.			

Yudenich in the west
General Yudenich's army was the smallest army, only some 15,000 men, but it reached the outskirts of Petrograd in October 1919 before being turned back by larger Bolshevik forces.

Denikin and Wrangel in the south
Denikin's southern army of 150,000 had a large contingent of Don Cossacks. His army made ground across the Don region, intending to join up with Kolchak. By the summer of 1918 it was besieging Tsaritsyn, a key city under the command of Joseph Stalin. The Bolsheviks had to hold this city at all costs to prevent the southern and eastern White armies from linking up, and to protect vital grain supplies that passed through Tsaritsyn en route to Bolshevik-held cities to the north and west. The successful defence of Tsaritsyn became a heroic story in Bolshevik mythology and the city was later renamed Stalingrad in Stalin's honour.

Denikin launched another offensive in the summer of 1919. Spectacularly successful, it came within 320 km of Moscow by October. But Trotsky organised a ferocious counter-attack, forcing a hasty and panic-stricken White retreat. The southern White army was pushed right back into the Crimean peninsula. Denikin was replaced by Wrangel. The Whites held out for much of 1920 but had to be evacuated by British and French ships in November of that year.

Makhno's Insurgent Army
The most dangerous of the Green armies was Makhno's Insurgent Army, which had successfully used guerrilla warfare against Whites and Reds and was strongly supported by the peasant population in the Ukraine. It had encouraged the growth of communes and soviets for peasants to run their own affairs without any central direction – a real challenge to the Bolshevik centralised state. Towards the end of the war, Makhno's army fought as an irregular division for the Reds. But as soon as the war was won, the Bolsheviks crushed his peasant-anarchist movement, although it proved no easy task. Makhno escaped to Romania.

Kolchak in the east
Admiral Kolchak headed an army of some 140,000, which came in from the east, building on the successes of the Czech Legion and linking up with it. Initially very successful, they took Kazan and Samara by June 1918. But the advance fell apart for several reasons:
• determined counter-attacks by the Red Army
• internal quarrels and apathy among the Czechs
• power struggles with the Socialist Revolutionaries (see Case Study 1, page 134), who staged revolts that weakened Kolchak's army.
By the autumn of 1919, the Reds had turned Kolchak's advance into a long retreat, throughout which they harassed his army. Eventually, in 1920, Kolchak was captured and shot.

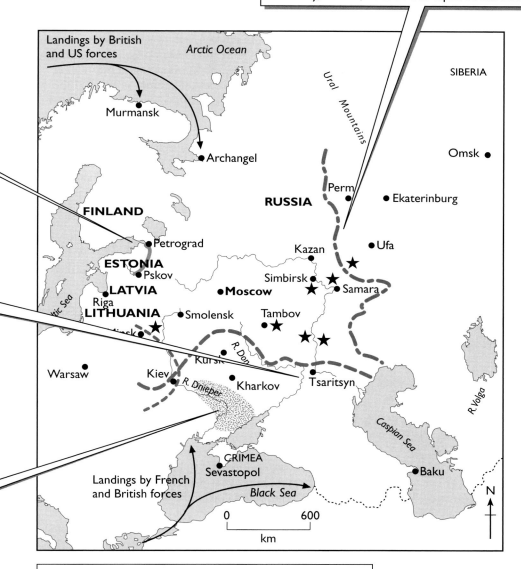

Landings by British and US forces

Arctic Ocean

SIBERIA

Ural Mountains

Murmansk

Archangel

Omsk

Perm

Ekaterinburg

RUSSIA

FINLAND

Petrograd

Kazan

Ufa

ESTONIA

Pskov

Simbirsk

Samara

LATVIA

Riga

•**Moscow**

LITHUANIA

Smolensk

Tambov

Warsaw

Kiev

Kursk

R. Don

Kharkov

Tsaritsyn

R. Volga

R. Dnieper

Caspian Sea

CRIMEA
Sevastopol

Baku

Landings by French and British forces

Black Sea

N

0   600
km

Key

———— Yudenich offensive against Petrograd

– – – – Furthest advance of Polish armies

▬ ▬ ▬ Furthest advance of Denikin and Wrangel's armies

▬ ▬ ▬ Furthest advance of Kolchak's armies

⬚ Area of activity by Makhno's partisans

★ Major peasant uprisings

ANNEXATION
Taking over the territory of other countries and joining it to own country.

C What was the role of other countries in the Civil War?

Allied troops were sent to Russia to help to reopen the Eastern Front against Germany. But before they could go into action the war ended, in November 1918. The troops stayed on, ostensibly to guard munitions dumps in Archangel and Murmansk.

Western countries, however, had other objectives. The British, encouraged by Winston Churchill, the War Secretary, were amongst the most active forces. They sent £100-million-worth of supplies to the Whites. Churchill saw the Whites as crusaders against Bolshevism; he dreaded the spread of Bolshevism to other countries in Western Europe. However, within Britain there was substantial opposition to involvement in the Russian Civil War. Lloyd George, the Prime Minister, feared disaffection of war-weary troops, and the small but increasingly influential Labour Party believed Britain should not fight the Russian working class.

A number of other countries sent small forces, but they were there for different reasons. The French were probably the most anti-Bolshevik because French investors had put millions of francs into Russia and the Bolsheviks had nationalised foreign-owned businesses without compensation. But the soldiers were not keen to fight and there were mutinies in the French fleet in the Black Sea. The Japanese sent a sizeable force into Siberia, especially around Vladivostok. But they were more interested in trying to grab some valuable territory than in fighting the Bolsheviks. The USA sent troops to the same area, largely to stop the Japanese ANNEXING any land. Other countries which sent small detachments included Italy, Serbia, Romania, Greece and Canada.

The involvement of the Allies was unenthusiastic and ineffective. The troops had had enough of war and there was no real support from the public in their home countries. The Allies provided the Whites with valuable supplies but that was about all. Allied soldiers got involved in a few skirmishes but took no part in serious military action.

■ 7D The Russo-Polish War, 1919–21

Key
—— Poland's established frontiers, June 1920
······ Eastern extent of Poland's conquests in Russia, June 1920
⟵ Russian counter-attacks
◠ Polish line of defence, August 1920
▨ Land annexed by Poland under Treaty of Riga, March 1921
----- Poland's eastern frontier, 1921–39

The Russo-Polish War 1919–21

In 1919, the Poles hoped to take advantage of the chaotic situation in Russia and to take territory which had once been part of the Polish empire. Their troops, under Pilsudski, were initially successful, capturing Kiev in May 1920. But by this time, the Bolsheviks had more or less defeated their Civil War enemies and the Polish invasion brought even non-Bolsheviks to the support of the Red banner – the Poles were an old enemy. In a daring campaign led by Tukhachevsky, the Poles were pushed right back to Warsaw.

Lenin hoped that the success of the Reds might encourage revolution in Germany. In fact this was the sort of revolutionary war – spreading the revolution by force – that left-wing Bolsheviks had wanted much earlier. Germany was unstable and some cities had set up 'red soviets'. However, the Reds had now overstretched their supply lines and, lacking support, were comprehensively defeated by the Poles. A settlement was reached in 1921. Under the Treaty of Riga, the Russians had to surrender large areas of White Russia and the Ukraine to the Poles.

FOCUS ROUTE

Using Sources 7.1–7.7 and the main text, note down the main ways in which you think Trotsky contributed to the Red victory.

D How important was the role of Trotsky in the Civil War?

When Trotsky was made Commissar for War in 1918, the army was on the point of disintegration. He restored discipline and professionalism to what was now called the 'Worker's and Peasants' Red Army' and turned it into an effective fighting force. He reorganised the army along strict hierarchical lines and brought back thousands of former tsarist officers to train and command army units. Many of these officers, who were unemployed, hungry and poor, seized the opportunity to get back into the world they knew best. To ensure their loyalty, Trotsky had their families held hostage.

The return to a traditional army was resented by other leading Bolsheviks, especially Stalin and Zinoviev. They had a different concept of a revolutionary army – one which was more like a militia and certainly not one that had tsarist officers in charge. Trotsky only managed to get his way with the support of Lenin, who saw that it was the only solution, given the state of the army and the urgency of the situation. To placate the party, and ensure the loyalty of the officers, Trotsky attached a political commissar to each army unit. The job of the commissar (who was often a fanatical Bolshevik) was to watch and report on the actions of the officers and make sure they were politically correct. They also fed back useful information to the central headquarters.

Soldiers' committees (which dominated army units) and the election of officers by soldiers were ended. This did not go down well with the soldiers, who also resented the reintroduction of ranks, saluting and pay differentials. But Trotsky went further – he re-established harsh military discipline, bringing back the death penalty for a range of offences (see Source 7.1). He thought this was essential to make men fight. He also formed labour battalions to help at the Front, comprised of men who could not fight or were seen as unreliable; many of these came from the ranks of the bourgeoisie, or 'former people' as they were now known.

Trotsky's strengths were his energy, passion and organisational abilities. According to Dmitri Volkogonov, a Soviet historian and ex-general, Trotsky was not much of a military strategist and the key military decisions were taken by others. But Trotsky never claimed to be an expert in military matters. His chief contribution was as the person in overall charge, holding things together and making the organisation work effectively; this was no small achievement in Russia between 1918 and 1920.

SOURCE 7.1 Orders to the Red Army from Trotsky, 1918

- *Every scoundrel who incites anyone to retreat, to desert, or not to fulfil a military order, will be shot.*
- *Every soldier who voluntarily deserts his post will be shot.*
- *Every soldier who throws away his rifle or sells part of his equipment will be shot.*

SOURCE 7.2 Trotsky used the special train to keep in constant contact with the Front and to take him and his special troops to the points where the fighting was fiercest. The arrival of the train was a great morale booster. It was his general headquarters and was fitted out as a munitions and uniform supply centre, a troop transporter and a radio-communications centre. It also had a garage and his own Rolls-Royce armoured car in which he drove to the Fronts.

There was not just one train and one set of carriages. In fact Trotsky had four locomotives and two whole sets of carriages at his disposal. Robert Service lists a staff of 369 by the end of 1918. 'This was no mere transport facility for the People's Commissar but a full military-political organisation.'
R. Service, *Trotsky*, 2009, pp. 230–1.

SOURCE 7.3 Trotsky reviewing troops. He used special forces to back up conventional forces, often marching his special forces, with machine guns, behind the ordinary troops. His special troops were kitted out in black leather and were a macho élite force. Trotsky remarked: 'I issue this warning. If any detachment retreats without orders, the first to be shot will be the commissar, the second will be the commander'

SOURCE 7.4 R. Service, *A History of Twentieth-Century Russia*, 1997, pp. 105–6

His [Trotsky's] brilliance had been proved before 1918. What took everyone aback was his organisational capacity and ruthlessness as he transformed the Red Army into a fighting force. He ordered deserters to be shot, and he did not give a damn if some of them were communist party activists; and in this fashion he endeared himself to Imperial Army officers whom he encouraged to join the Reds. He sped from unit to unit, rousing the troops with his revolutionary zeal.... His flair too paid dividends. He organised a competition to design a Red Army cap and tunic; he had his own railway carriage equipped with his own map room and printing press. He also had an eye for young talent, bringing on his protégés without regard for length of time and service.

However, this does not mean that Trotsky was just a backroom commander, far behind the front lines. Travelling in a specially equipped train (see Sources 7.2 and 7.5), he rushed to the points where the fighting was fiercest to provide support – although sometimes this involved his special troops making sure that Red forces did not retreat (see Source 7.3). His presence did seem to make a real difference and he genuinely seemed able to inspire men in a way that other leaders, especially White leaders, could not. It was Trotsky who decided to save Petrograd when it was under threat from Yudenich. The capital had been moved to Moscow and Lenin felt that they would have to give up Petrograd, the 'home of the revolution'. Trotsky disagreed, raced off with his train and, after fierce fighting, turned Yudenich's army away

The Red Army

It is easy to overplay the organisation of the Red Army in comparison to the Whites. Once the supply of urban workers ran out, the Reds conscripted peasants. Although they were willing to fight for their lands when the White armies approached, the peasants were generally unwilling conscripts. At harvest time, they would often desert. In protest at the mass conscription by the Reds and the seizure of their best horses and food for the army, the peasants staged uprisings which engulfed whole provinces. Many joined the independent Green armies. Rates of desertion were just as high for the Reds as for the Whites. By the end of 1919, the Red Army had around three million troops; the figure reached around five million by the end of 1920. But it is estimated that one million deserted in 1918 and nearly four million by 1921. The trouble was that when they deserted they took their weapons and uniforms with them, so even in the later stages of the war the Red Army was often poorly equipped (few had good boots), had a ragtag appearance and was short of ammunition. This is why Trotsky's train, which carried uniforms and supplies, was so important.

The Red Army also had its fair share of indiscipline. At worst, this became full-scale mutinies in which *burzhui* officers were murdered and new officers elected. There was festering resentment about *burzhui* officers and a great deal of anti-Semitism. Many of the commissars were Jews, including, of course, Trotsky himself..

SOURCE 7.5   V. Serge, *Memoirs of a Revolutionary 1901–1941*, translated and edited by
P. Sedwick, 1967, p. 92

*The news from the other fronts was so bad that Lenin was reluctant to sacrifice
the last available forces in the defence of the doomed city [Petrograd]. Trotsky
thought otherwise … He arrived at almost the last moment and his presence
changed the atmosphere … Trotsky arrived with a train, that famous train which
had been speeding to and fro along the different fronts … The train contained
excellent motor cars … a printing shop for propaganda, sanitary squads, and
specialists in engineering, provisioning, street fighting, all bound together by
friendship and trust, all kept to a strict vigorous discipline by a leader they
admired, all dressed in black leather, red stars on their peaked caps, all exhaling
energy. It was the nucleus of resolute and efficiently serviced organisers, who
hastened wherever danger demanded their presence.*

SOURCE 7.6   E. Mawdsley, *The Russian Civil War*, 1987, pp. 277–78

*The historian looking at Trotsky's Civil War career must beware of two myths.
The first is the Soviet view dominant ever since his disgrace in the late 1920s that
he played no beneficial role in the Civil War. ('History,' Comrade Stalin in fact
pointed out, 'shows that … Kolchak and Denikin were beaten by our troops in
spite of Trotsky's plans.') The second might be called the 'Trotskyist' myth that
exaggerates his importance. The truth lies in between the two, but given the state
of Western historiography it is perhaps the second myth that deserves the most
attention. Trotsky was, of course, the second best-known Soviet leader. But his
career in 1917–1920 was marked by spectacular failures. He made major mistakes
in foreign policy in early 1918 and in economic policy in 1920. Even his career
in the Red Army had the bitterness of the summer of 1919. Trotsky's vital step
was to support the creation of a regular army against much party opposition.*

*He also played an important agitational role, his famous
headquarters train covered 65,000 miles, and all this was
something that Lenin, as their comrade Lunacharsky
pointed out, could not have done. The fighting men needed
a figurehead to rally around, and Trotsky played his part
effectively. At the same time the other important leaders of
the Civil War should not be lost sight of. Sverdlov, who died
in early 1919, helped organize the state and the party, and
Rykov, disgraced in the 1930s, was the man in charge of the
war economy. Smilga, another future oppositionist, was the
chief political organizer of the Red Army. Something should
be said for Stalin, too, who had a most active career in the
Civil War; if he had been killed in 1920 he would certainly
be remembered as one of the great activists of the war. And
outside the party probably no one was as important as two
former Tsarist colonels, Vatsetis and Kamenev.*

SOURCE 7.7   Various contemporary images of Trotsky

ACTIVITY

1 Why does E. Mawdsley in Source 7.6 think that Trotsky's
importance has been overstated?

2 What do you consider was Trotsky's most important
contribution to the Red victory?

FOCUS ROUTE

1 List the key weaknesses in the White forces.
2 Provide an example or supporting argument for each weakness identified.

E Why were the Whites divided and lacking in support?

We can use two case studies to illustrate the weaknesses in the White camp.

Case study 1: divisions

In 1918, most of the Socialist Revolutionaries had fled to Samara on the Volga to set up the Komuch (the Committee of the Members of the Constituent Assembly). Later, they were pushed back by the Reds and linked up with the Omsk government run by Rightists (former tsarist officers and monarchists) who favoured a military dictatorship. Initially, they reached agreement and set up a joint government. But there were squabbles between the socialists, liberals and monarchists. The officers organised a coup and arrested Socialist Revolutionary ministers. They awarded Admiral Kolchak the title of 'Supreme Ruler'. Kolchak then had hundreds of Socialist Revolutionary activists arrested and many executed, including ten Socialist Revolutionary members of the original Constituent Assembly. As a result, the Socialist Revolutionaries later staged revolts against him and undermined the rest of his campaign, contributing to his defeat.

Case study 2: why the Whites could not get support

The Southern Volunteer Army that assembled on the Don was largely an army of officers who had lost much to the Bolsheviks, including their livelihoods and family estates. These officers thought that the Don Cossacks, who lived in the region, would fight with them for the old order. But the Don Cossacks only wanted independence for their own region. They agreed to fight to counter the Bolshevik threat, but throughout the war kept their units separate and would not always obey orders from the central command. They were very reluctant to go further into central Russia once their homeland had been secured from the Bolsheviks and this was a real problem for the Whites in 1919. Denikin, the leader of the Southern Volunteer Army, might have enlisted their support if he had promised them autonomy, but he had no time for separatists.

It was not just Denikin who would not make concessions to national aspirations. The Kadets would countenance nothing other than 'A Russia Great, United and Indivisible'. This was particularly crass since the southern White armies were operating in areas where people were demanding more autonomy or independence, such as the Ukraine and the Caucasus. If they had been prepared to make concessions, then they might have gained much more support.

The brutality of White armies antagonised the peasants. The Cossacks in the southern army were especially guilty of this. As their nationalistic feelings were heightened, they practised a sort of 'ethnic cleansing', driving out thousands of non-Cossack peasants (mainly Russians and Ukrainians) from their lands and treating them brutally. Outside their own lands, they were worse – looting, raping, and pillaging villages for food supplies; and conducting fiercesome pogroms against Jewish settlements. This drove the peasants into the arms of the Reds.

The peasants were, of course, the main source of soldiers for the White army. In White-held areas they were conscripted in their thousands and whenever they got the chance they deserted in their thousands. The Volunteer Army in the main treated the peasants with contempt. Denikin helped landowners recover their estates. His followers and the other White leaders made it clear that the peasants would have to give back most of the land they had seized in 1917. As a result, the peasants were always going to oppose the Whites.

The identification of the Whites with the old tsarist order remained a problem for them throughout the war. Many Rightists paid lip-service to free elections and democratic ideals but really wanted to turn the clock back to life as it had been before the revolution. The Kadets and the Rightists in the south wanted the old empire back, without any concessions to national minorities and little acknowledgement of the peasant revolution. But the urban workers and peasants had made too many gains from the revolution to go back.

TALKING POINT

Why do you think that in times of crisis and the collapse of centralised authority there is a growth in nationalist aspirations and 'ethnic cleansing'?

Improving your own performance

This activity has two aims. The first is to help you to record information about the Bolshevik victory in the Civil War. The second is to help you to develop your note-taking skills, keeping your notes as brief as possible and setting them out so they are easy to understand and/or learn for examinations. Two methods are suggested here. You can choose the one that suits your style of learning.

Method 1: Linear method

Draw up a table with Reds on one side and Whites on the other, as below. Then list the key points (using bullet points or numbers) under the appropriate heading. It is useful to treat the weaknesses of the Whites separately since some questions in exams focus specifically on this.

Factors favouring the Reds	Weaknesses of the Whites

Method 2: Spider or pattern diagrams

This method is particularly useful for seeing topics at a glance. The diagram below shows you how you might set out this one but it is best to follow your own logic as long as you split up the topic into coherent categories.

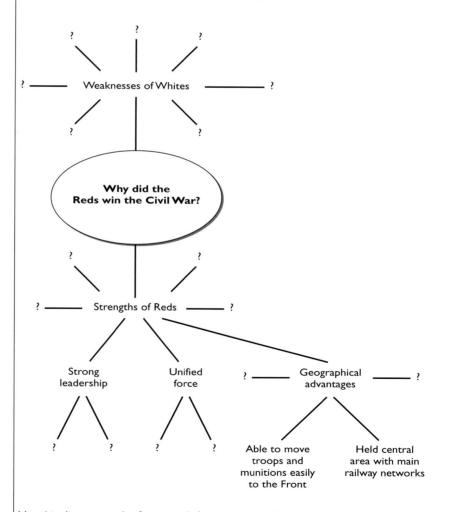

Use this diagram as the framework for your notes, but bring in any useful extra information from the Focus Route activities you have done in this chapter.

F   Why did the Reds win?

■ 7E Why did the Reds win?

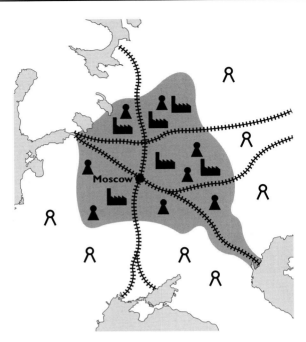

Geographical factors

- The Bolsheviks held the central area, which included Petrograd and Moscow. They moved their capital to Moscow, at the hub of the railway network. This made it easier to transport men and munitions to the battle fronts.
- This area also contained the main armament factories in Russia, so the Bolsheviks could carry on producing war materials. Much of the artillery, rifles and other military equipment of the old Russian army fell into Bolshevik hands.
- The central area was heavily populated (much more so than White-held areas), so the Bolsheviks were able to conscript large numbers to fight. Red armies often vastly outnumbered their White opponents.
- Whites were scattered around the edges of this central area, separated by large distances. This made communications difficult, especially moving men and weapons and co-ordinating the attacks of different White armies. They had no telephone links; they had to use officers on horseback to convey messages.

Unity and organisation

- The Bolsheviks had a single, unified command structure.
- Trotsky organised the Red Army into an effective fighting force. He turned it from a 'flabby, panicky mass' into a better organised army than the Whites.
- The Whites were made up of different groups who had entirely different aims and beliefs – they could not agree on whether they were fighting for monarchism, republicanism or for the Constituent Assembly. This made it hard for them to co-operate and impossible to develop a political strategy. They were also split by their views on national minorities.
- They had little chance of developing a co-ordinated military strategy. Often the White generals would not work together because they did not like or trust each other. For example, other generals were suspicious of Kolchak's motives and intentions.

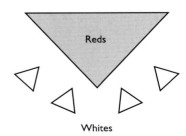

Leadership

- Trotsky proved himself to be a superb leader. Personally brave, he took his special forces to the parts of the Front where the fighting was fiercest. He was able to inspire and rally men.
- Discipline was very tough in the Red Army; the death penalty was used frequently. Unwilling peasant conscripts knew that certain death lay before them if they retreated in a battle – they would be machine-gunned by their own side.
- White leaders were, on the whole, second rate. Several were cruel and treated their men with contempt. They reminded the soldiers of the worst aspects of the Russian army and tsarist rule. Therefore, there was little natural warmth or support for the White leaders. Many soldiers deserted.
- The level of indiscipline and corruption in the White armies was extraordinary. Denikin said: 'I can do nothing with my army. I am glad when it carries out my combat orders.' In Omsk (Kolchak's base), uniforms and munitions supplied by foreign interventionist governments were sold on the black market, and officers lived in brothels in a haze of cocaine and vodka. Units of the Red Army sometimes ended up in English army uniforms and prostitutes in English nurses' uniforms.

Support

- The support of the peasants was crucial since they supplied the main body of soldiers for both sides. They had little love for either side and were just as inclined to desert from Red as from White armies into which they had been conscripted. But Lenin had legitimised their right to the land while the Whites made it clear that land would be restored to its former owners. Kolchak even gave estates to landlords who had not owned them before the revolution. So peasants were inclined to support the Reds.
- Whites lost the support of nationalist groups. White leaders wanted to restore the Russian empire with its pre-1917 borders. This antagonised national groups (separatists) such as the Ukrainians and Georgians who were looking for more autonomy in their affairs or complete independence. Therefore separatists would not support the Whites when White forces were based in their territory.
- The Bolsheviks had a core support group of some workers and soldiers but did not enjoy widespread popular support. War Communism and the way they managed the cities and food supply saw to that. But urban workers and peasants wanted to protect the gains of 1917 and the Reds seemed to offer them their best chance of doing this. The Whites were associated with the old system of government.

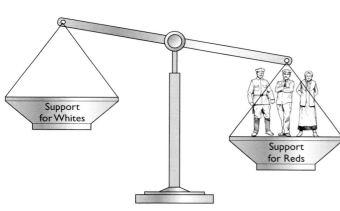

Other factors

- Foreign intervention should have worked in the Whites' favour and it certainly did bring them supplies and weapons. But it was half-hearted and largely ineffective. It also gave the Bolsheviks a propaganda coup because they could present themselves as the defenders of Russian soil against foreign forces.
- Both sides used propaganda but the Whites, particularly Denikin, did not see how valuable it was. The Reds used extremely imaginative and powerful images, including:
  - the Whites would take away land from the peasants
  - foreign invaders were supporting the Whites
  - the Reds offered a wonderful new society for workers and peasants.

FIGHT FOR YOUR LAND! FIGHT FOR THE RED ARMY!

ACTIVITY

Propaganda in the Civil War

Both Reds and Whites used propaganda, but it was the Reds who really understood its value and poured resources into its use. Practise your interpretative skills by examining the sources on pages 138–139. Analyse each poster in turn: look at its component parts and try to work out what each represents.

1 What message is each poster trying to put over?
2 How effectively do the posters convey their messages?
3 Do some work better than others?
4 Which do you think is the most effective poster?
5 Do you think that these political posters are useful historical evidence about the attitudes that people on both sides held at the time?
6 Why are these posters useful to historians?
7 Why do you think the Bolsheviks used agitprop trains, like the one in Source 7.10, and an agitprop boat?

SOURCE 7.8 A Soviet poster from 1918. It shows the sword of the Red Army cutting off the advance of the White forces, led by Wrangel

SOURCE 7.9 A Red poster showing the White generals Denikin, Kolchak and Yudenich as slavering dogs under the control of the Western interventionist leaders

SOURCE 7.10 An agitprop (*agit*ation and *prop*aganda) train. Trains richly decorated with Red propaganda images carried film crews, theatre groups and educational literature. They stopped at country stations where they set up stages and classrooms to bring literacy and new ideas to the peasants

SOURCE 7.11 This pro-Reds 1919 poster's caption reads 'To the defence of Petrograd'

SOURCE 7.12 An anti-Bolshevik poster depicts a Red as a huge, grotesque monster, faced by White guardsmen and their allies. An English officer is arriving bringing tanks and aeroplanes

SOURCE 7.13 A pro-Whites poster showing Red Army soldiers forcibly taking grain and possessions from peasants

G What was life like in Russia during the Civil War?

In the late twentieth century, civil wars in the Balkans and the Russian Federation showed how savage, brutal and chaotic such conflicts are. In the Russian Civil War, central authority disappeared and local areas were left to fend for themselves. The fighting fronts were rarely stable. Kiev in the Ukraine changed hands some sixteen times, so the inhabitants were not sure which army was approaching. It was also common for units of soldiers (the Cossacks in particular) to change sides, fighting at one time for the Whites and later for the Reds, depending on how they saw their interests and advantage. As Kolchak's army retreated, one whole regiment murdered its officers and went over to the Reds.

The Civil War in Russia was full of unspeakable atrocities committed by both sides out of fear and resentment. The Cossacks in the south raped and murdered whole villages of Jews in pogroms that may have taken 115,000 lives in the Ukraine alone. They claimed the Jews supported the Bolsheviks. In the Donbass region, the Whites routinely shot miners who did not produce enough coal. In one case in Rostov, they buried hundreds of Red miners alive. In Kharkov, the Reds nailed the epaulettes of officers to their shoulders while they were still alive.

The biggest killer of all was disease, especially typhus, which spread rapidly amongst the lice-ridden troops and the civilian population. Over one million people are thought to have died from typhus and typhoid in 1920. Estimates suggest that around 450,000 were killed by disease over the whole period while 350,000 were killed in the fighting.

One way to get an idea of what the Civil War was like is to look at novels written about this period by people who were personally involved. You can read extracts from Boris Pasternak's novel *Dr Zhivago* in Source 7.14. Pasternak had first-hand knowledge of the Civil War.

SOURCE 7.14 B. Pasternak, *Doctor Zhivago*, paperback edn 1975, pp. 407, 416. Zhivago has been captured by partisans. At one point they are surrounded by White forces and come across a man who has crawled into their camp

His right arm and left leg had been chopped off. It was inconceivable how, with his remaining arm and leg, he had crawled into the camp. The chopped-off arm and leg were tied in terrible bleeding chunks on to his back, together with a small wooden board; on it, a long inscription stated, with many words of abuse, that the atrocity was in reprisal for similar atrocities committed by such and such a Red unit ... It was added that the same treatment would be meted out to all the partisans unless, by a given date, they submitted and gave up their arms to the representatives of General Vitsyn's army corps.

[Zhivago escapes from the partisans and makes his way home.]
For a long time, for almost half his journey on foot, he had followed the railway, all of it out of action, neglected and covered with snow. Train after train, abandoned by the Whites, stood idle, stopped by the defeat of Kolchak, by running out of fuel ... they stretched ... for miles on end. Some of them served as fortresses for armed bands of robbers or as hide-outs for escaping criminals or political refugees – the involuntary vagrants of those days – but most of them were common mortuaries, mass graves of the victims of the cold and the typhus raging all along the railway line and mowing down whole villages ...

Half the villages were empty, the fields abandoned and unharvested as after an enemy invasion – such were the effects of the war: the Civil War ... In the abandoned field the ripe grain spilled and trickled on the ground.

SOURCE 7.15 I. Babel, *Collected Stories*, trans. D. McDuff, 1994, p. 136. Isaac Babel was born in Odessa in 1894, the son of a Jewish tradesman. He joined the Bolsheviks in 1917. In 1920 he joined the Red Army and served with the famous cavalry commander Budyonny as a war correspondent for ROSTA, the Soviet news agency. In 1925 he wrote the book *Red Cavalry*, a collection of stories based on his Civil War experiences, from which this extract was originally taken

Budyonny was standing by a tree, in red trousers with a silver stripe. The brigade commander had just been killed. In his place the army commander had appointed Kolesnikov. An hour ago Kolesnikov had been colonel of a regiment. A week ago Kolesnikov had been the leader of a squadron.

The new brigade commander was summoned to Budyonny . . . 'The curs are giving us the squeeze,' the commander said with a dazzling grin. 'Either we win or we die. There is no other way. Got it?'

'Got it,' Kolesnikov replied, his eyes bulging.

'And if you run, I will shoot you,' the commander said, smiling, and turned to look at the section leader.

'Very well,' said the section leader . . . He touched his peaked cap with five youthful red fingers, began to sweat and walked off . . . He walked with lowered head, his long and crooked legs moving with agonising slowness. The blaze of the sunset washed over him, crimson and improbable as approaching death . . . His orderly led up a horse for him. He leapt into the saddle and galloped off . . .

I happened to catch sight of him again that evening (after the battle in which the enemy was annihilated) . . . riding out in front of his brigade . . . his right arm in a sling . . . The front squadron was lazily leading the others in the singing of obscene couplets. In Kolesnikov's manner of sitting in the saddle that evening I saw the lordly indifference of a Tartar khan.

TALKING POINT

How useful do you think novels like these are to historians?

H Why did Lenin adopt War Communism?

FOCUS ROUTE

Make notes on:

a) the problems facing the Bolshevik government on the domestic front
b) the main features of War Communism as a solution to the Bolsheviks' problems and a means to develop socialism
c) the use of terror and class warfare to defeat elements in society hostile to the government
d) the arbitrary nature of the terror.

While Trotsky managed the Civil War, Lenin concentrated on building and consolidating the Bolshevik state. This is not to say that Lenin had no part in the Civil War. He and Trotsky took strategic decisions together and Trotsky needed Lenin's support on a number of occasions, for example, over the use of former tsarist officers in the army. But Lenin took charge of the day-to-day business of the Sovnarkom and the problems he faced were formidable. Chief amongst these was the rapid deterioration of the economy in the spring of 1918.

To ensure their survival in the first months after the October Revolution, the Bolsheviks had handed over control of the land to the peasants and control of the factories to the workers' committees. The pressure from peasants and workers had been irresistible. But it was not long before the shortcomings of both policies became apparent.

Industry fell apart as workers' committees proved incapable of running the factories (although the economic collapse was underway well before the workers took over, so they cannot be blamed entirely). This was compounded by acute shortages of raw materials created by the Civil War. Industrial output, particularly consumer goods, shrank in the Bolshevik-held central area. The shortage of goods led to soaring price inflation and the value of the rouble collapsed. Peasants would not supply food to the cities if there were no goods for which food could be exchanged and paper money was worthless. Moreover, the rich wheat areas of the Ukraine were outside Bolshevik control. So the food shortages got worse and as early as February 1918 the bread ration in Petrograd had reached an all-time low of only 50 grams per person per day. There were

THE PROBLEM OF FOOD SUPPLY

Getting food into the cities had been a problem since 1915 and had contributed significantly to the February and October Revolutions. For some time the peasants had been unco-operative. During 1917 they had been interested only in getting the land and once they had it they wanted to be left alone to farm it. Their main wish was to run their lives without outside interference. They were not really concerned about the problems of the cities, which had little to offer them in return for their grain. Added to this, large peasant households had split themselves into several smaller households to increase their claim for land and consequently the land had been divided up into small parcels. This encouraged a return to subsistence farming rather than production for the market. Yet Lenin had promised to give the workers 'bread' and this was a promise he could not afford to renege on.

SUMMARY OF KEY FEATURES OF WAR COMMUNISM

- Grain requisitioning
- Private trade banned
- State control of industry
- Single managers to replace workers' committees
- Passports to prevent workers leaving the towns
- Rationing

food riots in many cities in early 1918. Workers started to flee from the cities, leaving factories short of workers. The situation was desperate. Lenin was faced with two main problems:

- keeping the workers in the cities to produce munitions, essential war supplies and other desperately needed goods
- feeding the workers.

SOURCE 7.16 B. Williams, *The Russian Revolution 1917–21*, 1987, pp. 62–63

By the end of 1920 the proletariat, the class the revolution was all about, had shrunk to only half its pre-revolutionary size. Petrograd lost 60 per cent of its workforce by April 1918 and one million people had left the city by that June. In Russia as a whole the urban proletariat decreased from 3.6 million in January 1917 to 1.4 million two years later. Starving and unemployed workers left the towns to return to the villages, to join the Red Army, or to enter the ever-growing ranks of the bureaucracy. Hardest hit were the large state-owned metallurgical factories employing the very section of the working class which had provided the Bolsheviks with the core of their support in 1917. The Vyborg district of Petrograd saw its population fall from 69,000 to 5,000 by the summer of 1918.

It was not only economic problems that Lenin faced in the summer of 1918; he was also confronted by the full onslaught of the Civil War. From this point onwards, the Bolsheviks were fighting for their lives. As a result, the whole economy of the Red-held part of Russia was geared towards the needs of the army. The name given to the policies Lenin adopted from 1918 to 1921 is War Communism.

The main features of War Communism

Grain requisitioning
The Bolsheviks had been sending units of Red guards and soldiers out into the countryside to find grain for the hard-pressed cities. In May 1918 a Food-Supplies Dictatorship was set up to establish the forcible requisitioning of grain as the standard policy. Unsurprisingly, the peasants resisted bitterly.

Banning of private trade
All private trade and manufacture were banned. However, the state trading organisation was extremely chaotic and industry was simply not producing enough consumer goods. So an enormous black market developed, without which most people could not have survived.

Nationalisation of industry
All industry was brought under state control and administered by the Supreme Council of National Economy (Vesenkha). Workers' committees were replaced by single managers reporting to central authorities. These were often the old bourgeois managers now called 'specialists'. This was the only way to stop the chaos caused by the factory workers' committees who had voted themselves huge pay rises, intimidated management and stolen materials for illegal goods. Not all workers were against nationalisation: many, faced with the closure of their factory, urged that it be nationalised and kept open. They were desperate to keep their jobs.

Labour discipline
Discipline was brought back to the work place. There were fines for lateness and absenteeism. Internal passports were introduced to stop people fleeing to the countryside. Piece-work rates were brought back, along with bonuses and a work book that was needed to get rations.

Rationing
A class-based system of rationing was introduced. The labour force was given priority along with Red Army soldiers. Smaller rations were given to civil servants and professional people such as doctors. The smallest rations, barely enough to live on, were given to the *burzhui* or middle classes – or as they were now called, 'the former people'.

THE ASSASSINATION ATTEMPT ON LENIN AND THE BEGINNING OF THE LENIN CULT

After addressing a meeting of workers on 30 August, Lenin was shot in the neck and badly wounded. The culprit arrested on the spot was Fanya Kaplan, an ex-anarchist turned Socialist Revolutionary. She claimed that she was protesting about the signing of the Treaty of Brest-Litovsk. The Lenin cult began at this time. Eulogies appeared in the Bolshevik press giving him Christ-like qualities, unafraid to sacrifice his life for the revolution. Zinoviev made a long address of which 200,000 copies were published. Portraits and posters of him appeared in the streets (none had been produced up to this time) in a deliberate effort to promote his god-like leadership qualities. (See Chapter 9 for more about the Lenin cult.)

The Red Terror

Another crucial component of War Communism was the systematic use of terror to back up the new measures and deal with opposition. The Bolsheviks faced increased opposition inside the cities from:

- workers who were angry at their economic plight, low food rations and state violence. There were calls for new Soviet elections, a free press, the restoration of the Constituent Assembly and the overthrow of the Sovnarkom (only six months after the revolution). Signs appeared on city walls saying: 'Down with Lenin and horsemeat! Give us the Tsar and pork!'
- anarchists who rejected the authoritarian control of the government
- left-wing Socialist Revolutionaries who were protesting about the Treaty of Brest-Litovsk. They turned to terrorism, shooting the German ambassador in July 1918 to try to wreck the Russian relationship with the Germans. They captured Dzerzhinsky, the head of the Cheka, in May and managed to shoot Lenin in August 1918. Two other Bolshevik Party leaders were murdered. They put the regime under real pressure.

The assassination attempt on Lenin prompted the Cheka to launch the Red Terror in the summer of 1918, but this was simply an intensification of what was already happening. From June onwards, Socialist Revolutionaries had been arrested in large numbers, along with anarchists and members of other extreme left groups. Mensheviks and Socialist Revolutionaries were excluded from taking part in soviets. Many Kadets were already in prison, others had fled to the south.

The execution of the Tsar and his family

One of the most significant victims in this period was the Tsar. Nicholas, along with his family and servants, was shot on 17 July 1918 in Ekaterinburg in the Urals. Lenin and Sverdlov (Party Secretary 1918–19) claimed that it had been carried out by the local soviet against their wishes, but the weight of evidence now suggests that the order came from the centre. Lenin did not wish to antagonise the Germans at this point so he probably wanted to suggest that it was nothing to do with him. Alexandra, the Tsar's wife, was German and, of course, the Tsar was a blood relation to the other monarchs in Europe – for example, he was cousin to the German Kaiser. The stories about the possible survival of some of the Tsar's children may have been allowed to flourish for similar reasons: the Bolshevik leaders did not wish to accept responsibility in the international community for this horrific act. The truth must have been known to them: that the whole family had been shot and their bodies, having been drenched in acid, had been thrown into a disused mine shaft and later buried.

The Terror intensifies

When the Red Terror got underway, the change was one of scale and intensity. Execution, previously the exception, now became the rule. Prisoners in many cities were shot out of hand. Official records put the figure for deaths at the hands of the Cheka for the years 1918–20 at nearly 13,000, but estimates put the real figure at nearer 300,000. The Cheka fanned the flames of class warfare, as some Bolsheviks talked of wiping out the middle class completely. But the real purpose of the Terror was to terrify all hostile social groups. Its victims included large numbers of workers and peasants as well as princes and priests, prostitutes, judges, merchants, traders, even children (who made up five per cent of the population of Moscow prisons in 1920) – all guilty of 'bourgeois provocation' or counter-revolution. The problem was that no one was really sure who the counter-revolutionaries were.

THE CHEKA

The Cheka grew rapidly after occupying its new premises in the infamous Lubianka in Moscow at the end of March 1918. By June it had a thousand members and by September most provinces and districts had a Cheka branch. It worked outside of the law or justice system, reporting directly to Lenin and the politburo. As one of its founder members put it: 'The Cheka is not an investigating committee, a court or a tribunal. It is a fighting organ on the internal front of the Civil War ... It does not judge, it strikes.'

SOURCE 7.17   The Lubianka in Moscow, the headquarters of the Cheka. There was a prison inside the building

Felix Dzerzhinsky

The head of the Cheka was Felix Dzerzhinsky, a Pole from Lithuania. As a boy he had wanted to be a Jesuit priest and may have brought some of the Jesuit religious fanaticism into his political life. For he was a fanatic, and just the person Lenin needed to head up the Cheka. He was incorruptible and merciless. Having spent a great deal of his adult life in tsarist prisons, he knew a lot about how they worked and possessed the zeal to deal with the class that had put him there. He commented to the Sovnarkom: 'Do not think I seek forms of revolutionary justice; we are not in need of justice. It is war now – face to face, a fight to the finish. Life or death!'

In the cities, Cheka arrests had a terrifyingly random character (see Source 7.18). People were arrested for being near scenes of 'bourgeois provocation' or because they were acquaintances of suspects. Many were denounced as counter-revolutionaries following arguments or as a result of vendettas. In the provinces it was possibly worse, since local Cheka bosses controlled their own patch and acted as petty tyrants with no court of appeal. Some were very dubious characters who used their position to pursue long-term vendettas against sections of the local community. There was little central control.

The Cheka was particularly active in the countryside, helping requisitioning brigades to collect grain from the peasants. Quotas were filled even if this left peasants starving. It was little better than theft and some of the brigades were little more than bandits, taking much more than food. The peasants resisted in a wave of uprisings and attacked the collectors. Bolshevik party officials were murdered. One Cheka man was found with his stomach slit open and stuffed with grain as a lesson to others. In another village, the twelve members of a brigade were decapitated and their heads were put on poles.

The Cheka and Red Army units gave no quarter. They were supported by Lenin: in a telegram to Bolshevik leaders in Penza he wrote, 'Hang no fewer than a hundred well-known kulaks [richer peasants], rich-bags and blood-suckers and make sure the hanging takes place in full view of the people.' He tried to encourage the poorer peasants to attack the kulaks but he failed to ignite class warfare in the villages. Thousands of peasants were arrested. In retaliation, the peasants hid their grain and stopped planting for the next season. Wheat harvests went into serious decline. It would not be unfair to say that the Bolsheviks were at war with the peasants.

To house all these dissident workers, troublesome peasants and bourgeois saboteurs, the Bolsheviks set up concentration and labour camps. The machinery of terror and the police state were created under Lenin, not Stalin. It is almost certain that hundreds of thousands perished, although no accurate figures are available from a time when there was so much dislocation and disorder, and proper records were not kept or were lost.

■ **Learning trouble spot**

Were the Bolsheviks in control?

It may be assumed that because the Bolsheviks used terror ruthlessly they were firmly in control of the internal situation in the cities, especially Moscow and Petrograd. But this was far from the case. According to Robert Service, evidence from the Russian archives has confirmed that the situation between 1918 and 1920 was extremely chaotic and that Bolshevik control was limited. When Lenin was shot, his minders had to make sure that he had a Bolshevik doctor, fearing that any other doctor might be happy to see him perish. Bolshevik officials were in great danger of being shot by enemies. Lenin rarely ventured out on to the streets. A story is told that on one occasion his car was stopped, he was robbed by a gang (who did not recognise him) and marooned in a dangerous area of Moscow; when he went to a local party headquarters he was not allowed in because the doorman did not recognise him either. ('The consolidation of the Bolshevik State', R. Service, unpublished lecture, London, January 1999.)

SOURCE 7.18 O. Figes, *A People's Tragedy: The Russian Revolution 1891–1924*, 1997, pp. 643–44

Peshekhonov, Kerensky's Minister of Food, who was imprisoned in the Lubianka jail, recalls a conversation with a fellow prisoner, a trade unionist from Vladimir, who could not work out why he had been arrested. All he had done was to come to Moscow and check into a hotel. 'What is your name?' another prisoner asked. 'Smirnov,' he replied, one of the most common Russian names.

'The name, then, was the cause of your arrest,' said a man coming towards us. 'Let me introduce myself. My name too is Smirnov, and I am from Kaluga. At the Tagana there were seven of us Smirnovs ... they somehow managed to find out that a certain Smirnov, a Bolshevik from Kazan, had disappeared with a large sum of money. Moscow was notified and orders were issued to the militia to arrest all Smirnovs arriving in Moscow and send them to the Cheka. They are trying to catch the Smirnov from Kazan.'

'But I have never been to Kazan,' protested the Vladimir Smirnov. 'Neither have I,' replied the one from Kaluga. 'I am not even a Bolshevik, nor do I intend to become one. But here I am.'

Was War Communism just a reaction to the Civil War and the economic crisis?

It is clear that the Bolsheviks adopted more centralised systems of control to run the economy in order to carry on the war. They had to make sure the army was supplied: they needed the factories to produce munitions and other goods and they needed food to feed the workers. But War Communism was not just a reaction to these pressures. For Lenin, it was an extension of class warfare and no different from the waging of the Civil War against external enemies. In fact, the Bolsheviks called it the 'internal front'. Lenin wanted to squeeze out the counter-revolutionary forces whether they came from the left or the right – 'those not being with us are against us'. It was a way of wiping out old bourgeois attitudes and any lingering bourgeois power. Terror was an essential component of this.

Lenin was supported by other Bolsheviks. They hated the market system and were not unhappy to see it collapse in 1918. They thought centralised control was the way to develop socialism. They had always wanted the nationalisation of industry and state control. Their attachment to War Communism is shown by their reluctance to abandon it when the Civil War ended. Trotsky wanted to see the 'militarisation of labour', in which the discipline and practices of the army would be taken into civilian life to build the new socialist state. At the end of the Civil War, he wanted units of soldiers to be drafted into the factories and fields to work under military discipline.

1 What was life like in Bolshevik cities under War Communism?

Life in Russia between 1918 and 1921 was a matter of survival. Less than a third of the urban diet came from state-provided rations; the rest came from the black market. 'Bag-men' travelled between villages and cities selling their produce. The urban workers eked out their rations by selling or exchanging handmade or stolen goods for food. Many travelled into the countryside with goods to barter for food. This became known as 'cigarette lighterism' since cigarette lighters featured in the products they made, along with shoe soles made from conveyor belts, penknives, nails and ploughs made from iron bars. This movement of people created chaos in factories in 1918 because at any one time a high percentage of workers might be absent. The railway system was choked with bag-men moving between cities.

The Bolsheviks did try to stamp out the free market under War Communism, but it was futile. The Cheka raided trains to stop bag-men travelling, and they raided markets where the goods were sold. But they could not be everywhere and it was always easy to bribe officials. Anyway, the Bolsheviks had little choice but to tolerate the black market or see the cities starve. Everybody hunted for food as prices rocketed. Horses disappeared from the streets only to reappear as 'Civil War sausage'. Wages in 1919 were reckoned to be at two per cent of their 1913 level and on average an urban worker spent three-quarters of his income on food. Fuel for heating was also critically short. In the freezing winter of 1919–20, some 3000 wooden houses in Petrograd were stripped to provide fuel. Trees disappeared. Sanitary conditions were appalling and water had to be collected from pumps in the streets.

The middle classes were in a worse position than the workers. They were the class enemy and were not allowed to work, although some were drafted back as managers in the nationalised industries or to work in the civil service. Most survived by selling clothes and jewellery, in fact anything they owned, for bread. One study in the 1920s found that 42 per cent of prostitutes in Moscow were from bourgeois families. Emma Goldman found young girls 'selling themselves for a loaf of bread or a piece of soap or chocolate' (*My Disillusionment in Russia*, 1923, page 11). Members of the nobility fared no better: Princess Golitsyn sold homemade pies, Countess Witte cakes and pies. For the 'former people' life was arduous, queuing up with the poor for food and fuel.

SOURCE 7.19 Middle-class women selling items on the street in order to survive

EMIGRATION

By the end of the Civil War, many of the 'former people' had fled abroad. Two to three million emigrated in the first years after the revolution. Groups of Russians arrived in countries throughout the world. Many *émigrés* settled in Germany, France and other Western European countries while sizeable communities developed in the USA and Australia. Berlin was the *émigré* capital at first. Then they moved on to Paris where Tsar Cyril I was acclaimed by *émigré* monarchists. Restaurants and hotels were staffed by the old *burzhui* and there were thousands of Russian taxi drivers in Paris in the 1930s.

Soviet Russia lost a great deal of mercantile and managerial talent, along with scholars, scientists and other skilled groups. Much of the top educational élite fled, many becoming prominent in Western universities and industry, such as Sikorsky who developed the helicopter for the USA.

SOURCE 7.20 E. Goldman, *My Disillusionment in Russia*, 1923, pp. 8–9. Goldman is writing about the Petrograd she found on returning there in January 1920. She had lived there as a teenager in the 1880s but had gone to live in the USA. She was an anarchist with sympathies towards the Communist revolution

It was almost in ruins, as if a hurricane had swept over it ... The streets were dirty and deserted; all life had gone from them ... The people walked about like living corpses; the shortage of food and fuel was slowly sapping the city; grim death was clutching at its heart. Emaciated and frost-bitten men, women and children were being whipped by a common lash, the search for a piece of bread or a stick of wood. It was a heart-rending sight by day, an oppressive weight by night. It fairly haunted me, this oppressive silence broken only by the occasional shots.

The workers at least benefited from the social revolution insofar as the palaces and town houses of the rich were taken over and the living space divided up amongst poor families. One owner of a palace ended up living in his former bathroom. The houses were run by building committees, often under the control of former domestic servants who relished the opportunity to turn the tables on their former masters. There was a popular mood to humiliate the old bourgeoisie. City soviets rounded up army officers, civil servants, aristocrats, stockbrokers and other formerly wealthy people and made them clear rubbish or snow from the streets, much to the amusement of workers and soldiers passing by.

The workers were not so happy about the corruption that surrounded the Bolshevik Party. Many areas were run by local mafias of Bolshevik officials who lived well whilst others starved. It came from the top. Five thousand Bolsheviks and their families lived in the Kremlin and best hotels in Moscow with access to saunas, a hospital and three vast restaurants with cooks trained in France. In Petrograd, Zinoviev, the party boss of the city, lived at the Astoria Hotel, coming and going with his Cheka bodyguards and a string of prostitutes. The hotel, where many Bolsheviks lived, retained its old waiters, now 'comrade waiters', who served champagne and caviar in room service. Bribery and corruption was rife throughout the party. Almost anything could be had from corrupt Bolshevik officials: foodstuffs, tobacco, alcohol, fuel. The wives and mistresses of party bosses went around 'with a jeweller's shop window hanging round their necks'.

SOURCE 7.21 A. Ransome, *Six Weeks in Russia in 1919*, 1919, p. 19. Arthur Ransome was a British journalist who later went on to write the famous children's book *Swallows and Amazons*

Rooms are distributed on much the same plan as clothes. Housing is considered a State monopoly, and a general census of housing accommodation has been taken. In every district there are housing committees to whom everybody wanting rooms applies. They work on the rough and ready theory that until every man has one room no one has a right to two ... This plan has, of course, proved very hard on house-owners, and in some cases the new tenants have made a horrible mess of the houses, as might indeed have been expected, seeing that they had previously been of those who had suffered directly from the decivilizing influences of overcrowding.

SOURCE 7.22 L. de Robien, *The Diary of a Diplomat in Russia 1917–18*, 1969. De Robien was a French diplomat used to moving in court circles

Friday 8 February 1918
We are living in a madhouse, and in the last few days there have been an avalanche of decrees. First comes a decree cancelling all banking transactions, then comes another one confiscating houses. I have made no mention of taxes which continue to hit people from whom all source of income has been removed: 500 roubles for a servant, 500 roubles for a bathroom, 600 roubles for a dog and as much for a piano. All inhabitants under the age of 50 are forced to join the 'personal labour corps'. Princess Obolensky has been ordered to go and clear the snow off the Fontanka Quay. Others have to sweep the tramlines at night.

TALKING POINT

Why do you think Lenin's use of class warfare played so well with the workers and soldiers in Russian cities? Do you think the attitudes displayed by the workers and others towards the old bourgeoisie were reasonable and understandable?

ACTIVITY

1 What aspects of the experience of War Communism are revealed in Sources 7.20–7.22?
2 How reliable do you think these sources are? Consider the writers and their backgrounds. Do their backgrounds make them less or more reliable?

ACTIVITY

Either

1 a) Choose a small group (four or five students) to be Communist Party activists. This group prepares a speech which justifies the policies of War Communism. You could mention:

- the economic situation
- the needs of the military in order to conduct the Civil War
- the longer-term objectives of the Communist state and the workers' state that will develop
- why it is important to use terror to deal with the bourgeoisie, to 'loot the looters'
- why grain requisitioning is necessary
- why it is necessary to have central control of the economy
- the problems caused by the workers' committees.

b) The rest of the class are workers. In groups of three or four, list your complaints about the actions of the Communist (Bolshevik) Party since the October Revolution and the economic situation you find yourself in during 1920. You support the revolution but not necessarily the Bolsheviks. Explain how you expect to see things change now that the Civil War is coming to an end.

c) One or two members of the Communist group should present the speech. Workers from different groups should then make their points and a debate/argument can take place in role.

Or

2 a) Explain how the Communists would have justified War Communism and the use of terror.

b) Describe how workers fared under War Communism and their attitudes towards the Bolshevik government.

KEY POINTS FROM CHAPTER 7

How did the Bolsheviks win the Civil War?

1 The Civil War was very complex with many forces operating over a large territory. It was a very confusing period during which the sides were not clearly defined.

2 White forces made substantial gains in late 1918 and up to the autumn of 1919, putting the Bolsheviks in a crisis situation. By October 1919 the Bolsheviks had turned the tide, picking off White armies one by one, and thereafter pushed the Whites back until their final defeat at the end of 1920.

3 The Reds were in a better position geographically, and had better organisation, better communications and a clear line of command. However, the Red Army had problems, particularly the high desertion rate.

4 Trotsky made a significant individual contribution to winning the war by his organisational abilities (transforming the Red Army), his energy and his personal bravery.

5 The Whites lacked good leadership, unity and co-ordination between armies during campaigns. They were riven by internal divisions and squabbles.

6 The Whites lacked support from the peasants and national minorities because of their reactionary policies.

7 Lenin adopted War Communism to meet the needs of the army and to conduct a civil war on the 'internal front'.

8 Terror was an essential component of this internal civil war to defeat counter-revolution.

9 Communists saw War Communism as the route to socialism.

10 Most people's experience of War Communism was that it was a terrible time of privation and chaos.

How was the Bolshevik state consolidated between 1921 and 1924?

CHAPTER OVERVIEW

In 1921, Lenin and the Bolsheviks were on the edge of disaster. With the Civil War over, workers and peasants expected to see an improvement in their standard of living and an end to wartime policies. However, by the spring of 1921 economic conditions had deteriorated and there was open revolt against the Bolshevik government. Lenin was forced into making economic concessions in his New Economic Policy (NEP) to ensure the survival of the regime. The economy recovered and the Bolsheviks were reprieved. The NEP was accompanied by political repression and a strengthening of the centralised one-party state. By the time of Lenin's death in 1924, Bolshevik power had been consolidated and the foundations of the future Communist regime put in place.

A Why were the Bolsheviks in trouble in 1921? (pp. 149–153)

B How successful was the New Economic Policy? (pp. 154–159)

C How did the centralised state develop in Russia between 1918 and 1924? (pp. 160–166)

A Why were the Bolsheviks in trouble in 1921?

ACTIVITY

Why was 1921 a year of crisis for the Bolsheviks?

1 Use Sources 8.1–8.6 to identify and explain the difficulties in which the Bolsheviks found themselves in 1921.

2 Look at Source 8.2 carefully. Then draw a line graph showing what was happening in Petrograd between 1914 and 1920. You will need three different scales (for population, births and deaths).

3 **a)** What were the Kronstadt sailors calling for in Source 8.9 (p.152)?

   b) At what other time in the last ten years might the sailors have been making similar demands?

   c) Why was the Kronstadt rising so significant?

4 If you had to choose the most serious problem facing Lenin, which would it be and how would you deal with it?

SOURCE 8.1   Victims of the famine of 1921. This famine may have killed as many as five million people. It was partly caused by a drought in southern Russia which led to crop failures. But it was also caused by the Bolshevik requisitioning programme which had depleted the peasants' reserve stocks of grain and persuaded large numbers of peasants not to plant so much. The net result was one of the worst famines of the twentieth century. It was so bad that it attracted international aid, particularly from the USA. In some areas, there were reports of cannibalism

150

HOW WAS THE BOLSHEVIK STATE CONSOLIDATED BETWEEN 1921 AND 1924?

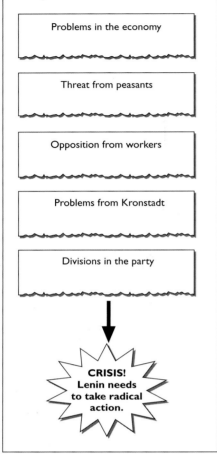

FOCUS ROUTE

Use a copy of the chart below to summarise the key reasons why Lenin had to make a radical change of policy in March 1921. Fill in the details under the headings in each box.

Problems in the economy

Threat from peasants

Opposition from workers

Problems from Kronstadt

Divisions in the party

CRISIS! Lenin needs to take radical action.

SOURCE 8.2 The population of Petrograd 1914–20, from L. A. and L. M. Vasilievski, *Kniga o golode*, 1922, pp. 64–65

Year	City population in millions	Births per thousand of population	Deaths per thousand of population
1914	2.2	25	21
1917	2.5	18	25
1918	1.5	15	44
1919	0.8	15.5	81.5
1920	0.6	12	uncertain – between 90 and 100

SOURCE 8.3 C. Read, *From Tsar to Soviets: The Russian People and their Revolution 1917–21*, 1996, p. 192

There is no word of strong enough force to use when one comes to the situation in Russia in those years. Total industrial output fell to around 20 per cent of pre-war levels ... Total output of finished products in 1921 was 16 per cent of 1912 levels. For unfinished products it was 12 per cent. Production in key sectors was down to around 29 per cent in mining; 36 per cent in oil; less than 10 per cent in the metal industries; 7 per cent in cotton textiles; 34 per cent in wool. Transport [mainly rail and river] also collapsed to about 20 per cent of the pre-war level. Agricultural production was more robust but it became centred on the subsistence of the producers. Surpluses became smaller and smaller. The grain harvest in 1921 was only 48 per cent of the 1913 figure.

SOURCE 8.4 S. Fitzpatrick, *The Russian Revolution 1917–1932*, 1994, p. 86

The worst blow to the new regime came in March 1921 when, after an outbreak of workers' strikes in Petrograd, the sailors at the nearby Kronstadt naval base rebelled. The Kronstadters, heroes of the July Days and supporters of the Bolsheviks in the October Revolution, had become almost legendary figures in Bolshevik mythology. Now they were repudiating the Bolsheviks' revolution, denouncing 'the arbitrary rule of the commissars' and calling for a true soviet republic of workers and peasants.

SOURCE 8.5 C. Read, *From Tsar to Soviets: The Russian People and their Revolution 1917–21*, 1996, p. 266, describing the Tambov rebellion

According to Cheka sources there were 118 separate risings throughout Soviet Russia in February 1921 ... But the best known and most widespread was the Tambov uprising [which] ... began in August 1920 and lasted until June 1921 ... At the height of the rebellion, large parts of the countryside of three [districts] of Tambov province were no-go areas for Soviet power and there were patches of rebellion elsewhere in the province.

SOURCE 8.6 O. Figes, *A People's Tragedy: The Russian Revolution 1891–1924*, 1997, p. 758

By March 1921 Soviet power in the countryside had virtually ceased to exist. Provincial Bolshevik organisations sent desperate telegrams to Moscow claiming they were powerless to resist the rebels and calling for immediate reinforcements. The consignment of grain to the cities had been brought to a virtual halt within the rebel strongholds. As the urban food crisis deepened and more and more workers went on strike, it became clear that the Bolsheviks were facing a revolutionary situation. Lenin was thrown into panic ... 'We are barely holding on,' he acknowledged in March. The peasant wars, he told the Tenth Party Congress on 8 March, were 'far more dangerous than all the Denikins, Yudeniches and Kolchaks put together'.

151

HOW WAS THE BOLSHEVIK STATE CONSOLIDATED BETWEEN 1921 AND 1924?

By 1921, the Soviet economy was in ruins. The transport system was on the point of total collapse. Factories could not get the materials they needed and most industrial enterprises had ceased production (see the figures in Source 8.3). Grain production had fallen to disastrously low levels. Famine was rampant in the south and hungry people walked the streets of the northern cities. Hundreds of thousands died from disease – typhus, cholera, dysentery and the influenza epidemic which raged across northern Europe. In these circumstances, large sections of Russian society were not willing to put up with the continuation of wartime policies.

The main threat to the Communist government came from the peasantry. Now that the Civil War was over and there was no possibility of a White victory, the hostility of the peasants to grain requisitioning (still continuing because no food was getting into the cities) erupted in a series of revolts which engulfed the countryside (see Source 8.5). The most serious revolt was in the Tambov region (1920–21) where for almost a year the Red Army was unable to deal with a peasant army led by Alexander Antonov. A poor harvest in 1920 had left peasants with almost no reserves of grain. When requisitioning brigades arrived to take what little they had, the peasants reacted violently. This story was repeated in other areas where the Bolsheviks had deliberately set the amount of grain to be procured at unreasonably high levels. The remnants of Green armies, supported by local peasant populations and deserters, proved tough nuts for the Red Army to crack and large areas of the countryside were in open revolt and outside of Moscow's control.

Nor was dissent restricted to the countryside. In the cities, the severe winter of 1920–21 brought repeated strikes. On 22 January 1921, the bread ration was cut by one-third in several cities, including Moscow and Petrograd. Food demonstrations had to be broken up by the Cheka and special troops because ordinary soldiers refused to fire on the crowds. The situation was not so very different from that of February 1917. Party spokesmen were howled down at workers' meetings and hostile resolutions were passed. Urban workers were particularly angry about:

- the food shortages
- the militarised factories – 'worse than a tsarist prison camp' – where workers could be imprisoned or shot if production targets were not reached
- the way the state had hijacked their unions, making them no more than instruments to keep the workers under control.

There were calls for 'soviets without Communists' and there was a revival in support for other socialist parties. Martial law was imposed in Moscow and Petrograd.

The strikers in Petrograd were supported by the sailors at the nearby Kronstadt naval base who were in close contact with workers. In March 1921, they mutinied in the hope of starting a general revolt against the Bolsheviks. They demanded multi-party democracy and civil rights. As the sailors were the heroes of the 1917 revolution their revolt was a great shock to the regime. Nevertheless, the sailors were roundly condemned and Marshal Tukhachevsky was sent to deal with the dissidents, who fought tooth and nail to defend their base. The ringleaders were rounded up and shot without trial; thousands of others were sent to Solovetsky, the first big labour camp, on the White Sea.

The situation in the cities and the position of the workers also led to divisions in the party. A group called the Workers' Opposition grew up under Alexander Shlyapnikov and Alexandra Kollontai. They wanted the workers to be given more control of their own affairs and supported complaints about the reintroduction of single managers and the militaristic organisation of the workplace. In particular, they criticised Trotsky's plan to make the trade unions agencies of the state, even to the extent that union officials should be appointed by the state. The trade union debate caused furious arguments inside the party at the end of 1920.

Lenin realised that concessions to the peasants and some measure of economic liberalisation were essential for the regime to survive. Popular

■ **Learning trouble spot**

Who were the Kronstadt sailors?

The Bolsheviks (and some books) claimed that most of the Kronstadt sailors of 1917 (see pages 96–97) had been killed in the Civil War, so the men who mutinied in 1921 were not the same sailors who had fought for the revolution. However, the historian Israel Getzler has shown that in fact they were, by and large, the same men (*Kronstadt 1917–1921: The Fate of Soviet Democracy*, 1983, page 226). Kronstadt had always had a large number of Socialist Revolutionaries and anarchists and was not always as Bolshevik as has been claimed. Many of the sailors were ex-peasants who had connections with the countryside and supported the peasant revolts. They also knew that the Bolshevik propaganda about the strikers in Petrograd was a pack of lies.

152

HOW WAS THE BOLSHEVIK STATE CONSOLIDATED BETWEEN 1921 AND 1924?

discontent could no longer be suppressed. He said that the Kronstadt revolt was the 'flash that lit up reality more than anything else'. It was clear to him that the government could not continue with its policy of War Communism, despite the desire of many Bolsheviks to do so. Some, including Trotsky, wanted to intensify War Communism by drafting the Red Army into a militarised labour force to build socialism by coercion. Lenin's problem was how to carry the party along with him and prevent a massive rift from opening up that might destroy the party altogether.

SOURCE 8.7 The attack on Kronstadt. Red Army troops under Tukhachevsky attacked Kronstadt across the ice linking the base to the mainland. The Cheka were lined up behind them to make sure no one retreated. Ten thousand bodies littered the ice after the first assault. It was a very bitter battle lasting eighteen hours

SOURCE 8.8 Kronstadt sailors guarding the Tauride Palace on the single occasion when the Constituent Assembly met, on 5 January 1918

SOURCE 8.9 Extracts from the manifesto of the Kronstadt Revolt of March 1921

Having heard the report of the representatives of the crews sent by the general meeting of ships' crews to Petrograd to investigate the state of affairs there, we demand:

1 *that in view of the fact that the present Soviets do not express the will of the workers and peasants, new elections by secret ballot be held immediately, with free preliminary propaganda for all workers and peasants before the elections;*

2 *freedom of speech and press for workers and peasants, anarchists and left socialist parties;*

5 *the liberation of all political prisoners of socialist parties, as well as all workers and peasants, Red Army soldiers and sailors imprisoned in connection with the working class and peasant movements;*

7 *the ending of the right of Communists to be the only permitted socialist political party;*

11 *that the peasants be given the right and freedom of action to do as they please with all the land and also the right to have cattle which they themselves must maintain and manage, that is without the use of hired labour.*

153

HOW WAS THE BOLSHEVIK STATE CONSOLIDATED BETWEEN 1921 AND 1924?

SOURCE 8.10   Extracts from *Izvestia* (the Kronstadt rebels' newspaper) quoted by W. Bruce Lincoln, *Red Victory: A History of the Russian Civil War*, 1989, p. 511

'For three years, the toilers of Soviet Russia have groaned in the torture chambers of the Cheka. The peasant has been transformed into the lowest form of farm labourer and the worker has become a mere wage slave in the factories of the state. The toiling intelligentsia has come to naught ... It has become impossible to breathe,' the Kronstadt rebels concluded. *'All of Soviet Russia has been turned into an all-Russian penal colony.'*

SOURCE 8.11   A group of soldiers who have just helped to put down the Kronstadt rising in March 1921. Lenin and Trotsky are in the centre of the group

SOURCE 8.12   *History of the All-Union Communist Party (Short Course)*, Moscow, 1938

Two circumstances facilitated the outbreak of the Kronstadt mutiny: the deterioration in the composition of the ships' crews, and the weakness of the Bolshevik organisation in Kronstadt. Nearly all the old sailors who had taken part in the October Revolution were at the front, heroically fighting in the ranks of the Red Army. The naval replenishments consisted of new men, who had not been schooled in the revolution. These were a perfectly raw peasant mass who gave expression to the peasantry's discontent with the surplus-appropriation system. As for the Bolshevik organisation in Kronstadt, it had been greatly weakened by a series of mobilizations for the front. This enabled the Socialist Revolutionaries, Mensheviks and White Guards to worm their way into Kronstadt and to seize control of it.

SOURCE 8.13   C. Read, *From Tsar to Soviets: The Russian People and their Revolution 1917–21*, 1996, p. 277. Read is using I. Getzler, *Kronstadt 1917–1921: The Fate of Soviet Democracy*, 1983, pp. 207–8

Getzler has convincingly argued for continuity of personnel at all levels. Data relating to the crews of Petropavlovsk and the Sevastopol show that of 2,028 sailors whose year of enlistment is known, 1,904 [93.9%] were recruited into the navy before the 1917 revolution. Only 137 [6.8%] had been recruited in the years 1918–21. According to Getzler, at least 75.5% of Baltic fleet sailors serving on 1st January 1921 were likely to have been drafted before 1918. 80% of them were Russian, 10% Ukrainian and only 9% from the Baltic States including Russian Poland and Finland. The majority of the Revolutionary Committee spearheading the revolt had also been participants in the 1917 revolution.

SOURCE 8.14   C. Read, *From Tsar to Soviets: The Russian People and their Revolution 1917–21*, 1996, p. 277

In his most famous comment Lenin said of Kronstadt, 'This was the flash which lit up reality better than anything else.' The tragic reality it lit up was that Bolshevism was not interested in listening to the political arguments of the ordinary people of Russia and had, irony of ironies, become the executioner of genuine soviet democracy. While much of the country had hoped for better once the civil war had ended, the Bolsheviks gave unconditional notice that they would continue to maintain political control on no other terms than their own.

154

HOW WAS THE BOLSHEVIK STATE CONSOLIDATED BETWEEN 1921 AND 1924?

B How successful was the New Economic Policy?

FOCUS ROUTE

1 What similarities and differences were there between War Communism and the New Economic Policy? Compare the two by completing a table like the one shown below as you work through this section.

	War Communism	New Economic Policy
Procuring grain from the peasants		
Private trading		
Rationing		
Small-scale industry		
Large-scale industry		
Transport and banking		

2 Develop a mnemonic so that you can learn the main features of the New Economic Policy for an exam, for example, ROTCOM (**R**equisitioning stopped. **O**wnership of small businesses allowed. **T**rade ban lifted. **COM**manding heights of industry with state).

In March 1921, faced with economic collapse and widespread rebellion, Lenin felt compelled to make a radical turnaround in economic policy, making significant concessions to private enterprise. This turnaround is called the New Economic Policy (NEP).

■ 8A Key features of the New Economic Policy

Grain requisitioning abolished
Grain requisitioning was replaced by a 'tax in kind'. Peasants had to give a fixed proportion of their grain to the state, but the amount that they had to hand over was much less than the amounts taken by requisitioning. They could sell any surpluses on the open market.

Small businesses reopened
Small-scale businesses under private ownership were allowed to reopen and make a profit. This included businesses like small workshops and factories that made goods such as shoes, nails and clothes. Lenin realised that peasants would not sell their produce unless there were goods that they wanted on sale.

Ban on private trade removed
The removal of the ban on private trade meant that food and goods could flow more easily between the countryside and the towns. Privately owned shops were reopened. Rationing was abolished and people had to buy food and goods from their own income. The money economy was back!

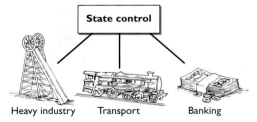

State control of heavy industry
The state kept control of large-scale heavy industries like coal, steel and oil. It also retained control of transport and the banking system. Industry was organised into trusts that had to buy materials and pay their workers from their own budgets. If they failed to manage their budgets efficiently, they could not expect the state to bail them out.

The details of the NEP were worked out among members of the Politburo (see page 160) and presented to the party with the full support of the heavy hitters. Zinoviev put the main Politburo line: 'I ask you, comrades, to be clear that the New Economic Policy is only a temporary deviation, a tactical retreat.' Bukharin rammed home the point: 'We are making economic concessions to avoid political concessions.' Lenin compared it to Brest-Litovsk, something that had to be done but which would not last for ever. This turnaround was hard for Lenin to justify: some party members considered the NEP to be a betrayal of the principles of the October Revolution. At the Tenth Party Congress in 1921, there was fierce debate. What finally persuaded the doubters was the Kronstadt revolt. They realised that splits in the party could result in their losing power altogether. There was a genuine desire for unity and they were prepared to fall in behind Lenin – as long as the NEP was a 'temporary' measure.

Economic recovery

By 1922, the results of the NEP were better than anyone expected. There was food in the markets in the cities and brisk trade in other goods. Shops, cafés and restaurants reopened and life began to flow back into the cities. By 1923, cereal production had increased by 23 per cent compared with 1920. Industrial production also made a rapid recovery as small-scale enterprises responded quickly to surging demand. From 1920 to 1923, factory output rose by almost 200 per cent, admittedly from a very low base. When there were profits to be made, it was amazing how quickly distribution systems began to operate, albeit in a haphazard and disorganised way. Larger-scale industry took longer to revive but the recovery was well underway by 1924.

One of the chief agents in the revival was the appearance of the private traders, or 'Nepmen' as they came to be called. They scoured the villages buying up produce – grain, meat, eggs, vegetables – to take into the markets in the cities. They travelled round the workshops picking up nails, shoes, clothes and hand tools to sell in the markets and to the peasants. Stalls turned into premises and then into much larger shops. By 1923, Nepmen handled as much as three-quarters of the retail trade.

The first three or four years of the NEP were the heyday of the Nepmen. Deals were made, corruption was rife and the rewards were high. Property speculators were back. You could get anything from officials if the bribe was big enough. This was a get-rich-quick society and the Nepmen, a much coarser breed than the old bourgeoisie, displayed their wealth conspicuously. They

SOURCE 8.15 A Moscow street market, packed with stalls and shoppers after the legalisation of private trading under the NEP

WHAT DID URBAN WORKERS THINK ABOUT THE NEP?

Urban workers were less happy than the peasants. In the first two years of the NEP unemployment rose steeply, particularly in the large state-controlled trusts; they cut their workforce because they had to make a profit. Wages remained generally low and workers found little protection in the market place. It seemed to them that the peasants were doing well at their expense. They also objected to the power of the single managers and bourgeois specialists who had more privileges than them. Some workers called the NEP the 'New Exploitation of the Proletariat'.

crowded the restaurants, where dinners with French wine cost $25 a head, and then went on to gaming clubs or brothels. Prostitution and crime flourished. The Moscow municipal government got most of its income from taxes on gambling clubs. Walter Duranty (see Source 8.16) claimed that only two years after the beginning of the NEP there were over 25,000 private traders in Moscow.

Progress was not even and there were problems. By 1923, so much food was flooding into the cities that the prices started to drop whilst the price of industrial goods rose because they were still in short supply. Trotsky called this the 'scissors crisis' (see Source 8.17). This imbalance was problematic because it made the peasants reluctant to supply food. But the crisis did not last long: the government took action to bring industrial prices down and started to take the peasant tax in cash rather than in kind to encourage the peasants to sell their produce. Meanwhile, industry made steady progress, reaching the production levels of 1913 by 1926 (see Source 8.18).

The peasants did well out of NEP. After the famine, there was rapid recovery in the villages. A great deal of the trade was between villages, in produce and in hand-crafted goods. Peasants could also make money on the side in the cities or through the Nepmen. It seemed to them that they had won back their villages to something like the situation in late 1917 – they could farm their land without too much interference from the government. The local branches of the soviets were, on the whole, still weak in the countryside and traditional forms of organisation around the communes were still much stronger.

Many people inside and outside Soviet Russia thought that the NEP marked the end of the Communist experiment. They believed that Lenin's government had realised that centrally directed industry and food supply could not work and had returned to the capitalist fold. Foreign powers wanted to encourage this trend and started to make trade agreements, Germany in 1922 and Britain in 1924. The NEP's success in lifting the economy and taking the steam out of the peasant revolts was not in doubt, but the Communist experiment was merely on hold; it was far from over.

SOURCE 8.16 W. Duranty, *I Write As I Please*, 1935, pp. 138–50. Duranty was an American journalist who spent long periods in Soviet Russia and was in Moscow during the NEP period. Malcolm Muggeridge, the English writer and journalist, called Duranty 'the greatest liar in history' when he subsequently became an apologist for the Stalinist regime. But there is no reason to doubt that his observations of the NEP reflect what was happening in the early 1920s. These are extracts from the section on the NEP in his book

Moscow had changed during my three weeks' absence on the Volga. Everywhere dilapidated and half-ruined buildings were being refurbished and restored, and the fronts of the houses cleaned and painted. Shops, cafés and restaurants were being opened in all directions.... The city was full of peasants selling fruit, vegetables and other produce, or transporting bricks, lumber and building materials in their clumsy, creaking carts. Suddenly goods began to appear from unexpected corners, hidden or hoarded ...

To the Communists and to the small group of proletarian leaders who had benefited by the Military Communist period NEP was doubtless repugnant, but to the mass of workers it brought jobs that would henceforth be paid in money instead of valueless paper or mouldy rations. To the traders NEP meant opportunity and the dawn of better days. Until August 9th it was a crime ... to buy and sell anything. It is true that buying and selling was practised more or less overtly, even in the public markets, but the latter were continually raided to 'suppress speculation' and any owner of valuables might find himself denounced, arrested, and his property confiscated. The NEP decree changed all that....

Ill-informed foreigners like myself naturally saw first the superficial phases of NEP, its reckless gambling, its corruption and license; which were not all the truth but real enough ... The restaurant proprietor was a typical case of the

157

HOW WAS THE BOLSHEVIK STATE CONSOLIDATED BETWEEN 1921 AND 1924?

earlier NEP-man. He began to speculate in apartments and furniture and made a lot of quick money. At one time he had a fine eight-room apartment of his own, no less than three automobiles, two mistresses and a large amount of gold. [He was going to escape abroad] when he was arrested by the Gay – pay – oo [GPU secret police], which made short work of him. All his property was confiscated and he was sentenced to ten years' imprisonment on the lonely isle of Solovetsky in the White Sea.

Without going so far as to say that the authorities approved or encouraged NEP's excesses, there is no doubt that they deliberately 'took the lid off' in many respects. Gambling halls and night clubs had no difficulty in getting licenses on condition that part of the receipts were reserved for the State. It was estimated that the receipts of the Moscow Soviet from this source were 4,000,000 gold roubles in the year 1922, which was used for much-needed repairs to the streets, sidewalks, drainage and lighting systems.

One morning at the top of my street I saw a man sitting on the sidewalk selling flour, sugar and rice on a little table ... at the end of a week his 'table' had doubled in size and he was selling fresh eggs and vegetables. That was October and by mid-November he had rented a tiny store across the street, handling milk, vegetables, chickens and the freshest eggs and apples in Moscow ... By the following May he had four salesmen in a fair-sized store, to which peasants brought fresh produce each morning ... In July he added hardware. In October, after a year's trading he sold out ... to buy a farm and live independently for the rest of his life ...

His enterprise stimulated scores of peasants to fatten chickens and little pigs, or plant vegetables, or fashion wooden bowls and platters and forks and spoons and produce clay pots and the rest of the village handcraft. In a single year the supply of food and goods jumped from starvation point to something nearly adequate and prices fell accordingly. This was the rich silt in NEP's flood, whereas the gambling and debauchery were only froth and scum.

SOURCE 8.17   The movement of agricultural and industrial prices that produced the 'scissors crisis' of 1923

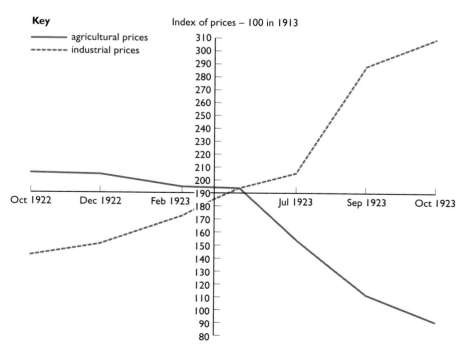

158

HOW WAS THE BOLSHEVIK STATE CONSOLIDATED BETWEEN 1921 AND 1924?

SOURCE 8.18 Agricultural and industrial production figures, 1913–26, taken from A. Nove, *An Economic History of the USSR, 1917–1991*, 1992, p. 89

	1913	1920	1921	1922	1923	1924	1925	1926
Grain harvest (million tons*)	80.1	46.1	37.6	50.3	56.6	51.4	72.5	76.8
Sown area (million ha.)	105.0	—	90.3	77.7	91.7	98.1	104.3	110.3
Industrial (factory) production (million roubles at 1926–27 values)	10,251	1,410	2,004	2,619	4,005	4,660	7,739	11,083
Coal (million tons)	29.0	8.7	8.9	9.5	13.7	16.1	18.1	27.6
Electricity (million kWhs)	1,945	—	520	775	1,146	1,562	2,925	3,508
Pig iron (thousand tons)	4,216	—	116	188	309	755	1,535	2,441
Steel (thousand tons)	4,231	—	183	392	709	1,140	2,135	3,141
Cotton fabrics (million metres)	2,582	—	105	349	691	963	1,688	2,286
Rail freight carried (million tons)	132.4	—	39.4	39.9	58.0	67.5	83.4	—

N.B. Tons (Imperial Measure) are used throughout. 1 ton = 1.016 tonnes (metric).

ACTIVITY

How successful was the NEP up to 1925?

1 Using Source 8.18 and the text, assemble figures to show the economic recovery up to 1925.
2 Why do you think the economy recovered so quickly after the introduction of NEP? (Refer to the text and Sources 8.15, 8.16 and 8.19.)
3 Describe the 'scissors crisis'.
4 What do you think Communists would find offensive about Nepmen and the NEP (see Source 8.16)?
5 Paragraphs form the building blocks of an essay. Usually a paragraph develops one clear point and provides supporting evidence or further explanation of that point.
  a) Write a paragraph on the economic successes of the NEP, using the evidence you have collected in your answers to questions 1 and 2 above.
  b) Write a second paragraph on the problems associated with the NEP, particularly for the workers and Communists.

SOURCE 8.19 A Soviet poster celebrating the electrification of Russia. Lenin saw electrification as a key factor in modernising Russia, bringing even the villages out of the dark ages, and the electrification programme expanded under the NEP. Lenin envisaged a network of power stations powering the large-scale industry that would build socialism. He said, 'Soviet power plus electrification equals Communism'

Did the liberalisation of the economy lead to political liberalisation?

The Bolsheviks had no intention of letting the limited capitalism of the NEP develop into a full-scale restoration of capitalism that might foster the emergence of a political system based on government by a number of political parties (pluralism). Political liberalisation was not on the cards. The NEP was a 'carrot' to buy off the peasants and workers economically, but it was accompanied by the 'stick' of political repression.

■ 8B Political repression during the period of the New Economic Policy

Attacks on political rivals

Political pressure on the rival socialist parties was intensified. The Mensheviks and Socialist Revolutionaries had become much more popular during the strikes and revolts and had played some part in encouraging them. The Bolsheviks used this as an excuse to arrest some 5000 Mensheviks in 1921 for counter-revolutionary activities. The Mensheviks and Socialist Revolutionaries were outlawed as political organisations.

Show trials

The show trial – a classic feature of the later Stalinist terror – made its appearance at the time of the NEP. The Communists rounded up a large number of Socialist Revolutionaries and held a show trial, during which former Socialist Revolutionaries who had collaborated with the secret police accused old colleagues of heinous crimes. Among the accusations was the claim that the Central Committee of the Socialist Revolutionaries had authorised assassination attempts on Lenin or had collaborated with Denikin. Many of those accused were already in jail when the alleged crimes had been committed. Nevertheless, 34 Socialist Revolutionary leaders were condemned as terrorists; eleven were executed.

Censorship

Censorship became more systematic. In the spring of 1922, dozens of outstanding Russian writers and scholars were deported to convince the intelligentsia that it was not a good idea to criticise the government.

In the same year, pre-publication censorship was introduced. Books, articles, poems and other writings had to be submitted to the Main Administration for Affairs of Literature and Publishing Houses (Glavlit) before they could be published.

Establishment of the GPU

The Cheka was renamed the GPU (Main Political Administration) in 1922.

The secret police actually grew in importance during the NEP. Arbitrary imprisonment and the death penalty continued to be applied after 1922 as an instrument of social policy.

The GPU periodically harassed and arrested Nepmen as speculators and class enemies in order to assure left Communists and the urban workers that they were keeping capitalistic tendencies under control.

Crushing of peasant revolts

The peasants who had staged revolts against the government were dealt with harshly.

The Tambov region, for instance, was swamped by Red Army troops in 1922. Whole rebel villages were destroyed in a brutal campaign.

Villages that supported the Reds were rewarded with salt – a vital commodity because it was needed for food preservation – and manufactured goods, and fed propaganda about the benefits that the NEP would bring them.

Attacks on the Church

The Communists also mounted a fierce attack on the Church, which they saw as a rival to their power and which was enjoying something of a revival at the beginning of the NEP.

Previously the war against the Church had mainly taken the form of propaganda, but in 1921 the Union of the Militant Godless was established to challenge the Church more directly.

In 1922, orders were sent out to strip churches of their precious items, ostensibly to help famine victims. When clergy and local people tried to protect their churches, there were violent clashes. Death penalties were handed out to leaders of the Russian Orthodox Church and thousands of priests were imprisoned.

FOCUS ROUTE

Before you read this section you might want to look back at Chapter 6, covering the setting up of the Bolshevik state. As you work through this section, make notes on:

a) the factors that led the Bolshevik state to become more centralised
b) how the Communist Party grew in importance at the expense of government bodies
c) how power became concentrated in the hands of the people at the top of the Communist Party.

■ 8C Politburo membership 1919–24

Name	Full member
V. I. Lenin	1919
L. B. Kamenev	1919
L. D. Trotsky	1919
J. V. Stalin	1919
N. N. Krestinsky	1919
G. A. Zinoviev	1921
A. Y. Rykov	1922
M. M. Tomsky	1922
N. I. Bukharin	1922

By 1924, Soviet Russia was governed by a centralised, one-party dictatorship which did not permit anyone to challenge its power. The party organisation dominated government institutions and the main decisions were taken by a Politburo which consisted of seven to nine senior party leaders. A large part of the economy – industry, banking, transport and foreign trade – was controlled by the government. How did this happen?

When the Bolsheviks came to power, they had no blueprint for government and almost no administrative experience. So they had to improvise a system to run the country. The urge to centralise control was clearly present from the beginning. The creation of the Sovnarkom, bypassing the Soviet (see pages 117–118), showed that the main decisions were going to be taken by the Bolshevik centre with little account taken of other political viewpoints. Nationalisation and state control were always part of their plan for the economy (despite having to give way to pressure for workers' control) and, as a step towards this, they had immediately nationalised banking.

However, it seems unlikely that Lenin would have moved so quickly towards a highly centralised state had it not been for the Civil War and the economic chaos in which the country found itself in 1918. Chart 8D (page 161) shows some of the main reasons for the growth of centralisation in this period.

The Bolshevik response to the desperate situation in 1918 was to centralise government control. The Sovnarkom accrued more and more power to itself to direct the course of the war and run the economy. But the centralising tendency did not stop there. Two other distinct trends were taking place during the Civil War:

- the Communist Party began to dominate government
- the Communist Party itself became more centralised, more bureaucratic and less democratic. Power was concentrated in the hands of a few people at the top.

How did the party come to dominate government bodies?

The Civil War saw the party organisation grow in importance at the expense of government bodies.

- In 1919, the Politburo was created, forming an inner ruling group of around seven people at the top of the Communist Party. The Politburo soon took precedence over the Sovnarkom as the key decision-making body. The Sovnarkom started to meet less frequently and was regarded as less important.
- At district and local level, the local Communist Party organisations took control of soviets across Russia (see the Learning trouble spot on page 162). Party officials ran the soviets and obeyed party orders above all else. So the soviets were now effectively subordinate to the party.
- From 1919 onwards, the Central Committee of the party began to appoint its own 'trusted' nominees to key positions in soviets (previously such positions had been filled by people elected by the members of the soviet). This was done to increase the centre's control over local party apparatus and local government.

There is a tendency, when talking about the growth of centralisation in the Bolshevik regime, to assume that the centre did have control of what was going on. But the Bolsheviks, as you know from the last chapter, were struggling to cope with the chaotic state of government during the Civil War. In Nizhniy-Novgorod, for example, everything was controlled by a local mafia of Bolsheviks and black marketeers who defied Moscow. So it is understandable that the regime should have used the party structure to gain more centralised control of government bodies and bring some sort of order out of the chaos.

Collapse of industry

The collapse in industrial output had become critical by the summer of 1918. It was essential to keep certain industries going to fight the Civil War, so the government nationalised industry and brought it under the control of the Supreme Economic Council (Vesenkha), which reported directly to the Sovnakom. Workers, desperate to keep their factories going and keep their jobs, literally begged the government to nationalise their workplaces. By the autumn of 1919, it was estimated that 80 per cent of all enterprises were part of a centrally directed economy.

Railways

The railway system – essential for the war effort and to maintain food supplies to cities – was collapsing, and the railway union was dominated by Mensheviks who could not be relied on. So transport, too, was taken under direct control.

INCREASING CENTRALISATION

Civil War

The very nature of the Civil War meant that there was little time to carry out consultation with the soviets and other bodies. Emergency decisions, by their very nature, needed to be taken quickly. So decision-making became more centralised.

Peasants

The peasants were obstinately unwilling to supply the cities with food. Since the market in food was not working, it became necessary to set up a food supplies directorate to organise the collection and distribution of food centrally.

■ Learning trouble spot

Pragmatism or ideology?

Left-wing historians tend to see the increasing tendency to centralisation as a practical response to the problems caused by the Civil War. Right-wing historians tend to see it as the result of Communist ideology, which entails central planning and state control. In their view, the Bolsheviks were a small minority who used terror and central control to impose their policies on an unwilling population.

It seems likely that centralisation was a mixture of ideology and pragmatism. The Bolsheviks considered centralised state control to be socialist and this justified War Communism. However, many of their actions were pragmatic responses to the problems the Civil War threw up. For example, they had to take control of the food supply and certain industries because they were collapsing. And at the end of the war, the Bolsheviks were prepared to adopt the pragmatic NEP instead of continuing with War Communism, which some, including Trotsky, believed was the correct ideological line to move towards socialism more quickly.

162

HOW WAS THE BOLSHEVIK STATE CONSOLIDATED BETWEEN 1921 AND 1924?

■ **Learning trouble spot**

Soviets and local Communist Parties

The relationship between the soviets and the Communist Party at local and district level can be confusing. After the revolution, the soviets took over the functions of local government. Many of the soviets were run by elected non-Bolshevik socialists. They often tried to remain independent of the central authorities and ignored instructions from Moscow. The Communists could not tolerate hostile or unco-operative soviets as they sought to marshal their resources to fight the Civil War. So they used ballot rigging or intimidation (in the form of the Cheka) to win soviet elections. They then installed a chairman and executive committee made up of Communists to run the soviet. The chairman of the soviet was often the chairman of the local Communist Party, too. Later on in the 1920s, people who were not Communist Party members were not even allowed to stand for election to the soviets.

■ **8E How did the Civil War make the party more centralised and less democratic?**

IMPACT OF CIVIL WAR, 1918–20

The membership had changed. Towards the end of 1919, the party was purged of undesirables. The new members recruited between 1920 and 1922 were mainly of peasant background. Few had any knowledge of Marx and some knew little about 1917. They had joined to improve their life chances. They were more prepared to do as they were told.

The party had lost its base in the proletarian workforce. Many of its earlier urban worker members had gone on to fight in the Civil War or join the party bureaucracy. By 1919, 39 per cent of party members were in the army and the majority of others were workers in offices, not factories.

Discussion and debate declined. In 1917 and in the months afterwards, the party had been characterised by passionate debate, disagreement and splits. But as the Civil War progressed, such debate declined as the need for unity grew.

The party became more centralised and hierarchical. The Politburo, with seven to nine members, took over the decision-making from the much larger and unwieldy Central Committee of around 40 members. Orders were passed out from the centre and party members were expected to carry them out.

The rank and file of the party generally accepted that the crisis caused by the Civil War and the state of the economy justified the increased centralisation and discipline in the party. A large proportion of party members had fought in the Red Army and a military discipline had been instilled in them. The Civil War became for them a heroic period during which they had been linked in camaraderie, and they were used to a pattern of command in which orders replaced consultation.

163

HOW WAS THE BOLSHEVIK STATE CONSOLIDATED BETWEEN 1921 AND 1924?

How did the party become more centralised and less democratic between 1921 and 1924?

This process of centralisation and bureaucratisation did not stop when the Civil War finished; it continued from 1921 to 1924. Two aspects of this are particularly significant.

The ban on factions 1921

The splits in the party during 1920 had angered Lenin. Groups like the Workers' Opposition and the Democratic Centralists (campaigning for more democracy in the party) seemed to him to be an unnecessary distraction given the crises they faced in 1921 (famine, revolts, Kronstadt mutiny). He called for unity and an end to splits and factionalism. As a result, in 1921, the Tenth Party Congress agreed to pass a 'ban on factions'. This meant that once party policy had been agreed by the Central Committee then everybody was expected to accept it and not form 'factions' to challenge the party line. The penalty for factionalism was expulsion from the party.

The *nomenklatura* system

This system was established from 1923 onwards. The Bolshevik leaders wanted to make sure that key personnel in public bodies were drawn from Bolsheviks or pro-Bolshevik workers. So a list of about 5500 designated party and governmental posts – the *nomenklatura* – was drawn up. The holders of these posts could only be appointed by the central party bodies. Overt loyalty counted for more than expertise; people who wanted promotion did what they were told. This tightened the one-party state internally. The people in the *nomenklatura* (key posts) became an elite.

By 1924, the net result of all these changes was a much more authoritarian and centralised Communist Party whose members, on the whole, were less likely to debate issues or challenge the leadership and more likely to carry out instructions through habits of discipline or the chance of promotion. Decision-making was concentrated in an increasingly small number of hands. The party had become more detached from its proletarian base and began to see the workers as 'uncultured' (Lenin) because they did not have the origins, experiences or education of the 1917 revolutionary proletariat. The party began to reinterpret its role: it saw itself as having the exclusive right to lead the people into the light of socialism – the party alone knew the right course to follow.

BUREAUCRACY V DEMOCRACY IN THE PARTY

The issues of bureaucracy, democracy and the power of the Secretariat in the party caused disagreements and arguments in the early 1920s. In 1923, Trotsky raised the issue of bureaucracy which he defined as the mindless and unthinking carrying out of duties laid down by superiors. He and his supporters felt the party was becoming too bureaucratised and that Stalin was killing the tradition of inner party democracy (a view shared by all of Stalin's opponents in the forthcoming power struggle). A bureaucratised party would exclude the main mass of the party from meaningful participation in economic and political decision making. Furthermore, the Secretariat was taking over from the top, appointing local party secretaries on the basis of loyalty to the 'centre' rather than merit; the principle of elections with local party secretaries responsible to their constituency was being lost. Ultimately, this meant the bureaucracy would become detached from the party base and the party would become estranged from the working class.

164

HOW WAS THE BOLSHEVIK STATE CONSOLIDATED BETWEEN 1921 AND 1924?

RSFSR

The Russian Soviet Federal Socialist Republic, created in 1918 after the Bolsheviks took control. In 1922 it became the main republic in the new USSR and in 1991 remained as the area we now call Russia after the break up of the USSR.

The government of the Soviet Union

The Russian Soviet Federal Socialist Republic (RSFSR) had been proclaimed in January 1918. Its constitution, introduced in July, defined the state as 'a dictatorship of the urban and rural proletariat'. Its job was to ensure transition to a socialist society. It employed the principle of 'he who does not work shall not eat'. The 'former people' (the middle classes) had no right to vote.

During the Civil War, areas conquered by the Red Army were taken into the RSFSR or, if it was a large area with a history of independence, such as the Ukraine, Belorussia or Georgia, it was made into a separate republic. The RSFSR was regarded as 'Russia' (since the majority of the population was Russian) and was far larger and more powerful than the other republics. The status of the smaller republics in relation to the RSFSR led to an acrimonious debate between Lenin and Stalin, the Commissar for Nationalities (see pages 172–173). Stalin wanted all the republics to be more directly controlled by Moscow. Lenin wanted a federation of soviet republics in which all were on a more or less equal footing. Lenin won the argument and at the end of 1922 the Union of the Soviet Socialist Republics (USSR) was formally established.

Despite Lenin's victory in the debate, the republics were never really free to govern themselves. The Communist Party organisations in the republics were regarded as regional branches of the Russian Communist Party and the commissariats (governments) of the republics were regarded as regional branches of the Sovnarkom. And, of course, both the Sovnarkom and the Central Committee were controlled by the Politburo.

The Communists were keen to avoid any suggestion that the way they controlled the republics was in any way similar to the tsarist empire, in case this led to national revolts. They tried to establish instead the idea that they were all part of a benign brotherhood of different ethnic groups. They deliberately fostered national consciousness, setting up native language schools and encouraging theatre and cultural events reflecting national traditions. Most members of the Communist Party were Russians, so they tried to bring in people of different ethnic groups to train as party officials and run their local party branches. This was called 'the planting down of roots'.

■ 8F The republics in 1922

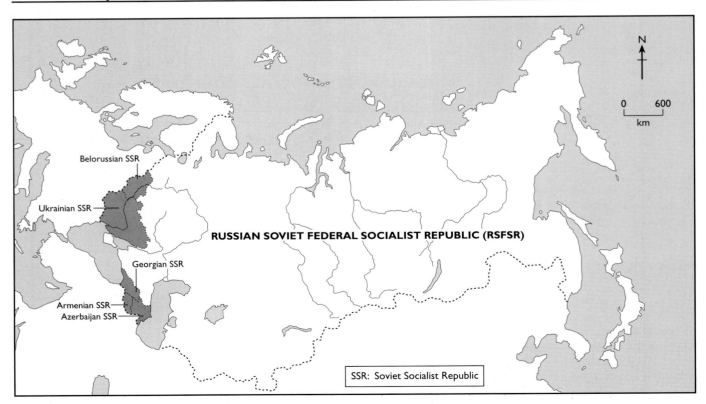

SSR: Soviet Socialist Republic

SOVIET GOVERNMENT

Council of People's Commissars (Sovnarkom) Membership: Around fifteen to twenty members under Lenin, who was chairman. Members came from the Central Executive Committee.
Role: Key decision-making body – it issued orders and decrees. It met daily and decided important aspects of policy. It became less important in the early 1920s as the Communist Party took more control.

Central Executive Committee (former executive of the Soviet) Membership: Elected by Congress of Soviets.
Role: It made laws and oversaw the administration of the government when the Congress was not meeting. Its functions overlapped with those of the Sovnarkom. In practice, it had little power.

All-Russian Congress of Soviets Membership: Delegates were elected by city and provincial soviets, although membership was weighted in favour of the cities. It met twice (later only once) a year.
Role: It was the supreme law-making authority.

Provincial and city soviets Membership: Members were elected from local and district soviets to the soviets representing regions or larger cities like Leningrad and Moscow.
Role: They oversaw administration of the cities and regions, and carried out policy decisions made at the centre. They also fed back to the centre the specific needs and problems of the regions and cities.

Local and district soviets Membership: This was the lowest level of soviet – made up of representatives from a local area elected by local people. In the later 1920s, only Communist Party members could be elected to soviets. Soviets became less important in relation to the local Communist Party.
Role: Local soviets were the point of contact for people who wanted to put their needs and wishes forward to higher levels of authority, who could take action on their behalf. They put policy decisions into action at district and local levels.

THE RELATIONSHIP OF THE GOVERNMENT TO THE COMMUNIST PARTY

Key officials in the government were members of the Communist Party. Senior members of the government were usually senior members of the party. Increasingly, government bodies became simply the instruments for carrying out the policies made in the Politburo and higher levels of the party.

COMMUNIST PARTY

Politburo Membership: Around seven to nine members chosen by the Central Committee. It met on an almost daily basis.
Role: This was the leading decision-making body of the Communist Party – the inner cabinet. Set up in 1919, it took over from the unwieldy Central Committee as the most influential body of the Communist Party. It increasingly took power from the Sovnarkom. The key decisions were made in the Politburo.

Central Committee Membership: Around 30–40 members.
Role: It ran party affairs when congresses were not sitting. It was the main party body until 1919 and continued to discuss and vote on key party issues, although power lay increasingly with the Politburo.

Congress Membership: Representatives were chosen from city and regional party organisations.
Role: It debated issues facing the party and voted on the main policies. In the 1920s, under Lenin, debates could be fierce and open, although the 'ban on factions' in 1921 meant that decisions could not be questioned once a vote had been taken. In practice, this gave more power to the centre. It elected members of the Central Committee and Politburo.

City and provincial parties
Party secretaries at this level were often very powerful. Kamenev and Zinoviev derived much of their support from their control of the Moscow and Leningrad parties. Whoever was party secretary of the Ukrainian Communist Party, for example, was often just a step away from joining the Politburo. The central party organisation took an interest in appointing party members to key posts at this level, especially after Stalin became the General Secretary. Delegates to the party congress came from this level.

Local parties
People often joined local parties for the advantages they could get from being a party member, such as election to the local or district soviet or other government jobs.

CENTRE AND PERIPHERY

Although there was a tendency towards the centralisation of power, the further you got away from Moscow, the more district and local party organisations tended to act independently. They would not always carry out orders from the centre. A culture of lying grew up in the lower levels of the party. Local party bodies protected their own areas of power and did not always feed back accurate information to the centre. The relationship between the centre and the 'periphery' (regional and local government) was often strained throughout the 1920s and the 1930s.

DEMOCRATIC CENTRALISM

It was on this idea that the Soviet claim to democracy rested. Town and village soviets were elected by the working people. Day-to-day administration was in the hands of an executive committee appointed by each soviet and directly responsible to it. Delegates were sent from the lower bodies progressively up the different levels to the top. The idea was that the system of soviets represented a real chain from people to government, through which the expressed ideas of the people could be carried to the highest level – this was the 'democratic' element. In this way, the centre could keep in contact with the people. Once decisions had been made at the centre they were passed down through the levels and carried out – the 'centralism' element.

This was how the system was supposed to work in theory. In practice, more and more power was accumulated at the centre during the Civil War. The Sovnarkom made most of the decisions and laws, and sent out its orders. The city and provincial soviets largely carried out the instructions from the centre and there was little democratic input from the lower levels of soviets.

KEY POINTS FROM CHAPTER 8

How was the Bolshevik state consolidated between 1921 and 1924?

1 The Bolsheviks were in serious trouble in 1921, facing massive peasant revolts, strikes and opposition from workers, a rising at the Kronstadt naval base, economic distress and famine. The Bolshevik regime was in jeopardy.

2 There were also factions inside the Communist Party, like the Workers' Opposition, who wanted changes in policy.

3 Lenin made economic concessions in the form of the New Economic Policy to ensure the survival of the regime.

4 The NEP was accompanied by repressive measures as the Communists asserted their control.

5 Between 1918 and 1924, the government of the Communist state became increasingly centralised. This was partly the result of pragmatic responses to fighting the Civil War and coping with an economy in dire circumstances, and partly the result of party ideology.

6 The Secretariat and party bureaucracy became particularly powerful. The party became increasingly important at the expense of government institutions.

7 The Communist Party itself became more centralised and controlled by a smaller number of people at the top. It became more used to obeying orders, there was less open debate and discussion, and a 'ban on factions' meant that party members were less likely to challenge the party leaders.

8 By 1924, the Soviet Union was a highly centralised, one-party state.

Section 3 Review: The consolidation of the Bolshevik state 1917–1924

■ A How did the Bolsheviks consolidate their power?

Pragmatic decisions to ensure survival

- They initially gave peasants and workers what they wanted, to get their support in the first months after the October Revolution. They realised they were not able to control the situation so they gave way to popular demands and aspirations. They passed a number of other measures that were popular with workers, for example the abolition of titles and ranks.
- They signed the Treaty of Brest-Litovsk to bring Russia's involvement in the First World War to an end and to honour their peace pledge.
- They employed the tough policy of War Communism to keep the regime afloat. They seized grain from a peasantry reluctant to supply it and took strong measures to keep workers in cities and towns so that they could continue to run industries essential to the war effort.
- They introduced the NEP; this was an economic concession to achieve political survival.

The Bolshevik grip on power tightens

Ruthless methods and terror

- They set up the Cheka (secret police) as an instrument of terror to deal with opposition. They arrested first Kadets, and then Socialist Revolutionary and Menshevik leaders. The Cheka was a formidable force that supported the Bolsheviks at every turn and helped them win the war against 'internal enemies'. Some historians see the Cheka as *the* key factor in the survival of the Bolshevik regime.
- They used force to break the civil service strikes and deal with demonstrations against them.
- Class warfare was used to terrorise the middle classes and all hostile social groups. This played well with workers and soldiers and made it difficult for people to criticise the new government.
- They used repressive measures during the NEP to consolidate their political position.

Staying in control

- They refused to take part in a socialist coalition government and crushed the Constituent Assembly, establishing one-party control.
- They exploited the weakness of the opposition, particularly the Socialist Revolutionaries and Mensheviks, who underestimated them and would not get involved in violent anti-Bolshevik protest.
- They defeated the Whites in the Civil War. People were more inclined to support the Bolsheviks to keep the 'gains of the revolution'.
- They developed a highly centralised state to make sure their policies were carried out.

ACTIVITY

How did the Bolsheviks consolidate their power? Chart A on page 167 provides one way of organising analytical points to answer this question.

Working in groups of three or four, draw up a detailed diagrammatic essay plan on a large piece of paper. You can go back to different parts of Section 3 to collect details to support the points you are making. Either use the organisation of points suggested in the diagram to form clear blocks of writing or organise them in a different way. For instance, you could organise them chronologically, explaining:

- how the Bolsheviks dealt with their enemies and built up their power base in the first six months; then

- how they won the Civil War and employed the methods of War Communism; and finally

- how, when threatened by revolts and collapse in 1921, they brought in the NEP and tightened their hold over the Soviet Union.

When you have finished, present your essay plan to the rest of the class, who can comment and add extra information or other ideas.

Some essays have two parts: the first part descriptive and the second part more analytical. For instance, part a) below is descriptive, part b) analytical.

a) What measures did the Bolsheviks adopt to maintain control of Russia from the revolution of October 1917 to the death of Lenin?

b) Why did the economic policies adopted between 1918 and 1924 arouse opposition within the Bolshevik Party and the USSR?

For part **a)** you simply describe the measures.

For part **b)** think about:

- the different views within the Bolshevik Party about the impact of War Communism on the workers, the control of the trade unions and the implementation of the NEP

- the views of non-Bolshevik workers and peasants (and Kronstadt sailors) towards the different elements of War Communism

- aspects of the NEP that would have antagonised some groups, particularly workers.

From Lenin to Stalin

Paintings

Paintings are a valuable source of historical information. They tell us a great deal about the period in which they were painted and often give us a vivid impression of the individuals and people involved in making history. But we have to be careful how we interpret them and what information we take from them. Many of the Soviet paintings you will see here were painted under strict controls, particularly in the 1930s, and were designed to convey a very specific impression. Here are a number of points to look out for:

- Who painted the picture – what do we know about him or her?
- When was it painted – what do we know about the period in which it was painted in regard to political control of the arts or the schools of painting that were prevalent at the time? Paintings of individuals and events were often done long after the person had died or the event had happened.
- Who paid for or commissioned the picture and what degree of control did they exercise over the finished product?
- What was the purpose behind the painting of the picture?
- Is it a painting of a real scene? Artists sometimes completely make up pictures, having not been at an event and having no clear idea of what went on. They import characters who could not have been there and put together people who could not possibly have been together.

Lenin died in 1924, leaving a huge gap at the top of the Communist leadership. He had held the party together since 1917 and been central to determining policy. His death did not come at a good time. Now that the economy had recovered after the crises of 1921 there were many issues to resolve concerning the route to socialism, democracy and leadership in the party, and the problems of a growing bureaucracy. These issues, as well as conflict between the key personalities, led to a struggle over power that lasted for the next five years. Eventually, it was Stalin who succeeded Lenin. In Chapter 9 we look at the relationship between Lenin and Stalin at the end of Lenin's life and assess Lenin's contribution to the Russian Revolution from 1917 to 1924. In Chapter 10 we look at how Stalin emerged as the sole leader of Soviet Russia by 1929.

ACTIVITY

Educating the workers in the spirit of Communism was to be achieved, in part, by producing images of the leaders. The chairman of Moscow's artists said: 'The task of the construction of images of Lenin and Stalin, the geniuses who created socialism, and their closest comrades, is one of the most responsible creative and ideological tasks that art has ever faced.'

There were several images of the leader that were acceptable:

a) Lenin/Stalin as *the* Leader – huge statues, majestic, impersonal, superhuman figures
b) The Leader as the Inspirer and Organiser of Victories, conveying energy, willpower, infectious leadership
c) The Leader as the Wise Teacher, emphasising the leader's intelligence and piercing understanding – portraits of Lenin and Stalin at work in their studies or speaking at meetings
d) The Leader as a Man, the Friend of children, workers, and so on – the Leader glows with tenderness, and the audience holds him in awe.

The lion's share of the Stalin Prizes awarded from 1934 to 1953 were for representations of the leaders.

Look at Sources 1–7. Put each source into one (or more) of the four categories of image (above). Refer to the detail in the images to explain your choice.

SOURCE 1 A painting of Lenin returning to Petrograd in April 1917. Made in the 1930s, it depicts Lenin as the engine driver of the revolution. It also includes Stalin in the background, although he was not on the train that brought Lenin back to Russia, nor in the party that greeted him at Finland Station

SOURCE 2 Lenin in his study, a painting by Isaak Brodsky

SOURCE 3 *Lenin on the Tribune*, a painting by Aleksandr Gerasimov

SOURCE 4 *Leader, Teacher, Friend,* a painting by G. Shegal, 1936–37

SOURCE 5 A painting (1926) showing Stalin addressing industrial workers

SOURCE 6 Merkurov's statue of Stalin, displayed at the Great Soviet Exhibition of 1939

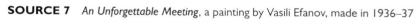

SOURCE 7 *An Unforgettable Meeting*, a painting by Vasili Efanov, made in 1936–37

9

How significant is Lenin's contribution to history?

CHAPTER OVERVIEW

Lenin died in January 1924, although for most of 1923 he was incapacitated by illness. In the last years of his life, he was concerned about the state of the party, the growing bureaucracy and the power of Stalin. His relationship with Stalin deteriorated in 1922 and it seemed likely that Stalin's power would be curtailed. But Lenin died before any changes could take place and it was Stalin who took the lead at his funeral and in developing the Lenin cult. Lenin's contribution to the Russian Revolution from 1917 to 1923 was enormous, but how significant is he in history? Did he really make a difference?

A Lenin's relationship with Stalin at the end of his life (pp. 172–173)

B Lenin's funeral and the Lenin cult (pp. 173–174)

C Summing up Lenin (pp. 175–176)

D Did Lenin make a difference? (pp. 177–180)

A Lenin's relationship with Stalin at the end of his life

THE GREAT RUSSIAN CHAUVINIST AND THE GEORGIAN AFFAIR

During the Civil War Georgia had been run by Mensheviks. At the end of the war, the Red Army took control by force and Stalin – himself a Georgian – was sent to visit the area and see how the Bolsheviks in Georgia were managing. However, Stalin was insulted and shouted down at meetings by the Mensheviks, and accused of betraying his birthplace. Stalin, who never took kindly to slights and insults, took the Bolsheviks to task for being too weak on opposition groups. He threatened and bullied them to adopt a more aggressive policy. In one incident, a local Bolshevik leader was struck by Ordzhonikidze, one of Stalin's henchmen. Stalin believed that Russians should govern the peoples of the USSR from Moscow rather like the tsars had done. This is why Lenin called him the 'Great Russian chauvinist'.

Lenin suffered a series of strokes from late 1921 until his death in January 1924. He was able to carry on working during 1922, but a major stroke in March 1923 left him without the power of speech. In 1922, he still had considerable influence but was removed from the onerous work of running the day-to-day business of government. He had time to think about the problems of the party. He became concerned about the extent of the party bureaucracy and increasingly aware of the power that Stalin had accrued to himself. He was particularly worried about the way Stalin had abused his power by intimidating and bullying the Communists who were governing Georgia. Lenin detected a dark side to Stalin that might present a danger to the party. He mounted an investigation into the Georgian affair that confirmed his fears. He also fell out with Stalin over the issue of the Soviet republics (see page 163).

After the second of his strokes in December 1922, Lenin wrote a testament, a 'Letter to the Party Congress' to be read after his death (see Source 9.1 on page 173). In it Lenin warned that Stalin had become too powerful and that he could not be trusted to use his power wisely. From this point onwards, Lenin did not trust the information with which Stalin provided him. How much Stalin knew about this is not certain, but he clearly perceived that relations with Lenin were not good and was anxious about the Georgian investigation.

Stalin's wife worked as a secretary for Lenin, living in his house while he was ill, and she provided a conduit of information about Lenin's contacts. Stalin found out about the increasingly warm correspondence between Trotsky and Lenin. They were working on plans to restore more democracy to the party and there seems little doubt that, if Lenin had survived a little longer, Stalin would have lost some of his key positions in the party. Stalin tried to see Lenin, but Krupskaya, Lenin's wife, would not let him visit. Stalin, in a telephone conversation, insulted her, using crude, abusive language. Lenin was upset by this and added a note to his testament which would have been very damaging to Stalin if made public.

According to the historian Robert Conquest, Lenin was more than upset: 'He was in fact prepared for open hostilities ... One of Lenin's secretaries told Trotsky that Lenin was now preparing "a bomb" against Stalin; and Kamenev learned from another of the secretaries that Lenin had decided "to crush Stalin politically" ' (*Stalin: Breaker of Nations*, 1991, page 104). But before this could happen, Lenin had another stroke on 7 March and never recovered the power of speech.

SOURCE 9.1   Extracts from Lenin's testament, 25 December 1922

Comrade Stalin, having become General Secretary, has immeasurable power concentrated in his hands, and I am not sure that he always knows how to use that power with sufficient caution. Comrade Trotsky, on the other hand ... is distinguished not only by his outstanding ability. He is personally perhaps the most capable man in the present C.C. [Central Committee], but he has displayed excessive self-assurance ... These two qualities of the two outstanding leaders of the present C.C. can inadvertently lead to a split ...

I shall not give further appraisals of the personal qualities of other members of the C.C. but recall that the October episode with Zinoviev and Kamenev was no accident, but neither can the blame for it be laid on them personally, any more than non-Bolshevism can upon Trotsky. Speaking of the young C.C. members I wish to say a few words about Bukharin ... Bukharin is not only a most valuable and major theorist of the Party; he is also rightly considered the favourite of the whole Party; but his theoretical views can only with the very greatest doubt be regarded as fully Marxist.
[Postscript added 4 January 1923]
Stalin is too rude, and this fault ... becomes unacceptable in the office of General Secretary. Therefore, I propose to the comrades that a way be found to remove Stalin from that post and replace him with someone else who differs from Stalin in all respects, someone more patient, more loyal, more polite, more considerate.

B Lenin's funeral and the Lenin cult

The unexpected news of Lenin's death led to widespread displays of public grief. Theatres and shops were closed for a week, while portraits of Lenin draped in red and black were displayed in windows. Over three days, three and a half million people queued for hours to file past his body lying in state. However much they hated the regime the people seemed to have a genuine affection for Lenin, much as they had had for the tsars.

Stalin made the most of Lenin's funeral to advance his position in the party. Just before Lenin's death, Trotsky was ill and had set out to the south of Russia for a rest-holiday. Stalin contacted him and told him that he (Trotsky) would not be able to get back in time for the funeral. So Trotsky did not attend and it looked as though he could not be bothered to turn up. His reputation and political prestige were severely damaged by his non-attendance. Stalin, on the other hand, acted as one of the pallbearers and made a speech in which he appeared to be taking on the mantle of Leninism (see Source 9.2 below). Stalin hoped to transfer to himself the prestige, respect and loyalty associated with Lenin. He set himself up as Lenin's disciple, the person who would carry on Lenin's work. He was already thinking of the looming power struggle.

SOURCE 9.2   J. V. Stalin, *Collected Works*. These are extracts from Stalin's speech at Lenin's funeral

There is nothing higher than the calling of the member of a Party whose founder and leader is Comrade Lenin ... Leaving us, Comrade Lenin ordered us to hold high and keep pure the great title of member of the Party. We vow to thee Comrade Lenin, that we shall honourably fulfil this commandment.... Leaving us, Comrade Lenin enjoined us to keep the unity of the Party like the apple of our eye. We vow to thee, Comrade Lenin. That we will honourably fulfil this, thy commandment ...

FOCUS ROUTE

Make notes on the relationship between Lenin and Stalin at the end of Lenin's life using these questions to guide you:

a) Why was Lenin concerned about Stalin?
b) What was the Georgian affair?
c) How did Lenin and Stalin's relationship deteriorate?
d) What appears to have been the purpose of Lenin's testament?
e) Who came out of the relationship the worst?

TALKING POINT

Chance or accident can be a significant factor in explaining events.

1 How does chance seem to have played a role in the succession to the Russian leadership?
2 Can you think of other examples when chance may have had a significant impact on historical events?

FOCUS ROUTE

Make notes to explain:

• how Stalin used Lenin's funeral to his advantage
• what the cult of Leninism was and why Stalin encouraged it.

SOURCE 9.3   Members of the Central Committee of the Communist Party carrying Lenin's coffin to Red Square on 27 January 1924. Stalin is on the left in the picture

SOURCE 9.4   Although the cult of Lenin is associated with Stalin, Zinoviev played a more important part initially. Here is an extract from a pamphlet he produced in 1918 in his typical overblown style:

On the horizon a new figure has appeared. He is the chosen one of millions. He is leader by the grace of God. Such a leader is born once in 500 years in the life of mankind.

SOURCE 9.5   Extract from a poem by V. Mayakovsky written to celebrate Lenin's fiftieth birthday, 1921

I know . . .
It is not the hero
Who precipitates the flow of revolution.
The story of heroes
Is the nonsense of the intelligentsia!
But who can restrain himself
And not sing
Of the glory of Il'ich?
Kindling the lands with fire
Everywhere . . .
Lenin! Lenin! Lenin!
I glorify in Lenin.

SOURCE 9.6   I. Deutscher, *Stalin*, rev. edn 1966, pp. 270–71. Deutscher demonstrates that Stalin's own 'Biographical Chronicle' shows how he orchestrated Lenin's funeral and put himself in the central role

21 January – *6.50a.m. Lenin dies at Gorky. 9.30a.m. Stalin and other members of Politburo arrive at Gorky.*
23 January – *9a.m. Stalin and other leaders carry coffin with Lenin's body from Lenin's home at Gorky . . . (they travel on by train) . . . to the House of Trade Unions in Moscow where Lenin lay in state for the next four days; 6.10p.m. Stalin stands in the guard of honour at the bier.*
25 January – *Stalin calls upon the party to collect relics of Lenin for the newly founded Lenin Institute.*
26 January – *At the second congress of the Soviets, Stalin reads an oath of allegiance to Lenin.*
27 January – *9a.m. Stalin and others carry the coffin out of the House of Trade Unions; 4p.m. End of the funeral procession at the Red Square – Stalin and others carry the coffin into the future mausoleum.*
28 January – *Stalin addresses a memorial meeting.*

The cult of Leninism

The Lenin cult had begun just after the attempt on his life in 1918 (see page 143). Stalin gave it new momentum at Lenin's funeral. The Lenin cult was a sort of quasi-religion in which Lenin's name could be invoked like a deity or his words trotted out, much as the Bible is used to justify actions. At least, Stalin used it this way. Lenin made it clear before he died that he did not want this kind of adulation. His wife, Krupskaya, publicly asked that there should be 'no external reverence for his person'. But under pressure from Stalin, Lenin was embalmed and his tomb turned into a shrine. Lenin's brain was sliced into 30,000 segments and stored so that scientists in the future could discover the secrets of his genius.

All sorts of Lenin memorabilia, from posters to matchboxes, were produced. Statues of Lenin appeared all over the Soviet Union. Petrograd was renamed Leningrad and many streets and institutions were named after him. Trotsky was sickened by the whole business, but it was difficult to speak out against it without being accused of disloyalty and disrespect.

C Summing up Lenin

Lenin had many qualities that proved invaluable in pushing through the October uprising in 1917 and ruling Russia in the post-revolutionary period. He had great organisational abilities and leadership skills, together with a strong personality to force through decisions in the Politburo and Central Committee. He was tough, hard and calculating, totally dedicated to politics and revolution. From October 1917 until his last major stroke in March 1923, he spent up to sixteen hours or more a day, running the Bolshevik government, making sure that the revolution survived.

Lenin was a good orator, though not brilliant in the way that Trotsky was. He did not bring his speeches to life with metaphors and well-crafted phrases. Rather his skill lay in his ability to express ideas simply and make his audience understand complicated political concepts. He was good in argument, bringing people around to his views, an essential quality in a leader. He was forceful and persuasive.

Lenin did not look for personal gain from the Revolution. He did not seek the pleasures of life like some other Bolshevik leaders. His one diversion was his romantic friendship with Inessa Armand. He lived simply with Krupskaya, whom he called 'comrade', and his sister in a three-bedroomed apartment in the Kremlin and often slept in a small room behind his offices. They ate their meals in the cafeteria. He continued the austere life of the revolutionary that he was used to. He liked things to be orderly and tidy with fixed hours for meals, sleep and work. He had little private life: his life was the Revolution.

Politics also dominated his personal friendships. He would cut off personal connections with people with whom he fell out over politics. Martov, who was a close personal friend in the early days of the Social Democratic Party, was cast off when he became a Menshevik and Lenin poured scorn upon him, something he regretted when Martov died. Lenin's attitude to political opponents was vitriolic. According to the Russian writer Maxim Gorky in 1918, Lenin's attitude was that 'who is not with us is against us'.

Lenin had a strong streak of ruthlessness and cruelty. In the late 1980s and 1990s, Soviet archives were opened up as the Communist regime came to an end. These revealed a much harder, more ruthless Lenin than the 'softer' image he had enjoyed amongst left-wing historians and groups. For instance, a memorandum, first published in 1990, reveals his ordering the extermination of the clergy in a place called Shuya after people there fought off officials who had come to raid the church. The Politburo voted to stop further raids on churches but Lenin countermanded them (see page 300). Similarly, he was vitriolic about the peasants, ordering the hanging of a hundred kulaks as a lesson to others (see page 144).

Lenin believed that revolutionaries had to be hard to carry out their role, which would inevitably involve spilling the blood of their opponents. Although hard and tough on others, it seems that Lenin was not personally brave. He was not a revolutionary who rushed to the barricades. He left the fighting to others. According to Valentinov, a revolutionary who knew him well, Lenin's rule was to 'get away while the going was good'.

Lenin's domination of the party is one of the key factors in his success. There were many disputes and splits in the party, such as the serious split over the Treaty of Brest-Litovsk, right into the 1920s. But in the end he always managed to bring the party behind him and keep it united. According to Beryl Williams (*Lenin*, 2000, page 13), Lenin's contemporaries attested to his 'hypnoptic influence'. His personal magnetism and charisma are not in doubt. But he also had tremendous political skills – of knowing when to persuade, when to cajole, when to give in, when to threaten to resign and when to get really tough and demanding. Above all, Lenin was convinced of his role and his destiny (see Source 9.8 on page 176). He never had any doubt that he knew the right path and could lead the party along it.

LENIN – THE ABSENT REVOLUTIONARY

It is strange to think that Lenin had been absent from Russia for seventeen years (apart from six months in 1905–6) before his return in April 1917. He was a professional revolutionary who knew very little about the people he had come to lead to revolution, and they knew virtually nothing about him. After the July Days he went into exile again and was not seen again until he returned secretly in October. Most people did not recognise him even in the period after the Bolsheviks took power. Trotsky was much better known and much more popular. Commentators have said that Lenin had no real knowledge of ordinary Russian people and no experience of their everyday working lives (he had only had a paid job for two years). Maxim Gorky said that his ignorance bred contempt for ordinary people and the suffering they endured.

ACTIVITY

Write a list of the aspects of Lenin's character and personality that you think contributed to his success.

TALKING POINT

On pages 173–4 you read about the displays of public grief after Lenin's death. What do you think were the main reasons for this reaction?

SOURCE 9.7   A. N. Potresov, a Menshevik, describing Lenin shortly after his death

Only Lenin was followed unquestioningly as the undisputed leader, as it was only Lenin who was that rare phenomenon, particularly in Russia – a man of iron will and indomitable energy, capable of instilling fanatical faith in the movement and the cause, and possessed of equal faith in himself . . .

No one could sweep people away so much by his plans, impress them by his strength of will, and then win them over by his personality as this man, who at first sight seemed so unprepossessing and crude, and, on the face of it had none of the things that make for personal charm. Neither Plekhanov nor Martov nor any one else had the secret of that hypnotic influence on, or rather ascendancy over, [other people] which Lenin radiated.

SOURCE 9.8   Chernov, the Socialist Revolutionary leader, on Lenin

Lenin possesses a devotion to the revolutionary cause which permeates his entire being. But to him the revolution is embodied in his person. Lenin possesses an outstanding mind, but it is a . . . mind of one dimension – more than that a unilinear mind . . . He is a man of one-sided will and consequently a man with a stunted moral sensitivity.

SOURCE 9.9   S. Nechayev, *Catechism of a Revolutionary*, 1869

The first article:
The revolutionary is a dedicated man. He has no personal feelings, no private affairs, no emotions, no attachments, no property, and no name. Everything in him is subordinated towards a single exclusive attachment, a single thought and a single passion – the revolution.

LENIN AND THE ORIGINS OF THE BOLSHEVIK PARTY

Some historians argue that Bolshevism itself is a Russian phenomenon. Lenin, it is claimed, merged Russian revolutionary thought with Marxism in the creation of the Bolshevik ideology and concept of the party. As a young man, Lenin had immersed himself in the revolutionary writings of an earlier period. He was profoundly influenced by the writer Chernyshevsky who considered that society could only be perfected by socialism. While in jail in 1862, Chernyshevsky wrote his famous novel *What Is To Be Done?* Its hero is a super-revolutionary who renounces all pleasure to harden himself physically and mentally in preparation for the coming revolution. Lenin read the book five times one summer, claiming that it had changed his life and shown him how to become a revolutionary. Lenin used the title *What Is To Be Done?* for his 1902 tract on the nature of a revolutionary party.

Lenin was also influenced by Nechayev's *Catechism of a Revolutionary*, which advocated that revolutionaries should be hard and ruthless, lacking in sentiment and dedicated (see Source 9.9). This was necessary to encourage the short-term misery required for long-term happiness: some revolutionaries believed they had to make conditions so bad for people that they would rise up against their rulers. Nechayev also planned a revolutionary organisation based on cells (three or four people) directed by a central committee. We can see from these writers where some of Lenin's key ideas about revolution and the Bolshevik Party originated.

D Did Lenin make a difference?

One of the big questions in history is to do with the role of the individual: how far have individuals influenced the course of history? This is sometimes called the 'great man' theory of history insofar as it appears that certain people, occupying positions of power, make decisions or initiate actions that change the course of history. Is Lenin one of these individuals?

To make a judgement about this we have to ask how significant Lenin was in creating the world's first Communist state. How different would the world have been if he had not arrived in Petrograd in April 1917? As we saw at the end of Section 2, circumstances helped the Bolsheviks enormously: the weakness of the opposition (liberal and other socialist parties); the collapse of the army; intense economic distress; the Kornilov affair; Kerensky's blunders. All of these factors meant that the opportunity to seize power literally fell into the Bolsheviks' laps. It seems likely that the Soviet would have taken power anyway and that a socialist government – albeit a very different one from the Communist regime of the 1920s – would have been formed, even if Lenin had not intervened.

So is there a good case for suggesting that Lenin really did make a difference and changed the course of the twentieth century? Charts 9A and 9B set out some of the main points for the argument that he did. The points refer back to pages where you can find more explanation or supporting argument.

■ 9A Lenin's personal qualities

Leader
He was an outstanding leader, who alone was able to hold the Bolshevik Party together when it might have fragmented, for example over the October uprising, the Red Army and the NEP.

No one else in the party had the prestige and standing to see them through these difficult periods.

He had great organisational abilities, demonstrated in his management of the country during War Communism, when he and Sverdlov made virtually all the day-to-day business decisions until the latter's death in 1919.

He was flexible and pragmatic, finding solutions to the problems that arose when building a government from scratch in 1917–18 (for instance, using 'bourgeois specialists' and single managers in the factories, introducing the NEP in 1921).

V. I. Lenin
1870–1924
LEADER
ORGANISER
PRAGMATIST

KEY IDEAS OF
MARXISM-
LENINISM

The revolutionary
élite

Bypassing bourgeois
democracy to achieve
the PROLETARIAN
REVOLUTION

Theorist
He was a brilliant theorist. His adaptations of Marxist theory have become known as Marxism–Leninism. His developments of Marxism had two important implications for the Russian Revolution:

1 His concept of a small, disciplined revolutionary party that could seize power as a vanguard on behalf of the working class was crucial in 1917 (see page 26).

2 His development, along with Trotsky, of the notion that the proletariat could carry through a socialist revolution without going through the 'bourgeois-democratic stage' (because the bourgeoisie was too weak) led to the April Theses, Bolshevik opposition to the Provisional Government and the October uprising.

HOW SIGNIFICANT IS LENIN'S CONTRIBUTION TO HISTORY?

KEY POINTS OF INTERVENTION

RUSSIAN REVOLUTION and the BOLSHEVIK STATE

New Economic Policy
He persuaded a very reluctant party to accept the economic compromises of the NEP, based on his record and standing in the party. There is a good chance that the Bolsheviks would have been overthrown if they had continued with War Communism (see page 146).

NEP

Treaty of Brest-Litovsk and the Red Army
Lenin pushed through the signing of the Treaty of Brest-Litovsk despite the opposition of the left Communists; he realised that they had to have peace to survive (see page 121). He supported Trotsky in creating a traditional hierarchical Red Army using ex-tsarist officers, against serious opposition in the party from leading Bolsheviks such as Stalin. Trotsky would not have got this through without Lenin and if he had not, then the Bolsheviks might well have lost the Civil War.

Brest-Litovsk and Red Army

Issue of socialist coalition
Lenin insisted that the Bolsheviks rule as a one-party state. He forced this through against the opposition of leading Bolsheviks who wanted a socialist coalition (see page 120). If this had happened, a very different Russia would have emerged and the Civil War would have taken a very different form, if it had taken place at all. Lenin crushed the Constituent Assembly, which was the legitimate government elected by Russians.

Socialist coalition

October uprising
Lenin pressurised the unwilling Bolshevik Central Committee into staging the October uprising. They resisted his demands on several occasions (he faced outright opposition from Zinoviev and Kamenev). It is very likely that the Bolsheviks would not have got into power if they had not acted when they did (see pages 104–105).

October uprising

April Theses
Lenin forced these through despite much opposition in the party, though he was in tune with the militant rank and file. The April Theses became the basis of party policy – uncompromising opposition to war, and the handing over of power to soviets – which brought the Bolsheviks much support and made them the only credible opposition party to the Provisional Government (see pages 82–84). The April Theses gave them a clear focus which cut through the indecisiveness of other socialist parties.

April Theses

ACTIVITY

How do Sources 9.10–9.14 support the case that Lenin made a difference? Refer in your answers to specific parts of the sources.

SOURCE 9.10   C. Read, *From Tsar to Soviets: The Russian People and their Revolution 1917–21*, 1996, p. 164

While the leadership [of the Bolshevik Party] continued to show that it was not fully disciplined by falling into warring groups over every major initiative from Lenin's April Theses, through the July Days, the seizure of power in October, the Brest-Litovsk Treaty, military and trade union policy during the Civil War and the adoption of NEP in 1921, it is essential to note that, despite the divisions, Lenin's line was eventually followed on all of these key questions. In other words, the 'Bolshevik' structure of the party boiled down to Lenin's domination of it. This is confirmed by the fact that, after his illness and death in 1924, the divisions were no longer able to be healed and the leadership fell into purging and, eventually, bloodletting.

SOURCE 9.11   A letter from Lenin to the Bolshevik Central Committee, 29 September 1917, in which he urges a Bolshevik takeover

To miss such a moment, to 'wait' for the Congress of Soviets, would be utter idiocy, or sheer treachery ... To refrain from taking power now ... is to doom the revolution to failure. In view of the fact that the Central Committee has even left unanswered the persistent demands I have been making ... I am compelled to regard this as a subtle hint that I should keep my mouth shut ... I am compelled to tender my resignation from the Central Committee ...

SOURCE 9.12   N. N. Sukhanov, quoted by J. Carmichael, *A Short History of the Revolution*, 1967, p. 83

Lenin was a very good orator – not an orator of the consummate, of the rounded phrase, or of the luminous image, or of absorbing pathos, or of the pointed witticism, but an orator of enormous impact and power, breaking down complicated systems into the simplest and most generally accessible elements, and hammering, hammering, hammering, them into the heads of his audience until he took them captive.

[Talking of the April Theses] Skobelev told Miliukov about his [Lenin's] lunatic ideas, appraising him as a completely lost man standing outside the movement. I agreed with his assessment of Lenin's ideas and said that in his present guise he was so unacceptable to everyone that he was not at all dangerous ... We refused to admit that Lenin might stick to his 'abstractions'. Still less did we admit that through these abstractions Lenin would be able to conquer not only the revolution, not only all its active masses, not only the whole Soviet – but even his own Bolsheviks. We were cruelly mistaken.

SOURCE 9.13   R. Service, 'Lenin: Individual and Politics in the October Revolution', *Modern History Review*, September 1990

The October Revolution has often and widely been held to have been predominantly Lenin's revolution. But was it? Certainly Lenin had a heavier impact on the course of events than anyone else. The point is, however, that great historical processes are wrought not only by individuals. There were other mighty factors at work as well in Russia in 1917. The conditions for a seizure of power with the sanction of exhausted workers, war-weary soldiers and angry peasants could hardly have been more favourable ... Lenin died before he had the chance to face up properly to the consequences of the kind of revolution he had led. He was a man who helped to shape his times: but his times also moulded him.

SOURCE 9.14   P. Kenez, *A History of the Soviet Union from the Beginning to the End*, 1999, pp. 27–28

Historians have asked whether the Bolshevik seizure of power in October was a coup d'état, carried out by the impetuous Bolsheviks, or a true revolution, the work of the radical workers and soldiers of Petrograd. But perhaps the most striking aspect of events was neither the Bolsheviks' daring, nor the behaviour of the workers, but the complete disintegration of governmental authority. Every politically aware person in Petrograd knew that the Bolsheviks were about to act, but the government could not defend itself. Under the circumstances one could hardly speak of a coup d'état, much less a conspiracy. The Bolsheviks seized power because the country was in the throes of anarchy.

TALKING POINT

Do you agree with Trotsky or Deutscher on Lenin's role in 1917? Would the twentieth century have been different without Lenin or Hitler or Churchill?

ACTIVITY

The key points picked out in Charts 9A and 9B are examples of an **analytical** approach to answering a question. When you analyse something, you break it down into its component parts and you select elements which are relevant to the statement you are making or the question you are answering. You can then use **descriptive** material to support your analytical points.

Here are some different styles of examination writing tasks. Pick one suitable for your purposes:

a) Using the sources and your own knowledge, examine the statement, 'Lenin's role in the Bolshevik seizure of power has been exaggerated.'

b) Lenin was a man who helped shape his times, but his times also moulded him.

c) i) Describe Lenin's role in the Bolshevik consolidation of power.
   ii) Was Lenin a dictator by intent or by circumstance?
   [First part is more descriptive, second part is more analytical.]

■ **Learning trouble spot**

Trotsky and the role of Lenin in the revolution

Trotsky, like Lenin, believed that politics and especially revolutions were about the involvement of the masses. He believed that the masses were the driving force that made Russian revolution possible, although they needed the Bolshevik Party to provide direction. He wrote, 'Without a guiding organisation the energy of the mass would dissipate like steam not enclosed in a piston box. But nevertheless what moves things is not the piston or the box but the steam.' However, Trotsky had no doubt about the importance of Lenin's role in April and October 1917 when the Bolshevik Party was divided and unclear on the direction to take. He wrote to Preobrazhensky in 1928, 'You know better than I do that had Lenin not managed to come to Petrograd in April 1917, the October Revolution would not have taken place.'

Trotsky is even more definite about October: 'Had I not been present in Petrograd in 1917 the October Revolution would still have taken place – on the condition that Lenin was present and in command. If neither Lenin nor I had been present in Petrograd, there would have been no October Revolution: the leadership of the Bolshevik Party would have prevented it from occurring – of this I have not the slightest doubt!'

This view is one that the Marxist historian Isaac Deutscher (Trotsky's biographer) cannot accept. For him the idea that without Lenin there would have been no revolution for many years is a startling one for a Marxist with a determinist view of history. He argues that the revolutionary trend will find or create its leader or leadership from whatever human material is available. The idea of the irreplaceable colossus is 'an optical illusion' (*The Prophet Outcast: Trotsky,1929–1940*, pages 240–246).

The role of the great man or woman in history is a perennial question. E.H. Carr discusses this in his book *What is History?* 1964, pages 54–55. He is anxious to dispel the idea that great men are jack-in-the-boxes who emerge miraculously from the unknown to interrupt the real continuity of history. For Carr the great man 'is at once a product and an agent of the historical process, at once the representative and the creator of social forces which change the shape of the world and the thoughts of men'. Carr distinguishes between those great men who, like Lenin and Cromwell, helped to mould the forces that carried them to greatness and those who, like Napoleon and Bismarck, rode to greatness on the back of already existing forces (*What is History?* 1964, pages 54–55).

KEY POINTS FROM CHAPTER 9

How significant is Lenin's contribution to history?

1 At the end of his life, Lenin's relationship with Stalin deteriorated.

2 It is likely that Stalin's power would have been curtailed if Lenin had lived just a little bit longer or if his testament had been made public.

3 Stalin used Lenin's funeral to portray himself as the disciple of Lenin and he started the cult of Leninism.

4 He tried to transfer Lenin's prestige and status to himself as the person pledged to continue Lenin's work.

5 Lenin had many qualities that made him a successful leader.

6 The 'soft' image of Lenin has been destroyed by new archive material which shows him to have been hard and ruthless.

7 There is a good case for saying that Lenin 'made a difference' as an individual in history.

10

How did Stalin emerge as the sole leader of Russia?

CHAPTER OVERVIEW

Finding a successor to Lenin was never going to be easy. He had played a unique role in holding the party together and giving it direction after the revolution. There was a real possibility that in-fighting and division could pull the Communist Party apart. For the five years after 1924, a power struggle took place in the USSR. The struggle was not just about which person should become leader, it was also about the policies the party should follow; and it was as much about keeping some people out of power. This has led some historians to call it a struggle 'over' power rather than 'for' power. The person who emerged in 1929 as the victor of this struggle was Joseph Stalin. In this chapter, we look at how this happened and why Stalin was able to defeat his opponents.

A Who were the contenders? (pp. 183–185)

B What were the main issues in the leadership struggle? (pp. 185–187)

C How did Stalin become party leader? (pp. 188–191)

D Why did Stalin become party leader? (pp. 192–195)

TALKING POINT

Why does the death of a powerful leader in countries with authoritarian governments cause problems in the period immediately afterwards? Can you think of other countries where this has happened?

ACTIVITY

In this chapter you are going to do an activity in three stages to help you to think about the personal attributes that might have helped someone to become leader of the USSR. The first stage is below. You will do Stages 2 and 3 later in the chapter.

Stage 1

From the list below, choose the six most important qualities/characteristics that you think would have been advantageous for a leader in the USSR to have in 1924. You can add one other of your own choice not on the list.

- Good Marxist theoretician, who could take over Lenin's mantle
- Good orator
- Capacity for organisation
- Decisiveness
- Capacity for action
- Able to melt into the background
- Boring and dull
- Good at carrying out routine tasks
- Good at doing the paperwork, a good bureaucrat
- Unwavering loyalty to the party
- Clear vision of the way to socialism and prepared to take on party members who did not share this vision
- An important player in the Revolution of 1917
- Somebody everybody could accept because he did not have strong views
- Good in discussion and debate
- Popular with the party
- Able to work with other leading party figures
- Able to be ruthless
- Good writer

Joseph Stalin

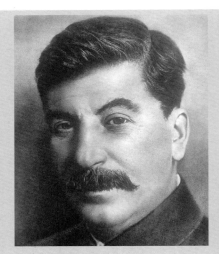

Joseph Dzhugashvili was born in Gori in Georgia in 1878 or 1879. He is one of the few leading revolutionaries who had a genuine working-class/peasant background. His mother was the daughter of serfs and very devout in her religious beliefs. His father was a shoemaker who worked mainly in Tiflis, some distance away. Stalin's mother brought him up virtually on her own, working hard as a seamstress and laundress to support Joseph. They were poor and he had a hard upbringing as she beat him severely for acts of disobedience. However, he did well at school and gained a place at a seminary in Tiflis to train as a priest. But the young Joseph found Marxism rather than God. He was drawn into the underground world of the revolutionaries, writing pamphlets and attending secret meetings. He particularly admired the writings of Lenin. He soon graduated to the full-time role of revolutionary, organising strikes and possibly becoming engaged in raiding banks to fill the Bolshevik Party coffers. The name he used as his first revolutionary pseudonym was Koba.

Between 1902 and 1913, he was arrested frequently and exiled to Siberia, escaping on five occasions. He was placed in a number of prisons where he gained a reputation for toughness. He became hardened, particularly after the death of his first wife in 1907. He later took on the pseudonym 'Stalin' which means 'man of steel'. In 1912, he was invited onto the Central Committee of the Bolshevik Party because they were short of working-class, leading members and Stalin remained in Russia as a point of contact, while most of the others were in exile in European countries. When the February Revolution broke in 1917, he was one of the first to arrive on the scene in Petrograd.

Stalin had not played a key role in the events of 1917. He was made editor of *Pravda*, the party newspaper, and given a seat on the Executive Committee of the Petrograd Soviet. Initially, he followed a pro-war line in accordance with the Soviet and other socialists. He changed his line when Lenin appeared on the scene and seems to have followed Lenin slavishly thereafter. Whilst close to the centre of the Party, he does not seem to have been given any discernible role. There is no evidence of Stalin taking charge of any of the events during the October Revolution. Sverdlov and Trotsky were the main organisers and Sverdlov did not like Stalin.

After the October Revolution, Stalin was made Commissar for Nationalities in the new government. His offices were close to Lenin's and it is likely that at this time he gained Lenin's trust as a devoted Bolshevik operator. In the Civil War, he was sent to Tsaritsyn (later renamed Stalingrad) to organise food supplies and defend this very important strategic position from the Whites. It was in doing this job that he came into conflict with Trotsky: Stalin did not like having to carry out Trotsky's orders and was removed from his military post for disobedience. On several occasions during the Civil War he had shown a tendency to disobey orders from the centre, even Lenin's, because he wanted to do things his own way. Lenin, however, set these 'mistakes' aside because he had other work for Stalin.

Good luck helped Stalin in his next advancements. In March 1919, Sverdlov, who had shown himself to be a great organiser, died of Spanish flu. Lenin was left with few top administrators and looked to Stalin. He appointed Stalin head of the Workers' and Peasants' Inspectorate, through which he became familiar with the work of different government departments. In May 1919, Lenin put him in charge of the Orgburo which controlled aspects of the party organisation. Stalin was also elected to the new Politburo, which from now on became the main organ of power. This was followed in 1922 by his appointment as the party's first General Secretary in charge of general organisation.

Stalin's appointment to these key positions showed how much his reputation had grown and how much trust Lenin placed in him. He gained a reputation for 'industrious mediocrity'. Other Bolsheviks saw these jobs as part of the dull routine of party bureaucracy. They were soon to find out otherwise.

Sukhanov, the diarist of the revolution, made this comment about Stalin in 1917: 'The Bolshevik Party … includes a whole series of great figures and able leaders in its general staff. Stalin, however, during the course of his modest activity in the Executive Committee gave me the impression – and I was not alone in this view – of a grey blur which flickered obscurely and left no trace. There is really nothing more to be said about him.' Stalin had his revenge. Sukhanov died in the camps in 1940.

FOCUS ROUTE

As you work through this chapter, compile a table like the one below to record information about the factors working for Stalin and against his opponents. You will be able to use this in the essay at the end of the chapter.

Factors that favoured Stalin	Weaknesses of Stalin's opponents

A Who were the contenders?

In retrospect, it is clear that the contest for the leadership was really between Trotsky and Stalin. But this was not apparent at the time. At first, Stalin was regarded as a minor player, with the chief contenders being Trotsky on the one hand and Zinoviev and Kamenev on the other. Also, in the early stages the power struggle was more about stopping others getting to the top rather than trying to come out on top oneself.

It is useful to place the contenders for party leadership in terms of their political position in the party of 1924. There was a clear split between the radical left wing led by Trotsky and the right wing headed by Bukharin. The majority of party members lay somewhere in between. Stalin fell into this group. The men shown in Chart 10A were in the Politburo elected in June 1924.

■ 10A Contenders for leadership of the Communist Party

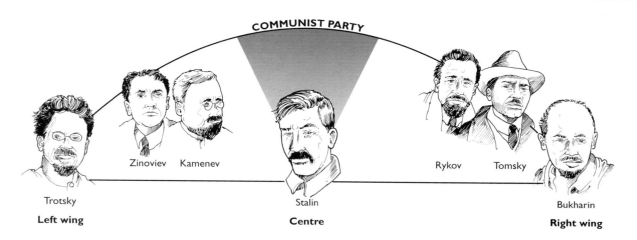

COMMUNIST PARTY

Trotsky — **Left wing**
Zinoviev — Kamenev
Stalin — **Centre**
Rykov — Tomsky
Bukharin — **Right wing**

Contenders

Leon Trotsky

Trotsky was the only member of the Communist Party who could rival Lenin in intellect and in his writings on Marxist theory. He was one of the Bolshevik's best orators, able to work crowds and bring them around to his point of view. He was particularly popular with the younger, more radical elements in the party. His contribution in the years 1917–24 had been second, if not equal, to that of Lenin himself. He had planned the October Revolution, persuading Lenin to wait until the end of October. His organisation of the Red Army and his drive and determination had played a significant part in bringing victory in the Civil War. His position as Commissar for War gave him a strong base in the army.

Working against him were his arrogance and aloofness. He seemed dismissive of other leading Bolsheviks, sometimes treating them with disdain and lack of respect. He was short and brusque with people who seemed to be wasting his time and he never went out of his way to endear himself to his colleagues. They felt his uncompromising views might lead to splits in the party. Many old Bolsheviks regarded Trotsky as an outsider since he had only joined the Bolshevik Party in 1917 and other party members were not convinced of his loyalty to the party. This perception was wrong: he was loyal, perhaps too loyal, and accepted decisions that he did not agree with because he did not want to damage the party.

Two other important factors worked against Trotsky in the power struggle. First, he did not like the business of political in-fighting, making deals and alliances. He preferred to work on a level where arguments were hammered out in debate or by the pen, where he was convinced of his natural superiority. This high-minded approach left him vulnerable to less scrupulous colleagues. Second, for three years from late 1923 Trotsky suffered attacks of an undiagnosed fever. This sapped his strength and left him less able to deal with the continuous political attacks mounted on him by his enemies. It also meant that he was absent for crucial votes in the Politburo, although meetings were sometimes held at his bedside.

Gregory Zinoviev

Zinoviev was an old Bolshevik, active in the party as early as 1903. He had worked closely with Lenin before the Revolution and was with Lenin on the train that pulled into Petrograd's Finland Station in 1917. However, Zinoviev opposed the armed uprising in October and fell out with Lenin about the construction of the new government; he favoured a socialist coalition. As a result, he was not given a major post in the Sovnarkom but he was made Party Secretary in Leningrad. This was an important position, allowing him to build up a strong power base. In 1919, he was made Chairman of the Comintern (see page 328) and became a full member of the Politburo in 1921. He was a good orator but not an intellectual. He was not popular, being seen by others as vain, incompetent and cowardly, making himself scarce when things got dangerous. No one seemed to like him. Victor Serge said he gave 'an impression of flabbiness … irresolution' and was 'simply a demagogue'. The historian E. H. Carr said he was 'weak, vain, ambitious [and] only too eager to occupy the empty throne' (*The Russian Revolution from Lenin to Stalin*, 1979, page 64).

Lev Kamenev

Kamenev was an active Bolshevik and full-time revolutionary from 1905. He was a close collaborator with Lenin abroad from 1907 to 1917. He was a major contributor to party doctrine and had heated debates with Lenin, who regarded him as able and reliable. In 1917, he opposed Lenin's April Theses on ideological grounds. With Zinoviev, he opposed the armed uprising in October 1917 and wanted a socialist coalition government. This lost him influence in the party but he was made Party Secretary in Moscow and later Commissar for Foreign Trade. This brought him into the Politburo and into a position to challenge for the leadership. He was a moderate, liked and well regarded. But he was much too soft to become a real leader. In his book *Socialism in One Country* (1958), E. H. Carr describes Kamenev as intellectually superior to Stalin and Zinoviev but 'by far the least effective of the three … Kamenev had neither the desire nor the capacity to lead men; he lacked any clear vision of a goal towards which he might have led them' (pages 161, 162).

Nikolai Bukharin

Bukharin was one of the younger generation of Bolsheviks. Born in 1888, the son of a schoolmaster, he was nearly a decade younger than Stalin. He had joined the Bolshevik Party in 1906, was arrested in 1912, and then escaped to Germany. He had become a major figure in the party before 1917, close to Lenin. He was an important theorist who argued with Lenin about political strategy. He took a leading role on *Pravda*, the party newspaper, during 1917. He led the left-wing opposition to the signing of the Treaty of Brest-Litovsk and between 1920 and 1921 criticised Trotsky and Lenin in the 'trade-union' controversy (see page 151). He did not become a full member of the Politburo until 1922.

Bukharin was intellectually inquisitive. He did not accept that only Marxists could contribute to knowledge about history and politics. He loved poetry and novels and was a talented painter. He liked to enjoy life and was very popular. Even his opponents found it hard to dislike him. Lenin called him 'the golden boy' of the Bolshevik Party. He was not a saint and could argue his points fiercely, especially on the NEP. He did not have the skills and political cunning of Stalin. In his testament, Lenin called Bukharin 'the biggest and most valuable theoretician in the Party' and 'the favourite of the whole Party'. But Lenin added, 'his theoretical views can only with the greatest doubt be regarded as fully Marxist'.

Alexei Rykov

Alexei Rykov, born in 1881 into a peasant family, became chairman of Vesenhka (Supreme Economic Council) in 1918 and later succeeded Lenin as Chairman of the Sovnarkom, having been his deputy from 1921. He was outspoken, frank and direct, not always endearing himself to his colleagues. He was a strong supporter of the NEP and opposed any return to War Communism. He was more statesmanlike than many of his colleagues but a notorious drinker: in some circles, vodka was known as Rykova.

Mikhail Tomsky

Mikhail Tomsky, born in 1880, was an important figure in the trade union movement, being an active member of the metalworkers' union before 1917. In 1918, he was made Chairman of the Central Council of Trade Unions. He was one of the few genuine workers in the party leadership. He fought hard for workers to have trade union rights and was dismayed by the reduction of trade unions to an 'appendage of the state'. He opposed Lenin in the trade union debate of 1920.

ACTIVITY

Stage 2
You have now read about the main contenders for the leadership of the Communist state. Which of them best meets the criteria that you drew up in Stage 1 of this Activity on page 181? Do you now wish to change your mind about the key characteristics/qualities the new leader should have?

TROTSKY – A DICTATOR?

Trotsky had no intention of becoming a dictator and had always been aware of the tendency for this to happen after a revolution. In 1904, he had warned that if a small party seized power, then: 'The organisation of the Party takes the place of the Party itself; the Central Committee takes the place of the organisation; and finally the dictator takes the place of the Central Committee.' He did not attempt to use the Red Army to secure his position. He was to argue for more democracy and openness in the party in the mid-1920s. However, some commentators have suggested that, whatever he said, he was dictatorial in style and may have acted accordingly if he had become leader.

B What were the main issues in the leadership struggle?

When we study power struggles in history we, quite naturally, focus on the personalities involved, their strengths and weaknesses, and why one emerged stronger than others. We see the struggle as a sort of contest of wills in which the contestants possess or do not possess certain qualities that allow one of them to come out on top. Whilst this is certainly important, we also have to look at the issues that were uppermost in people's minds when the struggle was taking place. These may be just as important in persuading people to support one candidate rather than another. This is particularly the case in the Soviet Union where there was a very real and contentious debate about government policy and the road to socialism. The key issues here were to do with leadership, industrialisation and party policy.

1 The nature of the leadership

Many party members did not want to see one person running the party and the government; they favoured 'collective leadership' or rule by committee. During the Civil War, the state had become highly centralised, with Lenin taking executive decisions. Now that the situation was more settled, it was thought that a collective leadership would be a more socialist way of running the state.

Party members feared that a 'dictator' could emerge to take control of the centralised state that had developed by 1924. This fear affected the decisions party members took between 1924 and 1926 – and the man they feared was Trotsky. As commander of the Red Army, he was in a strong position to crush opposition. His arrogant manner and conviction that he knew the direction the party should take seemed to confirm such fears.

Party members were also worried about the unity of the party after Lenin's death. They knew it was essential that the party stick together if it were to accomplish the huge task of transforming an unwilling population into good socialists. They therefore did not want a leader who might cause divisions among the different wings of the party and split it into warring factions. Again, it was Trotsky they feared.

2 The NEP and the industrialisation debate

The issue that dominated party conferences in the mid-1920s was the NEP and how the economy should be run. Everybody agreed on the need to industrialise. Industrialisation was the key to creating a large class of proletarian workers to build socialism. The question was how to do this in the most effective way. As the 1920s progressed, the NEP became increasingly unattractive to party members and they were deeply disturbed by its outward manifestations – the growth of a rich superclass, property dealing, land speculation, gambling and prostitution. These did not have any place in a socialist state. Also, after 1925 serious problems began to emerge:

- By 1925–26, industry had recovered to its pre-1913 levels. Some new impetus was needed to take it on but there was argument about where the resources to do this were going to come from.
- There was a high level of unemployment amongst workers. Wages for those in work did not keep pace with the rising prices of consumer goods, always in short supply. So many workers remained relatively poor and many could not get jobs – in the workers' society!
- Food shortages started to reappear. Peasants held on to their produce because they could not buy much for their money.

It was against this backdrop that the power struggle took place. It was a question not so much of whether party members supported the NEP – they had only accepted it as a stop-gap measure – but of when and how it should be ended. It was on this point that the two wings of the party diverged.

- The left wing of the party, led by Trotsky, Zinoviev and Kamenev, wanted to end the NEP and go for rapid industrialisation. This entailed the militarisation of labour, breaking the stranglehold the peasants had on the economy and squeezing more grain out of them to pay for industrialisation.
- The right wing, led by Bukharin, wanted to keep the NEP going and to encourage the peasants to become richer, so that they would spend more on consumer goods, which would, in turn, lead to the growth of manufacturing industry. They believed that conflict with the peasants might lead to economic collapse and endanger the Communist state.

(You can find out more about this debate and how it was resolved in Chapter 11.)

FOCUS ROUTE

1 Make notes summarising the key issues facing the party in the 1920s.
2 Which contender would be most hindered by the leadership issue?
3 How do you think the divisive NEP debate would affect the chances of particular contenders?
4 Which policy – 'Permanent Revolution' or 'Socialism in One Country' – do you think would most appeal to party members after so many years of conflict? Which contender would this help most?
5 Add any relevant information to the table you started on page 182.

ACTIVITY

Study Source 10.1.

1 What does the horse represent?
2 Who are the people on the sledge?
3 Why do you think the artist used the image of a horse and sledge?
4 How does this cartoon reveal the stance of Kamenev and the Left towards the NEP?

SOURCE 10.1 A 1924 cartoon showing Kamenev's stance on the NEP. The horse has the letters NEP on its collar

Why was the NEP so crucial to discussions in the party in the 1920s?

a) The NEP was crucial because economic policy was at the centre of the debate about the nature of the society the Communists were trying to create. It was a passionate issue. How long should they allow rich traders and peasants effectively to control the new workers' society? When could they push forward to industrialisation?

b) Attitudes in the party towards the NEP changed during the 1920s because economic circumstances were changing. In 1924, the NEP was still delivering economic recovery, but after 1925 problems started mounting. A threat of war in 1928 provided an added spur to industrialise more quickly, as did food shortages in the cities after 1927. So, party members, who had been prepared to go along with the NEP in the mid-1920s, might have adopted a different position in the late 1920s. The positions that the contenders took on this issue during the 1920s would therefore influence the amount of support they got from different sections of the party.

ACTIVITY

Stage 3

Having looked at the issues which divided the party, delete from the list you produced for the Activity on page 181 any characteristics/qualities that you think would **not** be useful in a new leader. Add new ones (or ones from the original list) that you now think would be helpful. In small groups, discuss your final lists and then compare them with other groups to see if you have reached any consensus.

3 'Permanent Revolution' versus 'Socialism in One Country'

Another important issue in the 1920s was the overall policy that the party should develop for the future, now that the USSR was the only Communist state in the world and world revolution had not taken place. Trotsky and Stalin developed different lines on this.

Permanent Revolution

Trotsky believed in 'Permanent Revolution'. He was convinced that the Communist revolution in Russia could not really succeed because the Russian working class was too small and the economy underdeveloped; it needed the support of the working class in the more industrialised countries of Europe. Trotsky felt therefore that the Russians should put energy and money into helping the working class in other countries to stage their own revolutions. He believed that the Russians should go on fighting a 'permanent revolution' until a world Communist revolution had been achieved.

Trotsky also wanted to subject the USSR to a continuing revolutionary process that would move society in the direction of socialism. He believed that measures such as compulsory labour units organised along military lines and forcing peasants into collective farms might be necessary to squeeze out old attitudes and create the economic base on which a socialist society could be built.

Socialism in One Country

Towards the end of 1924, Stalin put forward a different policy line that he called 'Socialism in One Country'. He said that the Communists had to accept that the world revolution had not happened and was not likely to take place in the immediate future. He proposed that the Russians build a socialist state in the USSR without the help of people from outside. Appealing to nationalism and patriotism, he said that they were in a unique position to show the world what socialism meant. They would solve their own problems and create a workers' society that was vastly superior to the capitalist West. They would be world leaders. It was optimistic as well as patriotic. Stalin argued that Permanent Revolution was defeatist and showed that Trotsky did not believe in Russia, its people and its mission. It was also a very flexible doctrine because it meant that the leaders of the Communist Party could say what was the best way to achieve socialism at any particular moment in time.

■ 10B Summary: Three key issues affecting the power struggle

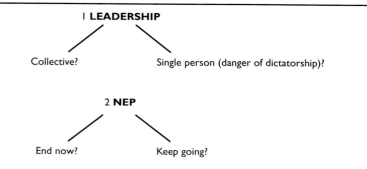

1 LEADERSHIP

Collective?   Single person (danger of dictatorship)?

2 NEP

End now?   Keep going?

3 PARTY POLICY ABOUT DIRECTION OF REVOLUTION

Permanent Revolution?   Socialism in One Country?

FOCUS ROUTE

1 Make notes on the way Stalin outmanoeuvred his opponents.
2 Add more details to your table of factors which helped Stalin and worked against his opponents, especially Trotsky.

C How did Stalin become party leader?

Did Stalin have a long-term plan to achieve power, carefully worked out from the beginning of the 1920s, or did he take advantage of opportunities that presented themselves between 1923 and 1929? As you can see from Source 10.2, Westwood does not think Stalin had a long-term plan. What we can be sure of is that he was determined to defend his position in the power stakes and be an important player at the top of the Communist Party, because he began building his power base in the party from 1922 onwards.

SOURCE 10.2 J. N. Westwood, *Endurance and Endeavour*, 1973, p. 287

For the most part, the intrigues and manoeuvres of the contestants were motivated not so much by desire to get to the top as by the desire to keep rivals away from the top. Although Stalin seemed to win every trick, it is unlikely that he followed a long-term plan. He did not need to, he could stand back and watch his rivals dig their own graves, occasionally offering his spade to one or other of them.

■ 10C How did Stalin build up his power base?

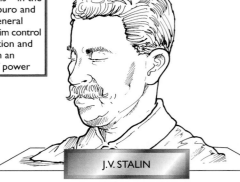

It was Stalin's position in all the key party organisations – in the Politburo, in the Orgburo and Secretariat, and as General Secretary – that gave him control of the party organisation and membership and such an enormous amount of power

J. V. STALIN

Party Secretary
This position gave him control, to some extent, of the business of the Politburo. For example, drawing up agendas and papers for the Politburo meetings gave him control over what was discussed and what information other members received.

Positions in Orgburo and the Secretariat
These gave him control of appointments to positions of responsibility in the party structure. He could put his supporters in key positions. In particular, the party secretaries from regional to local party level were increasingly Stalin's men: party secretaries of regions like the Ukraine were very powerful and at lower levels could virtually decide how party members voted.

Control of the party organisation
This meant that he could influence the selection of delegates who were sent to the annual party congress where major issues of policy were decided and the Central Committee was chosen. He could pack the congress with his supporters. This accounts for the hostile reception Trotsky received at conferences from 1924 onwards and the number of delegates who voted the way Stalin wanted. His ability to deliver votes in the congresses made him a valuable ally. This is why Zinoviev and Kamenev sought his support.

Control of party membership
This allowed him to get rid of the more radical elements – students and soldiers – who were likely to support Trotsky. Stalin supervised the 'Lenin Enrolment' of 1924 and 1925, in which the party almost doubled its membership to one million. The new members tended to be young urban workers, poorly educated ex-peasants who were not interested in ideological debate and were likely to do what their local party organiser told them to do. Stalin's practical policies based on nationalism appealed to them.

The other contenders had power bases but did not build up their support in the way Stalin did; they all made the mistake of underestimating Stalin.

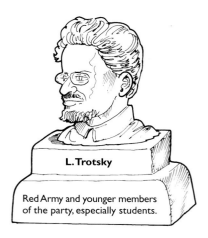

L. Trotsky

Red Army and younger members of the party, especially students.

L. Kamenev and G. Zinoviev

Zinoviev had a local power base in Leningrad and Kamenev one in Moscow. Both cities were well represented at the Party Congresses. Leningrad had always been a key city for the Bolsheviks. Zinoviev believed, erroneously, that his firm organisational base there made him too strong for Stalin.

N. Bukharin

He had some support in Moscow after Kamenev was defeated and he appealed to the youth of the party. But his main strength lay in his popularity and reputation as an outstanding theorist.

When studying how someone like Stalin came to power, there is a tendency to see the process as inevitable. We identify certain factors that helped the person to achieve power – for example, aspects of his character and personality, or weaknesses in, or wrong moves by, his opponents – and these seem to suggest that the end result was a foregone conclusion. But this is only with the benefit of hindsight. There were several points at which Stalin's ambitions might have been blocked. His position was not completely secure in 1929 and it was only by about 1937 that his position was virtually unassailable.

ACTIVITY

Can you identify any points at which Stalin's career might have been stopped:

a) when Lenin was alive
b) during the power struggle?

■ **10E The power struggle**

BEFORE THE BOUT BEGINS
- The positions Stalin held in the party administration – General Secretary from 1922, and member of the Orgburo and Secretariat – gave him enormous power over the policy and personnel of the party. This was the case even before Lenin died, but his rivals did not realise it and underestimated him.
- The ban on factions in 1921 was potentially a devastating weapon in the hands of the man who could control votes at party congresses.

Round 1: Stalin ahead on points
Stalin struck two significant blows at Lenin's funeral:
- He tricked Trotsky into not turning up for the funeral, severely damaging Trotsky's reputation and political prestige
- He made the most of the funeral, setting himself up as Lenin's disciple, the person who would carry on Lenin's work

Round 2: Stalin dodges a knock-out blow
Krupskaya gave Lenin's secret testament to the Central Committee in May 1924 just before the Thirteenth Party Congress. If read out to the congress, it would have spelt the end of Stalin's career. But Zinoviev and Kamenev urged that it should not become general knowledge, probably because
- it was not very flattering about them because of their opposition to Lenin in 1917; this was not something they wanted to bring to the congress's attention when they hoped to become its leading lights
- they thought that Stalin presented no real threat to them or the party and they wanted Stalin's help in defeating Trotsky
- they thought the testament might help Trotsky.
Trotsky remained silent, unwilling to become involved. This was a major mistake on his part and was to cost him dearly later.

Round 3: Trotsky on the ropes
The Thirteenth Congress in 1924 saw hostilities out in the open. Zinoviev, Kamenev and Stalin, now effectively a triumvirate leading the party, presented party policy at the congress. Trotsky criticised the party for becoming bureaucratic and less democratic. Despite making brilliant speeches, Trotsky was easily defeated in the votes because the congress was packed with 'well-instructed Stalinist delegates' as well as the powerful blocs controlled by Zinoviev and Kamenev. Trotsky could have appealed to supporters inside and outside the party, but he had approved the 'ban on factions' in 1921 and was unwilling to cause splits in the party.

Round 5: Knockout blow for the left

In 1925, Stalin's policy of 'Socialism in One Country' proved very popular with party members, attracting the right wing of the party because it seemed to fit in with the NEP – their own route to socialism. A new alliance emerged between Stalin in the centre of the party and Bukharin on the right, supporting NEP and co-operation with the peasants. At the Fourteenth Party Congress in 1925, Zinoviev and Kamenev attacked Stalin, calling for a vote of no confidence in him, the ending of the NEP and a tough line against the peasants. But Stalin's control of the party machine was now so complete that they gave him little trouble. They lost every vote because Stalin had control of the delegates.

In 1926, they joined Trotsky, their old enemy, to form a 'United Opposition' and made a direct appeal to the party masses and the workers, trying to organise demonstrations in Moscow. This was a mistake because they could now be accused of 'factionalism'. As a result, all three lost their positions of power (see page 195) and in 1927 were expelled from the party.

The winner

In December 1929, Stalin celebrated his fiftieth birthday. He was now the undisputed leader of the USSR.

Round 4: The left slugs it out

In 1924, Zinoviev and Kamenev mounted a vicious campaign against Trotsky, questioning his loyalty and raising his opposition to Lenin before 1917. Trotsky retaliated by attacking them in *Lessons of October*, in which he criticised their unwillingness to back Lenin in the 1917 revolution. Stalin stayed in the background, happy to see the left wing tearing itself apart while he continued to build his power base. He seemed to be the moderate peacemaker, anxious to maintain party unity. Zinoviev and Kamenev, still frightened of Trotsky, allowed Stalin to bring more of his supporters into key positions in the party organisation, forming the majorities on committees and at conferences.

Round 6: Knockout blow for the right

In 1928, Stalin turned against the NEP and attacked the right wing of the party. He now advocated rapid industrialisation and the use of force to make the peasants co-operate – the very policies of the left that he had just smashed! Bukharin mounted a strong defence of the NEP but at the congress of 1929 found himself outvoted by Stalin's supporters, who were joined by those on the left who supported the anti-NEP line. Bukharin and the other right-wing leaders, Rykov and Tomsky, were removed from the Politburo and other party bodies (Rykov had been Premier since Lenin's death and Bukharin had been head of the Comintern).

Why did Stalin become party leader?

ACTIVITY

1 You will already have developed your own ideas about why Stalin emerged as the leader of Soviet Russia by 1929. The writers of Sources 10.3–10.10 indicate some of the key reasons why they think Stalin won the power struggle and whether this was to do with his skills or the weaknesses of his opponents. Read the sources carefully. Decide which column of the table below they would fit into.

Importance of control of party organisation	Policies	Stalin's personal characteristics and political skills	Weaknesses of opponents, especially Trotsky	Luck

2 How do these sources suggest that perceptions of Stalin changed considerably between 1924 and 1928?
3 What does this tell us about how Stalin conducted his campaign for the leadership?
4 Add new information from these sources to the table of factors which helped Stalin and worked against his opponents (page 182).

SOURCE 10.3 G. Hosking, *A History of the Soviet Union*, 1985, p. 140

To his comrades in the Party leadership he [Stalin] was known, rather condescendingly, as 'Comrade Card-Index' (Tovarishch Kartotekov): they were content to leave him to assemble and classify the personnel files, not yet realising what power was accumulating therein. Most of them, being well read in the history of past revolutions, were obsessed by a very different danger: that of finding the revolutions hijacked by another Bonaparte.
*[**Note:** Bolsheviks were very knowledgeable about the French Revolution and expected, after the initial period of violent revolution, that a Napoleon Bonaparte figure would emerge as a dictator in Russia.]*

SOURCE 10.4 I. Deutscher, *The Prophet Unarmed: Trotsky 1921–29*, 1959, p. 93

The truth is that Trotsky refrained from attacking Stalin because he felt secure. No contemporary, and he least of all, saw in the Stalin of 1923 the menacing and towering figure he was to become. It seemed to Trotsky almost a bad joke that Stalin, the wilful and sly but shabby and inarticulate man in the background, should be his rival.

SOURCE 10.5 E. H. Carr, *Socialism in One Country*, 1958, p. 151

[Trotsky] ... the great intellectual, the great administrator, the great orator lacked one quality essential – at any rate in the conditions of the Russian Revolution – to the great political leader. Trotsky could fire masses of men to acclaim and follow him. But he had no talent for leadership among equals. He could not establish his authority among colleagues by the modest arts of persuasion or by sympathetic attention to the views of men of lesser intellectual calibre than himself.

SOURCE 10.6 Bukharin, at a secret meeting with Kamenev in July 1928

Stalin is a Genghis Khan, an unscrupulous intriguer, who sacrifices everything else to the preservation of power ... He changes his theories according to whom he needs to get rid of next.

SOURCE 10.7 I. Deutscher, *Stalin*, rev. edn, 1966, p. 277

In the Politburo, when matters of high policy were under debate, he [Stalin] never seemed to impose his views on his colleagues. He carefully followed the course of debate to see what way the wind was blowing and invariably voted with the majority, unless he had assured his majority beforehand. He was therefore always agreeable to the majority. To Party audiences he appeared as a man without personal grudge and rancour, as a detached Leninist, a guardian of the doctrine who criticised others only for the sake of the cause.

SOURCE 10.8 C. Ward, *Stalin's Russia*, 1993, pp. 35–36

All Bolshevik leaders were trying to find their feet in an unfamiliar and unanticipated world, and the doctrine of socialism in one country at least had the merit of describing things as they really were ... The theory evoked a sympathetic response from two groups: the new sub-elites advanced by the crises of the immediate post-evolutionary years and workers sickened by the manifold injustices and inequalities of the NEP. The latter were men and women indifferent to factional squabbles and impatient for socialist reconstruction; the former were people ... for whom the Revolution was primarily a Russian achievement – Soviet patriotism sat easily with the enjoyment of the fruits of offices. A Stalinist constituency was in the process of formation and Stalin's 'left turn' (rapid industrialisation and collectivisation) brought most of them round to his way of thinking.

SOURCE 10.9 R. Conquest, *Stalin: Breaker of Nations*, 1991, pp. 129–30

In 1923 Stalin had been on the point of political ruin. In 1924 he was one among equals, but without any outright supporters in the full membership of the Politburo. Six years later he would be in unchallenged power ... In six years Stalin outmanoeuvred a series of opponents; first in alliance with the rest of his colleagues, he opposed and demoted Trotsky. Then in alliance with the Bukharin–Rykov 'Right' he defeated the Zinoviev–Kamenev 'Left' bloc ... and finally he and his own following attacked their hitherto allies, the 'Rightists'.

SOURCE 10.10 M. McCauley, *Russia 1917–41*, 1997, p. 78

Stalin had luck on his side. Had Lenin not died Stalin would probably have been sent to the provinces to work for the Party. Dzerzhinsky, the head of the Cheka, from its inception to his death in 1926, was never one of Stalin's fans. His death allowed Stalin to infiltrate his supporters into the political police and eventually use them against his opponents.

ACTIVITY

Write an essay entitled: Why did Stalin rather than Trotsky emerge as the leader of the USSR in 1929?

You will have collected a lot of information to help you to answer this question as part of the Focus Route activity on page 182 but how are you going to structure your essay and deploy the information? The twenty-one cards on page 194 can help you to do this. Five of the cards are paragraph headings. They represent the **main points** which directly answer the essay question. The other cards represent points which **support** the main points.

1 Using your own copy of the cards and working in groups of three or four, find the **main points** and arrange them in a row. Then find the **supporting points** that go with each main point and put them in the correct column. The columns are not evenly balanced. Some main points have three cards, others have only two.

2 But how much weight should you give to each of the different explanations – which are the most important reasons? Try this: choose **nine** cards that you think are the most important in answering this question. Arrange them in the shape of a diamond like the one shown here. Put the one you think is the most important at the top, the next two most important on the second line and so on. (N.B. We have **not** shown a correct answer in the example.)

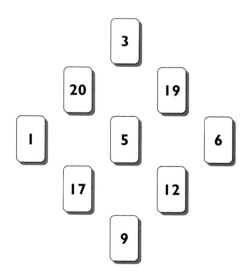

3 Discuss the cards you chose and the order you put them in with other members of the class. Argue the case for your ordering compared with theirs.

4 Now write your essay. Don't just use the information given on the cards. Use the rest of the information in this chapter to develop your points fully. You don't have to stick to our paragraph headings. The important thing is that you decide what your main points are to answer the question and how you are going to explain/support these main points.

1 Stalin had control of the party machine through his key positions in the Politburo and Orgburo and as General Secretary.	**2** Stalin stayed in the background pretending to be a moderate peacemaker. So no one realised he was a serious power player. He outmanoeuvred his opponents, playing them off against each other.	**3** Luck favoured Stalin rather than Trotsky.	**4** Socialism in One Country was more appealing to most party members than Permanent Revolution. It gave Russians a special historic role.
5 Stalin made full use of Lenin's funeral to advance his position. He tricked Trotsky into not attending the funeral. He took on the mantle of Leninism to transfer Lenin's prestige to himself.	**6** Stalin's personal characteristics and qualities helped him become leader of the party.	**7** Stalin was able to appoint his own supporters to key positions in the party. He controlled the membership of the party, using his power to expel members likely to support Trotsky and bring in new members likely to support him.	**8** Stalin was politically very skilful and cunning.
9 Stalin was perceived as dull and mediocre – the 'grey blur'. So no one saw him as a threat until it was too late. He was tough and ruthless. He was determined to protect his power base and make sure that he was not ousted.	**10** Trotsky himself was responsible for his own downfall. He had weaknesses that made him unfit for the power struggle.	**11** Lenin and Sverdlov died at the right time for Stalin.	**12** Trotsky had only joined the Bolsheviks in August 1917 and was not seen as a loyal member of the party. Many Bolsheviks did not trust him. They thought he might try to become a dictator.
13 Stalin's different positions on the NEP during the mid to late 1920s and his decision to go for rapid industrialisation at the end of the 1920s were supported by the majority of party members.	**14** Less high-minded, more down to earth and practical than other leading Bolsheviks, Stalin was ideally suited to managing the bureaucratic and centralised party that had developed.	**15** Trotsky was too high-minded and arrogant, dismissive of his colleagues. He was respected but did not engender affection or personal loyalty. He was seen as the person most likely to cause splits in the party.	**16** Stalin's control of appointments and the membership made him a useful ally. Other contenders wanted him on their side because he could deliver votes in the congresses.
17 Trotsky did not go out of his way to develop or build up his power base in the party and allowed Stalin to erode the one he already had. Like the other contenders, he underestimated Stalin and was outmanoeuvred by him.	**18** Stalin was a very loyal party member who was one of the few leaders with proletarian roots. It seemed he would not cause splits in the party.	**19** Stalin adopted policies that were broadly approved by the majority of the Communist Party. He was responsive to the mood of the times.	**20** Trotsky did not like getting involved in the 'drudgery of politics'. He was no good at political intrigue, making alliances and trade-offs.
			21 It was lucky for Stalin that Lenin's testament was not read out and that Trotsky was ill for most of the power struggle.

What happened to Trotsky and the other leadership contenders?

In January 1925, Trotsky lost his position as Commissar for Military Affairs; in December of the same year he lost his Politburo seat. Zinoviev was sacked as Leningrad Soviet Chairman in January 1926 and was ousted from the Politburo in July. Kamenev lost his Politburo seat at the same time and in October was removed as leader of the Comintern. In 1927, all three were expelled from the party because of their role in the United Opposition, when they campaigned for more democracy and openness in the party. Factionalism had been banned in 1921.

Kamenev and Zinoviev, demoralised, recanted their views and petitioned to be allowed to rejoin the party. They were readmitted in June 1928. Trotsky refused to recant and in 1928, on Stalin's orders, found himself being bundled in his pyjamas into a train heading for central Asia. He was allowed to go with his secretaries and around 30 other oppositionists to Alma-ata, almost 5000 km from Moscow. The following year he was deported to Turkey, where he started to write his account of the Russian Revolution and to mount what turned out to be a continuous attack on Stalin over the next decade. In 1933, he moved to France and then on to Norway, but his political activities did not make him welcome in Europe and in 1937 he went to live in Mexico. He was always under threat from Stalin's agents and in August 1940 was murdered by a hit man with an ice-pick.

Bukharin, Rykov and Tomsky suffered a similar fate. Accused of 'right deviation', in 1929 they lost their posts. Bukharin was ousted from the Politburo and lost his posts as editor of *Pravda* and President of the Comintern. All three later recanted their views and were allowed to remain in the party. Bukharin made a major contribution in writing the Soviet constitution of 1936 but this did not save him from trial and execution later in the 1930s (see page 247).

KEY POINTS FROM CHAPTER 10

How did Stalin emerge as the sole leader of Russia?

1 The main protagonists in the power struggle were Stalin and Trotsky. Zinoviev, Kamenev and Bukharin were also contenders.
2 Key issues – leadership, the NEP, policies – were as important as the personalities involved.
3 It was a struggle over power rather than a struggle for power. The contenders were anxious to prevent rivals from coming to power and pursuing policies with which they did not agree.
4 On the whole, party members tended to support Stalin's changes of policy line. They supported Socialism in One Country and his line on the peasants at the end of the 1920s.
5 Stalin's control of the party machine was a crucial factor in his success.
6 Stalin was a skilful politician who outmanoeuvred his opponents, but he was also lucky.
7 Trotsky's weaknesses and errors of judgement were important factors in his defeat.
8 All Stalin's opponents vastly underestimated him.

How did Stalin transform the economy of the USSR in the 1930s?

At the end of the 1920s, Stalin launched radical economic policies that literally changed the face of Russia, creating a new industrial and agricultural landscape. In Russia this was called the 'Great Turn'. Historians have talked about a second revolution (1917 being the first) and a 'revolution from above' since it was instigated by Stalin and the Communist leadership. The NEP was cast aside and Stalin introduced Five-Year Plans for industry and agriculture. Chapter 11 examines the reasons for the Great Turn. Chapter 12 looks at the collectivisation of Soviet agriculture and Chapter 13 looks at Stalin's programme for rapid industrialisation. A cultural revolution accompanied the Great Turn and this is covered later, in Chapter 17.

SOURCE 1   S. Fitzpatrick, *The Russian Revolution 1917–1932*, 1994, pp. 9–10

In theory, industrialization and economic modernization were only means to an end for Russian Marxists, the end being socialism. But the more clearly and single-mindedly the Bolsheviks focused on the means, the more foggy, distant and unreal the end became. When the term 'building socialism' came into common use in the 1930s, its meaning was hard to distinguish from the actual building of new factories and towns currently in progress.

SOURCE 3   R. W. Davies, 'Stalin and Soviet Industrialization', *History Sixth*, March 1991

This was the first attempt at the comprehensive planning of a major economy, and was thus an important turning point not only for Russian history, but also for the history of world industrialization ... In 1929, Stalin launched the so-called 'socialist offensive', which combined rapid industrialization with the forcible collectivization of peasant agriculture.

SOURCE 2   Stalin, writing in *Pravda*, 5 February 1931

To lower the tempo [of industrialisation] means falling behind and those who fall behind get beaten. But we don't want to be beaten ... The history of old Russia consisted, amongst other things, in her being beaten continually for her backwardness. She was beaten by the Mongol khans. She was beaten by the Turkish beys ... She was beaten by the Polish and Lithuanian gentry. She was beaten by the Anglo-French capitalists. She was beaten by the Japanese barons. She was beaten by all of them because of her backwardness, her military backwardness, cultural backwardness, political backwardness, industrial backwardness, agricultural backwardness ... We are fifty or a hundred years behind the advanced countries. We must make good this distance in ten years. Either we do it, or we shall be crushed.

SOURCE 4   Stalin, in an article entitled 'Year of the Great Breakthrough', *Pravda*, 7 November 1929

From small, backward, individual farming to large-scale, advanced, collective farming. The new and decisive feature of the peasant collective farm movement is that the peasants are joining the collective farms not in separate groups, but in whole villages, whole regions, whole districts, and even whole provinces ... We are becoming a country of metal, an automobilised country, a tractorised country. And when we have put the USSR on an automobile, and the muzhik [peasant] on a tractor, let the esteemed capitalists, who boast their 'civilisation', try to overtake us.

SOURCE 5 Uzbek peasants in Samarkand crowd around a tractor for a lesson in the new farming methods. The tractor came to symbolise the changes taking place in the countryside; children were even named 'Tractor' in honour of the new machines

SOURCE 6 Workers looking at a board showing production plans and targets

SOURCE 7 Workers digging in Magnitogorsk, an industrial centre that expanded rapidly in the early 1930s

SOURCE 8 A women's construction brigade, whose job was to build a factory in Moscow, 1931

197

HOW DID STALIN TRANSFORM THE ECONOMY OF THE USSR IN THE 1930S?

11 Why did Stalin make the Great Turn?

CHAPTER OVERVIEW

Under the NEP the Soviet Union had recovered from seven years of warfare (1914–21), but by 1927 it had not developed its industry much beyond the pre-1914 level and its agriculture was still backward. Also, by the late 1920s the NEP was presenting the Communists with a variety of economic and social problems. Stalin, with the support of the majority of the party, felt that the NEP was not delivering the economic performance or the type of society they had envisaged. They wanted to press ahead with rapid industrialisation to build a socialist society. In this chapter we look at the reasons for the Great Turn.

A What were the driving forces behind Stalin's economic policies? (pp. 198–199)

B Was the NEP working at the end of the 1920s? (pp. 200–202)

C The Great Turn (pp. 202–203)

FOCUS ROUTE

Make notes on the reasons why Stalin wanted to industrialise the USSR as rapidly as possible.

A What were the driving forces behind Stalin's economic policies?

The overriding aim of Stalin's policies was to industrialise and modernise the USSR as quickly as possible. He wanted backward Russia to become the 'Soviet America'. The Russians would beat the capitalists at their own game and become a force in the world to be reckoned with. Stalin had a number of reasons – practical and ideological – for wanting to force the pace.

Why did Stalin want to industrialise the USSR so quickly?

1 To increase military strength
Stalin knew that a country that was not industrialised was a weak country. To fight a modern war, a country had to have a well-developed industrial base to manufacture the huge quantities of weapons and munitions that would be required. There was a war scare in the late 1920s, and during the 1930s Stalin became increasingly convinced that the USSR would be attacked.

2 To achieve self-sufficiency
Stalin wanted to make the USSR much less dependent on Western manufactured goods, especially the heavy industrial plant that was needed for industrial production. It was important that the USSR had a strong industrial base to produce the goods its people needed. This would make it self-sufficient and more independent in the world.

3 To increase grain supplies
Stalin wanted to end the dependence of the economy on a backward agricultural system. In the past, this had created major problems whenever there was a bad harvest or the peasants did not produce enough food. He did not want the new socialist state to be at the mercy of the peasantry.

4 To move towards a socialist society

According to Marxist theoreticians, socialism could only be created in a highly industrialised state where the overwhelming majority of the population were workers. In 1928, only about twenty per cent of the population of the USSR were workers.

5 To establish his credentials

Stalin needed to prove to himself and other leading Bolsheviks that he was the successor and equal of Lenin. His economic policies were central to this. The economic transformation of the USSR, taking the revolution forward in a giant leap towards socialism, would establish him as a leader of historic importance.

6 To improve standards of living

Stalin wanted to catch up with the West, not just militarily, but also in terms of the standard of living that people enjoyed. Industrialisation created wealth for a society. The Communist life should be a good life and people in other parts of the world should appreciate what it had to offer working people.

■ **Learning trouble spot**

Why did industrialisation depend on agriculture in the USSR?

To industrialise a country you need to spend money on factories, machinery and equipment to produce goods. This is called capital investment. Initially, the machinery and equipment have to be bought from foreign countries. The USSR had gold, furs, timber, oil and a range of products to export, but these could not generate the sums of money needed to pay for heavy industrial equipment on the scale Stalin required.

The Soviet Union was not in a position to obtain loans from abroad (as the tsars had done); few Western capitalists would invest in a Communist state. The only source which could generate enough wealth was agriculture. Surplus grain could be exported to earn foreign currency to buy industrial capital equipment. On top of this, the peasants were required to produce extra grain to feed a growing workforce in the cities. This meant that every year the state had to obtain from the peasants food for the cities as well as grain for export. The problem for the Communist government was that agricultural production was in the hands of the millions of peasants who could hold the great socialist experiment to ransom. If they did not yield up sufficient grain, the push to industrialisation could not move forward.

COMMUNISTS AND PEASANTS

Lenin, Stalin and other leading Communists had never had much time for the peasants. The conservative tendencies of the peasants and their petty-bourgeois attitudes had no place in the new state. Lenin looked forward to huge factory farms where the agricultural workers would be no different from their industrial brothers, all part of the socialist utopia. The party never really managed to secure any real hold on the mass of the peasantry and the peasants, for their part, returned the hostility.

FOCUS ROUTE

Why did the majority of the party think a new approach to the peasantry was required?

ACTIVITY

Work in groups of three. Each person takes on one of the roles below and has a minute to clearly explain one of the following:

a) as a bureaucrat – why more grain is needed and why it isn't reaching the markets

b) as a government official – how you are going to persuade the peasants to get more grain to the markets

c) as a peasant – how and why you will avoid supplying more grain to the markets.

After each explanation, the other two members of the group summarise what they have heard by choosing two or three key points.

THE URALS–SIBERIAN METHOD

Stalin's visit to the Urals, in January 1928, lasted for only three weeks. It is said that this is the only time he visited an agricultural area in his life. During this period, the so-called 'Urals–Siberian method' was developed. This involved encouraging poor and middle-income peasants to denounce kulaks who were 'hoarding grain'. The grain would then be seized and the kulaks arrested. The Urals–Siberian method was identified with the coercion of the peasants.

B Was the NEP working at the end of the 1920s?

The 1926 Party Congress had charged the leadership with 'the transformation of our country from an agrarian into an industrial one, capable by its own efforts of producing the necessary means'. The push for industrialisation was on. However, at the end of the 1920s it seemed that the NEP had run out of 'push'. By 1926, the excess capacity in industry had been used up. This meant that all the factories, machinery and equipment that had existed pre-1914 had been put back into use as far as this was possible. A massive injection of capital investment was now needed to move the industrialisation process forward. To make matters worse, the economy was facing serious difficulties at the end of the 1920s.

The NEP and the peasants

Although the grain supply had increased enormously under the NEP and the fear of famine had receded, the peasants were not producing the quantities of grain the government needed for its industrialisation plans. In 1913, Russia exported twelve million tons of grain; in the best years of the NEP the amount never exceeded three million. This was having a devastating effect on foreign trade: in 1926–27 exports were at 33 per cent and imports at 38 per cent of their 1913 levels due to the decline in grain exports. So the Soviet Union could not bring in the technology (machinery, etc.) it needed for industrial expansion.

The grain was simply not reaching the market. There were a number of reasons for this:

- Agriculture was still very backward, relying on traditional methods of farming. For example, in 1927 over five million inefficient wooden ploughs were still in use.
- When the land was shared out after the revolution, peasant landholdings had tended to become smaller than before 1917. The large estates and large farms which supplied the cities had disappeared. They had been divided up amongst the land-hungry peasants. On the majority of these smaller holdings, people ate most of what they produced.
- The relationship between the government and the peasants deteriorated towards the end of the 1920s (you will find out more about this in Chapter 12).

The government tried a new tactic to encourage the peasants to put more grain on the market. It stopped collecting taxes from the peasants in the form of grain and made them pay a money tax. At the same time, the government clamped down on private traders who were paying the peasants around twice the price that the state was paying for grain. So the peasants had to sell at lower prices to the state and had to sell more than before to pay their taxes.

This worked initially, but the peasants soon got wise to the government's ploy. Since meat prices were still going up, they started to feed grain to their animals rather than sell it at low prices. Also, they found that there was not much point in having surplus money because there was little they could buy with it, since industrial consumer goods were still in short supply. So peasants started to hold back their grain from the market, hoping for the price to rise. As a result, the grain procured by the state at the end of 1927 was about three-quarters of what it had been in 1926.

Stalin sent out officials, backed by the police, to seize grain. In January 1928, he himself went to the Urals and Western Siberia on a requisitioning campaign. He got more grain, but the relationship between the peasants and the government was breaking down and there was substantial resistance to Stalin's actions. Despite resistance in the party to Stalin's methods, he used them again the following year after the poor harvest in 1928 forced the government to ration bread in the cities.

Was the NEP working for the urban workers?

The NEP had not brought great rewards for the urban workers. Although they were better off than at any time before the revolution, real wages had, by 1928, only just passed their pre-war level. True, they had an eight-hour working day and other social benefits, and in state-run factories they had some power: local trade-union representatives often sat on a panel running the factory alongside the specialist director (usually an old bourgeois manager). But most industrial organisations were still hierarchical and the trade unions tended to support government-appointed managers rather than their own members. Lenin himself had favoured schemes from the USA which used time and motion studies to speed up production.

Worse than this, thousands of workers did not have jobs at all. High unemployment persisted throughout the NEP. The workers complained bitterly about the gap between themselves and the better off. They complained about the high prices charged for food by the peasants and market traders and about the bourgeois specialists and officials who were paid so much more than they were.

Women had been particularly hard hit by the NEP. Many had been forced out of their jobs when the Red Army was demobilised or been forced to move from skilled to unskilled work. So large numbers of jobless, unsupported women ended up on the streets.

Housing was still a major problem and most workers lived in overcrowded, poor-quality houses and flats. For instance, in Smolensk in 1929, the factory committee of a cement works reported: 'Every day there are many complaints about apartments: many workers have families of six and seven people, and live in one room.' There was also a mounting crime problem in the cities. As a result of the turmoil of the war and civil war, thousands of young people were parentless and rootless, forming gangs which roamed the streets to find their victims. It was hardly the workers' paradise that the revolution had promised.

ACTIVITY

What would you advise?

You are one of Stalin's advisers. Everyone agrees on the need for industrialisation but you have to help him decide how to carry it out. Decide which policy you think is the better one for Stalin to follow. Give your reasons for choosing that policy and identify three points which would make the other policy less acceptable. You must take into account the circumstances at the end of the 1920s.

Policy 1

- Carry on with the NEP policies with some modifications. In particular, increase the price of grain to encourage the peasants, especially the best farmers, to produce more.
- This will give the peasants more money to spend on consumer goods, which will encourage growth in industry. This will increase employment and gradually improve wages.
- The state will be able to procure more grain for export and for the workers. However, in the short term there will not be so much money for investment, so industrialisation will have to proceed more slowly.
- Provide a programme of agricultural help, encouraging peasants to work together and share machinery, and even to join collective farms. The state will provide help with mechanisation, especially tractors, to increase grain production. Develop model farms for peasants to visit and educate them in modern agricultural methods.
- This is the only way to avoid a return to the days of War Communism and the conflict with the peasants that had such disastrous results in 1921. Workers will benefit in the long term.

Policy 2

- Go all out for rapid industrialisation because time is running out. Russia needs to move towards socialism and be able to defend itself. Organise workers into 'shock brigades' to achieve higher production, and keep their wages low so that all available resources can be invested in industry.
- Squeeze the peasants hard: keep the price the state pays for grain low and tax the peasants heavily. This will provide extra money to invest in industry, and grain for export in order to buy industrial machinery.
- If the peasants do not offer the grain for sale voluntarily, wring it out of them by force as in 1918.
- Encourage peasants to work on large collective farms which can be farmed more efficiently and productively. The government will provide tractors and other mechanised equipment. This will also release surplus labour to go to the cities to work in the new developing industries. Collective farms will socialise the peasants.
- Fast industrialisation will actually help the peasants because it will produce the tractors and equipment they need.

Discussion and review

The policies that you have considered in the Activity on page 201 broadly represent the positions of different groups in the Communist Party at the end of the 1920s, although they have been adapted for the purposes of this exercise.

Policy 1

The first policy is close to that of Bukharin and the right. Bukharin accepted that industrialisation was the main goal but believed that the best way to achieve this was with the co-operation of the peasantry. He thought that the 1905 Revolution had failed because there was no link between the workers and the peasants – 'the supreme lesson for us all' – and that they had been successful in 1917 because of the combination of '*a peasant war* against the landlord and a *proletarian revolution*'. It was not that he particularly liked the peasants. But he had been impressed by their fierce independence during 1920–21 and believed that trying to force the peasants to supply more grain might lead to the collapse of Soviet Russia and the end of all their revolutionary hopes.

The right, which included most of the party's agricultural experts, were prepared to take more time to achieve the desired ends. They believed it would take time to prepare Soviet agriculture for collectivisation and were not keen on Stalin's 'War Communist'-style methods of seizing grain.

Policy 2

The second policy is close to the ideas of Eugene Preobrazhensky, a leading left-wing economist. He argued that the USSR had to pass through a stage of 'primitive socialist accumulation' similar to the 'primitive accumulation' that Marx identified as a stage in the development of industrialised societies. In developing capitalist societies, workers had been exploited (for example, by low wages and poor conditions) and colonies had been raided (for cheap raw materials) to provide the capital for industrial growth. In the USSR, it was the peasantry who had to be exploited through taxation and prices so that the wealth they generated could be transferred to industrial investment. For example, if the government bought cheap grain from the peasants and sold it for higher prices, the surplus money that resulted could be 'pumped' into industry. The implication of this policy was that industrial development could be funded only at the expense of the peasants. However, Preobrazhensky did not advocate violence, confiscation or forced collectivisation.

FOCUS ROUTE

Draw up a chart. On one side, make the case for continuing the NEP. On the other, put the case for a more direct, forced approach.

Continuing the NEP	Ending the NEP/rapid industrialisation

C   The Great Turn

At the Fifteenth Party Congress in December 1927, the announcement of the First Five-Year Plan marked the end of the NEP. The plan demanded more rapid industrialisation, setting high targets for industry to achieve. In agriculture, the plan called for collectivisation – some fifteen per cent of peasant households were to be collectivised.

The NEP had provided a 'breathing space' while industry and agriculture recovered from the dismal depths of War Communism. But it was not developing an industrial, urban, proletarian, socialist society. From the Bolsheviks' point of view, it was creating the wrong type of society. The NEP encouraged private markets, private enterprise and Nepmen. The peasants, still the great mass of the population, showed no signs of becoming good socialists and could not be relied upon to produce the grain that the state needed for its industrialisation programme.

The majority of party members had accepted the constraints of the NEP but they had never liked it. They were itching to move forward towards the establishment of a socialist society. This could only, in their eyes, be achieved with the support of a largely proletarian workforce in a highly developed industrialised society. So they warmly welcomed Stalin's 'left turn' (adopting the ideas of the left wing of the party) in his policies for the modernisation and industrialisation of the USSR. The Five-Year Plans represented a significant step towards achieving the goals of the revolution.

There was also another factor which encouraged the party to support more rapid industrialisation – the fear of invasion. By 1927, relations with France and Poland had deteriorated, Britain had broken off diplomatic relations and there were suspicions about Japanese intentions. The USSR needed an industrial base to build armaments.

The change from the NEP to Five-Year Plans is called the Great Turn because it marks a major shift in the direction of the Soviet economy towards central planning – the 'command economy'. The land was to be socialised through collectivisation; no longer would it be owned by individual peasants. Industrialisation would lead to the growth of the proletariat, along with new cities and new wealth – the 'good society' that workers aspired to – and would build a strong, self-sufficient state. This was to be the big step forward towards the new socialist society. It indicated a significant cultural shift, in the process of which 'New Soviet Man' would emerge. You can read about this in Chapter 17.

Stalin's policies were not new. Planning by the centre had been an important feature of the Soviet economy since the revolution. Lenin had assumed direct control of industry after 1917 and had kept control of the 'commanding heights' of industry (large-scale industries, banking, etc.) under the NEP. It was the way Stalin carried out his policies that was new. He was to take the planning to a level unimaginable at the time of Lenin's death in 1924 and to implement his policies in a way that few could have foreseen.

Another reason why the Great Turn is significant is that these policies also wrought great changes in the Communist Party and the relationship between the party and the people. Some historians maintain that it is at this point that the Soviet Union 'went wrong' – that it now followed a path that led to totalitarianism, tyranny and inhumanity. These historians suggest that the USSR would have done better to have continued with the NEP (see page 243).

ACTIVITY

Use the information collected in your Focus Route activities to answer the following questions.

Either:

1 Write three or four paragraphs setting out the reasons why Stalin made the Great Turn. Each paragraph should make a key point and be backed up with further explanation or supporting evidence for the key point.

Or:

2 Draw a large annotated diagram showing the issues and debates surrounding the NEP and why Stalin and the Communist Party opted for the Five-Year Plans.

KEY POINTS FROM CHAPTER 11

Why did Stalin make the Great Turn?

1 The NEP was not producing the sort of society that many Communists wanted by the end of the 1920s.

2 There was a continuing debate about the NEP in the Communist Party throughout the 1920s: the right wing of the party wanted to keep it and the left wing wanted to end it.

3 No Communists liked the outward manifestations of the NEP – the Nepmen and the strength of the private market. Nor did they like being held to ransom by the peasants.

4 Urban workers and Communist Party members wanted to move forward to take the revolution on and build a socialist society.

5 The workers were suffering high unemployment rates and low wages.

6 The peasantry were starting to hold back food from the market and food shortages were serious in 1928 and 1929.

7 There was a war scare in 1928 that increased fears about the Soviet Union's vulnerability to attack and made the need to produce armaments more urgent.

8 In 1928, the decision was taken to end the NEP and to embark on a massive industrialisation programme in the Five-Year Plans.

9 This has been called the Great Turn and it marked a significant shift – economic, political and cultural – in the history of the Soviet Union.

12 Was collectivisation a success?

CHAPTER OVERVIEW

Stalin forced through collectivisation at an incredibly rapid pace. This caused chaos in agriculture as well as suffering and misery on a huge scale. At the end of the first wave of collectivisation, he appeared to relent and called a halt. But the next year he restarted the programme with increased vigour. Peasant attempts to resist the process proved futile. By 1932, collectivisation had resulted in an enormous drop in agricultural production and created a famine in which millions died. However, Stalin secured the surplus food he needed to feed the industrial workforce and, to some extent, to pay for industrialisation.

A Why collectivise? (pp. 204–206)

B Why was collectivisation carried out so rapidly? (p. 206–208)

C How was collectivisation carried out? (pp. 209–210)

D What impact did collectivisation have on the peasants? (pp. 210–216)

E Was collectivisation a success? (pp. 217–218)

A Why collectivise?

In mid-1929, less than five per cent of peasants were on collective or state farms. In January 1930, Stalin announced that around 25 per cent of the grain-producing areas were to be collectivised by the end of the year. This announcement took even his own officials by surprise. Most party members had assumed that collectivisation would be carried out on a voluntary basis and had not anticipated the speed at which it was going to take place. Some were horrified.

SOURCE 12.1 A mechanised harvester at work. The government promised that collective farms would bring modern agricultural machinery and methods to the peasants

SOURCE 12.2 Babies are settled into an outdoor nursery as their mothers march off to work in the fields of the collective farm

SOURCE 12.3 A literacy class on a collective farm

SOURCE 12.4 The slogan on this poster reads 'Come and join our kolkhoz, comrade!'

ACTIVITY

Examine Sources 12.1–12.4. They are examples of propaganda published to persuade peasants of the advantages of collectivisation. What messages do they contain about why the Communists thought collectivisation was a good thing?

FOCUS ROUTE

Make notes explaining:

a) why the Communists saw collectivisation as the solution to the problems facing Soviet agriculture

b) how a kolkhoz worked and its relationship with the towns and with machine and tractor stations (MTS).

What was a collective farm?

There were three main types of collective farm:

- the toz, where peasants owned their own land but shared machinery and co-operated in activities like sowing and harvesting. This type was more common before 1930
- the sovkhoz, which was owned and run by the state. The peasants who worked on this state farm were paid a regular wage, very much like factory workers
- the kolkhoz, where all the land was held in common and run by an elected committee. To form a kolkhoz, between 50 and 100 households were put together. All land, tools and livestock had to be pooled. Under the direction of the committee, the peasants farmed the land as one unit. However, each household was allowed to keep its own private plot of up to one acre. They could use this to grow vegetables and keep a cow, a pig and fowl.

The original aim of collectivisation was to create more sovkhozes, but the kolkhoz with private plots became the type most favoured by the Communists in the collectivisation process of the 1930s.

Why did the Communists think collectivisation was the solution to the USSR's agricultural problems?

1 Larger units of land could be farmed more efficiently through the use of mechanisation. Tractors and other machinery would be supplied by the state through huge machine and tractor stations (MTS). Experts could help peasants to farm in more modern ways using metal ploughs and fertilisers. The net result would be much higher food production.
2 Mechanised agriculture would require fewer peasants to work the land. This would release labour for the new industries.
3 It would be much easier for the state to procure the grain it needed for the cities and for export. There would be fewer collection points and each farm would have Communist supporters who would know how much had been produced.
4 Collectivisation was the socialist solution for agriculture. You could not build a socialist state when the majority of the population were private landholders who sold their products on the market. Collectivisation would socialise the peasantry. They would live in 'socialist agrotowns': living in apartment blocks instead of wooden huts, leaving their children in crèches, eating in restaurants, and visiting libraries and gymnasiums. They would be bussed out to the fields to work. They would learn to work together co-operatively and to live communally.

B Why was collectivisation carried out so rapidly?

The answer to this question lies in the grain procurement crisis of 1928–29. We saw on page 200 that Stalin had visited the Urals and sent officials into the countryside to seize grain in 1928. In 1929, even though the harvest was much better, the state was still finding it difficult to get grain out of the peasants. The peasants were resisting the government's policies and were not marketing their food. Matters were so bad that meat as well as bread had to be rationed in the cities. The cities were hungry. Stalin blamed kulaks (rich peasants) for hoarding grain (see Source 12.5). Large numbers were arrested and deported to Siberia.

MTS stations
There were 2500 machine and tractor stations (MTS). Established to support collective farms, they maintained and hired out machinery. Typically, peasants had to hand over twenty per cent of their produce for this service. But the MTS stations were also used to control the countryside. Each MTS had a political department. Its job was to root out anti-soviet elements and troublemakers, and establish party cells in local areas. It was also there to ensure that every kolkhoz handed over its quota of grain.

Relationship of the collective farm to the towns
The first priority of the collective farm was to deliver quotas of grain and other food products to the state. The state paid very low prices, then sold the produce to the towns at slightly higher prices. Once the state quota had been met, peasants could sell any surplus at the local market. This came mostly from the peasants' private plots and was the main source of milk, butter, eggs, etc., for the urban population.

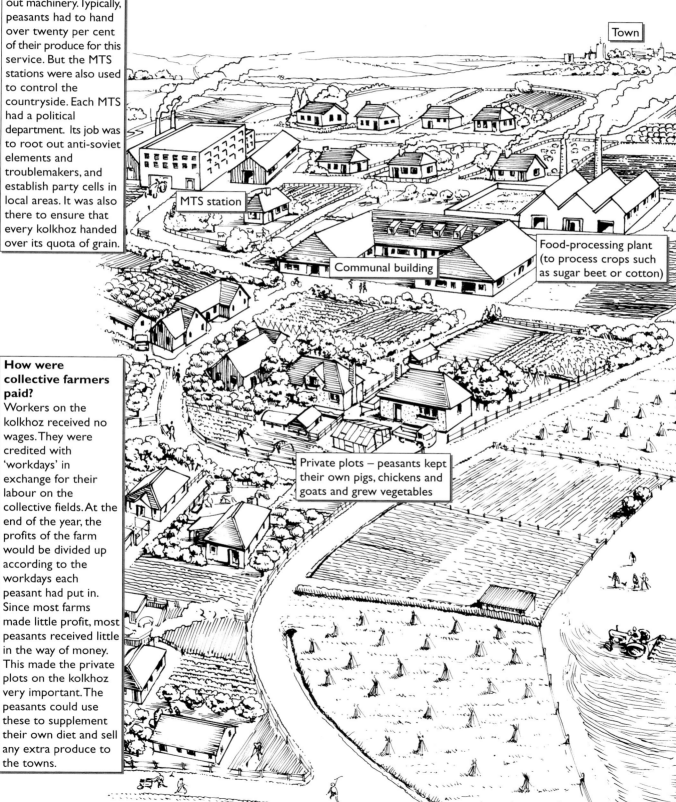

Town

MTS station

Communal building

Food-processing plant (to process crops such as sugar beet or cotton)

Private plots – peasants kept their own pigs, chickens and goats and grew vegetables

How were collective farmers paid?
Workers on the kolkhoz received no wages. They were credited with 'workdays' in exchange for their labour on the collective fields. At the end of the year, the profits of the farm would be divided up according to the workdays each peasant had put in. Since most farms made little profit, most peasants received little in the way of money. This made the private plots on the kolkhoz very important. The peasants could use these to supplement their own diet and sell any extra produce to the towns.

FOCUS ROUTE

1 How can you explain why Stalin decided to collectivise so rapidly?
2 Why was his policy so actively resisted by Bukharin and the right wing of the party?
3 What other pressures was Stalin under at the time when the decision to collectivise rapidly was taken?
4 Why is it difficult to explain the reasons for Stalin's decision?

SOURCE 12.5 J. V. Stalin, *Collected Works*, Vol. 11, 1955. Visiting Siberia in January 1928, Stalin is reported to have said the following to administrators

You have had a bumper harvest ... Your grain surpluses this year are bigger than ever before. Yet the plan for grain procurement is not being fulfilled. Why? ... Look at the kulak farms: their barns and sheds are crammed with grain ... You say that the kulaks are unwilling to deliver grain, that they are waiting for prices to rise, and prefer to engage in unbridled speculation. That is true. But the kulaks ... are demanding an increase in prices to three times those fixed by the government ...

But there is no guarantee that the kulaks will not again sabotage the grain procurements next year. More, it may be said with certainty that so long as there are kulaks, so long will there be sabotage of grain procurements.

Bukharin and the right wing of the party were worried that Stalin's methods would lead to the return of War Communism – a cycle of violence and rural unrest, shortages of bread and other foods, and rationing. Under pressure from the right, Stalin agreed to stop grain seizures in 1928 and to try raising the price of grain to encourage peasants to put more on the market. But with continuing food shortages in 1929, the party swung behind Stalin, and Bukharin and the rightists were removed from key posts. Shortly afterwards, Stalin announced a policy of forced mass collectivisation. He had decided to break the peasants' stranglehold on the economy.

It seems likely therefore that the decision to collectivise rapidly was an emergency decision taken to solve the procurement crisis of 1928–29 and to crack down on the resistance of the peasants. This conclusion is supported by the lack of preparation and planning for a revolution in Soviet agriculture. There were simply not enough tractors, combine harvesters, agricultural experts or supplies of fertiliser to carry out a high-speed collectivisation programme.

However, this decision should be seen in the context of the other factors mentioned at the end of Chapter 11. Stalin, the party and many others wanted to move forward. There was a genuine sense of crisis in urban Russia at the end of the 1920s. The 1927 war scare had made the perceived need for industrialisation all the more urgent and that meant getting more grain out of the peasants. The party broadly supported Stalin and wanted to force the pace of industrialisation and solve the peasant problem.

Historians have also shown that there was a lot of support for collectivisation among the urban working class. It was not only that they were hungry and angry at what they saw as the deliberate actions of peasants in holding back food. Many saw the socialisation of the land as a key part of the revolution and the way out of poverty towards the great society. Whether they, or indeed Stalin, had any idea of what this would entail is a different matter.

■ **Learning trouble spot**

Complicated explanations
It is sometimes difficult to explain the actions of politicians because they have to cope with a range of interrelated issues at any given time and under different political and economic pressures. When Stalin was deciding whether or not to opt for rapid forced collectivisation, he was also:
• trying to push forward rapid industrialisation plans upon which his credibility as a leader was staked
• dealing with the problem of feeding the workers, his natural supporters
• engaged in a power struggle to become leader of the party
• fighting a political battle with Bukharin and the right about the pace of industrialisation and how they should handle the peasants

• looking at the results of the Urals–Siberian method in 1929, which appeared to have been a successful way of getting grain from the peasants
• thinking about a long-term solution to allow the development of agriculture, which for Communists had always been collectivisation and agrotowns.
So when Stalin made his decision, he was playing with a range of factors. And it might also be the case that he decided he had had enough of the peasants and was going to break their resistance. His personality also has a role to play here and he had a history of taking revenge on people who thwarted him.

C How was collectivisation carried out?

FOCUS ROUTE

1 Explain the process by which collectivisation was carried out.
2 Describe how the peasants resisted this process.

WHO WERE THE KULAKS?

Soviet writers divided the peasants into three classes:

- kulaks, or better-off peasants
- middle peasants (those on moderate incomes)
- poor peasants and landless labourers.

An examination of Soviet data shows that the so-called kulak might own one or two horses, hire labour at times during the year and produce a small surplus for the market. There was no separate rich peasant stratum. Indeed, once the attack on kulaks began, many got rid of some of their animals and other resources so that they would be classed as middle peasants.

In practice, a kulak was anyone officials decided was one. Often the people they identified were the most enterprising peasants in a village, the better farmers, the ones who had a little machinery and a few animals. So, in getting rid of them, they were destroying the best chance for more successful agriculture.

Force, terror and propaganda were the main methods employed in carrying through collectivisation. Stalin returned to the familiar ideological weapon of the 'class enemy' as the mechanism to achieve his ends. It was not difficult to find a class enemy in the countryside – the kulak! In December 1929, he announced the 'liquidation of the kulaks as a class'. Molotov, one of Stalin's leading supporters, said that they would hit the kulaks so hard that the so-called 'middle peasants' would 'snap to attention before us'.

The aim of identifying the kulak as a class enemy was to frighten the middle and poor peasants into joining the kolkhozes. But villagers were often unwilling to identify kulaks, many of whom were relatives or friends, people who might have helped them out in difficult times or lent them animals to plough their land. Even if the kulaks were not liked, they were part of a village community in which the ties to fellow peasants were much stronger than those to the Communist state. In some villages, poor peasants wrote letters in support of their richer neighbours. Meanwhile, richer peasants quickly sold their animals and stopped hiring labourers so that they could slip into the ranks of the middle peasants.

Many local party officials opposed the policy of forced collectivisation, knowing that it was unworkable. They were unwilling to identify as kulaks good farmers who were valuable to the community. They also knew that collectivisation would tear the countryside apart. So Stalin enlisted an army of 25,000 urban party activists to help to revolutionise the countryside. After a two-week course, they were sent out in brigades to oversee the collectivisation process, backed by the local police, the OGPU (secret police) and the military. Their task was to root out the kulaks and persuade the middle and poor peasants to sign a register demanding to be collectivised. The land, animals, tools, equipment and buildings would be taken from the kulaks and used as the basis for the new collective farm, the creation of which the activists would then oversee.

The so-called 'Twenty-five Thousanders' had no real knowledge of how to organise or run a collective farm, but they did know how to wage class warfare. 'Dekulakisation' went ahead at full speed. Each region was given a number of kulaks to find and they found them whether they existed or not. The kulaks were divided into three categories: counter-revolutionaries who were to be shot or sent to forced-labour settlements; active opponents of collectivisation who were to be deported to other areas of the Soviet Union, often to Siberia; and those who were expelled from their farms and settled on poor land.

A decree of 1 February 1930 gave local party organisations the power to use 'necessary measures' against the kulaks. Whole families and sometimes whole villages were rounded up and deported. The head of the household might be shot and his family put on a train for Siberia or some distant part of Russia. Others would be sent off to the Gulag labour camps or to work in punishment brigades building canals, roads or the new industrial centres. Up to ten million people had been deported to Siberia or labour camps by the end of the collectivisation process.

The Communists also mounted a huge propaganda campaign to extol the advantages of collective farms and to inflame class hatred. In some areas this was effective. Many poorer peasants did denounce their neighbours as kulaks. Sometimes this was an act of revenge for past grievances but, of course, it was to the advantage of the poor peasants to get their hands on their neighbours' animals and equipment for the new collective. Children were encouraged to inform on their neighbours and even on their parents. One thirteen-year-old girl denounced her mother for stealing grain.

Peasant resistance

The peasants resisted collectivisation bitterly despite the mass deportations. There were riots and armed resistance. One riot lasted for five days and armoured cars had to be brought in to restore order. In many instances troops had to be brought in. Peasants burned crops, tools and houses rather than hand them over to the state. Raids were mounted to recapture animals that had already been taken into the collectives. Action by women often proved the most effective form of opposition. Women's revolts were reported in the press. Kaganovich, a member of the Politburo, recognised that 'women had played the most advanced role in the reaction against the collective farm'. The women's protests were carefully organised, with specific goals such as stopping grain requisitioning or retrieving collectivised horses. They reckoned, sometimes correctly, that it would be more difficult for troops to take action against all-women protests. The government found their tactics difficult to deal with.

One of the main forms of resistance was to slaughter animals and eat or sell the meat rather than hand over the beasts to the kolkhoz. Mikhail Sholokhov described this graphically in his novel *Virgin Soil Upturned* (1935):

'Kill, it's not ours any more ... Kill, they'll take it for meat anyway ... Kill, you won't get meat on the collective farm ... And they killed. They ate until they could eat no more. Young and old suffered from stomach ache. At dinner-time tables groaned under boiled and roasted meat. At dinner-time every one had a greasy mouth ... everyone blinked like an owl, as if drunk from eating.'

D What impact did collectivisation have on the peasants?

By the end of February 1930, the party claimed that half of all peasant households had been collectivised – a stunning success. In reality, it was an agricultural disaster on a huge scale. The most enterprising peasants had been shot or deported, agricultural production disrupted, and a huge number of animals slaughtered – around 25–30 per cent of all the cattle, pigs and sheep in the USSR (mostly eaten by the peasants). Peasants who had been forced into collectives were in no mood to begin the sowing season and the level of resistance was high. This was fed by rumours in some areas that women were about to be 'socialised' and that there were special machines to burn up old people.

Knowing that further peasant resistance could lead to the collapse of grain production, Stalin backtracked. He wrote an article for *Pravda* in March 1930 saying that his officials had moved too far too fast. They had, he said, become 'dizzy with success'. This was probably not far from the truth. Young, ferocious and militant urban activists had got carried away, competing with each other to see who could get the most households into collectives. Central government seemed to have little direct control over what was happening in the provinces. Stalin called for a return to the voluntary principle and an end to coercion. Given the choice, a huge number of peasants abandoned the new collective farms and went back to farming for themselves.

But once the harvest had been gathered in, Stalin restarted the campaign and it was just as vicious as before. Throughout 1931 peasants were forced back into the collectives they had left, so that by the end of the year large areas of the USSR had been collectivised, taking in over 50 per cent of peasant households. The peasants had already paid a terrible price for their resistance and lack of co-operation. But worse was to come.

The famine of 1932–34

While collectivisation proceeded apace, the state continued to requisition grain. The state had collected 22.8 million tons of grain by the end of 1931, enough to feed the cities and to export to finance the industrialisation drive. However, this had taken place against a huge drop in grain production, largely caused by the chaos and upheaval of collectivisation (see Source 12.16 on page 217). This was partly due to the activists' lack of farming knowledge and the skills to run collectives properly, but there were other reasons. For instance, there were not enough animals to pull the ploughs (because the peasants had eaten them) and tractors had not arrived in sufficient numbers to fill the gap. To make matters worse, there was a drought over a large area of the USSR during 1931.

By the spring of 1932, famine had appeared in parts of the Ukraine and, after a temporary respite following the harvest of 1932, it spread to other areas. From late 1932 until well into 1934, the USSR was subject to a famine which killed millions of peasants. In his exhaustive study *The Harvest of Sorrow* (1986), Robert Conquest puts the figure as high as seven million although other historians have suggested it was much lower. But all historians accept that the scale of human suffering was enormous. One reason why it is difficult to give exact numbers is that the scale of the famine was largely unacknowledged by the Soviet regime. It did not want to admit that collectivisation had failed to deliver. But it seemed to go further than this. According to Conquest, collectivisation had become the weapon to break peasant resistance and to deal once and for all with the 'accursed problem' as Communists called the peasant question.

Conquest cites the example of the Ukraine which was, he believes, singled out for special treatment because of the strength of Ukrainian nationalism and opposition to collectivisation. As the 'breadbasket' of Russia, the Ukraine had been set high targets for grain procurement in 1931 and 1932 (over seven million tons each year), even though the total amount being produced was falling rapidly. Thousands of extra officials, backed by detachments of OGPU, were drafted in to root out hidden stocks of grain held by peasants – and root it out they did, in brutal requisitioning gangs (see Source 12.14 on page 214). This condemned hundreds of thousands to starvation. Worse than this, Conquest claims that requisitioned grain was left rotting in huge dumps or in railway sidings while starving people could not get access to it. In some areas, groups did make attacks on grain dumps, only to be punished later. Many were shot while others were rounded up and deported to labour camps.

While other historians do not see the famine as being directly sought by Stalin, most acknowledge that the Communist government was determined to procure grain at any cost. This is borne out by the continued export of grain to other countries – 1.73 million tons in 1932 and only slightly less the following year – during the worst period of the famine.

The government brought in strict laws to ensure that grain was handed over. A law of 7 August 1932, which became known to many peasants as the Law of the Seventh-Eighths (passed on the seventh day of the eighth month), prescribed a ten-year sentence for stealing 'socialised' property, which could mean five ears of corn. This was later changed to the death sentence. Decrees in August and December laid down prison sentences of up to ten years for peasants selling meat and grain before quotas were fulfilled. Peasants tried to escape famine-hit areas by fleeing to the cities and other areas. The Soviet government brought in internal passports to control the vast movement of people.

The net result of the government's policy was the death of millions of peasants in the Ukraine, the north Caucasus, Kazakhstan and other parts of the USSR. It is difficult to reach any other conclusion than that the famine of 1932–34 was man-made. It was the direct result of the upheaval caused by collectivisation – the purging of the peasants who had the best farming expertise, the poor organisation of the new collective farms, the lack of machinery and fertilisers, the lack of know-how, and the resistance of peasants who slaughtered animals and refused to work hard on the land. This was compounded by government policy which continued to take excessive amounts of grain from the worst-hit areas and export it abroad to pay for industrial equipment.

SOURCE 12.6   V. Kravchenko, *I Chose Freedom: The Personal and Political Life of a Soviet Official*, 1947, p. 104. Kravchenko was a Communist who later fled the Soviet Union. Here he is an eyewitness to a round-up of kulaks

'What's happening?' I asked the constable.

'Another round-up of kulaks,' he replied. 'Seems the dirty business will never end. The OGPU and District Committee came this morning.'

A large crowd was gathered outside the building.... A number of women were weeping hysterically and calling the names of husbands and fathers. It was like a scene out of a nightmare ... In the background, guarded by the OGPU soldiers with drawn revolvers, stood about twenty peasants, young and old, with bundles on their backs. A few were weeping. The others stood there sullen, resigned, hopeless. So this was 'Liquidation of the kulaks as a class!' A lot of simple peasants being torn from their native soil, stripped of their worldly goods and shipped to some distant labour camps. Their outcries filled the air ... As I stood there, distressed, ashamed, helpless, I heard a woman shouting in an unearthly voice ... The woman, her hair streaming, held a flaming sheaf of grain in her hands. Before anyone could reach her, she had tossed the burning sheaf into the thatched roof of the house, which burst into flames instantaneously.

'Infidels! murderers!' the distraught woman was shrieking. 'We worked all our lives for our house. You won't have it. The flames will have it!' Her cries turned suddenly into bitter laughter. For some reason, on this occasion, most of the families were being left behind.

SOURCE 12.7   Peasants protesting against the kulaks. The Soviet version of the collectivisation process was that the poorer peasants themselves demanded that the kulaks be forced out and asked to be collectivised

SOURCE 12.8   V. Serge, *Memoirs of a Revolutionary 1901–1941*, translated and edited by P. Sedwick, 1967, p. 247

In a Kuban market town whose entire population was deported, the women undressed in their houses, thinking that no one would dare make them go out naked; they were driven out as they were to the cattle trucks, beaten with rifle butts ... Trainloads of deported peasants left for the icy north, the forests, the steppes, the deserts. These were whole populations, denuded of everything; the old folk starved to death in mid-journey, newborn babes were buried on the banks of the roadside, and each wilderness had its crop of little crosses.

ACTIVITY

Use Sources 12.6–12.14 on pages 212–214 to answer these questions.

1 What impression do you get of the dekulakisation and collectivisation process from Sources 12.6–12.11?
2 Given Sholokhov's background (Source 12.12), how valuable do you think his novel is as historical evidence?
3 Look at Sources 12.13 and 12.14. Do they change your answer?
4 What justification or explanation of the process is provided by Communists in Sources 12.12–12.14?
5 What value, if any, does a novel like Sholokhov's have for historians looking at collectivisation?

SOURCE 12.9 Peasants signing up to join a collective farm. Typically, party activists would call a village meeting and invite the villagers to set up and join a collective farm. They would offer inducements such as machinery, or make threats of increased taxes or forced exile

SOURCE 12.10 A famine victim, 1932

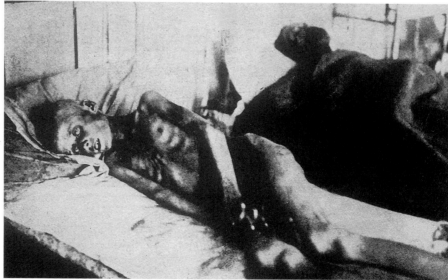

SOURCE 12.11 An OGPU colonel speaking to the historian I. Deutscher as they travelled to Kharkov, quoted in *Stalin*, rev. edn 1966, pp. 324–25

'I am an old Bolshevik,' he said almost sobbing, 'I worked in the underground against the Tsar and I fought in the civil war. Did I do all that in order that I should now surround villages with machine-guns and order my men to fire indiscriminately into crowds of peasants? Oh, no, no!'

SOURCE 12.12   M. Sholokhov, *Virgin Soil Upturned*, 1935, pp. 71–73. Sholokhov was an active Communist who wrote this pro-collectivisation novel. But he was horrified by what he saw of dekulakisation and wrote a letter to Stalin condemning the 'disgusting methods' that officials used. In his reply Stalin acknowledged that officials were guilty of crimes but claimed that Sholokhov did not appreciate the other side of the picture, that the peasants were engaged in sabotage and 'waging what was in essence a "quiet war" against the Soviet power – a war of starvation, Comrade Sholokhov'. In this extract from Sholokhov's novel, one of the main activists of the local soviet, Razmiotnov, at a meeting with other activists where they are adding up the totals of grain they have confiscated from kulaks, is making a surprise announcement

'I'm not going on.'

'What do you mean? "Not going on." ' Nagulnov pushed the abacus to one side. . . .

'I've not been trained! I've not been trained to fight against children! At the front was another matter. There you could cut down who you liked with your sword or what you liked . . . And you can all go to the devil! I'm not going on! . . . Do you call it right? What am I? An executioner? Or is my heart made of stone? I had enough at the war . . . Gayev's [a kulak] got eleven children. How they howled when we arrived! You'd have clutched your head. It made my hair stand on end. We began to drive them out of the kitchen . . . I screwed up my eyes, stopped my ears and ran into the yard. The women were all in a dead fright . . . the children . . . Oh, by God, you . . .'

. . . 'Snake!' [Nagulnov] gasped out in a penetrating whisper, clenching his fist. 'How are you serving the revolution? Having pity on them? Yes . . . You could line up thousands of old men, women and children, and tell me they'd got to be crushed into the dust for the sake of the revolution, and I'd shoot them all down with a machine gun.' Suddenly he screamed savagely, a frenzy glittered in his great, dilated pupils, and the foam seethed at the corners of his lips.

SOURCE 12.13   V. Kravchenko, *I Chose Freedom: The Personal and Political Life of a Soviet Official*, 1947, p. 130. Kravchenko, a party activist in the Ukraine, quotes the secretary of the Ukrainian Central Committee

A ruthless struggle is going on between the peasantry and our regime. It's a struggle to the death. This year was a test of our strength and their endurance. It took a famine to show them who is master here. It has cost millions of lives, but the collective farm system is here to stay. We've won the war.

SOURCE 12.14   L. Kopelev, an activist who later went into exile, quoted in R. Conquest, *The Harvest of Sorrow*, 1986, p. 233

With the rest of my generation, I firmly believed that the ends justified the means. Our great goal was the universal triumph of Communism . . .

I saw what 'total collectivisation' meant – how they mercilessly stripped the peasants in the winter of 1932–33. I took part in it myself, scouring the countryside . . . testing the earth with an iron rod for loose spots that might lead to buried grain. With the others, I emptied out the old folks' storage chests, stopping my ears to the children's crying and the women's wails. For I was convinced that I was accomplishing the great and necessary transformation of the countryside; that in the days to come the people who lived there would be better off . . .

In the terrible spring of 1933 I saw people dying of hunger. I saw women and children with distended bellies, turning blue, still breathing but with vacant lifeless eyes. And corpses – corpses in ragged sheepskin coats and cheap felt boots; corpses in the peasant huts . . . I saw all this and did not go out of my mind or commit suicide . . . Nor did I lose my faith. As before, I believed because I wanted to believe.

Collectivisation after 1934

At the end of 1934, it was announced that 70 per cent of peasant households were in collectives, rising to 90 per cent in 1936. Individual peasant landholdings were gradually squeezed out. Grain production began to recover slowly but did not exceed pre-collectivisation levels until 1935 (1930 being an exceptional year). Meat production did not pass pre-collectivisation levels until after 1953. Grain procurement continued at a high level throughout the 1930s, whatever the harvest.

The problem was lack of incentive – the peasants had nothing to work for. They were supposed to get a share in the profits of the farm at the end of the year but there never were any profits. They practised a form of passive resistance shown in apathy, neglect and petty insubordination on the newly created kolkhozes. The state could do little about it. On many farms the chairman (usually a Communist) was changed regularly because he could not get the peasants to perform.

This made the private plots on collectives very important. It was the only way peasants could earn something for themselves. Peasants could sell their products on the local market. The state did not hinder them because the economy desperately needed food. It has been estimated that these private plots provided 52 per cent of vegetables, 57 per cent of fruit, 70 per cent of meat and 71 per cent of milk as well as butter, honey and wool to Soviet consumers.

The peasants referred to collectivisation as the 'second serfdom'. They were tied to land they did not own. They could not leave the farms without the permission of the authorities. Draconian laws would punish them if they stepped out of line. However, Sheila Fitzpatrick in her book *Stalin's Peasants* (1994) maintains that the peasants developed all sorts of ways of subverting the farms and turning matters to their advantage. The peasants had been broken by collectivisation but they had not been totally crushed.

SOURCE 12.15 Extracts from peasants' letters to *Our Village*, a peasant newspaper, concerning the first collectivisation drive, 1929–30. These letters were not actually published in the newspaper

Ivan Trofimovitch

I am a poor peasant. I have one hut, one barn, one horse, three dessyatins of land . . . Isn't it true that all the poor peasants and middle peasants do not want to go into the kolkhoz at all, but you drive them in by force? . . . [In my village] poor peasants came out against it . . . they did not want serfdom.

Pyotr Gorky

Every day they send us lecturers asking us to sign up for such-and-such a kolkhoz for eternal slavery, but we don't want to leave our good homes. It may be a poor little hut, but it's mine, a poor horse, but it's mine. Among us, he who works more has something to eat . . . Let the peasant own property. Then we assure you that everyone will be able to put more surpluses on the market.

Unnamed peasant

Comrades, you write that all the middle peasants and poor peasants join the kolkhoz voluntarily, but it is not true. For example, in our village of Podbuzhye, all do not enter the kolkhoz willingly. When the register made the rounds, only 25 per cent signed it, while 75 per cent did not . . . If anyone spoke out against it, he was threatened with arrest and forced labour . . . Collective life can be created when the entire mass of the peasants goes voluntarily, and not by force . . . I beg you not to divulge my name, because the Party people will be angry.

COLLECTIVISATION CASE STUDY: SMOLENSK

The Smolensk Archive was seized from the Nazis by US troops in 1945, having been abandoned by Soviet forces in 1941. It contains a lot of information about changes in agriculture in the province of Smolensk. It tells the story of how collectivisation was carried out and how the peasants responded to it. The following account is a summary of the findings from the Smolensk Archive. Source 12.15 contains extracts from the archive.

Before collectivisation, 90 per cent of the population lived on the land. In 1927, five per cent of households were classified as kulaks, 70 per cent middle peasants and 25 per cent as poor peasants. During 1927–28, increasing pressure was applied to the kulaks. They were made to pay heavier taxes and higher wages for hired labourers; they were prosecuted for grain speculation and concealment.

After September 1929, activists were sent to the area to intensify the campaign against the kulaks and to speed up grain deliveries. But they found it difficult to get local support. Often the 'kulaks' were respected village leaders linked by blood ties to poor and middle peasants. The villagers maintained their solidarity against the Soviet authorities. Even more problematically, the activists found that local soviet members and party workers sided with the peasants.

As the activists could get little co-operation, they took harsher measures. All peasant households were required to deliver fixed quotas of grain, with penalties or even prison sentences for failure to do so. If households failed to deliver their quota, 'workers' brigades' would descend and seize their grain. The peasants responded by hiding grain and attacking activists. In October 1929, ten chairmen and eight party secretaries of village soviets were murdered. The OGPU were called in to support the activists and a 'pall of terror' enveloped the villages. In court cases it was found that almost half of the offenders were middle and poor peasants; they were condemned as ideological kulaks.

Shortly after this, Smolensk was hit by the first collectivisation drive (1929–30) characterised by 'storm' tactics. The local soviets and party workers could not be trusted to carry out effective dekulakisation or organise the kolkhozes, so brigades of urban workers, the 'Twenty-five Thousanders' (see page 209), were used.

OGPU reports reveal a picture of chaos and confusion.

There was a wave of panic in the villages. Kulaks were dekulakising themselves – selling all they owned, leaving their property to relatives and friends, even just abandoning their fields and homes. Growing numbers were fleeing east to Moscow and the Urals. There was a reported wave of suicides amongst richer households with well-to-do peasants killing their wives and children as well as themselves. While some poor peasants were pleased to see the attacks on the kulaks, other poor and middle peasants colluded with kulak friends to protect their lives and property. Petitions were collected testifying to the good character of kulaks who were on the lists.

There was also a lot of antagonism towards the kolkhozes, as the extracts from the letters in Source 12.15 show. In one incident in September 1929, 200 peasants attacked a kolkhoz, destroying equipment and clothes. The majority of the attackers were women armed with pitchforks, spades and axes. There were numerous instances of burned barns, haystacks and houses. The OGPU noted the heavy involvement of women in these outbursts against the collectives.

Generally, the halt to collectivisation in March 1930, after Stalin's 'dizzy with success' article in *Pravda* (see page 210), was well received. The archives show how the local officials and activists were really out of control, arresting whomever they pleased, including many middle peasants, often on the basis of vicious rumour. There were cases of activists blackmailing kulaks to take their names off the confiscation and deportation lists.

But by March 1931, Smolensk was again the subject of intense dekulakisation. Lists of kulaks were collected by village soviets. Activists set about liquidating kulak households and deporting whole families. The OGPU reported that there was much sympathy in the villages for the deported. Nevertheless, the process of collectivisation went ahead with over 90 per cent of peasant households in kolkhozes by the end of the 1930s.

Although there are gaps in the Smolensk Archive about how the collective farms operated, it is full of complaints about inefficiency, poor chairmen, lax working practices, drunkenness, thievery and worse abuses. The picture is one of apathy from the ordinary kolkhoz members and lack of enthusiasm for life on a collective farm.

ACTIVITY

1 Compare the material from the Smolensk Archive with what you have already read about collectivisation. List the points where the specific detail here agrees with the general picture and the points where it disagrees.

2 What does the archive tell us about the kulak response to the pre-collectivisation grain seizures?

3 What does the archive show us about the behaviour and actions of the activists and their relations with the kulaks?

4 Think about the value of the archive to historians. Remember, it was collected by the Soviet authorities.

   a) Do you think we can trust the general picture it presents of collectivisation?

   b) What view of the peasant response is clear from the unpublished letters?

   c) Do you think these letters are useful and reliable evidence for historians?

Assessing collectivisation

Draw up a table to make notes on your assessment of collectivisation. You can use the table shown here or make notes under your own headings. You might also like to design a more interesting way of setting out your notes, for example, in a flow diagram or spider diagram.

Use the sources and information which follow to complete your table or diagram. At the end of this section you are going to use these notes in an essay which considers the overall successes and failures of Stalin's economic policies in the 1930s.

Ways in which collectivisation was economically successful for the government	Ways in which collectivisation was politically successful for the government
Ways in which collectivisation was an economic failure	**The human cost of collectivisation**

SOURCE 12.16 Agricultural output and state procurement of grain, 1928–35, from A. Nove, *An Economic History of the USSR, 1917–91*, 1992, pp. 180, 186

	1928	1929	1930	1931	1932	1933	1934	1935
Grain harvest (million tons)	73.3	71.7	83.5	69.5	69.6	68.4	67.6	75.0
State procurement of grain (million tons)	10.8	16.1	22.1	22.8	18.5	22.6		
Grain exports (million tons)	0.03	0.18	4.76	5.06	1.73	1.69		
Cattle (million head)	70.5	67.1	52.3	47.9	40.1	38.4	42.4	49.3
Pigs (million head)	26.0	20.4	13.6	14.4	11.6	12.1	17.4	22.6
Sheep and goats (million head)	146.7	147.0	108.8	77.7	52.1	50.2	51.9	61.1

Study the figures in Source 12.16 and answer the following questions:

1 How can you explain the figures for grain harvests from 1928 to 1935?
2 What is the significance of the state procurement of grain in relation to the overall grain harvest over the same period?
3 Why are the grain export figures significant?
4 Analyse and explain the figures for animals over this period.

GREAT DEPRESSION
A world economic slump that began in 1929 with the Wall Street Crash and lasted until the beginning of the Second World War.

Any assessment of collectivisation reveals a very mixed picture. Economically, it appears to have been a disaster. The fact that grain harvests dropped dramatically in the early 1930s when grain was most needed and did not recover to their 1928 level (apart from 1930 which was an exceptional year) until the latter half of the 1930s is a damning indictment. This is an even worse performance when you compare the figures with the last harvest of tsarist Russia in 1913 (see Source 8.18 on page 158). The Soviet Union also lost a huge proportion of the animal population, a loss from which it did not really recover until after the Second World War.

However, although the overall grain harvest declined in the early 1930s, state procurements did not. The state collected the grain it needed to feed the rapidly growing workforce and to sell abroad to pay for industrial equipment. What is more, dispossessed peasants from the overpopulated countryside fled to the towns, so providing labour for the new factories. Collectivisation had succeeded in its main purpose – to provide the resources for industrialisation.

This view, however, has been challenged by several historians. They believe that valuable resources had to be diverted to agriculture: because of the need to build large numbers of tractors, for example, and to send out agronomists and large numbers of activists and secret police. Furthermore, the USSR did not get as much foreign money for its grain as it had hoped because the GREAT DEPRESSION had forced down world grain prices.

On top of this, the human costs were horrendous. The suffering cannot be quantified, particularly for those who not only lost their homes but ended up in the Gulag prison camps. Roy Medvedev estimates that some ten million peasants were dispossessed between 1929 and 1932, of whom around two or three million lost their lives. Then we must add the cost of the famine. Robert Conquest estimates around seven million died, five million of them in the Ukraine alone. Whatever the actual figure, it represents an inexcusable episode in Soviet history.

For the party, collectivisation was an essential part of its modernisation drive. The party did not want a sizeable sector of the economy to be dominated by the private market or to be at the mercy of the peasants who hoarded grain. In this sense, collectivisation was a political success. The party gained control of the villages and did not have to bargain with the peasants any more. It had established a system, using local soviets and MTS, of controlling the countryside and making agriculture serve the towns and workers.

SOURCE 12.17 C. Ward, *Stalin's Russia*, 1993, p. 47

What happened between November 1929 and December 1931 cannot be grasped merely by reciting statistics ... a socio-economic system in existence for five hundred years vanished for ever. But the whirlwind which swept across the countryside destroyed the way of life of the vast majority of the Soviet people, not just the Russians ... Early in 1930, countless individuals and families in entire regions and republics – the Russian, Ukrainian and Caucasian grain districts – were stigmatized as kulaks, driven from their land, forced into collectives, exiled or shot. Central Asian cotton growers and sugar beet farmers in the Central Black Earth region suffered the same fate in 1931.

SOURCE 12.18 R. Service, *A History of Twentieth-Century Russia*, 1997, pp. 181–82

With the exception of 1930, mass collectivisation meant that not until the mid-1950s did agriculture regain the level of output achieved in the last years before the Great War. Conditions in the countryside were so dire that the state had to pump additional resources into the country in order to maintain the new agrarian order ... to agronomists, surveyors, and farm chairmen but also to soldiers, policemen and informers. Moreover, 'machine-tractor stations' had to be built from 1929 to provide equipment for the introduction of technology.

Yet Stalin could draw up a balance sheet that, from his standpoint, was favourable. From collectivisation he acquired a reservoir of terrified peasants who would supply him with cheap industrial labour. To some extent, too, he secured his ability to export Soviet raw materials in order to pay for imports of industrial machinery ... Above all, he put an end to the recurrent crises faced by the state in relation to urban food supplies as the state's grain collections rose from 10.8 million tons in 1928–9 to 22.8 million tons in 1931–2. After collectivisation it was the countryside, not the towns, which went hungry if the harvest was bad.

TALKING POINT

Use the information and sources on pages 217–218 to discuss the statement: 'Collectivisation was a political success but an economic failure and a human disaster.'

KEY POINTS FOR CHAPTER 12

Was collectivisation a success?

1 Collective farms were the socialist solution for agriculture, changing individualistic peasants with capitalist tendencies into agroworkers.
2 Stalin also wanted to bring the peasants under control and ensure the food supply needed for his plans to industrialise the Soviet Union.
3 There was a lot of support for his programme amongst the urban working classes but a high level of resistance from the peasantry.
4 Stalin used force, terror and propaganda to collectivise Soviet agriculture at high speed. Brutal methods were used, including mass arrests, mass murder and the deportation of hundreds of thousands of peasants.
5 Peasants resisted by slaughtering and eating their animals and fighting the activists who carried out collectivisation.
6 The impact on agriculture was disastrous. Grain production fell and there was a tremendous drop in the number of animals.
7 In 1932–34 a famine, largely the result of government policies, killed millions of peasants.
8 Vast numbers of peasants fled the countryside to become industrial workers in the new booming industrial centres.

13

How well planned were the Five-Year Plans?

CHAPTER OVERVIEW

The Five-Year Plans for industry were ambitious and far-reaching. They envisaged nothing less than the transformation of the Soviet Union into a great industrial power. Central planning would replace the capitalist market as the main device for managing the economy.

The plans soon hit problems as the central planning system found it could not cope with the demands it had imposed on itself. The First Five-Year Plan was marked by its outrageous targets for INDUSTRIAL ENTERPRISES. The workers suffered as their needs were pushed to the bottom of the scale of priorities. Yet, despite all the problems, the plans were successful in many respects.

A How were the Five-Year Plans organised? (pp. 222–224)

B What did the Five-Year Plans achieve? (pp. 225–229)

C How did the workers fare under the plans? (pp. 230–239)

D Did urban living standards improve during the plans? (pp. 240–241)

E How successful were the Five-Year Plans for industry? (pp. 242–244)

> **INDUSTRIAL ENTERPRISE**
> Large factory, mine, etc. or collection of factories, mines, etc. run as one unit.

ACTIVITY

What do Sources 13.1–13.7 suggest about:
a) the attitudes of certain groups towards the big push for industrialisation
b) the scale and vision of the venture
c) the idea of socialism in comparison to capitalism in the 1930s?

SOURCE 13.1 S. Kotkin, *Magnetic Mountain: Stalinism as a Civilisation*, 1995, p. 35

The transformation of the old Russia into the USSR was viewed as tantamount to the discovery of a new continent by one contemporary geographer ... To the majority of people who participated in building it, socialism in the USSR afforded the means to acquire a niche, as well as a sense of pride, in a society that did seem to be qualitatively different – in comparison with capitalism, which was then synonymous not with wealth and freedom but poverty and exploitation, as well as imperialism and war.

SOURCE 13.2 A. Bullock, *Hitler and Stalin: Parallel Lives*, 1991, p. 298

A young Komsomol [Young Communist League] member leaped at the opportunity to organise a shock brigade [see page 227] in 1929. 'When we went to work in the factories, we lamented that nothing would be left for us to do, because the revolution was over, because the severe [but] romantic years of civil war would not come back, and because the older generation had left to our lot a boring, prosaic life that was devoid of struggle and excitement.'

SOURCE 13.3 A. Nove, *An Economic History of the USSR, 1917–91*, 1992, p. 193

There were, in the later years, all too many examples of phoney official superlatives, which gave rise to widespread cynicism. So it is all the more necessary to stress that thousands (of young people in particular) participated in the 'great construction projects of socialism' with a will to self-sacrifice, accepting hardship with a real sense of comradeship. Statistics will also be cited to show that others had very different attitudes to their work, not only prisoners and deportees but also peasants fleeing collectives.

SOURCE 13.4 S. Kotkin, *Magnetic Mountain: Stalinism as a Civilisation*, 1995, p. 93

A group of young enthusiasts, working double shifts, whole days without rest and with little food, met to discuss the work on blast furnace no. 2, 'their' furnace, the Komolska. One of them opened the meeting by asking, 'Does anybody have any suggestions?' Someone else was quoted as saying, 'What kind of suggestions could there be – everybody straight to the site for a subbotnik [any time extra time was performed without compensation].' If we are to believe the credible account from which this conversation is taken, the youths 'worked till dawn'. Such pathos was genuine and it was widespread. 'Everyone, even the labourers, felt that Magnitogorsk [steel works] was making history, and that he, personally, had a considerable part in it,' wrote John Scott [see case study, page 221], himself deeply affected by the enthusiasm of the crusade. 'This feeling was shared to some extent even by the exiled kulaks.'

SOURCE 13.5 The Dnieprostroi Dam, built in the 1930s, increased Soviet electric power output fivefold when it began operating

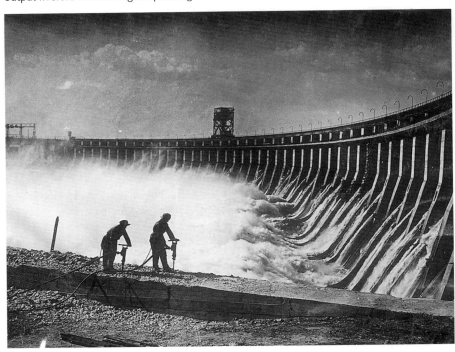

SOURCE 13.7 The Magnitogorsk steel works, 1932. Magnitogorsk rapidly developed into a major industrial centre in the early 1930s

SOURCE 13.6 The Moscow metro, built in the 1930s, was a showpiece of Soviet construction

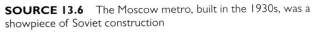
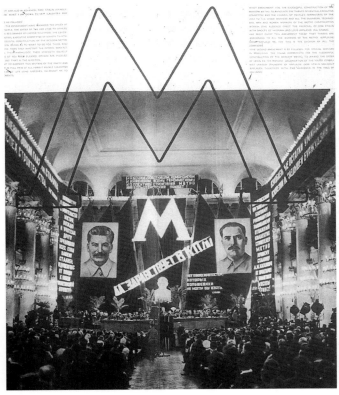

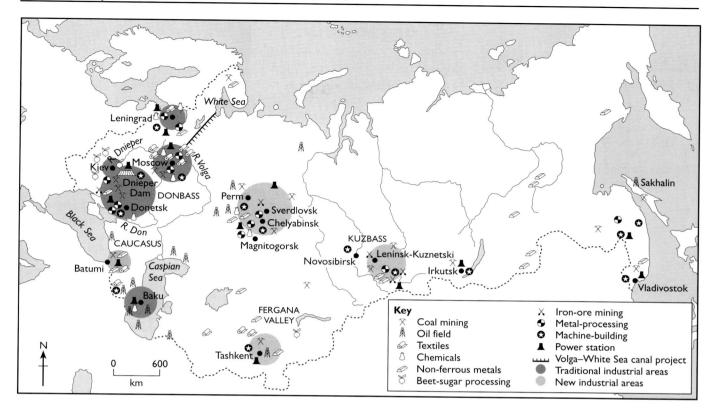

MAGNITOGORSK CASE STUDY

Throughout this chapter the development of the industrial centre at Magnitogorsk in the Urals, 'the most celebrated of the new, superior industrial age' (S. Kotkin, *Magnetic Mountain: Stalinism as a Civilisation*, 1995, pages 34–35), is used as a case study to show what general policies involved when translated into practice. Magnitogorsk was designed to be the socialist city of the future, inhabited by Soviet Socialist Man (*Homo Sovieticus*). Two main sources are used for the case study:

- Stephen Kotkin, *Magnetic Mountain: Stalinism as a Civilisation*, 1995. This outstanding study is an example of the recent trend among some Western historians of focusing on the experiences of the Russian people. Kotkin looks at the relationship between the authorities and the inhabitants of Magnitogorsk. The latter were not mere passive clay in the hands of the authorities; they knew how to make the best of their situation and which rules could be bent. So the people and the authorities influenced each other in the creation of the new city and the attempt to create new socialist citizens. He gives a vivid picture of the life of the newly urbanised Soviet workers of the 1930s that emphasises chaos and population movement. Thus the reintroduction of the tsarist internal passport system appears not as the culmination of a premeditated policy designed to establish total control over the populace, but rather as a typically heavy-handed Communist improvisation to combat a problem their policies had done so much to create.
- John Scott, *Behind the Urals*, 1942. Scott was an American college student who left the Depression-hit USA in 1932 to take part in the great experiment. He became a member of the Communist Party and spent several years as a volunteer worker at Magnitogorsk. Sympathetic to the aims of the socialist authorities, he nevertheless reveals the problems and hardships of life in the front-line of the industrial expansion. His book is regarded as the best eyewitness account by a Westerner.

The idea that the Soviet Union was at last on the road to socialism, via industrialisation, inspired party members and urban workers alike. There was a feeling that they were creating a new type of society that would be far superior to that of their capitalist neighbours. After the compromises of the NEP, there was a return to the war imagery of the Civil War and War Communism. There was talk of a 'socialist offensive', and of 'mobilising forces on all fronts'. There were 'campaigns' and 'breakthroughs', 'ambushes' by 'class enemies'. People who opposed or criticised the regime's policies thus became guilty of treachery.

The creation of this state of psychological warfare, with appeals to patriotism, was a useful device to push through policies, particularly since mistakes and failures could be blamed on the enemy. But many Communists did see the struggle as a war against backwardness and enemies inside and outside the Soviet Union. Industrialisation was the way to break through to socialism and to protect themselves from the hostile forces that appeared to be surrounding them.

■ **Learning trouble spot**

What is the difference between central planning and capitalism?

In a capitalist market economy, the production of goods and the allocation of resources and investment in industry are largely determined by supply and demand working through prices, that is, by the operation of the market. The demand for a product pushes up the price of that product. This encourages producers to enter the market to supply the product and make a profit. They bring the necessary investment in industrial plant and make decisions about the methods and techniques used to produce and distribute the goods. In this way, resources – raw materials, land and labour – flow to this particular industrial activity.

In a centrally planned system, state agencies co-ordinate the activities of the different branches of production. They make the decisions about the allocation of resources, where investment should be targeted, what methods of production should be used and what economic strategies should be followed.

A How were the Five-Year Plans organised?

The plans put central planning at the forefront of the Soviet economy. The state decided what was produced, where it was produced and when it was produced. The key feature of the plans was the setting of production and output targets which industrial enterprises had to achieve. Five-Year Plans set down broad directions and could be changed as they went along. There were also shorter one-year or even quarterly plans which set more specific targets for individual enterprises. The targets were backed by law, so failure to meet targets could be treated as a criminal offence. Bonuses were paid to enterprises that exceeded their plan target.

The party, acting through the government, set the priorities for the plans and the targets for key industries. The People's Commissariats (ministries or government departments) were responsible for working out more detailed plans for different regions and the enterprises under their control. Although there were varying numbers of industrial commissariats during the 1930s, four major ones had developed by 1934: heavy industry, light industry, timber and food. The most important of these was the Commissariat of Heavy Industry, which headed the industrialisation drive. By 1939, there were twenty commissariats.

In theory, industrial enterprises could have a say in formulating the plan but, in practice, instructions would be passed down through various bureaucratic layers to the managers of the enterprises. Chart 13B shows a simplified diagram of how the system worked using heavy industry as an example. However, this system emerged only as the plans developed and was not in place at the beginning. The planning of the First Five-Year Plan was much more chaotic.

■ **13B How the Five-Year Plans were administered using changes to heavy industry as an example**

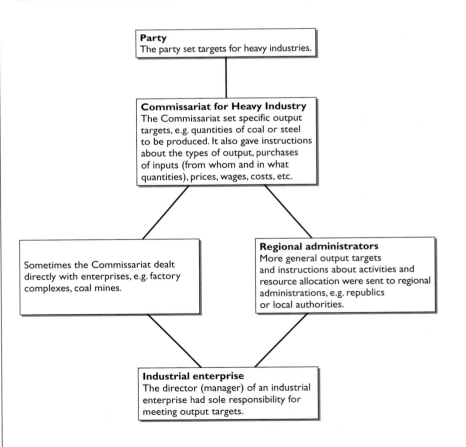

WHAT HAPPENED TO PRIVATE INDUSTRY?

The state already had control of large-scale industry (run by trusts) under the NEP, so these were brought into the new system. But there were quite a lot of small-scale private industries supplying consumer goods such as shoes and textiles. These were starved of supplies and resources and most collapsed during the First Five-Year Plan. This was a disaster for the Russian consumer who found it very hard to get clothing, shoes and other products. The situation was compounded by the collapse of cottage industries in the countryside due to collectivisation. Peasants had traditionally made clothes, tools and other products for a domestic market and these were swept away in the collectivisation upheaval. Most industrial enterprises of any size were under state control by the end of the 1930s.

Sergei Ordzhonikidze

'Sergo' had joined the Bolshevik Party in 1903 and became active in the underground political scene where he became friends with Stalin. Elected to the Central Committee, he played a prominent role in the revolution and the Civil War. He worked with Stalin in Georgia and it was he who struck the Bolshevik official in the incident which upset Lenin so much (see page 172). He was one of Stalin's staunchest supporters in the Politburo during the First Five-Year Plan. His key position as head of the Commissariat of Heavy Industry put him in the driving seat of the push for rapid industrialisation. He was reasonably popular in the party and was a moderating influence in the Politburo.

It was a top-down method of management which applied in the workplace as well. The principle of one-person management was established right at the beginning. The director of an industrial enterprise (for example, a large factory or several units of production) was in sole charge and responsible for seeing that the targets were achieved. The trade unions were told not to interfere and to focus on increasing worker productivity. Workers' control and influence over the factory floor, such as it had ever existed, receded as the plans progressed.

All this begs the question: who co-ordinated the activities of the different branches of industry to balance the system and make it work? For instance, if you decide to expand the railway, then you need to plan for enough steel to make the rails. Gosplan (the State Planning Commission), which had originally been set up in 1921 as a forecasting agency, was given the job of working out the figures – the inputs each industry would need and the output each had to produce – to meet overall targets for the plan (see the example in Chart 13C).

The party not only laid down basic priorities but interfered in the day-to-day running of enterprises. It had a grip on the economy at all levels. Senior party officials appointed and dismissed planners and senior managers, often for political rather than economic reasons. From 1930 to 1937, the Commissariat for Heavy Industry was led by Sergei Ordzhonikidze, who had a direct line to different factories and moved around people and resources as he wished. At the local level, the party got involved in checking whether enterprises were fulfilling the plans; party secretaries were held responsible if industrial enterprises in their area did badly.

■ 13C Planning required to achieve targets

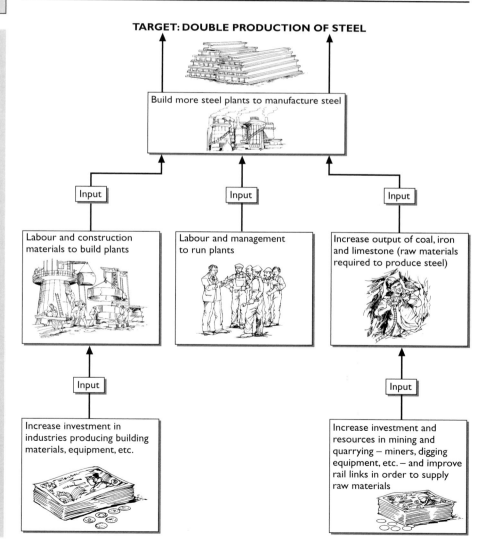

Features of the plans

The plans in the 1930s were dominated by an emphasis on the development of heavy industry. Stalin and the Supreme Economic Council (Vesenkha) agreed that the lion's share of investment should go into coal, iron, steel and other heavy industries. These would provide the power, capital equipment and machine tools that could be used to manufacture other products. The Soviet Union would then be less dependent on the West for these goods and could move towards self-sufficiency or 'autarky'. This decision meant that consumer industries producing clothes, shoes and similar products would be downgraded. Soviet citizens were asked to sacrifice their standard of living for longer-term objectives. There were two main reasons behind this:

1 It seemed to the Stalinists that Western industrial revolutions had been underpinned by the initial development in coal, iron and steel.
2 They were driven by the need to develop the sort of industries that could protect the Soviet Union should it be attacked from the West.

Three other features of the plans are worthy of note:

- The plans were always declared complete a year ahead of schedule. This denoted the superiority of Soviet planning over the Western capitalist economies which were, at this time, going through the worst throes of the Great Depression. It was also a psychological device to encourage the already hard-pressed workforce to even greater achievements.
- Huge new industrial centres were constructed virtually from nothing, for example at Magnitogorsk in the Urals and Kuznetz in western Siberia. Most of these were located east of the Ural mountains, a strategic decision to make them less vulnerable to attack from the West.
- Spectacular projects were conceived to demonstrate the might of the new Soviet industrial machine. This has been called 'gigantomania'. The Dnieprostroi Dam in eastern Russia (Source 13.5 on page 220) was, for two years, the world's largest construction site and it increased Soviet electric power output fivefold when it came on stream. Other projects included the Moscow–Volga canal and the prestigious Moscow metro with its elaborate stations and high vaulted ceilings (see Source 13.6 on page 220).

Foreign participation

A significant aspect of the industrial development of the USSR in the early 1930s was the involvement of foreign companies and individuals. A large number of companies sent specialists, engineers and skilled workers to help to erect new factories or exploit new resources. Henry Ford helped the Russians to develop a car industry. Russian engineers were trained by Ford in the USA and it was Ford-designed cars that were produced at the car plant in Gorky. Colonel Hugh Cooper, the engineer in charge of the Dnieprostroi Dam project, was an American. So was A. Ruckseyer, the man behind the huge growth in the asbestos industry at a remote place in the Urals called Asbest. Thousands of skilled workers – British, American and many other nationalities – came for a variety of reasons, some ideological and some because of unemployment in the West. The Great Depression convinced many people that capitalism was in its death throes and that the dynamic Soviet Union offered hope for the future of working people.

> **AT MAGNITOGORSK**
>
> Iron and steel were at the heart of Soviet industrialisation so the development of Magnitogorsk, with its huge reserves of iron ore, was at the forefront of the labour offensive. One contemporary Soviet pamphlet stated: 'Near Magnetic Mountain the steppe has been turned into a battlefield, the steppe is retreating.' The object of the battle was to build a gigantic steel plant capable of challenging the best in the capitalist world. In March 1929, 25 settlers arrived on horseback at the snow-covered site. By June 1930, the first train arrived with the banners 'The Steel Horse Breathes Life into the Magnitogorsk Giant. Long Live the Bolshevik Party!'

B What did the Five-Year Plans achieve?

■ 13D The achievements and weaknesses of the Five-Year Plans in the 1930s

FIRST FIVE-YEAR PLAN
October 1928 to December 1932

The emphasis was on heavy industries – coal, oil, iron and steel, electricity, cement, metals, timber. This accounted for 80 per cent of total investment; 1500 enterprises were opened.

Successful sectors
- Electricity – production trebled.
- Coal and iron – output doubled.
- Steel production – increased by one-third.
- Engineering industry developed and increased output of machine-tools, turbines, etc.
- Huge new industrial complexes were built or were in the process of being built.
- Huge new tractor works were built in Stalingrad, Kharkov and other places to meet the needs of mechanised agriculture.

Weaknesses
- There was very little growth, and even a decline, in consumer industries such as house-building, fertilisers, food processing and woollen textiles.
- Small workshops were squeezed out, partly because of the drive against Nepmen and partly because of shortages of materials and fuel.
- Chemicals targets were not fulfilled.
- The lack of skilled workers created major problems. Workers were constantly changing jobs, which created instability.

Comment

In reality, many targets were not met. The Great Depression had driven down the price of grain and raw materials, so the USSR could not earn enough from exports to pay for all the machinery it needed. Also, a good deal of investment had to go into agriculture because of the forced collectivisation programme. However, the Soviet economy was kick-started: there was impressive growth in certain sectors of the economy and there were substantial achievements.

SECOND FIVE-YEAR PLAN
January 1933 to December 1937

Heavy industries still featured strongly but new industries opened up and there was greater emphasis on communications, especially railways to link cities and industrial centres. Four and a half thousand enterprises opened. The plan benefited from some big projects, such as the Dnieprostroi Dam, coming into use.

Successful sectors
- Heavy industries benefited from plants which had been set up during the first plan and now came on stream. Electricity production expanded rapidly.
- By 1937, the USSR was virtually self-sufficient in machine-making and metal-working.
- Transport and communications grew rapidly.
- Chemical industries, such as fertiliser production, were growing.
- Metallurgy developed – minerals such as copper, zinc and tin were mined for the first time.

Weaknesses
- Consumer goods industries were still lagging, although they were showing signs of recovery. There was growth in footwear and food processing – modern bakeries, ice-cream production and meat-packing plants – but not enough.
- Oil production did not make the expected advances.

Comment

There was a feeling in the party that Stalin had overreached himself in the First Five-Year Plan, that targets had been too high. The second plan was more one of consolidation. The years 1934–36 were known as the 'three good years' since the pressure was not so intense, food rationing was ended and families had more disposable income.

THIRD FIVE-YEAR PLAN
January 1938 to June 1941

The third plan ran for only three and a half years because of the USSR's entry into the Second World War. Once again, heavy industry was emphasised as the need for armaments became increasingly urgent.

Successful sectors
- Heavy industry continued to grow, for example, machinery and engineering, but the picture was uneven and some areas did poorly.
- Defence and armaments grew rapidly as resources were diverted to them.

Weaknesses
- Steel output grew insignificantly.
- Oil production failed to meet targets and led to a fuel crisis.
- Consumer industries once again took a back seat.
- Many factories ran short of materials.

Comment

The third plan ran into difficulties at the beginning of 1938 due to an exceptionally hard winter and the diversion of materials to the military. Gosplan was thrown into chaos when the purges (see Chapter 14) created shortages of qualified personnel, such as important managers, engineers and officials, who linked industries and government.

FOCUS ROUTE

1 As you work through pages 225–229, collect evidence about the planning system and its effectiveness and record it in a table like the one shown here.

Evidence of success and achievements	Evidence of failures and weaknesses	Evidence that the Five-Year Plans were not well planned

2 Who were the 'bourgeois specialists' and why were they attacked by the party?
3 Why were officials and managers reluctant to admit to problems in the plans?

SOURCE 13.8 Industrial output 1913–40, from R. W. Davies, M. Harrison and S. G. Wheatcroft (eds), *The Economic Transformation of the Soviet Union, 1913–1945*, 1994

	1913	1928	1932	1933	1936	1937	1940
Electric power (billion kWh)	1.9	5.0	13.5	16.4	32.8	36.2	48.3
Crude oil (million tons)	9.2	11.6	21.4	21.5	27.4	28.5	31.1
Coal (million tons)	29.1	35.5	64.4	76.3	126.8	128.0	165.9
Pig-iron (million tons)	4.2	3.3	6.2	7.1	14.4	14.5	14.9
Rolled steel (million tons)	3.5	3.4	4.4	5.1	12.5	13.0	13.1
Quality steel (million tons)	0.04	0.09	0.68	0.89	2.06	2.39	2.79
Copper (thousand tons)	31.1	30.0	45.0	44.3	100.8	97.5	160.9
Cement (million tons)	1.52	1.85	3.48	2.71	5.87	5.45	5.68
Mineral fertilisers (million tons)	0.07	0.14	0.92	1.03	2.84	3.24	3.24
Sulphuric acid (million tons)	0.12	0.21	0.55	0.63	1.20	1.37	1.59
Metal-cutting machine tools (thousands)	1.5	2.0	19.7	21.0	44.4	48.5	58.4
Locomotives (standard units)	265	478	828	941	1566	1582	1220
Generators (thousand kW)	–	75	1085	587	–	561	468
Electric motors (thousand kW)	–	259	1658	1385	1653	1833	1848
Tractors (thousand 15 hp units)	–	1.8	50.8	79.9	173.2	66.5	66.2
Lorries (thousands)	–	0.7	23.7	39.1	131.5	180.3	136.0
Raw sugar (million tons)	1.35	1.28	0.83	1.00	2.00	2.42	2.17
Cigarettes (billions)	22.1	49.5	57.9	62.7	85.9	89.2	100.4
Vodka (million decalitres)	118.9	55.5	72.0	–	89.7	92.5	44.3
Cotton fabrics (million linear metres)	2582	2678	2694	2732	3270	3448	3954
Woollen fabrics (million linear metres)	105	101	89	86	102	108	120

SOURCE 13.9 A comparison of pig-iron and steel production in the USSR and in Magnitogorsk

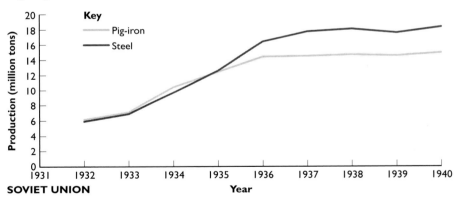

SOVIET UNION

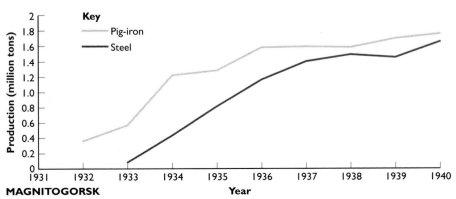

MAGNITOGORSK

ACTIVITY

Compare the two graphs in Source 13.9. The similarities in their pattern are striking. Study Source 13.8 also, and consider why there was a slowdown in production between 1936 and 1938.

AT MAGNITOGORSK

SOURCE 13.10 Changing production targets for pig-iron during the First Five-Year Plan

		Tons per year
	1928	656,000
Summer	1929	850,000
Late	1929	1,100,000
Early	1930	2,500,000

Raw materials Firms routinely requested far more than they required because they were never sure what they would be allocated. Interruptions in deliveries were so regular that firms hoarded what they could, while at the same time bombarding the centre with requests for more of everything. Coal supplies were often found to be short on arrival, having been pilfered on the way. The plant therefore had to request more coal than it needed and probably ended up buying the 'lost coal' on the black market.

Quality Significant amounts of pig-iron and steel were found to be unusable when the time came to count up output. But even if it was declared defective, it was still sent to metal-starved firms that had little choice but to use it.

SOURCE 13.12 A. Nove, *An Economic History of the USSR, 1917–91*, 1992, p. 191. Nove recounts a story told by Isaac Babel

'One old oil expert, given what he regarded as an absurd order to increase production, is said to have written to the Central Committee as follows: "I cease to be responsible for the planning department. The [plan] figure of 40 million tons I consider to be purely arbitrary. Over a third of the oil must come from unexplored areas … Furthermore the three cracking plants which now exist are to be turned into 120 plants by the end of the five-year plan. This despite the huge shortage of metal … and so on." '…

Needless to say the new targets were far beyond practical possibility. The rush, strain, shortages, pressures became intolerable, and caused great disorganization. Naturally, supplies of materials, fuels, goods wagons, fell short of requirements.

The First Five-Year Plan

As the First Five-Year Plan got underway, there was a wave of planning fervour or 'target mania'. There was a sort of competition between Gosplan and Vesenkha (the Supreme Economic Council), who were bidding each other up with higher targets. The original targets set in the first plan were optimistic, but almost before it was begun targets were revised upwards. In April 1929, two versions of the plan were produced – a 'basic' and a much higher 'optimum' version. The latter was chosen. This envisaged targets being increased by astonishing amounts, for instance, coal up from 35 to 75 million tons and iron ore from six to nineteen million tons. To many, these seemed hopelessly unachievable.

Some historians have suggested that planning was more in the realms of socialist fantasy than rational calculation. In *The Russian Revolution 1917–1932* (1994, pages 129–34), Sheila Fitzpatrick talks of this period as one in which the 'spirit of a Cultural Revolution' swept people along. Party leaders and members had a millennial vision of a country that would be transformed. They believed that in two or three years they would have a socialist rather than a market economy and money would be abandoned as the main means of rewarding workers. In this sense, the First Five-Year Plan can be seen more as a propaganda device to drive Soviet citizens forward and create a sense of urgency.

Setting targets is one thing; detailed planning, which involves the complex co-ordination of different branches of industry over a huge area, is something else. And this sort of detailed planning seemed to be notably absent from the First Five-Year Plan. The party handed out broad directives and priorities and it was left to officials and managers at regional and local levels to work out ways to achieve the production targets they had been set. This was bound to lead to problems.

SOURCE 13.11 Output targets for the First Five-Year Plan, from A. Nove, *An Economic History of the USSR, 1917–91*, 1992, p. 145

	Actual output in 1927–28	**1932–33 targets in first version of plan**	**1932–33 targets in 'optimum' version of plan**
Coal (million tons)	35	68	75
Iron ore (million tons)	6	15	19
Steel (million tons)	4	8	10

The high targets placed enormous strain on the economy. Materials of all sorts were in short supply and there was intense competition to get hold of them. At higher levels, powerful people in industrial commissariats pulled strings to make sure that their pet projects got the resources they needed for completion. Materials and workers – shock brigades – were rushed into key industries to do certain jobs, often on the order of a senior party official, despite the fact that this left other areas short and waiting for supplies. At the regional and local levels, factories competed with each other for scarce resources. Bribery and corruption were rife. Managers made illegal deals in their desperation to get the parts or supplies they needed to fulfil their targets. Some were known to hijack lorries and ambush trains to get supplies intended for other plants. Bottlenecks appeared everywhere due to shortages of materials and the inadequacy of the transport system. The railways could not cope with what they were expected to transport: it soon became clear that the planners had not invested enough in track or rolling stock.

The net result of this was twofold:

1 In some parts of the economy there was underproduction because factories were held up by shortages of materials. In other parts there was overproduction as factories rushed to exceed their targets.
2 There was a great deal of wastage because:
   a) overproduction created thousands of parts that other industries did not want
   b) much of the output was sub-standard, such as lorry tyres that lasted for only a few weeks.

What made matters worse was that few managers or officials were prepared to admit anything was wrong. They did not want to be accused of sabotaging the plans or criticising the party. So mistakes were covered up and problems were left unresolved. It was all buried in the colossal amount of paperwork that flowed around the USSR. All that mattered to managers and officials at different levels was that they could show they had achieved their targets, whether this was real or invented. In fact, there were extravagant claims of over-fulfilment in many areas. This seemed to confirm that the system was working and discouraged others from speaking out about problems.

Of course, not all the mistakes could be covered up and somebody had to be blamed. Class enemies were ready to hand and Stalin was not slow to use this political tool in the same way as he had in the collectivisation drive. The industrial equivalent of the kulak was the 'bourgeois specialist'. These were the old pre-1917 managers, engineers and technical staff who had survived the NEP in important jobs because of their skills and abilities. Now they were identified as saboteurs who were deliberately causing hold-ups, breakdowns and general problems in the supply industries. They were uncovered and imprisoned. Show trials were held to hammer home the point to other managers.

The attack on the bourgeois specialists was not just a cynical tool to frighten others and find a convenient scapegoat for errors and miscalculations. Many party members believed that this group did harbour bourgeois, anti-socialist attitudes that would scupper their revolution: they wanted proletarians in key technical positions. Unfortunately, the loss of valuable personnel so quickly caused so many problems that by 1931 the offensive against them was quietly dropped.

In the First Five-Year Plan, consumer goods industries, such as textiles, were sacrificed to the needs of heavy industry. Other areas suffered from the closure of small-scale enterprises and workshops. These were squeezed out for two main reasons:

• they had been largely run by Nepmen
• they could not get supplies of raw materials.

These small-scale operations might have been able to respond to consumer demand but there was no room for them in a centrally organised system.

WHY WERE OFFICIALS AND MANAGERS TOO FRIGHTENED TO ACKNOWLEDGE THE PROBLEMS OF THE PLANNING SYSTEM?

In March 1928, managerial and technical staff were accused of counter-revolutionary activities at the Shakhty coal mine in the Don Basin. Stalin was closely involved in the proceedings. The staff were forced to confess to subversive activities in a 'show trial' for all of the public to see. Five were executed and the rest were given long prison sentences.

The aim of this was clear – to intimidate managers and party officials who did not go along with the pace of industrialisation. The Shakhty trial created shock waves throughout the planning system. Gosplan was purged of pessimists and non-party members at the end of the 1920s. Statisticians who presented low targets were replaced by those who could paint a more optimistic picture.

In the early 1930s, trials of professionals and specialists were held in cities throughout the Soviet Union. In November 1930, the 'Industrial Party' show trial was held. This was a party of professionals who were supposedly organising the sabotage and wrecking of the Five-Year Plan. But this party was invented by Stalin. The accused were mainly industrialists, Mensheviks and Socialist Revolutionaries who worked for the government. In 1933, in the Metro-Vickers trial, British specialists were found guilty of sabotage.

It is therefore not surprising that managers were unwilling to admit to mistakes when it could lead to investigation and criminal charges.

The Second and Third Five-Year Plans

By the beginning of the Second Five-Year Plan, party leaders were prepared to acknowledge the problems that had resulted from the breakneck speed of industrialisation from 1929 to 1932. The severe shortages, disruptions in transport, lack of skilled workers and slower growth rates for certain industries were sufficient evidence of this. In 1932, the great leap forward seemed to be on the verge of collapse.

The second plan was revised and targets were scaled back. The emphasis was more on consolidation. The plan was worked out in greater detail for each industry and region. The People's Commissariats, which were more organised and clearly defined by 1934, gave specific targets for the enterprises under their control as well as estimates of costs, labour, prices, and so on. Investment was ploughed into the railway system, thus increasing enormously the amount of freight it was able to carry. There were new training schemes that encouraged workers to learn skills and master techniques to tackle the problem of skills shortages. There were still plenty of rough edges to the planning system – shortages, waste, and under/over-production continued – but not on the scale of the first plan.

Many of the schemes started in the first plan now came on stream, boosting industrial growth enormously. For instance, the USSR was almost self-sufficient in the production of machine tools and far less dependent on foreign imports of machinery. The Soviet Union enjoyed the 'three good years' of 1934–36 and the achievements by 1937 were impressive. The Second Five-Year Plan envisaged more resources going into consumer industries, since leaders had realised how badly the workers had suffered during the early 1930s through lack of goods and basic commodities. There were improvements in some areas, like footwear production and food processing, but as the plan progressed, resources were again diverted into other areas.

After 1937, the USSR witnessed an economic slowdown. Although there was a general increase in industrial output during the Third Five-Year Plan, some areas like iron and steel virtually stopped growing. There was a fuel crisis when the oil industry failed to meet its modest targets. As Europe moved towards war, resources were channelled into the armaments industry and this created shortages elsewhere. Alec Nove (Source 13.13) places much of the blame for this slowdown on the purges that were in full swing in 1936 and 1937 (see Chapter 14). Nove claims the purges deprived the economy of valuable personnel and paralysed the ability of administrators and party officials to take the initiative and solve problems. Also, many planners were purged with the result that the planning system was thrown into confusion.

The picture at the end of the Third Five-Year Plan shows planning once more in a confused and even chaotic state, with shortages, waste and bottlenecks as growing features of the economy. Indeed, looking back over the plans it is sometimes difficult to see where the word 'planned' fits into the 'planned economy' of the 1930s. Yet this rough-and-ready system worked and, by 1941, the USSR had succeeded in creating the industrial base for a powerful arms industry.

SOURCE 13.13 A. Nove, *An Economic History of the USSR, 1917–1991*, 1992, p. 239

[The purge] swept away ... managers, technicians, statisticians, planners, even foremen. Everywhere there were said to be spies, wreckers, diversionists. There was a grave shortage of qualified personnel, so the deportation of many thousands of engineers and technologists to distant concentration camps represented a severe loss. But perhaps equally serious was the psychological effect of this terror on the survivors. With any error or accident likely to be attributable to treasonable activities, the simplest thing to do was to avoid responsibility, to seek approval from one's superiors for any act, to obey mechanically any order received, regardless of local conditions.

C How did the workers fare under the plans?

Did the workers support the plans?

The urban working classes and young people in general were enthusiastic at the beginning of the plans. They were carried forward by the spirit of cultural revolution and wanted to move forward to a better society. Evidence of this enthusiasm can be found in the actions of the thousands of young people who volunteered to go and work on distant projects, often labouring in the most primitive of conditions. They were prepared to make sacrifices to build a new world which would probably bring real benefits only for their children. They were participating in the great construction projects of socialism (see Sources 13.5–13.7 on page 220).

On a more practical note, workers believed they would be better off. Their real wages had risen only slowly under the NEP and unemployment had been high in the late 1920s. Social historians have found evidence suggesting that shop-floor workers in the main supported the party hierarchy in its industrialisation push. They also approved of the attack on the bourgeois specialists. Young workers were tired of their 'old' managers still strutting around giving orders and engineers enjoying privileges while they slaved away.

The party had envisaged the creation of a proletarian intelligentsia with highly developed technical skills ('red specialists') who would fill the role of the old specialists and become loyal to the regime. To some extent this succeeded. The cohort of industrial workers of the late 1920s, possessing highly valued skills, quickly advanced to supervisory posts or became managers or party officials. There were great strides in higher technical education for more able and intelligent proletarians. This group did well on the whole when wage differentials were introduced and their standard of living was significantly higher than that of the broad mass of workers.

Workers who stayed in their jobs and observed labour discipline could do well in the 1930s. Training courses meant they could improve their qualifications and position, pay and prospects. Those who exceeded their targets were rewarded with higher pay, better working conditions and, with luck, better housing. They were celebrated in newspapers and on notice boards where they worked.

Women in the labour force

One of the most important sources of new labour was women. Some ten million women entered the workforce. Women dominated some professions, particularly medicine and school teaching. The less well educated, especially tough ex-peasant women, became labourers or factory workers. Generally, women were paid less and found it more difficult to gain advancement than men. However women were working in jobs that they had not done before, as Source 13.14 on page 231 shows.

Sarah Davies' survey of women workers in Leningrad in 1935 (*Popular Opinion in Stalin's Russia: Terror, Propaganda and Dissent 1934–41*, 1997) showed that women workers in the city made up 44 per cent of the workforce but were likely to be less well paid, less literate and less involved in political and

■ Learning trouble spot

Proletarianisation

Some students have difficulty understanding why the Communist Party was so anxious to 'proletarianise' the mass of the Russian people, that is, turn them into industrial workers. The Communists believed that the vast majority of the population had to be proletarians with the right attitudes before you could create a socialist state and then move on to establish Communism – the ultimate Marxist goal. This meant that you had to get rid of the old bourgeois capitalist attitudes connected to the selfishness of the free market economy – the notion of working for one's own self-interest with profit as the main incentive for economic activities. The people who held these attitudes were class enemies. Only when you got rid of these people could you proceed to the co-operation and sharing envisaged in the higher form of socialism.

To push forward proletarianisation, the party believed it had to:

- get rid of bourgeois specialists who made up the majority of the managers and engineers in industry and replace them with proletarians (red specialists)
- turn peasants flooding into the towns into good proletarians
- turn peasants remaining in the countryside into agricultural proletarians, hence the vision of factory farms and agrotowns.

technical education than their male counterparts. The issues that were most important to them were their children's needs, queues and fluctuating prices, not surprising as women had to look after the home as well as work. Their chances of reaching the top were limited. Of 328 factory directors, only twenty were women and seventeen of these were in textile and sewing factories where well over three-quarters of the workforce were women. There were only four women head doctors in hospitals, even though 50–60 per cent of all doctors were women.

SOURCE 13.14   Soviet women pilots in the 1930s

The quicksand society

The First Five-Year Plan required an enormous expansion of the labour force. The majority of the new workers were peasants who had been forced off the land by collectivisation. Around half the labour force by the end of the First Five-Year Plan was made up of peasants. They wandered in from the countryside, bemused and bewildered, looking for work, lodgings and adequate food. If they could find a better deal elsewhere, they moved on. There was a phenomenal turnover of labour. In the coal industry in 1930, the average worker moved jobs three times a year. These ex-peasants lacked the most elementary disciplines of time-keeping and punctuality. Their normal working pattern was entirely different from that required in a factory and they found it difficult to adapt to the monotonous hours of machine-based work. Many were resentful about being forced into industrial work anyway. This led to a high rate of absenteeism.

This turnover was not restricted to the peasants. Skilled and semi-skilled workers soon found that skills were at a premium and that managers, desperate to fulfil their targets, were anxious to attract them. They began to compete for skilled workers by offering higher wages or additional perks, such as extra food rations. These workers were able to move easily between jobs and this contributed to the destabilising effect of high labour turnover on industrial enterprises. One Communist leader talked of Russia being like a huge 'nomadic gypsy camp' and Moshe Lewin likened it to a 'quicksand society' (see Source 13.20 on page 234).

The skills shortage was one of the biggest problems the planners faced. In 1931, it was estimated that less than seven per cent of the workforce were skilled. A survey in 1933 showed that only seventeen per cent of those recruited to industry had any skills. In Elektrozavod, a $25,000 lathe from the USA lay unused for want of a minor repair which workers were unable to perform. Untrained, clumsy workers were doing an astonishing amount of damage to expensive imported machinery and were turning out poor-quality goods. Machines were not properly oiled and maintained. There were stories of whole production runs being ruined by ill-educated and untrained ex-peasants.

AT MAGNITOGORSK

Almost half of the workers in January 1932 were under 24 and typically ex-peasant, male, unskilled and illiterate. In 1933, about one-fifth (40,000) of the population were exiled peasants. John Scott (*Behind the Urals*, 1942) estimates that between 1928 and 1932 about three-quarters of new arrivals came of their own free will seeking work and the rest came under compulsion. Few of the engineers had real engineering experience. A colony of several hundred foreign engineers and specialists arrived to advise and direct the work.

SOURCE 13.15   S. Kotkin, *Magnetic Mountain: Stalinism as a Civilisation*, 1995, p. 95, writing about the fluidity of labour

By early 1934 almost ten times as many workers had passed through the site than were at hand. Indeed, who had not been to Magnitogorsk! You tell someone you're going to Magnitogorsk and everywhere you hear: 'Magnita, I'm going there,' or 'I just came from there.' Somebody says he has a brother there, somebody else is waiting for a letter from his son. You get the impression that the whole country either was there or is going there. Many people in fact came and left several times in the course of one year. In 1931 the average length of stay for a worker was 82 calendar days. Magnitogorsk became a revolving door.

1 Use the information in Sources 13.16 and 13.17 and a graph-drawing program to produce bar graphs illustrating the following:
   a) net gains or losses in the Magnitogorsk labour force for each month in 1931
   b) the overall pattern of gains and losses between 1930 and 1933.
2 Using ICT, produce a bar graph which shows:
   a) total number of workers on 1 January 1931
   b) total arrivals for 1931
   c) total departures for 1931
   d) total number of workers on 31 December 1931.
3 What do these graphs reveal about the turnover of labour in Magnitogorsk in 1931?

SOURCE 13.16   Labour turnover at Magnitogorsk, 1931

1st of month	Total workers	Arrived during the month	Left during the month
January	18,865	3,597	3,853
February	18,609	4,398	3,402
March	19,605	8,570	5,934
April	22,241	9,391	7,166
May	24,446	17,640	9,826
June	32,280	17,292	10,825
July	38,747	10,983	12,694
August	37,006	8,693	11,447
September	34,252	10,381	9,421
October	35,162	8,003	10,072
November	33,093	10,350	10,797
December	32,666	7,440	7,835

SOURCE 13.17   Workers arriving at and departing from Magnitogorsk, 1930–33

	Arrived	Left
1930	67,000*	45,000
1931	111,000	97,000
1932	62,000	70,000
1933	53,000	53,000
Total	**293,000**	**265,000**

* It is possible that the figure of 67,000 for 1930 is a typographical error and should have read 57,000

SOURCE 13.18   A. Nove, *An Economic History of the USSR, 1917–91*, 1992, p. 192. Nove quotes a future minister, talking about the birth of the Stalingrad tractor works

a) *A worker ... came to the Volga from a Moscow factory. Even he was full of wonder at the American lathes without belt transmission, with their own motors. He could not handle them. What is one to say of peasants fresh from the fields? They were sometimes illiterate.*

b) *The first director of the factory, Ivanov, wrote as follows: 'In the assembly shop I talked to a young man who was grinding sockets. I asked him how he measured, and he showed me how he used his fingers. We had no measuring instruments!'*

You are advisers to the Politburo. Working in groups of three, suggest at least one solution for each of the problems identified below. Then compare your solutions with those of other groups.
   Are you going to:

- use methods of intimidation to force the most out of the workers?
- find ways to encourage them to perform more satisfactorily?

Problems

1 Continuing shortage of labour – where can you get more workers for the ever-expanding factories?
2 Skills shortage – what can you do about the lack of technical skills?
3 Poor work habits amongst the ex-peasants – poor discipline and clumsiness.
4 Keeping the workforce stable – it is very hard to establish good practices if your workforce is constantly changing and moving to other places.
5 Absenteeism.
6 Motivating the workers to increase their productivity.
7 Keeping the existing skilled working class happy.

How did the party respond to its labour problems?

FOCUS ROUTE

1 Draw a diagram to record the main ways in which the Soviet government tried to deal with the problems it faced).
2 Compare these with the solutions you suggested in the second Activity on page 232.
3 What surprises you about some of the methods adopted by the Communists?

Wage differentials and incentives

To stop workers 'flitting' from job to job, wage differentials (i.e. paying some people more than others) were introduced to reward those who stayed put and acquired skills. Managers were allowed to pay bonuses. Other incentives were also used, such as awarding honours to outstanding workers; these were not just moral rewards but could bring perks and privileges such as access to closed shops, better housing and better clothes. Egalitarianism in wages was abandoned as early as 1931.

Piece work

Payment according to the pieces of work completed became common across industry, to try to drive up productivity.

Training

A massive training programme was brought into being. But many of the training programmes were poor and trainees were rushed through by poor instructors. The situation improved in the Second Five-Year Plan with fewer but better training schemes made available.

Tough measures

A series of measures were brought in between 1930 and 1933 to deal with absentees. These included dismissal, eviction from factory-owned homes or loss of various benefits. Causing damage or leaving a job without permission could lead to a prison sentence. The intimidation and terror applied to the bourgeois specialists were also applied to the workers.

   The degree of control increased during the Second and Third Five-Year Plans. In 1938, labour books were issued, along with internal passports. The labour book gave details of a worker's labour history, qualifications and any misdemeanours. It was very difficult to survive without one of these. In 1940, absenteeism became a crime, with two offences bringing a prison sentence.

Forced labour

Some labour shortages were solved by using forced labour, especially for the worst jobs in the worst conditions. Around 300,000 prisoners worked on the Baltic–White Sea Canal, many of them kulaks arrested during the collectivisation drive. After April 1930 all criminals sentenced to more than three years were sent to labour camps to provide cheap labour. The government decreed that these camps should be self-supporting. Lumber camps were set up in the forests of the frozen north and the timber produced was exported to help earn money for industrial investment. The number of forced labourers increased when the Great Purges got into full swing in the mid-1930s.

Propaganda and encouragement

A huge propaganda campaign was mounted to encourage workers to raise their productivity, which was outstandingly low during the First Five-Year Plan (see Sources 13.19 and 13.21). Shock-brigade campaigns (mounting intensive efforts to build structures such as dams) and 'socialist competition' were tried to raise work norms but they enjoyed only limited success. Probably the most significant propaganda initiative was the Stakhanovite movement (see pages 236–238). Although this caused some problems in the economy, productivity rates did improve.

AT MAGNITOGORSK

SOURCE 13.19 S. Kotkin, *Magnetic Mountain: Stalinism as a Civilisation*, 1995, pp. 90–92

In 1930 work began on a dam on the Ural River to supply the steel factory with water. Shock work began: 'Everyone to the dam! Everything for the dam!' There was socialist competition between left and right banks. The target date moved forward but the dam was built in a record 74 days, well ahead of schedule. One contemporary writer wrote: 'The Magnitogorsk dam was the school at which people began to respect Bolshevik miracles.' But it was not deep enough and the water froze, there was a chronic shortage of water, and a new dam five times as big was started almost immediately. When it was completed the first dam was submerged.

SOURCE 13.20 M. Lewin, 'Society, State and Ideology during the First Five-Year Plan', 1976, in C. Ward (ed.), *The Stalinist Dictatorship*, 1998, pp. 178–79. Lewin has an interesting background. Born in Poland in 1921, he became active in left-wing politics, escaping from the Nazis to work in the Soviet Union on a kolkhoz and in a mill. He was an officer in the Red Army for a brief time. After the Second World War he spent ten years in a kibbutz in Israel before holding academic positions in France, Britain and the USA

One of the results of this [mass influx of peasants to the cities] was the breakdown of labour discipline, which saddled the state with an enormous problem of education and disciplining the mass of the crude labour force. The battle against absenteeism, shirking, drinking in factories during working hours, and breaking tools was long, and the Soviet government played no 'humanistic' games in this fight. Very soon, methods such as denial of ration cards, eviction from lodgings, and even penal sentences for undisciplined workers were introduced.

Factories and mines in these years were transformed into railway stations – or as Ordzhonikidze [see page 223] exclaimed in despair – into one huge 'nomadic gypsy camp'. The cost of the turnover was incredible. Before they had managed to learn their job, people had already given their notice or done something in order to get fired. But the same process, and on a large scale, was going on among managers and administrators, specialists and officials. At all levels of the local administration and party apparat, people adopted the habit of leaving in good time, before they were penalized, recalled, brought in for questioning, downgraded, fired or arrested.

Thus workers, administrators, specialists, officials, party apparatus men, and, in great masses, peasants were all moving around and changing jobs, creating unwanted surpluses in some places and dearths in others, losing skills or failing to acquire them, creating streams and floods in which families were destroyed, children lost, and morality dissolved. Social, administrative, industrial and political structures were all in flux. The mighty dictatorial government found itself, as a result of its impetuous activity during those early years of accelerated industrialisation, presiding over a 'quicksand' society.

SOURCE 13.21 A Soviet propaganda poster, *In the Struggle for Fuel and Metal*, produced in 1933 with the aim of spurring on the workers to fulfil the Five-Year Plan. Gustav Klutsis, the creator of this poster, was a master of photo-montage techniques, and his posters were reproduced thousands of times. A party member since 1920, he was a loyal Stalinist, but neither this nor his work for the party could save him when he was denounced by a jealous rival during the purges; he was shot in 1938

SOURCE 13.22 J. Scott, *Behind the Urals*, 1942, p. 49. Scott describes aspects of the attempts to motivate workers in Magnitogorsk

In 1933 wage differentials were approximately as follows: the average monthly wage for an unskilled worker in Magnitogorsk was something in the neighbourhood of 100 roubles; a skilled workers' apprentice 200, a skilled worker, 300; an engineer with experience 600 to 800; administrators, directors etc., anywhere from 800 to 3000. The heavy differentiation plus the absence of unemployment and the consequent assurance of being able without difficulty to get any job in any profession learned, supplemented and stimulated the intellectual curiosity of the people. The two together were so potent that they created a student body in the Magnitogorsk night schools of 1933 willing to work eight, ten or even twelve hours on the job under the severest conditions, and then come back to night school, sometimes on an empty stomach and, sitting on a backless wooden bench, in a room so cold that you could see your breath a yard in front of you, study mathematics four hours straight....

... Competition between individuals, brigades and whole departments was encouraged ... The Stakhanov movement [see pages 190–192] hit Magnitogorsk in the autumn of 1935. Brigade and shop competition was intensified. Banners were awarded to the brigades who worked best, and monetary remuneration accompanied banners ... Wages rose. Production rose ...

ACTIVITY

Use the information in Sources 13.19–13.23 on pages 234–235 to answer the following questions.

1 Which of the measures the Soviet government brought in do not fit well with socialism and would be more at home in a capitalist system?

2 **a)** What does Moshe Lewin (Source 13.20) reveal about the problems facing the Soviet authorities and the actions they took?

  b) How reliable do you think Moshe Lewin's account is as a historical source?

3 What do Sources 13.19–13.22 tell you about the methods used to motivate workers?

4 **a)** Does John Scott's account (Source 13.22) suggest these were successful?

  b) How reliable do you think his account is?

5 **a)** Do you think the 'Dear Marfa' letter (Source 13.23) is solely the work of the author?

  b) Why did she write this letter or allow her name to be attached to it?

  c) What arguments does Anna use to persuade Marfa to reform her husband?

  d) Marfa was illiterate but the letter could have been read to her. How effective do you think it was?

SOURCE 13.23 Extracts from a letter preserved in the Magnitogorsk archives, from Anna Kovaleva to Marfa Gidzia, and quoted in S. Kotkin, *Magnetic Mountain: Stalinism as a Civilisation*, 1995, pp. 218–19

Dear Marfa!
We are both wives of locomotive drivers of the rail transport of Magnitka. You probably know that the rail transport workers of the MMK (Magnitogorsk Metallurgical Complex) are not fulfilling the plan, that they are disrupting the supply of the blast furnaces, open hearths and rolling shops ... All the workers of Magnita accuse our husbands ... Every day there are stoppages and breakdowns in rail transport ... [To fulfil the plan] it is necessary to work like the best workers of our country work. Among such shock workers is my husband, Aleksandr Panteleevich Kovalev. He always works like a shock worker, exceeding his norms, while economising on oil and lubricants ... My husband receives prizes every month ... My husband's locomotive is always clean and well taken care of....

Your husband, Iakov Stepanovich, does not fulfil the plan. He has frequent breakdowns on his locomotive, his locomotive is dirty, and he always overconsumes fuel ... all the rail workers of Magnita know him, for the wrong reasons, as the worst driver. By contrast, my husband is known as a shock worker. He is written up and praised in the newspapers ... He and I are honoured everywhere as shock workers. At the store we get everything without having to wait in queues. We moved to the building for shock workers. We get an apartment with rugs, a gramophone, a radio and other comforts ...

Therefore, I ask you, Marfa, to talk to your husband ... Persuade him that he must work honourably, conscientiously, like a shock worker. Teach him to understand the words of comrade Stalin, that work is a matter of honour, glory, valour and heroism....

STAKHANOVITES

Named after Alexei Stakhanov who produced an enormous amount of coal in one shift in 1935; the Stakhanovite movement was part of a government campaign to make workers produce more and put pressure on managers to make their operations more efficient; workers who gained the accolade 'Stakhanovite' enjoyed better food, accommodation and other privileges such as holidays.

ACTIVITY

You are going to take part in a STAKHANOVITE simulation. To do this you need to split your class into groups of four or five. Each group takes on one of the roles below. The crucial characters are starred.

- The manager*
- Assistant manager
- Would-be Stakhanovite*
- Local party secretary*
- At least one, but not more than three, ordinary workers

The scenario

A worker in a factory producing steel wants to make an attempt to gain Stakhanovite status by raising his production rate enormously. You have to decide whether your character will support this attempt. To do this you need to think about:

a) your position at the moment:
  - your aims
  - what you have to do to achieve these aims and be successful
  - the problems you face.

b) what the implications of a successful attempt will be for you and others.

Then decide whether you will or will not support the attempt, setting out your reasons clearly.

How to proceed

1 Read the material on pages 237–239 about Stakhanovites, working conditions and the pressures on a manager in 1936 in industry. Different members of your group can read different parts and then you can pool your knowledge.
2 Discuss in your group how your character will respond by considering the points in a) and b) above. Decide on your response (if possible, the whole group should agree) and prepare your case for a meeting of all the characters, to be held in the next lesson. Some groups may wish to consult with others before the meeting, for example the groups playing the workers or the groups playing the manager and assistant manager.
3 Hold the meeting of all the characters to decide if the attempt should go ahead. The characters should be prepared to argue their cases aggressively in an open meeting.
4 Come out of role and discuss the following questions:
   a) What decisions were made and why were they made?
   b) What does the simulation tell you about the tensions in Soviet society?
   c) What were the advantages/disadvantages of Stakhanovism for:
      i) the individual
      ii) the factory/mine/workplace?
   d) How effective was the Stakhanov movement as a mechanism for driving up productivity?
   e) What can we learn about the relationship between politics and economics in the USSR in the 1930s?

The Stakhanov record

SOURCE 13.24 Alexei Stakhanov, the coal miner whose astonishing output inspired countless other workers to copy his example

At ten o'clock on 30 August 1935, Alexei Stakhanov, a pneumatic-pick operator, began his special shift. After five hours of uninterrupted work he had cut 102 tons of coal, almost sixteen times the norm of 6.5 tons per shift. How was this done?

The idea came from Konstantin Petrov, party organiser at Central Ormino in the Don Basin. Central Ormino lagged behind its plan quota and Petrov wanted to do something about it. He knew Stakhanov usually produced above the norm results on his shift. Ideal conditions were set up: an uninterrupted supply of compressed air, a good pick, two carefully selected proppers (to prop up the roof as Stakhanov cut away the coal) and ample supplies of timber. Hauliers were on hand to take the coal away. Petrov was there, holding a lamp on the coal face. Normally, the miners working on the face that Stakhanov cut produced around 52 tons in total per shift, but they did their own propping. Stakhanov with his support team cut twice the amount that the eight miners would have produced.

Barely two hours after Stakhanov had finished, Petrov assembled a party committee at which Stakhanov was acclaimed for his world record for productivity – the correct path to 'guarantee the fulfilment of the annual plan ahead of schedule'. Stakhanov received 200 roubles (instead of the normal 30 roubles), a bonus equal to a month's wages, an apartment reserved for technical personnel with a telephone and comfortable furniture, passes to the cinema and live performances at the local workers' club, and places at a holiday resort. He also had his name prominently displayed on the mine's honour board.

A special meeting of coal hewers was called, with compulsory attendance of local party, union and managerial leaders. Sectional competitions were set up for miners to emulate Stakhanov's achievements. The party got the response it wanted. Several miners demanded the chance to beat the record, and by 5 September two had done so. Others were warned: 'All those who try to slander Stakhanov and his record will be considered by the party committee as the most vile enemies of the people.'

Ordzhonikidze, the Commissar for Heavy Industry, had Stakhanov, the 'Soviet Hercules', put on the front page of *Pravda*. He said, 'In our country, under socialism, heroes of labour must become the most famous.' On 11 September, *Pravda* used the term 'Stakhanovite movement' for the first time and in November Stalin called for Stakhanovism to spread 'widely and deeply' across the entire Soviet Union. Recordmania swept the country: by December 1935, the records achieved in heavy industry alone filled two volumes.

The Stakhanovite movement was seen as a way of compelling management to adopt new production methods and increase rates of production. Those reluctant to do so were branded as saboteurs, with the warning 'Such pseudo leaders must be removed immediately'. With pressure from above to meet increased targets and from below from workers wanting to be Stakhanovites, who would have wanted to be a manager in Soviet Russia at that time?

A MAGNITOGORSK STAKHANOVITE

V. P. Ogorodnikov was the son of a peasant from Smolensk. His name features four times in a list of eight record-breaking shifts in a Magnitogorsk steel mill between September 1935 and January 1936. The second-highest-earning worker in Magnitogorsk, he was rewarded with a brand-new motor cycle and an individual house with its own garden, 70 per cent paid for by the factory. Before the revolution perhaps only a factory owner could have afforded such a house. He became a household name.

SOURCE 13.25 A cartoon showing the leading 'Stakhanovite' blooming mill operators, featured in the Magnitogorsk newspaper. Left to right: Ogorodnikov, Chernysh, Bogatyrenko and Tishchenko

SOURCE 13.26 The output of the leading 'Stakhanovite' blooming mill operators in Magnitogorsk, 1935–36 *(In a blooming mill, melted metal is formed into steel ingots or bars.)*

Date/shift	Name	Steel ingots produced per shift
12 September 1935	Ogorodnikov	211
22 September	Tishchenko	214
25 September	Bogatyrenko	219
9 October	Ogorodnikov	230
? October	Bogatyrenko	239
29 October	Ogorodnikov	243
11 January 1936	Ogordnikov	251
11 January (next shift)	Chernysh	264

PARTY SECRETARIES

Party Secretaries were charged with overseeing the implementation of Moscow's orders. They were judged by the output of major industrial enterprises in their areas – over fulfilment of plan targets was demanded at any cost, and health and safety issues came a poor second. They would use their influence to help managers secure scarce supplies in competition with factories from other areas. Failure to meet a target might have serious consequences.

The Stakhanovite campaign gave them the chance to overcome inertia in industry and put pressure on managers to improve productivity and raise output.

WORKERS

Workers were anxious to improve their position. But they could not strike; the NKVD saw to that. They wanted to take advantage of any wage differentials in order to secure a better standard of living. Also, they tried to avoid harsh punishments for absenteeism or poor quality work – they did not want to be accused of wrecking. One way to get higher wages and to avoid accumulating a poor record was to move from one job to another so that the authorities could not keep track of them.

When Stakhanovism started, workers resented the increased norms (these went up by around 30 per cent in some enterprises) and there was increased tension between managers and workers. Some workers demanded to become Stakhanovites in order to gain increased pay and privileges. For example, they demanded good tools, but other workers resented that the would-be Stakhanovites got the best equipment.

MANAGERS

Managers had to fulfil their targets and would do anything, including bribery and corruption, to do it. They could only fulfil their targets with the co-operation of the workers. Managers were especially desperate to keep skilled workers: some managers registered non-existent workers on the payroll and distributed their ration cards to favoured workers. Harsh laws on absenteeism were not enforced, payments were made for work that had never been done and bonuses were paid wherever possible. Moscow attacked the overpayment of wages but managers were more worried about failing to meet production targets. They made up success stories to keep Moscow happy. Soviet managers had a saying: 'It's necessary not to work well but to account well.'

Stakhanovism presented managers with problems. Workers put them under a lot of pressure to be classified as Stakhanovites and wanted good tools to do the job more efficiently, but there were not enough of these to go around. Such shortages frustrated workers and could lead to them charging managers with wrecking by 'hindering us from working in a Stakhanovite fashion'. Managers also had to deal with other problems arising from Stakhanovism, such as:
- resentment from workers who did not want production norms to increase
- distortions in the production process caused by resources being focused on Stakhanovite workers. Managers were judged on total output, not output from specific areas within the enterprise.

■ 13E Pressures on a manager in 1936

PRESSURES FROM ABOVE

Targets
There was increasing pressure from party officials to fulfil targets. Failure could lead to savage attacks on managers.

Increased labour norms
These were increased on average by ten per cent in early 1936, and by up to 50 per cent in some areas. If managers applied the norms, workers often left. Some workers could not make the norms, which caused tension between workers and management. Managers who tried to lower norms could be accused of wrecking and arrested by the NKVD.

Books must balance
State subsidies to industry were cut substantially from 1936 onwards and enterprises were expected to pay for the fuel, raw materials and labour they needed from their own income. Managers who found themselves with a shortfall faced charges of wrecking.

Wage incentives
In 1936, rationing ended and there were more consumer goods to buy. Food became more expensive. Workers wanted better wages, especially when they had to work harder. But enterprises could not afford these because of cuts in subsidies and the need to balance the books (see left). However, at the same time the gap between ordinary workers' wages and that of managers and professionals increased.

ECONOMIC PRESSURES

Labour shortage
By 1936, the number of new workers coming into industry had declined by two-thirds because of better living conditions on collective farms and the drafting of young men into the armed forces. Mining and lumbering were hit hard.

Shortage of vital raw materials
There were shortages of oil, coal and timber (partly as a result of the lack of labourers to supply them) at a time when domestic consumption was expanding rapidly.

ECONOMIC PRESSURES

Competition from military spending
From 1936 onwards there was an unplanned increase in spending on the armed forces (from 3.4 per cent of the budget in 1931 to 16.1 per cent in 1936 and 32.5 per cent in 1940) and the military was given priority in the allocation of materials.

Fall in foreign trade
The worldwide slump in trade during the 1930s meant it was no longer possible to import technology such as new industrial machines.

D Did urban living standards improve during the plans?

Throughout the 1930s, the central planning system never managed to improve the standard of living of the very citizens for whom the plans were ostensibly designed. During the First Five-Year Plan, in particular, the workers suffered very badly. There was a profound lack of consumer goods, and food was rationed. It is estimated that in Leningrad and Moscow between 1928 and 1933 meat, milk and fruit consumption declined by two-thirds.

The pressures created by the expanding urban population were phenomenal. It is estimated that cities and towns were growing at a rate of 200,000 every month and there was very little provision for this wave of humanity pouring in from the countryside. The newcomers were mainly peasants who had suffered from the psychological upheaval of being uprooted from their rural lifestyle. Some of the towns in more remote areas were akin to frontier towns, with no paved roads and inadequate sanitary arrangements. They had been turned into huge construction sites, surrounded by a sea of mud. Workers lived in barracks in appalling conditions. Overcrowding was intense, and with it came its usual bedfellows – dirt and squalor. There was very little control and life was brutish, violent and crime-ridden.

In 1935, Stalin announced that 'Life has become better, comrades, life has become more joyous.' Just how joyous is open to question. The planners were not able to meet the needs of urban dwellers. Housing, in particular, remained abysmal; there was intense overcrowding in sub-standard accommodation as building materials were diverted to factory building. Town transport, mainly trams, was also invariably packed. There was a shortage of water, shops and catering facilities. Most workers ate in their factory canteens. There was some expansion of shops during the Second Five-Year Plan but the centralised distribution system was poor and the shops often lacked basic commodities. Long queues, seemingly a permanent feature of Russian life, had as much to do with the scarcity of shops as with lack of products. However, some industrial enterprises set up their own shops, bringing in food from farms, and the peasants supplied towns with milk, eggs, vegetables and meat from their private plots. It is difficult to generalise for all sections of society and some workers certainly became better off during this period.

AT MAGNITOGORSK

Only 15 per cent of Magnitogorsk's population lived in permanent brick apartment buildings, taking up 33 per cent of the city's space. Twenty-five per cent lived in mud huts they had built for themselves. Virtually everybody had at some time lived in the huge barrack-like workers' housing. By 1939, there were enough public bath-houses to allow every inhabitant to have seven baths a year. In *Behind the Urals* (1942, pages 184–88), John Scott records that there were different levels of housing: directors and top managers had houses with several rooms and gardens; skilled workers had small houses or apartments with basic facilities; unskilled workers had poor-quality housing or mud huts.

SOURCE 13.27 M. Lewin, 'Society, State and Ideology during the First Five-Year Plan', 1976, in C. Ward (ed.), *The Stalinist Dictatorship*, 1998, p. 177

In the cities, the inordinate and unanticipated growth transformed a strained housing situation into an appalling one, creating the specifically Soviet [or Stalinist] reality of chronically overcrowded lodgings, with consequent attrition of human relations, strained family life, destruction of privacy and personal life, and various forms of psychological strain. All this provided a propitious hunting ground for the ruthless, the primitive, the blackmailer, the hooligan, and the informer. The courts dealt with an incredible mass of cases testifying to the human destruction caused by this congestion of dwellings. The falling standards of living, the lines outside stores, and the proliferation of speculators suggest the depths of the tensions and hardships.

SOURCE 13.28 M. Fainsod, *Smolensk under Soviet Rule*, 1958, p. 322, describing living conditions for unskilled workers in 1937

The workers' barracks were described as overcrowded and in a state of extreme disrepair with water streaming from the ceiling 'straight on to workers' beds'. Heat was rarely provided in the barracks; bedding went unchanged; and sanitary work was almost non-existent. There were no kitchens and eating halls on the construction sites; hot food could not be obtained until the evening when workers had to walk a long distance to reach the dining hall. 'Many of the women', one female Party member reported, 'live practically on the street. No one pays any attention to them; some of those defenceless creatures threaten to commit suicide.' In addition, cases where wages were not paid on time were on the increase. All this 'neglect of the elementary needs of workers' as well as 'lack of care for them as human beings' resulted in 'fully justified dissatisfaction' and bitterness on the part of the workers.

SOURCE 13.29 H. Eekman, a Belgian diplomat, saw ordinary families in Moscow in the late 1930s cramped into small, shared living accommodation

They made pathetic efforts to isolate from their neighbours the few square feet of floor space allotted to their use. Every piece of furniture, every stick they owned, every ragged remnant saved from old curtains, was pressed into service to build some sort of fence or stockade around their cramped refuge.

URBAN HOUSING STATISTICS IN THE FIRST FIVE YEAR PLAN

Housing
- Plan 33% increase
- Actual 16% increase
- Result 50% shortfall

Urban population
- Plan 32.5 million
- Actual 38.7 million
- Result 20% higher than expected

Moscow population
- 1929 2.2 million
- 1932 3.7 million

By the end of the 1930s, 40% of the Soviet urban population were former peasants who had moved within the decade.

SOURCE 13.30 N. Mandelstam, *Hope Against Hope*, 1971. Nadezhda Mandelstam was the wife of one of Russia's greatest poets of the twentieth century, Osip Mandelstam, and a victim of Stalin's repression. She survived and wrote two volumes of memoirs: *Hope Against Hope* and *Hope Abandoned*

At the end of the twenties and in the thirties our authorities, making no concessions to 'egalitarianism', started to raise the living standard of those who had proved their usefulness. The resulting differentiation was very noticeable, and everybody was concerned to keep the material benefits he had worked so hard to earn – particularly now that the wretched poverty of the first post-revolutionary years was a thing of the past. Nobody wanted to go through that again, and a thin layer of privileged people gradually came into being – with 'packets', country villas, and cars. They realized only later how precarious it all was: in the period of the great purges they found they could be stripped of everything in a flash, and without any explanation. But in the meantime those who had been granted a share of the cake eagerly did everything demanded of them.

SOURCE 13.31 J. Scott, *Behind the Urals*, 1942, pp. 122–23. John Scott was an American volunteer working in Magnitogorsk (see page 221). Here, he writes about Masha the daughter of illiterate, poor peasants. Masha did not receive her first pair of shoes until she was fourteen years old. Her parents were very supportive and Masha studied at school, in a higher education institute in Moscow and at Magnitogorsk Teachers' College. She then taught adults in a party higher education college

From the incredible poverty and suffering of the civil-war period, the Russian people were working their way up to a higher standard. All Masha's family were enthusiastic. Several of the children joined the Komsomol, and after years of argument, the mother succumbed to the pressures of her children and took down the icons from the walls of the hut. Then she too decided to study. Masha's mother learned to read and write at the age of fifty-five. She was taught by her youngest daughter.

Masha went to the capital in 1929. At that time the industrialization of the country was just beginning. Russia's rapidly expanding economy was crying for every kind of professional skill, for engineers, chemists, teachers, economists, and doctors. The higher schools paid stipends to their students, and aided them in every way to get through their courses and out to factory and laboratory. Masha finished up her preparatory work, and then entered the Mendelyeyev Institute, where she worked part time as laboratory assistant to make a few roubles for bread.

Masha was very happy in Magnitogorsk. She felt that the world was at her feet. She slept on the divan of her sister and brother-in-law's tiny hotel room, she had two or three dresses, two pairs of shoes and one coat. In two more years, she would graduate from the teachers' college. Then she would teach, or perhaps take graduate work. Not only this, she was living in a town which had grown up from nothing just as she herself had. Living conditions were improving as the pig-iron production of the mill increased. She felt herself a part of a going concern. Hence her spontaneous pity for me, whom she first saw as a cast-off from a bankrupt and degenerating society.

ACTIVITY

How do Sources 13.27–13.31 confirm Stalin's claim of 1935 that 'Life has become better, comrades, life has become more joyous'?

Note: This activity requires you to interpret, evaluate and use source material in relation to its historical context.

1 Carefully analyse both the content and the provenance of the sources. Notice the differences in content and what this says about the experience of different sections of Soviet society and how experiences change in different parts of the country.

2 Examine the origins and purpose of the sources so you can judge their reliability and value.

3 Think about the different perspectives of the writers, for example, Lewin is a professional historian (see Source 13.20, page 234), and N. Mandelstam was a victim of Stalin's repression.

■ **Learning trouble spot**

Examining the statistics
The production figures for the Five-Year Plans can be seen in Source 13.8 on page 226. All of the figures are based on Soviet estimates. There are several ways in which the figures could be inaccurate:

- Managers of enterprises and factories had plenty of opportunity to manipulate the paperwork in order to inflate their successes and cover up their failures. It was not only their jobs that were on the line if they could not show that they had fulfilled their targets.
- Officials at regional levels also did not want to be seen to be failing to meet the targets set by the central administration. So they were likely to cover up failures and to accept good figures given to them by enterprises.
- Top officials did not want to be seen to be failing to achieve the key targets set for their industry. They wanted to show Stalin that they had been successful.

Western analysts, such as R. W. Davies, Alec Nove and Eugene Zaleski, have looked carefully at the Soviet figures and used different ways of calculating growth. Others have concluded that the Soviet statistics are often so contradictory that it is impossible to give an accurate picture of the achievements of the plans in the 1930s.

Conclusions

Despite the problems with the statistics, all commentators agree that there was substantial growth in heavy industry during this period, that there were impressive achievements, and that the Soviet Union was transformed on the industrial front. The command economy clearly had major weaknesses – unrealistic targets; the use of bribery, corruption and crooked deals to achieve targets; major shortages; and products of dubious quality. At best, the economy was ill-organised and badly co-ordinated, at worst it was chaotic. There were imbalances in the economy, with heavy industry taking priority over chemicals and transport and consumer goods being neglected throughout. The Russian people still spent an enormous amount of their time queuing and went short of essential commodities. Living conditions remained abysmal.

However, this has to be set against the state of Soviet Russia in 1928 and the massive steps forward that industry took in the 1930s. In a sense, the plans were trying to do the impossible in conditions of appalling backwardness. The targets were always unrealisable but they were designed to drive people forward to achieve the impossible. Resources were directed towards the areas of key priority and in a rough and crude way progress was made. Given the results, some historians have concluded that the type of command economy that emerged, with clearly set priorities, seemed reasonably well suited to the circumstances of the USSR in the 1930s. It got the Soviet industrial juggernaut rolling and that was no mean achievement.

SOURCE 13.32 C. Ward, *Stalin's Russia*, 1993, p. 81

When the first piateletka (Five-Year Plan) was declared complete in December 1932 no major targets had been reached, but there were some dramatic advances. In these four or five years the Soviet economy was fundamentally transformed. In the Urals, the Kuzbass, the Volga district and the Ukraine hundreds of mining, engineering and metallurgical enterprises were in the making. New factories materialised in the empty lands of the non-Russian republics scarcely touched by the modern world. More than half the machine tools on stream in the USSR by 1932 were fabricated or installed after 1928. Gigantic schemes like the Magnitogorsk combine (part of the Ural–Kuznetsk iron and steel complex) were built from scratch, the Truksib railway line opened in 1930 and the first of the Dnieprostroi's new turbines began to turn in 1932.

SOURCE 13.33 A. Bullock, *Hitler and Stalin: Parallel Lives*, 1991, pp. 295–96

After the grey compromises of the NEP, the Plan revived the flagging faith of the party. Here at last was the chance to pour their enthusiasm into building the New Jerusalem they had been promised. The boldness of the targets, the sacrifices demanded and the vision of what 'backward' Russia might achieve provided an inspiring contrast with an 'advanced' West with millions unemployed and resources left to waste because of the Slump. None of Stalin's targets might be achieved, but in every case output was raised: 6 million tons of steel was little more than half the 10 million allowed for, but 50 per cent up on the starting figure.

TALKING POINT

How well planned do you think the plans for industry were?

Would the Soviet Union have done better if it had continued with the NEP?

One question remains: would the Soviet Union have done better if it had continued with the NEP as Bukharin and the right wing of the party had wanted it to?

Some historians believe that the Soviet government could have avoided the human suffering and done just as well, probably better, by sticking with the NEP. Roy Medvedev (*Let History Judge*, 1972) and Stephen Cohen (*Bukharin and the Bolshevik Revolution*, 1974) were among the first historians to put forward this case. They contend that the modernisation of Russia could have been achieved by the continuation of the limited market economy of the 1920s. They accept that the pace would have been slower but maintain that the waste of resources would have been far less.

R. W. Davies, a leading British expert on the Russian economy, has a mixed view (*Soviet Economic Development From Lenin to Khrushchev*, 1998, pages 36–37). According to him, the NEP had delivered rapid recovery after the Civil War and the economy probably could have continued to expand at a moderate rate. But he acknowledges that the NEP had limitations for the Communists: serious unemployment and an unfavourable effect on other sectors of the economy, such as education and the railways. Also, Soviet officials were worried about the defence and armaments industries. He accepts that there were powerful arguments in favour of rapid industrialisation. He believes that in the end it is a political judgement of how essential it was for the USSR to establish a powerful heavy industry sector and an armaments industry in the space of a few years and whether the NEP was capable of doing that.

Alec Nove, in *Was Stalin Really Necessary?* (1964, page 23), argues that the party had reached an impasse at the end of the 1920s: the economy was stagnant and they needed to find a way forward. This was heightened by the sense of crisis caused by war threats. The policy of Bukharin – sometimes called 'riding towards socialism on a peasant nag' – was ideologically and politically unacceptable to the party. They could not base their industrialisation plans on the development of a prosperous peasantry who would voluntarily supply food. Rapid industrialisation and collectivisation were the way out of the impasse.

In his *An Economic History of the USSR, 1917–91* (1992), Alec Nove admits that there were colossal mistakes and disasters, but asserts that these should be seen in the context of the 1930s, when capitalism was in crisis in the rest of the world (this was the period of the Great Depression) and there were no models to follow. The command economy was inefficient but it concentrated resources in key areas and got the job done. Nove accepts there was a high price to pay for this, particularly the human suffering involved in collectivisation, and accepts that there might have been other ways of doing it. But he thinks that for Stalin and the Communist Party there was no real alternative. Without this 'leap forward', however crudely it took place, Nove doubts that the Russians would have created the sort of industrial base that helped them to win the Second World War.

TALKING POINT

Historians call the 'what if . . .?' approach counterfactual history. What do you think are the advantages and problems of asking 'what if . . .?' about the past. Can you suggest other topics where a counterfactual approach would be useful?

FOCUS ROUTE

In your Focus Route activities (pages 225 and 230), you should have collected information about the plans under these headings:

Evidence of success and achievements
Evidence of failures and weaknesses
Evidence that the Five-Year Plans were not well planned
Ways in which the plans benefited the workers
Ways in which the workers suffered or did not do well

1 Look back over the chapter and add any further information that you think should go in these categories.
2 Read pages 242–243, assessing the plans, then:
   a) add any more details
   b) note down any final comments.

KEY POINTS FROM CHAPTER 13

How well planned were the Five-Year Plans?

1 The party was convinced that the route to socialism was through industrialisation and the proletarianisation of the Russian people.
2 Although this was a 'revolution from above', there was a great deal of active support for the plans and for socialist construction from young urban workers.
3 The changes were administered through a 'command economy' which relied on centralised planning and control by government commissariats overseen by the Communist Party.
4 The mechanism chosen to deliver industrialisation was the Five-Year Plans, which set broad targets for all branches of industry. Most operational targets were contained in plans covering shorter periods such as one year.
5 Extremely ambitious targets were set to drive people to huge efforts. These had little to do with rational planning and more to do with propaganda.
6 Fulfilment and over-fulfilment of the plan targets became the overriding force driving the managers of industrial enterprises and officials.
7 Intimidation and fear permeated the system as managers strove to fulfil their targets. They, together with party officials, were evaluated on their target performance. This led to the falsification of figures and corruption.
8 The First Five-Year Plan was chaotic. There was an enormous amount of waste and many products were unusable. At the same time, remarkable progress was made in key heavy industries and huge-scale projects were undertaken.
9 Some workers did well out of the plans, particularly skilled urban workers. Other workers, particularly ex-peasants forced into cities by collectivisation, found themselves part of a 'quicksand society' trying to make a better living and avoiding harsh punishments by constantly moving from place to place and job to job.
10 The Second Five-Year Plan saw more developed planning and more reasonable targets. Workers enjoyed 'three good years' with more food and consumer goods but these were ended by the purges. The third plan saw a return to shortages and chaotic planning as resources were diverted to the military.
11 Generally, the standard of living for most workers during the plans was poor and improved marginally; housing standards remained abysmal.

Section 5 Review: How did Stalin transform the economy of the USSR in the 1930s?

ACTIVITY

Use the results of the Focus Route activities that you have completed in Chapters 12 and 13 to write the essay: How successful were Stalin's economic policies?

Work in groups to draw up a plan for the essay, using the skills you have learned in preceding essay-writing activities in this book.

a) Decide what the key points are and form these into your main paragraphs. Each point should directly answer the question posed in the essay title.

b) Work out what you are going to use as supporting points for each key point. These can be evidence that supports the key point or you can develop the argument around the key point.

In this essay, you have to weigh up the evidence for both sides of the argument. There is a debate about the economic issues and there is also a human dimension to take into account. You have to decide what line you are going to take. You could:

- deal with collectivisation first and then consider industrial policies
- deal with the economic aspects of agriculture and industry first and then look at the human dimension
- look at the successes of the agricultural and industrial plans first and then look at ways in which they were not successful
- take a different line altogether.

At the end, you need to write a concluding paragraph which draws the key points together and makes an overall assessment. Make sure that this is not a repetition of what you wrote in the introductory paragraph.

How did Stalin control the USSR?

During the 1930s, Stalin extended his control of the Communist Party and of the people of the Soviet Union. The machinery of state terror had been put in place in the early 1930s to push through the industrialisation and collectivisation drives. In the mid-1930s Stalin instituted the purges, which for the first time applied terror to the Communist Party itself. Stalin removed the old Bolsheviks from power and repressed other potential sources of opposition in the party, replacing them with an élite, the *nomenklatura*, who had a vested interest in supporting him. Terror was also applied to other sections of the population: anyone who showed signs of dissent or was critical of the regime was liable to arrest and imprisonment in the Gulag, the vast system of labour camps throughout the USSR.

At the same time Stalin, through the cult of the personality, was projected as a god-like leader. He alone could lead the people through present troubles to a glorious society – a socialist society – in the not too distant future. Stalin was feared but he was also loved. Chapter 14 looks at the causes of the Great Terror in the 1930s and considers Stalin's responsibility for the huge numbers who were killed. Chapter 15 examines the cult of the personality.

ACTIVITY

Terror, secret police and labour camps provide us with some of the most dramatic and enduring images of the Soviet Union in the 1930s: the knock on the door in the middle of the night . . . sleep deprivation and interrogation . . . show trials . . . hard labour in freezing conditions, or execution. A human tragedy on a huge scale lies behind these images. Read the case studies on pages 247–248.

1 For each case study explain:
   a) who the subject of the case study is
   b) what happened to him or her
   c) why you might be surprised that they were treated in the way they were.
2 What do you think these case studies show about what was happening in the USSR in the 1930s?
3 Draw up a list of questions that you would like to find the answers to – for example, how could it be that a party leader was purged?

PARTY LEADER

You have already met Nikolai Bukharin, the leading theorist of the right and the 'favourite of the whole party'. Although ousted by Stalin in the power struggle of 1929, he continued to work hard for the party. He edited *Isvestia* and was a major contributor to the 'Stalin Constitution' of 1936. But he was not safe. Arrested in February 1937, he was imprisoned for a year before becoming the 'star' of the third great show trial in March 1938. According to Sir Fitzroy McLean, a British diplomat, Bukharin dominated the proceedings in a most extraordinary way. Although forced to plead guilty, he showed his intellectual and moral superiority over Vyshinsky, the chief prosecutor. McLean adds that, by mistake, a flashlight revealed that Stalin was watching the proceedings from behind dark glass.

Before he was arrested, Bukharin wrote a 'last letter' dedicated to the future generation of party members, insisting that his young wife Anna Larina memorise it. In it he denounced the NKVD as the 'hellish machine [which] can transform any Party member into a terrorist or spy' and protested his innocence. He told Anna Larina that she was young and would live to see history clear his name. She did, but she had to wait 50 years: Bukharin was not REHABILITATED until 1988. Anna Larina herself spent twenty years in labour camps and in exile and did not see her baby son again until he was 21. Bukharin's disabled first wife was arrested in 1938 and interrogated at intervals until March 1940, when she was shot. Other members of her family were shot, disappeared or died in prison.

> **NKVD**
> The name of the secret police from 1934 to 1943.

> **REHABILITATED**
> Reputation restored. No longer treated as a traitor.

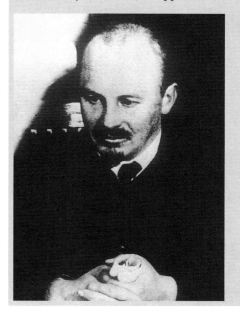

SOURCE 1 'Koba, why do you need me to die?' Bukharin wrote in a note to Stalin after the death sentence was pronounced on him. (Koba, meaning 'the Indomitable', was Stalin's revolutionary pseudonym. Its use here is a sign of how close Bukharin and Stalin had once been.) Two days later, Bukharin was shot

SOURCE 2 Anna Larina, Bukharin's wife

DAUGHTER OF A PARTY OFFICIAL

Seven-year-old Engelsina Cheshkova was bored, sitting with her bunch of flowers at a party meeting in 1936. So she got up and wandered towards the platform. Stalin picked her up, cameras clicked, and Engelsina became famous. A statue was erected in Moscow based on the picture: 'Thank you, Comrade Stalin, for my happy childhood.' But it did not turn out to be so happy. In December 1937, her father, a minor party official, disappeared. Engelsina, who was now 'the daughter of an enemy of the people', wrote a letter, dictated by her mother, to Stalin asking for help; she did not link her father's arrest with Stalin. The letter led to the arrest of her mother, who died in exile in Turkestan. Engelsina never saw her father again. Despite this, the adult Engelsina cried when she heard of Stalin's death because her eight-month-old daughter would never see Stalin alive – such was the effect of the cult of Stalin in the Soviet Union.

SOURCE 3 Stalin with Engelsina Cheshkova, 1936

WORKER AND MANAGER

You have already met the Stakhanovite Ogorodnikov, who worked in the steel mill in Magnitogorsk and had been praised as a hero of socialist labour. He had been refused entry to the party on the basis of his ex-kulak past and was soon to find himself caught up in the purges of the late 1930s. His boss at the mill, Golubitsky, seems to have resisted the scapegoating of subordinates when there were regular machine breakdowns at the plant, which were probably caused by Stakhanovites trying to break work norms. However, in doing so (or for other reasons), he incurred the resentment of the Procurator (Head of Justice in Magnitogorsk) who used the breakdowns to accuse Golubitsky of wrecking. Testimony from those below Golubitsky was needed and Ogorodnikov and two others were arrested and tortured in 1937. Golubitsky was arrested in March 1938, convicted in July 1938 and shot. Ogorodnikov was executed too, going from hero to villain in just two years.

SOURCE 4 A cartoon published in the *Magnitogorsk Worker*, the city newspaper, in September 1936. It shows factory bosses, including Golubitsky (top left), with piles of unusable products

14

How far was Stalin responsible for the Great Terror?

CHAPTER OVERVIEW

At the end of the First Five-Year Plan there was a great deal of hostility towards the Communist government and concerns within the party about the breakneck speed of industrialisation. There were growing signs of opposition to Stalin and a possibility that he would be replaced as leader. Then, in December 1934, Sergei Kirov, a leading member of the Politburo, was murdered. This triggered the wave of purges and terror, which reached its peak in 1937 and 1938. Thousands of members of the Communist Party were accused of being involved in conspiracies against Stalin and the party leadership. They were arrested and imprisoned or executed. The terror also engulfed other sections of the population, including the armed forces. Historians disagree about the causes of the purges and terror and the extent to which Stalin was personally responsible for them.

A What do we mean by the purges? (pp. 250–251)

B What sort of opposition to Stalin had developed before 1934? (pp. 252–253)

C The Kirov murder mystery (pp. 254–257)

D The Great Terror (pp. 258–266)

E Interpretations of the Great Terror (pp. 267–268)

F How far was Stalin's personality responsible for the purges and the Great Terror? (pp. 269–275)

NB Great Terror or Great Purges? Both of these terms are used by historians to cover the period of mass terror in the Soviet Union in 1937–38. According to Sheila Fitzpatrick, in *The Russian Revolution 1917–1932*, the term 'Great Purges' is a Western term, not a Soviet one. There was no public way to refer to it at the time; in private it was referred to as '1937'. Robert Conquest and other historians call this period the 'Great Terror'. Recent research has shifted the emphasis from elite and party victims to non-Communist victims who were, in numerical terms, a vastly larger group. The term Great Terror is therefore used more often than Great Purges and so in this second edition the authors have chosen to use it. You will, however, find references to the Great Purges in some of the sources.

FOCUS ROUTE

Make notes on the different sorts of purge. Make sure that you understand the differences between them.

A What do we mean by the purges?

The word 'purge' refers to 'cleaning out' or 'cleansing' an organism of impurities. The first purge of the Communist Party took place in 1918 and there were periodic purges or *chistki* (cleansings) throughout the 1920s. These usually took place at times when the leaders were seeking to exercise more control over the party or reshape it, as in the Lenin Enrolment of 1924 (see page 188). The party often took in more members (lowering entry standards) during periods of crisis such as the Civil War and collectivisation, and shed what it saw as undesirable elements when the crisis was over. But a *chistka* was, by and large, a non-violent process. Party members were required to exchange their party cards for new ones or to verify their party documents. In this process, people were refused new cards: they were expelled but not usually arrested.

After the murder of Sergei Kirov at the end of 1934 this changed. From 1936 and particularly in 1937–38, many old Bolshevik leaders were disposed of, the party was purged ruthlessly and violently, and other groups in society were swept up in the 'cleansing' process. This later period is called the Great Terror.

We can identify three phases in the purges of the 1930s:

1 The *chistka* of 1932–35 in which over twenty per cent of the party were expelled non-violently as part of a clearing-out process after collectivisation.
2 The show trials which saw prominent old Bolsheviks publicly tried and executed.
3 The Yezhovshchina, named after Yezhov, the head of the NKVD, which was a period of mass terror from 1937 to 1938 when thousands of party members, state officials, members of the armed forces, industrial directors, professionals and other sections of society were denounced, arrested and imprisoned. Many were executed; many more died in Soviet labour camps.

THE USE OF TERROR

Lenin used terror and class warfare to crush opposition. Stalin extended the use of terror and class warfare in the early 1930s to push through the Five-Year Plans. Millions of kulaks or 'class enemies' were killed or sent to labour camps. Many workers and engineers, accused of sabotage and wrecking, were sent to the growing Gulag. Government organisations, like Gosplan, were purged of ex-Mensheviks and the old bourgeois intelligentsia.

But Lenin and other Communists made a distinction between the methods to be used against opposition from outside the party and those for dealing with disagreements and opposition inside the party. There was a clear understanding that terror should not be used on party comrades. In the Great Terror, Stalin unleashed terror *inside* the party, which then engulfed an enormous number of people in the wider society.

■ Learning trouble spot

Why join the Communist Party?

Some Russians joined the party not for ideological reasons but for the considerable advantages and privileges that came with the party card. Party members could often get larger rations and access to scarce consumer goods. In some areas, belonging to the party gave members power over other groups. People were expelled from the party for all sorts of reasons such as drunkenness, corruption and not being an active member.

■ 14A Timeline of the purges

1932	Signs of opposition to Stalin's leadership. Ryutin, who had denounced Stalin as the 'evil genius of the Russian Revolution', was expelled from the party but not executed.
1932–34	Purge of 'undesirable elements' – mainly the more illiterate and inactive of the new working class and peasant recruits: 22 per cent of the party were expelled.
1934 February	Seventeenth Party Congress. Several provincial delegates urged Kirov to take over as General Secretary.
1 December	Murder of Kirov.
1935–36	Purge of the party resumed, with the focus now shifting to men who held more important posts. An 'exchange of party cards' led to half a million members being expelled.
1935 January	Zinoviev and Kamenev arrested.
1936 August	The first show trial, involving Zinoviev, Kamenev and fourteen others.
September	Yezhov replaced Yagoda as head of the NKVD.
1937 January	The second show trial, involving Radek, Pyatakov and fifteen others.
May	The purge of the Red Army began.
June	Tukhachevsky and leading army officers were shot.
July	NKVD Order No. 00447 against 'anti-Soviet elements'; social cleansing set in motion.
August	National sweeps began against ethnic minorities in border areas.
1938 March	The third show trial involving Bukharin, Rykov, Yagoda and eighteen others.
December	Beria replaced Yezhov as head of the NKVD.
1939 March	Eighteenth Party Congress. Stalin declared an end to the 'mass purges'.

THE STALIN CONSTITUTION OF 1936

As one of the worst periods of political repression in the history of the USSR was initiated, Stalin published the most 'democratic' constitution in the world (passed 5 December 1936). The rights it enshrined included:

- freedom from arbitrary arrest
- freedom of speech and the press
- the right to demonstrate
- respect for privacy of the home and personal correspondence
- employment for all
- universal suffrage for over-eighteens, free elections and secret ballots.

It was a hollow and cynical piece of propaganda since at that very time such rights were being systematically abused. However, the Constitution made it clear that all these rights were subordinate to the interests of the working classes and it was the role of the Communist Party to decide what those interests were. Also, only Communists could be put up for elections. So one-party dominance was assured.

The Constitution was written by a team headed by Bukharin and Radek, who were both to perish shortly afterwards in the purges. It was intended largely for international consumption, to show Communist sympathisers that the Soviet state was a democratic one at heart and provided the chief hope for the future of the world. Other important sections of the Constitution proclaimed that:

- the Soviet Union was a federal state with eleven autonomous republics
- ethnic groups would have local autonomy within the republics
- the old Congresses of Soviets were to be replaced by the Supreme Soviet, a single legislative body, filled by elected representatives from the Soviet republics
- the Council of the People's Commissars would continue as the chief executive authority
- the Soviet state embraced equality for all and joint ownership of the means of production.

Stalin claimed that his constitution was 'proof that socialism and democracy are invincible'.

B What sort of opposition to Stalin had developed before 1934?

By 1933, the Communist Party was extremely unpopular. Rapid industrialisation had created tension and stress in Soviet society which was putting a strain on relations between the party and the people. The violence of forced collectivisation and the famine of 1932–33 had alienated the peasantry, making the murder of rural Communists a regular event. Many urban workers were antagonised by the low wages, strict controls and harsh punishments in the workplace. There was upheaval and unrest in the overcrowded, insanitary and often violent cities with their constantly changing populations. Hatred was particularly high among the 'former people' such as priests, industrialists, traders and 'bourgeois specialists'. Russian society was unstable and volatile.

The majority of party members had supported the drive for industrialisation, but some had been deeply disturbed by the methods employed to push it through and were worried by the disaffection in the cities. Many were horrified by the terror methods used to collectivise agriculture, and the waging of a virtual war against the peasants. This was not the road to socialist construction that they had envisaged. Some, in despair at the events of these years, had committed suicide. Among these was Stalin's own wife, Nadezda Allilueva, who shot herself in November 1932. She was deeply depressed by the excesses of collectivisation, agreeing with Bukharin that the ravages of the countryside had gone too far.

SOURCE 14.1 Popular ditties expressed opposition to the regime in the early 1930s. The following examples are included in the Russian State Archive of Literature and Art (RGALI)

Stalin stands on a coffin
Gnawing meat from a cat's bones
Well, Soviet cows
are such disgusting creatures

How the collective farm had become
prosperous
There used to be thirty-three farms
and now there are five

We fulfilled the Five Year Plan
and are eating well
We ate all the horses
And are now chasing the dogs

O commune, O commune
You Commune of Satan
You seized everything
All in the soviet cause

STALIN'S WIFE

The story of Stalin's relationship with his wife is important because some historians suggest that it may have had an impact on the terror that was about to unfold. It is alleged that Stalin treated his wife badly, and that he was cold and impersonal. There have been allegations that he had affairs with other women; in *Stalin* (1997) Edward Radzinsky says 'he was unfaithful more and more frequently simply to hurt her'. According to Khrushchev, on the night of Nadezda's suicide it is claimed  that Stalin was so outrageously rude to his wife that she stormed out, knowing that he was with another woman, and that this finally prompted her to take her own life.

There are different interpretations of the significance of her suicide. Some writers say that Stalin showed little remorse and little interest in her funeral, and that he never visited her grave. They suggest that he saw her suicide as an act of betrayal. Other writers maintain that there is evidence to prove he loved his wife, despite a stormy relationship, and never got over her death. Radzinsky uses as evidence Bukharin's wife Anna, who said that Stalin asked for the lid of the coffin to stay open and sat by it for hours, and one of his bodyguards who recalled that Stalin spent hours by her graveside.

Most historians (including Bullock, Tucker and Medvedev) agree that the suicide made him draw more into himself and become more paranoid, less likely to trust those around him. In *Twenty Letters to a Friend* (1968), Svetlana Allilueva, Stalin's daughter, says inwardly things had changed catastrophically: 'something had snapped inside my father'. Robert Thurston suggests in *Life and Terror in Stalin's Russia 1934–41* (1996) that Nadezda's death, occurring at the same time that other groups were opposing him, may have filled him with hatred, suspicion and a desire to project his guilt over her death onto others.

Breakneck industrialisation and forced collectivisation brought dissension in the party at large. Throughout the First Five-Year Plan the central party in Moscow had had difficulties in getting local party secretaries and members to implement central policies and orders. They were unwilling to push forward, argued about high grain collection targets, were unwilling to identify kulaks and were reluctant to get rid of specialists and managers who might help them achieve their industrial production targets. Some were reluctant to implement the degree of terror the centre demanded.

This caused anger and some panic among party leaders who valued discipline above all else. So, in December 1932, Moscow launched a chistka to root out passive elements, violators of party and state discipline 'who do not carry out decisions, but cast doubt upon the decisions by calling them unrealistic and unrealisable' and 'turncoats who have allied themselves with bourgeois elements'. By 1935, around 22 per cent of members had lost their party cards. This was an attempt to re-establish control of the party in the regions, but it was also used to expel members critical of the party line laid down by Stalin.

And it was not just in the local party organisations that there were problems. In the early 1930s there were signs of growing opposition to Stalin's leadership at much higher levels. In 1932, a former Moscow party secretary, Ryutin, circulated to the Central Committee a 200-page document highly critical of Stalin. He called Stalin 'the evil genius of the Russian revolution'. Referring to his 'personal dictatorship', he urged Stalin's removal. This became known as the Ryutin platform.

Stalin wanted the death penalty for Ryutin. But other members of the Politburo, including Kirov and his friend Ordzhonikidze, opposed him. Ryutin was not executed. This was a blow to Stalin and a reminder that he was still subject to the majority of the Politburo.

Ryutin was not alone. The old Bolshevik A. P. Smirnov (a party member since 1896) was charged with forming an opposition group with several others looking to moderate the pace of industrialisation, make trade unions more independent and bring OGPU (the secret police) under party control. Again, Stalin wished to treat these oppositionists inside the party in the same way as those outside – to imprison or execute them – but again the majority of the Politburo would not support the execution of party members for purely political offences.

SOURCE 14.2 An extract from the Ryutin platform or memorandum

The rule of terror in the party and in the country under the clearly ruinous policy of Stalin has led to a situation where hypocrisy and two-facedness have become common phenomena ...

The most evil counter-revolutionary and provocateur could not have carried out the work of destroying the party and socialist construction better than Stalin has done. Stalin and his clique will not and cannot voluntarily give up their positions, so they must be removed by force.

KIROV TOPS POLL

There is evidence to suggest that provincial delegates asked Kirov to take over as General Secretary and that Stalin did badly in elections to the Central Committee: Kirov was supposed to have polled all but three of the 1225 votes, whereas 300 did not vote for Stalin. The result, it seems, was hushed up by Kaganovich, a staunch Stalinist, perhaps with the help of other senior party members.

The Seventeenth Party Congress

In January 1934, the front page of *Pravda* announced 'Socialism in Our Country has Won'. The Seventeenth Party Congress, which opened on 26 February 1934, was hailed as the 'Congress of Victors'. There was a feeling that the economic groundwork had been accomplished and it was now possible to slow down, stabilise, reduce the tensions caused by the breakneck pace of change, and give the workers some rewards – more food, more clothing and better living conditions. This seemed to have been recognised in the Second Five-Year Plan, which had been redrafted in 1933 with lower targets.

However, it became clear at the beginning of the congress that Stalin wished to push ahead energetically and not slacken the pace of industrialisation. A split opened between Stalin and other leading members of the Politburo. The popular, handsome Sergei Kirov, the Leningrad party boss, pointedly said 'The fundamental difficulties are behind us' and went on to talk about stopping forcible grain seizure from peasants and increasing rations for workers. He received long standing ovations from the congress, as long as those received by Stalin.

The title of General Secretary was done away with and Stalin and Kirov were both given the title of Secretary of Equal Rank. Stalin was by no means secure as leader. He commanded the unswerving loyalty of only two of the Politburo – Kaganovich and Molotov. He could be removed or demoted. On the sidelines stood Bukharin, who had always supported a more moderate line.

It was at this key point in the history of the Communist Party that Sergei Kirov was murdered.

C The Kirov murder mystery

The murder of Sergei Kirov is one of the great mysteries of Russian history in the 1930s. And it is an important murder. Robert Conquest argues in *The Great Terror: A Reassessment* (1990, page 37) that it was a turning point in history, which not only unleashed a terror that killed millions but also determined the future of Soviet Russia. But it is a strange mystery because we know who the murderer was. The mystery surrounds the motives for the murder and who, if anybody, arranged it.

SOURCE 14.3   Leading Communists attended Kirov's funeral. Many of them, including Stalin, were seen to weep

The murder

Just after 4pm on 1 December 1934, Sergei Kirov entered party headquarters in Leningrad – the Smolny Institute from where seventeen years previously Lenin and Trotsky had directed the October uprising. He left his personal bodyguard, Borisov, downstairs and went up to his offices on his own. He did not notice that the usual guards were absent from the corridors. Waiting, probably in a nearby toilet, was the assassin. As Kirov passed him in the corridor, he emerged from the shadows and shot Kirov in the back of the neck. He then fainted beside the body. Kirov died soon afterwards and the assassin was arrested.

The assassin

Leonid Nikolayev, aged 30, was a nervous man whose health was poor. He had joined the Communist Party in 1920 at the age of sixteen. After a troubled time in the party, he was expelled in March 1934 for a breach of discipline but later reinstated. He had never been linked to the left opposition of Trotsky, Zinoviev and others but had developed a hatred of the party bureaucracy which had not, he felt, recognised his worth and given him his due.

Nikolayev was married to Milde Draule who was a secretary at party headquarters and may have been having an affair with Kirov. A diary found in Nikolayev's briefcase showed he had planned the murder. A further statement found there claimed that the murder was 'a personal act of desperation and dissatisfaction arising out of his straitened material circumstances and as a protest against the unjust attitude of certain members of the government towards a live person'.

SOURCE 14.4 G. Lyushkov, deputy head of the NKVD Secret Political Department, one of Nikolayev's interrogators

Nikolayev lacked balance, he had many problems ... He was convinced that he was capable of any work ... and did not get on with people easily ... all his efforts led to him losing his official positions ... This drove him to the belief that the problem was not in his personal faults but in the institutions. This discontent in turn drove him into his scheme to assassinate some important figures in the Party.

DRAMATIS PERSONAE

Kirov – the victim
Nikolayev – the assassin
Yagoda – head of the NKVD
Medved – head of the NKVD in Leningrad
Zaporozhets – Yagoda's deputy
Stalin – the leader

Just before the murder

- Kirov had received a great deal of support at the Seventeenth Party Congress and more people had voted for him than for Stalin. He had opposed Stalin over the Ryutin affair and over the pace of industrialisation. He now wanted a relaxation of the terror and reconciliation with the peasantry. (This would have downgraded the role of the NKVD and reduced its profile and status.) By the summer of 1934, Kirov and Stalin had fallen out over a number of issues.
- The head of the NKVD in Leningrad was Medved; his deputy was Zaporozhets. It is alleged (but not proven) that just before the murder Zaporozhets brought in some personnel from Moscow and put them in key posts without Medved's permission, presumably on the orders of some higher authority. Medved wanted them removed and got Kirov's backing. When Kirov asked Stalin to have them removed, Stalin refused. Zaporozhets had previously worked with Yagoda, overall head of the NKVD.
- Prior to the murder, Nikolayev had twice been arrested in Kirov's neighbourhood and released both times on the order of Zaporozhets. It was also alleged that an NKVD man had posed earlier as a friend of Nikolayev and practised shooting his revolver with him.

What happened after the murder?

- Stalin came to Leningrad and carried out an interrogation of Nikolayev. When asked why he had murdered Kirov, Nikolayev pointed to the NKVD men, saying that Stalin should ask 'them' that question.
- A key witness was going to be Borisov, Kirov's bodyguard. But on the way to be questioned at the Smolny Institute, in a truck with several NKVD men, there was an accident in which he was killed and nobody else was hurt. The NKVD men were killed later.
- Very shortly afterwards, the first arrests were made on Stalin's instructions. Thousands in the Leningrad party were purged. This was the beginning of the Great Purges.
- The leading Leningrad NKVD men accused of negligence for not protecting Kirov were sentenced to labour camps but were given only short sentences. They were sent to the camps in special railway carriages and received privileged treatment, including regular gifts and the status of 'assistants' which gave them power over other prisoners. They were shot in the late 1930s.
- In the third show trial in 1938, Yagoda (by now the ex-head of the NKVD) was accused of involvement in the murder by making it easy for Nikolayev to get to Kirov. He pleaded guilty.

Sergei Kirov (1886–1934)

Born into a lower middle-class family, Kirov lost his parents early. He went to a vocational school to train as a mechanic, where he met radical activists from a nearby university. He moved to Tomsk in Siberia and joined the Social Democratic Party. In the 1905 Revolution he organised railway strikes, and was arrested in 1906. Released in 1909, he went to the Caucasus, worked on a newspaper and became committed to the Bolshevik wing of the party. He played an active part in the 1917 Revolution and in the Civil War as head of the Military Revolutionary Committee in Astrakhan. Later he was involved in bringing the Caucasus under Bolshevik control. After 1921 he became Secretary of the Azerbaijan Central Committee and in 1923 a member of the Central Committee.

When Zinoviev was ousted from his power base in Leningrad, Kirov became Party Secretary in Leningrad, which put him in a powerful position. He had not been particularly keen on forced collectivisation or on attacking Bukharin and the right, but in the end he threw in his lot with Stalin and was firmly committed to the rapid industrialisation policy. He was an excellent orator, the best in the party after Trotsky, and seemed to be popular in the party.

ACTIVITY

Conquest's account of the murder (summarised on pages 254–255) is based on evidence he has collected, much of it from memoirs and personal conversations. Not all of it is established fact, including exactly where everybody was at the time of the murder. Conquest also makes some inferences from the evidence that may or may not be true.

You are now going to consider a range of evidence from historians and other sources. You will have to judge whether you think their evidence is helpful, convincing and/or reliable. At the end you have to decide whether you think the murder was:

- carried out by Nikolayev alone
- carried out by Nikolayev with the help of the NKVD but without Stalin's knowledge
- ordered by Stalin, arranged by the NKVD and carried out by Nikolayev.

Write a paragraph explaining your decision. Say what you think is 'certain', 'highly likely', 'likely', 'probable', 'uncertain' or 'open to question'.
  You should bear these points in mind:

- Everyone agrees that Nikolayev did the murder and that he was a disgruntled and unstable man.
- So far no published evidence has been unearthed that directly links Stalin to the murder. Most of the evidence is second or third hand and has particular biases, for example, some of it is memoirs from people fleeing the USSR during the Cold War.

SOURCE 14.5   R. W. Thurston, *Life and Terror in Stalin's Russia 1934–41*, 1996, p. 20

There are many problems with the idea that he [Stalin] had Kirov killed. Evidence recently released from Russia shows that, contrary to many accounts, the police did not detain Nikolayev three times near Kirov, on each occasion mysteriously releasing him despite the fact that he was carrying a gun. He was stopped only once, and the circumstances were not suspicious. He had not received the gun from a Leningrad NKVD officer, as is typically claimed, but he had owned it since 1918 and had registered it legally in 1924 and 1930 (evidence from Pravda, 4 November 1991).

Nikolayev had a diary with him at the Smolny, but instead of showing that the party's enemies helped him in his attack, it indicated that he had acted alone. Kirov's bodyguard was not present at the fatal moment because his boss had called to say he would stay at home that day. Kirov went to his office anyway, only to meet Nikolayev by chance. The latter, who had a party card that would automatically admit him to the building, had gone there to ask for a pass to an upcoming conference.

SOURCE 14.6   J. Lewis and P. Whitehead, *Stalin: A Time for Judgement*, 1990, p. 63. A commission to look into the murder was held under Khrushchev, the Soviet leader after Stalin. This took place at a time when Stalin's record and reputation were being attacked. The commission did not produce a public report but one of its members, Olga Shatunovskaya, recalled events as follows

The NKVD latched on to this, that he [Nikolayev] was dissatisfied, and he wrote them a letter saying: 'I am ready for anything now. I hate Kirov' and they organised it. At the inquiry before Stalin he said: 'For four months the NKVD prepared me and convinced me that it was necessary for the Party and the country.'
  [On the question of the motive, she said:]
  When Stalin found out [that some delegates had approached Kirov to ask him to become General Secretary in Stalin's place] he decided to remove him and Kirov realised this. When he came back from the Seventeenth Congress he told his friends and family: 'My head is now on the block.' I had all these testimonies from his friends and family and now they have been destroyed ... It has been irrefutably proved that the murder of Kirov was organised by Stalin, through Yagoda and the NKVD.

SOURCE 14.7 R. W. Thurston, *Life and Terror in Stalin's Russia 1934–41*, 1996, p. 22, quoting the opinion in 1991 of A. Lakoviev, a Russian scholar and politician, who studied the available archives

L. V. Nikolayev planned and perpetrated the murder alone. [Files on the case] contain no information implicating J. V. Stalin and agencies of the NKVD. [Stalin] did not know of and had no relation to the attack on Kirov.

SOURCE 14.8 R. C. Tucker, *Stalin in Power: The Revolution from Above, 1928–1941*, 1992, p. 301

A young woman journalist then living and working in Rostov, Vera Panova, recalls in a posthumously published memoir that her husband, Boris Vakhtin, managing editor on another local paper, telephoned her late on 1 December and said: ' "Vera! In Leningrad they've killed Kirov!" Who killed him? I ask, no answer comes, but I know what will happen now: after all I've written about the burning of the Reichstag. And that night I have a dream but I don't dare tell it even to Boris: they themselves have killed Kirov so as to start a new terror. Against whom? Against the "lefts", against the "rights", against anyone they want. But I can't keep this dream from Boris for long. After vacillating, I tell it to him. He gives me a strange look and is silent.'

Even among ordinary Leningrad workers, a ditty was making its whispered rounds [and this might help explain the savage repressions soon to be visited upon the Leningrad working class]:

Oh cucumber, oh pomidor
Stalin killed Kirov
In the corridor.

SOURCE 14.9 J. Arch Getty and O. V. Naumov, *The Road to Terror: Stalin and the Self-Destruction of the Bolsheviks, 1932–39*, 1999, p. 145

Yagoda (through whom Stalin presumably worked to kill Kirov) was produced in open court and in front of the world press before his execution in 1938. Knowing that he was about to be shot in any event, he could have brought Stalin's entire house down with a single remark about the Kirov killing . . . such a risk would appear to be unacceptable for a complicit Stalin . . .

The Stalinists seemed unprepared for the assassination and panicked by it. Indeed it took them more than eighteen months after the assassination to frame their supposed targets – members of the anti-Stalin old Bolshevik opposition – for the killing.

POSSIBLE MOTIVES

- Stalin's motives are clear: to get rid of a rival and to use murder to get rid of opposition.
- Nikolayev, by all accounts, was disgruntled with the party but there is also a story that Kirov was having an affair with Nikolayev's wife, a secretary at party headquarters. This may have led him to transfer his disillusionment with the party onto Kirov.
- The motives of the NKVD are more difficult to identify. Conquest suggests there is no clear motive. Suggestions are:
  - they thought, or had been told, that Stalin wanted Kirov murdered
  - Kirov wanted to relax the terror, but the NKVD did not want to see this happen and did not want to see Kirov replace Stalin
  - they did not intend Nikolayev actually to kill Kirov; they intended to stop him before he could carry out the attack and use the attempted assassination as justification for their continuing role against enemies of the state.

FOCUS ROUTE

For the purposes of analysis, we are going to split up the Great Terror into a number of topics, but you should be aware that the purges were affecting the party, people and armed forces over the same period.

Make notes under the following headings:

a) the show trials
b) the Yezhovshchina –
  • purging the party
  • purging the armed forces
  • the wider terror.

ENEMY OF THE PEOPLE
This vague term now came into everyday use. It could be applied to anybody, covering any supposed offence that the authorities chose. Being identified as an enemy of the people meant arrest and imprisonment.

 The Great Terror

The show trials – getting rid of the old Bolsheviks

The Stalinist leadership used Kirov's murder as a pretext and justification for the Great Terror, which took place over the next four years. The murder was seen as evidence of a widespread conspiracy against the Soviet state and its leaders. There were enemies everywhere and they needed to be rooted out.

Within a few weeks there was an extensive purge of the Leningrad party, Kirov's power base. A 'Leningrad centre', plotting terrorist acts against the Soviet state, was uncovered. Thousands more, many outside the party, were soon accused of being Trotskyites involved in the plot to murder Kirov and other leading Communists. Kamenev and Zinoviev were arrested and put on trial in January 1935. Although no direct evidence could be produced against them, they were found guilty and given prison sentences.

It seems that few of those close to Stalin were demanding an extension of the terror at this point. But Stalin found out about communications between Trotsky and members of oppositionist groups in the party. He retaliated by sending out a Central Committee circular in June 1936 on the 'terrorist activities of the Trotskyist counter-revolutionary bloc'. This contained the crucial words 'the inalienable quality of every Bolshevik under present conditions should be the ability to recognise an ENEMY OF THE PEOPLE no matter how well he may be masked'. This was the sign that old Bolsheviks were going to be 'unmasked'.

Zinoviev and Kamenev were pulled out of prison and in August 1936 were put on trial in the full glare of the public. With them were fourteen others who had previously been members of the oppositionist groups in the party. These show trials were elaborately staged events in which the state prosecutor, Vyshinsky, proved the accused guilty of spying for foreign powers, as well as of being part of a counter-revolutionary bloc involved in Kirov's murder, with Stalin as the intended next victim. The idea of a show trial was not new. It was used in 1928 in the Shakhty trial (see page 228). It was an effective way to create an atmosphere of intimidation, a sense of danger and the feeling that there were enemies, spies and wreckers around. At the time, many accepted that such trials were genuine.

The accused confessed and were executed the next day. Zinoviev, according to police gossip, became so hysterical that his executioner panicked and shot him in a cell. These executions were significant because they were the first

SOURCE 14.10 A gallery of Stalin's victims put together by Trotsky's supporters. It shows what happened to leading Bolsheviks who had worked with Lenin

LEFT-WING OPPOSITION

The Bolsheviks in the first two major show trials were those who had formed the left-wing opposition in the 1920s. Many had supported Trotsky and had opposed Stalin's 'Socialism in One Country'. However, after their defeat in 1927 most had recanted and supported Stalin when he made his left turn to pursue what were, to all intents and purposes, their policies. Trotsky, in exile in the 1930s, was writing articles condemning Stalin as the 'grave digger of the revolution', claiming that his policies had brought the Soviet Union to ruin. Stalin was incensed by this. This is why he was so angry when he found out that Trotsky had been trying to communicate with members of the old left-wing opposition.

THE RIGHTISTS

The last big show trial featured the right wing of the Communist Party, people who had supported the NEP and opposed rapid industrialisation and forced collectivisation. Bukharin had recanted his views and worked on producing the 1936 Constitution. Tomsky, the other leading member of the right, did not wait for the show trial; once it was announced he was going to be investigated he committed suicide.

executions of people who had belonged to the Central Committee. The line had been crossed and many more executions were to follow. A second show trial took place in January 1937 in which Karl Radek, a well-known Trotskyite, and Pyatakov, a deputy in the Commissariat of Heavy Industry, were the main defendants. Needless to say they confessed and were found guilty.

The third and last great show trial was staged in March 1938. It was possibly the most dramatic because it involved Bukharin and he was able to make a more spirited defence of his actions. But in the end, he – along with twenty others, including old Bolsheviks like Rykov as well as the former head of the NKVD, Yagoda – confessed and was sentenced. Most were shot within a few hours, Bukharin and Rykov cursing Stalin as they died.

SOURCE 14.11   A show trial from the 1930s

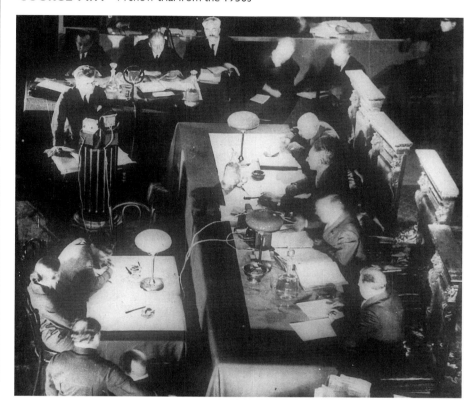

SOURCE 14.12   J. Arch Getty and O. V. Naumov, *The Road to Terror: Stalin and the Self-Destruction of the Bolsheviks, 1932–39*, 1999, p. 301. The authors quote this letter, which provides a good example of the sort of denunciations that flowed in after Bukharin had been named as a suspect

11 August 1936
Dear Comrade Yezhov
I would like to call your attention to the following:
Comrade N. I. Bukharin has been travelling to Leningrad frequently. While there, he has been staying at the apartment of Busygin, a former Trotskyite and now a counter-revolutionary. Comrade Bukharin has maintained a close relationship with him, both in person and by correspondence ... The fact was uncovered at a party meeting of this institute and reported by Zubkov, who was expelled from the party as a White Guard and abetter of counter-revolutionary work.
I consider it my duty to report this to you in view of the fact that a simple friendship with a sworn counter-revolutionary is hardly possible. It is my suspicion that Comrade Bukharin was aware of Busygin's work and, in particular, of his counter-revolutionary activities at the Institute of the Academy of Sciences.
With Communist greetings,
I. Kuchkin,
Official of the Vasileostrovsky Party District Committee, Leningrad

ACTIVITY

Read Source 14.12 and answer the following questions.

1 In what way are Bukharin's actions considered suspicious?
2 Why is Busygin identified as a counter-revolutionary?
3 What is interesting about Zubkov, the reporter of the association?
4 What does this letter tell you about denunciations and the way the purges spread?

ACTIVITY

Read the poem extract in Source 14.14 and answer the following questions.

1 Who is the hated Judas?
2 What crimes are they accused of?
3 Who do they seem to be serving?
4 How is Stalin portrayed?
5 Do you think this poem is useful historical evidence of the era of the show trials in Russia?

SOURCE 14.13 A speech by Vyshinsky, the prosecutor at the third show trial, March 1938

Our whole country is awaiting and demanding one thing. The traitors and spies who were selling our country must be shot like dirty dogs. Our people are demanding one thing. Crush the accursed reptile. Time will pass. The graves of the hateful traitors will grow over with weeds and thistles. But over us, over our happy country our sun will shine bright and luminous as before. Over the road cleared of the last scum and filth of the past, we, with our beloved leader and teacher, the great Stalin at our head, will march as before onwards and onwards towards communism.

SOURCE 14.14 The party poet was commissioned to write a poem for *Pravda* two days after the first show trial had started, although it was not published. Here is an extract:

Like flies stuck in glue
They carried out their villainous policies
And finally found
The place their villainy deserved . . .
Fascists . . . Himmler . . . how do you like that?
The incredible suddenly became clear fact,
Recorded in the transcript of the trial:
Betrayers of the Soviet motherland,
Pseudoparty traitors, liars,
Devoted clients of hostile offices,
Underground enemies, Fascist agents,
Murderers of Kirov . . .
Here are the ones who murdered Kirov!
They are going for Stalin! But they failed . . .
WE HAVE GUARDED STALIN
WE ARE UNABLE NOT TO GUARD HIM!
WE GUARD HIM AS OUR HEAD
WE GUARD HIM AS OUR HEART!
Where is Trotsky? Without him . . .
Your foredoomed group
Is lacking, empty,
But proletarian justice will pursue
The hated Judas everywhere . . .

STALIN'S FALCONS

Today's spin doctors would have had little to teach Stalin. It was important to contrast the good and heroic with the evil traitors. In 1933, he had challenged his pilots to fly 'farther than anyone, faster than anyone, higher than anyone'. At the time of the show trials, pioneering flights were being made by Soviet aviators over the Arctic. The first was greeted with a triumphal parade in Moscow on 15 August 1936, four days before the first show trial started. The second flight took place at the same time as the trial and execution of Tukhachevsky, the army general. And before the third great show trial, an Arctic explorer was literally kept on ice (on an Arctic ice-floe for nine months) so that he could arrive home to a mass welcome just after Bukharin and the others had been executed.

SOURCE 14.15 W. G. Krivitsky, *I Was Stalin's Agent*, 1939, p. 211

They made [their confessions] in the sincere conviction that this was their sole remaining service to the Party and the Revolution. They sacrificed honour as well as life to defend the hated regime of Stalin, because it contained the last gleam of hope for the better world to which they had consecrated themselves in early youth.

Why did they confess?

The show trials were a grotesque sham, although many inside and some outside the Soviet Union believed that the defendants were guilty. Some of the charges were ludicrous: plotting to assassinate Kirov, Stalin and even Lenin and the novelist Maxim Gorky; espionage on behalf of foreign powers; conspiring with Trotskyites, Mensheviks, rightists and other opposition groups; planning to restore capitalism and overthrow socialism. The evidence was clearly faked and some of it did not stand up: for example, one of the hotels the conspirators were supposed to have met at did not even exist; one of the accused was in prison when he was supposed to have committed an offence. So why did these tough and battle-hardened Bolsheviks confess?

The most obvious answer is that they were worn down by torture and interrogation (see pages 263–264) and this undoubtedly played a part. It is also clear that they agreed to confess as part of a deal in which their families would be spared. This is true of Bukharin, who wrote a last loving testament to his wife, and probably of Zinoviev and Kamenev. In the event, few of the family members escaped. But another clue is given by W. G. Krivitsky in Source 14.15.

The Yezhovshchina

Just after the first great show trial had ended in September 1936, Nicolai Yezhov replaced Yagoda as head of the NKVD (secret police). Yagoda was criticised for not finding enemies of the state quickly enough. This was a clear sign from Stalin that he wanted to advance the terror. Yezhov was about to initiate a period of terror – called the Yezhovshchina – which reached its height in mid-1937 and lasted until late 1938.

Nicolai Yezhov (1895–1939)

Yezhov (left) and Stalin in conversation

Yezhov had joined the party in 1917. Stalin brought him into the Central Committee in 1927 and gave him an investigative role before he made him head of the NKVD. He was responsible for the deaths of thousands of people. Only about 1.5 m tall, he was known as the 'Bloodthirsty Dwarf' or the 'Iron Hedgehog'. One old Communist remarked, 'In the whole of my long life I have never seen a more repellent personality than Yezhov's.' A Soviet account in 1988 in *Komsomolskaya Pravda* talks of Yezhov's 'low moral qualities' and 'sadistic inclinations'; that 'women working in the NKVD were frightened of meeting him even in the corridors' and that he lacked 'any trace of conscience or moral principles'. (All quoted in Robert Conquest, *The Great Terror: A Reassessment*, 1990, pages 14–15.)

THE STRANGE DEATH OF ORDZHONIKIDZE

SOURCE 14.16   Ordzhonikidze lies dead and high-ranking party members pay their respects. Left to right around the bed are his widow, Molotov, Yezhov, Stalin, Zhdanov, Kaganovich and Voroshilov

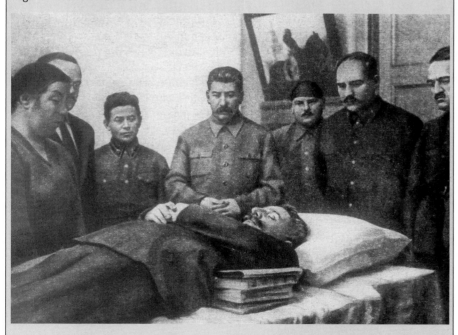

In February 1937, Sergei Ordzhonikidze died, after an angry confrontation with Stalin in which he pleaded for an end to the terror. He was particularly upset by the proceedings against Pyatakov who had worked closely with him at the Commissariat of Heavy Industry. Apparently, Ordzhonikidze was given the choice of suicide and a state funeral or being shot with no state funeral. He chose the former and Stalin said that it must be reported that he died of heart failure. Ordzhonikidze was buried with full honours. He was the last leading Politburo member to resist Stalin's policies. After this, the Great Terror of 1937–38 was unleashed.

SOURCE 14.17   R. Conquest, *The Great Terror: A Reassessment*, 1990, p. 257

It was not only this process of association that gave the Purge its increasingly mass character. In the 1930s, there were still hundreds of thousands who had been members of non-Bolshevik parties, the masses who had served in the White armies, nationalist elements in local intelligentsias, and so on. The increasingly virulent campaign for vigilance against the hidden enemy blanketed the whole country, not merely the Party, in a press and radio campaign. And while the destruction of hostile elements in the party was going forward, it must have seemed natural to use the occasion to break all remaining elements suspected of not being reconciled with the regime.

NKVD ORDER 00447

This notorious order was at the core of the Great Terror. Triggered by an instruction from Stalin, it was drawn up by Yezhov and sent out to the First Secretary of every republic and region. It set out categories to be dealt with – people with suspect political or social backgrounds – and quotas of people to be arrested in each area. These were always over fulfilled by the NKVD, in total up to 800,000 from summer 1937 to November 1938. But it was also part of a 'sweep of former kulaks and criminals', encompassing social marginals: recidivist criminals, hooligans, individuals who did not fit into the emerging Stalinist system. These, along with kulaks and workers formed, in numerical terms, the bulk of those repressed. It was social cleansing on a massive scale.

NATIONAL SWEEPS

From August 1937 a mass campaign was launched to uproot and deport national minorities from the USSR's western borders – Poles, Germans, Estonians and others – because of fears they might collude with an invader. Huge numbers were involved in this ethnic cleansing. This continued during and after the Second World War.

Purging the party

In the spring of 1937, Stalin made it clear that he thought traitors and spies had infiltrated the party at all levels in every locality. He encouraged lower-ranking party members to criticise and denounce those in higher positions. This resulted in a flood of accusations. Party members were 'unmasked' by colleagues for 'being part of the Bukharin Right in the 1920s' or 'authorising concessions to the peasants in 1925'. They were usually invited to confess before mass meetings and were then arrested. The flood turned into a torrent as more and more party members were dragged in. Some denounced fellow members in order to get their jobs or settle old scores, others to deflect criticism from themselves.

Denunciations were not directed only from the bottom of the party towards the top. Party secretaries and higher officials were anxious to find the counter-revolutionaries and 'fascist spies' in their local party network, if only to show how loyal they were to the regime. So they denounced people below them.

Mass terror

From spring the terror accelerated. Arrests of oppositionists increased dramatically. In July 1937, the Politburo passed a resolution condemning 'Anti-Soviet Elements'. This was elaborated by Yezhov in NKVD order 00447. He drew up an arrest list of over 250,000 of these 'elements', including scientists, artists, writers and musicians, as well as managers and administrators. The historian Chris Ward writes: 'An avalanche of monstrous charges, nightmarish allegations, incredible scenarios and random arrests overwhelmed swathes of the population while terrified, vindictive or simple-minded *apparatchiki* [party officials] flung denunciations at all and sundry . . . [for example] Boris Numerov, a distinguished scientist, supposedly organised a "counter-revolutionary astronomers' group" which engaged in wrecking, espionage and terror' (*Stalin's Russia*, 1993, pages 120–21). Historians were particularly vulnerable and many were accused of leading terrorist groups. One leading Bolshevik mentioned at his trial that 'arrests had begun among the historians'.

In practice, anybody could be arrested as an oppositionist. A quota system was applied to geographical areas and to public bodies. It went further than this: in July 1937, the proportion to be shot was fixed at 28 per cent, with the rest being sentenced to up to ten years' hard labour – and this was before the oppositionists had actually been arrested!

A huge media campaign was started, encouraging ordinary people to criticise party officials, bureaucrats and managers – to seek out the 'hidden enemies'. This harnessed popular dissatisfaction with officialdom and resulted in a huge number of denunciations and arrests. People were also encouraged to denounce workers and saboteurs in the workplace, so the rest of the population did not escape either. In *Let History Judge* (1972), Roy Medvedev mentions that over 1000 were arrested in a single factory. Conquest contends, in *The Great Terror: A Reassessment* (1990, page 258), that thousands of peasants, factory workers, shop girls and office clerks were swept up in the purges, although he accepts that the main target was 'officialdom, the intelligentsia'.

Once suspects had been arrested and subjected to interrogation by the NKVD, they always came up with names of accomplices. Workmates, friends, husbands and wives, sons and daughters – all could find themselves arrested because they had connections with someone who had been accused. The victims of the terror increased exponentially.

SOURCE 14.18 G. Gill, *Stalinism*, 1990, p. 32

People hoped to gain leniency for themselves or their families by co-operating with the NKVD, and were therefore willing to denounce others to the security organs. The circle of victims thereby widened.

SOURCE 14.19 Georgi Tsialadee, NKVD member

I asked him, Christopher Sergevich ... tell me honestly, how many people were executed in Georgia? I can tell you he said 80,000 ... we overfulfilled our plan.

SOURCE 14.20 R. Conquest, *The Great Terror: A Reassessment*, 1990, p. 253

Individual denouncers operated on an extraordinary scale. In one district in Kiev, 69 persons were denounced by one man, in another 100. In Odessa a single Communist denounced 230 people. In Poltava, a party member denounced his entire organisation.

ACTIVITY

Did the terror gain a momentum of its own?

1 Examine Sources 14.18–14.23. Explain what evidence each source provides to show how the terror gained its own momentum.

2 How do these sources agree/disagree with Conquest's suggestion, in Source 14.17, of the way that the mass terror spread?

SOURCE 14.21 J. Arch Getty, *The Origins of the Great Purges*, 1985, p. 178

Members denounced leaders [and each other] for dubious class origins, long-forgotten sins, and current misdeeds. Secretaries defended themselves and proved their vigilance by expelling and denouncing batches of rank and file members. Spetseedstvo [attacks on bourgeois specialists], antibureaucratism and class hatred re-emerged in strength against the backdrop of a full-blown spy scare. Panic-stricken local party officials even resorted to filling administrative positions with politically 'safe' employees of the NKVD.

SOURCE 14.22 A. Weissberg, *Conspiracy of Silence*, 1952, p.364. The physicist Alexander Weissberg, himself a victim of the purges, wrote of repeated purges of directors of the big foundries of the Ukraine

It was only the third or fourth batch who managed to keep their seats. They had not even the normal advantages of youth in their favour, for the choosing had been a very negative one. They were the men who had denounced others on innumerable occasions. They had bowed the knee whenever they had come up against higher authority. They were morally and intellectually crippled.

SOURCE 14.23 W. G. Krivitsky, *I Was Stalin's Agent*, 1939, p. 247. Krivitsky sheds some light on why Stalin purged the army

Stalin knew that Tukhachevsky and the other ranking generals could never be broken into the state of unquestioning obedience which he now required of all those about him. They were men of personal courage, and he remembered [that in] the days when his own prestige was at the lowest, these generals had enjoyed enormous popularity... He remembered too that at every critical stage of his rule – forcible collectivisation, hunger, rebellion – the generals had supported him reluctantly, had put difficulties in his path, had forced deals upon him. He felt no certainty now that ... they would continue to recognise his totalitarian authority.

Purging the armed forces

In 1937 it was the turn of the armed forces. Stalin was convinced that he could not count on the army to follow his policies. The leaders of the army were tough and difficult to intimidate. Marshall Tukhachevsky was the hero of the Civil War, but during this period he had come into conflict with Stalin. Stalin claimed that the army was plotting to overthrow him. Tukhachevsky and other generals had confessions beaten out of them (Tukhachevsky's written confession actually had blood stains on it) and were then executed. The NKVD then worked its way through the rest of the armed forces to devastating effect (see Chart 14B on page 266). That Stalin should risk wiping out his best commanders when the prospect of war loomed is a powerful indication of how far the terror had gone.

Arrest and interrogation

Many of the arrests came at night between 11pm and 3am. NKVD officers drove around in black vehicles called 'ravens', collecting their unwilling passengers. A knock at the door in the middle of the night inspired fear; some people kept a packed bag ready in case the knock was for them. In Moscow a sort of black humour developed during the purges. One joke told of a husband and wife being woken in the night by a loud noise. Terrified, the husband opened the door, then cheerfully called out to his wife: 'Don't worry, it's only bandits come to rob us.' A similar joke tells of a household being woken by bangs on the door. Eventually, one brave occupant opened it, calling up to the others: 'Don't worry comrades, it's just the fire brigade come to tell us the house is on fire.'

The reasons for arrest were arbitrary: criticising Stalin, telling a joke about Stalin, being a friend of someone who was arrested. Arrests were followed by the inevitable interrogation in which the victims were urged to confess their opposition to Stalin and involvement with counter-revolutionary groups. The theatre director Meyerhold, a prominent member of the avant-garde movement in the early Soviet Union, was forced to drink his own urine and then sign his confession with his left hand because his right arm had been broken.

Despite the pressure put on them, many Russians did refuse to confess and were executed quietly. Ryutin (see page 253) was brought from prison and tortured, but he refused to take part in a show trial and so he was executed. His wife and sons were also killed.

Confessions were important. They legitimised the arrests and proved that the state was right. It was a logical strategy when there was no real evidence to prove the accused guilty. The state prosecutor, Vyshinsky, thought a confession written by the accused looked more 'voluntary'. He said: 'I personally prefer a half confession in the defendant's own handwriting to a full confession in the investigator's writing' (see Sources 14.24 and 14.25).

Many Soviet citizens died in prison, either shot or dying from torture. Vans marked 'Meat' regularly arrived at Moscow cemeteries to deliver their loads – the naked bodies which filled the mass graves. People always knew when the female victims were Communist Party members because they had short hair. Those who did not die were sent to the Gulag, the network of labour camps that infested the USSR. Some of the most feared were in the north, in the Kolyma area, where the freezing weather made life intolerable. Relentless hard work and inadequate food and clothing killed many. Forced labour was also used on large building projects like the White Sea Canal, where it has been estimated that over 100,000 died because of the appalling conditions.

SOURCE 14.24 Mikhail Mindlin (arrested 1937), quoted in *The People's Century*, BBC TV, 1996

When the interrogation began, I was asked to sign some lies about myself and some good comrades from my region. They handed me a list of 47 people. They wanted me to sign a statement – I wouldn't. They kept me standing for five days, day and night. My legs were so swollen.

SOURCE 14.25 D. J. Dallin and B. I. Nicolaevsky, *Forced Labour in Soviet Russia*, 1948, p. 459

The basic mechanism and chief reliance of the extortion artists were physical torture . . . several basic techniques were common . . .

The 'parilka' or sweat room . . . several hundred men and women, standing close packed in a small room where all ventilation has been shut off, in heat that chokes and suffocates, in stink that asphyxiates . . . Many have stood thus two days . . . their feet are swollen, their bodies numb . . . they are not allowed to squat or sit. Every now and then, those who faint are dragged out into the corridor, revived and thrown back in the sweat room.

The so-called conveyor belt . . . examiners sit at desks in a long series of rooms, strung out along corridors, up and down stairs, back to the starting point: a sort of circle of OGPU agents. The victims run at a trot from one desk to the next, cursed, threatened, insulted, bullied, questioned by each agent in turn, round and round hour after hour. They weep and plead and deny and keep on running . . . If they fall they are kicked and beaten on their shins, stagger to their feet and resume the hellish relay. The agents, relieved at frequent intervals, are always fresh and keen while the victims grow weaker, more terrorised and degraded.

From the parilka to the conveyor, from the conveyor to the parilka, then periods in ugly cells when uncertainty and fear for one's loved ones outside demoralise the prisoner.

SOURCE 14.27 Baldeyev cartoon of labour camp prisoners

SOURCE 14.26 Baldeyev cartoon of corpses in a mass grave in a labour camp

SOURCE 14.28 D. Volkogonov, *Stalin*, 1988, p. 339. This is the testimony of Stepan Ivanovich Semenov, a Muscovite, who spent fifteen years in the camps. Two of his brothers were shot and his wife died in prison. He is now an old man without children or grandchildren

The worst thing is when you have no one waiting for you, when no one needs you. I and my brothers might have had children and grandchildren, families. The accursed Tamerlaine [Stalin] smashed and trampled everything. He took the future away from citizens who were not born because he killed their mothers and fathers. I'm living out my life alone and I still can't understand how it was that we didn't see that 'our' leader was a monster, how the people could let it happen.

The end of the terror

Stalin called a halt to the terror towards the end of 1938. By this time, Yezhov had been replaced by Beria. Arrests slowed down, although Central Committee members and army officers were purged well into 1939. The purges were destabilising Russian society. Administrative systems were falling apart with key personnel missing and this was having a negative impact on industrial production. Stalin blamed Yezhov and the NKVD for the excesses of the terror, which was probably true. In 1940, a hitman, on Stalin's orders, murdered Trotsky. Now indeed virtually all of the old Bolsheviks had been wiped out. However, the purges continued in a much-reduced form into the Second World War. For the victims, the terror never really ended, as Source 14.28 shows.

Osip Mandelstam

With a few notable exceptions, writers and artists suffered greatly during the terror. It was easy to step out of line and fall foul of the NKVD. In 1933 the poet Osip Mandelstam composed a sixteen-line poetic epigram about Stalin. It ran as follows:

> *We live, deaf to the land beneath us,*
> *Ten steps away no one hears our speeches,*
>
> *But where there's so much as half a conversation*
> *The Kremlin's mountaineer will get his mention,*
>
> *His fingers are as fat as grubs*
> *And the words, final as lead weights, fall from his lips,*
>
> *His cockroach whiskers leer*
> *And his boot tops gleam.*
>
> *Around him a rabble of thin necked leaders – fawning*
> *half men for him to play with.*
>
> *They whinny, purr or whine*
> *As he prates and points a finger,*
>
> *One by one forging his laws, to be flung*
> *Like horseshoes at the head, the eye or groin.*
>
> *And every killing is a treat*
> *for the broad-chested Ossete.*

The oral composition travelled from Muscovite mouth to mouth until it reached the police in a verse whose second stanza ran:

> *All we hear is the Kremlin mountaineer,*
> *the murderer and peasant slayer.*

Mandelstam read his poem to half a dozen friends, one of whom informed on him. Yagoda was so struck by the poem that he could recite it by heart and he did – to Stalin. Mandelstam was arrested and interrogated. Luckily, he was defended by Bukharin and exiled for three years rather than being shot or sent to a labour camp. When he returned, he tried to write a poem praising Stalin but it was never published. He was arrested in 1938 and his wife never saw him again. She later found out that he died in December 1938 of typhus: 'Silently, in pain, lying in the filth of a prison camp, Russia's greatest poet of the twentieth century died' (E. Radzinsky, *Stalin*, 1997, page 406).

■ 14B Who were the victims?

Leading party members
Khrushchev states that 98 out of 139 (70 per cent) members of the Central Committee elected at the Seventeenth Party Congress were arrested and shot. Of the 1966 delegates to the Congress, 1108 were arrested. This was the congress which favoured Kirov over Stalin.

Senior military officers
These included:
- Tukhachevsky, Chief of the General Staff, and seven other generals – all heroes of the Civil War
- all eleven war commissars and three out of five marshals of the USSR
- all admirals commanding fleets and their replacements
- all but one of the senior commanders of the air force.

In all, 35,000 officers were either imprisoned or shot – although over 11,000 were reinstated by the middle of 1940.

Managers, engineers and scientists
A high proportion of managers at all levels were purged. The railways were particularly hard hit. Leading physicists and biologists were arrested.

People related to those who had been purged
Colleagues, subordinates, relatives, wives, children, friends and associates.

Party and state leaders
In every national republic within the USSR, party and state leaders were charged with treason or bourgeois nationalism. In Georgia, two state prime ministers, four out of five of the regional party secretaries and thousands of lesser officials lost their posts.

NKVD
Yagoda, head of the NKVD, was arrested in 1937. According to figures given by D. Volkogonov in *Stalin* (1988, p. xxiv) more than 23,000 NKVD men perished at the end of the 1930s.

Mass terror 1937–38
- By far the largest group of all: kulaks, workers and various social marginals (recidivist criminals, the homeless, the unemployed, all those who deviated from Stalinist social norms)
- Anyone with contacts abroad, such as Comintern agents, diplomats, foreign trade officials, sportsmen
- Former Mensheviks and Socialist Revolutionaries
- Priests, members of religious groups and people holding unorthodox views of any sort
- People in the media, artists and historians.

National minorities
National minorities in Central and Eastern Europe were singled out but also Koreans, Chinese and Afghans.

How many were killed in the terror?
It is notoriously difficult to calculate the number of people killed in the terror when the evidence is full of gaps and inconsistencies. For instance, the results of a census taken in the Soviet Union in January 1937 were suppressed and the census organisers were shot as 'a serpent's nest of traitors in the apparatus of Soviet Statistics' who had exerted themselves to diminish the numbers of the population of the USSR. Also, the NKVD burned much of their archive as the Germans approached Moscow in 1941. Another problem is that historians calculate the number of victims over different periods of time and include peasants and workers repressed during collectivisation and the industrialisation drive of the early 1930s.

■ 14C Estimates of the number of victims of the Stalinist regime

Wheatcroft and Davies (1994) estimate that 10 million people died between 1927 and 1938. They believe that around 8.5 million of these died between 1927 and 1936, mostly from famine.

Dmitri Volkogonov claims that around 7 million people were executed between 1929 and 1953, with another 16.5 million imprisoned.

Estimates of victims of the Great Terror 1937–38 by **Robert Conquest** (1990):			
		Arrests	7–8 million
		Executions	1–1.5 million
		Population of camps	7–8 million
		Died in camps	2 million
	1932–1933:	Famine	7 million
	1929–1953:	Deaths (total)	20 million

E Interpretations of the Great Terror

There has been a vigorous debate between historians over the explanation of the Great Terror. The process that led to so many arrests and executions is not clear. Few documents were released under the Soviet regime and certain key archives, such as those of the KGB, have still not been opened. Those archives that have recently become available have provided a vast amount of information reflecting different experiences in different parts of the former USSR. So views might change as more archive material is examined and more becomes available.

Much of the debate between historians centres around:

- the role of Stalin in the terror and the extent of his personal control of the process
- the extent to which his actual personality shaped the terror.

The debate has been dominated by two broad approaches, outlined in Charts 14E and 14F (page 268).

Why do historians disagree about the terror?

The terror is a very political topic. It is not surprising that the 'totalitarian' view of the terror – that it was masterminded by an evil puppet master – should have been predominant in the Cold War period. Historians in the West wanted to demonstrate that it was a system where the leadership exercised totalitarian control over an unwilling population. However, the emergence of a new generation of historians in the 1970s and 1980s, who were not so anti-Soviet, and changes within the USSR itself, led to the totalitarian view being challenged. There are a number of reasons why historians disagree about the terror and these are summarised in Chart 14D. There has been an acrimonious debate over the use of sources.

■ 14D Why do historians disagree about the terror?

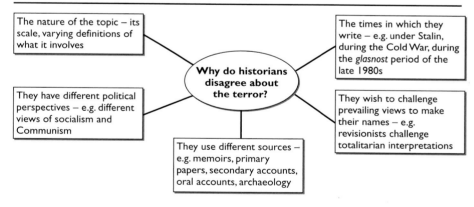

The nature of the topic – its scale, varying definitions of what it involves

The times in which they write – e.g. under Stalin, during the Cold War, during the *glasnost* period of the late 1980s

They have different political perspectives – e.g. different views of socialism and Communism

Why do historians disagree about the terror?

They wish to challenge prevailing views to make their names – e.g. revisionists challenge totalitarian interpretations

They use different sources – e.g. memoirs, primary papers, secondary accounts, oral accounts, archaeology

Debate over sources
In the context of the terror there has been an acrimonious debate over the use of sources. J. Arch Getty has criticised Western accounts that have relied on sources such as memoirs and accounts by people who fled the Soviet Union. He says they have a political bias that makes them unreliable and they are bound to attack Stalin as the central agent of terror. He places his emphasis on the use of archival records and official documents.

Other historians, including Alec Nove and Robert Conquest, accept that personal accounts should be treated with caution but make the point that archival materials and official reports can also be unreliable; officials simply reported what their superiors wanted to hear. They maintain that oral history and memoirs are indeed valuable sources.

■ 14E The totalitarian line

The totalitarian view has predominated in the West since the Second World War. It is sometimes called:

- the 'top down' view of the terror, because instructions were given by those at the top and carried out by those below, or
- the 'intentionalist' interpretation, because Stalin intended to kill his opponents and increase his personal power.

The prime exponent of this line in the West is Robert Conquest whose book, *The Great Terror: A Reassessment* (1990) sets out the case clearly with much supporting evidence. This view is also shared by liberal historians who were dissidents in the old Soviet regime, such as Roy Medvedev and Alexander Solzhenitsyn. But while Medvedev distinguishes between Lenin and Stalin, seeing the latter as the evil director of the terror, Solzhenitsyn sees a direct connection to the methods used by Lenin. He sees the terror of the 1930s as an escalation of the institutions (secret police, labour camps) put in place by Lenin.

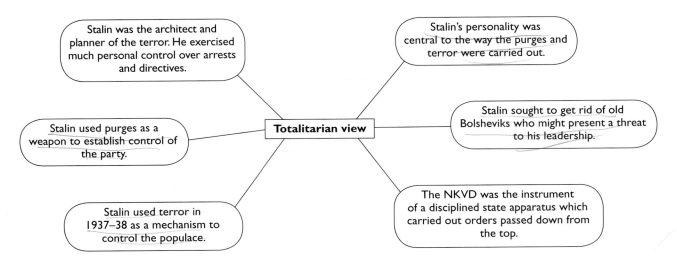

■ 14F The revisionist line

The totalitarian view has been challenged by revisionist historians from the 1970s onwards. This view is sometimes called 'decisionist' because it sees the terror as the result of decisions made by the Communist leadership in reaction to a series of crises in the mid-1930s. J. Arch Getty, in his book *The Origins of the Great Purges* (1985), put the most extreme case of the revisionists, seeming to take a lot of responsibility for the purges away from Stalin. He argues that focusing on Stalin alone has, for too long, provided simple and convenient interpretations when the real story is much more complicated. Other historians who have taken a revisionist or decisionist line on the terror are Sheila Fitzpatrick, Graeme Gill and Roberta Manning.

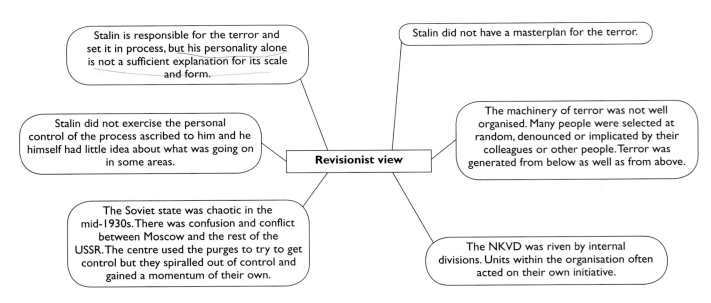

ACTIVITY

You are going to use this activity to help you to prepare for a major essay with the title 'How far was Stalin's personality responsible for the Great Terror?'

1 Read Sources 14.29–14.35. Decide how important each historian feels that Stalin's personality was to the Great Terror or the Great Purges and where each of them fits on the five-point scale below. Justify your choice by a brief reference to each source.

Absolutely central		Important		One of a number of factors
1	2	3	4	5

2 Make a list of the factors mentioned as causes of the terror.
3 Choose two sources which show markedly different interpretations of the terror. Explain how they are different.

SOURCE 14.29 R. Conquest, *The Great Terror: A Reassessment*, 1990, pp. 69–70

The one fundamental drive that can be found throughout is the strengthening of his own position. To this, for practical purposes, all else was subordinate. It led him to absolute power ...

He carried out a revolution which completely transformed the Party and the whole of society. Far more than the Bolshevik Revolution itself, this period marks the major gulf between modern Russia and the past ... It is true that only against the peculiar background of the Soviet past, and the extraordinary traditions of the All-Union Communist Party, could so radical a turn be put through. The totalitarian machinery, already in existence, was the fulcrum without which the world could not be moved. But the revolution of the Purges still remains, however we judge it, above all Stalin's personal achievement.

SOURCE 14.30 J. Arch Getty, *The Origins of the Great Purges*, 1985, p. 205

Western scholars have remained hypnotised by Stalin's cult of personality, and their obsession with him has led to studies of the Great Purges period that provide no detailed investigation of the political and institutional context. Rather than placing these events in these contexts, scholars have often discussed the Great Purges only against the background of Stalin's personality and categorised Stalinism simply as the undisputed rule of an omniscient [all-knowing] and omnipotent [all-powerful] dictator. Contradictions and confusion are seen as manifestations of Stalin's caprice, and too often the political history of the Stalin period has merely been the story of Stalin's supposed activities.

SOURCE 14.31 A. Nove (ed.), *The Stalin Phenomenon*, 1993, p. 32

No doubt there were rivalries and conflicts within the apparatus, and it is certainly useful to try to examine the relationships between elements of the apparatus and segments of society. But how can one avoid the conclusion that it was Stalin's decision to purge the party and society of what he regarded as suspect and unstable elements – even if one can accept that orders might have been distorted by [those who carried them out]? One is struck by the number of references to arrest plans, which zealous locals sought to fulfil or overfulfil. However, the whole process was set in motion from the top, and we do have the known telegram sent by Stalin and Zhdanov demanding the appointment of Yezhov to replace the apparently too lenient Yagoda.

SOURCE 14.32 R. Manning, 'The Soviet Economic Crisis of 1936–40 and the Great Purges', in J. Arch Getty and R. Manning (eds), *Stalinist Terror – New Perspectives*, 1993, pp. 140–41

In this way, the economic problems of 1936–41 and the Great Purges appear to be inexorably linked. The industrial showdown, which set in at a time when the USSR could least afford it, when a two-front war without allies seemed to be the Soviets' inevitable fate, shaped the course of the Great Purges at least as much, if not more so, as the terror in turn influenced the operation of the economy. When plans went awry, when deprivations, instead of disappearing, became more severe, when promised improvements in food supply did not materialise, the subconscious temptation to seek scapegoats became irresistible.

ASSESSING THE DIFFERENT INTERPRETATIONS

Source 14.29 Robert Conquest is the British author of *The Great Terror*, first published in 1968, with a second edition, *The Great Terror: A Reassessment*, published in 1990. This is a standard work on the subject. Conquest is regarded by some as a 'cold warrior'. He follows the 'totalitarian' line.

Source 14.30 J. Arch Getty, an American, is the leading revisionist historian on this topic – he attacks the 'totalitarian' view. He is a decisionist historian who concentrates on institutional rather than ideological, personal or social factors.

Source 14.31 Alec Nove (1915–94) was Russian-born – his father was a Menshevik. His family left the USSR for Britain in 1924. An expert on Soviet economic policy, he wrote extensively on Stalin and Stalinism.

Source 14.32 Roberta Manning, an American, is the mentor of J. Arch Getty with whom she worked closely and edited *Stalinist Terror – New Perspectives* (1993). She is a revisionist historian on Stalin.

Source 14.33 Stephen Cohen, a revisionist historian and biographer of Bukharin, sees a marked difference between the Leninist state and the Stalinist state. He suggests that Stalin led Soviet Russia along the wrong path and feels they would have done better to stick with Bukharin and the right.

Source 14.34 Isaac Deutscher (1907–67), a Polish Communist, was expelled from the party in 1932 because he was the leader of the anti-Stalinist group. He moved to England and became a journalist and historian. As well as his biography of Stalin, he wrote a three-volume biography of his hero, Trotsky.

Source 14.35 Alan Bullock was a distinguished liberal British historian, the author of *Hitler and Stalin: Parallel Lives* (1991).

SOURCE 14.33   S. Cohen, quoted in Thames TV documentary *Stalin*, 1990

Ultimately you cannot explain the great terror against the Party without focusing on Stalin's personality. For some reason Stalin had a need to rid himself of the old Bolshevik Party, the Party that remembered everything of Bolshevik history and knew in its heart of hearts that Stalin was not the Lenin of today. He had to rid himself of this party and he did. By the end of the thirties, it was a completely different party demographically, most of its members had joined since 1929. The older league had gone, there were a few tokens left but almost to a man/woman they were dead.

SOURCE 14.34   I. Deutscher, *Stalin*, rev. edn 1966, pp. 372–74

But why did Stalin need the abominable spectacle [in 1936]? It has been suggested that he sent the men of the old guard to their deaths as scapegoats for his economic failures. There is a grain of truth in this but no more. For one thing, there was a very marked improvement in the economic conditions of the country in the years of the trials. He certainly had no need for so many scapegoats; and, if he had needed them, penal servitude would have been enough – Stalin's real and much wider motive was to destroy the men who represented the potentiality of alternative government.

The question that must now be answered is why he set out to reach this objective in 1936? Considerations of domestic policy can hardly explain his timing. Widespread though popular dissatisfaction may have been, it was too amorphous [lacking focus] to constitute any immediate threat to his position. The opposition was pulverised, downtrodden, incapable of action. Only some sudden shock ... involving the whole machine of power might have enabled it to rally its scattered and disheartened troops. A danger of that kind was just then taking shape; and it threatened from abroad. The first of the great show trials, that of Zinoviev and Kamenev, took place a few months after Hitler's army had marched into the Rhineland ...

... In the supreme crisis of war, the leaders of opposition, if they had been alive, might indeed have been driven to action by a conviction, right or wrong, that Stalin's conduct of the war was incompetent and ruinous. At an earlier stage they might have been opposed to his deal with Hitler ... It is possible they would have then attempted to overthrow Stalin. Stalin was determined not to allow things to come to this ... It is not necessary to assume that he acted from sheer cruelty or lust for power. He may be given the dubious credit of the sincere conviction that what he did served the interests of the revolution and that he alone interpreted those interests aright ...

SOURCE 14.35   A. Bullock, *Hitler and Stalin: Parallel Lives*, 1991, pp. 496–97

I have already suggested the two most important features of Stalin's psychology. The first was his narcissistic personality, characterised by his total self absorption ... and his conviction that he was a genius marked out to play a unique historical role. The second was the paranoid tendency which led him to picture himself as a great man facing a hostile world peopled with jealous and treacherous enemies engaged in a conspiracy to pull him down, if he did not strike and destroy them first ...

Throughout his life Stalin had a psychological need to confirm and reassure himself about both those beliefs – about his historic mission and about the truth of the picture he had formed of himself in relation to the external world ... The same obsession which had provided the drive to defeat his rivals and match Lenin's revolution with his own now nerved him to outdo his predecessor by freeing himself from the constraints of the party and becoming the sole ruler of the Soviet state.

Even more striking is the coincidence between Stalin's second psychological need ... and his political aim, in the years 1934–9, to destroy the original Bolshevik Party created by Lenin and replace it with a new one, maintaining a façade of continuity but in fact remaking it in his own image.

SOURCE 14.36   Stalin in a photograph believed to show him signing death warrants

SOURCE 14.37   Two of Stalin's sayings

One death is a tragedy, a million is a statistic.

If there is a person, there is a problem; no person no problem.

What reasons have been put forward for the terror?

In this section we look at Stalin's personality and motives, and also at other reasons that have been put forward to explain the form the terror took.

The vast majority of historians accept Stalin's responsibility for the terror. He was at the centre of the decision-making process and cannot be absolved. However, some revisionists argue that focusing on Stalin alone has for too long provided simple interpretations when the real story is more complicated.

The role played by Stalin

A number of historians argue that Stalin's personality was the driving force behind the terror, and that without him there would have been no Great Terror in the form it took – for example, old Bolsheviks would not have been humiliated and executed. Chart 14G outlines the role that they think his personality played in the Terror.

■ 14G What role did Stalin's personality play?

Deeply suspicious of others, verging on paranoia. Khrushchev reports that Stalin was a very 'distrustful man, sickly suspicious, seeing everywhere about him "enemies", "double dealers" and "spies"'. The suicide of his wife seems to have made him even more convinced that those around him would betray him, so he wanted to get them before they got him.

These facets of his character – paranoia and vengefulness – might explain why his former comrades were killed rather than disgraced, demoted or exiled as they would have been under Lenin.

Vindictive and vengeful, a bearer of grudges, taking revenge on those who had belittled or thwarted him in the past. In the early days of the revolution, the old Bolsheviks had treated him in a condescending way as mediocre and dull.

Crude and brutal even for a Bolshevik, with a fascination for violence; when hard pushed, he resorted to violence as a solution to his problems

This might explain the violence of the terror carried out against party members and people who were causing him problems.

Limited abilities but unlimited ambitions; he had an inferiority complex.

This might explain why he had to get rid of the old Bolshevik party members who knew his limitations, would not accept his heroic pose and might try to thwart him. He may also have wanted to destroy those who were his intellectual superiors, especially in party doctrine and history.

Idealised view of himself as the hero of the revolution, a genius who alone could take Russia forward to socialism and effect the transformation of the country, and who therefore could not be thwarted. This is a view stressed by Alan Bullock (Source 14.35) and Robert Tucker. Those who refused to accept his vision Stalin defined as traitorous: 'Only by believing in the victims' treasonous designs or deed could he come to terms with their failure to share his grandiose beliefs about himself.' (R. Tucker, *Stalin in Power: The Revolution from Above*, 1992).

CONTROL OF THE PARTY

By 1939 the party had 1,589,000 full members (in a population of nearly 170 million). Only 8.3% had joined before the end of 1920; 70% had joined after 1929.

A comparison between the Party Congresses of 1934 and 1939:

- In 1934 81% of delegates had joined the party before 1920
- In 1939 19% of delegates had joined the party before 1920
- At the 1939 Congress, unlike 1934, there was no debate, criticism or discussion. It was, in Leonard Schapiro's words, 'a cowed and servile assembly'.

By 1939, 318 out of 385 regional party secretaries had been repressed and the overwhelming majority of secretaries of party committees all over the country were under 40, owing their education and advancement to Stalin. For them the revolution and civil war were little more than a legend.

- **Stalin's motives**

No one is suggesting that the purges were just a symptom of a dysfunctional personality. Many historians and commentators like Khrushchev believe that Stalin thought that he was acting in the interests of the party and the revolution. He thought that his removal or the reversal of his policies would be disastrous for the Soviet Union. We can identify several interrelated motives that have been suggested for his actions:

- Stalin felt threatened by the growing opposition to him in the early 1930s. He reacted to this by eliminating all possible rivals so that no one could form an alternative government.
- Stalin was determined to be in a position of absolute power:
  a) He wanted to bring the party under his total control so that they would carry out his policies and edicts without question. Keeping the party in a constant state of insecurity (who would be arrested or denounced next?) was a way of keeping control. This was particularly true of the *nomenklatura* around the Central Committee: it allowed Stalin to keep his lieutenants guessing about whom he would adopt as 'his people'.
  b) He wanted control of the people; the terror crushed opposition and any critics.
- By the late 1930s, Stalin was convinced that there was a good chance of war. He wanted to remove anybody who might oppose his foreign policy. He also did not want to allow anybody to slow down the pace of industrialisation because the Soviet Union would need weapons and armaments to fight the war. It was essential to make the revolution safe from external threats.

Other reasons for the terror

But do Stalin's personality and his motives fully explain the terror? Revisionist historians and others have suggested a variety of other reasons for the scope of the terror and the way it escalated out of control. These do not exclude Stalin but see him and his lieutenants as reacting to situations, rather than as the protagonists setting everything in motion. They also see the terror as being generated 'from below'. The categories below have been devised for clarity but they are closely interrelated.

- **Problems within the party**

The central party in Moscow was having real problems controlling the party in the regions and the localities. J. Arch Getty argues that on a local level political administration was marked by sloth and inertia. Also, edicts from the central party sometimes conflicted with other demands. The local party often did not want to 'find' kulaks because they were valuable men in the community. In industrial towns, local party bosses wanted to reach their production targets and so did not want to purge specialists. Party leaders reacted to this in two ways:

- They used coercive tactics, like the show trials, to create an atmosphere in which nobody in the party felt safe and everyone was therefore more likely to obey orders.
- They encouraged the lower levels of the party to criticise those higher up. This led to a rush of accusations which got out of control and developed a momentum of their own.

- **Economic difficulties**

In the mid-1930s production figures were levelling off and the Five-Year Plans were falling behind schedule. There was a downturn in the Soviet economy after 1936 as a result of technical problems, Stalin's management of the economy and a bad harvest in that year. This led to two responses by Stalin and the élite that contributed to the spiralling growth of the terror:

- The leadership needed to find scapegoats (amongst managers as well as workers) for these economic failures. Roberta Manning has argued (Source 14.32 on page 269) that difficulties were seen as being due to enemy sabotage and wrecking.

■ 14H Summary: other reasons for the terror

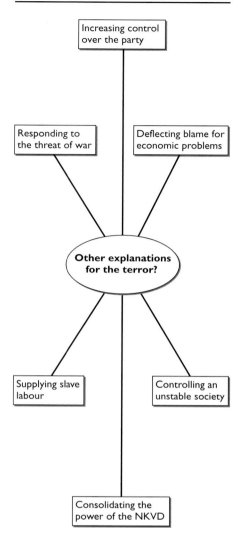

■ Learning trouble spot

Coercion and mobilisation

In response to both the problems in the party and the problems in the economy, the Communist leadership used the dual approach of coercion and mobilisation. Coercive techniques involved the show trials, arrests, imprisonment and the threat of the labour camps, which all induced fear and therefore compliance. Mass mobilisation involved getting those at the bottom of the social and economic hierarchy to criticise those above, to shake up officials and managers, make them more active and encourage their greater compliance with instructions from the centre.

– Stalin wanted to shake up managers and economic administrators, so encouraged criticism from below – attempting to 'mobilise the masses'. Workers were only too happy to identify managers and officials as the cause of their problems. What started as a genuine groundswell of grass-roots criticism of officials then got out of control in the heady, whipped-up atmosphere of the Great Terror.

This was tied in with the Stakhanovite campaign of 1936. The motive behind this was not only to encourage workers to be more productive but also to persuade would-be Stakhanovites to put pressure on their managers by demanding tools and materials to raise their production rates. Managers who did not respond were branded as wreckers by the workers.

- **Social instability**
  The disruption caused by the Five-Year Plans had created a terribly unstable society. Mass urbanisation had created social tension and violence in the overcrowded cities which lacked basic facilities and services. There was a great deal of hostility in the cities and countryside towards the Communist Party and the government was worried about the loss of control in the 'quicksand society' (M. Lewin). The government resorted to the terror of the purges to stifle criticism of the leadership, to control people and to keep them working. The campaign encouraging people to criticise officials (see above) was intended to deflect criticism and antagonism from the government.

- **The position of the NKVD**
  Some historians argue that the NKVD conducted the terror with such vigour because it was in the interests of the NKVD as an institution. Within the NKVD there were divisions and power struggles. Some units, especially in areas outside Moscow, operated their own fiefdoms, like a mafia, and used the terror to their own advantage. There may also have been a view that any slowdown after the rigours of enforced collectivisation and the First Five-Year Plan might make the NKVD appear less indispensable, but the terror would raise their profile and allow them to become the leading institution in the Soviet system. This is the argument of those who state that the NKVD was responsible for the murder of Kirov. The target fulfilment mentality (see Source 14.19 on page 263) contributed to the increasing number of victims. Forced confessions led to further denunciations.

- **The Gulag**
  By condemning vast numbers of people to the Gulag, the terror provided slave labour to carry out dangerous work such as logging and gold-mining in inhospitable regions. Stalin needed the money that these industries earned from foreign exports to buy in Western technology.

- **External threats**
  The prospect of war looked increasingly likely after Hitler became Chancellor of Germany. This increased enormously the pressure to develop an armaments industry based on heavy industry. Therefore an unwilling people, already suffering from the impact of the First Five-Year Plan, had to be pushed to even greater efforts. The terror was a mechanism to do this. Deutscher in Source 14.34 (page 270) also sees the threat of war as a spur to Stalin to purge the opposition who might interfere with his war plans. Anxiety about the security threat posed by ethnic minorities in Soviet border areas was behind the 'national sweeps' of 1937–38.

A final comment

It is still difficult to reach a final conclusion on the terror. Any explanation is likely to include a mix of the various factors mentioned here although it is a question of how much weight is given to them. Views are changing as more evidence, archival and oral, is coming into the public domain and more records become available. The records of the KGB – if they are ever released – will be of particular value. It is interesting to note that Arch Getty, in the light of new archival evidence, has revised his views in his book, with Oleg Naumov, *The Road to Terror: Stalin and the Self-Destruction of the Bolsheviks, 1932–39* (1999).

CASE STUDY: THE PURGES IN SVERDLOVSK

This case study is based on the work of James Harris ('The purging of local cliques in the Urals region 1936–7', in S. Fitzpatrick (ed.) *Stalinism: New Directions*, 2000, pages 267–71). He examined new archive material on Sverdlovsk, a large industrial centre and showed that the purges did not have a uniform cause.

Members of the regional party leadership had ensured an excellent standard of living for the ruling clique – large apartments, special access to consumer goods, high salaries – provided they remained loyal. Those who caused trouble or would not carry out instructions would lose these privileges. By 1935, all key positions were in their control; even the local NKVD man was a member of their inner circle. When faced with problems in fulfilling excessively high economic targets for the First Five-Year Plan, they manipulated the production figures, hid deficiencies in projects under construction, and found scapegoats outside the clique to explain underfulfilment.

But when it came to the Second Five-Year Plan, with more realistic targets, deficiencies could not be hidden because all the enterprises were supposed to be up and working. Poor management and machine breakdowns meant that there was serious underfulfilment as production fell. To make matters worse, a new NKVD man replaced the old one as the Great Terror got underway and there were demands to search for 'enemies everywhere'. The cosy coping mechanism had broken down.

The result was an avalanche of accusations, denunciations and incriminating information as members of the clique tried to save themselves. But each arrest led to further arrests as the NKVD followed the threads of the conspiracy. The use of terror grew in momentum and ferocity.

He now acknowledges that the 'fingerprints of Stalin' are all over the terror and that he played a central role in planning and executing it, although he still maintains that it did not happen as part of a master plan but rather as the response by Stalin and the Soviet élite to changing circumstances in Russia (see Source 14.39). However, as a result of research into recently opened archives, many historians identify Stalin as the chief mover, agent and director of the terror and link it clearly to his personality and his intentions – the outcomes he wanted to achieve.

SOURCE 14.38   R. Service, *A History of Twentieth Century Russia*, 1997, pp. 210–11

The Great Terror would not have taken place but for Stalin's personality and ideas. He it was who directed the state's punitive machinery against all those whom he identified as 'anti-Soviet elements' and 'enemies of the people'. Among his purposes was a desire to use his victims as scapegoats for the country's pain; and in order to sustain his mode of industrialisation he also needed to keep his mines, timber forests and construction sites constantly supplied with slave labour. It was probably also his intention to take pre-emptive measures against any 'fifth column' [internal dissidents] operating against him in the case of war. These considerations, furthermore, fitted into a larger scheme to build an efficient Soviet state subservient to his personal dictatorship – and to secure the state's total control over society. Such was the guiding rationale of the Great Terrorist.

SOURCE 14.39   J. Arch Getty and O. V. Naumov, *The Road to Terror: Stalin and the Self-Destruction of the Bolsheviks, 1932–39*, 1999, p. xiii

In spite of some misreadings and misunderstandings of earlier work, Stalin's guilt for the terror was never in question. We can now see his fingermarks all over the archives. Although he approved suggestions and draft documents from others as often as he launched his own initiatives, he played the leading role in the terror. But even with the new documents, the role remains problematic and hard to specify ... Stalin worked assiduously toward the goal of enhancing his power and centralizing authority in Moscow ... But even in Stalin's office, there were too many twists and turns, too many false starts and subsequent embarrassing backtrackings to support the idea that the terror was the culmination of a well-prepared and long-standing master design. Stalin was not sure exactly what kind of repression he wanted or how to get it until rather late in the story. He seems not to have decided on wholesale massacre until early in 1937.

ACTIVITY

Write an essay to answer the following question: Was Stalin's personality much the most important factor in explaining the Great Terror?

This kind of essay invites a number of responses:

a) a 'Yes' answer in which you argue that Stalin's personality was central to the terror and set out the evidence that supports your view

b) a 'Yes but . . . ' answer in which you argue his personality was important but suggest there were other reasons

c) a 'No' answer in which you suggest there were a variety of reasons for the terror. This answer does not exclude Stalin as a central player: you are saying that his other motives were more important than motives of personal vengeance, fuelled by paranoia and his own self-image. Or, you might want to argue that Stalin's role has been exaggerated.

You may wish to distinguish between the treatment of the old Bolsheviks in the show trials and the wider purges that drew in many thousands. You will probably want to give more weight to some factors than others. The diagram below may help.

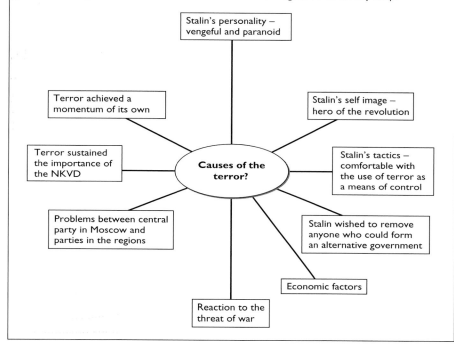

KEY POINTS FROM CHAPTER 14

How far was Stalin responsible for the Great Terror?

1. There was a difference between the earlier purges (*chistki*), which were non-violent, and the purges and show trials, which used terror against the party.
2. Terror had been a consistent feature of the Stalinist regime from its beginning.
3. There was marked opposition to Stalin before 1934 and at the Seventeenth Party Congress.
4. It has been argued that the murder of Sergei Kirov triggered the Great Terror.
5. Old Bolsheviks from both the left and the right wings of the party were disposed of in a series of show trials.
6. The party was purged from above and from below when members were encouraged to criticise and denounce others.
7. Mass terror engulfed other sections of the population who represented the bulk of those repressed. NKVD Order 00447 led to a campaign of 'social cleansing'. Millions died, or were imprisoned or deported.
8. Terror was used to deal with the instability caused by the 'quicksand society' and resolve the difficulties caused by impossibly high economic targets which were explained away as sabotage.
9. At the end of the process, Stalin emerged as dictator of the USSR with supreme control of a party that had been moulded by him and a populace that was, in the main, subservient to the leader and the party.

15 The cult of the personality

CHAPTER OVERVIEW

This chapter looks at the growth of the cult of the personality from the 1920s through to the end of the 1940s, when it was at its height. Stalin's image dominated the Soviet Union and he was seen as an omnipotent leader whom people should love and revere. The cult was not just about personal adulation of Stalin. It was also a response to a rapid period of change in the Soviet Union when many Russians were bewildered and confused about what was going on. The Stalin cult provided an image of purpose and solidity, giving people confidence and faith that someone could lead them out of their troubles to the good society.

A How did the cult of the personality develop? (pp. 276–279)

B Rewriting history (pp. 280–281)

C How did Russians react to the cult? (pp. 282–284)

A How did the cult of the personality develop?

ACTIVITY

1 The images in Sources 15.1–15.6 each carry a different message about Stalin. For each one, explain:
   a) the message it is designed to convey to the Russian people
   b) how you reached your interpretation.

2 a) What impression of Soviet Russia and of Stalin does Prokofiev's ode (Source 15.7) create?
   b) What are the religious overtones of this ode?

3 Does the fact that images of Stalin appeared everywhere, as described by Steinbeck in Source 15.8, prove that Stalin attracted genuine adulation?

SOURCE 15.1 A propaganda poster, made during the First Five-Year Plan, showing Stalin marching alongside miners

SOURCE 15.2   Stalin at the Helm, a poster from 1933

SOURCE 15.3   A 1937 photomontage of Stalin surrounded by a sea of children's faces

SOURCE 15.4   Grzelishvili's painting, *Comrade Stalin in his Early Years,* 1939

SOURCE 15.6   A painting by Kibrik: *On 24 October Lenin Arrived at Smolny During the Night.* In *Totalitarian Art* (1990), I. Golomstock points out that Lenin is motioning Stalin to go ahead of him, symbolically showing him the way to the bright future

SOURCE 15.5   The cover of *Ogonyok* magazine, December 1949, showing Stalin's godlike image projected into the sky, as part of the celebrations for his seventieth birthday

SOURCE 15.7   Ode to Stalin on his sixtieth birthday by the composer Prokofiev, 1939

Never have our fertile fields such a harvest shown,
Never have our villages such contentment known.
Never life has been so fair, spirits been so high,
Never to the present day grew so green the rye.
O'er the earth the rising sun sheds a warmer light,
Since it looked on Stalin's face it has grown more bright.
I am singing to my baby sleeping in my arms,
Grow like flowers in the meadow free from all alarm.
On your lips the name of Stalin will protect from harm.
You will learn the source of sunshine bathing all the land.
You will copy Stalin's portrait with your little hand.

SOURCE 15.8 John Steinbeck, the American novelist, visited the Soviet Union in 1947 and wrote the following entry in his diary (quoted in M. Cullerne Brown, *Art Under Stalin*, 1991, p. 175)

Everything in the Soviet Union takes place under the fixed stare of the plaster, bronze, drawn or embroidered eye of Stalin. His portrait does not just hang in every museum but in a museum's every room. Statues of him dignify the façade of every public building. His bust stands in front of all airports, railway and bus stations. A bust of Stalin stands in every classroom, and often his portrait hangs directly opposite. In parks he sits on plaster benches and discusses something or other with Lenin. In shops they sell million upon million of images of him, and in every home there is at least one portrait of him … He is everywhere, he sees everything … we doubt whether Caesar Augustus enjoyed during his life the prestige, the worship and the godlike power over the people of which Stalin disposes.

The personality cult and the adulation Stalin received are two of the most striking features of Soviet propaganda. By the end of the 1940s, Stalin dominated the USSR physically as well as politically. His image was literally everywhere, as Source 15.8 indicates. He was presented as the heir of Lenin and the sole infallible interpreter of party ideology. He acquired an almost god-like status. The unique position Stalin attained and the power he possessed to shape the Communist state and the lives of the people of the Soviet Union are called the 'cult of the personality'.

The origins of the cult can be seen in the late 1920s, but in this period the leadership was usually portrayed as an anonymous collective body making joint decisions; few pictures of the leaders appeared in the press. In 1929, Stalin was perceived as rather cold and distant. The full-blown cult really got going around 1933–34. Praise was heaped on Stalin personally and his link with Lenin and his role in the achievements of the First Five-Year Plan were emphasised. From 1935 onwards, it was possible to speak of Stalin only in glowing terms. He was portrayed as the *vozhd* (the leader), a genius with great wisdom and even prophetic powers.

The most likely explanation for the development of the cult lay in the economic and political circumstances of Soviet Russia in the mid-1930s. The disruption and disorientation brought about by the First Five-Year Plan and the terror meant that this was a bewildering and confusing time. Former heroes were revealed as traitors; wreckers and saboteurs were everywhere. The image of Stalin reassured the people that they had a strong leader to take them through these difficult and momentous times. There was a firm hand at the helm steering the ship, someone who knew where they were going. The cult of the personality was useful in holding Soviet society together.

Paintings, poetry and sculpture all served the cult. At the beginning of the cult the regime did not want people to be alienated by a remote leader, so they deliberately cultivated a more popular image of Stalin. Paintings and posters stressed Stalin's humanity and his active participation in the lives of ordinary people. He is seen marching alongside workers or in the fields with the peasants, or inspecting great projects. Stalin's relationship with children was emphasised: no nursery was without a 'Thank you, Stalin, for my happy childhood' painting. As the cult developed, operas and films glorified his role in the revolution or as the chief hero of the Civil War. By the end of the 1930s, paintings show him more detached and superior. Statues show him as more monumental, an all-powerful leader; this image could not be clearer than in the statue of Stalin at the Great Soviet Exhibition in 1939. Also in 1939, an exhibition entitled 'Stalin and the Soviet People' contained pictures of his childhood showing him as a natural leader or like a young Christ explaining the scriptures (see Source 15.4, page 277).

Success in the Second World War and the defeat of the Nazis enhanced Stalin's position and fed the cult, which reached its height at the end of the 1940s. Paintings show him in god-like solitude or with Lenin, sometimes even appearing to tell Lenin what to do. Stalin had lost his role as a disciple, now he was an equal or even the master. The omnipresent images of Stalin said to the Soviet people: 'Stalin is everywhere present and watching over you; he understands your hopes and has your best interests at heart.' During the celebrations of his seventieth birthday, a giant portrait of Stalin was suspended over Moscow and lit up at night by a battery of searchlights (see Source 15.5).

FOCUS ROUTE

1 Use the information on pages 276–279, including Chart 15A, to produce a diagram, mapping out the development of the cult.
2 Make brief notes describing the devices used to establish and spread the cult.
3 Why do you think the cult was used by the Soviet leadership when individual adulation was against their collective code?

1924–29	**ORIGINS OF THE CULT**
	• After Lenin's death in 1924, Stalin assumes a modest image. He wants to appear as a hard-working man of moderation. • He takes on the mantle of Lenin's disciple and servant of the party. 'Stalin is the Lenin of today' becomes a commonly used phrase. • Tsaritsyn is renamed Stalingrad in his honour in 1925.

1929–33	**CULT UNDERWAY**
	• For his fiftieth birthday in 1929, Stalin receives 350 greetings, including some from organisations that did not even exist. Stalin is portrayed as Lenin's faithful pupil and companion-in-arms. • The length of applause for Stalin at conferences gets longer. • By 1931, huge portraits of Marx, Engels, Lenin and Stalin appear on special occasions such as celebrations of the October Revolution. There are few individual portraits of Stalin.

1933–39	**CULT FULLY ESTABLISHED**
	• Stalin's image is used to reassure people that they have a strong leader to help them through the great disruption of the First Five-Year Plan and the confusion of the terror. • Paintings, poems and sculpture promote the Stalin cult. SOCIALIST REALIST art glorifies Stalin's role as leader. • The *History of the All-Union Communist Party* is published in 1938. History is reinterpreted in Stalin's favour. • As war looms, his image becomes more that of an all-powerful leader.

Post-1945	**HEIGHT OF THE CULT**
	• Stalin's image is everywhere; his power cemented by his success as war leader. • His childhood home becomes a shrine. • Increasingly, portraits show him in god-like solitude, superior and apart. • The celebrations of his seventieth birthday are extremely elaborate, organised by 75 leading figures including the whole Politburo. There are galas and greetings almost every day from 21 December 1949 to August 1951.

> SOCIALIST REALISM
> The ideological philosophy that guided Soviet literature and the arts after 1934; all creative writing and art had to celebrate the achievements of the proletarian in his struggle to make a contribution to the Soviet achievement.

STORIES ABOUT THE CULT
In his book *Stalin: Breaker of Nations* (1991, page 213), Robert Conquest tells of some of the more absurd effects of the cult:

■ At a provincial meeting there was an ovation when Stalin's name was mentioned and no one dared to sit down first. When one old man could stand no longer and sat down, his name was taken and he was arrested the next day.
■ When a speech of Stalin's was published on a series of gramophone records, one side of one of the records consisted entirely of applause.

Khrushchev cited the example of Stalin marking a 1948 edition of the *Short Biography* about his own life: he marked the points where he thought the praise was insufficient. Stalin wanted the following sentence to be added: 'Although he performed his task as leader of the people with consummate skill and enjoyed the unreserved support of the entire Soviet people, Stalin never allowed his work to be marred by the slightest hint of vanity, conceit or self-adulation.' (Khrushchev in his secret speech at the Twentieth Party Congress in which he denounced Stalin. Taken from S. Talbolt (ed.), *Khrushchev Remembers*, vol. 1, 1977, page 629.)

B Rewriting history

SOURCE 15.9 A famous photograph of Lenin addressing troops in 1920, with Trotsky and Kamenev on the steps to the right of the platform

SOURCE 15.10 After Trotsky's downfall, the same photograph was published with Trotsky and Kamenev painted out

SOURCE 15.11 In 1933, I. Brodsky painted the same scene on a giant canvas for the Central Lenin Museum in Moscow. Trotsky and Kamenev were replaced by two journalists. This photograph was taken for *Pravda* in 1940 and shows Red army and navy personnel staring at the work

FOCUS ROUTE

Why do you think Stalin found it necessary to rewrite the history of the revolution and the development of the Soviet state in the *Short Course*? Make a note of your answer.

Another significant aspect of the cult of the personality was the reinterpretation of history in Stalin's favour. In 1938, the *History of the All-Union Communist Party*, or *Short Course* as it was usually called, was published in the Soviet Union. In it, Stalin was given a much more important role in the October Revolution as chief companion to Lenin, his closest friend and disciple. Trotsky, on the other hand, was demoted to the role of bourgeois opportunist and given little credit. The other old Bolsheviks, especially Bukharin and his supporters, were designated 'enemies of the people' or were relegated to minor roles. All were dwarfed by the invincible heroes – Lenin and Stalin.

SOURCE 15.12 A photograph taken in April 1925 (above) and published again in 1939 (below)

The *Short Course* was not just another history book. It was *the* main history text for educational institutions across the USSR. It was the definitive version, replacing all the books that had had pages cut out or pasted over as leading Bolsheviks fell victim to the show trials and purges. According to the *Short Biography*, Stalin himself was the author of the *Short Course*. By 1948, it had sold 34 million copies in the Soviet Union and two million elsewhere.

As part of the process of reinterpretation, photographs were amended to support the new history. Stalin was added to photographs of Lenin to show that he had been his closest friend and adviser. Old 'heroes of the revolution' were airbrushed out of Soviet history. It was as if Stalin wanted them wiped from the collective memory of the period.

FOCUS ROUTE

1 Account for the relative success of the cult – why do you think it worked with the Russian people?
2 What conclusions can you reach about whether the adulation Stalin received was genuine? Make notes of your answers.

SOURCE 15.13 J. Gooding, *Socialism in Russia – Lenin and his Legacy, 1890–1991*, 2002, pp. 136–7

The 1917 revolutions had in rapid succession ousted both tsar and God, those age-old supports and foci for devotion…. The Soviet regime had been left with neither democratic legitimacy nor the power of a charismatic personality to sustain it. But one or other of these was indispensable; the regime under Stalin took the unBolshevik but deeply Russian course of restoring the charismatic element. So successfully did Stalin do this that by the late 1930s much of the population had become abjectly dependent upon him…. Instead of leading the Soviet people forward to democracy, he had led them back, amidst conditions of utter insecurity, to a culture in which childlike dependency mingled with a fierce rejection of anyone and anything alien – to a culture which the Bolsheviks themselves, as democrats and enlighteners, had once intended to liquidate.

C How did Russians react to the cult?

Stalin received adulation on a scale and intensity that few leaders have known and, according to Robert Service, he had a 'craving for adulation' (*A History of Twentieth-Century Russia*, 1997, pages 250–51). Although the cult was a carefully contrived propaganda campaign, it does not seem that the adulation was entirely manufactured. Service maintains that genuine enthusiasm for Stalin was limited until the end of the 1930s when the mass indoctrination campaign reached its peak. Such enthusiasm as had been aroused was then heightened by the grave threat to the Soviet Union presented by the war. Robert Thurston, the revisionist historian, is convinced that the people believed that the show trials were genuine and that Stalin was rooting out wreckers and saboteurs. They believed that Stalin was their true guide and the person who cared for them. Only this, he claims (in *Life and Terror in Stalin's Russia 1934–41*, 1996), can account for the huge affection that people had for Stalin. Testimony from people who lived through the Stalinist period after 1945 seems to support this view, but it is more difficult to assess before 1939.

Sarah Davies, in her book *Popular Opinion in Stalin's Russia: Terror, Propaganda and Dissent 1934–41* (1997), identifies three ways in which people reacted to the Stalin cult. They viewed Stalin as:

1 Benefactor. Many, including Stakhanovites, some soldiers and the young intelligentsia, had reason to be grateful to Stalin because they had acquired power and status despite often humble origins. Khrushchev, who followed Stalin as leader of Russia, was an example of such a person. Stalin was admired as the prime agent in achieving the astounding changes brought about by industrialisation and collectivisation. A letter from one woman said: 'I live very well and I think that I will live even better. Why? Because I live in the Stalin epoch. May Stalin live longer than me! … All my children had and are having education thanks to the state and, I would say, thanks to the party, and especially comrade Stalin, for he, along with Lenin, opened the way for us simple people … I myself, an old woman, am ready to die for Stalin and the Bolshevik cause.'

2 Traditional defender of the people. In this Stalin played a role very similar to that of the tsars. Millions of petitions and letters were sent to him and other Communist leaders asking for help against misfortunes or the actions of local officials or bureaucrats. As in tsarist times, criticism was directed against local officials while the leaders were praised. Letters often began with cult-style greetings: 'Dear comrade Stalin! Our beloved *vozhd*, teacher and friend of the whole happy Soviet country'. Stalin and other leaders were often referred to as 'uncle' or seen as 'like a father'. The petitioners affirmed their loyalty while criticising the actions of the regime's agents on the ground. This was in line with Stalin's own message that officialdom was riddled with corruption and that the great father, Stalin, was on the people's side. It seems that this populist aspect of the cult was in tune with people's traditional ideas.

3 Charismatic leader. According to Davies, Stalin was perceived as a demi-god possessing superhuman abilities and superhuman wisdom. This was reflected in the icons and symbols of the *vozhd* that appeared in houses and in processions, very similar to the honouring of saints in the Christian tradition. Statues and images of Stalin abounded (see Source 15.8 on page 278), as did references to him as the 'sun' or the 'man-god' (see Source 15.16 on page 284). How far ordinary Russians actually believed this is difficult to say, but it does seem that this charismatic aspect of the cult was a significant feature for a large number, especially after the Second World War.

There was, of course, a substantial section of the population – intellectuals, experienced party members and workers – who were aware of the absurdities of the cult. There was active criticism, particularly early on, about the way Stalin had been elevated to some sort of mystical status. Some workers in the mid-1930s objected to the incessant declarations of love for Stalin. Many in the party felt that this was not how Lenin would have acted and still favoured collective leadership of a more anonymous nature – the dictatorship of the party, not an individual. Such criticism was less likely to be expressed after the purges got underway. But there is evidence that by 1938 the excessive propaganda was becoming counterproductive and that people were becoming cynical. Sarah Davies gives the following examples from 1938:

- a leaflet ridiculing the Supreme Soviet, where the 'people's elect' were allowed to shout out 'Hurray' a thousand times in honour of the *vozhd* and his stooges
- an anonymous letter from a Communist supporter complaining about the use of Stalin's name: 'Everything is Stalin, Stalin, Stalin. You only have to listen to a radio programme about our achievements, and every fifth or tenth word will be the name of comrade Stalin. In the end this sacred and beloved name – Stalin – may make so much noise in people's heads that it is very possible that it will have the opposite effect.'

However, even amongst those who did not like him, and there were very many, there was often respect and even admiration. There was a feeling that Stalin was a great leader in the Russian tradition, like one of the great tsars such as Peter the Great. He was tough and he was hard but he had achieved a great deal, industrialised the USSR and made it into a great world power that other countries respected. And on his death in 1953, there were many who wept, even those whose relatives had suffered persecution or died under his rule. The cult of the personality may not always have had a lot of depth, but it had penetrated all areas of Soviet society and played an important role in popularising Stalin and bringing solidity, confidence and coherence to that society during a period of rapid change and instability.

SOURCE 15.14 J. Lewis and P. Whitehead, *Stalin: A Time for Judgement*, 1990, pp. 66, 121, quoting two Russians who grew up in the 1940s

Alexander Avdeyenko

Looking back on my life, I now see that period as one of sincere enthusiasm, as genuine human happiness … It would have been impossible for a common mortal to withstand the onslaught of Stalin, of the apparatus which was Stalin's, or the pressure which was put on people's reason, heart and soul. Day and night radio told us that Stalin was the greatest man on earth – the greatest statesman, the father of the nation, the genius of all time … Man wants to believe in something great.

Pavel Litvinov

Stalin was like a god for us. We just believed he was an absolutely perfect individual, and he lived somewhere in the Kremlin, a light always in his window, and he was thinking about us, about each of us. That was how we felt. For example, somebody told me he was the best surgeon. He could perform a brain operation better than anyone else, and I believed it. I knew that he was busy with other things, but if he wanted to do it he would be better.

ACTIVITY

Sources 15.15 and 15.16, one a poem from 1917 and the other from 1936, give us some insight into how attitudes changed from the time of the October Revolution to the era of the Stalinist state.

1 **a)** What is the message in the first poem?

b) How does the poet put over his message?

c) Why might this be a poem you could march to?

d) What insight does it give us into how some people might have felt in 1917?

2 **a)** What is the message in the second poem?

b) What images of Stalin does the poet create?

c) How does this message compare with the one in the first poem?

d) What does it suggest about the way in which people viewed how Communism moved forward?

3 Are these poems useful for historians of this period?

SOURCE 15.15 Extracts from a poem by V. Kirilov, a young proletarian in 1917. Young Communists chanted or marched to poems like these

We are the countless, awesome legions of Labour . . .
Our proud souls burn with the fire of revolt . . .
In the name of our Tomorrow we shall burn Raphael,
Destroy museums, trample the flowers of art.
We have thrown off the heavy crushing legacy . . .
Our muscles crave gigantic work,
Creative pangs seethe in our collective breast . . .
For our new planet we shall find a new dazzling path.
We love life, its intoxicating wild ecstasy,
Our spirit is tempered by fierce struggle and suffering.
We are everybody, we are everything, we are the flame and the victorious light,
We are our own Deity, and Judge and Law.

SOURCE 15.16 Extracts from 'Song About Stalin' by M. Izakvosky, 1936. This is a typical poem from the late 1930s

For the sake of our happiness
He marched through all storms.
He carried our holy banner
Over our enormous land.
And fields and factories rose,
And tribes and people responded
To the call of our leader.

He gave us for ever and ever
Youth, glory and power.
He has lit the clear dawn of spring
Over our homes.
Let us sing, comrades, a song
About the dearest person,
About our sun, about the truth of nations,
About our Stalin let's sing a song.

KEY POINTS FROM CHAPTER 15

The cult of the personality

1 In the cult of the personality, Stalin was presented as a god-like figure, omniscient and omnipresent.

2 The cult was at its height at the end of the 1930s. Images of Stalin on posters and paintings, in books and as statues were everywhere in the Soviet Union.

3 Stalin enjoyed this adulation and encouraged the view of himself as a great hero of the past. He had history rewritten to reflect this view.

4 The cult also served an important purpose: it gave the Russian people a sense of confidence in troubled times – Stalin would see them through to a better society.

Soviet society in the 1920s and 1930s

16 Were Soviet culture and society transformed by the October Revolution?

CHAPTER OVERVIEW

The Bolsheviks wanted to change society. Wherever revolutionaries seek to remake society, they challenge deep-rooted social institutions: the family, education and religion. In this chapter we focus on the experience of women after the revolution and also ask how much change there was in the family, religion, education and the arts. The first decade of Communism (1917–27) saw more equality for women, the most liberal divorce and abortion laws in Europe, an explosion of the arts, a fierce attack on religion and changes in education. But things did not always turn out as the revolutionary leaders intended.

A How much did life change for women and the family? (pp. 286–291)

B How did the Bolsheviks use artists and film-makers between 1918 and 1928? (pp. 292–297)

C How much change occurred in education? (pp. 298–299)

D What impact did the Bolsheviks have on religion? (pp. 300–301)

A How much did life change for women and the family?

ACTIVITY

Match up statements 1–5 with the seven depictions of women in Soviet art shown on pages 286–287. Think about the messages the artists are trying to convey.

1 Women hold prestigious positions and are not just simple workers.
2 Building Communism and love can come together and reach greater heights.
3 Soviet woman is physically robust and does jobs only men do in the West.
4 Men and women both play a full part in Soviet economic progress.
5 In the USSR motherhood and work can be combined joyfully.

SOURCE 16.1 *Industrial Worker and Collective Farm Girl*, a statue by Vera Mukhina, 1935

SOURCE 16.2 Georgie Ryazhsky's portrait, *The Chairwoman*, 1928

287

WERE SOVIET CULTURE AND SOCIETY TRANSFORMED BY THE OCTOBER REVOLUTION?

SOURCE 16.3 *Higher and Higher*, a painting by Serafima Ryangina, 1934

SOURCE 16.4 *Woman Metro-Builder with a Pneumatic Drill* by Aleksandr Samokhvalov, 1937

SOURCE 16.5 Gaponenko's *To Dine With the Mothers*, 1935

288

WERE SOVIET CULTURE AND SOCIETY TRANSFORMED BY THE OCTOBER REVOLUTION?

■ 16A Legislation on marriage and childcare

1917

- New divorce law – either partner could terminate a marriage on grounds of incompatibility. If one partner was not present at the divorce hearing, he or she was notified of the divorce by postcard.
- People's Commissar for Social Welfare passed laws which:
  - guaranteed paid maternity leave for two months before and after the birth
  - allowed nursing mothers to work shorter hours and take time to breastfeed their babies at work
  - excused women from heavy work or night work
  - set up a commission for the protection of mothers and infants, which made plans for maternity clinics, milk points and nurseries.

1920

Law passed allowing abortion to be performed under medical supervision. The Soviet state became the first country to legalise abortion on demand.

SOURCE 16.6 O. Figes, *A People's Tragedy: The Russian Revolution, 1891–1924*, 1997, p. 197, writing of Russia before the revolution

For centuries peasants had claimed the right to beat their wives. Russian peasant proverbs were full of advice on the wisdom of such beatings: 'The more you beat the old women, the tastier the soup will be.'

A rival proverb [was] 'Women can do everything; men can do the rest.'

Women and the family

The new Communist state intended to bring about fundamental changes in the position of women in society. The key to this was economic independence: women should be able to have a job outside of the crushing drudgery of looking after a home and family (see the views of Alexandra Kollontai in Chart 16B, page 290). Lenin regarded the traditional bourgeois marriage as akin to slavery, with the woman the property of her husband and subjugated to his will. It was economic and sexual exploitation. Freeing women from their domestic role required the large-scale provision of facilities such as canteens, laundries, kindergartens and crèches; in other words, the socialisation of domestic services. This was a requirement which Lenin understood and supported.

Changes to women's role in the home also implied a fundamental change in the relationship between men and women. Once freed from the constraints of bourgeois marriage, there would be more equality between the sexes and sexual liberation because people would be freer to choose their partners. Therefore laws were passed immediately to make divorce easier and later, in 1920, to allow abortion on demand. The Bolsheviks had set the socialist dream for women in motion, but this soon collided with the economic realities of life in the Soviet state in the 1920s.

In 1919, the USSR had the highest marriage rate and, by the mid-1920s, the highest divorce rate in Europe, twenty-five times higher than in Britain. This situation did not work in women's favour. With easy divorce available, women were abandoned when they became pregnant. There were reports of young men registering more than fifteen short-lived 'marriages'. One survey of broken marriages from the end of the 1920s indicated that in 70 per cent of cases divorces were initiated by the men and in only seven per cent by mutual consent. By 1927, two-thirds of marriages in Moscow ended in divorce; across the country the figure was one-half. Due to the housing shortage, divorced couples often still lived together and domestic violence and rape were common.

The government was neither willing nor able to fund enough crèches or public canteens to free women from childcare and housework. When, in 1922, the idea of state provision for crèches, kitchens and laundries was costed, it added up to more than the entire national budget. The reality for many Russian children was not a network of socialist kindergartens but life in gangs that survived by begging, scrounging, stealing and prostitution. Hundreds of thousands had been made orphans by war and civil war. Malcolm Muggeridge, the English journalist and writer, reported seeing orphans 'going around in packs, barely articulate and recognisably human, with pinched faces, tangled hair and empty eyes. I saw them in Moscow and Leningrad, clustered under bridges, lurking in railway stations, suddenly emerging like a pack of wild monkeys, and scattering and disappearing' (quoted in R. Pipes, *A Concise History of the Russian Revolution*, 1995, page 326). Contemporaries estimated that in the 1920s there were between seven and nine million orphans, most of whom were under the age of thirteen.

SOURCE 16.7 B. Williams, unpublished correspondence describing Soviet Russia in the inter-war years

It was a macho world for all the talk of equality. The nineteenth-century scientific ideas of in-built gender differences were still influential. Women cared and supported. Men built socialism. The iconography of the new state showed women with children or represented as peasants. The high-status proletarian was male, a metal worker or a blacksmith.

SOURCE 16.8 B. Williams, 'Kollontai and After: Women in the Russian Revolution' (unpublished lecture), quoting a Communist observer

In principle we separated marriage from economics, in principle we destroyed the family hearth, but we carried out the resolution on marriage in such a manner that only the man benefited from it ... The woman remains tied with chains to the destroyed family hearth. The man, happily whistling, can leave it, abandoning the women and children.

289

WERE SOVIET CULTURE AND SOCIETY TRANSFORMED BY THE OCTOBER REVOLUTION?

TALKING POINT

How important do you think employment is in changing the status of women in society today? Have increased economic independence, and higher positions in companies and public bodies, affected the lives of women and their relationships with men?

FOCUS ROUTE

Make notes on the following to prepare for a discussion:

- changes in the social and legal position of women after October 1917, including changes to the laws on divorce and abortion
- the difference between the socialist dream and the reality of childcare
- women's employment 1917–29
- the extent of women's political activity
- Alexandra Kollontai's ideas on women's emancipation, sex and marriage, and childcare.

Employment

During the First World War, the percentage of women in the urban workforce doubled; by 1917 it was about 47 per cent. After the Civil War, when five million men were discharged from military service, women suffered as men were given preference in jobs. Although women were paid less than men, employers regarded women as more expensive due to the time they took off work because of their home responsibilities. With the growth of urban unemployment during the NEP, women were forced from skilled to unskilled work – still predominantly in textiles and domestic service, and then from work to unemployment and into prostitution and crime. There were all-women gangs of thieves and 39 per cent of proletarian men used prostitutes in the 1920s. The result of all this was that the percentage of women in industrial labour by 1929 was practically the same as it had been in 1913. According to a survey in the 1920s, women in proletarian families worked an eight-hour day outside the home plus an extra five hours in domestic tasks; men did not help with the domestic work.

Participation in politics

You would imagine that a party that stressed the equality of women would promote this within their own party. But women's participation in the Communist Party did not make great strides in the 1920s. In 1917, women formed ten per cent of the party membership; in 1928, 12.8 per cent (156,000 women). At the party congress in 1918, only five per cent of the voting delegates were women and this percentage went down rather than up in succeeding years. Young, unmarried women had more time to be activists and female membership of the Komsomol (the Young Communist League) was much higher than party membership.

Women were up against two problems: Russian male chauvinism and the Marxist dislike of any separatist activity that could be interpreted as weakening the class struggle and proletarian unity. Traditional attitudes to women excluded them from party activities, as Sources 16.9 and 16.10 show. There were even reports of women being attacked or beaten by their husbands for being involved in party work.

In 1919, the party set up a women's department, Zhenotdel, to make women active defenders of the revolution through propaganda and agitation. However, in practice it focused on practical help such as social services, education and training, and making sure that new laws protecting women in factories were enforced, rather than on Alexandra Kollontai's more radical ideas about transforming women's role in society (see Chart 16B on page 290). Zhenotdel was abolished suddenly in 1930 on the grounds that it was no longer necessary.

SOURCE 16.9 J. McDermid and A. Hillyer, *Women and Work in Russia, 1880–1930*, 1998, p. 132

Before the revolution Kollontai tried to organise a meeting of women workers. Despite the promise of the St Petersburg committee of the party to provide a venue, when Kollontai and the women arrived, they found a sign on the door which read: 'The meeting for women only has been cancelled; tomorrow there will be a meeting for men only.'

SOURCE 16.10 B. Williams, 'Kollontai and After: Women in the Russian Revolution' (unpublished lecture), quoting a woman delegate who complained at a party congress that her activist husband forbade her to take part in public life

And in those very meetings which he forbids me to attend because he is afraid I will become a real person – what he needs is a cook and mistress wife – in those very meetings where I have to slip in secretly, he makes thunderous speeches about the role of women in the revolution, calls women to a more active role.

290

WERE SOVIET CULTURE AND SOCIETY TRANSFORMED BY THE OCTOBER REVOLUTION?

■ **16B The views of Alexandra Kollontai**

Paid work
Paid work outside the home should be the centre of women's lives. It would make them independent and personally fulfilled. As a good Marxist, she believed that a woman's rights and position in society 'always follow from her role in the economy and in production'. Capitalism oppressed women with the double burden of waged work and housework.

Marriage
The new marriage would be based on love, not on economic considerations or purely on sex, and would be unhindered by inequality, dependence or family ties. It need be neither monogamous nor long-lasting but it would be a true love relationship – the 'winged Eros' she writes about in her much misunderstood *Letter to Soviet Youth*. Like Lenin, she disapproved of the casual attitudes towards sex displayed by some Soviet youth in the 1920s.

Family life
The family could be transformed into something new: a network of collectives made up of a group of people working and living co-operatively together. Kitchens, dining rooms, laundries and childcare would be provided by the state.

Children
Motherhood was a duty but it ought not to be a burden. Once weaned, children would be the joint possession of the collective and possessiveness towards children would end. In the nurseries and kindergartens the new generation would learn to value the beauties of sociability, sharing and togetherness, and become accustomed to looking at the world from the perspective of the group and not through selfish eyes.

Workers' participation
Her belief in participation was not confined to women. The new society must be created from below. Trade unions must be preferred to the party bureaucracy. The party should return to the ideas of 1917. Trade unions, soviets and other elected workers' organisations should be trusted to run industry and create socialism themselves. Every party member should spend three months of every year working in factories or villages.

Alexandra Kollontai (1872–1952)

Alexandra Kollontai dominated Bolshevik theory and practice about 'the woman question' in 1906–22. The daughter of a wealthy general, her life was changed in 1896 after she visited a large factory. Shocked by the plight of the workers, which she saw as enslavement, she committed herself wholeheartedly to improving their living and working conditions. She plunged into revolutionary Marxism, leaving her husband and son. She was drawn into the Social Democratic Party, leaning towards the Mensheviks, but after the beginning of the First World War she committed herself to Lenin and the Bolsheviks. In 1917, she was on both the Central Committee of the Bolshevik Party and the Central Executive Committee of the Petrograd Soviet. She was appointed Commissar for Social Welfare after the revolution and drafted much of the 1917 legislation in this area. She resigned in protest over the Treaty of Brest-Litovsk.

After the Civil War, Kollontai was one of the leaders of the Workers' Opposition (see page 151) and clashed with Lenin. He stooped to a personal attack on her lifestyle. She had a succession of husbands and lovers: Shlyapnikov, the other leader of the Workers' Opposition, was her lover and she was married to Dybenko, a huge, black-bearded Bolshevik sailor and revolutionary hero seventeen years her junior.

The defeat of the Workers' Opposition effectively ended her political career. After this she was exiled to become a diplomat and in 1930–45 she was Soviet ambassador to Sweden; the King of Sweden was reported to be her lover. She wrote semi-autobiographical novels such as *Red Love* and *Love of Worker Bees*, putting forward her views on sex and the new woman. She retired to Moscow, the only surviving leading member of the opposition, and died in 1952 aged 80.

Enthusiasts to the left of Kollontai talked of free love, the abolition of marriage and forcibly removing children from the harmful influence of their parents to be brought up by the state. Kollontai did not, or at least did so with caution. Nevertheless, the pressure of the 'new morality' on girls led to 'liberty, equality and maternity!' Kollontai was increasingly associated with the corruption of Soviet youth rather than the liberation of Soviet women. There were some experimental communes but only one survived until the end of the 1920s. It had 168 members, only sixteen of whom were men. Student communes pooled all grants, books, even underclothes. One in Moscow forbade individual friendships. The fear of the 'new woman', prepared to sacrifice family, home and sometimes children for the cause, was widespread.

It is easy to overestimate the impact of these new ideas on Russian society in the 1920s. Although the family had been challenged by 'free' (unregistered) marriages, postcard divorces and abortion, the social radicalism of the decade can be exaggerated. Soviet law strongly emphasised the mutual responsibility of family members for each other's financial welfare and, as the state lacked the resources to provide social welfare, the family remained a key institution. There was an increase in promiscuity, but surveys in the 1920s suggest the increase was not as great as young men claimed. The majority held to traditional attitudes towards relationships and a large number dreamt of long-lasting partnerships based on love and marriage. Also, such change as did occur tended to be in the cities and not in the countryside, where the vast majority of the population remained unaffected by the concept of the new woman and freer sexual relations, as Source 16.11 indicates.

SOURCE 16.11 M. Hindus, *Black Earth*, 1926, pp. 165–67. In 1926 Maurice Hindus, an American academic, went back to the village in Russia where he had been born and talked to young people in the village

And what I asked, of the morality of young people? Had there been any changes since the Revolution? None, they replied. Girls were as strict as ever their mothers and grandmothers had been. Of course, a fellow could flirt with a girl, put his arm around her, hold her hand, kiss her, but only on the cheek, not on the lips – unless she was his fiancée. Otherwise – well – our girls were quite strong, a blow of their fists might even draw blood. Lapses in conduct were as rare as in the old times . . . it was the worst thing for a girl to submit to a man. Her betrayer is likely to abandon her, and no other man would have her as his wife. The girls knew that and took care of themselves.

And what, I further enquired, of the Young Communists? They laughed uproariously. Ekh, the Young Communists . . . some of them were against kissing and dancing, said it was all the invention of the capitalists to corrupt the peasant and the proletarian . . . and besides it was too much responsibility to be a Young Communist.

TALKING POINT

How far had women's lives and their position in society improved between 1917 and 1929?

LENIN'S VIEWS ON KOLLONTAI'S IDEAS

For Lenin, participation in the labour force plus socialisation of domestic duties equalled female emancipation. However, he thought that Kollontai's views on sex were completely unMarxist and anti-social. 'Of course . . . thirst must be quenched. But will the normal man, in normal circumstances, lie down in the gutter and drink out of a puddle, or out of a glass with a rim greasy from many lips?' was his attitude to casual sexual relationships – he deplored promiscuity. As far as he was concerned, young people required healthy sports and exercise rather than 'endless lectures and discussions on sex problems'. Lenin also condemned the Workers' Opposition as a deviation and radically wrong in theory.

FOCUS ROUTE

Make notes on:
- Proletkult
- the Bolshevik use of arts as propaganda
- cinema.

Anatoly Lunacharsky (1875–1933)

Lunacharsky was an intellectual, playwright and literary critic who was Commissar for Popular Enlightenment between 1917 and 1929. In the revolution he was a prominent and popular leader, second only to Trotsky as a crowd orator. He was creative and open-minded and encouraged artists, poets and musicians to work with the Bolsheviks. Although promoting proletarian culture, he also respected the cultural achievements of the past and was able to ensure that many historical buildings survived. At different times he was criticised by Lenin for his support of the avant-garde and Proletkult, and for trying to protect the Bolshoi theatre rather than using the money to set up reading rooms as part of the literacy campaign. Lunacharsky believed in allowing some artistic freedom and different schools of painting, literature and the performing arts did exist in the 1920s. He was replaced as Commissar in 1929.

LENIN'S VIEWS ON ART AND PROLETKULT

Lenin attacked all modern art as Futurism and was not keen on it. He believed that freedom in art was the freedom to 'elevate the masses, teach them and strengthen them'. He had no time for individual self-expression which he called 'bourgeois-anarchist individualism'. Lenin attacked the Futurist Mayakovsky's poem '150 Millions' as 'Rubbish, double-dyed stupidity and pretentiousness', declaiming 'And flog Lunacharsky for futurism'. Nor was he keen on Proletkult. He did not believe that you could invent a new proletarian culture; rather you should develop the best models and traditions from the existing culture from a Marxist world outlook.

B How did the Bolsheviks use artists and film-makers between 1918 and 1928?

Proletkult

Following the October Revolution, the Bolshevik government set up the Commissariat of Popular Enlightenment (Ministry of Education and Culture) headed by Anatoly Lunacharsky. The focus moved away from 'high art' – ballet, opera, fine art and museums – which was regarded as bourgeois and élitist, to 'popular culture' – art directed at the mass audience. Workers and peasants were encouraged to produce their own culture – Proletkult (proletarian cultural movement). This was to be a collective culture in which the 'I' of bourgeois culture would give way to 'we'. Some of the more extreme members of the Proletkult movement wanted to do away with existing libraries and art galleries, jettisoning the bourgeois culture of the past.

Proletkult was the idea of Alexander Bogdanov, Lunacharsky's brother-in-law. Bogdanov wanted to make art responsive to the needs of the working class and encouraged the masses to participate actively in making art. He set up studios, poetry circles, folk theatres and exhibitions. By 1920, there were around 400,000 Proletkult members, including 80,000 active in art studios and clubs. Bogdanov believed that proletarian art would move people towards Communism.

Lunacharksy was sympathetic to these ideas and believed that Proletkult should be independent of political control. Initially it was exempt from supervision. But it seemed to be developing as an independent working-class organisation, something the Bolsheviks would not tolerate, and so Lenin, antagonistic to the philosophy of Proletkult, had its regional and central offices shut down during 1921 and 1922.

How did the Bolsheviks use art in propaganda?

The Bolsheviks were anxious to harness art to the service of the new state. There had been a flowering of creativity in the arts in Russia in the years just before the revolution and this lasted into the 1920s. Innovators in the arts, the 'avant-garde', rejected the art of the past as linked with the bourgeois way of life which was to be destroyed. In the years immediately after the revolution, many of Russia's finest artists took part in the Soviet cultural experiment. The Bolsheviks wanted to keep well-known artists on their side if possible, and many artists, for their part, were encouraged by the ending of tsarist censorship. Indeed, artistic freedom was one area which the Bolsheviks encouraged in the first years after the revolution.

Artists of the avant-garde were excited by the revolution and embraced it. They wanted to communicate directly with the masses. Futurists like Mayakovsky and Malevich revolted against the boring old world. Like many fellow artists elsewhere in Europe, they were fascinated by machines and modern technology and wanted to reflect this in their art. Constructivists like Rodchenko, Tatlin and Lissitsky wanted to create a new proletarian culture based on the worker and on industrial technology. They concentrated on designing clothes, furniture, offices and everyday objects in an 'industrial style', using straight lines and geometrical shapes which they thought would liberate people. These two avant-garde schools influenced each other and sometimes it was difficult to tell a Futurist from a Constructivist.

Kasimir Malevich (1878–1935)

Malevich believed in the supremacy of geometric forms over realism and created his own system of art, Suprematism. Malevich is seen now as an important figure in the development of modern art though his work would have made a limited impact on workers, peasants and most Bolsheviks. He was regarded with suspicion and arrested in 1930. On his release he returned to more figurative painting but he did not toe the line completely. When he was buried in 1935, it was in a coffin decorated with Suprematist designs he had painted himself.

SOURCE 16.12 *Three Female Figures* K. S. Malevich, 1928–32

Vladimir Mayakovsky (1893–1930)

Mayakovsky was a young poet, playwright and artist of great energy who had joined the Social Democrats at the age of fifteen and was repeatedly jailed as a teenager for subversive activity. He was a Futurist and naturally welcomed the revolution wholeheartedly. He worked with the Bolsheviks producing posters and 3000 captions or slogans on a wide range of topics, from encouraging resistance during the Civil War to getting people to drink boiled water during an epidemic.

His play *The Mystery Bouffe* was a parody of the Biblical flood in which the unclean (proletariat) triumph over the clean (bourgeoisie). This was produced by Meyerhold (see page 313) as were the satires *The Bedbug* and *The Bath House*, fierce attacks on the smugness of petty leaders which exposed Communist bureaucracy. Both plays were soon withdrawn.

Mayakovsky was very egotistical: his first play was *Vladimir Mayakovsky* and his first book of poems *'I'*. His autobiography *I Myself* hardly showed him as the collective man. By 1930, he had grown disillusioned with the Communists. Always emotionally volatile, unhappy in love and denied a visa to go abroad, he committed suicide in April 1930. In 1935, when Mayakovsky was safely dead, Stalin proclaimed him 'the best and most gifted poet of our Soviet epoch'. Study of his work became compulsory in schools but his satires were not mentioned and neither was his interest in Futurism nor his suicide.

SOURCE 16.13 A ROSTA window poster produced by Mayakovsky to mark 'Remember Red Army Barracks Day' in 1920. The slogans read as follows:

1) We've finished off Russia's White Guards. That's not enough.
2) The ogre of world capitalism is still alive.
3) That means we still need the Red Army.
4) And that means we've got to help it out – the task is clear

SOURCE 16.14 Mayakovsky in front of propaganda posters in the window of ROSTA, the Petrograd telegraph office

Vladimir Tatlin (1885–1953)

Tatlin's 'Monument to the Third International' (the Comintern) was to be a tower twice the height of the Empire State Building. It was to be made of glass and iron and contain revolving glass shapes – cylinder, hemisphere, pyramid and cube – which would revolve at different rates: once a year, once a month or once a day. It was also to contain a propaganda centre equipped with telegraphy, telephone and radio, and a vast open-air screen. It was completely impractical and never got beyond the model stage.

SOURCE 16.15
Tatlin's Monument to the Third International 1919–20

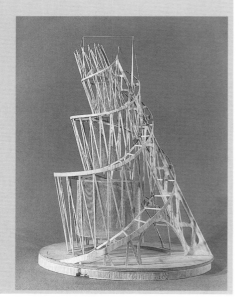

SOURCE 16.16 A classic image of Soviet industrial art from the mid-1920s. The caption reads 'Lenin is Steel and Granite'

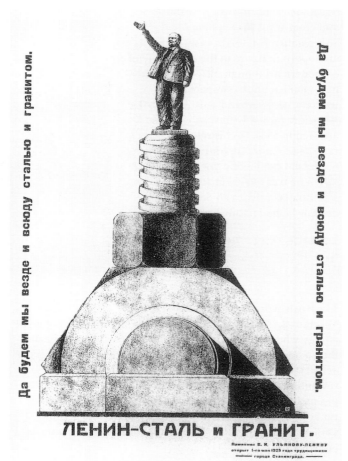

SOURCE 16.17 A Soviet poster celebrating the electrification of Russia

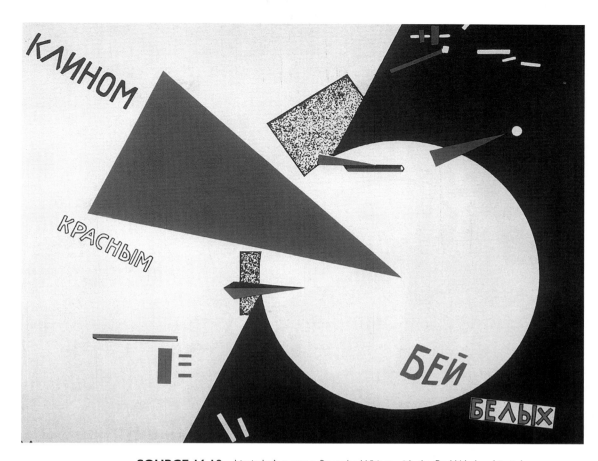

SOURCE 16.18 Lissitsky's poster, *Beat the Whites with the Red Wedge*. Lissitsky was influenced by Malevich and the belief that the pure geometric form was superior to representational art. In this poster he expressed a political idea clearly and simply through an arrangement of geometric shapes

Agitational art

The avant-garde artists were drawn into producing propaganda for the Bolsheviks. Malevich and Lissitsky produced 'agitprop art' and their designs were reproduced on agitprop trains (mobile propaganda centres; see Source 7.10, page 138), ships and banners, and above all, on posters displayed in the Petrograd ROSTA (Russian Telegraph Agency) windows. More than 1000 ROSTA posters were created over a two-year period. Agitprop theatre broke down barriers between actors and audience, encouraging the audience to respond vocally to the actions of the play. Meyerhold and other directors produced street plays designed to stir up hatred of the old bourgeoisie and encourage people to support the new regime.

Lenin wanted to take art into the streets and had a plan for monumental propaganda. He proposed that the streets of the major cities should display posters and slogans to educate the citizens 'in the most basic Marxist principles and slogans'. So Moscow City Soviet was draped with the huge banner 'The proletariat has nothing to lose but its chains'. Even more important than these slogans, in Lenin's view, were statues 'of great figures of social and revolutionary activity'. He provided a list of 66 names and personally unveiled the joint statue of Marx and Engels on the first anniversary of the revolution.

SOURCE 16.19 Lenin makes a speech at the unveiling of the memorial to Marx and Engels in Moscow, on the first anniversary of the October Revolution, in 1918

SOURCE 16.20 A detail from a ROSTA window poster. The early posters were done as single copies but later ones were stencilled and reproduced hundreds of times. The posters were not always easy to interpret but the message of this one is very clear

Another element of mass agitational art was street processions. These built on a rich tradition of public festivals and, in the Orthodox tradition, icons were carried across the village or town, though now they were Communist rather than religious icons. May Day and the anniversary of the October Revolution became the great ritual festivals of the new atheist Marxist-Leninist state. Lenin encouraged popular revolutionary celebrations but he wanted them to be carefully organised and controlled rather than spontaneous.

Probably the best example of mass street theatre was the great re-enactment of the storming of the Winter Palace in November 1920. It involved 10,000 people and included the Winter Palace itself as, in the words of the director, 'a gigantic actor and a vast character in the play ... each one of the 50 windows of the first floor will in turn show a moment of the development of the battle inside.' There were fireworks and music – indeed it was far more dramatic and more damaging to the building than the original event. It was a stage-managed October as it should have happened, with Lenin directing.

Cinema

The shortage of supplies of film equipment made film production very difficult during the Civil War, but by the summer of 1918 the agitproptrains were in action and equipped to spread political propaganda through films, plays and other media far and wide. In the early 1920s a special unit, Proletkino, was formed specifically for the production of political films in line with party ideology.

In 1925, however, the Politburo's decision not to intervene in matters of form and style in the arts allowed the Soviet cinema a brief period of great creativity. The most outstanding film-maker of this period was Eisenstein, who was anxious to show the power of the people acting together, as in his famous film of the Bolshevik revolution, *October*. However, Soviet audiences tended to prefer Hollywood comedies to his sophisticated work. Although the number of cinemas grew fast, and 300 million tickets were sold in 1928, the cinemas were almost entirely restricted to the towns. In 1928, the first All-Union Party Congress on Film Questions met and tighter control was imposed. It ruled that films should be accessible to the mass audience, and emphasised socialist ideas along strict party lines.

SOURCE 16.21 B. Williams, *Lenin*, 2000, p. 162

Cinema was, in theory, the ideal medium of propaganda, visual, technological, controllable. Lenin was especially keen for it to be used in areas where cinemas 'are novelties, and where therefore our propaganda will be particularly successful'. He recommended concentration on documentary film and newsreels, the making of short agitki on scientific topics, and encouraged the use of cinemas on agit-trains. He agreed that capital should be sought from private sources at home and abroad, 'on the condition that there should be complete guarantee of ideological direction and control by the government and the party', a statement which summed up his whole approach to the cultural revolution he so much desired. For Lenin propaganda, education and cultural development were not peripheral aims but absolutely central to the building of socialism.

Sergei Eisenstein (1898–1948)

SOURCE 16.22 Still from Eisenstein's film *Battleship Potemkin*

Eisenstein was the best-known Soviet film director of the twentieth century. He worked with the Bolsheviks and for the Moscow Workers' Theatre before moving into the film industry. His first film was *Strike* (1924), with a clear message about how the workers were oppressed and how they could resist. Two of his best-known films were commissioned by the Central Committee: *Battleship Potemkin* (1925) and *October* (1928). His radical new filming techniques, editing together different images to build tension and produce a dramatic climax, are seen most famously in the 'Odessa Steps' scene in *Battleship Potemkin* and contributed to its huge international success.

October provided the classic heroic images of the revolution, but was far more dramatic than the reality; more people were killed and more damage was done to the Winter Palace than in the real event. However, the film was strongly criticised by the party leadership. The first All-Union Party Congress on Film Questions ruled that Socialist Realism was the only acceptable artistic style. In 1926, Stalin proposed that Eisenstein should make a film on the need for collectivisation. Eisenstein relied on his experimental style and focused on tractors and a cream separator to symbolise the transition from primitive farming to the mechanised modern agriculture. The film was excessively re-edited on Stalin's orders and re-titled *The Old and the New*. It was released in 1929.

Eisenstein was attacked during the Cultural Revolution of 1928 to 1931 (see page 302) and fell out of favour. He did not come back into favour until he made *Alexander Nevsky* in 1938. This film was commissioned by Stalin. It featured the Russian prince Alexander Nevsky who defeated invading German knights in a battle in 1242. The film was intended to strengthen Russian nationalism in the face of the growing threat from Nazi Germany. It ended with Nevsky saying 'Go tell everyone in foreign parts, anyone who comes to us with a sword will perish by the sword.' It was withdrawn after the Nazi–Soviet Pact in 1939 but became required viewing once Germany had invaded the USSR. Eisenstein was later to make a two-part film on Ivan the Terrible, one of Stalin's heroes.

TALKING POINT

What does the rise, fall and rise again of Eisenstein tell us about the relationship between the government and the cinema?

298

WERE SOVIET CULTURE AND SOCIETY TRANSFORMED BY THE OCTOBER REVOLUTION?

FOCUS ROUTE

Make notes on:
- the aims of Communist education
- changes in schooling
- the liquidation of illiteracy
- the role of youth organisations.

TALKING POINT

Before reading this section, discuss ways you would expect the Communist regime to change education, particularly the school curriculum.

How much change occurred in education?

For Lenin, education was an essential building block in creating a socialist society. Each child was to receive nine years of free, universal education. The aim was to combine education and political propaganda; Lenin did not believe that education could be 'politically neutral'. The 1919 Party Programme defined schools as 'an instrument for the Communist transformation of society'. Even learning the alphabet could carry a political message: A = All power to the soviets, B = Bolsheviks, C = Communist; and simple rhymes spelt out the achievements of Soviet power. Pupils were to be cleansed of 'bourgeois' ideas. Religious teaching was to be replaced by an emphasis on Communist values and atheism.

Schools were placed under the Commissariat for Enlightenment. The head of the Commissariat, Lunacharsky, was interested in progressive Western teaching ideas, such as those of John Dewey which stressed 'learning by doing' and the importance of work and play. So between 1919 and 1920, schools were encouraged to follow a more liberal line focusing on the development of the child's personality. The authority of teachers was reduced and they were designated as 'school workers' who shared administrative control with committees drawn from older pupils and factory workers. Teachers were forbidden to discipline pupils or set homework and examinations. Some radicals wanted to do away with schools altogether.

On the whole, schooling was a disaster area. The new school system failed, although in many areas it was never put into use. The vast majority of teachers were not Communists (3.1 per cent in primary schools and 5.5 per cent in secondary schools), had a poor understanding of progressive methods and did not know what was expected of them. Teaching went on much as it had done before the revolution, only worse because teachers had lost their authority. As a result, this more liberal approach was abandoned and more traditional methods restored with the introduction of the NEP in 1921.

Matters did not, however, improve much. Under the NEP, financial pressures meant that the idea of universal schooling had to be abandoned. Many children left school: by 1923, the numbers of schools and pupils were barely half the totals of two years earlier. Schools did not have the proper resources and the teachers were very badly paid (in 1925, a teacher received a fraction of an industrial worker's pay). There was also a lasting legacy of falling standards and failure of authority in many schools (see Source 16.25).

SOURCE 16.25 R. Pipes, *A Concise History of the Russian Revolution*, 1995, p. 315. Pipes believes that the following extract, written in the style of a fifteen-year-old boy's diary, reflects the atmosphere of the early Soviet classroom

October 5
Our whole school group was outraged today. This is what happened. A new school worker came to teach natural science, Elena Nikitishna Kaurova, whom we named Elnikitka. She handed out our assignments and told the group: 'Children!'

Then I got up and said: 'We are not children.'

To which she: 'Of course you are children, and I won't call you any other way.'

I replied: 'Please be more polite or we may send you to the devil.'

Elnikitka turned red and said: 'In that case be so good as to leave the classroom.'

I replied: 'In the first place, this is not a classroom but a laboratory and we are not expelled from it . . . you are more like a teacher of the old school. Only they had such rights.'

That was all. The whole group stood up for me. Elnikitka ran off like she was scalded.

In the 1920s there were two main strands in the school curriculum:

- general education, which included learning about Communism and the history of the revolution
- practical education, focusing on technical subjects and industrial training, with visits to factories, state farms and power stations.

The Bolsheviks wanted to increase the number of party members, especially those from working class or peasant backgrounds, who had engineering and technical skills. However, the new Soviet citizen was also to have a knowledge of culture as well as industrial skills. The emphasis on indoctrination remained throughout the 1920s, but a survey in 1927 of schoolchildren aged eleven to fifteen showed that they had become increasingly negative towards Communist values as they got older, and nearly 50 per cent still believed in God.

Literacy

Before the revolution, the illiteracy rate was about 65 per cent. This explains some of the Bolshevik emphasis on visual propaganda, and sending agitprop trains all over the country. The Bolsheviks attached great importance to universal literacy so that all citizens could be both exposed to their propaganda and taught modern industrial skills. In December 1919, the 'liquidation of illiteracy' was decreed for all citizens aged between eight and 50. Illiterates who refused to learn faced criminal prosecution. Tens of thousands of 'liquidation points' were set up in cities and villages and between 1920 and 1926 some five million people in European Russia went through literacy courses.

Youth organisations

The Bolsheviks did not leave indoctrination to non-Communist teachers. They had a mission to capture the hearts and minds of the young. Two youth organisations were set up: the Pioneers for children under fifteen and the Komsomol for those from the age of fourteen or fifteen into their twenties. The duty of these organisations was to inculcate Communist values and to promote loyalty to the working class. In later years, they were used as instruments as social control and to promote discipline in schools. The Pioneers were much like the Boy Scouts, with activities, trips and camping. The Komsomol was much more serious and was used by the Communist Party to take propaganda into the towns and villages and to attack religious beliefs and bourgeois values. Komsomol membership was seen as a preparation for entry into the Communist Party. The Komsomol played a very important role in the Cultural Revolution of 1928–31 (see pages 302–303).

SOURCE 16.26 *He Who is Illiterate is Like a Blind Man. Failure and Misfortune Lie in Wait for Him on All Sides.* A poster promoting literacy from 1920

SOURCE 16.27 A member of the Komsomol

300

WERE SOVIET CULTURE AND SOCIETY TRANSFORMED BY THE OCTOBER REVOLUTION?

FOCUS ROUTE

Make notes on these key areas:

• Bolshevik policy towards the Church
• the Church's response
• the significance of the 1921–22 famine
• Lenin's attitude to the campaign against the Church during the famine
• the impact of Communist policies by 1929.

D What impact did the Bolsheviks have on religion?

The Bolsheviks were aggressively atheistic. They saw religion as a sign of backwardness. Lenin declared that the party's aim was to 'destroy the ties between the exploiting classes and the organisation of religious propaganda', and replace it with scientific education. Lenin forecast that 'Electricity will take the place of God. Let the peasant pray to electricity; he is going to feel the power of the central authorities more than that of heaven.' This attitude brought the Bolsheviks into direct conflict with the Orthodox Church, which was central to the lives of millions of peasants and an integral part of the village community.

In January 1918, the Bolsheviks issued the Decree on the Separation of Church and State which declared that the Church could not own property, church buildings had to be rented and religious instruction in schools was outlawed. Priests and clerics were declared 'servants of the bourgeoisie'. This meant that they were not allowed to vote and did not receive ration cards, or got those of the lowest category. Patriarch Tikhon, the head of the Orthodox Church, denounced the Bolsheviks and called upon the faithful to resist them by all possible spiritual means. The battle was on for the people's soul.

The Bolsheviks mounted an enormous propaganda onslaught. In 1921, the Union of the Militant Godless was established, with branches across the country. It held events such as debates to prove that God did not exist. It had its own newspaper which attacked the clergy as fat parasites living off the peasantry. Relics and icons were ridiculed – for example, weeping icons were shown to be operated by rubber squeezers. Peasants were taken for rides in planes to show there was no God in the sky. Atheist art showed a pregnant Virgin Mary longing for a Soviet abortion. At the same time, Communism was promoted as the new 'religion'. Public and private religious rituals were Bolshevised: Christmas and Easter became Komsomol Christmas and Easter; instead of baptisms, children were 'Octobered', with new names such as Revolyutsiya and Ninel (Lenin spelt backwards); Red weddings were conducted in front of a portrait of Lenin rather than an altar, with the couple making their vows both to each other and to the principles of Communism.

This anti-clerical propaganda was accompanied by more direct action, particularly after 1921. Lenin used the famine of 1921–22 to demand that the Church surrender its valuables, including consecrated vessels used in rituals, for famine relief. Instructions were sent to local soviets to seize the valuables. But there was bitter resistance. Unarmed civilians, often old men and women, fought soldiers equipped with machine guns. More than 8000 people were executed or killed in 1922 in the anti-Church campaign, including the Metropolitan of Petrograd (a leading churchman only just below the Patriarch in rank), 28 bishops and 1215 priests.

The Politburo was alarmed by this level of resistance and decided to suspend the action. But Lenin, who saw this as the opportunity to smash the Church, overruled them. The Russian historian Volkogonov, who has enjoyed unrestricted access to Russia's archives, has seen in Lenin's papers an order from him demanding to be informed, on a daily basis, about how many priests had been shot.

SOURCE 16.28 Red Army soldiers looting a church

SOURCE 16.29 Lenin, quoted in R. Pipes, *A Concise History of the Russian Revolution*, 1995, p. 338

It is now and only now, when in regions afflicted by the famine there is cannibalism and the roads are littered with hundreds if not thousands of corpses, that we can (and therefore must) pursue the acquisition of [church] valuables with the most ferocious and merciless energy, stopping at nothing in suppressing all resistance . . . The greater the number of representatives of the reactionary bourgeoisie and reactionary clergy we will manage to execute in this affair, the better . . .

There was also a campaign to split the Church from within. The 'Living Church' movement, backed by the OGPU (which had replaced the Cheka), hailed the revolution of October 1917 as a 'Christian deed' and denied that the Communists persecuted the Church. The Soviet government, it declared, alone in the world was striving to realise 'the ideal of the Kingdom of God'. Tikhon gave in, frightened that the Church would be split permanently. The Orthodox Church leadership gave no more trouble to the Communists.

Nevertheless, the Orthodox religion was not destroyed. Surveys of the peasantry in the mid-1920s revealed that 55 per cent were still active Christians. They continued to support priests with voluntary donations and carried out centuries-old religious practices. It is a mark of the durability of the Orthodox faith that the collapse of Communism in 1991 saw the immediate revival of the Church and large congregations for services.

KEY POINTS FROM CHAPTER 16

Were Soviet culture and society transformed by the October Revolution?

1 Soviet Russia had the most liberal divorce and abortion laws in Europe, but generally they worked against women. Childcare was supposed to become the collective responsibility of the state; in reality seven to nine million children lived on the streets in gangs of orphans.

2 Alexandra Kollontai was the only woman among the leading Bolsheviks, but the impact of her radical feminist ideas was limited.

3 The Bolsheviks believed in mass art that had to serve the new state. Some avant-garde artists were initially attracted to the regime but the relationship soured as political control increased.

4 Lenin was especially keen on the cinema and Eisenstein was an outstanding film-maker, but political control curbed his freedom later on.

5 Education was an essential element in building socialism but schools in the 1920s were not one of the Bolsheviks' successes.

6 The campaign to liquidate adult illiteracy had a higher success rate.

7 The Bolsheviks were aggressively atheistic and over 8000 believers were killed in the anti-Church campaign of 1922. However, religious belief persisted, especially amongst the peasants.

17

Culture and society in a decade of turmoil

CHAPTER OVERVIEW

The second decade of Communist rule began with the Cultural Revolution of 1928–31. It involved a return to the class struggle of the Civil War, with attacks on bourgeois specialists in the industrial workplace and on kulaks in the countryside. Its radical programme had an impact on the arts, education and religion. It was followed by a 'Great Retreat': a return to traditional values in the family, an emphasis on academic standards and discipline at school, and a more conservative style in the arts.

A What was the impact of the Cultural Revolution? (pp. 302–305)

B Women and the family in the 1930s – was there a 'Great Retreat' back to family values? (pp. 305–309)

C What was the impact of Socialist Realism in the arts? (pp. 310–315)

D What happened in education after the Cultural Revolution? (pp. 315–316)

E Soviet society at the end of the 1930s: had 'a new type of man' been created? (pp. 317–320)

A What was the impact of the Cultural Revolution?

FOCUS ROUTE

Make notes on the impact of the Cultural Revolution in different parts of Soviet life by examining:

- religion
- education
- the arts.

The Cultural Revolution was part of a great upheaval in the USSR associated with the 'socialist offensive' which began at the end of the 1920s with the First Five-Year Plan. There was a return to the class warfare of the Civil War and a repudiation of everything that had gone with the compromise of the NEP. This was seen in the attack on bourgeois specialists in industry, the Nepmen and the kulaks. It was accompanied by an attack on the old intelligentsia and bourgeois cultural values. Non-Marxists working in academic subjects such as history, philosophy and science, in the cinema, the arts and literature, in schools, in architecture and in town planning were denounced. There was an attempt to find truly 'proletarian' approaches in all these fields. So it was labelled the 'Cultural Revolution'.

The Cultural Revolution was more than an attack on bourgeois values. There was a vision of what the socialist future might be like, of a society transformed. People believed great changes were imminent. They had visions of new cities with large communal living spaces where money was no longer the main means of rewarding people and transacting exchanges. There would be a 'new Soviet Man'.

Young Communists, in particular, enthusiastically took up the challenge and took the lead in taking the attack forward on many fronts. They mounted a fierce attack on religion in the villages, broke up 'bourgeois' plays by booing and criticised painters and writers who did not follow the party line. The activists had been itching to move forward towards a more proletarian society with proletarian values. They pushed matters further than the leadership wanted. The Cultural Revolution was not simply a manipulation from above; it gained a momentum of its own.

SOURCE 17.1 A Komsomol activist interviewed in Munich after the war and quoted in S. Fitzpatrick, *Everyday Stalinism*, 1999, p. 37

I saw that the older generation, worn out after years of the war and the postwar chaos, were no longer in a position to withstand the difficulties involved in the construction of socialism. I thus came to the conclusion that the success in transforming the country depended entirely on the physical exertions and the will of people like myself.

The role of the Komsomols in the Cultural Revolution

The Komsomol (Young Communist League) had been set up in 1918 to help the party. Its members were aged fourteen to twenty-eight and by 1927 it had two million members. It was an exclusive club: many applicants were rejected on grounds of immaturity or insufficiently proletarian social origins. The membership was enthusiastic and leapt at the opportunity to drive the Cultural Revolution. They were to fulfil a number of roles between 1929 and 1933:

- being 'soldiers of production' in the industrial drive; one of the first directors of the Magnitogorsk site described the local Komsomol as 'the most reliable and powerful organising force of the construction'
- imposing labour discipline; leading and joining shock brigades
- enforcing collectivisation and collecting state procurements of grain, etc.
- leading the campaign against religion
- keeping an eye on bureaucracy, exposing official abuses, unmasking hidden enemies
- weeding out students whose families had been members of the 'former people', attacking non-party professors and teachers, with the aim of making the intelligentsia proletarian
- reporting on the popular mood.

SOURCE 17.2 R. Service, *A History of Twentieth-Century Russia*, 1997, p. 199

There is no doubt that many young members of the party and the Komsomol responded positively to the propaganda. The construction of towns, mines and dams was an enormously attractive project for them. Several such enthusiasts altruistically devoted their lives to the communist cause. They idolised Stalin, and all of them – whether they were building the city of Magnitogorsk or tunnelling under Moscow to lay the lines for the metro or were simply teaching kolkhozniki (collectivised peasants) how to read and write – thought themselves to be agents of progress for Soviet society and for humanity as a whole. Stalin had his active supporters in their hundreds of thousands, perhaps even their millions ... Stalin's rule in the early 1930s depended crucially upon the presence of enthusiastic supporters in society.

ACTIVITY

Study Sources 17.1–17.3. What was the role of the Komsomols in the Cultural Revolution?

SOURCE 17.3 A Soviet slogan

The future belongs to the Komsomols.

TALKING POINT

Does any Cultural Revolution require a body of people like the Komsomols in order to carry it through?

CASE STUDY: KOMSOMOL ACTIVITIES IN SMOLENSK

The worker and student Komsomols in Smolensk were given a major role in leading the collectivisation drive and overseeing all aspects of the harvest. The Smolensk archive contains the following resolutions passed at a Komsomol committee meeting for the whole area in April 1931:

1 Participation in the collectivisation drive, universal Komsomol enrolment in kolkhozes, and active leadership in preparation for the spring sowing
2 A major role in fulfilling the figures for industrial production during the year
3 An intensified campaign to enlist industrial and farm workers in the Komsomol and to establish a Komsomol cell in every kolkhoz and sovkhoz (state farm)
4 Prepare for military service, help to liquidate illiteracy among draftees, and provide political instructors for them.

The Komsomol members were also called upon to serve as pace-setters in industry and transport. They were required to enrol in technical courses to improve their qualifications, to organise shock brigades, and to encourage competition between different groups of workers. They were also expected to conduct campaigns to shame the laggards and discourage loitering on the job.

Impact on religion

The Cultural Revolution produced another onslaught on the Church and the priests who were part of the 'old world'. The Soviet government stressed the link between kulaks and churchgoers, accusing priests of supporting the peasants in their resistance to collectivisation. Priests were hounded out of the villages, churches were raided and church bells were melted down for industrialisation funds. The state imposed punitive taxes on churches and their priests. Peasants resisted, especially women, and were prepared to pay the taxes if they possibly could. But, by the end of 1930, 80 per cent of the country's village churches were closed.

Only one in 40 churches was functioning by the end of the 1930s, the others had either been knocked down or were being used for secular purposes. No churches were allowed in the new cities and towns. The number of active Orthodox priests fell from around 60,000 in the 1920s to only 5665 by 1941. More priests, mullahs and rabbis were killed during this period than during the Civil War. By 1939, only twelve out of 168 bishops active in 1930 were still at liberty.

Impact on education

Traditional teaching and discipline came under attack, as did textbooks, homework and testing an individual's academic achievement. Shulgin, a radical who headed an education research institute, put forward his theory of 'the withering away of the school'. He favoured the project method where education focused on 'socially useful work' which meant both practical production work and public activism. He said that a child could be socially useful by gathering firewood, working in a factory, teaching peasants to read or distributing anti-religious literature. The child could not, however, be socially useful by sitting in a classroom reading books or solving mathematical problems.

Shulgin believed schools should be directly linked to factories. This could lead to a very narrow education: at one school all the children in the upper years were trained to be 'poultry breeding technicians' and in central Asia children aged eleven to thirteen were exploited as cotton pickers for weeks on end. On the other hand, factory managers were not very happy about having untrained and undisciplined children getting in the way of their production targets.

Although the Cultural Revolution in schools did not last long, it had a lasting effect on the teachers. Many older non-party teachers were driven out, branded as 'bourgeois specialists', and replaced by 'red specialists'. The drive to create 'red specialists' can be seen, too, in the order from the Central Committee to send 1000 party members to technical colleges to study for higher degrees. Sheila Fitzpatrick has calculated that during the First Five-Year Plan, 150,000 workers and Communists, making up nearly a quarter of all students in higher education, began technical and political courses (*The Russian Revolution 1917–1932*, 1994, page 84).

SOURCE 17.4 Shulgin, quoted by S. Fitzpatrick in 'Revolution and Counter-Revolution in the Schools' in R. V. Daniels (ed.), *The Stalin Revolution*, 1990

You go into the classroom. Everyone stands up. Why do they need to do that? … Why? Well, it is the old residual past; the old dying order; the old type of relationship between adults and children, 'bosses' and 'subordinates', the 'teacher' and 'pupil'. An awful fart, a fart of the past … It must be driven out of the school, driven out.

■ 17A Key events

1929	Lunacharsky replaced as Commissar for Popular Enlightenment. Cultural Revolution coincides with the industrialisation drive.
1930	Mayakovsky commits suicide; Malevich under arrest for three months in 1930.
1931	Stalin's speech about the value of the tsarist-educated intelligentsia indicates that the Cultural Revolution is at an end.
1932	The RAPP abolished.

Impact on the arts

Art

With the intensification of the class war associated with the Cultural Revolution, some old master paintings were vandalised as products of bourgeois culture, and some galleries began to label exhibits according to the class origins of the artists. The major artist association changed its name to Association of Artists of the Revolution in 1928 and then to the Russian Association of Proletarian Artists in 1931. The emphasis was on the proletarian background of artists; more traditional artists like Aleksandr Gerasimov and Isaak Brodsky (see page 314), two of the leading realist painters, were attacked. Realist painters left the organisation, unable to adapt to the new demands.

Literature

The RAPP (Russian Association of Proletarian Writers) was the radical left-wing organisation which became the dominating force in literature during the Cultural Revolution. The RAPP was used to control Soviet writers and to fight 'deviations in literature' and 'fellow travellers' (non-party writers) who did not toe the proletarian line. Socialist construction and class struggle had to be at the heart of literature. Artistic brigades were organised, such as the 'First Writers' Brigade in the Urals', which sang the praises of industrialisation and collectivisation. For some writers it was too much: after witnessing the horrors of collectivisation Boris Pasternak was unable to write at all for a year.

Cinema

In an article 'We have no Soviet cinema', written by film director Pavel Petro Bytor in April 1929, film-makers including Eisenstein were accused of doing nothing for the workers and peasants. The principal task of Soviet cinema, according to the article, was to raise the cultural level of the masses. To do this, 'You must either be from the masses yourself or have studied them thoroughly' by spending two years living their lives. Straightforward, realistic films must be made with a simple story and plot. Films must deal with cows that are sick with tuberculosis, must be 'about the dirty cowshed that must be transformed into one that is clean and bright', must be about crèches for children and collective farms. 'Every film must be useful, intelligible and familiar to the millions – otherwise neither it nor the artist who made it are worth twopence' (quoted in R. Taylor, trans. and ed., *The Film Factory: Soviet Cinema in Documents, 1936–1939*, 1988, pages 261–62).

B Women and the family in the 1930s – was there a 'Great Retreat' back to family values?

FOCUS ROUTE

1 Draw and complete a table like the one below.

	Attitudes in 1920s	Attitudes in 1930s
Family		
Marriage		

2 What were the main reasons for the Great Retreat? Make a note of your answer.

Although in the 1920s the family had been described as 'bourgeois' and 'patriarchal' it had remained a key institution. The Soviet urban marriage rate remained very high by both pre-war and contemporary European standards. However, the impact of radical policies – unregistered marriages, postcard divorces and abortion – had noticeably weakened the family. The American sociologist Nicholas Timasheff claimed that 'Millions of girls saw their lives ruined by Don Juans in Communist garb, and millions of children had never known parental homes' (*The Great Retreat: The Growth and Decline of Communism in Russia*, 1946).

The upheavals caused by collectivisation, with millions of families uprooted, and the 'quicksand society' created by rapid industrialisation, with thousands of workers constantly on the move, had added to the growing problem of social instability. There was concern over the falling birth rate, and juvenile crime was increasing as a result of the huge numbers of homeless children on the streets. Soviet society needed some anchors and the mid-1930s saw a positive move to pro-family, pro-discipline and anti-abortion policies.

This change in attitude has been called the 'Great Retreat': marriage was to be taken seriously, and children urged to love and respect their parents, 'even if they are old-fashioned and do not like the Komsomol' (*Pravda*, 1935). The change in emphasis can be seen in the new Family Code of May 1936 in which:

- abortion was outlawed except where there was a threat to the woman's life and health, and for women with hereditary diseases
- divorce was made harder: both parties were required to attend divorce proceedings and the fee for registering a divorce was raised to 50 roubles for the first divorce, 150 for the second and 300 for any subsequent divorce
- child support payments were fixed at a quarter of wages or salary for one child, a third for two, and 50–60 per cent for three or more children
- mothers with six children were to receive cash payments of 2000 roubles a year – a really substantial amount – for five years, with additional payments for each child up to the eleventh.

Around the same time, laws were passed against prostitution and homosexuality, and having illegitimate children was stigmatised.

The birth rate did rise from under 25 per 1000 in 1935 to almost 31 per 1000 in 1940. Newspapers reported prosecutions of doctors for performing abortions and some women were imprisoned for having abortions, although the punishment for women in these circumstances was supposed to be public contempt, rather than prosecution.

SOURCE 17.5   A poster with the slogan 'The wide development of a network of crèches, kindergartens, canteens and laundries will ensure the participation of women in socialist reconstruction'

■ 17B Abortion rates in Leningrad, 1930–34

By the early 1930s, Soviet doctors were performing 1.5 million abortions a year. Abortion rates were highest in the cities. Statistics, especially for illegal abortions, are notoriously unreliable, but in *Popular Opinion in Stalin's Russia: Terror, Propaganda and Dissent 1939–41*, (1997, p. 65) S. Davies provides some figures for Leningrad

Year	Births (per thousand of population)	Abortions (per thousand of population)
1930	21.3	33.9
1931	21.3	36.3
1932	20.7	34.0
1933	17.0	36.7
1934	15.9	42.0

Divorce declined in Leningrad, but so too did marriage and by 1939 the marriage/divorce ratio was not much better than in 1934 – about 3.5 marriages for every divorce. Because of the high rate of desertion by husbands, many women ended up as the sole breadwinner for families which often consisted of a mother, one or two children, and the irreplaceable *babushka* (grandmother) who ran the household. At all levels of society, though most notably at its lower levels, it was women who bore the brunt of the many problems of everyday life in the USSR. However research, including interviews with refugees carried out by Harvard University's Russian Research Center, shows that the family was resilient and the state's change of attitude to the family in the middle of the 1930s was positively received.

TALKING POINT

A draft of the Family Code was published for public discussion. In the debate on abortion in the USSR there was nothing about the foetus's 'right to life' and little on women's right to control their own bodies (unlike the debate in the USA in the late twentieth century). The big issue was whether women whose material circumstances were very poor should be allowed to have abortions. The shortage of urban housing, which forced families into miserably confined spaces, and the high rate of desertion by husbands were major factors in this. While almost all participants in the discussion agreed that access to abortion should be restricted, total prohibition was deeply unpopular with urban women. How important do you think abortion on demand is to women's rights?

Juvenile crime was perceived as an increasing problem in the first half of the 1930s. For juvenile offenders, the law was relatively mild and rehabilitation was preferred. In 1935, Voroshilov, a member of the Politburo, signalled a change when he urged that the NKVD should be instructed to clear Moscow immediately not only of homeless adolescents but also of delinquents out of parental control. 'I don't understand why we don't shoot these scoundrels,' he concluded. A Politburo decree in April 1935 allowed just that. It made violent crimes committed by juveniles from twelve years of age punishable in the same way as those committed by adults, though the archives show no examples of actual executions of adolescent hooligans. This was followed by a law 'on the liquidation of child homelessness and lack of supervision', which increased NKVD involvement in attempting to get children off the streets and into appropriate institutions. Parents could be fined for the hooliganism of their children and risked having them taken away and placed in orphanages where parents would have to pay for their maintenance.

SOURCE 17.6   S. Fitzpatrick, *The Russian Revolution 1917–1932*, 1994, p. 151

The old-style liberated woman, assertively independent and ideologically committed on issues like abortion, was no longer in favour. The new message was that the family came first, despite the growing numbers of women who were receiving education and entering professional careers. No achievement could be greater than that of the successful wife and mother. In a campaign inconceivable in the 1920s, wives of members of the new Soviet élite were directed into voluntary community activities that bore a strong resemblance to the upper-class charitable work that Russian socialist and even liberal feminists had always despised. At a 'national meeting for wives' in 1936, the wives of industrial managers and engineers described their successes in cleaning up factory kitchens, hanging curtains in the workers' hostels, advising the working girls on personal hygiene and how to keep out of trouble, and so on.

SOURCE 17.7   S. Kotkin, *Magnetic Mountain: Stalinism as a Civilisation*, 1995, p. 179

In the Magnitogorsk newspaper in May 1936 abortion was pronounced 'an evil holdover from the order whereby an individual lived according to narrow, personal interests and not in the interests of the collective. In our life there is no such gap between personal and collective life. For us it seems that even such ultimate questions as the family and the birth of children are transformed from personal to social issues.' This was a long way from the 'abolition of the family as the basic cell of society' announced in the Magnitogorsk newspaper back in 1930.

SOURCE 17.8   A statement in the Soviet press in 1934, quoted in N. Timasheff, *The Great Retreat: The Growth and Decline of Communism in Russia*, 1946

There are people who dare to assert that the Revolution destroys the family; this is entirely wrong: the family is an especially important phase of social relations in socialist society ... One of the basic rules of Communist morals is that of strengthening the family ... The right to divorce is not a right to sexual laxity. A poor husband and father cannot be a good citizen. People who abuse the freedom of divorce should be punished.

SOURCE 17.9   *Pravda*, 28 May 1936

When we talk of strengthening the Soviet family we mean the fight against the wrong attitudes towards marriage, women and children. Free love and a disorderly sex life have nothing in common with Socialist principles or the normal behaviour of a Soviet citizen ... The outstanding citizens of our country, the best of Soviet youth, are almost always devoted to their families.

SOURCE 17.10   Extracts from letters sent to *Rabonitsa*, a women's magazine, in 1936. These letters would have been carefully selected for publication

From Tatanya Koval of the Lubchenko collective farm, Kiev district
I can't find the words to express my gratitude to the Party and the Government, to dear comrade Stalin for his care of us women ... My children are my joy. I've never had an abortion, and I'm not going to have any. I've borne children and I shall go on bearing them.

From Nina Ershova, Moscow
If a mother has seven children one has to be sent to school, another to the kindergarten, the third to a crèche; and then in the evening Mother has to collect them all, give them supper, look after their clothes, put them to bed ... Well, then that mother ... won't have a single minute left to herself. This surely means that women will be unable to take part in public life, unable to work.

This new law undoubtedly has much in its favour, but it is still too early to talk of prohibiting abortion. We must first develop our communal restaurants so that a woman does not have to bother about dinners, suppers and breakfast ... We must have more and better crèches and kindergartens, more laundries.

ACTIVITY

Study Sources 17.6–17.10.

1 What change do these sources suggest is taking place in attitudes to the family?
2 How do Sources 17.7–17.10 show how the Soviet regime was managing this change in attitudes?
3 Which letter writer in Source 17.10 is closest to the original revolutionary view about abortion and the role of women in society?

FAMILY LOYALTY OR CONSCIENCE OF THE NATION?
THE CASE OF PAVLIK MOROZOV

The real Pavlik

In a trial in 1932, thirteen-year-old Pavlik testified that his father, a poor peasant who had become chairman of the village soviet, had taken property confiscated from the kulaks. Pavlik's furious grandfather and cousin later stabbed him and his younger brother to death in the woods.

The legend of Pavlik

Pavlik's father secretly helped local kulaks by selling them false documents. In court Pavlik denounced him as a traitor. When Pavlik later denounced kulaks in the village for hiding and spoiling their grain, some of them ambushed him and killed him in the woods. They received the death sentence.

His symbolic importance

The legendary Pavlik was celebrated in song, statue and story. Those who were young in the 1930s recall being told at Pioneer and Komsomol meetings that it was their duty to report all suspicious events, following Pavlik's example.

Pavlik embodied the 'good' Soviet citizen who was 'above all, a member of the Soviet community, and only incidentally of the family group with which he could only identify himself if the group was in tune with the whole Soviet group. In rejecting his family and in denouncing his father, Pavlik Morozov was simply turning towards the group of which he was fundamentally a member. With the years, his story assumed a more definite content. More than towards the group, it was towards the Father of the group that he turned, towards Stalin ... Is it surprising that in the years of the purges his example was followed by countless children? ... the constantly presented influence of this example must not be underestimated for it had gradually placed the whole of society under Stalin's parental authority.' (Helene Carrère D'Encause, *Stalin: Order Through Terror*, 1981, pages 76–77)

TALKING POINT

1 How do you explain the differences between the real and the legendary Pavlik?
2 It has been argued that in the 1930s, in some respects, families drew closer for self-protection. 'We talked freely only in our own family. In difficult times we came together' (Harvard Project quoted in S. Fitzpatrick, *Everyday Stalinism*, 1999, page 140). Do you think this was more likely to happen than children following Pavlik's example?

C What was the impact of Socialist Realism in the arts?

FOCUS ROUTE

Make notes on what happened in the 1930s in the following areas:

• painting
• music
• literature
• cinema.

■ 17C Key events in the arts, 1931–38

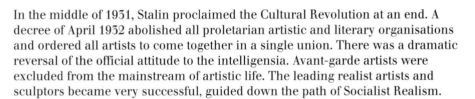

1931	Stalin makes a speech emphasising the value of the tsarist-educated intelligentsia.
1932	A party resolution is passed abolishing aggressive and competing proletarian organisations. RAPP is abolished and the Union of Composers and the Union of Architects are formed.
1933	Union of Writers formed. Zhdanov outlines the doctrine of 'Socialist Realism'.
1934	Architectural competition to design the 'Palace of Soviets' is won by a plan to build a 300-metre tower (taller than the Empire State Building) topped by a 100-metre statue of Lenin (taller than the Statue of Liberty). (It is never built.)
1936	Stalin criticises Shostakovich's opera *Lady Macbeth of Mtsensk*. The party issues decrees against 'formalism' in architecture and painting. (Formalism is defined as 'non-accessible, non-realistic, non-socialist'.)
1937–39	Purges hit the arts: around 1500 writers are killed, including the poet Mandelstam, the theatre director Meyerhold and the short story writer Babel.
1938	Eisenstein makes the film *Alexander Nevsky* which is in tune with growing nationalism and concern about impending war.

In the middle of 1931, Stalin proclaimed the Cultural Revolution at an end. A decree of April 1932 abolished all proletarian artistic and literary organisations and ordered all artists to come together in a single union. There was a dramatic reversal of the official attitude to the intelligensia. Avant-garde artists were excluded from the mainstream of artistic life. The leading realist artists and sculptors became very successful, guided down the path of Socialist Realism.

SOURCE 17.11 *Industrial Worker and Collective Farm Girl*, a sculpture by Vera Mukhina exhibited at the Paris Fair in 1937

What was Socialist Realism?

Although the origins of 'Socialist Realism' lay with Lenin's view that art and literature must educate the workers in the spirit of Communism, the term appears for the first time in 1932. In 1934, the newly founded Union of Writers proclaimed Socialist Realism to be the 'definitive Soviet artistic method'. Stalin liked realism – art which could be easily understood by the masses and which told a story. It would be a good vehicle for propaganda. Zhdanov said that 'Soviet literature must be able to show our heroes, must be able to glimpse our tomorrow.' Socialist Realism meant seeing life as it was becoming and ought to be, rather than as it was. Its subjects were men and women, inspired by the ideals of socialism, building the glowing future.

Art

From the beginning of the 1930s, Soviet paintings swarmed with tractors, threshing machines and combine harvesters or else peasants beaming out of scenes with tables groaning with food. It was at the height of the purges that Vera Mukhina's famous *Industrial Worker and Collective Farm Girl* (Source 17.11) was sculpted – a massive image of the Soviet people striding into a joyful future.

SOURCE 17.12 *A Collective Farm Feast*, a painting by Alesandr Gerasimov, 1937. Paintings like these were intended to reflect 'the "typical" or exceptional characteristics of the new life: i.e. the Party's concern for the labourers, which transformed inordinately heavy work into a joyful festival. Reality was very different. But such paintings were given the name in the USSR not of surrealism but of socialist realism' (I. Golomstock, *Totalitarian Art*, 1990)

■ 17D Some other titles of Socialist Realist art

Expulsion of the Kulaks (1931)
Construction of a Railway Bridge in Armenia (1933)
In the Struggle for Fuel and Metal (1933), a poster
Stakhanovites in a Box at the Bolshoi Theatre (1937)
The Factory Party Committee (1937)
Collective Farmers Greeting a Tank (1937)
Stalin and Voroshilov in the Kremlin (1938)

Anna Akhmatova (1888–1966)
Akhmatova is considered to be one of the greatest poets in Russian history. Much of her work was banned in the 1920s for being bourgeois and individualistic and she stopped writing for publication in the 1930s. It was not until after Stalin's death in 1953 that her work was published again in the Soviet Union.

The content of pictures was more tightly controlled. Artists were now given quite detailed guidelines when they were commissioned to produce specific works on a given subject. There were almost no pictures of domestic and family scenes. 'To judge from art alone Soviet man passed his entire existence in the factories, on the fields of collective farms, at party meetings and demonstrations, or surrounded by the marble of the Moscow metro!' (I. Golomstock, *Totalitarian Art*, 1990, page 193). Museum directors and their staffs received bonuses if they exceeded their targets for visitors – a big incentive to organise mass visits to their exhibitions. This ensured that more people were exposed to the message of Socialist Realism.

Music

Socialist Realism extended to music, too. Music was to be joyous and positive. Symphonies should be in a major key. Folk songs and dances and 'songs in praise of the happy life of onward-marching Soviet Man' were the acceptable sounds of music. Shostakovich's new opera *Lady Macbeth of Mtsensk* was attended by Stalin. He did not like it. It was criticised in *Pravda* in an article entitled 'Muddle instead of Music' and banned. Shostakovich never composed another opera.

Literature

By mid-1932, Stalin decided that the RAPP (Russian Association of Proletarian Writers) had served its purpose: it was criticised as being too narrow and was abolished. It was replaced by the Union of Soviet Writers which included non-proletarian and non-party writers and had Maxim Gorky (see page 315), himself a non-party member, as its first head. The degree of state control, however, was just as strong and Socialist Realism was proclaimed to be the basic principle of literary creation. In this climate, some great writers like Isaac Babel, Boris Pasternak and the poet Anna Akhmatova practised 'the genre of silence' and gave up serious writing altogether. According to Robert Service, 'No great work of literature was published in the 1930s and all artistic figures went in fear of their lives' (*A History of Twentieth-Century Russia*, 1997, page 248).

What were Socialist Realist novels like?

For Stalin, writers were the 'engineers of human souls', and Socialist Realism was 'the guiding principle': 'Literature should not be a single step away from the practical affairs of socialist construction.' From late 1929, many literary organisations began to organise writers into brigades and sent them to construction sites, kolkhozes and factories. Simple, direct language and cheap mass editions were demanded to make books accessible to a newly literate readership. There was nothing subtle about the titles: *Cement*, *The Driving Axle*, *How the Steel was Tempered*, and *The Great Conveyor Belt*.

Boris Pasternak (1890–1960)

Pasternak published his first collection of poems, which showed the influence of Futurism, in 1913. By 1917, he was established as a leading lyrical poet. Although he initially welcomed the Revolution, he soon became disillusioned by the excesses of the Bolsheviks. He was criticised as 'bourgeois' for writing about the individual, love and nature. He would not compromise with Socialist Realism in the 1930s and earned his living as a translator of classics, including Georgian works that Stalin liked. There is a story that Stalin crossed his name off an arrest list in the purges, saying, 'Don't touch this cloud dweller.' During the war he worked on his semi-autobiographical novel *Doctor Zhivago.* He could not get it published in the USSR but it was published in the West in 1957 and in 1958 he was awarded the Nobel Prize for Literature. The publication of *Doctor Zhivago* with its implicit criticism of the Communist regime led to his being persecuted inside the Soviet Union until he died in 1960. His book was finally published in the USSR in 1987.

As early as 1925, Gladkov wrote *Cement*, in which Gleb Chunalov, Soviet literature's first major hero of socialist construction, battled to bring a cement factory back into production against bureaucratic obstacles. Initially praised, by 1929 the hero was seen as too individualistic. Gladkov revised the novel after 1930 to bring it into line with the prevailing orthodoxy. The demand between 1929 and 1932 was to celebrate the little man, so Gladkov in his 1932 novel *Energy* had as his heroes a small group of construction workers.

In 1932 (after the RAPP had been closed down), the little man gave way to the hero. At the first congress of the Union of Soviet Writers in 1934 Zhdanov argued: 'It was in the decaying West that one found a preference for little heroes, minor writers and modest themes. Soviet literature, in contrast, reflected the great themes and heroism of the Soviet construction achievement.' The hallmark of the new Soviet literature, according to Zhdanov, was to be 'heroisation'.

Nikolai Ostrovsky's book *How the Steel was Tempered* fitted in well with this. Criticised when the first part came out in 1932, after 1934 it was praised as a classic work of Socialist Realism. It was the most frequently borrowed book from Magnitogorsk libraries. This book was not Stalin-centred but Ilin's *The Great Conveyor Belt* (1934) was. One of its heroes, a tractor-plant executive, in despair at the failure to get production going after the plant is built, resigns. But then he attends a Kremlin conference of economic executives at which Stalin explains the causes of current difficulties and how to overcome them. He is transformed and energised and demands, 'Send me where you will!'

HOW THE STEEL WAS TEMPERED

Nikolai Ostrovsky's hero Pavel Korchagin lives a life of self-sacrifice for 'common betterment'. After a humiliating childhood before the revolution he goes off to fight in the Civil War. Always seeking dangerous assignments, he emerges with a cracked skull and severely damaged spine but he plays his part in reconstruction after the war. He takes a correspondence course from the Red university to become a writer. Women fall in love with him but he chooses a mousy, ideologically 'unawakened' girl who works as a dishwasher. He encourages her to train to become a party member and when at last she gains admission it is a day of great happiness for him. Dying, blind and paralysed, he writes: 'I still believe that I shall return into the ranks and that in the attacking columns there will be my bayonet … For ten years the party and the Komsomol educated me in the art of resistance and the words of our leader were meant for me: "There are no fortresses that the Bolsheviks cannot take." '

The popularity of Pavel Korchagin took on cult proportions before, during and even for a few years after the Second World War. *How the Steel was Tempered* was an autobiographical novel. Ostrovsky suffered just as much as his hero but never despaired. When he wrote it, he was blind and could hardly move his hands and arms – he composed it half-writing, half-dictating – but writing it allowed him to make a contribution still.

TALKING POINT

How well does the development of the novel in these years illustrate the changes in Soviet society?

Cinema

Under the First Five-Year Plan, Stalin ordered increased production of documentaries supporting the plan's industrial objectives. Film-making came under the control of the Politburo's economic department and films had to be presented 'in a form that can be understood by the millions'. Film-makers were controlled by the 'cast-iron' scenario system. Under it, elaborately detailed scripts for new films – the subjects of which were often prescribed by Stalin – had to be precensored in the State Committee for Cinematography, and the film director had to work with colleagues whose task it was to ensure strict execution of the approved plan. No wonder there was not the same creativity and originality that there had been between 1925 and 1928.

Stalin loved watching films and had his own cinema in the Kremlin and in his *dacha* (country lodge) where he previewed new films before they could be released for the public. He particularly enjoyed musical comedy (musicals and literary adaptations dominated the film industry's output) and films which showed him as the main hero in the Civil War. He thoroughly enjoyed Charlie Chaplin films and imported Westerns. The mass audience preferred Hollywood films: Douglas Fairbanks was more popular than Eisenstein. The Bolsheviks had believed that film would be peculiarly effective and that the mass audience would be incapable of rejecting its message. Some very famous films were made, but film was much less effective than it aspired to be. The myth that the film was so powerful was more influential than the films themselves.

What were the experiences of leading figures in the arts in the 1930s?

In 1939, Isaak Brodsky, a very able draughtsman but with no great reputation outside the USSR, died honoured by the Soviet state. In the same year Vsevelod Meyerhold, who did have an international reputation, lay on the floor with a fractured hip and blood streaming from his battered face while his interrogator urinated on him. Why had they suffered such different fates?

SOURCE 17.13 Meyerhold, quoted in R. C. Tucker, *Stalin in Power: The Revolution from Above, 1928–1941*, 1992, p. 563

I, for one, find the work of our theatres at present pitiful and terrifying. This pitiful and sterile something that aspires to the title of socialist realism has nothing in common with art ... Go to the Moscow theatres and look at the colourless, boring productions which are all so alike and differ only in their degree of worthlessness ... In your efforts to eradicate formalism, you have destroyed art!

Case study: Vsevelod Meyerhold (1873–1940)

Meyerhold was a renowned theatre director and founder of the avant-garde theatre; his writings on the theatre are still read in the West today. He welcomed the revolution, became a Bolshevik, and proclaimed the beginning of a 'theatrical October'. The teacher of Eisenstein (see page 297) and the producer of Mayakovsky's satirical plays (see page 293), his Meyerhold Theatre in Moscow had an international reputation.

During the Cultural Revolution, Meyerhold and Mayakovsky were heavily criticised by the RAPP. In 1937, Meyerhold decided to produce a play based on the Five-Year Plan novel *How the Steel was Tempered* (see page 312) to celebrate the twentieth anniversary of the revolution. The horrors of the Civil War had never been shown so graphically on the stage, but it was optimistic Socialist Realism rather than genuine realism that was required and so the play was rejected. In December 1937, he was attacked in *Pravda* for failing to depict the problems which concerned every Soviet citizen. His theatre was closed in January 1938. He was accused of formalism but, at the conference of theatre directors in June 1939, said he preferred to be called a formalist than be forced into Socialist Realism.

Unsurprisingly, Meyerhold was arrested a few days later. His wife, a beautiful actress, was savagely stabbed to death in their apartment soon after. Meyerhold was horribly tortured to drag out a confession that he was a foreign spy and Trotskyite and he was shot in January 1940.

Case study: Isaak Brodsky (1884–1939)

Brodsky first came to notice when his picture of Lenin won the painting section of a competition held in Petrograd. Lenin was to remain Brodsky's main subject and his style that of the documentary photograph. His pictures, such as *Lenin's Speech at a Workers' Meeting*, portray both Lenin and the masses – two idealised elements of the USSR. The famous *Lenin at Smolny* shows Lenin absorbed in his work and his simple lifestyle despite the Civil War raging outside.

Brodsky's reputation grew in the 1920s but his style – 'too photographic' – fell out of favour during the Cultural Revolution. He was expelled from the Association of Proletarian Artists. By 1932, the Cultural Revolution was over and Brodsky was one of Stalin's favourite artists. His picture of Lenin in front of the Kremlin was the basis for the massive May Day decorations in 1932, in which Lenin and Stalin were paired as they were to be so often in the 1930s. Brodsky slavishly declared, 'A painting must be living and comprehensible. I have remembered these words of Comrade Stalin for ever.' In 1934, Brodsky was made director of the All Russian Academy of Arts and became the first artist to be awarded the Order of Lenin. He died in 1939.

SOURCE 17.15 *Lenin in Smolny* by Isaak Brodsky

ACTIVITY

1 Why was Meyerhold so criticised?
2 How well do Brodsky's paintings and methods illustrate Socialist Realism?
3 What do the experiences of Brodsky, Gorky and Meyerhold tell us about the relationship between artists and the Bolsheviks?

Case study: Maxim Gorky (pen name of A. M. Peshkov; 1868–1936)

Gorky's novels and plays gave him an international reputation and earnings which were large enough to be one of the Bolsheviks' main sources of income before 1917, although he was never actually a member of the party. The pseudonym he adopted means 'bitter' and, sent out to work at the age of eight, he knew more about the seamy side of life than almost any other Russian author. He was a humane and democratic socialist. He was critical of Lenin's seizure of power in 1917 and deeply distressed by the terror during the Civil War. The destruction appalled him and he helped to preserve both works of art and artists and intellectuals in the aftermath of the revolution. He became increasingly disillusioned with the Bolsheviks: even as early as the beginning of 1918 he wrote, 'It is clear Russia is heading for a new and even more savage autocracy.' Gorky left the country in 1921.

Stalin was desperately anxious for Gorky to return so that he could demonstrate that the most celebrated living Russian author was an admirer of the system. Gorky returned for a visit in 1928 when his sixtieth birthday was celebrated and he became a permanent resident in 1931. In 1934, he was made the first president of the Soviet Writers' Union. Former colleagues who had criticised the Bolsheviks felt he had sold out. He was flattered on a grand scale – the main street of Moscow was renamed after him, as was his birthplace Nizhny Novgorod – but he was never to be allowed to leave the Soviet Union again. By the end of his life, he regarded himself as under house arrest.

Although Gorky's health had been deteriorating, the circumstances and timing of his death have been regarded with suspicion. He died in June 1936 while receiving medical treatment. This was very convenient for Stalin, coming two months before the first show trial which Gorky was bound to have criticised openly. At his show trial in 1938 Yagoda, who was head of the NKVD in 1936, confessed to having ordered Gorky's death.

SOURCE 17.16 Gorky (left) with Stalin

In his notebooks, found after his death, Gorky compared Stalin to 'a monstrous flea which propaganda and the hypnosis of fear had enlarged to incredible proportions'. Stalin, though, led the mourners at his funeral and Gorky's ashes were placed in a niche in the Kremlin wall.

D What happened in education after the Cultural Revolution?

In the middle of 1931, the Cultural Revolution came to an end. A Central Committee resolution criticised the project method and the 'withering away of the school'. Compare the extract in Source 17.17 with Shulgin's ideas (page 304).

Stalin was outraged by the state of schools in 1931. The Komsomol's 'Cultural Army' had done enormous damage to local education authorities and wreaked havoc in the schools. Stalin needed educated workers to work in skilled jobs and be able to take advantage of the higher education and training schemes that were now on offer. The Central Committee ordered a fundamental shift in educational policy. The core recommendation was that the teaching of physics, chemistry and mathematics in particular 'must be based on strictly delineated and carefully worked out programmes and study plans', and that classes should be organised on a firm timetable. Examinations, homework, textbooks and rote learning reappeared. Discipline was emphasised and the authority of parents and teachers over pupils was supported; in the late 1930s school uniforms reappeared.

SOURCE 17.17 Central Committee resolution of 25 August 1931

[The school's basic failing is that it] does not give a sufficient amount of general knowledge, and does not adequately solve the problem of training fully literate persons with a good grasp of the bases of sciences (physics, chemistry, mathematics, native language, geography and so on) for entrance to the technicums and higher schools.

FOCUS ROUTE

Make notes answering the following questions:

I Did the Cultural Revolution have any lasting impact?

2 How far was radical change replaced by conservatism?

3 What was the impact of the changes on one subject: history?

In universities, there was also a return to something much more like the situation before the revolution. Entrance to university was based more on academic success than on class or political criteria. Examinations, degrees and academic titles were restored.

History, nationalism and education

'I like your book immensely,' wrote Lenin in the preface to M. N. Pokrovsky's *Brief History of Russia*. Published in 1920, it became *the* Soviet school text book. Pokrovsky was a historian who had been a Bolshevik since 1915 and became Deputy Commissar for Education. It was a straightforward Marxist work, which saw the whole of Russian history in terms of class struggle and included long descriptions of the brutal beatings of serfs by their owners and the dreadful working and living conditions of industrial workers. Economic forces drove history onwards, leading inevitably to socialism. Tsars and generals were barely mentioned, as Pokrovsky believed personality mattered very little in history.

The two most famous first-hand Bolshevik accounts of the revolution, John Reed's *Ten Days that Shook the World* (1919) and Trotsky's *History of the Russian Revolution*, presented the revolution as a popular rising and emphasised the role of the proletariat rather than the party in making the revolution. Lenin wrote in the foreword to Reed's book that he wanted to see millions of copies published in all languages – Stalin was much less keen, perhaps because he was not mentioned, and no Russian editions were published between 1930 and 1956.

Soon after the revolution, history was banished as a school subject because it was seen as irrelevant to contemporary life and had been used under the tsars to develop patriotism and reinforce the values of the ruling class. In the Cultural Revolution one notable historian, Professor Tarle, a non-Marxist historian and Russian patriot, who had written about Peter the Great and Ivan the Terrible, was attacked for glorifying the idea of monarchy and imprisoned. Professors could be identified as bourgeois specialists, too.

For Stalin, the Cultural Revolution was part of the great transformation of the USSR, but it did not reflect his ideas on history. By 1934, Pokrovsky had come under attack for reducing history to an abstract record of class conflict without names, dates, heroes or stirring emotions. Historians were now required to write about the imperial past in positive terms and Ivan the Terrible and Peter the Great, who expanded that empire, were looked on particularly favourably by Stalin. The term *rodina* (motherland), despised by the old Bolshevik internationalists, came back into common use. In May 1934, a decree on history teaching was issued declaring that the old ways must be replaced with 'mandatory consolidation in pupils' memories of important historical events, historical personages and chronological dates'. History faculties were restored in the universities of Moscow and Leningrad. Professor Tarle was released from prison to reoccupy his university chair in Moscow. In the new school history texts, which appeared in 1937, the years 1917–37 are 'presented as the finale of embattled Russia's long march through history from humble beginnings in the tenth century to world leadership and greatness under Lenin–Stalin' (R. C. Tucker, *Stalin in Power: The Revolution from Above, 1928–1941*, 1992, page 53). The past and its interpretation was important to Stalin. In Soviet history books, he emerged as one of the main architects of the revolution, the close companion and adviser to Lenin, and a hero of the Civil War.

TALKING POINT

What are the advantages and disadvantages of schools following a national curriculum in history and other subjects?

ACTIVITY

I How did interpretations of history change between the 1920s and the mid-1930s?

2 How did individual historians fare?

3 Did this add up to a 'Great Retreat' in history?

E Soviet society at the end of the 1930s: had 'a new type of man' been created?

Socialist construction involved not only building the structures of the socialist state but also creating the right sort of citizens to live in it. New Soviet Man would embody the morality, values and characteristics that a good Soviet citizen should possess. He would be a willing servant of the state with the right attitudes, far removed from the illiterate, uneducated peasant who exemplified the backwardness which had cursed the USSR in the past. New man was part of new modern industrial society, above all a proletarian with a sense of social responsibility and moral virtue. Creating citizens like this was the objective of the proletarianisation that was such an important part of the Cultural Revolution of 1929–31 (see page 302). The changes were aimed mainly at the young through the education system and the Komsomol youth organisation but all sorts of pressures were also brought to bear on adult workers in order to make them conform (see Chart 17E on page 318).

Pavel Korchagin, the hero of Nikolai Ostrovsky's novel *How the Steel was Tempered* (see page 312), is the archetypal new man who puts the interests of his comrades, the Bolsheviks and the revolution before himself – an example of self-sacrifice and moral virtue. Soviet writers from the mid-1920s onwards presented to the public new Soviet heroes who overcame hardship and obstacles in the cause of the construction of the new socialist society.

The idea that people could be programmed in this way drew support from the spurious theories of the Soviet scientist Trofim Lysenko, who believed that human beings could acquire characteristics that could be passed on from one generation to the next. Stalin was very much influenced by Lysenko's thinking and came to believe that socialist characteristics could be passed on if people were taught the right habits and attitudes. It was this notion of socialist programming that appalled writers such as George Orwell and Aldous Huxley, who in their books *1984* and *Brave New World* put the case against totalitarianism and its apparent need to crush individuality and the human spirit.

THE FORERUNNER OF ORWELL AND HUXLEY

Yevgeny Zamyatin is not as well known in the West as Orwell and Huxley but his novel *We*, written in 1924, was the forerunner of their books. In this Dystopia (a nightmare Utopia) the people are robot-like, known by numbers and have lives programmed in every detail. The story of D503's 'pitiful struggle against the ruler – the bald-headed Benefactor – is a plea for the right of the individual to live his life without oppressive interference from the state' (Robert Service in *A History of Twentieth Century Russia*, page 139). Zamyatin's book was banned in the USSR for sixty years.

Was a new type of man produced in Magnitogorsk?

If the new man were to be created, surely it would be at a place like Magnitogorsk where a great steel plant and a town of 150,000 people were created from nothing between 1929 and 1939? Stephen Kotkin, in his book *Magnetic Mountain: Stalinism as a Civilisation* (1995), has produced a remarkable study of the town, and what follows is based on his research. The aim at Magnitogorsk was to build not only an industrial giant but also a socialist paradise (see Chart 17E).

FOCUS ROUTE

Make notes on the forces trying to create the new man in Magnitogorsk and the evidence that the creation of a new man still had some way to go. What conclusion would you reach – had a new type of man been created?

Housing
In Magnitogorsk housing was not just for shelter; it was also designed to mould people. It was largely communal, and in every barracks there was a 'Red corner' with the barracks wall newspaper, shock-worker banners and pictures of Lenin and Stalin. It was intended to be a cultural training ground in which the dwellers could read, listen to lectures, watch films and discuss political issues.

Education
Virtually everyone in Magnitogorsk, even those who worked full time, attended some form of schooling, which reinforced the socialisation and politicisation being experienced at work. The school curriculum combined basic education with technical subjects and 'the spirit of socialism'. Compulsory courses in Marxism-Leninism began at an early age.

Public holidays
These took place on the anniversary of the October Revolution and on 1 May. The May Day parade was a highly organised procession, based on people's different places of work, with numerous floats, portraits of the leaders and Communist slogans.

Speaking Bolshevik
In Magnitogorsk you identified yourself as a 'Soviet worker' and learned to say the right things in the right way. The 'Dear Marfa!' letter (Source 13.23 on page 235) is a classic example. Kotkin found that workers in Magnitogorsk still spoke in the same way as they had in the 1930s, fifty years later.

Shock workers and socialist competition
An individual's work history recorded his or her profession, party status, record on absenteeism, study or course attendance, production achievements and how often their equipment broke down. The work histories of the shock worker, the award winner, and those who succeeded in socialist competition were made public and used to decide the distribution of material rewards.

Entertainment
More than 600,000 seats a year were sold at the cinema in Magnitogorsk: it was easily the most popular form of entertainment and a key mechanism for spreading socialist values. All Soviet films shown there carried forceful political messages. Foreign films were for pure entertainment, but no recognisably anti-socialist or overtly pro-capitalist popular culture was permitted. Newsreels were shown before and after every film. The inhabitants of Magnitogorsk read avidly: 40,000 books were sold in January 1936 and 10,000 people held library cards. Nikolai Ostrovsky's novel *How the Steel was Tempered* was the most frequently borrowed book from the Magnitogorsk libraries.

Censorship
'Censors were quintessential "social engineers", with the media serving as their instruments – or weapons, as Lenin wrote – in the battle to construct a Communist society. The instructional messages emanating from reading matter, radio, and, especially, films were paralleled by training received in schools' (S. Kotkin, *Magnetic Mountain: Stalinism as a Civilisation*, 1995)

Campaigns to improve behaviour
There were campaigns to improve men's behaviour towards women and to discourage alcohol consumption.

Use of agitators
In 1936, 214 agitators were employed to discuss political issues and present interpretations of domestic and international events.

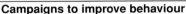

EVIDENCE THAT THE CREATION OF NEW SOVIET MAN STILL HAD SOME WAY TO GO

Housing
Private housing was never entirely eliminated, even in 1938. Privately owned mud huts (which had no 'Red corners') made up 17.5 per cent of the living space in Magnitogorsk. In the latter half of the 1930s, there was a shift away from barracks to providing apartments for families, as part of the pro-family policies then being adopted.

Preferences in entertainment
Next to the cinema, the most popular entertainment was performances of French wrestling (scripted wrestling). Attempts were made to use the circus at Magnitogorsk as a vehicle for propaganda about the Five-Year Plans and socialist construction but such attempts failed miserably – in *Beyond the Urals* (1942) John Scott describes such attempts as 'ludicrous'.

Limited success in campaigns to improve behaviour
The campaigns to improve men's behaviour towards women and to discourage alcohol consumption had very limited success.

Opposition to Stakhanovites
The case of the Magnitogorsk Stakhanovite (see page 238) shows the resentment that could be aroused. One worker remarked that Stakhanovism was an attempt to enslave the working class – he was arrested and sentenced to forced labour. Anti-Stakhanovite jokes show this resentment was felt all over the country.

The leverage that workers had
There was a perpetual labour shortage. Managers, desperate to meet their targets, could not afford to sack workers for breaking the rules on absenteeism and so on, and were prepared to take on workers sacked elsewhere. As we have seen, Magnitogorsk was a revolving door.

What was the national picture?

Magnitogorsk is just one example of the massive change that took place in the USSR in the 1930s. The regime was committed to economic, social and cultural transformation. In the First Five-Year Plan, there was massive social dislocation as ten million peasants changed occupations and moved into the towns.

By 1939, the combination of the technical education opportunities granted by the Cultural Revolution and the opportunities for upward mobility created as a result of rapid industrialisation and the purges meant that a working class/ peasant governing élite had been virtually achieved. Khrushchev, Brezhnev and Kosygin, who became key Soviet leaders in the 1950s, 1960s and 1970s, were among the 150,000 workers and Communists entering higher education during the First Five-Year Plan.

But was the mass of the people transformed? The attitude of the people to the regime is one way of assessing this. The historian John Barber estimated that one-fifth of all workers enthusiastically supported the regime and its politics, while another minority opposed, although not overtly. This left the great mass of workers, who were neither supporters nor opponents but nonetheless more or less 'accepted' the regime for its social welfare policies. NKVD soundings of popular opinion in the 1930s indicate that the regime was relatively, though not desperately, unpopular in Russian towns but much more unpopular in the villages, especially in the first half of the 1930s. The post-NEP situation was compared unfavourably with the NEP and Stalin was compared unfavourably with Lenin, mainly because living standards had fallen. The arbitrary nature of terror and rewards encouraged fatalism and passivity in the population. The historian Sheila Fitzpatrick in her book *Everyday Stalinism* (1999) has found that 'a degree of scepticism, even a refusal to take the regime's most serious pronouncements fully seriously, was the norm'. *Homo Sovieticus*, who emerges in the 1930s, may or may not be a new man, but he had to be a survivor and one 'whose most developed skill involved the hunting and gathering of scarce goods in an urban environment'.

ACTIVITY

Make a presentation to the rest of the class. Your presentation will cover changes in Soviet culture and society in the 1920s and 1930s. This can be done in groups or individually.

1 In a group, divide up the topics. Some topics are bigger than others, so two students might cover women and the family, one education, and so on.
2 Subdivide topics for individual presentations, e.g. the arts could be divided into painting, street theatre and agit-prop, literature, film and music. Students could research and report on individuals such as Malevich, Shostakovich and Mayakovsky.

WAS THERE A 'GREAT RETREAT'?

Trotsky denounced Stalin as the leader of a new privileged class and saw this as part of Stalin's betrayal of the revolution. The 1930s were a time of great shortage so access to special food rations and other scarce goods at low prices in special élite stores, together with access to better services and housing, was at the heart of privilege.

Does this inequality, combined with the change by the middle of the 1930s to more conservative policies on family values, divorce, abortion, education and the arts which we have already noticed, signify a retreat? Historians have debated this issue. Some, like Sheila Fitzpatrick, argue that there was a retreat, contrasting the revolutionary spirit of the Civil War and Cultural Revolution with the mid-1930s. They point to:

- the acceptance of hierarchy and social privilege
- respect for authority and tradition
- the return to traditional values in education, the family and the arts.

Historians who challenge this interpretation, like Stephen Kotkin and Ewan Mawdsley, argue that the creation of the new working class and the new intelligentsia meant that:

- there was no retreat on private ownership of land and the means of production, or on hiring labour
- the rest of the world saw Communist Russia as still distinctly anti-capitalist
- Stalinist culture may have embraced many of the traditions of nineteenth-century Russian realism but the content was 'modern': it was promoted to achieve objectives which the regime chose to stress – economic activity, the socialist utopia, national defence and adulation of the leader. It reflected a changing and advancing rather than a retreating society.

KEY POINTS FROM CHAPTER 17

Culture and society in a decade of turmoil

1 The Cultural Revolution of 1928–31 coincided with industrialisation and collectivisation. It saw a return to the class struggle of the Civil War.
2 The Komsomols were particularly active in enforcing the Cultural Revolution in education and art and intensifying the attack on religion.
3 After the Cultural Revolution there was a return to traditional values in many areas of Soviet society. This has been called the Great Retreat.
4 Abortion was outlawed and divorce was made harder after the introduction of the 1936 Family Code, which emphasised the value of family life.
5 In education, discipline, exams and traditional procedures were brought back.
6 Socialist Realism was the guiding principle for all artists from 1932 onwards.
7 Art was even more tightly controlled than it had been in the 1920s. Artists rose, like Brodsky, or fell, like Meyerhold, depending on how closely they followed the dictates of Socialist Realism.
8 Great writers like Pasternak were silent; lesser ones produced novels about the Five-Year Plans.
9 The Soviets were trying to produce a new type of man.
10 Their success was very limited. In spite of Stalin's terror, the Soviet people were survivors and remained sceptical.
11 There has been a debate among historians about whether there was a Great Retreat or not.

From pariah to saviour: the Soviet Union and Europe 1921–1945

SOURCE I A Communist cartoon of 1920. The caption reads 'Comrade Lenin cleans the world of filth'

ТОВ. ЛЕНИН ОЧИЩАЕТ ЗЕМЛЮ ОТ НЕЧИСТИ.

According to the orthodox Marxist view, revolution in the advanced states of Europe was essential for the success of the revolution in Russia. But this had failed to materialise. The Red Army had been defeated in the war against Poland, which Lenin had hoped would spark a European-wide revolution. All attempts at revolution in Germany and Hungary had failed. The Soviet Union was alone in a generally hostile capitalist world. Moreover, the ravages of war, revolution and civil war had left the country drained and famine stricken by 1921. The Soviet Union desperately needed to trade with capitalist countries and get economic help, so it was crucial to establish stable, working diplomatic relations with those countries. This posed a serious dilemma for Soviet foreign policy-makers since they were also committed to undermining capitalist governments.

In Chapter 18 we examine Soviet relations with Europe between 1917–1941 and why the Soviet Union came to terms with Hitler and signed a non-aggression pact with Germany. Chapter 19 looks at the Great Patriotic War and seeks to explain why a war that started disastrously ended in triumph.

SOURCE 2   Lenin, February 1921

We have always and repeatedly pointed out to the workers that the underlying chief task and basic condition of our victory is the propagation of revolution at least to several of the more advanced countries.

SOURCE 3   Lenin explaining why the Soviet Union was attending the international conference at Genoa in 1922

We go to it because trade with capitalist countries (so long as they have not altogether collapsed) is unconditionally necessary for us.

SOURCE 4   Litvinov (Commissar for Foreign Affairs), December 1933

The ensuring of peace cannot depend on our efforts alone, it requires the collaboration and co-operation of other states. While therefore trying to establish and maintain relations with all states, we are giving special attention to strengthening and making close our relations with those which, like us, give proof of their sincere desire to maintain peace and are ready to resist those who break the peace.

SOURCE 5   Stalin, speaking at the Seventeenth Party Congress, 1934

The USSR would never be swayed by alliances with this or that foreign power, be it France, Poland or Germany, but would always base her policy on self-interest.

ACTIVITY

What were the aims of Soviet foreign policy?

1   Study Sources 1–8. On your own copy of the table below, indicate which sources provide evidence of:
   a) the desire to spread revolution
   b) attempts to establish working relationships with other countries
   c) the desire to protect the Soviet Union's interests and ensure it could defend itself.

Source	Date	Desire to spread revolution	Establishment of working relationships	Defence of Soviet interests

2   What do these sources suggest about changes in Soviet foreign policy between 1920 and 1939?

SOURCE 6   Litvinov, May 1938, to the Director General of the Czech Foreign Office, comparing the situation with 1914–17

This time we shall observe the contest between Germany and the Western powers and shall not intervene in the conflict until we ourselves feel it fit to do so in order to bring about the decision.

SOURCE 7   Stalin at the Eighteenth Party Congress, March 1939

England and France have rejected the policy of collective security . . . and taken a position of non-intervention . . . the policy of non-intervention reveals an eagerness not to hinder Germany . . . from embroiling herself in a war with the Soviet Union . . .

. . . Be cautious and [do] not allow Soviet Russia to be drawn into the conflicts by warmongers who are accustomed to have others pull the chestnuts out of the fire.

SOURCE 8   The front page of a German weekly magazine, published after the Nazi–Soviet non-aggression treaty of 23 August 1939. It shows Stalin shaking hands with Ribbentrop, the German foreign minister

FOCUS ROUTE

Note the differences between the three commissars under the following headings:

- background and experience of foreign countries
- status in the party
- attitude to Germany
- other policy differences.

■ A Commissars for Foreign Affairs

Lenin kept foreign policy very much in his own hands. As in the 1930s under Stalin, the leader and the Politburo made the crucial decisions. However, the Commissar for Foreign Affairs worked out the style and delivery of policy.

G. V. CHICHERIN (1872–1936)
Foreign Commissar April 1918–July 1930
An ex-Menshevik and an aristocrat by birth, Chicherin was a highly educated but rather emotional, chaotic man. He had been employed by the tsarist foreign ministry and had extensive experience working abroad. He was in jail in Britain from August 1917 to January 1918. Lenin described him as 'an excellent worker, extremely conscientious, intelligent and learned'. He was not a member of the Politburo.

The policies he is identified with
- He always favoured close relations with Germany and helped to bring about the Treaty of Rapallo.
- He was anti-British.
- Like Lenin, he believed that the USSR was most secure when the capitalist powers were disunited, and that if the USSR were involved in, rather than isolated from, the system of capitalist international relations then this would be more likely to occur. So he pursued a policy of *peaceful coexistence*.

M. M. LITVINOV (1876–1951)
Foreign Commissar July 1930–May 1939 (Deputy Commissar 1921–30 and 1941–46)
Litvinov was an ex-Menshevik, with a Jewish background. He had spent a long time abroad, including ten years in Britain; his wife was British. He was an exceptionally talented negotiator and very good at establishing friendly relations with statesmen and opinion leaders in the democracies; a model of organisation. His influence was restricted to foreign affairs: he was not a member of the Politburo.

The policies he is identified with
- He believed that preventing all wars was in the USSR's interest. Unlike Chicherin, he favoured disarmament and signing the Kellogg Pact to outlaw war. He was a familiar figure at Geneva once the USSR had joined the League of Nations.
- He was pro-British and deeply suspicious of Germany, even in the 1920s, and he only grudgingly accepted the Treaty of Rapallo.
- He favoured collective security against fascism.

V. M. MOLOTOV (1890–1986)
Foreign Commissar May 1939–March 1949
Molotov means hammer, quite an apt name. A Bolshevik from his youth, he was never exiled abroad and had no direct experience of the world outside Russia. A member of the Politburo from 1925 (unlike Chicherin and Litvinov), he was made leader of the Comintern in 1929. He became Stalin's deputy and together they signed many death sentences during the purges. Trotsky called Molotov a 'blockhead' and other colleagues referred to him as 'stone arse' but he did exert some influence over Stalin in foreign policy and has been called 'one of the toughest negotiators of the twentieth century'. His appointment as Commissar (replacing the anti-German Litvinov) in May 1939 has been seen as sending out an encouraging signal to Germany.

The policies he is identified with
He favoured improved relations with Germany. The Nazi–Soviet pact of 1939 is often referred to as the Ribbentrop–Molotov Pact.

■ B Factors that helped to determine Soviet foreign policy during the inter-war years

When politicians make foreign policy, they are influenced by a number of different factors. For any given country, some factors are relatively constant while others vary according to the individuals involved and the circumstances in which they were operating. Here are some of the factors influencing Soviet foreign policy in the 1920s and 1930s.

Security – fear of invasion
Worries about security were increased by Russia's geography. Its frontier in the north-west and west was 3200 km long and lacked natural boundaries. As the only Communist state it was not unnatural for the Russians to fear invasion by the capitalist states. The list of invaders of Russia over the previous 800 years read like a Who's Who of military aggression and was referred to by Stalin to justify the need for rapid industrialisation under the Five-Year Plans.

Ideology
Orthodox Marxism stressed the need for revolution in other countries if socialism was to survive in the USSR. The USSR's desire to spread the revolution both at home and abroad threatened the West. Ideological differences did not rule out normal diplomacy, but they did provide the basis for mistrust. The existence of the Comintern and foreign intervention in the Civil War produced mistrust from the outset.

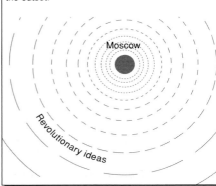

Economic backwardness
Soviet leaders were well aware of the perceived and actual technological inferiority of the Soviet state and the need for Western technological help in building Soviet industry.

FACTORS DETERMINING SOVIET FOREIGN POLICY DURING THE INTER-WAR YEARS

Attitudes of other countries
Not even the most powerful country can make policy totally uninfluenced by the actions of other countries. Foreign intervention in the Civil War left a legacy of suspicion, and the rise of Hitler and the failure of the British and French to act against him could not be ignored.

USSR, POLAND, GERMANY

The background and views of those making Soviet policy
The leaders of the country – Lenin, Trotsky and Stalin – and their Commissars for Foreign Affairs – Chicherin, Litvinov and Molotov – had an influence on policy.

The internal situation
At any given time, the internal situation was bound to impact on foreign policy. Thus the state of the country at the end of the Civil War, the power struggle to succeed Lenin, the Five-Year Plans and collectivisation all had an influence on foreign policy.

FOCUS ROUTE

Which of the factors in Chart B do you think was most important in influencing Soviet foreign policy between 1920 and 1939? Place the factors in order of importance.

Alone in a hostile world: how did Soviet foreign policy develop between 1921 and 1941?

CHAPTER OVERVIEW

In March 1919, the Comintern was set up to promote world revolution. But the Soviet Union also needed to establish diplomatic relations with countries in the capitalist world. This chapter explores Soviet relations with Britain, France and Germany. It looks first at how Lenin, and later Stalin, sought to prevent the capitalist countries ganging up against the USSR. Then it examines how Soviet policy-makers tried to deal with the threat of Hitler, initially promoting collective security against fascism. Finally, it explores the reasons why in 1939 Stalin decided to sign the Nazi Soviet Pact.

A What were the aims of Soviet foreign policy under Lenin? (p. 327)

B Why did the Comintern exist and what problems did it present? (pp. 328–329)

C What were the Soviet Union's relations with Britain and Germany between 1921 and 1933? (pp. 330–331)

D How did Stalin change Soviet foreign policy between 1924 and 1932? (pp. 332–333)

E What was collective security against fascism? (pp. 333–334)

F Why did the USSR make an agreement with Germany rather than with Britain and France in 1939? (pp. 334–341)

PHASE ONE	**Extricating Russia from the war: October 1917–March 1918**
October 1917	Decree on Peace
February 1918	Bolshevik cancellation of foreign debts
March 1918	Treaty of Brest-Litovsk

PHASE TWO	**The Civil War: 1918–20**
April 1918–September 1919	Foreign intervention in the Civil War
March 1919	Comintern (Third Communist International) set up to guide, co-ordinate and promote the Communist parties of the world.
April–October 1920	Russo-Polish war. Attempt to spread world revolution by arms defeated outside Warsaw in August.
July 1920	Second Congress of Comintern – laid on other Communist parties the overriding duty to protect the USSR.

PHASE THREE	**The need for recovery and peace: 1921–27**
March 1921	The treaty of Riga gave Poland parts of Belorussia and the Ukraine.
1921	Secret discussions with Germany on military and economic co-operation. Anglo-Soviet trade agreement.
1922	Rapallo agreement with Germany – the two countries recognise each other diplomatically. Secret military co-operation.
1924	Official recognition of USSR by Britain, France and Italy. 'Zinoviev letter' published in *The Times* newspaper in Britain.
1926	Treaty of Berlin with Germany extends the Treaty of Rapallo.
1927	Diplomatic relations between Britain and the USSR suspended (restored by Ramsay MacDonald in 1929).

PHASE FOUR	**The left turn of the Comintern: 1928–33**
1928	New, more radical Comintern line. Social Democrats (SPD) in Germany attacked as 'social fascists'. Foreign Communist party leaders suspected of following a line of their own are expelled from the Comintern and discredited. They are replaced by leaders obedient to Moscow. War scares: propaganda stressed the imminent danger of invasion.
1928–32	Rise in economic and military collaboration between the USSR and Germany.

PHASE FIVE	**Collective security against fascism: 1934–39**
March 1934	Trade agreement with Germany.
September 1934	Soviet entry into the League of Nations. Litvinov promotes a 'collective security' policy.
May 1935	Pacts with France and Czechoslovakia.
August 1935	Reversal of policy by the Comintern: now supports popular fronts.
1936–39	Soviet Union intervenes in Spanish Civil War.
November 1936	Anti-Comintern Pact involving Germany and Japan and, a year later, Italy.
September 1938	Munich agreement, Soviet Union excluded.
1938–39	Japanese attacks on Soviet territory in the Far East.
April 1939	Litvinov proposes a triple military alliance between the Soviet Union, Britain and France.
May 1939	Molotov replaces Litvinov as Commissar for Foreign Affairs.

PHASE SIX	**The Nazi–Soviet Pact 1939**
August 1939	Soviet-Anglo-French talks in Moscow.
23 August	Ribbentrop and Molotov sign the Nazi–Soviet non-aggression pact and a secret protocol dividing Eastern Europe into spheres of influence.
	(See the separate timeline – Chart 18E on page 338 – for the events leading to the pact of 1939.)

PHASE SEVEN	**The aftermath of the Nazi–Soviet Pact 1939–41**
1 September 1939	German troops invade Poland.
17 September 1939	Red Army enters Poland from the east.
30 November 1939	Soviet Union invades Finland.
12 March 1940	Finland signs peace treaty with USSR ceding territory.
17–23 June 1940	Soviet Union occupies the Baltic States.
22 June 1941	Germany invades the Soviet Union.

THE COMINTERN (THIRD COMMUNIST INTERNATIONAL)

The Comintern is described as the 'Third Communist International' because two previous organisations had been set up to encourage the spread of socialist ideas. The first was set up by Karl Marx in London in 1864 but was so riven by disputes that it soon fell apart. The second was a much looser association set up in Paris in 1889. It held international conferences to discuss Marxist theory but ceased to meet after the outbreak of the First World War.

A What were the aims of Soviet foreign policy under Lenin?

FOCUS ROUTE

Make notes in answer to the following questions:

1 What were Lenin's aims and what changes in policy did he make?
2 What evidence is there of the tension between the desire to spread revolution and the demands of political realism?
3 How did the Bolsheviks adapt their foreign policy to changing circumstances?

In the new Bolshevik government, Trotsky was made Commissar for Foreign Affairs. Initially, the Bolsheviks saw this as a minor post and Trotsky chose it to give himself more time for party work. But he was soon embroiled in difficult peace negotiations. Taking Russia out of the First World War had been a major Bolshevik pledge and the Decree on Peace, which called for an immediate truce and a just peace, was issued as early as 26 October 1917. But it brought no response from the major powers fighting the war. So a separate peace had to be made with Germany and the Treaty of Brest-Litovsk was signed on Lenin's insistence (see page 121). In no sphere of policy was Lenin's leadership more decisive and discernible than in foreign affairs. Over Brest-Litovsk he showed a much clearer understanding of the realities of 1918 than Trotsky with his policy of 'neither peace nor war' or Bukharin with his impractical idea of transforming the war into a revolutionary war.

Hopes of world revolution were put on hold as the Bolsheviks fought for their survival in the Civil War. Nevertheless, Lenin was confident that the revolution would spread. He told the first meeting of the Comintern that 'the victory of the proletarian revolution on a world scale is assured, the founding of an international Soviet republic is on the way'. The opposite appeared to be true when foreign governments intervened on behalf of the Whites in the Civil War, but their intervention did not have a major impact on the outcome of the war. It even helped the Bolsheviks insofar as it allowed them to brand the Whites as agents of foreign imperialists.

In 1920 the Poles, hoping to gain territory, invaded Russia but the Red Army drove the Polish army back (see Chart 7D on page 130). Lenin saw the chance to use Poland as 'the red bridge into Europe' and for Russia to aid the expected revolution in Germany. It did not happen. The failure to take Warsaw was one of the major disappointments of his life. The decision to carry on the fight after the Poles had been chased out of Russia was very much his own, against the wishes of the majority of his colleagues, and although Lenin had to admit that the policy had failed he never admitted that it was wrong.

The realisation that the Poles had fought against the Red Army invaders rather than rising with them to embrace the revolution forced Lenin to accept reluctantly that peaceful coexistence rather than spreading revolution was the only option in Europe for some time. Lenin was ever the pragmatist and ready to adapt policy to changing situations. Alone in a hostile world, the Soviet Union was vulnerable to attack and Lenin sought to counter this. His main aim was to divide the imperialist countries and prevent them from forming a capitalist bloc against Soviet Russia. He worked on exploiting the differences between them. He made moves towards Germany, another outcast nation, which resulted in the Treaty of Rapallo in 1922 (see page 330). He used conventional diplomacy to begin negotiating a trade agreement with Britain in 1921 (see page 330). However, establishing foreign relationships through diplomacy was complicated by the existence of the Comintern.

■ **Learning trouble spot**

Bolshevik objectives

It can be difficult to work out the objectives of the Bolsheviks in this period because they were contradictory. Lenin, interested in survival, was willing to compromise in conventional diplomacy but, as Beryl Williams makes clear in her book *Lenin* (2000, page 171), 'Peaceful coexistence [for Lenin] was a means to an end ... the goal remained a European, indeed a world Communist state'. So although the Bolsheviks were prepared to work within the normal diplomatic framework, they hoped that they would be able to foment revolution in other countries through the Comintern.

328

ALONE IN A HOSTILE WORLD: HOW DID SOVIET FOREIGN POLICY DEVELOP BETWEEN 1921 AND 1941?

Note your answers to the following questions:

1 What was the Comintern?
2 What happened at the second Congress and with what result?
3 What problems did the Comintern cause?

SOURCE 18.1 'Workers of the world unite!': the title page of *The Communist International*, a pamphlet published in Moscow in May 1919 and printed in several languages

SOURCE 18.2 A propaganda poster produced in Germany in 1919 by the Association for the Fight Against Bolshevism. The association was formed with support from the government and businesses to counter the threat of revolutionary influences on Germany

B ■ Why did the Comintern exist and what problems did it present?

In January 1919, when the revolutionary wave in Europe was at its peak, Lenin had called for an international congress of revolutionary socialists. In March 1919, a motley collection from 35 groups did meet in Moscow and the Comintern – the Communist International – was formed. The Comintern appealed at its first meeting to the workers of all countries to support the Soviet regime by all available means, including, if necessary, 'revolutionary means'. Such an appeal was likely to fuel fears in Western Europe (see the German propaganda poster in Source 18.2). As Map 18B on page 329 shows, attempts to stir up revolution in Europe were singularly unsuccessful.

The failure of revolutionary attempts in Berlin and Munich and of Bela Kun's Soviet Republic in Hungary, which lasted less than four months, convinced Lenin that success could only be achieved if foreign Communist parties adopted the Bolshevik model. One of the main aims of the Second International Congress organised by the Comintern in 1920 was to bring foreign Communist parties under its control. Twenty-one conditions were drawn up for membership of the Comintern, including the following:

- Communist parties had to be organised on Leninist principles of centralisation and discipline. (The British and Spanish delegates had demanded freedom of action for their Communist parties but it was not granted.)
- Parties had to prepare for civil war by establishing an underground organisation, by spreading revolutionary propaganda among the proletariat, peasantry and armed forces, and by setting up cells in trade unions and other worker organisations.
- Party programmes had to be approved by the Comintern; disobedience could mean expulsion.

This policy had two very important and damaging results:

1 Moscow insisted upon centralised control and discipline and made the national security of the USSR the top priority for all Communist parties in other countries. But this reduced the appeal of the Communist Party to the rank and file of workers in other countries.
2 The stated intentions of the Comintern and the financial support (real and imagined) it gave to its members seriously weakened the Soviet Union's chances of achieving reliable and stable commercial and diplomatic relations with the European countries.

Here is one example of how the activities of the Comintern damaged diplomatic relations with Britain.

- In 1924, the 'Zinoviev letter' – a letter supposedly from the Comintern to the British Communist Party instructing the latter to conduct propaganda in the armed forces and elsewhere – was published just before the British general election. It was a forgery, but it indicated how British opinion perceived the threat presented by the Comintern. The new Conservative government virtually suspended all dealings with the Soviet government throughout 1925.

Throughout his time in office, Chicherin petitioned the Politburo to separate the personnel, policies and activities of the Comintern from those of the Soviet government. In practice this did not happen. Key players like Zinoviev, Trotsky and Bukharin were all involved in the Comintern at different times and they could not be ignored.

Stalin abolished the Comintern in 1943 as a goodwill gesture to his wartime allies.

Key

Attempts by non-Russian Communists to seize power (all put down by armed forces)

■ Centres believed by Western powers to be training non-Russian Communists to carry out revolutionary activity in their own countries (countries affected shown in brackets)

★ Propaganda centres funded by the USSR to encourage revolutionary activity

Countries with strong anti-Communist policies after 1926, forming a barrier between Russia and Western Europe

ALONE IN A HOSTILE WORLD: HOW DID SOVIET FOREIGN POLICY DEVELOP BETWEEN 1921 AND 1941?

330

ALONE IN A HOSTILE WORLD: HOW DID SOVIET FOREIGN POLICY DEVELOP BETWEEN 1921 AND 1941?

C What were the Soviet Union's relations with Britain and Germany between 1921 and 1933?

Soviet Russia could not afford to remain isolated. It needed to trade with other countries and to bring in capital goods to help to revive its industry. There were also all sorts of other matters, such as the movement of people in and out of Russia, which needed to be sorted out by the normal round of diplomatic relations. These matters were handled largely by men working in the Commissariat for Foreign Affairs who had some diplomatic experience, like Chicherin, or by the new intake who soon became specialists in the field. There was often tension between these men and the revolutionary agitators working for the Comintern. What progress was made by conventional diplomacy?

FOCUS ROUTE

Draw a table with four columns and these headings:

Moves that strengthened/ maintained relations with Britain 1921–33	Moves that weakened relations with Britain	Moves that strengthened/ maintained relations with Germany 1921–33	Moves that weakened relations with Germany

As you work through this section, enter events/actions in each column.

Relations with Britain

The Anglo-Soviet trade agreement of 1921 marked the first positive contact with the Soviet Union (trade was mutually profitable) although relations between the two countries were never easy. The Conservatives dominated British governments for most of the 1920s and 1930s and were particularly suspicious of Soviet activity in Britain and the empire.

Diplomatic relations were strained in 1926 by what the British government saw as subversive Soviet behaviour during the General Strike. The Soviet leadership saw the strike as a political act and the beginning of a proletarian revolution. In reality, it was a dispute about wages. The Russian Central Council of Trade Unions sent a cheque for £26,000 (a considerable sum) to the Trades Union Congress (TUC), the national leadership of the trade unions. The TUC leadership sent it back to prevent the British government from claiming that they were in the pay of the Bolsheviks. All that Soviet policy had achieved was to encourage anti-Soviet die-hards in Britain.

Relations with Germany

It has been said that Germany and the USSR were natural allies in the 1920s. Both were outcast nations: Germany because it had been defeated in and blamed for the First World War, the USSR because of its Communist ideology and its refusal to support the Western powers in the First World War. The Rapallo Treaty of 1922 between the two countries was central to the Soviet Union's security. Although on paper it amounted to no more than the re-establishment of diplomatic relations, a renunciation of financial claims on each side and a promise of economic co-operation, it ended the isolation that both countries were experiencing. In the years that followed, it was underpinned by significant economic and military collaboration. In spite of the tensions caused by the activities of the Comintern, especially its involvement in Communist risings in Germany in 1921 and 1923, co-operation was mutually beneficial (see Chart 18C on page 331).

331

ALONE IN A HOSTILE WORLD: HOW DID SOVIET FOREIGN POLICY DEVELOP BETWEEN 1921 AND 1941?

After 1923 the chances of a Communist rising in Germany faded, removing the cause of tension between the two countries. However, in 1925 the Locarno treaties (a set of treaties between Western powers, which guaranteed the existing frontiers of Western Europe) indicated better relations between Germany, Britain and France. This worried Russia: would Locarno reintegrate Germany into the Western world and isolate the USSR? As a result, a whole clutch of trade treaties were signed between Germany and Russia on the eve of Locarno to reassure the Soviets. The Treaty of Berlin, signed in 1926, had the same purpose. It reaffirmed the terms of the Treaty of Rapallo and was to remain in force for five years. The USSR and Germany pledged neutrality if either were attacked by another power. Militarily and economically, though not politically, ties between the two countries grew stronger.

SOURCE 18.3 The German President, Hindenburg, welcomes Marshal Tukhachevsky (right) and a Soviet delegation in 1932. The Soviet army officers had come to observe German army manoeuvres

■ 18C Advantages of mutual co-operation between the USSR and Germany, 1922–32

Diplomatic advantages
Both ceased to be isolated outcasts. The USSR avoided the nightmare prospect of capitalist countries combining against it and Germany strengthened its bargaining position with Britain and France.

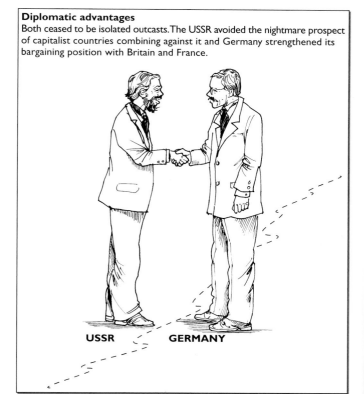

Military co-operation
German officers trained the Red Army in tank warfare and military aviation. The German army was able to train and experiment with weapons forbidden by the Treaty of Versailles – especially tanks, aircraft and gas. Co-operation reached its high point at the beginning of the 1930s.

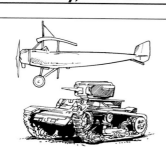

Economic co-operation
Germany was the only major country to make significant long-term loans to the USSR. German financial and technical help was important during the NEP and the First Five-Year Plan. The USSR supplied markets for German heavy industry. By 1932, 47 per cent of total Russian imports came from Germany. German firms in the USSR manufactured guns, shells, aircraft and tanks.

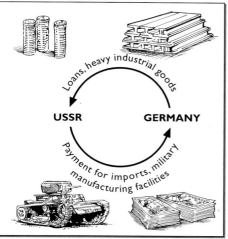

332

ALONE IN A HOSTILE WORLD: HOW DID SOVIET FOREIGN POLICY DEVELOP BETWEEN 1921 AND 1941?

 How did Stalin change Soviet foreign policy between 1924 and 1932?

FOCUS ROUTE

Make notes to prepare for a discussion on the following issues:

1 How did Stalin and Trotsky differ on foreign policy?
2 How did internal concerns shape Stalin's attitude towards the Comintern?

Stalin was not internationally minded like Lenin and he was not particularly interested in the activities of the Comintern. Stalin did not believe that the Comintern would bring about a revolution, even in 90 years. Stalin was committed to 'Socialism In One Country' – the idea that socialism could be built successfully in the Soviet Union without the necessity for revolution elsewhere. He thought it would be utter folly to risk the socialist transformation of Soviet Russia for the sake of possible revolution abroad. He dismissed the potential of foreign Communists to achieve revolutionary change. In his view, 'One Soviet tractor is worth ten good foreign Communists.'

This policy line brought splits in the party over foreign affairs for the first time since the Treaty of Brest-Litovsk. Many sided with Trotsky and his idea of 'Permanent Revolution'. Trotsky believed that revolution could not survive long in one country. Only when revolution had spread to Western Europe could socialism be established. If it did not spread it would, in time, succumb to a conservative Europe or be undermined by Russian backwardness. Trotsky and his supporters were alarmed by the way Stalin was sidelining the Comintern. Trotsky argued that under Stalin foreign Communist parties changed from being 'vanguards of world revolution' to the more or less pacifist 'frontier guards' of Soviet Russia.

Stalin, it seemed, was changing the focus of the Comintern from promoting world revolution to protecting the interests of the Soviet state.

How did the Comintern change?

The leadership of the Comintern reflected the situation in the Soviet Union. Zinoviev was president from 1919 to 1926. When the United Opposition – Trotsky, Zinoviev and Kamenev – was defeated, Bukharin, Stalin's ally, succeeded Zinoviev. When Bukharin in turn was forced out, the loyal Stalinist Molotov succeeded him.

In the late 1920s, Stalin's attention was fixed very much on the struggle for the leadership of the Communist Party. In 1928, he made his 'left turn' (opting for extreme left-wing policies of rapid industrialisation) and moved against Bukharin and the right wing of the party. As Stalin moved to the left, so did the policy of the Comintern. Foreign Communist parties were instructed to denounce social democratic parties as 'social FASCISTS' because they co-operated with bourgeois parties and governments (mirroring the attack on Bukharin for his co-operation with the bourgeois elements of the peasantry and the NEP).

Probably the most damaging consequences of this new policy direction were felt in Germany where the KPD (the Communist Party) was instructed to attack the SPD (the Social Democrats) as 'social fascists'. This divided the left just at the time when the Nazis and fascism were beginning to grow stronger. Stalin rejected pleas for joint action by the left in Germany against the Nazis and thereby contributed to Hitler's rise to power.

FASCISM
Extreme nationalist political movement, originating in Italy in the 1920s and taken up by Nazi Germany in the 1930s.

What was achieved in Soviet foreign policy between 1921 and 1933?

Between 1921 and 1933 conventional diplomacy had been much more successful than had the Comintern:

- the USSR was regarded as a European power once more
- there was no united capitalist front against the USSR
- foreign governments had begun to think they might be able to do business with the USSR
- valuable military and industrial gains had come from co-operation with Germany
- in 1933 the USA gave the USSR official recognition.

FOCUS ROUTE

To help to write your report you will need to explain what collective security against fascism meant. Make notes on its limited success.

ACTIVITY

It is 10 August 1939; Stalin wants your advice. He has asked you to write a report on whether the USSR should make an agreement with Germany or with Britain and France. Your report will have two parts:

1 Factual information for the main body of the report. You will find help for this in the Focus Route tasks in sections E–F.
2 Your recommendations. This will involve you drawing conclusions and giving your opinion, making the points that you think will weigh most heavily with Stalin.

You will find guidance on how to set out your report on page 337.

 # What was collective security against fascism?

In 1933, Hitler came to power in Germany. This changed international relations in Europe profoundly, especially in regard to the Soviet Union. Hitler's anti-Communist intentions were well known and the makers of Soviet foreign policy were going to have to re-adjust. One option was to work with other states to stop fascist expansion, i.e. collective security against fascism. In the USSR, the shift towards this can be seen in Litvinov's speech in December 1933 (Source 4 on page 322) and he is identified with this policy. However, relations with Germany were never broken off and behind the scenes between 1935 and 1937 there were negotiations on improving economic and political relations. Molotov, in particular, wanted improved relations with Germany and was openly critical of the policy of collective security.

In September 1934, the USSR became a member of the League of Nations, once referred to by Lenin as the 'robbers' den'. Litvinov was active in the League and had hopes that it could be an effective body. He denounced appeasement towards Germany as suicidal and urged the League to act decisively and resolutely to stop German aggression.

In May 1935, the Soviet Union signed mutual assistance pacts with France and Czechoslovakia. The Soviet Union was obliged to help the Czechs only if France came in, too. Although these pacts were good for the USSR's reputation as a supporter of collective security, neither was backed by military talks. Litvinov had no illusions: 'One should not place any serious hopes on the pact in the sense of real military aid in the event of war. Our security will still remain exclusively in the hands of the Red Army.' The French saw the pact as a political measure to scare Hitler and not an agreement which would require any military action on their part.

334

ALONE IN A HOSTILE WORLD: HOW DID SOVIET FOREIGN POLICY DEVELOP BETWEEN 1921 AND 1941?

In August 1935, the Comintern line of attacking Western social democratic and labour parties as 'social fascists' was completely overturned. Communists sought the help of such parties in the creation of 'popular fronts' that aimed to contain the spread of fascism. Soviet policy was to support governments that pursued an anti-German, pro-Soviet foreign line.

Two popular governments were formed in France and Spain, but they were not successful. In Spain it proved an excuse for the right-wing rebellion, which began the Spanish Civil War. The Nationalists, whose supporters included the Spanish fascists, could not accept the election of the Republicans, a left-wing popular front government, and civil war broke out in 1936. The Spanish Civil War was really about Spanish issues but foreigners saw it as a battle between left and right. This made it difficult for Stalin to ignore, especially as fascist Germany and Italy were helping the Nationalists. In the end, the Soviets decided to intervene but the aid given was limited: advisors were sent rather than regular units, and equipment was supplied – planes, tanks, machine guns, clothes and medical supplies – for which the Republic was systematically overcharged. However, this was still more than neutral France and Britain provided. Their failure to help the Republic alongside the USSR offered no encouragement for those like Litvinov who saw collective security against fascism as the way forward.

 Why did the USSR make an agreement with Germany rather than with Britain and France in 1939?

In 1936, Hitler had marched German troops into the Rhineland. In March 1938, he had forced the Anschluss with Austria. Reacting to these aggressive moves, Litvinov stressed the grave dangers lying in the future and the readiness of the Soviet government to join in a conference of the great powers to 'check the further development of aggression'. Litvinov specified Czechoslovakia as the area threatened. His proposal was rejected by the British government.

The Soviet Union was not invited to the Munich Conference in September 1938 in spite of its pact to join France in defence of Czechoslovakia. The Soviets always claimed they would stand by their treaty obligations, but had probably realised that they were unlikely to be called upon to do so. In any case, it would have been impossible to help Czechoslovakia without going through either Poland or Romania, neither of which was likely to agree to having Russian troops on their soil.

The Munich Conference and its concessions to Hitler must have made the Soviets wonder whether Britain and France would ever stand up to Hitler. However, the USSR did not drop its contact with Britain, although by March 1939 it was beginning to make some overtures to Germany. Whatever Stalin's preference, better terms would be achieved by being known to be negotiating with both sides.

Whether Stalin always preferred an agreement with Germany to one with Britain and France, or whether this was a last resort after the failure to reach agreement on collective security with Britain and France in August 1939, is a matter of debate. It could be argued that the cagey Stalin had no preferred option, was very flexible and was looking for the alliance which would be of most benefit to the USSR. Negotiating with both sides would drive up the terms; Stalin was interested in what each side had to offer.

FOCUS ROUTE

You will need to do the following in preparation for your report:

1 Assess the significance of the Munich Conference – how does it affect your view about whether the Soviet Union should make an agreement with Britain and France? Make notes on this.

2 Note down important points from Chart 18D on page 336. This should help you to weigh up the arguments over which side was the more attractive to the Soviets.

3 Don't forget the Japanese factor, which had a significant influence on Soviet policy. Which direction is it pushing you in – towards Germany or Britain and France?

335

ALONE IN A HOSTILE WORLD: HOW DID SOVIET FOREIGN POLICY DEVELOP BETWEEN 1921 AND 1941?

SOURCE 18.4 'What, no chair for me?', a Low cartoon published in 1938. At the Munich Conference attended by (left to right) Hitler, the British Prime Minister Chamberlain, Daladier (Prime Minister of France) and Mussolini, Hitler's demands were acceded to and the Sudetenland and one-third of the population of Czechoslovakia were transferred to Germany. War was avoided for the time being. Neither the USSR nor Czechoslovakia was invited to attend the conference

SOURCE 18.5 The Russian view of the Munich Conference: Chamberlain and Daladier direct German expansion east. The left-hand sign points to Western Europe; the right-hand sign to the USSR

336

ALONE IN A HOSTILE WORLD: HOW DID SOVIET FOREIGN POLICY DEVELOP BETWEEN 1921 AND 1941?

■ 18D Which side should the USSR make an agreement with – Britain and France or Germany?

The British and French perspective

- They were parliamentary democracies. They greatly distrusted the USSR and saw Communism as a threat to their empires.
- They were happy to preserve the situation in Europe that had been established under the terms of the Treaty of Versailles which ended the war with Germany in 1919.
- Britain believed the Red Army had been seriously weakened by the purges.
- They gave a guarantee to Poland, the most anti-Soviet of the eastern states, in March 1939. Britain would not put pressure on the Poles to give Soviet troops rights of passage across Poland, although France by August 1939 was prepared to do this. It was the stumbling block in the August 1939 negotiations in Moscow.
- Britain and France did not anticipate a deal between Germany and the USSR.
- They were prepared to give a guarantee to Poland in response to demands from the British parliament and public to take action.

The Soviet perspective on agreement with Britain and France

- The Soviets suspected that Britain wanted to turn German aggression on to the USSR while it watched from the sidelines, happy to see the Nazis and Communists destroy each other.
- Britain and France had repeatedly appeased Hitler and shown little enthusiasm for collective security against fascism.
- They had excluded the USSR from the Munich Conference, even though the USSR had treaty obligations to Czechoslovakia.
- Britain and France had dragged their feet over the triple alliance negotiations proposed by Litvinov in April 1939.
- Alliance with Britain and France might not prevent war with Germany and, if it did not, the USSR might bear the brunt of the fighting.
- Britain and France were not prepared to accept the USSR taking territory or having a sphere of influence across eastern Europe.

AGREEMENT?

AGREEMENT?

The German perspective on an agreement with the USSR

- Hitler wanted to avoid a war on two fronts.
- A non-aggression pact with Russia would scare off Britain and France; they would not intervene to defend Poland.
- A non-aggression pact that included promises of Soviet economic help would overcome any Anglo-French blockade – the Allied blockade had been important in Germany's defeat in the First World War.
- Agreement was needed in August so that Poland could be defeated before the autumn rains.
- Hitler had no qualms about conceding other countries' territory to Stalin.
- It would appear to be an ideological somersault – next to anti-semitism, anti-Communism was Hitler's strongest feeling. But Hitler was very flexible in his tactics; his ultimate aim of defeating the USSR had not changed.

The Soviet perspective on an agreement with Germany

- A pact with Germany was the only way to be sure of avoiding war in the West – Soviet security was Stalin's main concern.
- It would avoid a war on two fronts – the USSR was involved in hostilities with Japan, and Germany had influence with Japan through the Anti-Comintern Pact.
- Soviet armed forces had been hit by the purges and the rearmament programme was nowhere near completion. A pact with Germany would at least buy Russia more time.
- Russia would gain half of Poland and a sphere of influence from Finland to Romania, including the Baltic states.
- Agreement with Germany would be in line with the Treaty of Rapallo and the good relations of 1922 to 1934.
- Germany was still the USSR's major trading partner.
- It was in Stalin's interests to stand aside while the capitalist nations fought each other.
- It would appear to be an ideological somersault – a reversal of collective security against fascism.

ACTIVITY

It is now time to write your report to Stalin. Use the notes you have made in the Focus Route activities in this chapter. Do you recommend that he make terms with Germany or side with Britain and France against Germany?

Note: How to set out your report.

1 Title page
Title: Should the Soviet Union make an agreement with Britain and France or with Germany?
From: Yourself   Date: 10 August 1939
For: J.V. Stalin

2 Introduction
- Explain why the report is being written – the danger of war, both Britain and France and Germany were negotiating.
- Explain the need to calculate the best option for the Soviet Union.
- Method: evaluate the success of the policy of collective security against fascism in the light of events 1936–39. Analyse the attitudes and actions of the three countries. Offer an assessment of what each side can offer the Soviet Union.

3 Main text
Headings:
- The policy of collective security against fascism
- Spanish Civil War – extent and results of Soviet involvement
                    – British and French policy
- Munich Conference
- Key arguments for and against an agreement with Britain and France
- Key arguments for and against an agreement with Germany

4 Conclusions
Draw conclusions on how the collective security policy has worked and suggest which side has most to offer.

5 Recommendations
In the light of all the above, make recommendations to Stalin on what he should do.

■ Learning trouble spot

The Japanese influence

The Soviet Union's concern about Japan is often neglected when considering Stalin's actions. Stalin, like Hitler, wanted to avoid a war on two fronts. In the war scare of 1928, Stalin saw Japanese aggression as a significant danger. The Japanese invasion of Manchuria in 1931 was a direct threat to Soviet railway interests there and a potential threat to Mongolia (a Soviet satellite) and to Siberia in the Soviet Union itself. A further worry was the Anti-Comintern Pact signed by Germany and Japan in November 1936 and directed solely against the Soviet Union. The Japanese ambassador in Berlin was the architect of the pact, and Italy became its third member in 1937. In 1938 and 1939, there were major battles ending in Soviet victories when the Japanese tested Soviet defences: in July and August 1939 the Japanese suffered 61,000 casualties.

If Soviet Russia signed a pact with Germany, then Hitler could persuade the Japanese to cease their attacks on the Soviet Union and the danger of war on two fronts would be removed.

Date	Relations with Britain and France	Relations with Germany
10 March	Stalin's speech at Eighteenth Party Congress warns that the USSR will not 'be drawn into conflicts by warmongers who are accustomed to have others pull the chestnuts out of the fire'.	
16 April	Litvinov proposes a triple pact of mutual assistance between Britain, France and the USSR.	
17 April		The Soviet ambassador in Berlin proposes a resumption of trade talks between the USSR and Germany.
28 April		Hitler omits the usual attack on the USSR from a major foreign policy speech in which he denounces the German–Polish Non-Aggression Treaty and the Anglo-German Naval Agreement.
3 May	Litvinov (a Jew, identified with collective security against fascism, and married to an Englishwoman) replaced as Foreign Commissar by Molotov.	
8 May	Britain rejects Soviet proposals for a military alliance.	
20–30 May		Germany puts out feelers for renewed trade talks with the USSR.
27 May	Chamberlain instructs British ambassador in Moscow to open talks with the USSR on a mutual assistance pact.	
31 May		In a major foreign policy speech, Molotov questions the commitment of the Western powers to negotiations with the USSR and shows a readiness to continue trade talks with Germany.
12 June	Ambassador Maisky (Soviet ambassador in London) proposes a visit to Moscow by Lord Halifax (British Foreign Secretary).	
18 July		Soviets offer Germany a favourable trade agreement.
23 July	Britain and France agree to military talks with the USSR.	
5 August	Drax (the admiral heading the British military mission) leaves London for Leningrad by slow boat.	
11 August	Drax mission arrives in Moscow. Military talks begin.	
14 August		Ribbentrop instructs the German ambassador in Moscow to request, on his behalf, an audience with Stalin so that Ribbentrop could tell Stalin of Germany's proposals at first hand.
19 August	Breakdown of Anglo-Soviet negotiations.	German–Soviet trade agreement announced.
20 August		Molotov agrees to Ribbentrop's visiting Moscow on 26 or 27 August. Hitler cables Stalin asking him to receive Ribbentrop by 23 August at the latest (no European statesman had ever addressed Stalin directly before).
21 August		Stalin agrees.
22 August		Ribbentrop flies to Moscow.
23 August		Ribbentrop and Molotov sign the Nazi–Soviet non-aggression pact and a secret protocol dividing Eastern Europe into spheres of influence. Stalin had led the discussions.

339

ALONE IN A HOSTILE WORLD: HOW DID SOVIET FOREIGN POLICY DEVELOP BETWEEN 1921 AND 1941?

What were the attitudes of Germany, Britain and France?

Naturally we are focusing on Stalin's thinking, but the attitudes of German, British and French policy-makers are important, too.

Germany

Hitler's attitude to the USSR is not hard to understand. He needed to defeat Poland before the autumn rain and this is reflected in an increasing sense of urgency during August. Look at Chart 18D on page 336 to see what Germany could gain from a pact with the USSR. Hitler revealed his thoughts when talking to a League of Nations diplomat on 11 August 1939: 'Everything that I have in mind is directed against Russia; if the West is too stupid and too blind to grasp this then I will be forced to come to terms with the Russians, to smash the West and after its defeat to turn against Russia with all my forces. I need the Ukraine so that we can't be starved out as in the last war.' He did what he said. It did not contradict his anti-Bolshevism and shows his flexibility in approaching long-held objectives.

Britain and France

When Hitler took over the rest of Czechoslovakia in March 1939, the gravity of the situation forced Britain and France into guaranteeing Poland on 31 March. The Anglo-French guarantee to Poland was important. They were now bound to a country determined that the Red Army should not cross its borders again, as it had in 1920. The attitude of the Poles was a major stumbling block in the Anglo-French negotiations with the USSR, and one reason why the British spun things out was to delay reaching the sticking point of Soviet rights of passage through Poland.

British public opinion was in favour of a military alliance with France and Russia (84 per cent in favour according to a Gallup opinion poll) and there was support for it in the House of Commons (see Source 18.6). Chamberlain's attitude was rather different (see Source 18.7). He was strongly anti-Communist, and he wanted only as much Russian support as would be convenient to the British, would not alarm the Poles, and would not annoy the Germans. Molotov, on the other hand, was looking for an unbreakable alliance covering every possibility of Soviet–German conflict. The British also had concerns about how useful an alliance with the USSR would prove to be. In the wake of the purges, the British General Staff did not have a high opinion of Soviet military might and advised the Cabinet that Soviet intervention in a European war was likely to be 'an embarrassment rather than a help'.

The guarantee to Poland meant, in effect, that Britain and France had chosen Poland rather than the USSR. This situation was not as serious for the Soviets as it might appear; it had significant advantages for the Soviet Union. If an isolated Poland were to be attacked, the USSR would be vulnerable because Hitler might not stop at the Soviet–Polish border. But if Hitler attacked Poland now, Germany would face Britain and France. Both sides would want the Soviet Union, if not on their side, at least to remain neutral, and a long war between the three Western powers could allow a neutral USSR to achieve long-term gains.

There has been argument over the extent to which Chamberlain was responsible for the breakdown of the talks. It can be argued that however enthusiastically Britain had negotiated, it could not offer the Soviet Union as much as Germany – look at Chart 18D (page 336). On the other hand, it cannot be denied that Chamberlain was consistently sending out negative messages to the Russians. We cannot be certain of the intentions and assumptions of Stalin and Soviet policy-makers, but Chamberlain's attitude and the British lack of urgency provided a series of justifications, if not the true reasons, for Soviet rejection of any alliance.

SOURCE 18.6 P. Kennedy, *The Realities Behind Diplomacy*, 1981, p. 308, quoting a speech by Commander Bower, a backbench Conservative MP, to the House of Commons, March 1939

I am not prepared to regard Soviet Russia as a freedom-loving nation but we cannot do without her now. I know they have shot a lot of the people but there are some 170,000,000 of them left.

SOURCE 18.7 Neville Chamberlain, in a letter to his sister on 26 March 1939

I must confess to the most profound distrust of Russia. I have no belief whatever in her ability to maintain an effective offensive, even if she wanted to. And I distrust her motives, which seem to me to have little connection with our ideas of liberty, and to be concerned only with getting everyone else by the ears.

ACTIVITY

1 Look at Chart 18E on page 338. What does it tell you about which power was most eager to make an agreement with the Soviet Union?
2 How does your understanding of the perspectives of Germany, Britain and France influence your own views about why Stalin chose Germany?

TALKING POINT

Do you think that Chamberlain, together with the British and French negotiators, was just as responsible for the Nazi–Soviet Pact as Stalin and Hitler? Do you think that the British and French seriously blundered or do you think that whatever they did they were never going to make any difference to the outcome?

SOURCE 18.8 P. M. H. Bell, *The Origins of the Second World War in Europe*, 1987, pp. 261–62

The Soviets held a central position, and could judge which set of talks would better serve their interests. It is reasonable to assume that these were twofold: to keep out of a European war, especially when they were actually engaged in serious fighting with the Japanese in the Far East – they did not seek a war on two fronts; and to secure territory – a sphere of influence which would add to Soviet security, internal as well as external. It would be advantageous to bring the Ukrainians in Poland under Stalin's control. The British and French offered nothing substantial under either heading.

The Germans on the other hand were able to meet both Soviet interests. Instead of a risk of war, they could offer certain neutrality. In terms of territory and spheres of influence, they came bearing gifts, ready to carve up Poland and to yield at once when Stalin asked for the whole of Latvia to be in his sphere instead of only a part, as Ribbentrop at first proposed. Moreover the Germans could deliver the goods forthwith, whereas the British and French could deliver nothing.

Between the two sides, the Soviet choice could hardly be in doubt. It is only surprising that so much obloquy [criticism] has been heaped upon Stalin's head for making the best deal he could get, and that so much criticism has been levelled at the British for their dilatoriness [lack of urgency] when nothing could have enabled them to match the German offers. The competition was decided on substance, not on method.

The Nazi–Soviet Pact, August 1939 and its aftermath

This pact referred directly to the Treaty of Berlin of 1926, which committed both countries to refrain from aggression and to observe neutrality in conflicts involving third parties. A secret protocol (whose existence was denied until 1991 by the USSR) defined future spheres of influence, with part of east Poland, plus Estonia, Latvia and Bessarabia (part of Romania) passing to the USSR.

Germany invaded Poland on 1 September 1939 and advanced very rapidly. The Soviet Union joined in on 17 September, attacking from the east. Poland was soon overrun. A new Nazi–Soviet treaty was agreed on 28 September: in return for giving Germany slightly more of Poland than was originally agreed, Lithuania was transferred to the Soviet sphere of influence. Important economic concessions were made by the Soviets to Germany, and the economic agreements made in October were crucial to Hitler's plans. The amount of grain and raw materials he gained from the USSR, together with the rubber from the Far East which came through the USSR, enabled Hitler to get round any Allied blockade. Without these supplies of natural rubber, neither the western campaigns of 1940 nor the later campaigns in the USSR could have been fought.

Stalin moved to turn spheres of influence into a more solid defensive buffer. When Finland refused to make the concessions he wanted, the Red Army invaded at the end of November. The Finns resisted the incompetent Soviet forces and inflicted heavy casualties on them. As a result, the Soviets accepted Finnish requests for an armistice. The USSR gained territory around Leningrad and further protection for the Leningrad to Murmansk railway. In June 1940, on the pretext of dealing with acts of provocation, half a million Soviet troops were sent into the Baltic States. Estonia, Latvia and Lithuania were bullied into petitioning for incorporation into the USSR. Later in the month, more former Tsarist territory was taken when Romania was forced to hand back Bessarabia.

After the invasion of eastern Poland in 1939, political, economic and cultural élites were rounded up and 400,000 ethnic Poles were arrested, deported and/ or executed. This included the 22,000 officers Stalin notoriously ordered to be shot and buried at Katyn. Similarly, the occupation of the Baltic States led to the murder or deportation of several hundreds of thousands of 'anti-Soviet elements'.

Stalin had hoped for a long war in which Germany and the West exhausted each other; Germany's spectacular success and France's rapid collapse in the summer of 1940 was deeply worrying, especially when contrasted with the Soviets dismal performance in the Winter War against Finland. This had revealed gross defects in organisation and planning and the war with Japan had shown up weaknesses in the air force. Stalin admitted in November 1940 that, 'We're not ready for war of the kind being fought between Germany and England.' Hitler would have to be appeased.

ACTIVITY

Write an essay: Why did Stalin make an agreement with Germany in 1939 rather than with Britain and France?

As well as using the material in this section, you could look a little more closely at Hitler's motives. He was the one in a hurry!

KEY POINTS FROM CHAPTER 18

Alone in a hostile world: how did Soviet foreign policy develop between 1921 and 1941?

1 Soviet foreign policy had two tracks: strengthening the security of the USSR, and promoting world socialist revolution, for which purpose the Comintern was designed. However, failure to spread revolution meant that Soviet security became the top priority.

2 The USSR felt very vulnerable after the Civil War and needed economic help and foreign trade. In spite of a trade agreement with Britain (1921) relations were strained. The Treaty of Rapallo and good relations with Germany were central to foreign policy up to the end of 1932.

3 Stalin's policy of 'Socialism in One Country' advanced the interests of the USSR above those of world revolution. Switches in Soviet foreign policy were often determined by Stalin's domestic priorities.

4 By the end of 1932, the USSR was recognised as a European power again and there was no united front against her, but Hitler's aggressive nationalism changed the situation.

5 Litvinov is particularly associated with collective security against fascism. Joining the League of Nations and joining the popular fronts was part of this.

6 Contact with Germany was never lost in the 1930s and the exclusion of the USSR from the Munich conference was a blow to the collective security policy.

7 During 1939, the Soviets negotiated with Britain and France and with Germany.

8 In May 1939, Molotov replaced Litvinov as Commissar for Foreign Affairs, a sign that the Soviets were moving away from collective security.

9 Stalin made the Nazi–Soviet Pact because Hitler could offer much more than Britain and France.

10 The USSR took half of Poland and occupied a swath of territory from Finland to Romania. Several hundreds of thousands of 'anti-Soviet elements' were murdered or deported.

19 How was the Soviet Union able to turn disaster into victory in the Great Patriotic War?

CHAPTER OVERVIEW

When the Germans invaded the USSR in June 1941, they swept all before them. This chapter looks at the extent of the disaster that hit an unprepared Soviet Union, why it happened and how the situation was turned around. Stalin's role was central and controversial, but the massive economic effort, the development of the Red Army and the endeavour and resilience of the Russian people all contributed to the final victory. The horrors inflicted by the Germans in their war of annihilation made the Russian people receptive to wartime propaganda and there was an upsurge of patriotism. The Soviet Union made a major contribution to the defeat of Hitler.

A An outline of the war on the Eastern Front (pp. 343–346)

B Stalin's role (pp. 347–351)

C The Soviet war economy – 'Everything for the Front!' (pp. 352–353)

D The resilience of the Soviet people (pp. 354–356)

E Soviet wartime propaganda: drumming up support and maintaining morale (pp. 357–361)

F Why was the Soviet Union able to turn disaster into victory? (pp. 361–363)

THE GREAT PATRIOTIC WAR

In his first speech to the Soviet people after the German invasion, Stalin spoke of a 'patriotic war of all the people'. He wanted to motivate the population to drive out the Germans with a deliberate echo of the war against Napoleon in 1812, which was known as the 'Patriotic War'. The term 'Great Patriotic War' soon appeared in Pravda and is still used today. It refers to the war between the USSR and Germany and her allies from 22 June 1941 to 9 May 1945.

The GREAT PATRIOTIC WAR was the greatest war in history. More troops were engaged for the longest period of continuous fighting along the longest front. Twice as many combatants died as those of all nations killed on all fronts in the First World War. Too often, especially during the Cold War, the Soviet contribution to the defeat of Hitler has been underestimated. At no time were less than two thirds of Germany's forces committed to the Eastern Front. The sufferings of the Soviet people were enormous. It was here that the war was won and lost.

Comparing Soviet losses with other countries (including both soldiers and civilians), for every Briton or American who died, the Japanese lost 7 people, the Germans 20 and the Soviets 85.

SIEGE OF LENINGRAD

As the birth place of the Russian Empire and the Revolution, Leningrad was a city of symbolic rather than military importance. Hitler planned to flatten it. The siege, which lasted 900 days, began in September 1941.

The extraordinary resilience of the people, despite massive loss of life, made it typical of the Soviet war effort. In the bitterly cold starvation winter of 1941, about 800,000 Leningraders starved to death as rations fell to 8 ounces a day of adulterated bread for soldiers and workers, and 4 ounces for everyone else. There were 1,500 arrests for 'banditry' (cannibalism). The factories continued to make tanks, guns and shells until December when they ran out of electricity, water and raw materials. Typhus and scurvy were widespread.

In January 1942, Lake Lagoda froze sufficiently to allow trucks to bring in supplies and to evacuate half a million exhausted and emaciated Leningraders. Ships took over when the ice melted but death rates remained high until July 1942.

Anna Akhmatova and Dimitri Shostakovich (see page 311) were fully engaged in Leningrad's resistance. Both joined the Civil Defence and broadcast to the city on the radio before they were evacuated (see page 355). Shostakovich had worked by candlelight on his seventh symphony which he dedicated 'To the city of Leningrad'. On 9 July 1942, it was performed by a motley collection of musicians in the bombed Great Hall of the Leningrad Philharmonia and piped through loudspeakers in the streets. It had an overwhelming emotional effect. The people felt united in their conviction that the city would be saved.

The siege was lifted at the end of January 1944.

A An outline of the war on the Eastern Front

Outline of the war

On 22 June 1941, the German army, the most powerful army ever assembled in Europe, launched Operation Barbarossa against the Soviet Union, taking the Russians completely by surprise. Most of the Soviet aircraft were destroyed on the ground on the first day. There was chaos as the Germans swept eastwards. Red Army soldiers, finding themselves surrounded and outgunned, put up limited resistance and deserted in large numbers. Between June and December, the Red Army lost 2,663,000 killed in action and 3,350,000 taken prisoner (two million of whom were dead from starvation, disease and maltreatment by February 1942). By September, the siege of Leningrad had begun and Kiev had fallen with the loss of half a million men – encircled because Stalin refused to make a strategic withdrawal. By mid-October, there was panic in Moscow and government offices were evacuated to Kuibyshev (see map, page 345). Stalin, however, refused to leave the city. The areas lost in 1941 were some of the most industrially developed and fertile in the USSR, containing two fifths of the total population.

However, after the initial shock, Russian resistance stiffened and the Germans began to take casualties at a far higher rate than they had experienced before. In December 1941, a Soviet counter-offensive near Moscow pushed them back 150–200 kilometres, their first major setback. It meant that Russia could not be conquered in a single, lightning campaign before winter set in. The German forces were poorly prepared for the cold but Hitler ordered them to stand firm. Other factors started to work in the Russians' favour although not immediately. The German declaration of war on the USA would, in time, bring help to the beleaguered USSR. In the west, factories vulnerable to German takeover were being dismantled and moved along with their workers, to the east – a process that began only two days after the German attack. During 1942–43, their output would help the USSR to out-produce Germany in military hardware.

SOURCE 19.1
Dineka's painting, *The Defence of Sevastopol*, 1942. Although the fall of Sevastopol was one of the low points of the war, this painting expresses the idea of victory despite the hopeless position.

THE BATTLE OF STALINGRAD

The German commander, Paulus, and the 6th Army reached the outskirts of Stalingrad at the end of August 1942. From September to November, in a desperate struggle inside Stalingrad, a few thousand courageous Soviet men and women held up the Germans in spite of 75 per cent casualties. The railway station changed hands 15 times and a giant grain elevator was besieged for 58 days with Soviet troops holding out floor by floor against German tanks and guns. Red Army street fighting was very effective. Their forces preferred to fight at close quarters at night with snipers active by day, and they were backed by a barrage of artillery and rocket fire from the east bank of the Volga. This heroic resistance was vital and allowed their commander, Zhukov, to plan the encircling counteroffensive. This was the first time the Soviet military machine had been able to prepare and execute a large-scale operation involving millions of men and sustain it under the pressure of war – something Hitler did not believe possible. It began on 19 November and was a great success – it trapped the German 6th Army in a huge pocket. Hitler ordered Paulus to stand fast in Stalingrad, rather than attempt a break out. The pocket was reduced gradually and Paulus surrendered on 31 January 1943. In the whole operation, 800,000 German troops were lost. Ilya Ehrenburg wrote, 'Up till then one believed in victory as an act of faith, but now there was no shadow of a doubt: victory was assured.'

Nevertheless, in the spring and summer of 1942 the Germans continued to advance in the south. This was the hardest year of the war for the Soviets. Over ambitious Soviet offensives pushed through by Stalin led to more heavy losses, notably near Kharkov, where the Germans encircled and captured the equivalent of three Soviet armies. All of the Crimea and most of the Ukraine were in German hands. The fall of Rostov, with little resistance, marked the Russian army's lowest point and Stalin issued Order 227: 'Not a step back!' (see page 349). Hitler was so confident that he divided his forces in the south between conquering the Caucasus, to gain economic resources especially oil, and taking Stalingrad. Both sides came to see the struggle for Stalingrad as decisive.

The strength of Soviet economic and human resources began to make an impression. By the end of 1942, what has been called a third generation Red Army was emerging; the pre-war army had been destroyed in 1941 and the summer battles of 1942 had largely destroyed the hastily produced replacements. At all levels, command and control were becoming more effective and techniques were developed for conducting mechanised warfare on a grand scale. The Lend-Lease programme from the Americans contributed too. The supply of raw materials, food and transport was essential. From 1943 it allowed Soviet industry to concentrate on producing weapons. Without the half a million vehicles the USA supplied, every Soviet offensive would have stalled earlier.

General Zhukov predicted that the Germans would launch a huge and well prepared attack at Kursk. Stalin was persuaded to sit tight and wait. The Red Army and the local population dug 3,000 miles of trenches and laid over 400,000 mines. Forty per cent of the Red Army's manpower and 75 per cent of its armoured forces, backed by airpower, were crowded into the battle zone ready for the German attack. The largest and fiercest set-piece battle in history began on 5 July 1943. The German attack lasted nearly a week but, although Soviet losses of 70,000 men and 1,600 tanks were greater than those of the Germans, it was repulsed. Any realistic prospect of German victory in the east was snuffed out.

The following year, in a massive offensive beginning on 22 June, Operation Bagration (named by Stalin after a Georgian commander in the Napoleonic wars) showed just how well the revamped Red Army had learned the lessons of the first two years of the war. It was prepared in the utmost secrecy and used massed aircraft and tanks. It focused on Minsk and surprised the Germans completely with its scale and ferocity. The right wing historian Andrew Roberts, unlikely to exaggerate the Soviet contribution, described it 'as decisive as anything in the history of warfare, and [it] utterly dwarfed the contemporaneous Operation Overlord campaign'. In 68 days the 1.2 million strong German Army Group Centre was destroyed, the Germans suffering four times the number of casualties that were being sustained in the west. It was complete revenge for Barbarossa and the Germans were driven from Soviet territory and the Red Army entered Eastern Europe.

Stalin was determined to reach Berlin first. He selected his best field commanders to do so and encouraged professional rivalry between Zhukov and Konev in the race for Berlin. They faced a skilled and tenacious enemy and suffered 300,000 casualties including 78,000 dead. They lost 2000 tanks in three weeks as men and tanks were thrown at the problem. It is understandable, though, that having borne the brunt of the war, Stalin and the Soviet commanders felt that they and not their Western allies should capture the symbolic prize of Berlin. On 2 May 1945, Berlin surrendered.

Arctic convoys bring aid from Britain and USA

Legend:
- **1941 frontier** (dotted line)
- **1939 frontier** (grey band)
- **Furthest German advance 1941/42** (solid black line)
- **Operation Bagration** (shaded area)
- □ **Operation Barbarossa launched with over 3.5 million soldiers in three separate armies**

Pacific route from US west coast to Siberian ports, then aid brought overland

Kuibyshev (Samara) Government offices evacuated here

US aid coming up from Persian Gulf

Petsamo · Murmansk · Archangel · White Sea · Arctic Circle · URAL MOUNTAINS · FINLAND · Gulf of Bothnia · L. Onega · SWEDEN · Helsinki · L. Ladoga · Vyborg · Leningrad · ESTONIA · Kronstadt · Kazan · Magnitogorsk · LATVIA · Riga · 1941 · Moscow · LITHUANIA · Kaliningrad (Konigsberg) · Smolensk · Volga · Warsaw · Minsk · POLAND · Orel · Dnieper · Kursk · Voronezh · Kiev · Kharkov · 1942 · Don · BESSARABIA · Stalingrad · Odessa · Rostov · Gurev · ROMANIA · CRIMEA · Kerch · Astrakhan · Sevastopol · Yalta · CASPIAN SEA · BULGARIA · BLACK SEA · CAUCASUS MOUNTAINS · Constantinople · Batum · Tbilisi · Baku · Dardanelles · TURKEY

N

0   300
km

PHASE ONE	June–Dec 1941 German advance
22 June	Operation Barbarossa: Germany invades the USSR
28 June	Germans capture Minsk
3 July	Stalin's first wartime broadcast to the Soviet people
16 Aug	Stalin's order 270: Soldiers who allow themselves to fall into captivity are traitors to the Motherland
19 Sept	Fall of Kiev
26 Sept	Siege of Leningrad begins
30 Sept	Beginning of the Battle of Moscow
1 Oct	Evacuation of government to Kuibyshev 500 miles east. Lenin's body moved. Stalin stays
16 Oct	Height of the 'Moscow panic'
7 Nov	Stalin addresses Red Square parade
6 Dec	Soviet counter-offensive begins near Moscow

PHASE TWO	Jan 1942–Jan 1943 Stalemate until the decisive victory
8 May	Germans attack eastern Crimea
12 May	Unsuccessful Soviet offensive opened near Kharkov
4 July	Fall of Sevastopol
28 July	Stalin's order 227 issued: 'Not a step back!'
26 Aug	Zhukov appointed Deputy Supreme Commander of the Soviet Armed Forces
13 Sept	Launch of German offensive to take Stalingrad
19 Nov	Launch of Soviet counter-offensive, Stalingrad encircled by 23 Nov
1943	
31 Jan	Paulus surrenders at Stalingrad

PHASE THREE	Feb 1943–Aug 1944 Germans chased out of Soviet territory
March	Soviet setback, troops advance too rapidly and Germans counterattack and occupy Kharkov
12–15 July	Battle of Kursk
23 Aug	Red Army recaptures Kharkov
6 Nov	Soviets recapture Kiev
1944	To be known as the year of Stalin's 'ten great victories'
27 Jan	Leningrad blockade lifted; end of the '900 days'
13 May	Final defeat of Germans in the Crimea
6 June	Allies invade Normandy
22 June	Launch of Operation Bagration in Belorussia
3 July	Soviets recapture Minsk and take 100,000 German prisoners
18 July	Red Army troops enter Poland
29 Aug	Operation Bagration ends successfully after 68 days, 1.2 million strong Germany Army Group Centre destroyed

PHASE FOUR	Aug 1944–May 1945 The drive to Berlin
1945	
17 Jan	Soviet troops take the ruined city of Warsaw
13 Feb	Budapest falls to Soviet troops
13 April	Soviet troops take Vienna
23 April	Soviet troops reach Berlin
2 May	Berlin surrenders

SOURCE 19.2 This is one of the most famous photographs of the war and communicates the message of victory emphatically. It shows a Red Army soldier planting the Soviet flag on top of the Reichstag in Berlin. In fact it is a re-enactment. The first party had neither flag nor photographer and hoisted a red rag. The flag itself is called 'the holy of holies' and is displayed in a museum in Moscow dedicated to the victory in the Great Patriotic War. Look closely at this photograph – the soldier holding his colleague's legs is wearing two wrist watches. When this evidence of looting was noticed a few months later the photographer was ordered to paint out the watch on the soldier's right wrist

B Stalin's role

'The genius organiser of our victories' and 'the great captain of the Soviet people,' was how *Pravda* characterised Stalin, even in July 1941. However, opinions differ over whether Soviet soldiers really charged into battle yelling 'For the Motherland, for Stalin!' His cult grew even stronger after the victory at Stalingrad. Praise for him was not confined to the Soviet Union: in the USA he was made Man of the Year 1942 by *Time* magazine. Its editorial declared, 'Only Joseph Stalin fully knew how close Russia stood to defeat in 1942, and only Joseph Stalin fully knew how he brought Russia through'.

FOCUS ROUTE

Draw up a chart about Stalin's contribution to the war effort.

Positive contribution	Negative contribution

Impact of Stalin's pre-war purges of the armed forces

In May 1937, Stalin had launched a vast purge of high-ranking Red Army officers, beginning with Marshal Tukhachevsky. In all, 35,000 officers were arrested (see page 263). The purges had a traumatic effect on the army:

- Trained leaders were lost at a time when the Red Army was expanding rapidly.
- Political control of the military was strengthened with political officers brought back to oversee military commanders. This stifled initiative and independence of action. Commanders waited passively for decisions from above which, especially in the early days of the war, often came too late to make a positive difference to the situation on the ground. Rigid conformity led to frontal assaults that incurred enormous losses of men and equipment.
- The purges made foreign governments – potential allies as well as the Germans – assume that the Red Army was a broken shell.
- The military–industrial complex was purged too. This led to poor decision making on technical matters so that when war began, good quality, modern tanks and aircraft were not yet fully in mass production.

The effect of purges on personnel may have been exaggerated. Not all the executed Red Army commanders were proven military leaders in a mechanised war and many able middle-level commanders survived. Nevertheless, the overall impact at the beginning of the war was very detrimental to the Soviet armed forces.

TUKHACHEVSKY: A SERIOUS LOSS

Marshal Mikhail Tukhachevsky was the leading military thinker in the Soviet Union. In 1928 in a military review, The Future War, he put forward the idea of a grand offensive involving thousands of tanks, armoured vehicles and aircraft advancing at great speed to deliver a knockout blow – 'deep operations'. He foresaw that this highly mechanised war would require the mobilisation of economic resources on a huge scale which meant that the build-up of heavy industry was essential. 'It will be a war which will embrace multi-million-strong masses and the majority of the population of the combatant nations. The frontiers between the front and the rear will be erased more and more.' Tukhachevsky to the Communist Academy July 1930 (quoted in C. Bellamy, *Absolute War*, 2007 p. 37).

Tukhachevsky was a central figure in the military collaboration with Germany in the 1920s and early 1930s but, whereas many of the Germans involved in the collaboration played leading parts in the war, he and most Soviet military leaders participating were wiped out by the purges. Fortunately, his ideas of 'deep operations' were put into practice effectively from mid-1943 onwards.

Responsibility for initial losses

Stalin was convinced that the Germans would not attack the USSR until Britain was defeated. He believed that war with Germany was inevitable but thought that the Soviet Union would not be ready to fight until 1942. The poor performance of the Red Army in the war against Finland in 1940 confirmed him in this view. Therefore, Stalin's priorities in 1941 were to build up the Red Army and avoid doing anything that might provoke Hitler. So, for instance, deliveries of raw materials under the Nazi–Soviet Treaty, 28 September 1939, were met in full. Eighty warnings in eight months of German intentions and the build-up of troops, and repeated reconnaissance flights over Soviet territory were ignored. In the week before the invasion, Stalin refused the requests of Red Army commanders to have troops at battle readiness and in better defensive positions.

The German attack could not have come at a worst time. The Red Army and air force were in transition, changing their organisation, leadership, equipment, training, troop dispositions and defensive plans. The territorial gains after the Nazi–Soviet Pact meant that Stalin had ordered the abandonment of the old defensive lines in favour of positions on the new frontier, but by June 1941 the Russians had hardly any heavy guns, radio equipment or minefields in place on the new lines. Stalin also grossly underestimated the scale of the attack. The results were huge losses of men, territory and industrial and agricultural capacity (see page 352). 'Lenin left us a great legacy, but we, his heirs, have f----d it up,' Stalin admitted to a small group of his closest associates six days after the German invasion. It was as close as he came to admitting responsibility.

As a rallying force

'Comrades! Citizens! Brothers and Sisters! Fighters of our Army and Fleet! I address you, my friends!' So began Stalin's speech to the Russian people on 3 July 1941. This was his first speech since the German invasion and he had never addressed the Russian people in such terms before. 'All those years we had suffered from a lack of friendship and the words "my friends" moved us to tears', Konstantin Simonov recalled. Stalin spoke of a 'patriotic war of all the people' that would involve all-out support for the Red Army, defence of Russian cities with the help of a People's Militia, and partisan activity behind the German lines. Stalin realised, as he told Averell Harriman, the American diplomat, in September 1941, 'the Russian people are fighting for their homeland not for us'.

Stalin's finest hour was in October/November 1941. He stayed put during the Moscow panic. He addressed the eve of the anniversary of the Revolution rally, which had to be held in the ornate hall of the Mayakovsky metro station. 'If they want a war of extermination they shall have it! (*Prolonged and tumultuous applause.*) Our task now will be to destroy every German to the very last man! Death to the German invaders!' The parade in Red Square took place even though the distant rumble of guns could be heard – heavy snow meant it was safe from German bombers. On a film recorded in the Kremlin, Stalin spoke to the troops with a passionate appeal to a sense of Russian history (Source 19.3). Even a critic like the historian Volkogonov called this 'a bold and far-sighted move, reflecting the sure hand with which Stalin influenced public opinion and guided the people's mental state, and this at a time when many were doubtful about the outcome of the war'. Stalin has not been thought of as a great orator and only addressed the Soviet people nine times during the war, but his speeches in 1941 can be compared to those of Churchill in 1940–41 in their effect. Both leaders inspired their armed forces and civilians to fight on. Both leaders showed the leadership qualities expected in desperate times.

SOURCE 19.3   Stalin, 7 November 1941, to the armed forces in Red Square (authors' explanations in brackets)

The whole world is looking to you as the force capable of destroying the plundering hordes of the German invaders. The enslaved peoples of Europe . . . look to you as their liberators. A great liberation mission has fallen to your lot. Be worthy of this mission! The war you are waging is a war of liberation, a just war. In this war, may you draw inspiration from the valiant example of our great ancestors – Alexander Nevsky, [who defeated German knights in 1242], *Dimitry Donskoy* [who beat the Tartars in 1380], *Kuzma Minin and Dimitry Pozharsky* [who drove the Poles out of Moscow to end the Time of Troubles in 1612], *Alexander Suvorov and Mikhail Kutuzov* [heroic generals during the Napoleonic wars]. *May the victorious banner of Lenin be your lodestar.*

Stalin's ruthlessness

There is no evidence to suggest that Stalin suffered even the slightest remorse about sending millions to their deaths in battle and costly frontal assaults were often made. In 1941–42, his inflexible, standfast mentality prevented tactical withdrawals that would have avoided the catastrophic losses sustained when Kiev was encircled. Harsh discipline was imposed and scapegoats were sought for the initial disasters. General Pavlov, who had tried to hold the front line in the first week of the war, was arrested, accused of involvement in an anti-Soviet conspiracy, tortured and sentenced to death by a military tribunal for 'cowardice, panic-mongering, criminal negligence and unauthorised retreats'. He was shot along with three of his key subordinates. A number of high-ranking officers of the Red Air Force were arrested and blamed for the devastating attacks on Soviet airfields on 22 June. A special department of the NKVD was set up to lead the struggle against spies and traitors in the Red Army and had the authority to execute deserters on the spot.

Order 270 16 August 1941
Issued after the surrender of 100,000 encircled men at Uman in northwest Ukraine.

'Commanders and commissars who leave the front or surrender will be considered deserters and their families liable to arrest. The families of Red Army men surrendering to captivity will be deprived of state entitlements and assistance.'

Order 227 28 July 1942
Issued at the low point of the war after Rostov had fallen with barely a fight and when army discipline began to break down.

'Not a step back! This must now be our chief slogan. It is necessary to defend to the last drop of blood every position, every metre of Soviet territory, to cling on to every shred of Soviet earth and defend it to the utmost.'

Orders 270 and 227 were distributed to all fighting units in the army. They highlight the dilemma of the Red Army soldier: he was a deserter if he surrendered and a traitor if he retreated. Any officer caught infringing the order would be shot on the spot or sent to the punishment companies. Any soldiers guilty of cowardice or wavering would be shot or sent to the punishment companies. Over 430,000 men served in punishment companies, their numbers swollen by Gulag inmates and criminals. They were sent through minefields and on other almost suicidal missions. Blocking detachments were placed behind unsteady units 'to shoot on the spot panic-mongers and cowards'.

ACTIVITIES OF NKVD ON THE DON AND STALINGRAD FRONT BETWEEN 1 AUGUST AND 15 OCTOBER 1942:

- More than 40,000 people detained
- 900 arrested
- 700 shot
- 1300 sent to penal battalions
- Remainder returned to their units

ETHNIC CLEANSING

The Soviet takeover of eastern Poland and the Baltic States in 1939–40 involved mass deportations, executions and the infamous Katyn massacre. In 1943 and 1944, as the Red Army pushed westwards, this behaviour went even further. Exaggerated reports that some members of the population had collaborated with the Germans infuriated Stalin and were used as a pretext to punish entire nations. Only the Chechen-Ligush began an anti-Soviet rebellion as the Germans approached. Two million members of ethnic minorities – Crimean Tartars, Chechens and other Transcaucasian populations – were deported to the Soviet interior. Volga Germans had been deported in 1941 – although there were no grounds for regarding them as Nazi spies. A quarter of the deported nationalities died in transit or in the first five years in special settlements.

Alexander Samsonov, the leading Soviet historian of World War II, and a harsh critic of Stalin's leadership in many respects, wrote, 'The order [227], of course, was extremely severe, but necessary at that terrible moment.' He quoted an ordinary soldier's account of his reaction: 'All my life I will remember what Stalin's order meant . . . Not the letter, but the spirit and content of the order definitely made possible the moral, psychological and spiritual break-through in the hearts and minds of all to whom it was read . . . The chief thing was that they had the courage to tell people the whole and bitter truth about the abyss to whose edge we had slid.' Stalin later admitted that the Soviets were in a desperate situation having lost 70 million people and vast resources of grain and materials in the first months of the war and he needed to stop further retreats.

Stalin was also psychologically preparing the troops to make a final stand at Stalingrad and elsewhere. The sanctions against 'waverers' were not only to encourage discipline but also to bolster those who inclined to heroism. At the Battle of Stalingrad an estimated 13,500 Soviet troops were shot in the space of a few weeks. However, at less desperate times the order was frequently ignored. On balance, reports suggest that it had a positive effect but its impact can be exaggerated. It was aimed primarily at officers and political commissars and applied only to unauthorised retreats. Blocking detachments were abolished in October 1942 but the NKVD continued to carry out the same role.

Stalin and his generals

Stalin had been involved in major campaigns during the Civil War as a Politburo representative at the Front, but he was essentially an amateur in strategic and operational matters. Nevertheless, he exercised greater control over the country's war effort than any other national leader and was involved in the detailed planning and direction of military operations. His decisions, often made against good military advice, were responsible for some of the worst disasters of 1941–42. The over-ambitious counter offensives of the first half of 1942 which led to further big losses of men and territory had a sobering effect on Stalin. After this, Geoffrey Roberts writes, 'He listened more to the advice of his High Command, the advice got better and he got better at taking it.' The Red Army was learning and developing too. Both factors were important for victory at Stalingrad and beyond. Stalin demoted civil war cronies, like Voroshilov, and in early October 1942 the political officers were downgraded, increasing the prestige and power of the Red Army officer corps.

Stalin came to rely increasingly on three very able men: Vasilevsky, appointed Chief of the General Staff; Antonov (his deputy); and Zhukov, the hero of Leningrad and Moscow, whom he appointed as his Deputy Supreme Commander of the Soviet Armed Forces. Zhukov and Vasilevsky, conferring with Stalin at each stage, planned the deep, double encirclement of the German 6th Army at Stalingrad, which was the key to success. Although Hitler made mistakes, the Battle of Stalingrad was won by the Red Army rather than lost by the Germans.

Victory helped transform relations between Stalin and his generals and led to a better balance between his power and their expertise. Stalin accepted Zhukov's rejection of his plans for a 'pre-emptive offensive' in favour of the latter's defence in depth at Kursk – also backed by Vasilevsky and Antonov. This saved the Red Army from another disastrous summer campaign and instead ended any realistic prospect of German victory. In 1944, Operation Bagration (named by Stalin after a Georgian commander in the Napoleonic wars) was carefully prepared by Zhukov and Vasilevsky. Stalin had the last word on all strategic decisions but had learned to trust his High Command on many operational matters and to concentrate his energies on troop morale and battle readiness, supplies issues and the work of political officers in the Red Army. After meeting him in October 1944, General Sir Alan Brooke, Chief of the Imperial General Staff and the ablest British strategist of World War II, came away 'more than ever impressed by the dictator's military ability'.

ACTIVITY

Using Sources 19.4–19.8 and the chart you have made as you have gone through this section, prepare for a class discussion on the topic: Do you agree with Volkogonov that the Soviet Union triumphed not because of Stalin but in spite of him?

The verdict on Stalin's contribution

There is a great deal of debate about Stalin's contribution to the war. Would Hitler have been defeated without Stalin? Does Soviet victory prove that the whole Stalinist line – collectivisation, industrial growth, the destruction of the opposition – was correct? Or, was it due to Stalin's policies that the Germans got as far as Stalingrad? Stalin had no doubts himself, as Khrushchev informs us in Source 19.5.

SOURCE 19.4   D. Volkogonov, 'Stalin as Supreme Commander', in B. Wegner (ed.) *From Peace to War*, 1997, pp. 463–4 and 477

His (Stalin's) highly amateurish and incompetent military leadership, especially during the first year and a half of the war, manifested itself in catastrophic losses in terms of material and manpower. But the Soviet people were able to withstand this, not because of Stalin's genius but in spite of it . . . As Supreme Commander of the armed forces, Stalin led them to victory, but at the cost of unimaginable losses.

SOURCE 19.5   Khrushchev's 20th Party Congress speech, 1956

*Stalin very energetically popularised himself as a great leader; in various ways he tried to inculcate in the people the version that all the victories gained by the Soviet nation during the Great Patriotic War were due to the courage, daring and genius of Stalin and to no one else . . . Not Stalin, but the party as a whole, the Soviet Government, our heroic army, its talented leaders and brave soldiers, the whole Soviet nation – these are the ones who assured the victory in the Great Patriotic War. (*Tempestuous and prolonged applause.*)*

SOURCE 19.6   Roy Medvedev, *Let History Judge: The Origins and Consequences of Stalinism*, 1973, p. 455. Medvedev was a dissident and one of the severest critics of Stalinism

Stalin's name became a sort of symbol existing in the popular mentality independently of its actual bearer. During the war years, as the Soviet people were battered by unbelievable miseries, the name of Stalin and faith in him to some degree pulled the Soviet people together, giving them hope of victory.

SOURCE 19.7   Averell Harriman, US Ambassador in Moscow 1943–45, probably had more direct dealings with Stalin than any other foreigner during the war. W. Averell Harriman, 'Stalin At War', in G.R. Urban (ed.) *Stalinism*, 1982, pp. 41–42

Stalin the War Leader . . . was popular, and there can be no doubt that he was the one who held the Soviet Union together . . . I do not think anyone else could have done it . . . I'd like to emphasise my great admiration for Stalin the national leader in an emergency – one of those historical occasions when one man made such a difference. This in no sense minimises my revulsion against his cruelties; but I have to give you the constructive side as well as the other.

SOURCE 19.8   R. Overy, *Russia's War*, 1997, p. 328

At least part of the answer (to Soviet victory) must lie with Stalin and, below him, the political system which ran the Soviet war effort. Stalin supplied more than a capricious despotism. His willingness to bow to the military experts, hard though it must have been to do, showed in the end a sensible awareness of the limits of despotism. The image of Stalin supplied to the public – of a leader who was brave, all-seeing, steadfast – was a necessary one, however distant it was from reality. The contrast between his intervention in the war effort and that of the Tsar thirty years earlier is illuminating: Stalin became a necessary part of the machinery of re-conquest; Nicholas remained superfluous to it.

FOCUS ROUTE

As you work through this section make notes on:

- The impact of the German invasion
- The relocation and conversion of industry
- The success of mass production
- Why the Soviet economy did not collapse
- The contribution of Lend-Lease
- Agriculture

C The Soviet war economy – 'Everything for the Front!'

The Stalinist system came into its own during the war. Even before the war, the USSR could be represented as a garrison state making use of extraordinary forms of administration and control. One of the most important reasons why the Red Army was able to defeat the Germans was that in 1942–43 Soviet factories were producing aircraft, tanks, guns and shells faster than German factories. They were able to do this in spite of the terrible losses wrought by Operation Barbarossa, which took place in one of the country's most industrially developed regions containing so much of the country's defence capacity (see table below). In November 1941, industrial production was only 51.7 per cent the output of November 1940.

SOURCE 19.9 What the Russians lost in the area occupied by the Germans by the end of November 1941

85%+	of pre-war aircraft factories
70%+	of the capacity for coking coal and iron ore
60%+	of the capacity for pig iron, coal and aluminium and factories for making armaments and explosive powder
50%+	of the capacity for steel making and steel rolling, including the key rolling mill for armour steel
300+	armament factories including nine big tank factories
40%	of the capacity for electric power and railway freight
40%	of pre-war grain harvests and cattle stocks
60%	of pre-war pig herds
84%	of the domestic sugar producing capacity

The Russians set up an evacuation committee two days after the German attack to relocate machines, equipment and manpower vital for the war effort to the east. By the end of 1941, 1523 factories had been moved (their size and nature meant their economic significance was much greater than their number), including more than 100 aircraft factories. And along with the plant and machinery went hundreds of thousands of workers. There were up to a million and a half railway wagon loads of cargo. All this was done in conditions of haste, enemy harassment and shortages of railway trucks. In the summer of 1942, 150 large factories were evacuated from the Don and Volga regions. Between eight and ten per cent of the USSR's productive capacity was moved. In addition, 3500 new factories were created, most of them dedicated to armaments, and manufacturing industry was converted to war production.

Industry was geared almost entirely to the needs of the armed forces. The USSR out-produced Germany in the second half of 1942 by making considerably more effective use of its limited industrial resources. The key to this was the application of mass production methods. Soviet industry produced fewer models of each type of weapon, and subjected them to less modification. The famous T-34 tank underwent just one major wartime modification and the number of man-hours required to produce it fell from 8000 in 1941 to only 3700 in 1943. Production was concentrated in regions. For example, six sites produced 90 per cent of all tanks; a similar situation existed with aircraft.

Because of this focus, the civilian economy was neglected and living standards fell on average by two-fifths. Millions were severely overworked, under-nourished and very cold. Factory discipline was fierce with severe punishments for lateness and absenteeism (there were 7.5 million convictions for those 'crimes' during the war). The concentration on war production had become so great that the economic historian Mark Harrison argues that without Allied help the authorities would have been compelled in 1943 to withdraw major resources from fighting in order to avoid economic collapse. This help came in the form of Lend-Lease.

SELECTED STATISTICS FOR SUPPLIES OF EQUIPMENT SENT TO USSR 1941–45

- 363,080 trucks
- 43,728 jeeps
- 14,203 aircraft
- 380,135 field telephones
- 14,793,000 pairs of boots
- 782,973 tons of canned meat (spam)
- 339,599 tons of copper
- 261,311 tons of aluminium

SPAM
Pre-cooked canned meat, consisting primarily of chopped pork and ham

Lend-Lease

Despite isolationist feeling in the United States, the Lend-Lease Act of March 1941 empowered President Roosevelt (who was keen to help) to give military aid to Britain and to extend help to the USSR in October. The great bulk of supplies came from the USA but Britain and the Commonwealth also contributed. Initially, the effect was small, amounting to some five per cent of Soviet GNP in 1942, but this was crucial in the balance of overall resources. Imported trucks, jeeps and railway resources gave the Red Army vital mobility which, as Khrushchev admitted in his memoirs, was crucial: 'Without them our losses would have been colossal because we would have had no manoeuvrability.' One third of all Soviet vehicles came from abroad and were generally of better quality and more durable than home-produced ones. Studebaker trucks were particularly popular with the Red Army. American locomotives, railway wagons and rails were vital in the rebuilding or redirecting of Soviet railways – firstly to connect the new industrial bases in the east with military fronts, and then to replace those destroyed by the Germans. Whereas in the First World War railways had contributed to the collapse of the Tsarist regime, now they carried the men and *matériel* that enabled the Soviet armed forces to defeat the Nazis. Khrushchev admitted, too, that, 'without SPAM we wouldn't have been able to feed our army'. In 1943 and 1944 Lend-Lease contributed 10 per cent of the GDP of the USSR. Without it the defeat of the Wehrmacht would have taken 12 to 18 months longer.

There were three main routes by which Lend-Lease goods arrived:
- the hazardous Arctic convoy route, from Britain and the American east coast to Murmansk and Archangel in North Russia
- the Pacific route from the west coast of America to the Siberian ports
- the overland route via the Persian Gulf and through Iran.

Agriculture

Life was incredibly hard for the peasants. The countryside had been stripped of men, horses and machinery so that by the end of the war four out of five collective farmers were women, and carts and ploughs were increasingly pulled by human beings. The worst year for agriculture was 1943 with total output 38 per cent of the 1940 level. Malnutrition was general and pervasive. Under the rationing system only combat soldiers and manual workers in the most difficult and hazardous occupations were guaranteed sufficient food to maintain health. Half the population – the farming families – did not receive state rations at all. Consequently, the peasant's private plot was vital. The peasants had to consume most of what it produced to stay alive (their diet was dominated by potatoes and cabbage) and they could trade any surplus. Private trade revived for the first time since the NEP and town inhabitants travelled to the countryside in search of food. The state procurement of food from collective farms was probably even more ruthless than during the Civil War, but patriotism overrode the peasants' hatred of the collective farm system. Alec Nove summed up the situation: 'There was much that was genuinely heroic in the conduct of millions of overworked and underfed peasants, mostly women, who somehow kept the towns and soldiers fed under conditions that we have difficulty even imagining.'

ПЕРЕДОВЫМ КОЛХОЗАМ -ФРОНТОВОЕ СПАСИБО!

SOURCE 19.10 Victor Ivanov and Olga Burova's poster *'Frontline thanks to leading collective farms!'*, 1944

FOCUS ROUTE

As you work through this section make a note of key examples of resilience which you could use in an essay.

D The resilience of the Soviet people

On the day after the Victory Parade at a reception in the Kremlin, Stalin offered a toast 'to those simple, ordinary, modest people, to the "little cogs" who keep our great state mechanism in an active condition in all fields of science, economy and military affairs'. Soviet victory was won by the people, both men and women, but at enormous cost. They fought and worked to defend their homeland in a war for national survival against an utterly ruthless enemy.

Women and the war

When Stalin praised the contribution of Soviet women to the war effort he only mentioned those at the home front; the million women who had served in the armed forces were omitted and were not allowed to participate in the Great Moscow Victory Parade. After the war any image of Soviet woman as a military officer or pilot was buried by the overwhelming official emphasis on the Soviet woman as mother, wife and builder of society. In one sense this emphasis is a useful corrective. Women snipers and the flyers have attracted most attention, but it was the perseverance and determination of women in occupied zones and behind the front lines that contributed just as much, if not more, to their country's survival and ultimate triumph.

Partisans

Stalin demanded the creation of partisan units in the territory occupied by the Germans, operating 'anywhere and everywhere' to cause havoc by guerrilla warfare. A murderous struggle ensued between the partisans and the Germans and their collaborators. The Germans were ruthless. In September 1941, the order was issued that between 50 and 100 Communists should be killed for every German victim of a partisan attack: 250,000 were killed in anti-partisan operations in Belorussia – the area of greatest partisan activity. In the later part of 1941, members of the party and Komsomol activists were sent to help the partisans (see Zoya below). It was important for the Soviet leadership as it kept the occupied area in touch with Moscow and by mid-1942 each partisan unit had an NKVD cell attached to it to keep the group in line. Overall, Evan Mawdsley judges that the partisans probably reduced collaboration with the Germans by the local population and were responsible for the largest and most successful guerrilla campaign of the Second World War.

Zoya Kosmodemyanskaya
Zoya was an 18-year-old school girl Komsomol volunteer from Moscow. She was known as Tanya among the partisans and was captured by the Germans in the village of Petrishchevo at the end of November 1941, having set fire to stables used by the Germans. She did not break under torture and interrogation and had gone defiantly to her public hanging. There are various versions of her last words, including 'Stalin is with us', but all agree that she urged her comrades to fight on and told the Germans that she was not alone – there were 'one hundred and ninety million of us and you can't hang us all!' When the Red Army recaptured the place a few days later, her frozen, mutilated body was found. Her story was reported in *Pravda* and she became a powerful propaganda symbol; she was made a hero of the Soviet Union in February 1942. A long poem was written about her that year and the three artists who made up the Kukryniksy (see page 358) began the painting in Source 19.11 (page 356).

In the front line

Fractionally under 500,000 women served in the ranks of the armed forces and 500,000 in civilian support staff. Eventually all childless women aged 18–25 not engaged in work vital for the war effort were called to arms.

Women were particularly good snipers. The Central Women's School for Sniper Training turned out 1061 snipers and 407 instructors; its 'graduates' killed 12,000 German soldiers.

There were three separate women's air regiments: night bombers, day bombers and fighters. The feared 'night witches' (night bombers) flew 23,672 sorties in flimsy biplanes and 23 received the Hero of the Soviet Union award.

Women also fought as machine-gunners and in tanks, but they were most valued by fellow male soldiers as medics and signallers. 100 per cent of the nurses and over 40 per cent of doctors and field surgeons at the front were women and they suffered heavy casualties. Being a sapper or radio operator during the Battle of Stalingrad was very dangerous.

In the occupied areas, women made up 25 per cent of active partisans (see Zoya page 354).

The economic contribution

'Men to the front, women to the factories!'

In industry women had made up 41 per cent of the workforce before the war and between 51 and 53 per cent during the years 1942–45. In light industry 80–90 per cent of the workforce were women but even in heavy industry the proportion grew sharply. In 1942, in power stations over half of the turbine operators were women. By the end of 1944, 41 per cent of workers in the restored Donbass mines were women.

In one relocated tank factory, 8000 female workers lived in holes in the ground. But there was no wartime increase in women's share of managerial or administrative posts.

In the countryside able-bodied women outnumbered men by almost 4:1. The proportion of female labour employed in agriculture rose from 40 per cent in 1940 to over 80 per cent by the end of the war, all working predominantly by hand.

The home front

Urban sieges, rural deprivation, mass evacuation and mass deportation all played havoc with the well-being of millions of families and so hit women very hard.

With men at the front or evacuated with their factories, women made up 75 per cent of the population of Leningrad for most of the siege and so endured most of the hardship. (See Anna Akhamatova's broadcast, right.) By the end of 1942, 80 per cent of Leningrad's industrial workers were women.

Malnutrition, breakdown of public services, shortages and a 66-hour working week took its toll on women who were also having to run a home on their own.

ANNA AKHAMATOVA'S FAMOUS BROADCAST TO LENINGRAD IN 1941 ENDED LIKE THIS:

Our descendants will honour every mother who lived at the time of the war, but their gaze will be caught and held fast by the image of the Leningrad woman standing during an air raid on the roof of a house, with a boat hook and fire-tongs in her hands, protecting the city from fire; the Leningrad girl volunteer giving aid to the wounded among the still smoking ruins of a building . . . No, a city which has bred women like these cannot be conquered.

356

HOW WAS THE SOVIET UNION ABLE TO TURN DISASTER INTO VICTORY IN THE GREAT PATRIOTIC WAR?

SOURCE 19.11 The Kukryniksy, *Tanya* (1942–47)

At the front

In August 1941, a German general, Heinrici, in letters to his wife expressed his amazement at the Russians' 'astonishing strength to resist' and their astounding 'toughness'. 'Their units are all half-destroyed, but they just fill them with new people and they attack again. How the Russians manage is beyond me.' David Glantz, the leading Western historian of the Red Army, has analysed why Red Army soldiers fought so hard. 'Although naked fear of the enemy and their own officers and commissars, pervasive and constant propaganda and political agitation, threats of severe disciplinary measures and outright intimidation motivated Red Army soldiers to fight, they also fought and endured because they were patriotic.' This patriotism had a number of different sources – traditional Russian nationalism, some sort of loyalty to the Soviet state or sheer hatred of the German invaders – but it provided a powerful bond and motive force within the Red Army. This is backed up by the writer Kondratyev who was a young soldier with the Red Army and was wounded a number of times. He believed that the revival of morale had little to do with Stalin and the Party: 'It was a pure burst of love for our fatherland. That sacrificial incandescence and readiness to give one's life for it are unforgettable. Nothing like it ever happened again.' Another young soldier who made a detailed study of the culture and beliefs of the Red Army rank and file found that it was hatred of the Germans, more than anything else, which made the soldiers fight. This was reinforced in the summer of hate in 1942 by writers like Simonov and Ehrenburg (see page 358).

Orlando Figes singles out the readiness for personal sacrifice as the Soviet Union's greatest weapon. The ethos for personal sacrifice was particularly intense in the generation of 1941 – people born in the 1910s and early 1920s. The war for them was their civil war or First Five-Year Plan – represented as episodes of great collective enterprise and sacrifice. They fought with great bravery and paid the ultimate price. Only three per cent of the male cohort of soldiers born in 1923 survived until 1945. Comradeship was crucial for military cohesion and effectiveness. When, in 1942–43, military units began to stabilise, the comradeship that men found within their unit became a decisive factor in motivating them to fight.

357

HOW WAS THE SOVIET UNION ABLE TO TURN DISASTER INTO VICTORY IN THE GREAT PATRIOTIC WAR?

FOCUS ROUTE

As you work through the section and interrogate the different examples of propaganda, identify the different messages put forward.

E Soviet wartime propaganda: drumming up support and maintaining morale

The military oath on the poster begins: 'I, a citizen of the Union of Soviet Socialist Republics, entering the ranks of the Worker-Peasant Army, take an oath and solemnly swear to be an honest, brave, disciplined and vigilant fighter, to strictly protect military and state secrecy, unquestioningly to fulfil all military regulations and orders of commanders and bosses.' It ends: 'If, by malicious intent, I break this solemn vow, then let the severe punishment of the Soviet law overtake me: the universal hatred and contempt of the toilers'

SOURCE 19.12 I. Toidze, *Motherland Calls!* (1941).

As well as two mighty armies, two powerful propaganda machines were in action on the Eastern Front. In the Soviet Union, propaganda was particularly intense in the armed forces. Over 1000 writers and artists joined the campaign to report on the front, 400 of whom would die in the fighting. Their work was controlled by the Sovinformburo. Everything from *Pravda* to the news-sheets that soldiers were given at the front was monitored for ideological mistakes. Catherine Merridale in her study of the war from the perspective of an ordinary Russian soldier writes about the early months of the war (Source 19.13).

This tight control was not confined to journalism. People were imprisoned for loose 'defeatist talk' about the situation at the front. One woman was sentenced to seven years for telling a friend about the bombing of Smolensk. A network of political officers acted as agitators and teachers in every regiment. There was no escape from their lectures and slogans. They were ordered, 'to teach them implacable hatred and rage against the enemy, ardently to crush the fascist cur, to grind his face into the earth, to be prepared to fight to the last drop of their blood for every inch of Soviet soil'. Two of the Sovinformburo's most talented writers were Konstantin Simonov and Ilya Ehrenburg (see page 358).

SOURCE 19.13 Catherine Merridale, *Ivan's War*, 2005, pp. 94–96

Red Army troops were presented, effectively, with two wars simultaneously. The first, the one that they alone could know, was the war of the battlefield, the screaming war of shells and smoke, the shameful one of terror and retreat. But the other war . . . was the one the propaganda created. Soldiers and civilians alike could learn about it in newspapers, the most popular of which, Red Star, *was read aloud to small groups at the front. Serving troops saw film shows that included newsreel, some of which, because it was carefully staged, could seem more vivid than their own fragmented memories of combat . . . Stalin's official war unfolded with an epic certainty, in regular and well-planned episodes. Each captured or disabled German tank and plane were recorded . . . but the blank space where Soviet losses should have been, padded with slogans and even short verse, was noticed by newspaper readers everywhere.*

Konstantin Simonov

Simonov was an outstanding war correspondent, poet and novelist. He wrote in *Red Star* from all the critical fronts and accepted that he had a propaganda role. His reports aimed to strengthen morale and discipline, foster love of Stalin and hatred of the enemy. His poem 'Kill Him' was published in the same week as Ehrenburg's article (Source 19.14) and contributed to the summer of hate in 1942. Officers would read it to their men before they went into battle. This was partly because of the huge success of his poem 'Wait For Me', written in the summer of 1941. It voiced both the soldiers' romantic yearnings and their anxieties about the fidelity of their wives and girlfriends. Many Red Army soldiers kept Simonov's poem in their pockets. During the war Simonov did not do too much waiting. He was particularly attracted to women in military uniforms and liked to have sex on a Nazi flag, which he had recovered from the front. Simonov became part of the Stalinist élite after the war and a leading member of the Writers' Union. However, at the end of the 1950s he began to reassess Stalin's role, eventually taking the view that it was the people who had won the war and done so in spite of Stalin, and he addressed the regime's appalling waste of human life.

SOURCE 19.14 Ilya Ehrenburg, 'Kill the Germans', *Red Star*, 13 August 1942. This was typical of Ehrenburg's anti-German writings in *Red Star*. Stalin said they were 'worth two divisions'

The Germans are not human beings. Henceforth the word German means to us the most terrible curse. From now on the word German will trigger your rifle . . . If you have not killed at least one German a day, you have wasted that day . . . If you cannot kill your German with a bullet, kill him with your bayonet . . . If you leave a German alive, the German will hang a Russian and rape a Russian woman. If you kill one German, kill another – there is nothing jollier for us than a heap of German corpses. Do not count days; do not count miles. Count only the number of Germans you have killed. Kill the German – this is your old mother's prayer. Kill the German – this is what your children beseech you to do. Kill the German – this is the cry of your Russian earth. Do not waver. Do not let up. Kill.

When Stalin addressed the Red Army's State Parade in Red Square on the anniversary of the Revolution, he called on the soldiers to emulate their ancestors (see Source 19.3 page 349). It connected seamlessly with Soviet patriotic identity and the leader's own cult of personality. Political officers carried pocket-sized paperbacks describing outstanding Russian military leaders. Films were made about Suvorov and Kutuzov. Eisenstein's *Alexander Nevsky* ends, 'Whosoever comes against us by the sword shall perish by the sword. Such is the law of the Russian land and such it will always be.' Just the right note for the time!

Soviet artists were thoroughly involved too. The Kukryniksy was the collective name for three graphic artists who had worked together since they were students in the early 1920s. They wrote of their work: 'We aim at arousing in the Red Army, and among the workers on the Home Front, wrath and contempt for the enemy. We aim at amusing them, because what can raise the spirits like wholesome laughter? . . . From day to day we brand and expose and ridicule the enemy in hundreds of cartoons, for that is how we understand the artist's and satirist's task in wartime.' They were among 200 artists in Moscow alone who worked on posters displayed in Tass windows and were distributed throughout the country. (Tass was the news agency which superseded ROSTA in 1925.)

SOURCE 19.15 The Kukryniksy, *Smash and Destroy the Enemy Without Mercy!*, produced two days after the launch of Operation Barbarossa. Hitler's face pokes through the torn-up non-aggression treaty and the discarded mask of peace

SOURCE 19.16 V. Koretsky, *Red Army Serviceman, Save!* (1941)

SOURCE 19.17 The Kukryniksy, *Transformation of fritzes* (The TASS Window No. 640) (1942)

SOURCE 19.18 P. Korin, *Alexander Nevsky* (1942–3)

359

HOW WAS THE SOVIET UNION ABLE TO TURN DISASTER INTO VICTORY IN THE GREAT PATRIOTIC WAR?

SOURCE 19.19 Metropolitan Sergei, 22 June 1941

The Fascist brigands have fallen upon our native land . . . Our Orthodox Church has always shared the destiny of the people, bearing their trials, rejoicing in their successes, and this time too it is not going to forsake its people, bestowing as it does, the blessing of Heaven upon the forthcoming heroic exploit of the whole people.

SOURCE 19.20 *Pravda*, 20 July 1941

At a menacing time, when over our motherland hung grave danger, all the thoughts of the Soviet people turned to the glorious Bolshevik Party, to the father and friend of all toilers – comrade Stalin. 'For the Motherland, for Stalin!' With this fighting cry, soldiers, commanders and political workers of the Red Army accomplished marvels of bravery, destroying fascists . . . Comrade Stalin's name is a symbol of great victories, a symbol of the unity of the Soviet people.

The role of the Orthodox Church

The war was described as a 'Holy War' by the regime. Despite the best efforts of the Communists, in the 1937 census, 55 per cent of the people declared themselves religious believers. Stalin did not ignore this source of popular support. The Orthodox Church played its part: Metropolitan Sergei responded immediately to the German invasion (see Source 19.19). Nevertheless, it was not until September 1943 that Stalin met Metropolitan Sergei, abolished the League of the Godless, permitted the restricted publication of church literature within the USSR, the restoration of churches, and the publication of statements by Orthodox clergy in the Russian-language Soviet press. This was more than two years after the German attack and when the tide had very definitely turned. The overwhelming majority of the 15,000 Orthodox Church re-openings, which occurred by the end of the war, were in Ukraine and other western border areas, rather than in Russia itself. Stalin wanted to use the Orthodox Church to help re-establish Soviet power in non-Russian areas, where anti-Soviet nationalists had often been supported by local clerics. The Church could help the Kremlin by taming or removing rebellious clerics and could contribute to the Russification of the borderlands as it had in tsarist times. For its part, the Church acknowledged Stalin as 'the divinely anointed leader of our armed forces leading us to victory over the barbarian invasion'.

How effective was the propaganda?

The aim of any wartime government is to maintain morale, to persuade the people to make the effort and sacrifice required to achieve victory and to build confidence in the government's (and especially its leader's) ability to defeat the enemy. There was little chance that the Soviet government would neglect the last point. John Barber in his essay, *The Image of Stalin in Soviet Propaganda*, points out that from the start of the war Stalin was identified with the motherland (rodina). The early disasters did not lead to any suspension of the Stalin cult (see Source 19.20). Ehrenburg wrote that the soldiers fervently believed in him: 'On the walls I saw his photograph cut out of newspapers.' John Barber concludes that, 'perhaps what Stalin represented for ordinary people more than anything else during the war was hope – hope of victory, hope of survival, hope against hope that those in power cared about the millions they ruled.' David Glantz argues that 'pervasive and constant propaganda and political agitation' was one of the factors which helped make the Red Army fight so hard.

The propaganda had a darker side too. When the Red Army entered East Prussia, Ehrenburg announced that the hour of revenge had struck and this was reinforced by political officers and posters. They told their men that 'on German soil there is only one master – the Soviet soldier, that he is both the judge and punisher for the torments of his fathers and mothers, for the destroyed cities and villages.' Lev Kopelev was horrified by the looting, rape and plunder and in part blamed the Soviet propaganda machine. 'Millions of people had been brutalised and corrupted by the war and by our propaganda – bellicose, jingoistic and false. I had believed such propaganda necessary . . . but had also come to understand that from seeds like these come poisoned fruit.'

ACTIVITY

Analyse the examples of Soviet propaganda by identifying the message and assessing its effectiveness.

	Message	Effectiveness
Posters		
Source 19.10 *Frontline thanks to leading collective farms!*		
Source 19.12 *Motherland Calls!*		
Source 19.15 *Smash and Destroy the Enemy Without Mercy!*		
Source 19.16 *Red Army Serviceman, Save!*		
Source 19.17 *Transformation of fritzes*		
Paintings		
Source 19.11 *Tanya*		
Source 19.18 *Alexander Nevsky*		
Speeches, writing		
Source 19.3 Stalin, 7 November 1941		
Source 19.14 'Kill the Germans'		
Source 19.19 Metropolitan Sergei		
Source 19.20 *Pravda*, 20 July 1941		

F Why was the Soviet Union able to turn disaster into victory?

In Russia, this question has been answered in different ways over the years. At first the leadership of Stalin was the crucial factor and when this was attacked by Khrushchev, the war was seen as a triumph of communist discipline and leadership. Later the emphasis was on the Soviet people and their patriotism, resilience and endurance. None of these is a sufficient explanation although they all combined together to help defeat the most formidable army of the day.

The patriotism of the Soviet people cannot be overestimated. It was spontaneous: they were not just reacting to the horrors of Nazi occupation and the reinvigoration of nationalism and Orthodoxy by the Soviet government. The war brought people together in a way that the revolution and civil war had never done. The American Hedrick Smith recalls a Jewish scientist shocking his friends in conversation in the early 1970s by saying that the war was 'the best time of our lives ... because at that time we all felt closer to our government than at any other time in our lives. It was not their country then, but our country. It was not they who wanted this or that to be done, but we who wanted to do it. It was not their war, but our war. It was our country we were defending, our war effort.' (H. Smith, *The Russians*, 1976, p. 369.)

The war was a great test of the Stalinist system. Two comparisons with the First World War, when patriotism did not prevail, are instructive. First, even though there was not enough food, the priorities of Soviet food distribution were maintained and the more highly developed transport system meant that there were never the sort of problems and resistance in the towns that brought down tsarism. Second, heavy casualties meant that the personnel in the army changed greatly during the course of the war. In the First World War the army became less loyal and in the end would not support the Tsar; in the Great Patriotic War, by the end of 1942 the third generation Red Army had been created and became an effective modern army and Stalin's position was unassailable.

In this chapter the emphasis has been on the actions of the Soviet people and their leaders, but three other factors should be considered:

1 The Soviet Union was not alone. Stalin himself said that it was 'the coalition of the USSR, Great Britain and the USA against the German-fascist imperialists' that made the defeat of Hitler inevitable. He also acknowledged the value of Lend-Lease to his close associates: 'If we had had to deal with Germany one-to-one we could not have coped because we had lost so much of our industry.' Further, the Allied landings in Europe and the impact of their strategic bombing of Germany contributed to the comparative ease of the Red Army's advance in the second half of 1944.

2 Geography and weather. The sheer size of the USSR and the difficult climate contributed to the Russian victory. Stalin referred to 'General Winter', which played a part in defeating the Germans who were ill-prepared for the winter conditions. The Red Army coped much better with the climate and, as they drove the Germans back to Berlin, the distances.

3 Mistakes by Hitler and the Germans. After the war, German generals were quick to blame Hitler, but historians have argued that they should take their share of the responsibility. Nazi ideology led to the biggest mistakes: a serious underestimation of the strength of the USSR and the genocidal intent towards the people of the USSR. Hitler had promised a war of annihilation 'conducted with unprecedented, unmerciful and unrelenting harshness.' All captured Jews, party and state functionaries and intellectuals were to be killed. Hitler designated the Slavs as sub-human. Even the nationalities in the Baltic States and the western Ukraine who had welcomed the Germans as liberators were quickly alienated. By 1942 the Soviet people, particularly the soldiers at the front who entered recaptured territory, could have had no doubts about the horrors the Germans had in store for them. (By February 1942, the Germans had let two million of the three million prisoners of war captured in 1941 die.) This played its part in the mobilisation of the people to defeat the enemy. Robert Service goes as far as to say: 'If it had not been for Hitler's fanatical racism, the USSR would not have won the struggle on the Eastern Front. Stalin's repressiveness towards his own citizens would have cost him the war against Nazi Germany.'

The first six months of the war were an almost unmitigated disaster for the unprepared USSR. But the Red Army first halted and then inflicted the first major defeat on the German army without which it is difficult to see how the Western democracies, Britain and the USA, could have expelled Germany from its new Empire. The reasons for this turnaround have been explored in this chapter. The British historians John Barber and Mark Harrison provide a comprehensive answer (Source 19.21).

SOURCE 19.21   J. Barber and M. Harrison, *The Soviet Home Front 1941–1945*, 1991, p. 211

What enabled the Russians to wage such a terrible war and emerge victorious? The answer to these questions is the same – everything in their history, their revolutionary and national traditions, their cultural ties and family roles, the social, economic and administrative webs which defined their place in Soviet life, the organs of state, the Party and its leaders, and Stalin too. All these are indispensable elements of the explanation of what made them fight, and why victory cost them so much.

363

HOW WAS THE SOVIET UNION ABLE TO TURN DISASTER INTO VICTORY IN THE GREAT PATRIOTIC WAR?

ACTIVITY

Using the information you have gathered in this section, write an essay to answer the question: Why was the Soviet Union able to turn disaster into triumph in the Great Patriotic War?

Use this diamond nine activity to think about the relative importance you wish to give the different explanations. For instance, would you put Stalin's contribution at the top?

Make your own copy of the cards below. Choose the nine cards that you think are the most important in answering the question. Arrange them in the shape of a diamond like the one shown here. Put the one you think is most important at the top, the next two most important ones on the second line and so on.

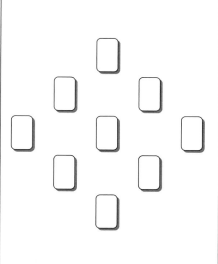

1 If it had not been for Hitler's fanatical racism, the USSR would not have won the struggle on the Eastern front	2 Geography and weather: The USSR was so huge and the climate so harsh that it was very difficult to invade successfully	3 The USSR was part of a superior coalition; Germany's allies were of little help	4 The USSR was able to raise huge armies in spite of suffering 10 million deaths in the armed forces
5 Stalin proved to be an effective military executive who was right at the centre of running the war. He learned; Hitler didn't	6 The population fused together so that the patriotism and endurance of the Soviet people won the war	7 Victory was a triumph for the system and the result of communist discipline and leadership	8 An economy geared almost exclusively to armaments out-produced Germany
9 Soviet propaganda, particularly intense in the armed forces, played its part in the patriotic response	10 Stalin was popular, as a war leader he held the Soviet Union together	11 Lend-Lease was crucial in the balance of overall resources and gave the Red Army vital mobility	12 The strategic mistakes of Hitler and his generals contributed to the German defeat

KEY POINTS FROM CHAPTER 19

How was the Soviet Union able to turn disaster into victory in the Great Patriotic War?

1 Stalin's purge of the military in the 1930s weakened the army, damaged morale and stifled initiative. It contributed to the disaster of June 1941.

2 The first few months of Germany's Operation Barbarossa were a disaster for the Soviet Union, but it was checked outside Leningrad and Moscow and had not achieved its objectives by the end of the year.

3 By 1943 the Red Army had developed into an effective modern army. Victory at Stalingrad was a turning point in the war.

4 Stalin's contribution was influential, but there is debate over whether the USSR defeated Germany because of, or in spite of, him.

5 The economy was seriously hit by early territorial losses The Soviet command economy came into its own during the war, enabling it to produce more military hardware than Germany.

6 The strain of the war effort brought the economy close to collapse by the end of 1942. Lend-Lease made a significant contribution to preventing a collapse. It underlines the point that the USSR was part of a superior coalition; Germany's allies were of little help.

7 Women's perseverance and determination played a vital and underestimated role in the USSR's survival and triumph.

8 In a people's war, patriotism and readiness for self sacrifice were key factors in Soviet success.

9 An appeal to patriotism, Russian history and hatred of the Germans were the key themes in wartime propaganda.

10 Invading the USSR was a huge undertaking. Hitler's fanatical racism alienated the Soviet people and contributed to his defeat.

11 The Soviet contribution to the defeat of Hitler has been underestimated. At no time were less than two thirds of Germany's forces committed to the Eastern Front. It was here that the war was won and lost.

Stalin's final years and Conclusion

20   Stalin's final years 1945–1953

CHAPTER OVERVIEW

Russia had suffered unimaginable loss of life and material damage as a result of the war and the final years of Stalin's rule were taken up with reconstruction. To achieve this, he returned to the centrally planned economy of the 1930s to manage industry and agriculture. He also returned to pre-war methods of control despite the desire of Soviet citizens for a more relaxed and humane society. He mounted a campaign of Russian nationalism and anti-Westernism to prevent the USSR being contaminated by 'democratic' ideas from the West. This was combined with a drive for ideological and cultural purity to bring the intelligentsia into line and push the USSR towards the Communist Utopia. He remained supreme leader of the one-party state and manipulated the main contenders for the leadership to ensure that he stayed in power and achieved the outcomes he wanted. He died in 1953.

A Tightening control (pp. 365–367)

B Post-war reconstruction (pp. 368–369)

C Stalin and the party (pp. 370–371)

D The end of Stalin (pp. 372–373)

E How can we explain Stalinism? (pp. 373–375)

F Was Stalinism Lenin's baby? (pp. 376–381)

G Assessing Stalin (pp. 382–386)

SOURCE 20.1 *The Morning of our Motherland*, a painting by F. Shurpin, 1948

FOCUS ROUTE

Make notes on:
- the losses suffered by the Soviet Union
- the treatment of the army and POWs
- the treatment of people in the newly annexed territories and repatriated communities
- the policies adopted by Stalin.

REPATRIATION

Under the Yalta agreement signed by Stalin, Roosevelt and Churchill in 1945, it was agreed that Soviet citizens in the areas liberated by the Americans and British should be repatriated to the USSR. As well as POWs, a substantial number had fought for the German army. But there were also Soviet citizens who had lived in German-held areas, many of whom were punished for real or suspected collaboration with the Germans. Many were repatriated by force. In one infamous episode in 1945, the British forced some 32,000 Cossacks, men, women and children, onto trucks and returned them to the USSR. The Cossacks knew that when they got back to the USSR they would suffer imprisonment, deportation to a remote area or execution; some committed suicide.

THE STORY OF P. M. GAVRILO (adapted from C. Merridale, *Ivan's War*)

Wounded in the Battle of Brest in June 1941 and certain he would die, Gavrilo fought to his last bullet, saving one grenade to hurl at the enemy before he passed out from loss of blood. His courage so impressed the Germans that, most unusually, they carried his body to a dressing station, then took him to a prisoner of war camp. It was for this act of 'surrender' that he stood accused after the liberation of his German camp in May 1945. His next home was a Soviet camp.

A Tightening control

The aftermath of the war

Russia had paid a terrible price for the war in human lives lost and people incapacitated. Some estimates put combined deaths – armed forces (over 8 million) and civilians (17 million) – at around 26–27 million, although it is difficult to be accurate; other estimates are much higher. Over 1700 towns and about 70,000 villages in the western part of the Soviet Union had been virtually obliterated as the war moved back and forth over them. The Germans had deliberately and systematically destroyed everything – houses, hospitals, factories, mills, schools, libraries, farms and farm buildings – as they retreated. Stalingrad had been a victory for the USSR but it was a heap of rubble. Around 25 million Russians were homeless. Millions were wounded and disabled and had to be looked after. Families had been pulled apart or destroyed leaving hundreds of thousands of widows and orphans. This was a physical and psychological shock of almost unimaginable proportions.

Amidst all this material and social damage, the situation in the USSR in 1945 was chaotic and unstable. Outside of the Russian Republic (RSFSR), many national groups bitterly resented being under Russian control, especially in the western Ukraine, Poland and the newly annexed Baltic States, where nationalist groups fought guerrilla-style actions against the Russian government for several years. Stalin ordered mass deportations of opponents and members of leading political élites in these countries. But also inside the RSFSR, Soviet citizens questioned whether their sacrifice and suffering had been worthwhile. Most peasants did not want to be brought back into collective farms with the low remuneration and restrictions this entailed. Workers grumbled about low pay, food rationing and a life of privation.

According to Robert Service, 'Stalin's discomfort was sharpened by the reports that broad segments of society yearned for him to abandon the policies and methods of the past.' Many Russians wanted a continuation of the more relaxed atmosphere at the end of the war; there had been rumours that things were going to get better. But any hopes of change were swiftly crushed. In 1946, Stalin announced that the victory had demonstrated the vitality of the Soviet socialist system. The 1930s model of Soviet society was re-imposed and Stalin returned to the tried and trusted pre-war methods to tighten his control. He believed that any relaxation would have imperilled his personal supremacy and vision for society.

The army was a potential threat to Stalin: it was powerful and popular after its wartime success. Stalin made sure the top generals did not receive too much praise, he reserved this for himself. He removed generals who might turn on him or side with other leaders in a power struggle. Marshall Zhukov, the war hero and master strategist, was accused of being involved in a plot against Stalin and sent to distant Odessa as commander, where he was out of the way. Top generals, such as Antonov, shared a similar fate; others fared worse, being executed or given long prison sentences. Returning Red Army soldiers were regarded with suspicion as they had seen countries in the West with standards of living way above that of the USSR. They might infect Russian society with ideas of 'democracy' and their experiences of different ways of living (see anti-Westernism, page 367). The worst treatment was reserved for former Red Army soldiers who had been prisoners of war (POWs) – Order No. 270 had declared them traitors. About half were condemned to the Gulag, even though many had already suffered horribly in German concentration camps. Numbers in the Gulag swelled to about 2.5 million. This suited Stalin who wanted to use their labour to rebuild Russia.

SOURCE 20.2 Khmelko's *The Triumph of the Victorious Motherland* (1949). The painting shows the Victory Parade in Red Square and the captured German standards laid out in front of Lenin's tomb with Stalin *et al* looking on

ACTIVITY

Compare Stalin's drive on Russian nationalism with the tsarist policy of Russification (see page 19). What are the similarities and differences?

SOURCE 20.3 Robert Service, *A History of Modern Russia, From Nicholas II to Putin*, Penguin, 2003, p. 315–5

Stalin placed the Russian nation on a pedestal: 'Among all peoples of our country it is the leading people.' Official favour for things Russian went beyond precedent. The lexicographers were told to remove foreign loan words from the dictionaries. For instance, the Latin-American tango was renamed the 'slow dance'. The history of nineteenth-century science was ransacked and – glory be! – it was found that practically every major invention from the bicycle to the television had been the brainchild of an ethnic Russian.

Russian nationalism

Stalin mounted a drive to emphasise the superiority of ethnic Russians over other nationalities, despite the fact that he was a Georgian (see Source 20.3). He had been called a 'Great russian chauvinist' before, by Lenin. Stalin was a genuine believer in Russian nationalism but this policy sat well with ethnic Russians and helped to secure their support for the regime. It was also an effective way of controlling other nationalities. In the non-Russian republics the top jobs, particularly party secretaries and police chiefs, went to Russians. Soviet central planning, collective farms and other institutions and practices were imposed on the newly annexed countries. The cultures of minorities like the Latvians and Lithuanians were denigrated. The Moldavian language had Russian words added and it had to be written in Cyrillic letters. Ukrainian was decreasingly taught to Ukrainian-speaking children in the Russian Republic.

Stalin reserved particular venom for the Jews, initiating a vicious campaign of anti-Semitism. In 1948, the Jewish anti-Fascist committee, which had helped send thousands of Russian Jews to fight the Nazis, was closed down and its leaders arrested. Jewish Soviet politicians disappeared and others in important positions lost their jobs. Jewish writers and artists were arrested. Jewish schools and synagogues closed. Textbooks did not refer to the fact that Karl Marx was a Jew. Stalin talked about setting up a special area for Jews in the Soviet Union in eastern Siberia. There were a series of trials in which Zionist conspiracies were exposed, culminating in the Doctors' Plot just before Stalin died (see page 371). The reason for the campaign lay in Jewish connections to the West. Many Jews had relatives in the USA, other Western countries and the new state of Israel, which was heavily backed by the Americans. Stalin called them 'rootless cosmopolitans' who owed more loyalty to Jewish internationalism and Israel than to the Soviet state. They were suspected of being agents for the West and more particularly America, Stalin's main enemy in the Cold War.

SOURCE 20.4 Quoted in J. N. Westward, *Endurance and Endeavour, Russian History 1812–2001*, 5th edn, 2002

Zhdanov in 1947 said: 'Is it appropriate for Soviet Patriots like us, representatives of progressive Soviet culture, to take the role of admirers or disciples of bourgeois culture? Our literature reflects a society which is on a higher level than any bourgeois-democratic society, a culture which is obviously superior to bourgeois culture and therefore, it need hardly be said, has the right to teach others the new, universal morals.'

ADVENTURES OF A MONKEY

In Mikhail Zoshchenko's *Adventures of a Monkey*, during the war the hero escapes a bombed zoo but samples Soviet life and then decides to go back to his cage where he can breathe more freely. Zhdanov called the author 'the scum of the literary world'.

Anti-Westernism and cultural purity

Stalin was determined to cut access to political and cultural ideas from the West – ideas that might pollute the socialist state. People who had been in contact with the democracies of the West were screened. Few foreigners were allowed in. Russians were not allowed to travel abroad and special permission was required to travel widely inside Russia. Relatives of people who had spent time outside the Soviet Union became suspects. Western books, films and music were vilified. Information from the outside world was cut off. Internal censorship was more rigorously applied, harking back to tsarist times. Officials met newspaper editors to plan news content that was censored twice – before printing and before distribution.

This anti-Westernism fed into the field of culture which had to be subservient to the state-party line. Soviet culture was to be seen as superior to liberal, Western culture (see Source 20.4). Zhdanov was Stalin's mouthpiece in the drive for ideological and cultural purity (known as the Zhdanovshchina) and he was given the job of bringing the Russian intelligentsia into line. The arts took the first hit. Hundreds of writers, condemned for kow-towing to the West, were expelled from the Writers' Union, which meant their works could not be published. This included Anna Akhmatova, the famous poet, whom Zhdanov denounced as 'half-nun, half-whore'. Theatres were attacked for staging too many Western plays. Soviet composers were attacked because their work was supposedly corrupted by bourgeois values and did not reflect Soviet virtues and musical traditions. Shostakovich's symphonies could no longer be performed; musicians needed a special pass to listen to Stravinsky. Painters and film directors had to follow the regime's dictats. Stalin himself intervened in Eisenstein's film of Ivan the Terrible urging the director to show 'that it was necessary to be ruthless'. Stalin praised Russian literary classics although here nationalism was more important than class; he wanted Soviet schoolchildren to read Pushkin despite his aristocratic background. Similarly, Stalin took a particular interest in linguistics, dismissing class theories of linguistics and the development of the Russian language, tracing its origins to places in the RSFSR (Russian Republic) rather than Kiev in the Ukraine where academics had previously located it.

Scientists also had to adhere to the guidelines set down by the state if they wanted to survive. Crude interventions were made into science such as party acceptance of the theories of the biologist Lysenko in agriculture which held back progress in Soviet biology and led to the arrest of leading biologists who did not agree with his theory. Chemistry also suffered. Physics was different. Although Einstein's theory of relativity was dismissed as it did not fit with Marxism/Leninism, Russian scientists could not ignore it or quantum mechanics if they wished to develop the atom bomb – so the state decided to leave physicists in peace.

TROFIM LYSENKO

Lysenko was a biologist and agronomist. He claimed heritable changes in plants could be achieved by changes in the environment, rather than by genetic factors alone. So, wheat subjected to refrigeration would produce seeds that could be sown in colder climates. This suited the need to grow crops in different regions of the Soviet Union but also seemed to be Marxist since it suggested that people, subjected to the right influences, could develop socialist tendencies that could be passed on. He was appointed head of the Academy of Agricultural Sciences in 1938. The work of other biologists was discarded, including the work of some renowned geneticists, some of whom were removed from their posts and arrested. Lysenko's ideas held back the development of work on genetics in the Soviet Union until after Stalin's death.

B Post-war reconstruction

Alec Nove, the famous economic historian, calls these years an 'oddly shapeless period' because economic policy, ideas and policies were 'frozen into their pre-war mould'.

FOCUS ROUTE

Copy and complete this table to help you answer the essay question at the end of this section.

	Loss/damage: problems after war	Main policies	Positive results	Negative results
Industry				
Agriculture				

Industry

Industry had been badly affected during the war. Factories were left in ruins, mines flooded and thousands of kilometres of rail track and a great deal of rolling stock were destroyed. Added to this was the dislocation caused by moving factories to the east and changing to war production. Something like 70 per cent of industrial production had been lost in the western regions that had been occupied and these had previously been the most developed areas. As recompense, the Soviet Union had stripped defeated countries, especially Germany, of factory materials, machinery and rolling stock; it also obtained reparations from these countries. But the task of rebuilding industry presented a huge challenge.

In 1946, Stalin announced the Fourth Five-Year Plan (1946–50). The centrally planned economy was back in full force. In the chaotic circumstances of 1945, central planning was probably a useful tool. The plan was a repeat of earlier versions. Eighty-five per cent of investment was devoted to heavy industry and capital goods (which included armaments) while consumer goods took a back seat. The target was to exceed pre-war industrial levels. To achieve this, the population was mobilised – everybody was to be involved in reconstruction work. For instance, in Leningrad, workers had to contribute 30 hours a month on top of their eight-hour working day. Citizens not working had to put in 60 hours and students 10 hours. Other cities probably had similar schemes. Extra labour was provided by prisoners of war (around 2 million) and the inmates of labour camps (around 2.5 million) – the populations of which had grown exponentially after the war. They were exploited mercilessly as slave labour on the most unpleasant work, particularly in the inhospitable north, cutting timber, and mining gold and, importantly, uranium for the new atom bomb.

The results were remarkable and undoubtedly owed much to the efforts of the Russian people who were prepared to endure privation, food rationing and long hours for low pay. Factories and steel works were rebuilt and mines re-opened at astonishing rates. The great Dnieper dam was back in operation and generating electricity by 1947. The same old problems resurfaced – bottlenecks and shortages of raw materials and component parts – but the end product was impressive. Production of coal and steel passed pre-war figures and, according to Alec Nove, industrial production in general passed pre-1940 levels, although the statistics emanating from Soviet sources have to be treated with caution.

Because of the Cold War and the expansion of Russian control of Eastern Europe there was a concentration on producing armaments. In 1949, the first Soviet atomic bomb was tested, which indicated that the USSR was catching up on technical achievement – in part due to captured German scientists. However, with the focus on heavy industry, this meant that even fewer resources were devoted to consumer industries, so goods like clothes, shoes and furniture were in short supply. But there were improvements in areas such as woollen goods, cotton fabrics and sugar. The details of the Fifth Five-Year Plan which was meant to have begun in 1951 were not announced until 1952. The plan followed similar lines to the fourth and had not progressed very far before Stalin's death in 1953.

SOURCE 20.5 A. Nove, *Industrial Growth in An Economic History of the USSR 1917–1991*, 1992, p. 298

	1940	**1945**	**1950**
Coal (million tons)	165.9	149.3	261.1
Electricity (million kWhs)	48.3	43.2	91.2
Oil (million tons)	31.1	19.4	37.9
Pig iron (million tons)	14.9	8.8	19.2
Steel (million tons)	18.3	12.3	27.3
Tractors (thousands)	66.2	14.7	242.5
Cement (million tons)	5.7	1.8	10.2
Cotton fabrics (million tons)	3,900	1,617	3,899
Wool fabrics	119.7	53.6	155.2
Leather footwear (million tons)	211.0	63	203.4

Agriculture

Agriculture was in a very poor state at the end of the war:

- Whole rural districts had been wrecked. Nearly 100,000 collective farms or kolkhozes had stopped functioning. Many peasants had returned to farming the land privately.
- There was a shortage of agricultural labour since most of Red Army had been peasants and there had been a heavy loss of life. In addition, many peasant soldiers had learnt skills in the army and went into industry rather than return to the villages.
- A large amount of arable land had not been cultivated for some time and had to be brought back into production.
- There was a shortage of tractors, horses, fuel and seeds.
- Livestock had been slaughtered and stock levels were low.

All these problems, combined with a severe drought, made 1946 a dreadful year. The grain harvest was down from 47.3 million tons in 1945 to 39.6 million in 1946, approximately half the amount produced in 1940. Grain procurements to feed the people in the cities and towns took up to 70 per cent of the yield leaving barely enough for the peasants to feed themselves and keep the animals alive. In some areas, notably the Ukraine, famine reared its head again.

Agriculture as a sector remained weak throughout the rest of the time Stalin was in power. According to Alec Nove, this was largely because of over centralised control and ill-judged policy. The kolkhozes were reconstituted and all land returned to them. Strict central controls were brought in, e.g. directives on sowing and crop selection. Crop rotation schemes using particular grasses were enforced in areas unsuited to them. The ideas of the biologist, Lysenko (see page 367), were taken up and pressed on farms to disastrous effect. Stalin intended to squeeze the peasants much as the regime had done in the past. Payments for their produce were kept very low, sometimes barely covering costs. To make matters worse, taxes were increased. Since the top priority had been given to industry, the villages were not allowed electricity from state power stations and were not provided with building materials to rebuild their houses. The only thing that kept the peasants afloat was their private plots but their ability to sell surplus produce on the market was stopped in 1948. With few incentives, motivation was at rock bottom and agricultural production suffered as a result. In the Fifth Five-Year Plan, there were announcements of large projected increases in grain and meat production but nothing was done to facilitate this. At the time of Stalin's death, Soviet agriculture was still in a mess.

SOURCE 20.6 Grain production (million tons), from A. Nove, above.

1940	95.6
1945	47.3
1946	39.6
1947	65.9
1949	70.2
1952	92.2

ACTIVITY

Write a short essay to answer the question: How effective were Stalin's policies to reconstruct Russia after the war?

C Stalin and the party

SOURCE 20.7 Stalin and other Politburo members, 1945. From left: Khrushchev, Stalin, Malenkov (white uniform), Beria, Molotov

PRACTICAL JOKES

The Politburo leaders were often subjected to practical jokes. Mikoyan dressed smartly in well-cut suits. Stalin teased him about his 'fancy airs', while Beria used to slip tomatoes into his pockets and then press him against a wall till they exploded.

During the festivities for the Victory Parade at the end of the war, much to Stalin's amusement, one of his aides secretly removed the ceremonial dagger from the scabbard of (ex-Prosecutor General) Vyshinsky's diplomatic uniform and replaced it with a pickle. For the rest of the day, the others laughed at the pompous Vyshinsky strutting around wearing his pickle.

Beria wrote the word 'prick' on a piece of paper and stuck it on Khrushchev's back, without his knowing. Khrushchev never forgot this humiliation.

At the end of the war Stalin was still the all-powerful leader – the *Vozhd* – and the one party state was intact. He was accorded the title 'Generalissimo' for his defeat of the Germans and his position had been strengthened by the war. He was 66 years old and held the two top posts of Head of Government and Party Chairman. The cult of the personality was at its height. He was probably more popular than he had ever been and his image was seen as vital for national security and rebuilding the USSR's shattered economy. Yet Stalin still needed the support of the party élites and he still worried about being supplanted. He was as paranoid as ever.

The Politburo in 1945 was almost the same as it had been in 1939, with key roles for Molotov, Kaganovich, Khrushchev, Zhdanov, Malenkov and Mikoyan. Stalin controlled decision-making although he left the details to others. He used the same pre-war technique of playing people off against each other and encouraging rivalry between contenders for the leadership and party influence. He did this to protect himself but also to make sure that the members of the Politburo worked hard to produce the outcomes he wanted. It was bear-pit politics. Zhdanov was Stalin's favourite and a loyal Stalinist henchman. He had led the defence of Leningrad when it had been besieged by the Germans during the war. He fronted the campaign against Western bourgeois influences. Beria (see opposite) was Stalin's secret police chief and enforcer. In the post-war period the MVD exercised enormous and terrifying power.

SOURCE 20.8 Stalin in the background working at his dacha on the Black Sea coast. In the foreground, Svetlana, Stalin's daughter, is sitting rather uncomfortably on Beria's knee

LAVRENTI BERIA

Beria was appointed head of the NKVD in 1938 and remained so until 1953. The NKVD was renamed the MVD in 1946 and, under Beria's leadership, became more powerful than ever. Beria was highly intelligent and totally unscrupulous. He was loathed by his colleagues; he made snide comments and jokes at their expense. According to Simon Sebag Montifiore, his main interests were: 'power, terror and sex. In his office, Beria kept blackjack clubs for torturing people and the array of female underwear, sex toys and pornography that seemed to be obligatory for secret-police chiefs.' He had an extensive sex life. If he could not seduce women, he had them kidnapped and then raped them. Many were later arrested and sent to labour camps. His excesses were worse than his predecessors. Stalin came to dislike him, warning his daughter Svetlana to leave Beria's house when he discovered she was there. The leaders' wives hated Beria, fearing for their daughters.

Zhdanov's power base in Leningrad had become influential and his two lieutenants, Kuznetsov and Voznesensky, were touted as potential leaders. But Zhdanov, a heavy drinker, died suddenly in 1948 of a heart attack, although rumours spread that he had been killed by his doctors. There followed a savage purge of the Leningrad party organisation, engineered by Beria and Malenkov, probably to gain influence and deal with potential rivals. It is also likely that Stalin thought that the Leningraders were becoming a little too confident and independent. Leading Leningrad party and government officials, including Kuznetsov and Voznesensky, were arrested, forced to confess, put on trial and executed. It was a carbon copy of the pre-war purges. This made everybody at the top feel insecure. This feeling was heightened by the arrest of Molotov's wife, a Jew, for supposedly annoying Stalin by giving too warm a welcome to the Israeli ambassador; she was imprisoned.

During the Second World War the party had grown from four to six million members, with a large number under the age of 45. Many of the new intake had little knowledge of the outside world, old revolutionary history or traditions, and tended to follow directives without question. Just as before the war, the party was put in charge of co-ordinating economic activity. However, the party was not so significant in initiating policies and actions. The Politburo rarely met and a Party Congress was not convened until 1952. Stalin preferred to rule more informally, sending out his orders by telegram or convening small groups to discuss key policy issues.

In 1952, at the 19th Party Congress, Stalin took little direct part and contented himself with sitting and watching the proceedings. But at a meeting of the Central Committee after the conference he made his last speech, in which he appeared to attack some of the current leadership. It seemed likely that a purge affecting all ranks of the party and the Soviet security organisation was about to take place. Beria felt he was at risk and Molotov was certain he was in danger. Nobody felt safe. Stalin seemed to be indicating that he wanted the leadership to be passed on to the younger generation.

How paranoid and dangerous was Stalin in his last years?

Stalin's health deteriorated after the war. He appeared much less frequently in public and retreated to his private residences. Some contemporaries and historians claim that he was becoming more detached from reality and paranoid, seeing enemies everywhere. His meals were tasted for poison and his routes of travel regularly changed. His 'hysterical' anti-Semitism, seeing Jews as American Fifth Columnists, seems to bear this out. Party leaders feared his mood swings. He organised parties for them, which involved heavy drinking and making his guests seem ridiculous, e.g. forcing them to sing and dance. He used these events to test them, get information out of them and inspire jealousy. Other historians have suggested that these were the same personality traits that he had displayed throughout his life. However, most agree that he had become more morose, vindictive and unpredictable. He was becoming frail and he suffered from arthritis, high blood pressure and probably mental deterioration – so this might account for his temperamental and sometimes petulant behaviour. He grew more suspicious towards the end of his life, even turning against his daughter, personal bodyguards and loyal retainers. And he certainly remained very dangerous, as the members of the Politburo would testify.

THE DOCTORS' PLOT

In January 1953, *Pravda* announced that 13 doctors, several of whom were Jewish, who treated top party officials, were accused of conspiring with the USA and killing Zhdanov and other high-ranking officials. It was said that they planned to wipe out the top Soviet leadership. Confessions were obtained under torture, during which two of the doctors died. But before they could be executed, Stalin died. Subsequently, the plot was declared a fabrication and MVD officers were executed.

ACTIVITY

What does Source 20.9 suggest about:
- the impact of the Stalin cult
- how genuine/artificial it was?

SOURCE 20.9 Vladimir Bukovsky, *To Build a Castle*, 1978, pp. 81–3

Stalin's death shook our life to its foundations. Lessons in school virtually came to a halt, the teachers wept openly . . . Enormous unorganised crowds streamed through the streets to the Hall of Columns, where Stalin sat in state. There was something awe-inspiring about those immense, silent, gloomy masses of people. The authorities hesitated to try and curb them and simply blocked some of the side streets with buses and lorries . . . The crowd below us surged forwards and backwards, like waves in the sea, and then suddenly, on one of the side streets, a bus shivered, toppled over and fell, like an elephant rolling on its side. This vast procession continued for several days and thousands of people perished in the crush . . .

But the years passed . . . Stalin was mentioned less and less. And I was bewildered: hadn't God died, without whom nothing was supposed to take place? . . . Another rumour spread like an obscure muttering: 'The biggest enemy of the people of them all was – Stalin!' It was amazing how quickly people believed this, people who two years before had stampeded to his funeral and been ready to die for him . . . All those people whose business it had been to praise Stalin for so many years now assured us that they had known nothing about the Terror or, if they had, had been afraid to say so. I didn't believe the ones who said they had never known: how could you fail to notice the deaths of millions of people, the deaths of your neighbours and friends? Nor did I believe the ones who said they had been afraid – their fear had brought them too many promotions.

D The end of Stalin

SOURCE 20.10 Stalin lying in state, 1953

Stalin's death

Stalin died in a way that fitted the atmosphere of fear he had created. After a night of heavy drinking he did not come out of his rooms the following day. Used to him staying in bed late and frightened to disturb him, his security guards left him alone until the evening, when they found him conscious but unable to speak. They called Beria and Malenkov who did not arrive until 3 a.m. the following morning. There was a long delay before the doctors were called; possibly the leaders hoped he would die before he could act against them. The doctors were reluctant to treat Stalin in case they would be associated with some sort of plot. Paradoxically, Stalin's personal physician was in prison because of the Doctors' Plot (page 371) and had to be consulted by telephone. Everybody was terrified they would be blamed. In fact, Stalin had suffered a stroke, was partially paralysed, and unable to speak. He died a few days later. At his deathbed, the Politburo leaders were mostly sad although relieved. But Beria appeared 'radiant' and 'regenerated' as he saw an opportunity to become the power broker in the USSR.

There was a genuine outpouring of grief when Stalin's death was announced to the wider Russian public. People were shocked and wept openly in the streets. He had been their saviour in the Second World War and represented stability and order in a changing and confusing world. Crowds flocked into Moscow to see his body and pay their respects, some being crushed to death in an eerie echo of Nicholas II's coronation disaster at Khodynka fields. Of course, not everybody felt sorry, particularly in the countryside, but it was better not to express negative views about Stalin. Stalin's body was embalmed and laid in the Mausoleum next to Lenin's.

De-Stalinisation

Stalin had not nominated any successor and had cultivated discord between the leadership contenders. However, there were some things that the new leaders did agree about: they wanted less violence and arbitrariness in political life and they wanted to get rid of Beria. Most were fearful of his power, his brutality and the information he had acquired, quite apart for their personal loathing of him. He was arrested by army generals and, after a secret trial, was executed along with six of his colleagues. It later emerged that at a secret meeting of the Central Committee in July 1953, Beria and the MVD were accused of having undue influence on the party and the government which had resulted in the Soviet Union taking the wrong direction on important matters. They were really attacking Stalin but it was too soon to accuse him at this point. This came later when, in 1956, Khrushchev, who had emerged as the new leader, in his 'secret speech' at the 20th Party Congress:

- attacked the 'cult of the personality' in which Stalin was given unquestioning adulation
- read out Lenin's testament emphasising the part criticising Stalin (see page 173)
- cast doubts on the executions of old Bolsheviks like Zinoviev and Bukharin
- criticised the role of the NKVD in the purges, especially the use of torture to extract confessions
- criticised the performance of Stalin during the war, holding him responsible for the disasters of 1941
- demonstrated that Stalin's 'grave abuse of power' continued after the war with the purge of the Leningrad party and the Doctors' Plot.

The speech was soon leaked to the outside world. It was a tremendous shock to Soviet citizens who had been brought up under Stalin and seen him as the foundation of everything good and correct. It was also a shock to party members. It was not until 1961 that an open attack on Stalin was made at the 22nd Party Congress, where the suffering of millions of ordinary Russians was acknowledged. Stalin's embalmed body was removed from the Mausoleum and buried next to the Kremlin wall.

While this was going on, a process of 'de-Stalinisation' had been taking place even before the secret speech. Inmates of labour camps were released. The MVD had been brought under party control and there was a new emphasis on 'legality'. There was now a move to develop the consumer goods industries to improve the lives of ordinary people. The control of literature was relaxed a little and it was easier to move around within the country. Prices paid for kolkhoz grain were increased. Khrushchev ushered in a period of reform but it only lasted until 1964 when he was removed from power.

E | How can we explain Stalinism?

Some historians call the period after the war up until Stalin's death 'high Stalinism' because it contains all the features that define Stalinism: personalised and centralised control, stifling bureaucracy, cult of the personality, the use of terror and enhanced role for the secret police, effective propaganda and cultural uniformity (see Chart 20A). Robert Service, however, does not think it is sensible to call it high Stalinism since it really was the same old Soviet order of the 1930s – the same amalgam of regimentation and chaos. Moreover, he says, Stalin did not control everything: there was even unrest in the Gulag, indicating there is something wrong when a totalitarian state cannot keep order in detention centres. Also, young people wanted to get on with their lives free of state interference and skilled workers, aware of their value to the economy, were not likely to be subject to the sort of labour discipline enforced before the war.

FOCUS ROUTE

Make notes on:
- the main features of Stalinism
- different explanations of Stalinism.

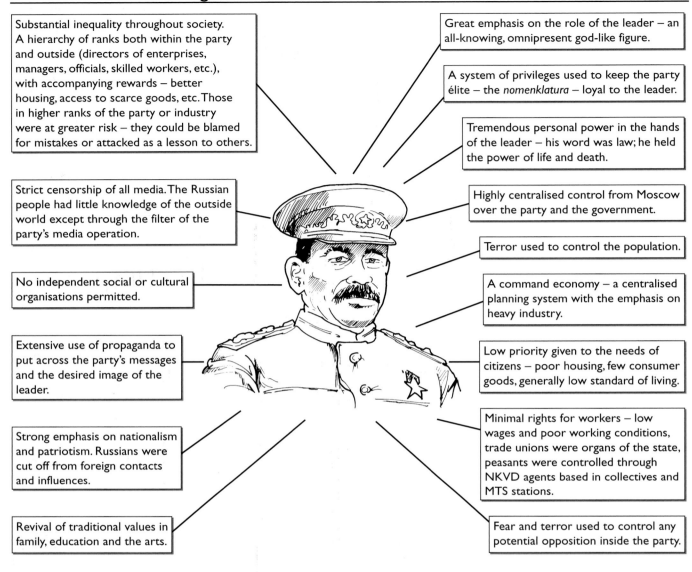

Substantial inequality throughout society. A hierarchy of ranks both within the party and outside (directors of enterprises, managers, officials, skilled workers, etc.), with accompanying rewards – better housing, access to scarce goods, etc. Those in higher ranks of the party or industry were at greater risk – they could be blamed for mistakes or attacked as a lesson to others.

Strict censorship of all media. The Russian people had little knowledge of the outside world except through the filter of the party's media operation.

No independent social or cultural organisations permitted.

Extensive use of propaganda to put across the party's messages and the desired image of the leader.

Strong emphasis on nationalism and patriotism. Russians were cut off from foreign contacts and influences.

Revival of traditional values in family, education and the arts.

Great emphasis on the role of the leader – an all-knowing, omnipresent god-like figure.

A system of privileges used to keep the party élite – the *nomenklatura* – loyal to the leader.

Tremendous personal power in the hands of the leader – his word was law; he held the power of life and death.

Highly centralised control from Moscow over the party and the government.

Terror used to control the population.

A command economy – a centralised planning system with the emphasis on heavy industry.

Low priority given to the needs of citizens – poor housing, few consumer goods, generally low standard of living.

Minimal rights for workers – low wages and poor working conditions, trade unions were organs of the state, peasants were controlled through NKVD agents based in collectives and MTS stations.

Fear and terror used to control any potential opposition inside the party.

What explanations have been put forward for the Stalinist dictatorship?

Stalinism in the 1930s seems to have little to do with the original aims and ideals of the 1917 revolution – freedom, equality between men and women, democracy and a good lifestyle for all based on sharing and co-operation. Commentators condemn the terror and atrocities committed during the Stalinist dictatorship and claim that Stalin betrayed the revolution and its ideals. So, how can we explain the Stalin dictatorship and the form it took? Some of the main explanations are given below.

1 Stalin's personality

Stalin's desire to dominate and be the hero of the revolution, his love of adulation, his conviction that he knew the right policies to follow and must not be thwarted, his paranoid behaviour and desire to get rid of individuals and groups who stood in his way, his tendency to use violence and terror to crush opposition and pursue his policies – all these traits influenced the system that emerged, particularly the nature of the purges and the use of terror. Stalin's personality is more fully considered in Chapter 15 and on page 385.

2 The circumstances surrounding the revolution and the Civil War

Lenin and a small minority had seized power in October 1917. They had refused to work with other socialist parties and had become isolated. Also, the country was in ruins after the war and there was a chaotic situation rapidly running out of control. To stay in power, to keep a lid on the explosive situation and suppress disorder, the Bolsheviks were ruthless – they launched the Red Terror, set up the Cheka and created an increasingly authoritarian state.

The Civil War also had a profound effect on the Bolshevik Party. It enforced on them military discipline, which demanded party unity above all else and strict obedience. It led to the development of a combative and a siege mentality that made them see enemies and conspiracies everywhere. It was a life-and-death struggle which saw them become hardened, pitiless and intolerant in their dealings with opposition. This mentality continued into the 1930s. The regime was not confident it could hold on to power and still saw enemies all around. Faced with this fear and insecurity, it resorted to terror and violence to resolve its problems. All this fed into Stalinism.

3 Economic reasons – was Stalin necessary?

Alec Nove argues (see page 243) that Soviet Russia was in an economic impasse at the end of the 1920s. It was still a backward country dependent on a peasantry unwilling to support the state's industrialisation and modernisation plans. Also, the anticipated world revolution had failed to materialise, leaving it isolated in the world and without the support of other countries to develop its industry and build socialism. For the majority of Bolsheviks, the only way out of this impasse was the 'socialist offensive' of 1928 and the launching of the rapid industrialisation and collectivisation programme.

Nove believes that once the decision had been taken to industrialise rapidly, it was bound to bring the party into conflict with the people because it would inevitably mean that their living standards would be hit and the party would be unpopular. The party would therefore have to use coercive methods 'on a grand scale' with a strong police state and 'party members fully employed in enforcing these drastic policies' (*Was Stalin Really Necessary?* 1964, pages 25–26). The socialist offensive would also involve the mass mobilisation of society – the use of wartime allusions and appeals to patriotism, warnings about the dangers of enemies and wreckers within and without, the encouragement of criticism of officials – which was a key feature of Stalinism. In these sorts of circumstance, Nove contends, a leader like Stalin was the one the party wanted because he had the qualities to carry them through this tough period.

4 The nature of the central planning system

The command economy requires the hierarchical organisation of society into ranks and levels with a 'supremo' at the top. With such a complex process to co-ordinate, involving thousands of products and hundreds of economic enterprises, there has to be an authority that issues instructions from the top. These are passed down to people at different levels who have to take decisions about the allocation of scarce supplies and materials. Then instructions are passed down from above to lower levels. Stalin used a system of rewards and wage differentials to encourage people at different levels to do their jobs, develop their skills and keep the workers' production rate up.

5 Russian history

Russia had a history of autocracy, with officials whose duty it was to serve the state and the tsar. State control over the people was normal and the state had played a commanding role in the growth of capitalism and industry in tsarist Russia. There were no habits or traditions of democratic political institutions. People were used to the idea of a strong leader who prevented anarchy and disorder. So Stalin tapped into a strong tradition in the role he adopted as a godlike figure who would provide strong leadership and see the Russian people through a difficult time. He seemed to see himself as a modernising leader in the style of Peter the Great (see page 387).

6 Stalinism was inherent in Leninism

All the apparatus of the Stalinist state – rule by one party, centralised control, central planning, secret police and the use of terror – was in place before Stalin became leader. Stalin used and extended these to their logical conclusion (see pages 376–381 for a fuller discussion).

Was Stalinism Lenin's baby?

There is an important debate about the extent to which Stalinism was a natural continuation of the ideas, policies and institutions of Lenin's regime. We can identify two clear schools of thought amongst historians, as outlined in Chart 20B.

ACTIVITY

1 Read the short extracts from different historians writing about the continuity between Lenin and Stalin (Sources 20.11–20.16).
2 The line below represents the two extremes in the debate. Decide where on the line the views of each historian should be placed. Some will be at the ends of the line, others will go part-way along the line, closer to one end than the other. Mark the source numbers in the relevant position on your own copy of the line.

Continuity between |———————————| **Clear break between**
Leninism and Stalinism   **Leninism and Stalinism**

SOURCE 20.11 R. Medvedev, 'The Political Biography of Stalin' in R. C. Tucker (ed.), *Stalinism, Essays in Historical Interpretation,* 1977

One could list the various measures carried out by Stalin that were actually a continuation of anti-democratic trends and measures implemented under Lenin, although it could be said that here we presume that Lenin never could have gone so far in this direction. In most respects, however, there is no continuity between Stalinism and Leninism. In pursuing a course aimed at abolishing NEP, in putting through a hasty policy of forced collectivisation, carrying out mass terror against the well-to-do peasants in the countryside and against the so-called bourgeois specialists in the cities, employing mainly administrative rather than economic methods to carry out industrialisation, categorically forbidding any opposition inside or outside of the party, and thus reviving, under other circumstances, the methods of War Communism, in all this, as in so many other ways, Stalin acted, not in line with Lenin's clear instructions, but in defiance of them, especially of Lenin's last writings of 1921–2, where he laid out the path of the construction of the socialist society.

■ 20B Contrasting views of historians

SOURCE 20.12   R. Pipes, *Three Whys of the Russian Revolution*, 1998, pp. 83–84

I believe that Stalin sincerely regarded himself as a disciple of Lenin, a man destined to carry out his agenda to a successful conclusion. With one exception, the killing of fellow Communists – a crime Lenin did not commit – he faithfully implemented Lenin's domestic and foreign programmes. He prevented the party from being riven by factionalism; he liquidated the 'noxious' intelligentsia; he collectivised agriculture, as Lenin had desired; he subjected the Russian economy to a single plan; he industrialised Russia; he built a powerful Red Army ... and he helped unleash the Second World War, which had been one of Lenin's objectives as well.

SOURCE 20.13   O. Figes, *A People's Tragedy: The Russian Revolution 1891–1924*, 1997, p. 807

On the one hand, it seems clear that the basic elements of the Stalinist regime – the one-party state, the system of terror and the cult of the personality – were all in place by 1924. The party apparatus was for the most part an obedient tool in Stalin's hands. The majority of its provincial bosses had been appointed by Stalin himself ... On the other hand, there were fundamental differences between Lenin's regime and that of Stalin. Fewer people were murdered from the start. And, despite the ban on factions, the party still made room for comradely debate.

SOURCE 20.14   G. Gill, *Stalinism*, 1990, pp 62–63

What is important is that these events were not a natural flow-on of earlier developments; they were sharp breaks resulting from conscious decisions by leading political actors. This means that those arguments that see Stalinism as the inevitable product of the 1917 revolution or of Leninism/Bolshevism are mistaken. Both the revolution and the corpus of theory which the Bolsheviks carried with them had elements which were consistent with the Soviet phenomenon (just as they had elements which were totally inconsistent with it). However, it needed the direct intervention on the part of the political actors in introducing the revolution from above and the terror to realise the Stalinist phenomenon in Soviet society.

SOURCE 20.15   I. Deutscher, *The Prophet Unarmed: Trotsky 1921–29*, 1959, pp. 464–65

Trotsky did not perceive the ascendancy of Stalinism as an inevitable result of the Bolshevik monopoly of power. On the contrary, he saw it as the virtual end of the Bolshevik government. We have traced the transitions through which the rule of the single party had become the rule of the single faction and through which Leninism had given way to Stalinism. We have seen that the things that had been implicit in the opening phase of this evolution had become explicit and found an extreme exaggerated expression in the closing phase ... Only the blind and the deaf could be unaware of the contrast between Stalinism and Leninism. The contrast shows in the field of ideas and in the intellectual climate of Bolshevism even more strongly than in the matters of organisation and discipline.

SOURCE 20.16   R. Service, 'Lenin: Individual and Politics in the October Revolution', *Modern History Review*, September 1990

Lenin was not the Devil incarnate. He genuinely adhered to at least some ideals which even non-socialists can see as having been designed to benefit the mass of humanity. Lenin wanted to bring about not a permanent dictatorship, but a dictatorship of the proletariat which would eventually eradicate all distinctions of social and material conditions and would rely decreasingly upon authoritarian methods. Ultimately Lenin wanted to abolish not only the secret police and the army but the whole state as such. If Lenin was therefore to be miraculously brought back to life from under the glass case in his mausoleum, he would be appalled at the use made of his doctrines by Stalin. Lenin was no political saint. Without him Stalin could not have imposed Stalinism. Institutionally and ideologically, Lenin laid the foundations for a Stalin. But the passage from Leninism to the worse horrors of Stalinism was not smooth and inevitable.

CONTINUITY BETWEEN LENIN AND STALIN

• One-party state
Lenin created the one-party state. He dealt ruthlessly with other socialist parties – Mensheviks and Socialist Revolutionaries – and was intolerant of opposing views. Stalin's control of the one-party state allowed him to crush all those who opposed or criticised him.

• Use of terror
Lenin was ruthless and used terror to achieve his ends. He was a 'class warrior' and waged 'class warfare'. He mercilessly attacked the bourgeoisie, the 'former people'. One of his first actions was to create the Cheka. Stalin likewise pursued 'class warfare' against the kulaks to force through collectivisation. Stalin used the methods he had learnt from Lenin. Lenin had set up labour camps for oppositionists in the early 1920s.

• Centralised and bureaucratic state
Lenin created a highly centralised and authoritarian state. This may in part be due to the circumstances after the revolution, particularly during the Civil War, but he had not dismantled the apparatus of the state in any way before he died. Stalinism is rooted in centralism: he extended the power of the centre to an enormous degree.

Lenin created a bureaucratic state that needed a bureaucrat and administrator to run it. Stalin was just the sort of wily operator required to prevent it collapsing. He revelled in bureaucracy and in running the party and government machine.

• Party and the people
Under Lenin the party became detached from the people. Lenin considered that the workers in the early 1920s were 'uncultured' and ill-educated (the older members of the working class had died in the Civil War or were in the party already). Lenin and the party leadership decided that the party alone knew the right path to follow and that they would have to lead and cajole the people along this path. Once this decision had been taken, dictatorship was ensured. Stalin simply continued this process and took it to its logical conclusion.

• Party democracy and control
Lenin destroyed democracy in the party with the 'ban on factions' in 1921. He used this to end the problem of splits during the crisis of 1921, but it created a situation whereby the party leadership could do what it wanted and dismiss any opposition within the party.

Also, most of the new generation of party members in the 'Lenin Enrolment' of 1924–25 were a 'green and callow mass' (Trotsky) who knew little about Marxism and were more inclined to follow orders than take an active part in democratic debate. The Civil War had also encouraged centralisation and military-style discipline within the party. So under Lenin, power was concentrated at the top and this facilitated Stalin's policies in the 1930s.

• Purges
Lenin instigated purges in the party to weed out elements he did not approve of.

• The economy
The economy under Lenin was largely in the hands of the state. Central planning had always been a feature of Bolshevik economic policy. During the NEP, the state controlled key industries and banking. It also regulated agriculture, e.g. by fixing prices. Lenin wanted to increase the power of the state to direct the economy. Stalin did just this.

• Mass mobilisation
Both Lenin and Stalin mobilised the workers to carry out their policies. Lenin did this for the October Revolution and during the Civil War. Stalin mobilised the workers to carry through rapid industrialisation and collectivisation in the early 1930s and again in the Stakhanovite campaign in the mid-1930s.

A CLEAR BREAK BETWEEN LENIN AND STALIN

• Centralised state
Authoritarian, centralised control was forced on Lenin by circumstances after the Revolution; it was not his choice. It is unlikely that he would have extended it to the degree that Stalin did.

• Cult of the personality
Stalin developed the cult of the personality and the idea of the supreme leader, the fount of wisdom in the party. Lenin would have deeply objected to this. This aspect of the Stalinist state was not built on Leninism.

• Purges
The party purges instigated by Lenin were non-violent, involving the withdrawal of party cards. Stalin used terror inside the party, which Lenin was always against. Lenin would never have countenanced the killing of leading Bolsheviks and other party members. This was the result of Stalin's personality and motives – he wanted to crush his enemies, remove all opposition and impose his vision of the future on the Soviet Union.

• Use of terror
Stalin employed terror as part of the fabric of his personality. He had a brutal streak and resorted to terror when threatened or thwarted. Lenin would never have set in motion the mass terror of the 1930s, particularly the mass enforced collectivisation of the peasants.

• Leninism
Lenin always objected to the term Leninism. He regarded himself as a Marxist. He saw Marxist theory as progressive, leading the way to socialism. Stalin developed the cult of Leninism and used it as an ideological orthodoxy to justify his actions.

• National minorities
Lenin wanted the national minorities to stay in the Soviet Union by choice. Stalin wanted to bend them to the will of Moscow, mould them to Russian control and make them adopt a style of Communist life as laid down from the centre. Lenin would not have crushed the national minorities in the way Stalin did.

• Party, government and bureaucracy
Lenin was very worried by the power of the party and the bureaucracy. He originally conceived of the government, the Sovnakom, running the country with the Politburo as a court of appeal for decisions. In practice, the party filled key posts in government and soviets. Lenin wanted to dismantle the stranglehold of the party machine and increase internal democracy but died before this could take place. Stalin reinforced bureaucracy in party and government.

• Peasantry
Lenin had stated clearly that the peasantry should not be coerced into collective farms.

Developing the argument

To a large extent, the debate hinges on the view you take of Lenin. If you see Lenin as a ruthless tyrant who seized power for his own political purposes, who used terror as a matter of course, and imposed his will on the people through an authoritarian one-party state, then you are likely to take the view that Stalinism was the logical extension of Leninism. This is the view taken by anti-Communist historians during the Cold War.

If, however, you take the view that Lenin was forced by circumstances – the Civil War, terrible economic conditions and the failure of world revolution to materialise – to develop a highly centralised state after the revolution then you are likely to see a break between Lenin and Stalin. The Bolsheviks could not have anticipated the problems they would face, they were changed by the Civil War and they became more authoritarian to cope with the situation as it developed. In this view, Lenin, if he had lived, would have allowed a more enlightened state to develop, would have encouraged more democracy in the party and would not have supported forced collectivisation or the purges of the 1930s. This has been described as the 'cuddly' view of Lenin and is more likely to be taken by left-wing historians and by revisionist historians.

In 'The Passage from Leninism to Stalinism' (unpublished lecture, January 1999), Robert Service draws on research from newly opened archives to suggest that Lenin was more ruthless than has sometimes been supposed. He actively encouraged terror to smash his enemies and was a fierce class warrior. We can see this in his attitudes towards the peasants and the Church (see pages 300–301). This is a long way from the cuddly view of Lenin. He moulded the state out of chaos after the First World War and it was a one-party authoritarian state. It is this that pushes Robert Service to the continuity side of the argument. However, Service is keen to point out that Lenin did have a vision of a utopian state where there would be no violence and terror and where the Russian people would enjoy the fruits of socialism. For Lenin, violence was a means to an end.

Of course, the problem with these arguments is that we cannot know what Lenin would have done. It may well be that, faced with the same situation as Stalin at the end of the 1920s, he would have become impatient and forced the pace. He was no great lover of the peasants and might have been prepared to use more forceful tactics. However, before he died he emphasised that coercion should not be used against the peasants. It is also clear that he was worried by the extent of bureaucracy and the lack of democracy in the party and intended to do something (though we don't know what) about this. And it is unthinkable that he would have killed his Bolshevik comrades and adopted the leadership style, entailed in the cult of the personality, that Stalin adopted.

Where does this leave us? We can definitely identify features of Stalinism in Leninism. Stalin fell back on tried and trusted methods used by Lenin – class warfare against peasants and terror against political opponents. Also, the way in which Lenin had organised the party and the state facilitated Stalinism and made it likely that control would fall into the hands of the best manipulator of the apparatus. The ban on factions provided Stalin with a mechanism to deal with opposition inside the party.

On the other hand, it is also clear that the 'Great Turn' initiated and implemented by Stalin, wrought great changes on the party and the people of the USSR – political, economic and cultural changes. The Soviet state of the 1930s was very much his construction. Also, Stalin extended and intensified Leninist methods, like class warfare and terror, to a degree unimaginable under Lenin. He was the executioner of Lenin's comrades and was responsible for the deaths of millions.

It is probably fair to say that Stalinism was built on the foundations of the Leninist state, even though it took a shape of which Lenin probably would not have approved.

FOCUS ROUTE

Make notes on the historiographical debate about the continuity between the Leninist and Stalinist states.

The historiographical debate

The debate about the continuity between the regimes of Lenin and Stalin is more than just of academic interest to historians; it has influenced the recent history of Russia. But first we need to look at the story of the way historians have viewed this topic.

Post-war consensus – the traditional view

The post-1945 interpretation amongst historians in the West, found in the works of Leonard Schapiro and Adam Ulam and developed more recently by Richard Pipes, reflects the 'traditional' view of totalitarianism. For these writers, Lenin and a small group of Bolsheviks seized power and imposed their will on an unwilling populace. To stay in power, they applied a regime of terror within the framework of a highly centralised state. The October Revolution was a malignant process which would always end in political dictatorship. For them, Lenin and Stalin are virtually the same: Stalin carries on what Lenin started and Stalinism is simply the fully developed version of Lenin's repressive creed of revolution. However, most of these historians, such as Schapiro, hold Stalin personally responsible for the excesses of the 1930s and the level of human suffering endured by the Russian people.

This view was held not only in the West. The prominent Soviet dissident Alexander Solzhenitsyn held that there was a direct link between Stalinism and the institutions set up by Lenin. He says that the apparatus of Stalinism – the one-party state, the secret police, the ban on factionalism – were all in place before Stalin assumed the leadership.

Clear break between Lenin and Stalin

The idea that Stalin was the natural heir of Lenin was challenged right from the beginning. As far as Trotsky was concerned, Stalinism was a perverted form of Leninism which arose as a result of Stalin's personality. For Trotsky, the purges marked the clear division between Bolshevik philosophy and Stalinism: 'The present purge draws between Bolshevism and Stalinism a whole river of blood' (Trotsky, 1937). Isaac Deutscher, the biographer of Stalin and Trotsky, takes a similar line, believing that Stalin perverted the basically democratic nature of Leninism into a personal dictatorship. He sees the terror, party dictatorship and ideological intolerance as products of the Civil War.

The main challenge to the post-1945 traditional view arrived in the 1970s. The Russian dissident historian and Leninist, Roy Medvedev, argued (*Let History Judge*, 1972) that Stalin distorted Lenin's noble vision and is alone responsible for the mass murder and terror of the 1930s. He claims that things went badly awry when Stalin took over and launched the rapid industrialisation drive and forced collectivisation. He believes that if Lenin had lived a little longer, the NEP would have survived and the USSR would have taken a slower, more humane route to socialism. Medvedev attaches a great deal of importance to Stalin's personality because he believes that the Soviet system of the 1930s would have been quite different under a different leader.

Revisionist historians in the West in the 1970s and 1980s have taken a similar line. Probably the best exponent of the revisionist position in this debate is Stephen Cohen. In *Rethinking the Soviet Experience* (1985, pages 38–70) he acknowledges that the Bolshevism of 1921–28 contained the 'seeds' of Stalinism, but he suggests that the seeds of Stalinism can also be found in other areas of the Russian historical and cultural tradition, and in events like the Civil War and the international situation the USSR found itself in at the end of the 1920s. Cohen stresses the differences between Stalinism and Leninism. He says that the authoritarianism before 1929 was very different from that of the 1930s, when it went to extremes. He sees, for example, the policies towards the peasants as a virtual civil war, the terror as a holocaust that victimised tens of millions of people, and the leader cult as the 'deification of a despot'. For him, the difference in degree divides Stalinism from Leninism.

Reviewing Lenin

Towards the end of the Communist period, Gorbachev had initiated what he called *glasnost* or openness. Novels that had been banned were made available to the public; for example, Alexander Solzhenitsyn's *Gulag Archipelago* (a study of the Soviet labour camp system) was published in 1989. Part of this *glasnost* process was a re-evaluation of the Soviet past. Russian archives began to open up in a way they had not before. There was a comprehensive attack on Stalin, and many of his victims, such as Bukharin, were rehabilitated.

But it was not long before Lenin himself came under scrutiny. As more documents about Lenin were uncovered so his ruthlessness and cruelty became more apparent. He was attacked, in particular, for his use of terror, for his callousness in the Civil War and as the originator of the labour camps and forced labour. In *The Unknown Lenin* (1996), a collection of documents from the Lenin archive in Russia, released after the fall of Communism, Richard Pipes revealed more details about Lenin's repressive policies in the Civil War period. The Russian historian Dimitri Volkogonov (a former general in the Red Army) changed his position. In his earlier biography of Stalin in 1988, Volkogonov argued that Lenin was trying to build democracy back into the state and break down bureaucracy, and that the failure to remove Stalin in 1924 condemned the Soviet Union to dictatorship and totalitarianism. However, by the time he came to write his biography of Lenin in 1994, having gained access to new archival evidence, he identified Lenin as the chief architect of the Communist state based on terror and coercion.

TALKING POINT

How is a knowledge of history important to today's politicians? Can a little knowledge do more harm than good?

Can you think of any examples where past events have influenced British politicians or been used by them to justify their policies?

ACTIVITY

Write an essay answering the following question: Was Stalinism Lenin's baby?

In your essay, refer to the historiographical debate surrounding this issue and mention the views of historians.

When you are writing essays, you have to develop a line of argument. This means arguing a particular case and supporting it with evidence. Often you can take one of the three approaches below:

1 'Yes' – you agree with the essay title and supply the points and supporting argument (with evidence) to show why you agree.
2 'No' – you take the opposite view, arguing against the essay title. In this case you would argue that Stalin changed the course of Soviet Russia, creating a system that was more to do with his priorities and personality than with Lenin's.
3 'Yes . . . but' – where you can argue the case for the proposition in the essay title (supplying supporting evidence) but also put the case against the proposition. At the end, you weigh up the argument and come down on one side or the other.

G Assessing Stalin

Whatever view historians take of Stalin in respect of Lenin's legacy – as betrayer or heir – or to what extent the Stalinist state was built on Leninist foundations, none would disagree that Stalin had a huge personal impact on the USSR. He created the architecture of the Soviet state in the 1930s and shaped its institutions. It was he who set up the command economy that drove forward the programmes of industrialisation and collectivisation. After the war, he made the key choices internally (continuing the old model) and externally, which made the USSR into a superpower. Kevin McDermott, in his biography of Stalin, puts it thus: 'Stalin stamped his ugly personality on Soviet state and society'. Volkogonov, in Source 20.17, says his mark could be seen everywhere. In assessing Stalin we have to consider his achievements and weigh up how far the changes he wrought were for good or ill. There are many Russians today who look back with some affection at the period of Stalin's dictatorship when Russia transformed itself and took a leading role in the world.

SOURCE 20.17 D. Volkogonov, *The Rise and Fall of the Soviet Empire*, 1998, p. 81

The marks left by Stalin cannot easily be wiped away. Whether the thousands of buildings in the 'Stalinist' style of architecture, the canals, the highways, blast furnaces, mines and factories – built to a large extent by the anonymous inmates of his Gulag – or nuclear weapons, his traces are steeped in blood. Between 1929 and 1953 the state created by Lenin and set in motion by Stalin deprived 21.5 million Soviet citizens of their lives.

■ 20D Assessing Stalin

The case for Stalin	The case against Stalin
Created the Soviet system and state of the 1930s and 1940s.	Developed the one-party state into a rigid and unrelenting system, which controlled Soviet citizens by fear and terror.
Led the drive in changing a backward rural country into a modern industrialised country.	Millions of Soviet citizens, probably over 20 million, died as a result of his policies.
There were great advances in fields such as medicine and education.	Expanded the Gulag system of labour camps.
Forced through the industrialisation pro-gramme at rapid pace so that the USSR was in a position to fight and win the Second World War.	Imposed ideological uniformity which had a negative effect on the life and culture of the USSR.
Set in place a centrally planned economy that was well suited to initial capital accumulation and developing heavy industry. Also a good tool for managing wartime economy and recovery afterwards.	The command economy was unable to cope with technological advances and a rapidly changing world.
Provided strong leadership and held the country together when tremendous social and economic change was taking place.	Collectivisation had only limited success and agriculture was in a poor state when Stalin died.
Played a significant role in leading his country to victory in the Second World War. Became a focus for loyalty and resistance. Was highly regarded by Russians for this.	The purge of army officers before the Second World War and mistakes at the beginning of the war nearly led to disaster: the Soviet Union lost a huge amount of territory and industrial capacity.
Extended the boundaries of the Soviet Empire after the Second World War and dominated Eastern Europe, spreading the Communist ideology.	He did enormous hurt to the non-Russian ethnic groups in the USSR, executing and deporting large numbers of them to remote regions and, in the process, destroying their political and cultural élites.
Turned the USSR into a major superpower.	Contributed to creating a dangerous and hostile world in the Cold War after the Second World War. Placed the world in great danger through his espousal of nuclear weapons.

The main claim for Stalinist achievement is the transformation of the USSR into a modern state with industry capable of providing the armaments that enabled the USSR to defeat Germany in the Second World War. There is no doubt that the growth of heavy industry in the 1930s was impressive and it was Stalin who drove the pace relentlessly when others wanted to slow down industrialisation. This allowed the Soviet Union to be in a much better position to take on the Germans and turn out weapons, such as T-34 tanks, in huge numbers. The

structure of the command economy meant that it could concentrate a major part of its economic strength on the war effort – much more than a market economy could have achieved. But the command economy had major weaknesses, such as production bottlenecks, shortages, poor quality goods, waste, corruption, etc. It was a rough and ready system that initially worked well to kick start industrialisation in the 1930s, to fight a war, and to generate recovery in the 1940s. But it was rigid and inflexible and unable to cope with changes in technology. Also, it never produced sufficient consumer goods – shoes, clothing and household goods of reasonable quality – to meet the needs of Soviet citizens. Some historians think that the Soviet Union would have done better to have continued with NEP, especially in respect of consumer goods, although others do not think the Soviets would have been able to make the advance in heavy industry that helped them win the war.

Stalin's polices for agriculture were unsuccessful. Collectivisation produced enough food to meet the needs of the industrialisation programme, and to that extent it succeeded. But in most other respects it was a disaster. Most particularly, it failed to produce enough food to feed adequately the people of the USSR. The peasants were never keen on collectivisation and paid a very high price in terms of lives, deportation and imprisonment for resisting its implementation. Agriculture did become more mechanised but not enough resources were devoted to this sector. Stalin was never very interested in well-being of the peasants and made no real attempts to provide them with incentives. This was particularly evident after the war and resulted in disastrous levels of production, which worried other Soviet leaders. Stalin saddled the USSR with an inefficient agricultural system.

Stalin could claim credit for the defeat of Germany in the war. He played a leading role in raising morale and strengthening resistance to the Nazis. Orders 270 and 227 were very harsh but some would maintain that Order 227 stiffened resistance at the lowest point of the war. His purge of the top echelons of the army in 1937–38 and mistakes in 1941 nearly led to disaster. This allowed the Germans to overrun large parts of western Russia, which contained much of the industry of the Soviet Union. However, unlike Hitler, Stalin did eventually hand control of the war to more talented generals who made the right strategic decisions. The victory gave the Russians immense pride and earned Stalin respect, if not affection. This sense of pride was enhanced when Stalin made decisions in foreign affairs that transformed the USSR into one of the world's superpowers. Russians liked being a major force on the world stage and it was Stalin who enabled this. Moreover, the Soviet Union was the model for a number of countries in the world that set up Communist regimes.

A key question in any assessment of Stalin is: were people better off? More particularly, were workers better off in what was ostensibly a workers' state? Standards of living remained low throughout the 1930s with shortages of food and consumer goods as well as poor quality, overcrowded housing. There was little improvement by 1941 and from then on things went downhill as a result of the war; the effect on housing was cataclysmic. After 1947, there was a slow, general improvement but it was only by 1952 that average workers reached the 1940 standard of living. Robert Conquest maintains that living standards at the time of Stalin's death were not much higher than they had been in 1928. At the same time, there had been real advances in health care (more doctors, hospitals, etc.) and education (schools, literacy) available to the mass of the population. After 1928, some workers were better off, particularly those in skilled technical jobs (see page 230). They could be rewarded with higher wages and better quality housing and had opportunities they would not have had under the tsarist regime. Middle ranking bureaucrats in the party and government, and higher ranks in the army and the security services, also did well in terms of wages, working conditions, preferment for houses, holidays, etc. Those who did best were the new ruling class within the USSR – the nomenclatura – who depended on Stalin for their position and jobs. They enjoyed a wide range of privileges in their guarded, prestigious apartment blocks and dachas. But generally, the workers' paradise and classless society was very far from being realised by the time of Stalin's death.

Against any of Stalin's achievements has to be set the dark side of Stalin's Russia. Stalin presided over a fearful and suspicious society that had a detrimental effect on human relationships. Terror was the main instrument of control and it emanated from Stalin himself. He was prepared to imprison, deport or execute any individual or group of people who threatened his position or obstructed the path he had determined the USSR would follow. He set the purges of the 1930s in motion and archive evidence shows that he was involved throughout. Underpinning the terror were the activities of the secret police who generated an atmosphere of fear and mistrust – you never knew who might be informing against you. And lurking behind them was the inhuman Gulag, the system of labour camps, which destroyed the human spirit along with millions of lives. Also, Stalin did immense damage to the cultural life of the USSR. Writers and artists were arrested and executed; books and poetry were not written; and films and other creative works were constrained by the demands for ideological purity and socialist realism.

To this account must be added the deaths of over 20 million Soviet citizens in the forced collectivisation programme of the 1930s (which created a famine in the Ukraine) and the Great Terror of the late 1930s. Alongside these sit the mass deportations of peasants during collectivisation, of national groups during the war, and of the political and military élites of the Baltic States and western Ukraine after the war – millions of people condemned to remote regions of the USSR whose lives were uprooted and often destroyed. Stalin traumatised a generation.

STALIN THE MICRO MANAGER

Stalin took two- to three-month vacations at his dacha on the Black Sea coast, but there was no let up in his control of affairs. He communicated his political will through confidential letters and coded telegrams to his key henchmen Molotov and Kaganovich as there was no reliable telephone link between Sochi and Moscow until 1935. These letters are valuable new sources: Stalin's letters to Molotov cover chiefly the years 1925–1930 and the Stalin-Kaganovich correspondence covers 1931–1936. Molotov acted as Stalin's deputy in the party in the 1920s and Kaganovich took over that role in 1930.

The letters show Stalin's determination to force through his policies and his angry and vindictive nature. In one he refers to Zinovieites and Trotskyites as scum three times in four lines. The letters are pervaded by exhortations to put pressure on people and check up on them: 'you cannot daydream and sleep when you are in power!' There are regular instructions to fulfil decisions with 'unrelenting firmness and ruthlessness' and attacks on bureaucracy. In July 1932, he wrote to Kaganovich:

'There are abominations in the supply of metal for the Stalingrad Tractor Plant and the Moscow and Gorky auto plants. It is a disgrace that the windbags at the People's Commissariat of Heavy Industry have still not gotten around to straightening out the supply system. Let the Central Committee place under its *continuous* supervision, without delay, the plants that are supplying them and make up for this disruption.'

In another, the following year, he wrote:

'The situation with artillery is very bad. Sergo [Ordzhonikidze] should be flogged for entrusting a major section to two or three of his favourite fools, showing that he is prepared to sacrifice the state's interest to these fools.'

The letters show us how Stalin micro-managed the struggle against his opponents in the 1920s and the show trial of Zinoviev and Kamenev in 1936. His ruthlessness in economic affairs is demonstrated by his pressing for the notorious 'law on five ears of grain' decree of 7 August 1932 to stop theft from collective farms, introduced in a time of famine and largely directed against starving peasants. In the five months after its introduction, 4880 death sentences were handed out. However, for all his power over life and death, the angry frustration of many of the letters reveals that people did not always do what Stalin wanted them to do.

SOURCE 20.19   Richard Overy, 'The Dictators', p. 13, quoted in *Stalin*, Kevin McDermott, 2006, Palgrave Macmillan, p. 12

The one consistent strand in all his activity was the survival of the revolution and the defence of the first socialist state. Power with Stalin seems to have been power to preserve and enlarge the revolution and the state that represented it, not just power for its own sake. The ambition to save the revolution became for Stalin a personal ambition, for at some point in the 1920s . . . Stalin came to see himself as the one Bolshevik leader who could steer the way with sufficient ruthlessness and singleness of purpose. His instinct for survival, his unfeeling destruction of thousands of his party comrades, his Machiavellian politics, point not to a personality warped by self-centred sadism, but to a man who used the weapons he understood to achieve the central purpose to which his life had been devoted since he was a teenager . . . (the) overriding historical imperative to construct Communism.

Stalin's motives

Was Stalin motivated purely by a lust for power and a paranoid suspicion of others? Our views of him have been influenced by Trotsky who saw Stalin as a bureaucrat, a mediocrity, who got control of the party machine and took Russia along a path dictated by his personality – a particularly evil one. Stalin was certainly ruthless and murderous in his desire for power. He was determined to sustain his supremacy by using terror and the secret police to crush opposition. He manipulated those around him to ensure that no one would be in a position to supplant him. He was vengeful and saw himself surrounded by enemies. It was this paranoid streak that seems to have become worse after the war. Bulganin confessed to Khrushchev: 'It has happened that a man goes to Stalin on his invitation as a friend. And when he sits with Stalin he does not know where he will be sent next, home or to gaol.'

However, it is too easy to explain away Stalin simply as an evil, power-mad dictator who behaved in a capricious manner. Historians like Kevin McDermott have pointed out that there was logic in his management style. Stalin was a bureaucrat: he favoured the practical and pragmatic. He used his Machiavellian methods – fear, playing people off against each other, creating insecurity and an atmosphere of suspicion and recrimination – to ensure that his subordinates achieved the outcomes that he wanted. This also protected himself from being supplanted. He had been shaped by life in an underground party, revolution, and civil war in a world of constant struggle, threat and intrigue – the world of Konspiratsia. There had always been genuine enemies from within and without. In some ways, it is not surprising that his methods were harsh and brutal.

Lust for power, personality defects and paranoia are important in explaining Stalin's brutal actions and personal politics but he was also motivated by ideas. He was an intellectual. He read widely and was interested in culture, linguistics and science, as well as political science. He looked at the world through a Marxist–Leninist prism but he was selective about the ideas he chose. He fused these ideologies with ideas of Russian nationalism, xenophobic pride and Soviet patriotism and turned them into policies. The Bolshevik Revolution had been cut off from and rejected by the rest of the world and Stalin knew that Russia on its own had to safeguard the Revolution and build socialism through a national effort. He was also influenced by ideas of empire and wanted to turn the USSR into a global power. He saw himself in the mould of a Peter the Great moderniser and was convinced that he was the person who could take the USSR along the road to the socialist and Communist Utopia. This, according to Richard Overy (see Source 20.19), helps to explain Stalin's motives.

SOURCE 20.20   A French poster from the 1930s, depicting Stalin dominating the masses

KEY POINTS FROM CHAPTER 20

Stalin's final years 1945–1953

1 The loss of life – up to 27 million Soviet citizens – and physical damage done to the USSR during the war was on an unimaginable scale.

2 Stalin returned to pre-war methods of control despite the desire for a more relaxed society.

3 Prisoners of war and Soviet citizens who had been trapped in the occupied areas were treated harshly, many sent to the Gulag or executed.

4 Stalin mounted a campaign of nationalism and anti-Westernism to help unite society and prevent the Soviet Union from being contaminated by any democratic ideas. Zhdanov led a drive for ideological and cultural purity (the Zhdanovshchina), which included a clampdown on the arts and sciences.

5 Stalin returned to the centrally planned economy and Five-Year Plans with an emphasis on heavy industry and armaments. Industrial recovery and growth was impressive.

6 The agricultural sector remained the weakest aspect of the Soviet economy.

7 Stalin's position as the all-powerful leader of the one-party state was strengthened by the war. He used the same manipulative politics to maintain his grip on power and control contenders for the leadership.

8 The period from 1945 to 1953 had been called 'high Stalinism'. Historians have put forward a number of explanations for why this developed.

9 Historians debate the extent to which the Stalinist state was built on Leninist foundations. Some believe there is a clear break between Lenin and Stalin, others think there is a clear line of continuity between the two.

10 Any assessment of Stalin must acknowledge that he drove the programme of industrialisation that modernised the USSR and enabled it to defeat Germany in the Second World War. However, a terrible price was paid for this – some 20 million people's deaths and a society poisoned by fear and terror.

21 Conclusion

CHAPTER OVERVIEW

The beginning of this chapter looks at the similarities between Stalinism and tsarism, bringing the book full circle. It then explores the nature of the totalitarian Stalinist state, which was full of contradictions and inefficiencies and did not exercise the total control of mind and action that the word 'totalitarian' implies. Finally, it provides a brief overview of the Soviet Union until the collapse of Communism in 1991 and the changes in the new Russia thereafter.

A Comparing tsarism with Stalinism (pp. 387–389)

B An imperfect totalitarian state (pp. 389–390)

C From Stalin to the modern day – a brief overview (pp. 391–393)

A Comparing tsarism with Stalinism

At the beginning of this book we looked at the tsarist regime in pre-revolutionary Russia. The Communist Revolution of 1917 was intended to bring about radical change and create a modern society in which social relations and the relationship between state and people were completely different from those of the tsarist system. Yet the Stalinist state that emerged in the 1930s and 1940s had many features in common with its tsarist predecessor. The system of personalised control in Stalin's dictatorship was very similar to that of the Tsar: the notion of a god-like leader, the chief benefactor and protector of the people, who knows the right course to follow and can lead the Russian people out of darkness into the light; the culture of blaming officials for problems instead of the person at the top. The icons of tsarism and Stalinism – the pictures, statues and imagery – are very similar in the way they portray the leader.

This is not to say that Stalinism was somehow inevitable. But there is a strong case for arguing that the traditions of Russian history played an important role in determining the shape and characteristics of Stalinism. In the difficult and sometimes chaotic circumstances in which the Russians found themselves, they retreated or slipped into traditional solutions that they understood well and with which they were comfortable. Traditional patterns of control found their way easily into the Stalinist repertoire and one school of thought sees Stalin as a Red tsar who pursued some of the tsars' traditional goals such as promoting nationalism and Russification and extending the boundaries of the empire. Stalin certainly saw himself as a moderniser in the tradition of Peter the Great. It is reported that in 1935 Stalin himself said that ordinary people needed a tsar to worship.

In chart 21A (see pages 388–389), the similarities of the two systems – tsarism and Stalinism – are compared. The three guiding principles of tsarism, autocracy, orthodoxy and nationalism, are used as a basis for comparison along with aspects of economic policy.

■ 21A Similarities between tsarism and Stalinism

Tsarism	Stalinism
Autocracy	
Rule by a supreme leader, the Tsar, who makes major decisions and has power of life and death over his subjects. He was given divine status.	Stalin was supreme leader of the Soviet Union, with power to sign death warrants. He was portrayed as a god-like figure in the cult of the personality.
The Tsar was supported by an élite – the nobility whose prime role was to serve the Tsar. Their positions of influence in the government, armed forces and civil service were held through the patronage of the Tsar.	Stalin was supported by the *nomenklatura* – an élite who held the top positions in the party, government, armed forces, etc., through the patronage of Stalin. He kept their support by the threat of removing privileges – access to scarce goods, best apartments, etc.
There was a huge government bureaucracy, slow, unwieldy and im-penetrable, with corruption at lower levels.	There was a huge, faceless bureaucracy in government and party which led to 'death by paper'. In local areas 'inner circles' of govern-ment and party officials and industrial managers cooked up deals to suit themselves, often ignoring instructions from the centre.
There was a well-developed system of ranks and privileges.	A system of ranks developed in the 1930s from the *nomenklatura* downwards. Being a party official or member brought power and privileges commensurate with the level. The command economy demanded there be officials and managers at different levels and wage differentials between workers.
The secret police – the Okhrana – were used to support the state and deal with critics and opposition. Many oppositionists were arrested and exiled to Siberia. The Okhrana had an extensive network of agents penetrating all areas of society.	There was extensive use of the secret police (OGPU, then NKVD) in all aspects of Soviet life – government, party, economic spheres and prison system (the Gulag) – and at all levels. They performed a moni-toring role, with power to root out opposition to party leadership.
Internal passports, residence permits and visas were used to control the movement of the population.	Internal passports, residence permits and visas were used to control the movement of the population.
There was lack of free speech – censorship of the press and banning of political parties (except between 1906 and 1914).	There was lack of free speech – censorship of the press and banning of rival political parties.
There was no tradition of democratic political institutions.	There were no genuinely democratic institutions although soviets were designed to be a purer form of democratic participation.
Tsars like Peter the Great and Ivan the Terrible saw themselves as leaders who were enforcing change on the nobility and others to create a strong Russian state. Peter also saw himself as a moderniser bringing Russia out of the dark ages. Ivan broke the nobility, torturing them and executing them on suspicion of treason, ensuring their loyalty to the state. His agents, the Oprichniks, wore black uniforms; their insignia was a dog's head on a broom, signifying their dog-like devotion to the Tsar and their duty to sweep away treason.	Stalin saw himself as being in the same tradition as Peter the Great and Ivan the Terrible, taking the Soviet Union towards socialism and making it into a great industrial power, respected in the world. He praised Peter in 1928, on the eve of the Great Turn, for building mills and factories to strengthen the defences of the country. When watching Eisenstein's film about Ivan he remarked that Ivan's fault lay in not annihilating enough of his enemies. Like Ivan, Stalin was prepared to deal harshly with any opposition. He believed he was acting in the interests of his country and its people.
Orthodoxy	
The Tsar's power was underpinned by the Russian Orthodox Church, a branch of Christianity. Russians saw their Orthodox beliefs as special and believed they had a mission to spread their beliefs to other parts of the world. They believed they were the upholders of the 'true' Christian faith.	Stalinism was underpinned by Marxism–Leninism which became an orthodoxy trotted out by Stalin to justify his actions. It was treated as a quasi-religion. Russians believed they had a mission to spread Com-munist beliefs throughout the world by encouraging world revolution.

Nationalism	
There was a strong emphasis on Russian nationalism and patriotism. There were attempts to export the Russian way of life to other parts of the empire through the policy of Russification. Tsars throughout the nineteenth century were looking to expand their empire and to become a major dominant power in European affairs.	Stalin emphasised nationalism in 'Socialism in One Country' – the idea that Russians could build socialism on their own without outside help. There were appeals to nationalism and patriotism in the Five-Year Plans. People who did not co-operate were denounced as traitors and 'enemies within'. Stalin mounted a drive on nationalism and Soviet patriotism in the 1940s. This included a policy of Russification.
	Stalin was keen on Russian domination of both government and party in the other Soviet republics, although some concessions were made to regions developing their own national traditions.
	In foreign policy, Stalin pursued a very nationalistic line, putting Soviet security above everything else, even to the point of doing a deal with Hitler. Any tsar would have been proud of Stalin's foreign policy, particularly the successful expansion after the Second World War, with the USSR's becoming a superpower.
Economic policy	
Under Nicholas, economic change was led from above, largely because the middle classes were too weak. It was a state-sponsored model with the government promoting industrial growth in conjunction with the development of the railways. The main emphasis was on the development of heavy industry at the expense of consumer goods. The driving force behind this was the need to be able to produce weapons and armaments so that Russia could remain a major power in the world. To get money for investment the state borrowed money from abroad and squeezed the peasantry very hard through taxation.	In 1928, Stalin initiated a programme of rapid industrialisation. This was driven from above through the command economy and Five-Year Plans. Targets were set by the planners at the top, which those below had to achieve. The main emphasis was on heavy industry at the expense of consumer goods. One of the main reasons for this was to build up a powerful armaments industry with which to fight the USSR's enemies, before and after the Second World War. To get the resources to invest in this, Stalin squeezed the peasantry very hard through taxation and by taking grain to feed workers and sell abroad.

ACTIVITY

Write a short essay under the title: Stalin the Red Tsar. Decide how far you think this statement is fair and what the main similarities between the tsarist state and the Stalinist state were. Draw on material from the beginning and end of this book and your own knowledge.

 # An imperfect totalitarian state

The image of the totalitarian state is that of a well-oiled, efficient machine in which commands and instructions from the top are passed down to those below and diligently carried out. But the Stalinist state was far from this. It was much messier and full of contradictions and inefficiencies. It was a totalitarian state but control was far from perfect. Stalin was dependent on the party élites and regional subordinates to get his policies put into action and they had to interact with society as a whole. Outwardly there was obedience to orders but under the surface there was often considerable disorderliness. The Soviet people were not just passive agents subject to the instructions, mobilisation and manipulations of the people at the top. They were participants who developed a way of coping with the Stalinist state – what has been called a 'Stalinist culture'. Sometimes this involved taking up Communist Party ideas and values and interpreting them in their own interests; sometimes it involved resistance and avoidance. Some, of course, took up the Soviet *mentalité* and tried to eradicate anti-Soviet elements in their life. Above all, *Homo Sovieticus* (see page 319) was a survivor.

There was a gulf between the centre and the periphery: cliques in regions far away from Moscow ran their own fiefdoms for their own interests while paying lip service to the central government. Many joined the Communist Party for their own advancement rather than ideological commitment, and fraud was common. Some ignored official policies or were deliberately obstructive. A lot of this type of action was kept secret from those higher up the chain of command. One reason for the purges was to try to gain control of outlying regions and make them carry out central policies more effectively.

In the centrally planned system, targets were set from the centre and the different parts of the system were supposed to work in harmony to achieve the desired outcomes. But 'the imperatives of meeting production targets of the Five-Year Plans led regional party and economic leaders into self protective practices that involved a systematic deception of the Centre' (S. Fitzpatrick (ed.), *Stalinism New Directions*, page 10). Desperate to fulfil targets, people sought to bribe or steal from others to get raw materials; factories turned out sub-standard or useless products or fiddled the figures. Party members often colluded in this because they did not want to be held responsible for unfulfilled targets. Even party bosses, desperate to carry out their own pet projects, manipulated the system for their own ends. Corruption was rife throughout the whole system. Workers also subverted the system, making use of the 'revolving door' in the early to mid-1930s to move on to other jobs to avoid trouble or to evade being caught by the authorities. Skilled workers, before and particularly after the war, were in such short supply that they could put pressure on managers to give them better wages and conditions and escape stringent labour discipline.

The peasants found all sorts of ways of subverting the running of the kolkhozes, turning matters to their advantage despite the draconian laws. Non-cooperation, lack of effort or insubordination all contributed to poor performance and this often led to mangers being replaced because they failed to reach targets. Party or local officials were caught by contradictions in policy, e.g. they were supposed to identify and remove kulaks but these were the very people who were most productive and most useful in fulfilling targets. Even a Politburo commission referred to the whole dekulakisation programme as a 'dreadful mess'.

As Chris Read has written, 'In many ways Soviet Russia remained a fluid and mobile society filtering through the fingers of those trying to control it.' Party and police authorities became obsessed by fear of social disorder from the uncontrolled migration of millions of peasants into towns and cities. Socially marginal elements and petty criminals roamed their outskirts. NKVD Order 00447 of July 1937 was designed to eliminate the 'socially harmful elements'. What Pasternak called 'the unprecedented cruelty of Yezhov's time' was in part an attempt to control the 'quicksand society'.

Stalin's Russia was a heavily centralised and controlled state and there was much tighter control of the average person's existence. Conformity to a formulated state view was insisted upon. But it was not the total control that the word 'totalitarian' implies. The non-Communist intelligentsia were intimidated by the authorities but did not always toe the party line; many of them stopped writing or creating art and kept their heads down. The cult of the personality and propaganda were effective but many saw though the fabrication. In the final years of Stalin's rule, there were many problems in the economy and difficulties in controlling the wider population. For example, young people wanted a more liberated lifestyle. The party leaders and their subordinates knew about the problems and knew that reform was needed but nobody would tell Stalin. There were also other contradictions: Communist Russia was supposed to be an egalitarian society but it was hierarchically ordered with a self-interested ruling class; it was meant to be a workers' paradise but for much of Stalin's rule there were dire shortages, rationing and poverty.

Khrushchev 1953–1964

Nikita Khrushchev, who emerged as leader after Stalin, realised the need to reform the Stalinist system (see De-Stalinisation page 372). He inherited all the problems of the over-centralised economy and was anxious to bring in changes. He wanted to reward collective farmers more generously and increase the supply of food; he also wanted to produce more consumer goods – telephones, televisions, fridges and the like – to improve the basic standard of living. Khrushchev commented in 1953: 'What sort of Communism is it that cannot provide sausage?' Indeed under him the quality of life did improve significantly. However, too many of his schemes, labelled 'hare-brained' by his opponents, did not work. This, together with perceived failures on the international front, notably the Cuban missile crisis, saw him removed from power in 1964. Interestingly, however, he was not executed or imprisoned.

There was a thaw in cultural life during the Khrushchev era. Many writers who had been banned were rehabilitated, like Anna Akhmatova. Writers tested the limit of state censorship: prose or poems critical of Stalin were acceptable but works that denounced the party or belittled the present Soviet way of life were off limits – they were denounced or left unpublished. Boris Pasternak's *Dr Zhivago* was refused publication in the Soviet Union but was published in Italy in 1957 and in 1958 Pasternak was awarded the Nobel Prize for literature. Illegal copies circulated in the USSR and Pasternak was expelled from the Writers' Union, although subsequently he was reinstated. In 1962, Solzhenitsyn published *One Day in the Life of Ivan Denisovich*, the first time that the full truth of what went on in the camps had been revealed in Soviet literature. On 21 October, *Pravda* published Yevgeny Yevtoshenko's poem 'The Heirs of Stalin'. The poem attacked Stalin and his followers and warned against a resurgence of Stalinism. It began with the removal of Stalin's coffin from the Lenin Mausoleum for reburial and contained the lines:

And I appeal to our government with the request:
to double,
to treble
the guard at this tombstone,
So that Stalin may not rise,
and together with Stalin –
the past.

These two publishing events were a high watermark for reform; conservatives were outraged. Solzhenitsyn was unable to publish his next novels and Yevtoshenko's poem was not printed again for a quarter of a century.

SOURCE 21.1 Khrushchev

SOURCE 21.2 Brezhnev

SOURCE 21.3 Gorbachev

Brezhnev 1964–1982

After Khrushchev there was a reversion to Stalinism but in a modified, less severe form. The new Secretary General of the Party, Leonid Brezhnev, never considered using mass terror or individual despotism but there was less tolerance of criticism or dissent. Writers could be sentenced to hard labour for criticising the Soviet state and persistent dissidents were confined in mental asylums. Compromises were made with the people as long as they accepted the status quo. The trusted were given greater access to forbidden literature and foreign goods in special shops; they were even allowed to travel abroad, usually to Eastern Europe. The party became complacent and there were jobs for life for the nomenclatura. Ordinary people shared in the job security and there were pensions, free health care, access to education and other social security benefits, and more food was made available at controlled prices. Life was better for most people. However, compared with the West, their standard of living was still low and there was a serious shortage of housing. Trade with the West grew: the Russians had gas, oil and gold that were in high demand and for which prices increased rapidly in the 1970s. This tended to obscure the fact that the old central planning system was decaying from the inside. Much of the capital machinery used in industry was becoming obsolete and needed replacement, which required massive investment. But the main problem was that the planning system could not adapt to the scientific and technological advances of the second half of the twentieth century. Modern industry was simply getting too complex to have an over-centralised, top-heavy structure determining all its constituent parts. The command economy was not capable of producing a creative élite able to take on the dynamic competition from the West where the microchip revolution and computer industry were racing ahead.

Aware of changes in the West, the urbanised, more educated middle classes of the Soviet Union were becoming increasingly disenchanted with their stagnant regime. The two sick old men – Andropov and Chernenko – who led the USSR for the next three years did not change much.

Gorbachev 1985–1991

During the Brezhnev era, ideology had become fossilised and virtually meaningless. By the 1980s, an unlikely alliance of hardliners in the Communist Party and modernisers, who coalesced around Mikhail Gorbachev, attempted to inject some life into the Soviet system. They began a process of restructuring (*perestroika*). They did not know it at the time, but this was to be the last throes of the Communist regime. Gorbachev and the modernisers were influenced in their thinking about the direction the regime should take by the debate about the continuity between Lenin and Stalin. They were reading Medvedev and Cohen (see page 380) and came to the conclusion that things had gone wrong in the USSR at the point when Lenin died and Stalin took over. They thought that if they could return to the NEP-style economy of 1924–25 and inject elements of market capitalism back into the economy, then they could set the Soviet Union on the way to a more humane and socially just form of Communism. In the economy that emerged in the mid-1980s there was a considerable amount of decentralisation, some state enterprises were allowed to manage themselves and targets were no longer imposed; small-scale private enterprises were allowed. But this did not deliver the economic growth required and there were shortages of basic household goods, medicines and foodstuffs. Soviet citizens began to lose faith in *perestroika*. The dismantling of the one-party, centralised state offended hard-line traditionalists in the Communist Party who were generally unhappy with the direction the regime had taken domestically and in foreign affairs. In Eastern Europe, Communism appeared to be collapsing and, with republics asserting their independence, it looked as though a break-up of the USSR was inevitable. Eventually, these traditional conservative elements planned a coup to overthrow Gorbachev. When this failed, the Communist Party was discredited and its days became numbered. On 31 December 1991, the USSR ceased to exist and the Communist experiment in Russia which started with the Bolshevik Revolution of 1917 was ended.

After Communism

The USSR was broken up and some former republics – Georgia and the three Baltic States – became independent states. Initially, other regions agreed to remain in the Commonwealth of Independent States (CIS) although increasingly they began to go their separate ways and some, like the Ukraine, subsequently left the CIS. The problems were compounded by the large number of ethnic Russians who lived in these areas, e.g. the Baltic States and the Crimea, and this created a great deal of tension.

The Russian Federation (RSFSR), or more simply Russia, entered a turbulent period in the 1990s as the new President, Boris Yeltsin, attempted to reform the economic and political systems. He initiated a programme of democratisation. Most dramatically, the government embarked on rapid change from the planned economy to a market economy, which involved the privatisation of industry and the end of price controls and government subsidies. The results were disastrous – rising prices, unemployment, wages and pensions unpaid, homelessness and poverty. Unchecked crime and corruption were a massive problem as mafia-style gangs moved in on the big cities and gained influence over businesses and banks. The privatisation process led to the emergence of 'robber capitalists', industrial/financial 'oligarchs' who made huge profits out of the selling off of state industry, often in dubious circumstances. A large proportion of these profits went into foreign banks rather than being re-invested in Russian industry. Russia became dependent on loans from the West and began to look weak on the world stage as its armed forces went into decline. It is not surprising that Soviet citizens began to look with fondness at the 'safety-net' society of the Communist era where they were provided with guaranteed employment, food, shelter and health care.

According to Robert Service, it is the unpleasantness of life in the period after the collapse of Communism that in part accounts for a revival in popularity of Stalin. Stalin gave people order, pride and predictability, which reassured them and allowed them to overlook the systematic oppression. In December 2008, Stalin was voted third in the 'Name of Russia' poll conducted by a state-owned Russian television channel, although doubts have been expressed about the veracity of the voting. Vladimir Putin, who replaced Yeltsin as President, took the line that the achievements of the Soviet era should be acknowledged, in particular the Soviet effort in the Second World War – one of the key building blocks of a new national pride. Victory Day, 9 May, has become one of Russia's most important national holidays. 'We won the Great Patriotic War', said Putin in 2009. 'Even if we look back at the casualties, you know that no one can throw a stone at those who organised and led that victory, because if we had lost that war, the aftermath would have been much more catastrophic.'

Of course, it should be acknowledged that millions hated Stalin and his memory. In May 2010, an exhibition to raise awareness of the dictator's purges opened in Moscow, hitting back at what the organisers say is Stalin's rehabilitation. In the new Russia, the tsars do not get such a bad press and the Russian Orthodox Church has made a strong comeback. There has also been growing authoritarianism. It remains to be seen how far the traditional elements of Russian history influence its development in the 21st century.

Bibliography and Selected Reading

Dates in brackets are dates of first publication.

Abraham, R., *Alexander Kerensky, The First Love of the Revolution*, Columbia University Press, 1987

Acton, E., *Rethinking the Russian Revolution*, Edward Arnold, 1990

Acton, E. and Stableford, T., *The Soviet Union: A Documentary History, Vol. I 1917–1940*, University of Exeter Press, 2005

Alliluyeva, S., *Twenty Letters to a Friend*, Penguin, 1968

Ascher, A., *P. A. Stolypin: The Search for Stability in Late Imperial Russia*, Stanford, 2001

Ascher, A., *The Revolution of 1905*, Stanford, 2004

Avrich, P., *Kronstadt 1921*, Princeton University Press, 1970

Babel, I., *Collected Stories*, trans. D. McDuff, Penguin, 1994

Badcock, S., 'Autocracy in Crisis: Nicholas the Last' in Thatcher, I. D. (ed.), *Late Imperial Russia: Problems and Perspectives*, Manchester University Press, 2005

Barber, J. and Harrison, M., *The Soviet Home Front 1941–1945*, Longman, 1991

Bell, P. M. H., *The Origins of the Second World War in Europe*, Longman, 1987

Bellamy, C., *Absolute War*, Macmillan, 2007

Brandenberger, D., *National Bolshevism: Stalinist Mass Culture and the Formation of Modern Russian National Identity, 1931–1956*, Harvard University Press, 2002

Bullock, A., *Hitler and Stalin: Parallel Lives*, Harper Collins, 1991

Bushnell, J., *Mutiny amid Repression: Russian Soldiers in the Revolution of 1905–1906*, Indiana University Press, 1985

Carmichael, J., *A Short History of the Revolution*, Sphere Books, 1967

Carr, E. H., *The Russian Revolution from Lenin to Stalin*, Macmillan, 1979

Carr, E. H., *Socialism in One Country*, Macmillan, 1958

Carrère D'Encause, H., *Stalin: Order Through Terror*, Longman, 1981

Chamberlain, W. H., *The Russian Revolution 1917–21*, Macmillan, 1935

Cohen, S., *Bukharin and the Bolshevik Revolution*, OUP, 1974

Cohen, S., *Rethinking the Soviet Experience*, OUP, 1985

Conquest, R., *The Great Terror: A Reassessment*, Pimlico, 1990

Conquest, R., *The Harvest of Sorrow*, Hutchinson, 1986

Conquest, R., *Lenin*, Fontana, 1972

Conquest, R., *Stalin and the Kirov Murder*, Hutchinson, 1989

Conquest, R., *Stalin: Breaker of Nations*, Weidenfeld & Nicolson, 1991

Corin, C., 'Zinoviev and Kamenev: From Lenin's closest collaborators to Yagoda's trophies', *History Review* No 54, March 2006

Corin, C., 'Police, Spies and Double Agents: Russia 1881–1914', *History Review* No 64, September 2009

Corin, C., 'Sources: Stalin, Molotov, Kaganovich and Russia', *New Perspective*, Vol 116, No 1, September 2010

Cullerne Brown, M., *Art under Stalin*, Phaidon Press, 1991

Dallin, D. J. and Nikolaevsky, B. I., *Forced Labour in Soviet Russia*, Hollis & Carter, 1948

Daniels, R. V. (ed.), *The Stalin Revolution*, Heath, 1990

Davies, R. W., *Soviet Economic Development from Lenin to Khrushchev*, CUP, 1998

Davies, R. W., Khlevniuk, O. and Rees, E. A. (eds), *The Stalin – Kaganovich Correspondence 1931–1936*, Yale University Press, 2003

Davies, R. W., 'Stalin and Soviet Industrialization', *History Sixth*, March 1991

Davies, R. W., Harrison, M. and Wheatcroft, S. G. (eds), *The Economic Transformation of the Soviet Union, 1913–1945*, CUP, 1994

Davies, S., *Popular Opinion in Stalin's Russia: Terror, Propaganda and Dissent 1934–41*, CUP, 1997

De Robien, L., *The Diary of a Diplomat in Russia, 1917–18*, Praeger Pubishers, 1969

Deutscher, I., *Stalin*, rev. edn, Pelican, 1966

Deutscher, I., *The Prophet Unarmed: Trotsky 1921–29*, OUP, 1959

Deutscher, I., *The Prophet Outcast: Trotsky 1929–40*, OUP, 1963

Duranty, W., *I Write as I Please*, Simon & Schuster Inc., 1935

Erickson, J., 'Soviet Women at War' in Read, C. (ed.), *The Stalin Years: A Reader*, Palgrave, 2002

Fainsod, M., *Smolensk Under Soviet Rule*, Harvard University Press, 1958

Farmborough, F., *Nurse at the Russian Front*, Futura, 1977

Ferro, M., *Nicholas II: The Last of the Tsars*, Viking, 1991

Figes, O., *A People's Tragedy: The Russian Revolution 1891–1924*, Pimlico, 1997 (1996)

Figes, O., *Natasha's Dance: A Cultural History of Russia*, Allen Lane, 2002

Figes, O., *The Whisperers: Private Life in Stalin's Russia*, Allen Lane, 2007

Fitzpatrick, S., *Everday Stalinism*, OUP, 1999

Fitzpatrick, S., 'Revolution and Counter-Revolution in the Schools' in Daniels, R. V. (ed.), *The Stalin Revolution*, Heath, 1990

Fitzpatrick, S., *The Russian Revolution 1917–1932*, OUP, 1994 (1982)

Fitzpatrick, S. (ed.), *Stalinism: New Directions*, Routledge, 2000

Fitzpatrick, S., *Stalin's Peasants*, OUP, 1994

Garrard, J. and Garrard, C., *World War II and the Soviet People*, St Martin's Press, New York, 1993

Geifman, A., *Entangled in Terror; The Azef Affair and the Russian Revolution*, SR Books, 2000

Getty, J. A., *The Origins of the Great Purges*, CUP, 1985

Getty, J. A., 'The Politics of Stalinism' in Nove, A. (ed.), *The Stalin Phenomenon*, Weidenfeld and Nicolson, 1993

Getty, J. A. and Manning, R. (eds), *Stalinist Terror – New Perspectives*, CUP, 1993

Getty, J. A. and Naumov, O. V., *The Road to Terror: Stalin and the Self-Destruction of the Bolsheviks, 1932–39*, Yale University Press, 1999

Getzler, I., *Kronstadt 1917–1921: The Fate of Soviet Democracy*, CUP, 1983

Gill, G., *Stalinism*, Macmillan, 1990

Glantz, D., *Colossus Reborn: The Red Army at War, 1941–1943* University Press of Kansas, 2005

Goldman, E., *My Disillusionment in Russia*, Garden City, 1923

Goldman, E., *My Further Disillusionment in Russia*, Garden City, 1924

Golomstock, I., *Totalitarian Art*, Harper Collins, 1990

Harris, J., 'The purging of local cliques in the Urals region 1936–7' in Fitzpatrick, S. (ed.), *Stalinism: New Directions*, Routledge, 2000

Haslam, J., *The Soviet Union and the Struggle for Collective Security in Europe*, Macmillan, 1984

Haslam, J., *The Soviet Union and the Threat from the East, 1933–41*, Macmillan, 1992

Hiden, J., *Germany and Europe, 1919–39*, Longman, 1993 (1977)

Hindus, M., *Black Earth*, T. Fisher Unwin, 1926

Hosking, G., *A History of the Soviet Union*, Fontana, 1985

Hosking, G., *Russia and the Russians*, Penguin, 2001

Howson, G., *Arms for Spain*, John Murray, 1998

Kenez, P., *A History of the Soviet Union from the Beginning to the End*, CUP, 1999

Kennedy, P., *The Realities Behind Diplomacy*, Fontana, 1981

Kershaw, I., *Fateful Choices: Ten Decisions That Changed the World, 1940–1941*, Allen Lane, 2007

Khrushchev, N., *Khrushchev Remembers*, Vol. 1, ed. S. Talbot, Penguin, 1971

Khrushchev, N., *Khrushchev Remembers: The Glasnost Tapes*, 1990

Kotkin, S., *Magnetic Mountain: Stalinism as a Civilisation*, University of California Press, 1995

Kravchenko, V., *I Chose Freedom: The Personal and Political Life of a Soviet Official*, Robert Hale, 1947

Krivitsky, W. G., *I Was Stalin's Agent*, Hamish Hamilton, 1939

Laver, J., *Russia 1914–41*, Hodder, 1991

Lewin, M., 'Society, State and Ideology during the First Five-Year Plan', 1976, in Ward, C. (ed.), *The Stalinist Dictatorship*, Edward Arnold, 1998

Lewis, J. and Whitehead, P., *Stalin: A Time for Judgement*, Methuen, 1990

Lieven, D., *Nicholas II Emperor of all the Russias*, John Murray, 1993

Lih, L., Naumov, O. and Khlevniuk, O. (eds), *Stalin's letters to Molotov*, Yale University Press, 1995

Lincoln, B., *Red Victory: A History of the Russian Civil War*, Simon & Schuster, 1989

Linz, S. J. (ed.), *The Impact of World War II on the Soviet Union*, Totowa, New Jersey, 1985

McCauley, M., *Russia 1917–41*, Sempringham, 1997

McDermid, J. and Hillyer, A., *Women and Work in Russia, 1880–1930*, Longman, 1998

McDermott, K., *Stalin*, Palgrave Macmillan, 2006

McKean, R.B., *The Russian Constitutional Monarchy, 1907–1917*, Historical Association, 1977

McKean, R.B., *St Petersburg Between the Revolutions: Workers and Revolutionaries June 1907–February 1917*, Yale University Press, 1990

Mandelstam, N., *Hope Against Hope*, Collins/Harvill, 1971

Manning, R., 'The Soviet Economic Crisis of 1936–40 and the Great Purges' in Arch Getty, J. and Manning, R. (eds), *Stalinist Terror – New Perspectives*, CUP, 1993

Mawdsley, E., *The Russian Civil War*, Birlinn, 2000 (1987)

Mawdsley, E., *The Stalin Years*, University of Manchester Press, 1998

Mawdsley, E., *Thunder in the East*, Hodder Arnold, 2005

Medvedev, R., *Let History Judge*, Macmillan, 1972 (1971)

Medvedev, R., 'The Political Biography of Stalin' in Tucker, R. C. (ed.), *Stalinism: Essays in Historical Interpretation*, Norton, 1977

Merridale, C., *Ivan's War*, Faber and Faber, 2005

Montifore, S.S., *Stalin, The Court of the Red Tsar*, Weidenfeld and Nicolson, 2003

Montifore, S. S., *Young Stalin*, Weidenfeld and Nicolson, 2007

Moynahan, B., *The Russian Century*, Random House, 1994

Nove, A., *An Economic History of the USSR, 1917–91*, Penguin, 1992 (1969)

Nove, A., *Was Stalin Really Necessary?*, Allen & Unwin, 1964

Nove, A. (ed.), *The Stalin Phenomenon*, Weidenfeld and Nicolson, 1993

Orlov, A., *The Secret History of Stalin's Crimes*, Jarrold, 1954

Ostrovsky, N., *How the Steel Was Tempered*, Moscow, 1932

Overy, R., *Russia's War*, Penguin, 1997

Pallot, J., *Land Reform in Russia 1906–1917*, Oxford University Press, 1999

Pankrashova, M. and Sipols, V., *Why War was not Prevented*, Novosti Press, Moscow, 1970

Pasternak, B., *Doctor Zhivago*, Collins Fontana, 1975 (first published in English 1958)

Pipes, R., *A Concise History of the Russian Revolution*, Harvill Press, 1995

Pipes, R., *Russia Under the Bolshevik Regime, 1919–24*, Harvill Press, 1994

Pipes, R., *Three Whys of the Russian Revolution*, Pimlico, 1998

Pipes, R., 'The Great October Revolution as a clandestine coup d'état', *Times Literary Supplement*, November 1992

Pipes, R., *The Degaev Affair: Terror and Treason in Tsarist Russia*, Yale University Press, 2005

Pipes, R. (ed.), *The Unknown Lenin*, Yale University Press, 1996

Pomonarev, B. N., *History of the Communist Party of the Soviet Union*, Moscow, 1960

Radzinsky, E., *Stalin*, Sceptre, 1997 (1996)

Ransome, A., *Six Weeks in Russia in 1919*, George Allen and Unwin, 1919

Rappaport, H., *Joseph Stalin: A Biographical Companion*, 1999

Read, C., *From Tsar to Soviets: The Russian People and their Revolution 1917–21*, UCL Press, 1996

Read, C., *In Search of Liberal Tsarism: The historiography of autocratic decline*, The Historical Journal 45, 2005

Reed, J., *Ten Days that Shook the World*, Penguin, 1977 (1919)

Roberts, G., *Stalin's Wars*, Yale University Press, 2006

Roberts, G., *The Soviet Union and the Origins of the Second World War*, Macmillan, 1995

Roberts, G., *Victory at Stalingrad*, Longman, 2002

Rogger, H., *Russia in the Age of Modernisation and Revolution 1881–1917*, Longman, 1983

Sakwa, R., *The Rise and Fall of the Soviet Union 1917–1991*, Routledge, 1999

Schapiro, L., *1917*, Temple Smith, 1984

Schleifman, N., *Undercover Agents in the Russian Revolutionary Movement: The SR Party 1902–1914*, Macmillan, 1988

Schneiderman, J., *Sergei Zubatov and Revolutionary Marxism*, Cornell University Press, 1976

Scott, J., *Behind the Urals*, Secker and Warburg, 1942

Serge, V., trans. and ed. P. Sedwick, *Memoirs of a Revolutionary 1901–1941*, OUP, 1967 (1963)

Service, R, *A History of Modern Russia: From Nicholas II to Putin*, 2nd edn, Harvard University Press, 2005

Service, R., *A History of Twentieth-Century Russia*, Penguin, 1997

Service, R., *Lenin, A Biography*, Macmillan, 2000

Service, R., 'Lenin: Individual and Politics in the October Revolution', *Modern History Review*, September 1990

Service, R., *Stalin, A Biography*, Macmillan, 2004

Service, R., *The Russian Revolution 1900–1927*, 2nd edn, Macmillan 1991 (1986)

Service, R., *The Russian Revolution 1900–1927*, 4th edn, Macmillan, 2009

Service, R., *Trotsky*, Macmillian, 2009

Sholokhov, M., *Virgin Soil Upturned*, Penguin (1935)

Smith, S., *Red Petrograd: Revolution in the Factories 1917–1918*, CUP, 1983

Solzhenitsyn, A., *The Gulag Archipelago*, Vols 1–2, Collins/Harvill, 1974, 1975

Sukhanov, N. N., *Notes on the Revolution*, 1922; trans. and ed. J. Carmichael, *The Russian Revolution 1917: A Personal Record*, OUP, 1955

Talbott, S. (ed.), *Khrushchev Remembers*, Vol. 1, Penguin, 1977

Taubman, W., *Khrushchev The Man and his Era*, W. W. Norton, 2003

Taylor, A. J. P., *Origins of the Second World War*, 2nd edn, Penguin, 1963 (1961)

Taylor, R. (trans. and ed.), *The Film Factory: Soviet Cinema in Documents, 1936–1939*, Routledge and Kegan Paul, 1988

Thomas, H., *The Spanish Civil War*, 3rd edn, Penguin, 1977

Thurston, R., *Life and Terror in Stalin's Russia 1934–41*, Yale University Press, 1996

Timasheff, N., *The Great Retreat: The Growth and Decline of Communism in Russia*, Dutton, New York, 1946

Trotsky, L., *The History of the Russian Revolution*, 3 vols, Victor Gollancz, 1932–33

Tucker, R. C., 'The Emergence of Stalin's Foreign Policy' in *Slavic Review*, 1977

Tucker, R. C., *Stalin in Power: The Revolution from Above, 1928–1941*, Norton, 1992

Tucker, R. C. (ed.), *Stalinism: Essays in Historical Interpretation*, Norton, 1977

Ulam, A., *Expansionism and Coexistence*, 2nd edn, Praeger, 1974

Urban, G.R. (ed.), *Stalinism*, Temple Smith, 1982

Vasilievski, L. A. and L. M., *Kniga o golode*, 1922

Vernadsky, G., *A Source Book of Russian History*, Vol. 3, Yale University Press, 1972

Volkogonov, D., *Lenin: Life and Legacy*, Harper Collins, 1994

Volkogonov, D., *Stalin*, Weidenfeld and Nicolson, 1988

Volkogonov, D., *The Rise and Fall of the Soviet Empire*, Harper Collins, 1998

Volkogonov, V., 'Stalin as Supreme Commander' in Wegner, B. (ed.), *From Peace to War*, Berghahn Books, 1997

Waldron, P., *Between Two Revolutions: Stolypin and the Politics of Renewal in Russia*, UCL Press, 1997

Waldron, P., *Governing Tsarist Russia*, Palgrave Macmillan, 2007

Waldron, P., *The End of Imperial Russia, 1855–1917*, Palgrave Macmillan, 1997

Ward, C., *Stalin's Russia*, Edward Arnold, 1993

Ward, C. (ed.), *The Stalinist Dictatorship*, Edward Arnold, 1998

Watt, D. C., *How War Came*, Heinemann, 1989

Weinberg, G., *World in the Balance*, Hammer, 1981

Weissberg, A., *Conspiracy of Silence*, Hamish Hamilton, 1952

Westwood, J., *Endurance and Endeavour*, OUP, 1973

Westwood, J. N., *Endurance and Endeavour, Russian History 1812–2001*, 5th edn, Oxford University Press, 2002

Williams, B., *Lenin*, Longman, 2000

Williams, B., *Russia 1905*, History Today, May 2005

Williams, B., *The Russian Revolution 1917–21*, Historical Association Studies, 1987

Acknowledgements

Photo credits
Cover *l & r* © Bettmann/Corbis, *c* © Hulton-Deutsch Collection/Corbis, *background* © David King Collection; **p.v** © Illustrated London News; **p.vi** *l & r* © David King Collection; **p.1** *t & b* © David King Collection; **p.2** *l* © Topham Picturepoint/TopFoto, *r* © MosFilms/Ronald Grant Archive; **p.6** © David King Collection; **p.7** *t & b* © David King Collection; **p.9** © David King Collection; **p.11** © superclic/Alamy; **p.12** © David King Collection; **p.13** © Illustrated London News; **p.21** © Hulton Archive/Getty Images; **p.26** © David King Collection; **p.27** © David King Collection; **p.30** © David King Collection; **p.34** © RIA Novosti/TopFoto; **p.36** © Topham Picturepoint/TopFoto; **p.39** © David King Collection; **p.41** *b* © David King Collection; **p.47** © Hulton Archive/Getty Images; **p.58** *t* © David King Collection, *b* © Walter Daran/Time Life Pictures/Getty Images; **p.60** *r* © TopFoto; **p.63** *t & b* © David King Collection; **p.67** © David King Collection; **p.76** © David King Collection; **p.77** © David King Collection; **p.82** © David King Collection; **p.87** *t & b* © David King Collection; **p.91** *t* © David King Collection, *b* © Popperfoto/Getty Images; **p.92** © Mary Evans Picture Library; **p.93** © Portrait of Alexander Kerensky: Harry Ransom Humanities Research Center, The University of Texas at Austin; **p.97** © David King Collection; **p.99** © Portrait of Alexander Kerensky: Harry Ransom Humanities Research Center, The University of Texas at Austin; **p.100** © Print Collector/HIP/TopFoto; **p.101** © David King Collection; **p.103** © David King Collection; **p.109** © MosFilms/Ronald Grant Archive; **p.131** © David King Collection; **p.132** © David King Collection; **p.133** © David King Collection; **p.138** *tr, tl & b* © David King Collection; **p.139** *t* © David King Collection, *c* © The British Library Board (85/1856.g.812), *b* © The British Library Board (85/1856.g.828); **p.144** © Popperfoto/Getty Images, *b* © David King Collection; **p.146** © David King Collection; **p.149** © David King Collection; **p.152** *t* © David King Collection, *b* © Hulton Archive/Getty Images; **p.153** © David King Collection; **p.155** © Hulton Archive/Getty Images; **p.158** © David King Collection; **p.170** *tl & tr* © David King Collection, *bl* © David King Collection/DACS 2010, *br* © State Russian Museum, St Petersburg; **p.171** *t & bl* © David King Collection, *br* © David King Collection/DACS 2010; **p.174** © Hulton Archive/Getty Images; **p.175** © David King Collection; **p.182** © David King Collection; **p.183** © David King Collection; **p.184** *t, c & b* © David King Collection; **p.185** *l & r* © David King Collection; **p.186** © David King Collection; **p.197** *tl, tr & bl* © David King Collection, *br* © Bettmann/Corbis; **p.204** © RIA Novosti/TopFoto; **p.205** *t & bl* © David King Collection, *c* © Roger-Viollet/Topfoto; **p.212** © David King Collection; **p.213** *t* © RIA Novosti/TopFoto, *b* © David King Collection; **p.220** *t, bl & br* © David King Collection; **p.223** © David King Collection; **p.231** © David King Collection; **p.234** © David King Collection; **p.237** © David King Collection; **p.238** © David King Collection; **p.247** *tl, tr & br* © David King Collection; **p.248** © David King Collection; **p.252** © David King Collection; **p.254** © Popperfoto/Getty Images; **p.255** © David King Collection; **p.258** © David King Collection; **p.259** © David King Collection; **p.261** *l & r* © David King Collection; **p.264** *l & r* Drawing from: Dancik Sergejewitsch Baldajew "Gulag Zeichnungen", published by Bℤffgen, Klahn & Klamt © 1993 www.Zweitausendeins.de; **p.271** © David King Collection; **p.276** © David King Collection; **p.277** *all* © David King Collection; **p.280** *tl, tr & b* © David King Collection; **p.281** *t & b* © David King Collection; **p.286** *tl & br* © David King Collection; **p.287** *tl & b* © David King Collection, *tr* © State Russian Museum/DACS 2010; **p.290** © David King Collection; **p.293** *t* Three Female Figures, 1928–32 (oil on canvas), Malevich, Kazimir Severinovich (1878–1935)/State Russian Museum, St. Petersburg, Russia/The Bridgeman Art Library, *cr & bl* © David King Collection; **p.294** *tl* © SCRSS PHOTO LIBRARY www.scrss.org.uk, *b* © David King Collection; **p.295** *t & b* © David King Collection; **p.296** © David King Collection; **p.297** © MosFilms/Ronald Grant Archive; **p.299** *l & r* © David King Collection; **p.300** © David King Collection; **p.306** From collection International Institute of Social History (Amsterdam); **p.309** © ITAR-TASS/Anatoly Grakhov; **p.310** © SCRSS PHOTO LIBRARY www.scrss.org.uk; **p.311** *t* © David King Collection/DACS 2010, *b* © David King Collection; **p.312** © David King Collection; **p.314** *t & b* © David King Collection; **p.315** © David King Collection; **p.321** © David King Collection; **p.322** © David King Collection; **p.323** *t, c & b* © David King Collection; **p.328** *t & b* © David King Collection; **p.331** © Ullsteinbild/Topfoto; **p.335** *t* © Evening Standard/Solo Syndication, *b* © David King Collection; **p.343** The Defence of Sevastopol, 1942 (oil on canvas), Dejneka (Deineka), Aleksandr Aleksandrovic (1899–1969)/State Russian Museum, St. Petersburg, Russia/© DACS/RIA Novosti/The Bridgeman Art Library/DACS 2010; **p.346** © akg-images/Voller Ernst; **p.353** © RIA Novosti/TopFoto; **p.356** © RIA Novosti/TopFoto; **p.357** © RIA Novosti/TopFoto; **p.359** *tl, tr & bl* © RIA Novosti/TopFoto, *br* © World History Archive/TopFoto; **p.364** © David King Collection/DACS 2010; **p.366** Credit: The Triumph of the Victorious Motherland, 1949 (oil on canvas) by Khmelko, Mikhail Ivanovich (1919–75) © Private Collection/The Bridgeman Art Library; **p.370** *t* © 2006 RIA Novosti/TopFoto, *b* © Gamma-Keystone via Getty Images; **p.371** © 2004 Topham Picturepoint/TopFoto; **p.372** © Popperfoto/Getty Images; **p.385** © AP/Press Association Images; **p.385** © David King Collection; **p.391** © TopFoto; **p.392** *t* © AFP/Getty Images, *b* © RIA Novosti/TopFoto.

c = centre, *l* = left, *r* = right, *t* = top, *b* = bottom

Text credits
A. Ascher: extracts from *The Revolution of 1905* (Stanford University Press, 2004), reprinted by permission of the publisher; **Alan Bullock:** extracts from *Hitler and Stalin: Parallel Lives* (HarperCollins, 1991); **R.W. Davies et. al. (editors):** text extracts and graph from *The Economic Transformation of the Soviet Union 1913-1945* (Cambridge University Press, 1994), © Cambridge University Press 1994, reproduced with permission; **Isaac Deutscher:** extracts from *Stalin*, Revised edition (Oxford University Press, 1961; Pelican Books, 1966); **Orlando Figes:** extracts from *A People's Tragedy: The Russian Revolution 1891-1924* (Pimlico, 1997), reprinted by permission of The Random House Group Ltd; **Stephen Kotkin:** extracts from *Magnetic Mountain: Stalinism as a Civilisation* (University of California Press, 1995); **Moshe Lewin:** extracts from 'Society, State and Ideology during the First Five-Year Plan', from *Cultural Revolution in Russia 1928-31*, edited by S. Fitzpatrick (Indiana University Press, 1978), reprinted by permission of the publisher; **Osip Mandelstam:** 'Stalin Epigram' from Nadezhda Mandelstam, *Hope Against Hope: A Memoir*, translated by Max Hayward (HarperCollins, 1971); **E. Mawdsley:** extract from *The Russian Civil War* (HarperCollins, 1987); **Alec Nove:** text extracts and two graphs from *An Economic History of the USSR, 1917-91* (Allen Lane The Penguin Press, Third edition, 1992), copyright © Alec Nove, 1969, 1972, 1976, 1982, 1989, 1992, reprinted by permission of the publisher); **C. Read:** extracts from *From Tsar to Soviets: The Russian People and their Revolution 1917-21* (Routledge/UCL Press, 1996); **J. Scott:** extracts from *Behind the Urals* (Secker & Warburg, 1942); **Robert Service:** extracts from *A History of Twentieth-Century Russia* (Allen Lane, 1997), reprinted by permission of the author; **R. C. Tucker:** extracts from *Stalin in Power: The Revolution from Above, 1928-1941* (W.W.Norton, 1992); **Chris Ward:** extracts from *Stalin's Russia* (Hodder & Stoughton, 1993); **Beryl Williams:** extracts from *The Russian Revolution 1917-21* (Wiley-Blackwell, 1987), reprinted by permission of the publisher.

Every effort has been made to establish copyright and contact copyright holders prior to publication. If contacted, the publishers will be pleased to rectify any omissions or errors at the earliest opportunity.

Index

Note: Entries in **bold** refer to the historical terms explained in the glossary boxes and the pages on which those glossary boxes occur.

abortion 288, 306, 307, 308
agitprop art 138, 295–6
agriculture 16, 18, 158, 199
    poor harvests 29, 88, 150, 151
    post-war reconstruction 369
    reforms 47, 48, 52–3, 56
    during Second World War 353
    see also collectivisation
Akhmatova, Anna 311, 343, 355, 367
Alexander I, Tsar 15
Alexander II, Tsar 3–4, 10
Alexander III, Tsar 10, 11, 12, 19
Alexandra, Tsarina 14, 61, 62, 63, 64
All-Russian Congress of Soviets 165
anarchy 119
annexation 130
anti-Semitism 12, 19–20, 40, 140, 366
anti-Westernism 367
Antonov, Alexander 151, 350
April Theses 83, 178
armed forces
    army 9, 12, 38, 57, 69, 76, 93, 131
        in First World War 59–60
    and Kornilov affair 99–100
    mutinies 35, 38, 50, 57, 67–8, 151–3
    navy 96
    and Petrograd Soviet 78
arts 305, 310–11, 342, 366
    agitprop art 138, 295–6
    Cultural Revolution and 305
    Lenin in 170, 171, 276–7, 280
    paintings as historical sources 169–71
    and propaganda 292–6, 295
    Socialist Realism and 310–15
    Stalin in 284, 386
    Winter Palace 2
    women in 286–7
autocracy of tsars v, 9, 11, 48, 70–1, 388
Azef, Evno 34, 58

Babel, Isaac 141, 310, 311
bag-men 146
Beria, Lavrenti 251, 370, 371, 372, 373
Black Hundreds 36, 40
Bloody Sunday 28, 32, 33–5
Bochareva, Maria 86, 87
Bogdanov, Alexander 292
Bolsheviks 24, 26, 27, 57, 81
    consolidation of power 167
    and corruption 147
    popularity of 96–8, 100, 107–8, 110
    Red Guard 99–100
    retention of power 124
    strengths 112
    threats from opposition 119
    see also Red Army
bourgeois revolution 23

Brest-Litovsk Treaty 121, 122, 178, 327
Brezhnev, Leonid 392
Britain 156, 329, 330, 334, 336, 338, 339, 340
Brodsky, Isaak 305, 313, 314
Bukharin, Nikolai 58, 121, 183, 184, 195, 247, 253
    and industrialisation 202
    and leadership struggle 189, 191, 192
    on New Economic Policy 155
    and 1936 constitution 251
    show trial 247, 259, 261
Bunge, Nikolai 11

capitalism vi, 21, 23, 222
censorship 8, 159, 318
Central Committee 160, 162, 164, 165, 178
central planning 222, 228: see also command economy; Five-Year Plans
centralisation: development of 160–6
Cheka 118, 119, 143–4, 146
Chernov, Victor 21, 81, 87–8, 96, 97, 176
Chicherin, G.V. 117, 323, 328
Chkheidze, Nikolai 76, 77, 82, 97
cinema 292–7, 305, 313, 318
    Bolsheviks and 292–6
    as propaganda 297, 318
Civil War 126–48
    Bolshevik victory, reasons for 136–9
    Communist Party, impact on 162
    course of 127–9
    key events 127
    life in Russia during 140–1
    and nationalisation 161
    role of other countries 130
    Trotsky and 131–3
coalition 85, 120, 178
Cold War v, **105**
collectivisation 196–7, 223, 383
    assessment of 217–18
    and famine 211, 214
    impact on peasants 210–16
    implementation of 209–10
    opposition to 210
    plan of collectivised farm 207
    post-1934: 215
    reasons for 206
    Smolensk 216
    speed of 206–8
Comintern 326, 328–9, 332
command economy 203, 375, 382–3, 389: see also central planning; Five-Year Plans
communism v, 22–3
Communist Internationals 326

Communist Party
    impact of Civil War on 162
    leadership battle 183–7
    membership benefits 250
    and peasants 199
    and soviets 162
    structure of 165
Constituent Assembly 76, 81, 108, 120
corruption 8, 147, 155
Cossacks 9, 38, 67, 109, 134, 140, 365
counter-revolution 78, 143
coup d'état **69**
crime 93, 156, 201, 289, 307
Crimean War 15
Cultural Revolution 302–5, 316
culture 304, 367, 390–1: see also arts; cinema; literature
Czech Legion 127, 129
Czechoslovakia 333, 334, 335, 339

Dagaev, Sergei (Alexander Pell) 10
Decree on Peace 121, 327
democratic centralism 166
Denikin, General Anton 126, 127, 128, 134, 137
de-stalinisation 373
dictatorship of the proletariat 118
divorce 288, 306, 307, 308
Doctors' Plot 366, 371, 372
Dumas
    constitutional experiment 48–52
    and end of Romanovs 69
    Nicholas II and 52, 61, 64
    Progressive Bloc 61–2, 64
    Stolypin and 47–8, 50
Durnovo, P. N. 39, 40
Dzerzhinsky, Felix 117, 122, 144, 193

Eastern Front 343–6
economy 11, 16, 389
    deterioration in 88–9, 150–1
    foreign participation 224
    improvements in 52–5
    recovery of 155–8
    Stalin and 198–9
    transformation of 196–7
education 10, 17, 37, 241, 298–9, 304, 315–16, 318
Ehrenburg, Ilya 344, 356, 357, 358, 360
Eisenstein, Sergei 35, 297, 305, 310, 358
    October 109, 296, 297
emigration 146
employment
    women and 7, 230–1, 289
    see also unemployment
enemies of the people 258
ethnic cleansing 350

factionalism 163, 191, 195
famine 149, 151, 211–14
Fascism 332
  collective security against 333–4
February Revolution 65–9, 73–4, 89
feudalism 22
First World War 85–6
  impact of 59–64
Five-Year Plans 202–3, 389
  First 225, 227–8, 231–3, 240, 241, 242, 319
  Second 225, 229, 233
  Third 225, 229, 233
  Fourth 368–9
  Fifth 369
  achievements 225–9
  evaluation of 242–3
  and Great Purges 272–3
  heavy industry and 222, 223, 225, 242
  living standards during 240–1
  organisation of 222–4
  workers and 230–9
food rationing 108, 141, 142, 151, 154, 206, 240
food shortages 88, 141–2, 149, 186, 208
food supply issues 161, 198: see also grain requisitioning policies
foreign investment 16, 42
foreign policy 322–4, 326–41
  Lenin and 322, 327
  Stalin and 322, 332–3
France
  and Russian Empire 16, 42
  and USSR 333, 334, 336, 338, 339, 340

Gapon, Father 33, 34
Gerasimov, Aleksandr 305, 311
Germany
  First World War 59, 121
  trade agreements 156
  and USSR 330–1, 332, 333, 334, 336, 338, 339, 340
Gorbachev, Mikhail 381, 392
Gorky, Maxim 79, 119, 175, 311, 315
Gosplan 223, 225, 227, 228
GPU (secret police) 159
grain exports 53
grain requisitioning policies 142, 149, 151, 200, 211, 217
  end of 154, 208
Great Depression 217, 224, 225
Great Purges, see Great Terror
Great Retreat 305–9
Great Terror 250–1, 258–74
  Five-Year Plans and 229, 272–3
  interpretations of 267–74
  NKVD and 266, 273, 274
  Stalin's personality and 269–74
  in Sverdlovsk 274
  timeline 251
  victims 266
Great Turn 202–3
Green armies 126, 128, 132
Guchkov, Alexander 49, 57, 69

Gulag, see labour camps

heavy industry 15, 154, 222–5, 242
  iron and steel 16, 29, 54
historiography 104
History of the All-Union Communist Party (Short Course) 279, 280–1
Homo Sovieticus, see New Soviet Man
housing 201, 240, 241, 318
Huxley, Aldous 317

industrial enterprises 219, 222, 223
  labour turnover 231–2
industrialisation 15–16, 55, 74, 186, 196–7, 202
  and agriculture 199
  and Great Turn 203
  and NEP 200–1
  Stalin's economic policies 198–9
  see also industry
industry 158
  deterioration in 88
  development 54–5
  nationalisation 116, 142, 161
  post-war reconstruction 368–9
  recovery of 155
  workers 55–6
  workers' committees and 141
  workers' control decree 117
  see also heavy industry; industrialisation; light industry
International Women's Day march 65, 67
internationalists 81

Iskra (newspaper) 26, 27, 29
Izvestia (newspaper) 35, 98, 153, 247

Japan
  and Russia 30–1, 32, 37, 130
  and USSR 336, 337
July Days 86, 96–8
juvenile crime 201, 307

Kadet Party (Constitutional Democratic Party) 37, 49, 50, 51, 57, 90, 94, 100, 119, 134
  and Duma 52
  policies (March 1917) 81
Kaganovich, Lazar 253, 391
Kamenev, Lev 101, 120, 133, 165, 183, 184, 195, 251
  and July Days 97
  and leadership struggle 189, 190–1
  show trial 258–9, 261
Kerensky, Alexander 51, 76, 77, 78, 86, 90–3
  and Kornilov affair 99–100
  mistakes by 111
  and October Revolution 101–2
  problems facing 93
Khodynka Field 13, 42
Khrushchev, Nikita 252, 256, 279, 282, 351, 370, 373

culture under 391
  on Lend-Lease 355
  on Stalin 271
Kirov, Sergei 251, 253, 254–7
Kolchak, Admiral 126, 127, 129, 134, 137
Kollontai, Alexandra 113, 117, 151, 289–91
Komsomol 299, 303
Komuch 126, 134
Konspiratsia (secret police) 10
Kornilov, Lavr 99–100, 126
Kornilov affair 99–100
Kosmodemyanskaya, Zoya 354, 356
Kronstadt 96–8, 150, 151, 152–3
Kronstadt revolt 151–3
Kukryniksy 354, 356, 358, 359
kulaks 7, 18, 209, 389–90
  action against 212, 216
  and grain production 206, 208

labour camps 151, 264, 273, 365, 373, 378
labour problems 233
  turnover 231–2, 234
League of Nations 333
Left Socialist Revolutionaries (Left SRs) 120, 121, 122
Lena Goldfields Massacre 55, 57
Lend-Lease 344, 353, 362
Lenin (Vladimir Ilyich Ulyanov) vi, 23, 26, 27, 57, 58, 79, 169–70
  April Theses 83
  and art 292, 295
  in art 280, 314
  assassination attempts 143, 145
  assessments of 175–6
  and Bolsheviks 24, 98
  contribution to history 177–9
  cult of 143, 174
  escape from Petrograd 98
  and foreign policy 322, 327
  funeral of 173–4
  and New Economic Policy 155
  and October Revolution 101, 180
  and problems caused by ending the war 121–2
  return of 82–4
  and St Petersburg Soviet 39
  and Sovnarkom 117
  and Stalin 172–3
  and Stalinism 376–81
  and threat from other Socialists 120
  and War Communism 141–5, 151–2
Leningrad: siege of 343
liberalism 20, 57, 81: see also Kadet Party; Octobrists
libertarianism 106
Liebknecht, Karl 41
light industry 16, 19, 33, 54
Lissitsky, Lazar Markovich (El Lissitsky) 292, 295
literacy 19, 55, 299
literature 305, 311–12
Litvinov, M. M. 322, 323, 333, 334, 338

living standards 383
  during Five-Year Plans 240–1
  at Magnitogorsk 240
  for peasants 7, 56
  during Second World War 352
  for workers 7, 19
Lunacharsky, Anatoly 117, 292, 298
Lvov, Prince G. E. 76, 77, 80, 90
Lysenko, Trofim 317, 367, 369

Magnitogorsk 197, 220, 221, 224, 226,
  227, 231–2, 234, 235, 308
  labour turnover 232
  living standards at 240
  New Soviet Man 317–18
  Stakhanovite movement 238
Makhno, Nestor 126, 128
Malevich, Kasimir 292, 293, 295
Malinovsky, Roman 58
Mandelstam, Osip 265, 310
Martov (Julius Tsederbaum) 26, 27, 83,
  97, 175
Marx, Karl vi, 21
Marxism 21
Marxism-Leninism 23
Mayakovsky, Vladimir 292, 293, 294
Mensheviks 24, 26, 27, 35, 57, 100, 119
  and Duma 51
  and 1905 revolution 38
  outlawing of 159
  and Petrograd Soviet 76
  policies (March 1917) 81
  reaction to April Theses 83
  and St Petersburg Soviet 38–9
  and soviets 36
Meyerhold, Vsevolod 263, 293, 295, 310,
  313
middle classes 7, 17, 40, 42
Milyukov, Paul 49, 62, 76, 81, 85
modernisation v, 15–17, 70, 74
Molotov, Vyacheslav M. 58, 209, 253, 323,
  333, 339, 391
Morozov, Pavlik 309
Munich Conference 334–5
music 311
MVD (secret police) 370, 371, 373

Narodnaya Volya (People's Will) 4, 10, 20
national identity 9
national minorities 14, 80, 81, 88, 164,
  365, 366, 378
  and 1905 revolution 38
  resignations over concessions to 90
  and Russification 19–20
  self-determination 117, 137
nationalisation 116, 142, 161
nationalism: Russian 366, 389
Nazi-Soviet Pact 340–1, 348
New Economic Policy (NEP) 154–9,
  178, 186–7
  evaluation of 243
  industrialisation and 200–1
  peasants and 156, 200

political repression during 159
New Soviet Man 203, 317–20, 389
Nicholas II, Tsar v, 12–14, 19
  assessment of 13–14
  downfall of 64, 73
  and Duma 51, 61, 64
  execution of 143
  and First World War 61–2, 64
  and October Manifesto 36
  and Russo-Japanese War 30
  survival of 1905 revolution 42
Nikolayev, Leonid 254, 255, 256–7
1905 revolution 26, 28–39
  causes of 28–32
  course of 37
  interpretation of 43–4
  peasants and 40
  restoration of order 40–42
NKVD (secret police) 247, 251, 255,
  265
  and Great Purges 263, 266, 273, 274
  and juvenile crime 307
  during Second World War 350
nobility 6, 28
nomenklatura system 163, 383

October Manifesto 17, 36, 37, 42
October Revolution v, vi, 178
  assessments of 104–9
  Bolsheviks and 101–3, 109
  Cossacks and 109
  Lenin and 101, 180
  reactions to 113–14
  storming of Winter Palace 109
  timeline leading to 96
Octobrists 49, 51, 52, 57
Ogorodnikov, V. P. 238, 248
OGPU (secret police) 209, 216, 251,
  301
oil industry 16, 29, 54
Okhrana (secret police) 8, 29, 34, 40,
  57, 58
Operation Bagration 344, 350
Operation Barbarossa 343–4, 345, 346,
  348, 352
Ordzhonikidze, Sergei 58, 223, 237, 261
Orthodox Church 9, 300–1, 388, 393
  attacks on 159
  reforms 50, 52
  during Second World War 360
Orwell, George 317
Ostrovsky, Nikolai 312, 317, 318

partisans 354, 355
party secretaries 238
Parvus (Alexander Helphand) 27
Pasternak, Boris 140, 305, 311, 312,
  390–1
peasants 6, 7, 18, 87–8
  and agrarian reforms 52–3, 56
  and Bolsheviks 144, 149–50, 151
  collectivisation, impact of 210–16
  Communist Party and 199

and land reform 87–8
  and nationalisation 161
  and NEP 156, 200
  and 1905 revolution 40
  and Urals-Siberian method 200
  and White army 134
Pell, Alexander (Sergei Dagaev) 10
People's Will (Narodnaya Volya) 4, 10, 20
permanent revolution 187, 332: see also
  world revolution
Petrograd Soviet 76–8, 93, 98, 100, 108,
  182
  and Kornilov affair 99
  Military Revolutionary Committee
    (MRC) 101
  policies (March 1917) 81
Pioneers 299
Plehve, Vyacheslav von 30, 32, 58
Pobedonostsev, Konstantin 12, 13
Pokrovsky, M. N. 316
Poland 339, 340–1
police 10, 68: see also secret police
police trade unions 29
Politburo 117, 160, 162, 165, 370
popular revolution 2
populism 20
Potemkin mutiny 35, 38
Pravda (newspaper) 57, 58, 182, 184
Preobrazhensky, Eugene 202
private industry 223
private enterprise 202, 206, 207, 215:
  see also New Economic Policy
proletarianisation 230
Proletkult 292
propaganda 234
  art in 292–6
  cinema as 297
  in Civil War 137, 138–9
  cult of Stalin 276–84
  during Second World War 357–60
protest actions 8, 20, 67
  peasants and 18, 210
  urban workers and 19
  see also strikes
Provisional Government 76–9, 80–1,
  85–9, 94, 111
purges 347, 378: see also Great Purges
Putilov engineering works 19, 33, 65
Putin, Vladimir 393
Pyatakov, G. L. 251, 259

Radek, Karl 251, 259
railway industry 4, 15–16, 29
  in First World War 61
  and nationalisation 161
  during Second World War 353
  strikes 37
  see also Trans-Siberian Railway
Rapallo Treaty 327, 330
RAPP (Russian Association of Proletarian
  Writers) 304, 305, 311
Rasputin, Grigory Yefimovich 62, 63, 64
rearmament 54

Red Army 126, 131, 132, 136, 137, 178
    patriotism of 356
    purges 251, 347
Red Terror 143–5
Reds, see Bolsheviks
rehabilitation 247
religion 19, 300–1, 304: see also anti-
    Semitism; Orthodox Church
Rodchenko, Alexander 292, 294
Rodzianko, Mikhail 49, 60, 69
**RSFSR (Russian Soviet Federal
    Socialist Republic) 163**, 393
Russian calendar 65, 121
Russian Empire
    communications 4
    modernisation of 15–17
    recession 29
    social structure 6–7
    under tsarism 8–11
Russification 9, 12, 19–20
Russo-Japanese War 17, 30–1, 33, 37
Russo-Polish War 130
Rykov, Alexei 117, 133, 183, 185, 191,
    195, 259
Ryutin, Martemyan 251, 253, 264

Second World War (Great Patriotic War)
    aftermath of 365–7
    agriculture during 353
    Eastern Front 343–6
    living standards during 352
    NKVD during 350
    Orthodox Church during 360
    propaganda during 357–60
    railway industry during 353
    Stalin and 347, 348–51
    victory 361–2
    women during 354–5
secret police 62, 79
    Cheka 118, 119, 143–4, 146
    GPU 159
    Konspiratsia 10
    MVD 370, 371, 373
    OGPU 209, 216, 251, 301
    Okhrana 8, 29, 34, 40, 57, 58
    see also NKVD
self-determination 116, 117
Serge, Victor 133, 184, 212
Sergei, Grand Duke 36, 58
shock brigades 219, 227, 233
Sholokhov, Mikhail 210, 214
Shostakovich, Dmitri 311, 343, 367
show trials 159, 228, 247, 251, 255,
    258–9, 261, 315
Simonov, Konstantin 348, 356, 357, 358
Smolensk 216, 303
Social Democratic Labour Party (SDs)
    24, 29, 38: see also Bolsheviks;
    Mensheviks
socialism *vi*, 22, 219–21
Socialism in One Country policy 187,
    191, 193, 332
Socialist Realism 279, 297, 310–15

socialist revolution 23
Socialist Revolutionary Party (SRs) 20,
    21, 29, 57, 100, 119
    Combat Organisation 58
    and land issues 87–8
    and 1905 revolution 38
    outlawing of 159
    policies (March 1917) 81
    and St Petersburg Soviet 38–9
Solzhenitsyn, Alexander 268, 380, 381,
    391
Southern Volunteer Army 126, 134
Soviet aviators 260
soviets 35, 36, 77, 100, 108, 118, 162
    post-October revolution 160, 165
    Second All-Russian Congress 101,
    102
**Sovnarkom (Council of People's
    Commissars) 117**, 117–18,
    120, 160, 164, 165
Spanish Civil War 334
St Petersburg Soviet 35, 37, 38–9
Stakhanov, Alexei 236, 237
Stakhanovites 236, 237–9, 318
Stalin (Joseph Dzhugashvili) *vi*, 58, 121,
    133, 182, 316
    in artwork 171, 276–7, 364, 385
    assessments of 351, 382–5
    and collectivisation 208
    and Comintern 332
    cult of 247, 276–84, 378
    death of 372
    economic policies 198–9
    foreign policy 322, 332–3
    and Great Purges 269–74
    and Great Turn 202–3
    last years 371
    and leadership struggle 188–95
    and Lenin 172–3, 190
    letters to Molotov and Kaganovich
    384
    and modernisation 17
    1936 constitution 251
    opposition to 259, 270
    poetry about 284
    and Politburo 370
    power base 188
    pre-1934 opposition to 252–3
    and Second World War 348–51
    and Socialism in One Country policy
    187, 191, 193, 332
    and Sovnarkom 117
    and transformation of economy 196
    view of army 131
Stalingrad: battle of 344, 350
Stalinism
    explanation of 373–5
    Lenin and 376–81
    tsarism and 387–9
Stolypin, Peter 40, 47–8, 50, 52–3, 56
strikes 19, 151
    general strikes 29, 35, 55–6, 67
    and 1905 revolution 33–4

railway industry 37
    textile workers 19
    wartime 61
students 38, 55–6
Sudeikin, Georgii 10
Sukhanov, N. N. 83, 96, 97, 98, 108, 179,
    182
Supreme Economic Council (Vesenkha)
    142, 161, 224, 227
Sverdlov, Yakov 58, 102, 117, 133, 182
Sverdlovsk 274

Tambov region revolt 40, 150, 151, 159
Tatlin, Vladimir 292, 294
taxation 11, 16, 147, 156, 200, 304
terror 119, 378, 379, 384: see also Great
    Terror
terrorism 39, 143
Tocqueville, Alexander de 29
Tomsky, Mikhail 183, 185, 191, 195, 259
totalitarianism *vi*, 389–90
trade unions 57, 120, 151, 185, 201, 290,
    330
Trans-Siberian Railway 4, 15, 31, 33, 127
Trotsky, Leon 25, 27, 35, 83, 121, 128,
    183, 195
    and Civil War 127, 131–3
    death of 265
    and dictatorship 185
    and July Days 96, 97
    and leadership struggle 189, 190–1,
    192
    and Lenin's funeral 173
    on Nicholas II 13
    and October Revolution 101, 102,
    103, 109, 180
    and permanent revolution 187
    and Red Army 136, 178
    and St Petersburg/Petrograd Soviet
    39, 100
    and Sovnarkom 117
    on Stalin 259
    views on revolution 332
    and War Communism 152
Trudoviki 49, 51, 52, 90
tsarism: and Stalinism 387–9
tsarist state 8–11
    constitutional experiment 48–52
    end of 70–2
    political opposition to 20–7
    principles of tsarist rule 9
    structure of 8
Tsereteli, Irakli 81, 85, 117
Tukhachevsky, Marshal Mikhail 127, 130,
    151, 251, 260, 263, 347
Twenty-five Thousanders 209, 216

unemployment 29, 186, 201
Union of Russian People 40
urban workers, see workers
USSR (Union of Soviet Socialist
    Republics)
    creation of 163–4

foreign trade   200
government structure   165–6
post-war reconstruction   368–9
war economy   352–3

Vatsetis, I. I.   122, 133
Vyshinsky, Andrei   258, 260, 264, 370

War Communism   141–7, 151–2
War Industries Committees (WICs)   61
White armies   126, 128, 130, 134, 137
Witte, Sergei   11, 15–16, 17, 36, 42
women
    in artwork   286–7
    and collectivisation, resistance to   210,
        216
    and employment   7, 201, 230–1, 289,
        355
    and family   288, 305–8
    participation in politics   289–91
    during Second World War   354–5
Women's Death Battalion   86, 87, 109
workers   7, 18–19, 156, 201
    and Five-Year Plans   230–9
    and industry   55–6
    and Stakhanovite movement   238
Workers' Opposition   151, 163, 290, 291
working classes   17
working conditions   18–19, 55
world revolution   121, 187, 327: *see also*
        permanent revolution

Yagoda, Genrikh   255, 257, 259, 261, 315
Yeltsin, Boris   393
Yevtoshenko, Yevgeny   391
Yezhov, Nicolai   250, 251, 261, 262, 265
Yezhovshchina   250, 261
youth organisations   299
Yudenich, General Nikolai   126, 127, 128

Zamyatin, Yevgeny   317
zemstva   10, 11, 20, 28–9
zemstvo congresses   32, 36
Zhdanov, Andrei   310, 312, 367, 370–1
Zhukov, Marshal Georgi   350, 365
Zinoviev, Grigory   58, 101, 120, 147, 165,
        174, 183, 184, 195, 251
    and leadership struggle   189, 190–1
    on New Economic Policy   155
    show trial   258–9, 261
    view of army   131
Zinoviev letter   329
Zubatov, Sergei   29